Praise for *Seeking SRE*

"Reading this book is like being a fly on the wall as SREs discuss the challenges and successes they've had implementing SRE strategies outside of Google. A must-read for everyone in tech!"

—*Thomas A. Limoncelli*
SRE Manager, Stack Overflow, Inc. Google SRE Alum

"A fantastic collection of SRE insights and principles from engineers at Google, Netflix, Dropbox, SoundCloud, Spotify, Amazon, and more. Seeking SRE shares the secrets to high availability and durability for many of the most popular products we all know and use."

—*Tammy Butow*
Principle SRE, Gremlin

"Imagine you invited all your favorite SREs to a big dinner party where you just walked around all night quietly eavesdropping. What would you hear? This book is that. These are the conversations that happen between the sessions at conferences or over lunch. These are the (sometimes animated, but always principled) debates we have among ourselves. This book is your seat at the SRE family kitchen table."

—*Dave Rensin*
Director of Google CRE

"Although Google's two SRE books have been a force for good in the industry, they primarily frame the SRE narrative in the context of the solutions Google decided upon, and those may or may not work for every organization. *Seeking SRE* does an excellent job of demonstrating how SRE tenets can be adopted (or adapted) in various contexts across different organizations, while still staying true to the core principles championed by Google. In addition to providing the rationale and technical underpinning behind several of the infrastructural paradigms du jour that are required to build resilient systems, *Seeking SRE* also underscores the cultural scaffolding needed to ensure their successful implementation. The result is an actionable blueprint that the reader can use to make informed choices about when, why, and how to introduce these changes into existing infrastructures and organizations."

—Cindy Sridharan
Distributed Systems Engineer

Seeking SRE

*Conversations About Running
Production Systems at Scale*

Curated and edited by David N. Blank-Edelman

Beijing · Boston · Farnham · Sebastopol · Tokyo

Table of Contents

Part II.   Near Edge SRE

Part III.   SRE Best Practices and Technologies

Part IV.   The Human Side of SRE

Introduction

David N. Blank-Edelman, curator/editor

And So It Begins...

Conversations. That's the most important word in the title of this book, so pardon the lack of subtlety I'm demonstrating by making it the first and last word of this book.

Why is it so important? That's where the "Seeking" part of *Seeking SRE* comes in. The people I respect in the Site Reliability Engineering (SRE) field all believe that the field itself is still evolving, expanding, changing, and being discovered. We are all in some sense still seeking SRE.

In my experience, fields like ours grow best when the people in that field—the actual practitioners—talk to one another. Bring people together, let them talk, argue, laugh, share their experiences (success and failures) and their unsolved problems. A smart, kind, diverse, inclusive, and respectful community in conversation can catalyze a field like nothing else.

Origin Story

It was at SREcon16 Europe, one of the gatherings of the SRE community, that this book was born. (Full disclosure: I'm one of the cofounders of SREcon.) Brian Anderson, the original O'Reilly editor for this book, was on the hunt. The splendid book by Google called *Site Reliability Engineering* (*https://landing.google.com/sre/book.html*) had recently met with much-deserved commercial success and the publisher was on the lookout for more SRE content to publish. He and I were talking about the possibilities during a break when I realized what didn't exist for SRE. There was no volume I knew of that could bring people into some of the more interesting conversations that were happening in the field (like those that were happening at SREcon). I was seeing people discuss subjects like these:

- New implementations of SRE that didn't have a book yet. SRE has blossomed in new and exciting ways as it has taken root in different (sometimes brownfield) contexts.

- Innovative ways to learn how to practice SRE.

- What gets in the way of adopting SRE.

- The best practices people had discovered as they adopted, adapted, and lived it.

- Where the field was going next, including the subjects that are new now in the field but will be commonplace in short order.

- Finally—and maybe most important—what about the humans in the picture? What is SRE doing for them? What is SRE doing to them? Are humans really the problem in operations (that need to be automated away) or is that short sighted? Can SRE improve more than just operations?

And, so, the idea for *Seeking SRE* was born. Much to my surprise and delight, close to 40 authors from all over the field and all over the world liked the idea and decided to join me on this little project. I can't thank them enough.

Voices

Besides a wee bit of meta matter like what you are reading now, I've tried to keep my voice soft in the book so that we could stand together and hear what its amazing contributors have to say. You'll likely notice that this book doesn't have a single consistent textual voice (mine or any other editor's). There's no attempt made to put the material into a blender and homogenize the chapters into a beige "technical book register." I intentionally wanted you to hear the different voices from the different contributors just the way they talk. The only instruction they were given on tone was this:

> Pretend you are at lunch at a conference like SREcon. You are sitting with a bunch of smart SREs at lunch you don't know, and one of them says to you, "So, what are you working on? What's interesting to you these days?"
>
> You begin to answer the question…
>
> Now write that down.

Even further in this direction is the crowdsourced chapter on the relationship between DevOps and SRE (Chapter 12). When I realized that there are likely many answers to this question and that no one I knew had the only right answer, I put the question out to my social networks (and people were kind enough to broadcast it even further). I'm very grateful for everyone who answered the call. And just for fun, there are also little "You Know You're an SRE" tidbits scattered throughout the book from anonymous contributors (I promised anonymity when I asked the internet for them, but thanks to everyone who provided one or several!)

In addition to a variety of milieu, there's also a variety of opinions and viewpoints. Are you going to agree with everything you read in this volume? Gosh, I hope not. I don't agree with everything, so I don't see why you should. That would make for a really boring set of conversations, no? I strongly recommend that you remember that there are one or more humans behind every chapter who were brave enough to put their opinions out there, so we all could have a good confab. The SRE community's capacity to engage with respect is something I've come to appreciate over the years, and I know you'll follow in that tradition.

As the editor/curator of this book, which I'm very proud of, I do want to mention one regret up front. Our field has a real problem with diversity and inclusion of underrepresented minorities. We can't have all of the important conversations if not everyone is in the room. Despite my attempts to address this lack of representation, this book doesn't go far enough to work against this situation. I take full responsibility for that failure.

Forward in All Directions![1]

Are these the only interesting conversations to be had in SRE? Not by a long shot. These are just the ones that could be assembled into a book in finite time. By the time you are done reading, I am sure you will have your own list of omissions (don't hesitate to send them to me). There are definitely subjects that didn't make it into the book for a whole host of reasons (time, author availability, no one thought of it in time, etc.). I'm keenly interested in hearing what you think should be in a book like this that isn't already. If this book is a hit and there are future editions/volumes, your suggestions will be a great start for future conversations.

And finally, if this book is just a good passive read for you, dear reader, it is either a partial success or a partial failure depending on your disposition. At the very best, it hasn't met its Service-Level Objective. If you take it as the invitation it is meant to be and join the conversation—and by doing so you help us push the field forward—it will have met its objective.

Welcome.

Acknowledgments

Drop a stone into a pond and you get these lovely ripples undulating out and back into the center. Drop a book idea into the world and the same thing happens.

---

1 Apologies to 3 Mustaphas 3.

This means there are these concentric circles of people I need to thank. In the middle are all of the contributors who were willing to bring their time, energy and brilliance to the project. Thank you authors, one and all.

The authors created fabulous content, and then the tech reviewers told us all how to make it even better. Thank you to Patrick Cable, Susan J. Fowler, Thomas A. Limoncelli, James Meickle, Niall Richard Murphy, Amy Nguyen, Grace Petegorsky, and Yonatan Zunger.

The next ring are the O'Reilly editors, past and present who were willing to take this book in, tolerate the chaotic deadline-defying maelstrom inherent in a contributed volume of brilliant people, and refine its contents into the splendid shape you see now. Thank you Brian Anderson, Virginia Wilson, Kristen Brown, Melanie Yarbrough, Nick Adams, and Nikki McDonald. Thanks to the proofreaders Bob Russell and Rachel Monaghan. Also, thank you to Karen Montgomery and the O'Reilly design department for providing the cuddly animal for the cover. Now the sea otter on my bookshelf has a friend.

And finally, thank you to Cindy and Elijah, my family, and all my friends who were willing to tolerate yet another book project with good cheer. They are the people that provided the support I needed to drop the stone into the pond in the first place.

## PART I

SRE Implementation

- Can you build an SRE practice by giving people the context they need?
- How do you find and hire good SREs?
- How do you build an SRE team?
- Is it possible to improve a team itself through metrics?
- How do you do SRE when you don't own your systems?
- Is it possible to implement SRE principles at your organization without a dedicated SRE team?
- How does an SRE implementation unlike any other evolve over time?
- What does it take to grow SRE in a brownfield setting at a large enterprise?
- How do you transition from sysadmin to SRE?
- What do you need to eliminate in your organization to be able to do SRE?
- What does the DevOps world think about SRE?
- What is the relationship between DevOps and SRE?
- What is SRE like at other organizations that serve billions of people daily?

Discuss.

You Know You're an SRE When...

...your children tell you to stop bugging them about doing their homework because, "I'm within SLO!"

...you have to justify the difference between ops, SRE, DevOps, and so on, and you confuse even yourself sometimes.

...your first question is "how are you measuring that?"

...you erase the word "blame" from your vocabulary.

## CHAPTER 1

Context Versus Control in SRE

*A discussion with Coburn Watson, Microsoft (formerly Netflix)
and David N. Blank-Edelman*

David: We've had the pleasure of talking about a lot of things in the time we've known each other. One of the most interesting things I've heard you speak about is a way of doing SRE that focuses on providing context instead of using processes that are centered around control (the more common way SRE is practiced). Can we dig some more into this? Can you explain what you mean by context versus control and what a good example of each would be?

Coburn: I think of context as providing additional, pertinent information, which allows someone to better understand the rationale behind a given request or statement. At the highest level, availability-related context as shared at Netflix with an engineering team would be the trended availability of their microservice[s] and how that relates to the desired goal, including availability of downstream dependencies. With this domain-specific context, an engineering team has the responsibility (and context) to take the necessary steps to improve their availability.

In a control-based model a team will be aware of their microservice[s] availability goal, but if they fail to achieve that goal there might be a punitive action. This action might involve removing their ability to push code to production. At Netflix, we err toward the former model, sharing context on microservice-level availability, then working with teams when needed to help improve availability.

The challenge is making sure sufficient context is provided to teams. When someone makes a nonideal operational decision at Netflix, the first question to ask is whether that person had sufficient context to make a better decision. Quite often, the SRE team will find that a hit to availability is a result of insufficient context being passed to the team, in particular context related to reliability. Those are the gaps we seek to close as an SRE team to improve overall availability.

In a very large organization, it can be challenging to provide enough context such that, based on context alone, people can achieve the desired availability goals for their services. In organizations of this scale, you often have to fall back on more processes to achieve your availability goals. One example is the Google error budget model.[1] Another case for a more control-based model is when lives are on the line. If someone frequently writes unsafe software for an airplane autopilot system, that person (and company) probably has a very low tolerance for a primarily context-based approach. They don't want to get together and figure out how to improve their availability through additional context if planes are falling out of the sky. It's up to each SRE organization to determine how much risk they can assume as one factor in finding the split between a context- versus control-based model.

I believe there is a difference between information and context. In systems monitoring, information could just be a bunch of availability metrics I jam into a dashboard and email to the team. A typical engineer receiving such an email would ignore it because, 1) they are in charge of writing business logic for a service, and 2) they lack the expertise to digest and understand resource and availability metrics presented as time series.

At Netflix we have hundreds of thousands of operational metrics available to us. In order to support a context-driven model to improve availability, we have to bring specific domain knowledge to bear on the data. This requires taking the information and massaging it into a format that tells a story about availability. By applying such a transformation, we are able to push this context to teams on an as-needed basis so they can measure if availability improves for the given microservice. As an example, one key availability metric is the trended success rate from dependent services on a given microservice (as measured from the client side and breaking down failure rates based on cause).

My team doesn't own availability, but our job is to improve it over time. Why? Because someone can always blow a tire off the car. Oftentimes teams reach out and say, "I'm not quite sure why my availability dropped; can we talk about that?" While investigating the situation, it could be discovered that someone modified a client library or changed a timeout setting. As mentioned earlier, it is important to start from the principle that people are not operating in a negligent manner; they're just lacking the context to make the better decisions. We also don't forget that the systems can be overly complex and the operational bar required to avoid incidents is both too high or unnecessary. An example in this latter category is the tuning of static timeouts in a dynamic system.

---

1 See Chapter 4, "Service Level Objectives" (*https://landing.google.com/sre/book/chapters/service-level-objectives.html*), from Google's first *Site Reliability Engineering* book.

Though a context driven model is ideal, you can drift toward the needed control when you see a team having repeated incidents. They have been provided the same effective availability context as other teams, yet their availability continues to suffer. In some companies, control takes the form of prohibiting code from being pushed to production, and then of course engineers come to management because they need to push code to production. At Netflix I'll lead with the "you're on my list" discussion with an engineering manager, which involves in-person additional level-setting around expectations of service availability. If there is a common view, then I'll mention that they are developing a lot of features, but not addressing the necessary changes required to improve availability. I end by asking, "How do we get those on your list?" In my mind, that's about the extent of control I really want. I am lucky to work in a company with a mature set of individuals who recognize the importance of availability to the business and prioritize efforts appropriately. I find this type of discussion typically gets the needle pointing in the right direction.

Mentioned previously, but worth calling out again, before I make context-versus-control seem like a utopia that everyone can achieve, just remember that we run a business where if we have a failure, maybe streams don't get delivered. We don't have planes falling out of the sky or people's heart machines stopping. That gives us more flexibility about where we fall on the context-versus-control spectrum.

David: Does this mean that a context-based approach works at smaller scales but not nearly as well at larger scales?

Coburn: I believe the "scale" at which context over control works has little to do with the size of the production environment or customer base. It's more about the organization size and how they operate between teams. As you grow an organization, the effective use of context for availability can be challenging. A key factor may be less one-on-one communication or face-to-face time as the company grows.

At Netflix, I have the luxury of all the engineering teams I engage with residing on one campus. I can have coffee with any manager at Netflix. I've worked at large companies like HP with teams sitting on the other side of the globe. In that global situation, I still get them appropriate context, but it requires more work to give effective context. My assumption is if a company leans in and starts with control it's primarily because (regardless of scale) they're much more comfortable leading with process and control.

David: Is there a way that infrastructure plays into reliability as related to context?

Coburn: We consider ourselves in our push-model perspective to have great reliability because we're immutable in nature. I think we've all worked at companies where we upgrade something, and it turns out it was bad and we spend the night firefighting it because we're trying to get the site back up because the patch didn't work. When we go to put new code into production, we never upgrade anything, we just push a new version alongside the current code base. It's that red/black or blue/green—whatever people call it at their company. The new version of code goes in, and if something breaks in the canary, we just take it back out and we immediately roll back, or we don't even go through with the full deployment. This brings recovery down from possibly hours to minutes.

Although we have immutable code deployments, we also have something called Fast Properties. This means we can go into production with a later ability to dynamically update an application property. Since this breaks our immutable model but is often required, we see this capability being overused and leading to production incidents. Much like other common problems in production, if we see a team or collection of teams stumbling over the problem of dynamic property management, we look for ways to remove the risk through improved tooling. In our production environment, we now use Spinnaker, our continuous delivery platform, to manage staggered rollouts of dynamic properties to minimize blast radius and identify issues early. We refer to this general strategy as a "guardrail."

Even once we've done that, sometimes teams still go change something manually instead of going through a fast property pipeline and break production. If it happens again, we're like, "OK, they clearly haven't gotten the message. We need to go meet with them and say, 'please don't push this button'." We try at all costs to not take away the button, but at some point, we probably will.

David: This brings up a question about feedback loops. It sounds like some of your feedback signals are "did the site go down?", "did something trend positive?", or in terms of money "did it trend negative in the way you wanted it to?" Is there a more direct way to get an understanding from the humans whether they got the context they needed besides observing the system in a black box fashion and seeing whether the indicators you were looking at changed?

Coburn: That's one of the evolutions we've made as our company's grown. At Netflix we probably have 2,000 engineers, and that covers all different product domains. I could be building an internal tools UI, an encoding engine, standing up an infrastructure stack, or something to give you better recommendations. Some of those efforts have a more significant impact on customer-facing availability than others. From a numbers perspective, probably 50% of our engineering teams on a given day can do whatever they want in production and it has no possible risk to our service availability in any way whatsoever.

Initially we used to walk around the hall banging the virtual pan and yelling, "Hey, our availability is at three-nines; this is a problem!" The problem is it's a very diffuse message and 50% of the people are like, "OK, great, um, you're saying availability is not good, but what can I do about it as my services can't impact availability?"

Then, we changed our messaging to focus the hinging of the pain on the teams that actually affect availability, which might be the other 50% of the population. So, now, at least our message about service availability is hitting the right audience. The next step is to funnel context, which is specific to each engineering team and allows them to evaluate if they have substandard availability.

But even figuring out who to provide this information to isn't always easy. In a microservice architecture, there might be 40-plus teams that actually have microservices running at any given time, which can impact availability on the service critical path. If we're measuring availability at the edge of our service and determine that one-tenth of 1% of users couldn't play movies in a given hour, it's quite challenging to identify which team might have actually driven that outage. Even more challenging is that, in many cases, it's externally driven. As one example, think of an online gaming platform that needs to be available to play a title on the service. In that case perhaps I have to go to the UI team at Netflix that depends on that service and see if they can build resiliency to the external vendor service failure (which we have done).

I find it helpful to be clear within your organization when referring to the terms "availability" and "reliability." As an analogy to how we use these terms at Netflix in the context of our streaming service, I refer to a disk array which might be part of a Storage-Area Network. If the disk array represents the service, the underlying disk drives in the array would represent microservices. The design of the disk array takes into account that individual drives might fail, but the array should still function to both serve and persist data. Using this model, you would calculate availability as the percentage of time the disk array (the Netflix streaming service, in my world) is able to provide service to a client. The rate at which drives fail in the array represents the reliability of the drive (in my case, a microservice).

Much as with disk array configurations (RAID configuration, caching, etc.), you can apply operational patterns in a microservice architecture to improve overall service availability in light of possible microservice failures. One such example in use at Netflix is the Hystrix framework, based on the bulkhead pattern, which opens up "circuits" between microservices when a downstream microservice fails. The framework serves a fallback experience when possible to still provide service to an end user.

In conclusion, setting and measuring reliability goals at the microservice level lets you move toward a desired aggregate service-level availability. Different organizations might use the terms availability and reliability differently, but this is how we define them in light of our operational model.

David: So, what sort of info can you give to that team that would be actionable?

Coburn: Another company I talked to had a microservice availability report. They looked at the rate at which services were providing successful calls to their neighbor. If I'm a service that handles subscriber or member information and I have 30 services talking to me, my primary measure of availability should be the rate of success my dependencies have. Many times, teams will focus on their service-side view of being up and running. This doesn't guarantee you are servicing requests successfully at the desired rate, but it all comes down to the measures.

We liked the model from the other company and looked to see how we could apply it to our own infrastructure. Luckily, we have a common IPC [interprocess communication] framework and we have metrics around Hystrix and other commands that record the rate at which a client (dependent service) is having successful calls. We aggregate this information for all our critical microservices and compare the trend to the previous 30 days. It isn't meant to be near real time, it's meant to be more operational—are you getting better or worse.

Let's say a team owns three microservices, and the goal is for the microservices to have four-nines availability for calls from clients. If these microservices stay above four-nines, the team will never receive an email (availability report). If the last 7 days compared to the previous 21 have a deviation in a negative manner, or if the microservices are failing to achieve the four-nines, a report will be sent to the team. The report shows week over week as a bar chart. Green indicates you're achieving the goal for a given week. Red or yellow means you're failing to achieve the goal. Yellow means improvement over the previous week; red indicates degradation. Clicking on a bar in the graph will deliver a detailed report that shows for the entire window call rates of upstream (client) services talking to the microservice and the availability to those calls. On the right panel is a view of downstream dependency call and success rates, which is helpful as the microservice availability might be reduced by downstream dependency. We call this internal implementation the "microservice availability scorecard framework." At this point, the SRE team (working with Data Analytics) has provided information to a team about the microservices they own, and in particular their microservice availability to dependent client services, independent of Netflix service availability. This should be very actionable information. When dashboards are continually pushed to engineers, they can stop looking at them relatively quickly. The SRE solution at Netflix is to only push a scorecard when something changes that a team might need to pay attention to.

David: So, this sounds pretty *reactive*, right? You send them a scorecard because you'd like to see something that already happened be different in the future. What's the *proactive* side of this? How do you help someone who is trying to make a good decision well before they would get a scorecard?

Coburn: A good analogy for the scorecard is a message on your car dash indicating "your right front tire is losing pressure." It doesn't tell you what to do about it, just provides information that a trend is going in the wrong direction. When thinking about how to best inform people, I leveraged experience from past work in the performance domain, where we're not as worried about catching large performance deviations. We have committees that evaluate a system looking for significant deviations, so if CPU demand happens to jump 20% on a push, alarms start going off. What ends up getting you in the long run is the five-millisecond increase week over week for a six-month period. At the end of which you say, "Wow, I'm suddenly running with three times as much capacity for that service; what happened?" The role of the scorecard is to catch smaller deviations as well to avoid that slow and dangerous drift. I think the analogous situation for reliability is if you ignore the small deviations and fail to proactively address them, you're just waiting for the big outage.

David: OK, so what do you do from a contextual perspective to allow people to make the right decisions in the moment? In theory, the error budget concept means that at any time T, I have a way to determine at that moment whether I should do or not do something like launch a new version. What is the contextual version of that? Is the theory that people look at a scorecard synchronously and then make the right decision?

Coburn: If someone is having a problem where they're significantly impacting actual production availability, such as consistently having production incidents that result in customers not being able to stream content, then the microservice availability scorecard context is probably not the way to solve that problem. In that case, they have most likely been receiving the report but not acting on it. The way to solve that problem is to gather in a room and figure a path forward. It still doesn't mean they should stop pushing code, because they have a lot of other services dependent on them.

To your question about more real-time inputs to help engineers make better deployment decisions in the moment, we strive to put the information inside of the tools they are working with. Spinnaker now exposes availability trends at the cluster (the AWS term is Autoscaling Group) and it is right in front of the engineer if they are making a change via the UI.

When we look at continually improving availability, the target falls into two primary categories: avoiding all incidents, regardless of type, and a specific failure pattern someone has that's causing an incident or repeated outage.

From a context perspective, if they're having a problem where they're making a set of decisions over and over that result in production-impacting incidents, that requires a human-delivered versus a system-delivered report. At Netflix, the Core SRE team doesn't have the responsibility to step in and troubleshoot and resolve microservice-specific issues, but the team is instead considered the "central nervous system of Netflix." Taking the central nervous system analogy a bit further, this is the only team at Netflix that sees all the failures, whether external, internal, CDN [Content Delivery Network], network, etc., with the resultant responsibility to determine which teams to reach out to and engage.

David: Viewing your group as the nervous system of Netflix, what process do you have for propagating information throughout the org so that people in one part can learn from the other parts (either a good way to do something or not to repeat a bad experience)?

Coburn: Based on the specific shortcoming in operational risk we would like to address, we have a couple of channels to get the best practice applied: drive to get the necessary enhancements into our operational tools (for example, Spinnaker, canary analysis) to seamlessly expose it to all teams or socialize the suggested change via an availability newsletter which is published monthly. In some cases, the suggested best practice is one of the tooling extensions previously incorporated into tooling.

Both of these are methods to help move the needle on availability in an aggregate manner.

Some changes that we incorporate into tooling might be referred to as a guardrail. A concrete example is an additional step in deployment added to Spinnaker that detects when someone attempts to remove all cluster capacity while still taking significant amounts of traffic. This guardrail helps call attention to a possibly dangerous action, which the engineer was unaware was risky. This is a method of "just in time" context.

David: What about cases where somebody uses one of your tools like Hystrix in a way that is a perfectly valid way to use it, but experience has shown that this way yields negative results? It's not the case that you want to change the tool because the tool is just fine. How do you propagate experience like this through the org once you've learned that lesson? It sounds like the availability reports would be one of the examples of that?

Coburn: That's right. The availability report is actually challenging to interpret. Once you receive it, you need to click in three to four strategic (and often hidden) places on the report just to get to actionable data. This was a fairly significant barrier to adoption, and so we created a four-minute video to function as an onboarding tutorial for report usage. When people get the report, it says please watch this four-minute video to understand how to use this report. It didn't move the needle fully but definitely improved the actionability of the report for those who took the time to use it.

David: Let's talk about the limitations of context versus control. Do you think that a context-based system works as well in an environment where the product and the metrics for it are more complex than Netflix? Is it the simplicity of the Netflix product that makes it work so well for you?

Coburn: First I would point out that in aggregate the Netflix service (in terms of its interacting parts) is as complex as you might find anywhere else. There are a number of factors that allow context to be more broadly effective at Netflix versus other companies. It ties directly to a lack of complexity in the engineering organization and the structure of our service. The following are some of the key factors:

- We have all the engineers sitting in one location. Common engineering principles are easily socialized and additional tribal knowledge of best practices is implicitly socialized and discussed.
- We have one dominant version of the software running in a given region at a given time. We additionally have control over that software stack and we can change it whenever we want (not shipped to customers, with the exception of device applications).
- We have a service where people don't die if it breaks.
- We have a little bit of runway and we have an SRE team who is willing to take a bunch of bullets if availability gets worse and say "my job is to fix it."

For this last bullet point, it can be somewhat of a difficult situation for the reliability organization to say they're responsible for improving availability, but at the same time don't have total control over the factors that impact availability. A lot of people aren't comfortable with saying they're responsible for improving something they don't necessarily have absolute control over.

At a company where you ship a product to the field (for example, self-driving car software), this model might not work. You wouldn't want to wait and say, "Wow, look, that car drove off the road. That was an error. Who wrote that? Well, let's get it right next year." In contrast, the space we operate in allows a fair amount of room to leverage context over control, as we don't put lives at risk and can make changes quickly to the aggregate product environment. That said, I think you can see situations when companies start to scale where they started with context but move over time to have a bit more control as warranted by the needs of the customer and reliability. You could generalize this perspective in that you will eventually move more toward the other end of the spectrum from which you started, if even only a little bit.

David: In the past we've talked a bit about context versus control from an engineering investment perspective. Can you say a bit more about this?

Coburn: I think about four primary dimensions: rate of innovation, security, reliability, and efficiency (infrastructure/operations). Depending on how your organization is structured, you could own one or more of the dimensions. Even if you don't own a given dimension, the decisions you make in your own space can have significant impacts on the others. I'm in a situation where I own at least two, reliability and efficiency, because I also own capacity planning. When I think about how hard I want to push on teams to improve those dimensions I want to try as little as possible to reduce drag on the others (rate of innovation, security). Keeping this model top-of-mind allows us as an SRE organization to be more thoughtful in our asks of other engineering teams.

Somewhat related, we also make explicit trade-offs in order to improve one dimension at the cost of another. We have cases where we run significantly inefficient (over-provisioned) for a given microservice for the purposes of increased rate of innovation or reliability. If we have a service that needs to run with twice as much headroom because of bursty traffic, I don't care if that costs me an additional tens of thousands of dollars a year, because all I need is one big outage to quickly burn that amount of engineering effort/time.

David: OK, so how do you connect that back to context versus control?

Coburn: With control as an example, let's say I actually take away the ability for someone to push code because I need to increase this dimension of reliability. On the one hand it stops the near-term breakage, but it slows down innovation. The goal is to try to provide more context to avoid forcibly slowing down other dimensions and let the owner of a given service determine which dimension to optimize for, taking into account their current demands. In contrast, control has a much more binary effect on other dimensions.

David: Does context have a positive or negative effect on any of those dimensions? Control clearly does, as you just mentioned, but what about context?

Coburn: Context does have a strong upside and track record, at least in our case. In the past five years, our customer population has grown six times, our streaming has grown six times, our availability has improved every year, our number of teams has increased every year, and our rate of innovation has gone up every year. That's without applying control to improve availability, but rather predominantly by improving through context combined with improvement of the platform so engineers spend less time working on operational aspects that shouldn't be required in their role (such as determining how to configure pipelines to have staggered pushes across regions).

David: If control can have a negative effect on those dimensions, can context can have a similar adverse effect?

Coburn: It can, but I have yet to see where the context we provide to teams results in an undesired behavior that actually harms availability. One area in which this can be a risk is infrastructure efficiency. Although we provide detailed infrastructure cost context to teams, we don't have or enforce cloud cost budgets on teams. Case in point, engineers simply deploy whatever infrastructure they need and receive a cost report each month that provides them context about their cost. With this context one team chose to try and optimize efficiency by staying on an older and less reliable instance type, which was of course much less expensive. We then had an outage due to poorly performing and less reliable instances, often running underprovisioned. In this case, we provided cost context, the decision was to overindex on efficiency, and as a result reliability took a hit. We decided to socialize with teams that we would rather run less efficient than compromise reliability, aligned with our explicit prioritization of domain concerns.

Coburn Watson is currently a partner in the Production Infrastructure Engineering organization at Microsoft. He recently concluded a six year adventure at Netflix where he led the organization responsible for site reliability, performance engineering, and cloud infrastructure. His 20+ years of experience in the technology domain spans systems management through application development and large-scale site reliability and performance.

## CHAPTER 2

Interviewing Site Reliability Engineers

Andrew Fong, Dropbox, Inc.

There are two phrases you continually hear about why projects are successful: "My engineers made it possible" or "My engineers did the impossible."

Much of this book is about technology and how to apply it to problems. That technology is completely useless without the right people. This chapter is dedicated to the softer side of our jobs: hiring those right people. Every one of these hires will operate and build the technology that is used to solve problems, disrupt industries, and achieve feats that no one thought were possible.

It all begins with the engineer.

Interviewing 101

Before we get into the specifics of SRE hiring, it is useful to build a common understanding of how interviewing typically works. This is a general overview based on experiences working at companies such as AOL, Google, YouTube, and Dropbox.

Who Is Involved

Generally, there is a minimum of three parties involved: the candidate, the recruiter, and the hiring manager.

Industry Versus University

Usually, there are two types of candidate profiles that hiring managers recruit: industry and university (which includes masters and PhDs). Industry candidates are engineers who have worked in similar positions at other companies. University candidates are exactly what it sounds like—students. Compared to recruiting software engineers, recruiting SREs from universities is significantly harder and more specialized. The major reason for this is that you will first need to educate university students on what SRE is before they will even apply for the role. In this book, we focus exclusively on industry recruiting.

Biases

Before we go too deep into the interviewing content, it is important to recognize that we are all humans and thus have biases. We do not cover how to avoid all biases within this chapter. However, we do call out two specific ways to combat biases that organizations starting to build out SRE teams should seek to implement. The first is to do a blind résumé review, and the second is to standardize your hiring processes. Both of these are simple enough tweaks to existing processes or are simply best practices for building a new interview process.

Blind résumé review means that you are attempting to remove biases from the résumé review by obfuscating identifying information within the résumé. You will need to understand what matters to your organization and calibrate the blind review process accordingly.

Helping you to standardize the hiring process is a goal of this chapter. By the end of this chapter you will have learned a systematic way of evaluating candidates, both at scale as well as for a limited number of positions.

At the end of this chapter, there are links to further reading on the topic of conscious and unconscious biases.

The Funnel

Most companies think of hiring as a funnel that has stages through which candidates pass until they either fall out at a given stage or receive an offer. Figure 2-1 illustrates what a typical funnel looks like.

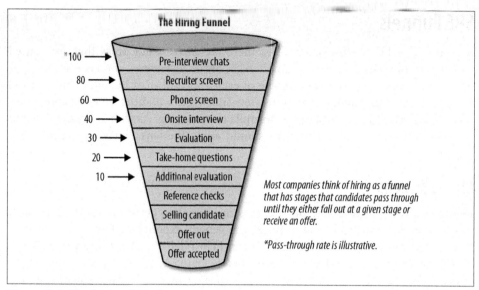

Figure 2-1. The hiring funnel

Let's take a look at the individual steps involved:

1. Pre-interview chats
2. Recruiter screen
3. Phone screen
4. Onsite interview
5. Evaluation
6. Take-home questions
7. Additional evaluation
8. Reference checks
9. Selling candidates
10. Offer out
11. Offer accepted

Each of these stages serves a unique purpose. Measuring the stages of the funnel will help you to refine the process and hire world-class candidates. What and how you measure is a topic for another book. What's important here is that you know the funnel exists and some of its basic stages.

SRE Funnels

Now that you know what a funnel is, there are three major areas that are crafted specifically for hiring SREs: the phone screen, onsite interviews, and take-home questions. This section lays out the purpose of each area and what technical and cultural areas it covers. The content of the interview and stages will differ between companies and is not meant to be a prescriptive formula to recruiting. As with all areas related to talent within your organization, you should apply the lens that your organization requires.

Phone Screens

Before you bring a candidate on site, it is important to get some basic signal with respect to motivation, technical aptitude, and general experience. The phone screen is done at the top of the funnel because it can help filter out candidates who will not make it through the interview. This prevents incurring a high expense at later stages, in the candidate's time as well as your engineering team's time. Also, you can use the phone screen to touch on a variety of topics to help form a hypothesis of where this engineer would fit or would not fit into your organization. If you are unable to formulate this hypothesis, you might want to walk away after the phone screen.

Conducting a phone screen

A good format that has been tested at multiple companies is to have phone-screen questions that are specific and concrete enough that the candidate is able to get to a solution within 20 minutes. For example, having a coding and a process or troubleshooting question allows you to determine someone's technical breadth and experience.

Coding, which is pragmatic and simple enough to do in a shared online coding tool, works well and usually results in reasonable signal regarding the candidate's technical depth.

Troubleshooting or process questions should aim at understanding how the candidate reasons through problems that do not involve code. A simple rule of thumb can be aiming for two 20-minute questions along with a 10- to 15-minute discussion about the role, company, and expectations; this combination typically fills a one-hour phone screen.

You will want to have a few phone-screen questions in your tool chest and be willing to pivot depending on the candidate's experience. Having an easy question that allows you to keep the conversation going is perfectly fine at this stage.

It's important that the candidate walks away from the conversation with a positive view of your organization, even if you are not moving on to the next stage.

The Onsite Interview

Before you bring a candidate into your office to interview, you should formulate an explicit hypothesis around the candidate. This allows you to do the following:

- Set expectations for the interview panel
- Fully understand what your organization is looking to hire
- Craft an interview loop that will fairly evaluate the candidate

A good hypothesis will include the expected seniority, growth path, and leadership skill set, which you can validate via the interview process. For example:

> The systems engineering team, which works on Linux automation, is looking to hire a senior engineer with strong distributed systems knowledge that will grow into a technical leader, either formal or informal, of a team of mostly junior engineers.

Teasing this apart, you can identify what the team is looking for in a candidate:

- Senior engineer
- Systems knowledge
- Distributed systems
- Technical leadership
- Mentorship

Taking this data and combining it with other baseline requirements that you might have, such as coding, you can create an interview loop that accurately evaluates the candidate for the role. In this case, to evaluate these skills, you want to understand the candidate's working knowledge of Linux, how that person operates distributed systems, and how well they can mentor and set technical direction on a team as well as whether the candidate possesses the baseline coding requirement.

A good loop for a candidate that is being evaluated for that hypothesis would include the following:

- Two medium-to-difficult coding questions that involve understanding of system designs
- Deep dive or architecture
- A focused interview on leadership, mentorship, and working with others

Coding and system questions

Good questions that can test coding and systems tend to be those that are real world and are bounded by your organization's size against a scaling factor of 10. For example, consider the following question:

> Design and code a system that can distribute a package in parallel to N servers.

You want to select an N that is realistic for the scenario that you expect the candidate to face. If your organization has 100 servers, it's realistic to expect it will grow to 1,000 but not 100,000. You will expect the SRE to solve the problem at hand when on the job, so ask the question in a way that is realistic for the working environment.

Deep dives and architecture questions

Deep dives and architecture test similar attributes of a candidate—namely, their ability to reason about technical trade-offs. However, you will want to set up the interviews in a slightly different way. Deep dives tend to work better when you ask the candidate to select the space ahead of time. This allows you to place an engineer with the candidate who has thought about the problem ahead of time. Architecture questions do not require this advance preparation. However, similar to the coding question, you want to set bounding parameters. An example of a bounding parameter can be to specify an initial scale and then increase the scale at various stages. By starting small, you can assess attributes of the candidate, such as their bias toward simple versus complex solutions as well as how they think about trade-offs at each stage of the problem.

Cultural interviews

All cultural fit interviews are a way of ascertaining how well a candidate will fit into your organization's cultural value system. This is not a "would I like to hang out with this person?" interview. Rather, it is a properly crafted set of questions that dig into the way an engineer works with others, whether the person focuses on the right areas, and whether they are able to articulate problems.

Cultural fit can even offset technical weaknesses depending on the size and structure of your organization. For example, an extremely talented engineer who cannot operate in a large company might be a pass, whereas someone who understands organizational leverage but has small technical gaps might be much more valuable at scale. You can determine this fit by posing questions that dig into the candidate's working style, such as asking for examples of how the person approached a certain project and what reflections and learnings they took from the experience. Good candidates will typically be able to articulate the "why's" behind their thought process and what they would do differently given your environment.

Take-Home Questions

Occasionally, you will have a scenario in which you want to get additional technical signal after you have looked at the interview feedback. You can choose to have the candidate return for another technical interview or use a take-home question. Take-home questions have positives and negatives. Let's explore both before examining what makes a good take-home question.

On the positive side, take-home questions allow a candidate to fully showcase their ability to write software in a more real-world scenario. The candidate has access to their own development environment, access to their favorite search engine, and the ability to pace themselves. All of this results in much higher signal, including aspects around collaboration via clarifying questions, if needed, with the proctor.

However, take-home questions are not without drawbacks. The major disadvantages of take-home questions involve the time commitment required of both the candidate and an engineer from your company. A typical scenario requires a three-day window for both parties to be available and will delay the potential offer. You should be very judicious in the use of a take-home question.

Good take-home questions should be built in a way that can provide signal for the area or areas for which you lacked signal from the initial interviews. At this stage of the funnel, you will have very few candidates, and it will also be hard to calibrate your organization on the questions. To counteract this, having another hypothesis on what the take-home will validate is very important. It is equally important to not discount the onsite interview if parts of the take-home are not on par with the onsite. Remember, you are looking to validate something you did *not* get signal on during the initial onsite interview.

Advice for Hiring Managers

The hiring manager, or the person responsible for staffing the role, has three major responsibilities during the interview process:

- Building the hypothesis (covered in "The Onsite Interview" on page 19)
- Convincing or selling the candidate to join your organization
- Knowing when to walk away from a candidate

Selling candidates

From the first minute you meet and talk to a candidate, you should be selling them on your organization. How you do this will vary from person to person. You want to know the answer to three questions in order to to effectively sell a candidate:

- What motivates the candidate?
- What is their value system?
- What type of environment brings out their strengths?

By understanding these dimensions, you can craft a compelling narrative for a candidate to join your organization.

Walking away

Walking away from a candidate is one of the hardest things to do during the process. You, and potentially your team and organization, will have made a time and emotional investment into a candidate. Walking away is also something that can occur at any stage, not just after you decide to pass because of interview performance.

The core reason for walking away from a candidate comes down to organizational fit. Each time you learn something new about a candidate is an opportunity to reevaluate. Just as in engineering, the hiring process is about trade-offs. A perfect candidate might demand a salary that you cannot afford, or they might have the perfect technical skills but none of the leadership skills you are looking for. Walking away is hard, but know that making the wrong hire is almost always worse in the long run. Optimize your pipeline to avoid false positives. If you are willing to take risks, be explicit and have a strong performance management program in place.

Final Thoughts on Interviewing SREs

People form the backbone of your organization, and you should use your interviewing process to ensure that you have found the very best people for your organization. Be prepared to take risks and place bets on people just as you would if they were internal to your organization, because you will never know everything you want to know in such a short time with a candidate. This is an imperfect process attempting to get a perfect output, and thus you will need to iterate and be open-minded as well as take risks.

At the end of the day, even if you decide to not make an offer based on the interview performance, make sure that the candidate walks away feeling the process was fair and they had a good experience. Wouldn't that be what you would want if you were in their shoes?

Further Reading

- Hiring Site Reliability Engineers (*https://www.usenix.org/system/files/login/arti cles/login_june_07_jones.pdf*)
- 7 Practical Ways to Reduce Bias in Your Hiring Process (*https://hbr.org/ 2017/06/7-practical-ways-to-reduce-bias-in-your-hiring-process*)
- Hiring Your First SRE (*https://sreally.com/hiring-your-first-sre-bdda38ee175d*)

Andrew Fong is an engineering director at Dropbox. He is also one of the first members of the SRECon steering committee and helped cochair the inaugural conferences. He has spent his career in infrastructure at companies such as AOL, YouTube/Google, and Dropbox.

## CHAPTER 3

So, You Want to Build an SRE Team?

Luke Stone, Google

This chapter is for leaders in organizations that are not practicing Site Reliability Engineering (SRE). It's for the IT managers who are facing disruption from the cloud. It's for operations directors who are dealing with more and more complexity every day. It's for CTOs who are building new technical capabilities. You might be thinking about building an SRE team. Is it a good fit for your organization? I want to help you decide.

Since 2014, I've worked in Google Cloud Platform, and I've met at least a hundred leaders in this situation. My first job at Google was before SRE existed, and today I work with cloud customers who are applying SRE in their organizations. I've seen SRE teams grow from seeds in many environments. I've also seen teams that struggled to find energy and nutrition.

So, let's assume that you want to build an SRE team. Why? I've heard some themes that come up over and over. These made-up quotes illustrate the themes:

- "My friends think SRE is cool and it would look nifty on my résumé."
- "I got yelled at the last time we had an outage."
- "My organization wants more predictable reliability and is willing to pay for it."

They are cheeky distillations of more nuanced situations, but they might resonate with you. Each one points to several opportunities and pitfalls. Understanding them will help you to figure out how SRE would fit into your organization. Let's take a look at the real meaning of each one.

Choose SRE for the Right Reasons

"My friends think SRE is cool and it would look nifty on my résumé."

The first point is about avoiding misconceptions: your organization must understand SRE at a deeper level.

If SRE seems cool to you, congratulations on your excellent taste! It is pretty cool to take something as theoretical as an error budget and apply it to a real-world problem…and to see results. It's science! It's engineering!

However, in the long run, SRE is not going to thrive in your organization based purely on its current popularity. Every outage will be a test of the team's ability to deliver real value. The bad news is that it takes a lot of work to build trust around a team that is highly visible when things go disastrously wrong. The good news is that SRE is well designed, detailed, and tested in the real world. It can be the backbone of your plan to achieve the reliability that you need.

So, you can't count on the coolness to take you very far. A well-functioning SRE team has a culture that develops over time, and it's going to be a long-term, high-effort project to start a team in your organization. We're talking months to years. If this is not your idea of fun, you can still get some quick results by adopting a few SRE practices. For example, you can practice consistently writing postmortems and reviewing them with your team. This can be useful, but don't expect it to have the same impact as adopting the full set of SRE principles.

Similarly, don't expect to have impact from your SRE team if it is not practicing the SRE approach to production engineering all day, every day. It's tempting to slap the SRE label on an existing team, change a few job titles, and claim that you've taken the first steps. You can probably guess that this is unlikely to succeed because it doesn't actually change anything about the systems themselves. An SRE team is fundamentally a team of software engineers who are pointed at the reliability problem, so if your organization doesn't sustain software engineers, it's not right for SRE. If you have software engineers but can't focus their energy on an SRE approach to production reliability, you'll have another flavor of "SRE in name only."

An effective SRE team requires a certain environment. There must be support from the ground up, also from the sides and above. You'll need to get buy-in from the SRE team members themselves, their peers (development teams and other SRE teams), and management. The team will not thrive in isolation. It needs to be integrated into your company's technical core. Ease of communication matters, so consider physical colocation with development teams or investing in high-quality video conferencing. SRE needs to be at the table for high-level decisions about reliability needs and levels of investment in people and redundant infrastructure.

The members of the team must be dedicated and trustworthy to one another. They must be skilled at automation and technical troubleshooting. They must possess the generosity necessary to continually build one another up because SRE is really a team effort and there is a saying: "No heroes." Avoid teams that have been scraped together from far-flung individuals. It might be better to repurpose a well-functioning team to bootstrap your SRE team.

SRE teams interact with other teams, particularly development teams, so these need to be bought in, too. For example, it's hard to create a blameless postmortem culture if developers or managers are pointing fingers. When paired with an SRE team, a development team should put something of value into the partnership. Here are some examples:

- Fund the team
- Agree to take some on-call shifts
- Give SRE a mechanism to prioritize SRE needs
- Dedicate the best software engineers to the SRE team

Here's a recipe for disaster: when the dev team expects the SRE team to "just fix it." SRE should be empowered to ensure that the software can be operated reliably, and the dev team should be interested in collaborating toward that goal. The developers should be expected to actively participate in production operations—for example, by pairing with SREs or taking a small slice of the SRE team's operational duties. This will make them aware of the value of the SRE team and also gives some firsthand data about what it's like to operate the system. It's also very important for business continuity in case the SRE team needs to "hand back the pager" and stop supporting the system. If the developers cannot or will not take responsibility for some portion of the production engineering tasks, SRE is not going to work.

SRE thrives in an environment of open, effective communication. It will be very difficult if the SRE team is excluded from the conversations about the future of the product or service. This can be unintentional friction, for example if the SRE team is in a remote location, works in a different time zone, or uses another language (spoken or programming language, that is). It's even worse if the SRE team is local but excluded from planning or social events.

But wait, I thought SRE was obviously cool! I mean, look at SREcon attendance growing every year, and the SRE book's a best-seller. At Google, SREs wear awesome bomber jackets and they have a logo with a dragon on it. Super cool!

If you want to make SRE successful in your organization, it definitely helps to make it cool. That doesn't mean it needs to be elitist or exclusive. There will be a tendency for other teams to reject SRE if they don't understand it, so it's very important to get all technical leaders to introduce the concepts and the people into their teams. You might be willing to try a rotation program between dev and SRE, or a policy whereby people can freely transfer between dev and SRE teams. It's about building personal relationships and treating SRE as equals.

At a higher level, the executive leadership must be willing to back up the SRE team when it is acting according to its principles, even when the world appears to be on fire. Leadership must defer to SREs who are managing a live incident. They must be willing to sign off on Service-Level Objectives (SLOs) (*https://landing.google.com/sre/book/chapters/service-level-objectives.html*), meaning that they are taking responsibility for defending some amount of downtime as acceptable. They must be willing to enforce error budgets, meaning enforcing consequences like feature freezes when budgets are exceeded.

Orienting to a Data-Driven Approach

"I got yelled at the last time we had an outage."

This point is about recognizing that an organization is compatible with SRE only if it's driven by facts and data.

My grandfather was not an SRE. He was a truck driver and an entrepreneur. At one point in the 1950s he invested in a novel gadget: an alarm clock that turns off when the user screams. Very effective for getting everyone up in the morning. It's the only machine I've ever seen that does the right thing when you yell at it.

If your organization reacts to engineering problems by applying emotion, it's not ready for SRE. People will need to keep cool heads in order to get to the bottom of increasingly difficult reliability problems. When people feel threatened, they are motivated to hide information, and SRE requires an open and collaborative atmosphere. For example, some teams give awards, not punishment, to people who take responsibility for causing an outage, *if* they follow up with an appropriate incident response and postmortem.

Be alert for signs of maturity like focus on long-term benefits, incremental improvement, and acknowledgment of existing problems. If people can face problems, a blameless postmortem culture can take root. If they want to measure the pace of improvement, SLOs and error budgets will work. If they are willing to invest, automation will thrive and toil melts away.

A good sign is the use of objective metrics to drive business discussions. People agree ahead of time on the desired, measurable outcomes, and then periodic reviews check the numbers and adjust as necessary. If you have seen a scenario in which someone's review was full of bad news, and the group's reaction was to offer help, the culture might be right for SRE.

Another good sign of maturity is when the organization can reward "landings" (e.g., automation in production providing measurable savings) instead of "launches" (like a new, shiny tool). Do you reward significant clean-ups and grunge work that improves maintainability and operational effectiveness?

SRE relies on a fact-based approach, like hard science. It can take time to get some difficult facts, like the root cause of an outage or an analysis of when the current capacity will be inadequate. It's very important that these facts get the respect they deserve. Look for people who are patient about gathering the facts. Look for people who question assumptions and demand hard evidence. Avoid people who don't have the focus or the interest to get to the bottom of a complex technical situation.

People across your organization will need to put their trust in the SRE process as their chosen tool for managing reliability. They will need to stick to the process and live with the reliability goals that they originally agreed to. An SLO and an error budget are like a contract with performance targets and consequences. Sticking to this contract in the face of an incident requires a cool head. It needs to be OK for SRE to say, "errors increased, but stayed within SLO, so this is not an emergency."

Commitment to SRE

"My organization wants more predictable reliability and is willing to pay for it."

This brings us to the last point: your organization must be willing to invest the attention and resources required to sustain an SRE team.

SRE can be expensive. You'll want to be sure about what you're getting from it. A sustainable SRE team needs enough people to cover on-call duties without getting burned out, and enough people to have cycles for automation, tooling, and other production engineering projects. They will also need enough people to respond to the service's myriad operational needs that come up. If the team is understaffed, even by a little, the most talented people will leave and you won't achieve your goal. There is a minimum team size necessary to carry SRE responsibilities for a system. This doesn't make sense for smaller systems, so some things will be out of scope for the SRE team. They are not expected to solve everyone's problems.

Many people think that SRE is about continually increasing reliability, forever, asymptotically approaching 100%. That could be your goal, but at some point, you'll get diminishing returns on your resources. SRE is really about managing your reliability so that it doesn't get in the way of other business goals. The organization must be able to accept reliability under 100%—because no systems are perfect. Some amount of downtime must be anticipated, accepted, and even embraced. Reluctance to face this reality is the single most significant barrier to adopting SRE.

What goals would be more important than reliability? When technology is a differentiator to the business. Where innovation is important. In these cases, you might want a product development team going as fast as possible—and it would be worthwhile to have an SRE team providing some reliability guardrails. For example, SRE could provide a deployment system with canary servers and easy rollbacks.

SRE can fit into your organization if you have enough discipline to trust the process. At first, it seems like SRE establishes another set of constraints. But, actually, people gain freedom when they adopt practices like SLOs and blameless postmortems. An SLO is a codification of clear expectations. It allows local optimizations and empowers people to reason about the reliability impacts of their decisions. A blameless postmortem is explicit permission to point out things that went wrong. It allows you to begin to address the root cause of your reliability issues. These are powerful tools. Like all good tools, they require training and maintenance. And, of course, they should be used according to their design and best purpose.

Making a Decision About SRE

I hope this chapter has given you some perspective on whether SRE is a good fit for your organization. The steps for actually starting the team can be covered in another chapter, or perhaps another book! If you're still not sure whether SRE is right for you, here are some ideas for gathering more information:

- Find some influential people in your organization (leaders and old-timers, for example) and have them read the first few chapters of the original SRE book (*https://landing.google.com/sre/book/index.html*). Do the ideas resonate? Does SRE seem realistic?

- Brainstorm some SLOs for your service. Test them with the people who are responsible for the user experience. Play "what if" with a few scenarios, like unplanned outages of various durations, planned maintenance for a feature, and degraded service.

- Try to think of a mature, important system with which to start. Are there clear reliability metrics? Is it clear who would decide on the SLOs and error budget?

- Imagine that you've built an SRE team. How do you tell if it's working well? More reliability with fewer people? At greater release velocity? Something that's measurable.

You are now well armed with questions to help you evaluate the possibility of SRE in your organization. Be sure to include your colleagues and stakeholders while you are gathering data and deliberating. This decision is too big to be taken by one person. Working together, you can make a wise decision on starting your SRE team. Good luck!

Luke Stone joined Google in 2002 as the first technical support engineer for AdSense. He witnessed SRE's impact on Google from the beginning and joined Google SRE as a founding member of the Customer Reliability Engineering team. Before Google, Luke was a system administrator and developer in academic and nonprofit organizations, and studied computer science at Stanford.

## CHAPTER 4

Using Incident Metrics to Improve SRE at Scale

Martin Check, Microsoft

Whether your service is looking to add its next dozen users or its next billion users, sooner or later you'll end up in a conversation about how much to invest in which areas to stay reliable as the service scales up. In this chapter, we take a look how to use incident metrics to focus investments by way of a case study from Microsoft Azure. It applies lessons we've learned working on service reliability on a variety of services, ranging from startups to enterprise services all the way to cloud scale. Azure makes a particularly good case study, as the tremendous scale, growth, and diversity of product offerings amplify the typical reliability themes. We show how using data and some innovative techniques to analyze and report on these themes helped us to drive improvements.

The Virtuous Cycle to the Rescue: If You Don't Measure It...

As with any problem management effort, we began by looking at the data. However, when we went to do so, it turned out that we had thousands of data sources, service telemetry, incident management metrics, deployment metrics, and on and on. In fact, we had so many data sources to look at that it made deciding what data to look at and in which order to tackle the problems tricky. After looking at the best practices in the industry and consulting with experts, we ultimately landed on a system called *the virtuous cycle*, shown in Figure 4-1, to underpin our improvement efforts. The virtuous cycle created a framework that we could use to see how effective our monitoring was by how quickly we detected outages, how well we were learning from outages by measuring the root-cause analysis (RCA) process and repairs, and how quickly those bugs were getting fixed. We could then look at our code quality and deployment velocity to see how quickly we'd run through the full cycle.

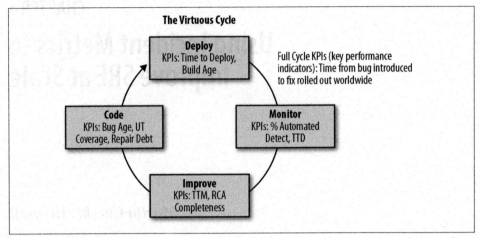

Figure 4-1. The virtuous cycle

As SREs, we know that every minute of downtime matters, so we began by finding the key metrics that told us how effective we were at responding to and repairing incidents. This meant that first we had to define the metrics that were representative and then get agreement on definitions and start/end times. Let's dive into the metrics that we picked and why we thought they were so important:

Time to Detect (TTD)

Time to Detect is the time from the impact start to the time that an incident is visible to an operator. We start the counter when impact first becomes visible to the customer, even if our monitoring didn't detect it. This is often the same as the time that the Service-Level Agreement (SLA) is breached.

Believe it or not, TTD is the most important metric for incidents that require manual mitigation action. This measure determines the quality and accuracy of your monitoring. If you don't know about your customer pain, you can't begin the process of recovery, and you certainly can't actuate automation to respond or mitigate. Maybe even more important, you can't communicate to your customers that you know about the problem and are working on it. The challenge with TTD is balancing the monitoring sensitivity such that you find all of the customer issues quickly and accurately, without constantly interrupting your engineers for issues that don't impact customers.

Time to Engage (TTE)

This is the time from detection until the appropriate engineer is engaged. This can be difficult to determine during the event, and sometimes even afterward. It can be hard to look back through the log of war to pin this down on a single engineer, so it's OK to approximate with the first engineer on the scene. This metric is very important to look at how effectively we're able to mobilize the response, and accounts for both the triage time (determining severity and ownership) as well as the time to escalate and mobilize the responders. There are a lot of ways in which you can improve this; automated escalation and paging systems, clear expectations for on-call, follow-the-sun support models, and even improved monitoring can help ensure the alert goes to the right on-call engineer the first time.

Time to Fix (TTF)

This is the time that it takes the responder to mitigate the issue.

All of these metrics, when added together (TTD + TTE + TTF) are represented by Time to Mitigate (TTM), the full-cycle time through the outage, as represented in Figure 4-2.

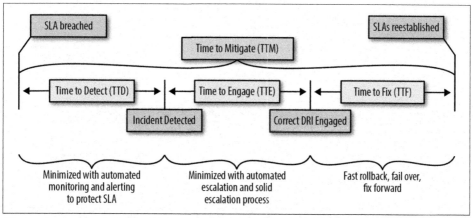

Figure 4-2. Example of an outage mitigation time breakdown

You might have different metrics, definitions, or thresholds, but all that matters is that your group agrees on the common taxonomy and measures. The agreement on taxonomy is particularly important because if the mitigation event is not agreed upon, we can have disconnects, as some teams could try to disengage before the incident is fully resolved. These become especially critical after the incident to ensure a common taxonomy during the incident review meetings to talk about where there are opportunities for improvements.

Metrics Review: If a Metric Falls in the Forest…

After we had these metrics defined, we brought our engineering leaders together to look at the key metrics that we identified as crucial to drive the virtuous cycle. We then could track how we're progressing and derive insights and create action plans in areas where we weren't hitting our goals. After defining and agreeing on metrics, we began collecting and reporting on per-service aggregates of the data to determine how we're doing, find areas and common themes for improvement, and measure the impact of improvements we made. Figure 4-3 shows an example of a dashboard to measure incident and deployment metrics. This allowed us to track metrics trends for our incident response cycle and engineer improvements just the way we engineer features into the product.

	Period 1	Period 2	Period 3	Period 4	Period 5	Period 6	Trend	Goal
Σ Incidents	XX	XX	XX	XX	XX	XX.XXX%		
Σ Major Incidents	X	X	X	X	X	X		
SLO	XX.XXX%	XX.XXX%	XX.XXX%	XX.XXX%	XX.XXX%	XX.XXX%		XX.XX%
TTD @ XX%ile	XX	XX	XX	XX	XX	XX		<X min
TTE @ XX%ile	XX	XX	XX	XX	XX	XX		<XX min
TTF @ XX%ile	XX	XXX	XX	XXX	XX	XX		<XX min
TTM @ XX%ile	XX	XXX	XX	XXX	XX	XX		<XX min
% Outages autodetected	XX%	XX%	XX%	XX%	XX%	XX%		XX%
# DRIs engaged per Bridge	XX	X	XX	X	XX	XX		X
DRI Hops	X	X	X	X	X	X		X

Top Incidents			Cause	TTD (mins)	TTM (mins)	Repair Items	Impact (reported)	Impact (Actual)
Incident in North Europe due to Code Bug			Code Bug	XX	XX	1	2	XXX Accounts impacted
Network Incident due to Configuration			Config	X	XX	4	0	X,XXX Accounts impacted

Deployment		95% of clusters		100% of clusters	
	Build Age	Build Age Trend	Build Age	Build Age Trend	
Service A	XX		XXX		
Service B	XX		XX		

Figure 4-3. SRE metrics dashboard

Notice that the incident response metrics we discussed earlier show up here: TTD, TTE, TTF, and TTM, trending by time period, and measured against goals that we had set and agreed on with service owners. If we found data was sparse, had high variability, or had major outliers, we would apply percentiles to the data to normalize it enough. We then could look at the outliers to understand them better and drive the percentiles toward 100%.

Surrogate Metrics

If you look closely at the SRE metrics dashboard, you'll notice a few metrics like Directly Responsible Individual (DRI) hops (how many on-call engineers are needed to resolve an incident) and autodetection (how many incidents are detected via monitoring). These are surrogate metrics, which are sometimes related to the top-level "Time to" metric that are more specific and actionable than the high-level metrics, but don't by themselves indicate success. We found that using surrogate metrics led to faster, more durable improvements because giving engineering managers specific action items and submetrics was a more effective way to drive action than just telling teams to "do better" and "try harder."

Exploring your data is a great way to find surrogate metrics. Looking at TTE as an example, as we investigated incidents with long engagement times, we found factors that correlated with or led to high engagement times, such as engaging many engineers to resolve a single incident. This would occur due to knowledge gaps, instrumentation gaps, or even inconsistent expectations for on-call response. To address this, we added the "#DRIs engaged per bridge" submetric, which lets us see how many DRIs are engaged on any given incident. Having fewer DRIs engaged could still result in a long response time, especially if they don't engage additional resources when they should. However, when taken together with the TTD and TTE, this is a good indication of how effective our monitoring and diagnostics are at getting the alert to the right responder early.

Similarly, while working to improve TTD, we noticed that it was 10 times higher when the outage was detected by our customers instead of being caught by monitoring. To measure this, we instrumented the autodetect rate as a surrogate metric for TTD. This doesn't mean that all autodetect incidents have good TTD, but automated detection is required to get good TTD. As is typical for surrogate metrics, automated detection is necessary, but not sufficient to achieve world-class TTD.

This is not a complete list of surrogate metrics, but just a few examples to get you started.

Repair Debt

Some of the best insight we derived during the metrics review came from the post-incident review process. There is a lot of great material out there already, so I'm not going to go deep into how to do a good postmortem (see "Further Reading" on page 41 for a few examples). I'll skip to what matters most to our metric reviews: every time we identify a bug or improvement opportunity, we log it and track it as a repair. Repair items are technology or process fixes that either prevent an outage from recurring or reduce its duration. Typically, these are broken down into short-term items and long-term items. Short-term items should be rolled out quickly (within a week) and might be a process, a script, or a hotfix. Long-term items are more durable fixes, such as more thorough code fixes (i.e., fixing a class of issue versus an instance of an issue, or fixing a class of issue across multiple product lines), creating broader process change (i.e., building and delivering incident management training across multiple organizations), or building tooling like chat bots or autoescalation/mitigation. Repair items are typically tracked in the same work management system you use for tracking product work items, but what matters is that they are recorded and reportable and distinguishable from standard product backlog.

Tracking repair items lets us incorporate operational debt into the standard engineering process and treat it just like feature work. The diagram in Figure 4-4 is a good example of what happens when we first began tracking repairs. There is usually an initial spike in debt as we start to expose previously unknown or unfocused repair actions. Then, the team adjusts its practices to incorporate repair debt into its normal rhythm of business, and the repair debt comes down. Tracking repair debt is important because these problems always existed, but until they were tracked, measured, and shared, the engineering team couldn't take action to improve the service. This helps to provide a signal for the team, together with the error budget, for how to prioritize service reliability work against feature work.

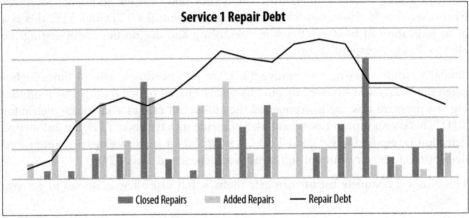

Figure 4-4. An example repair debt graph

Virtual Repair Debt: Exorcising the Ghost in the Machine

Not every movie has a Hollywood ending, and we found that not every service saw the fruits of repair item rigor. In some cases, even though repair debt was stable, the reliability month over month wasn't necessarily getting better. For these services that had stable repair debt but weren't seeing reliability improvements, we were baffled. Why weren't they improving if the repair debt was stable and appeared well attended? We dug deep into some of the data that we hadn't yet curated, did our best Sherlock Holmes impression, and found a surprising insight. Some services weren't doing a thorough RCA, and as a result they had either low RCA completion rates or RCAs without enough repairs. This meant that the repair items never made it into the backlog and the service didn't have the opportunity to improve.

This brought about a new challenge: how do we maximize the quality of a postmortem? Not only do we need to measure whether repair items were getting fixed, we also need to measure whether they were getting created in the first place. Most postmortems include a lot of text describing the problem and what was done to mitigate. We could certainly apply some machine learning to the text and try to parse out intent, but that would take a significant investment and would not be deterministic.

The simplest solution was sitting right in front of us all along in the form of the "Time to" metrics that we attach to every incident and every postmortem. Any incident that missed a time to detect, engage, or mitigate goal should have a corresponding repair item. This meant that we had to have a taxonomy in the repair process to attach engagement, diagnosis, and detection flags so that we could programmatically extract "missed repair items." We then used all of the missed repair items to measure what we called "virtual repair debt."

Visualizing virtual repair debt became a powerful tool to drive improvements. As seen in Figure 4-5, the gray line representing repair debt makes it look like the team is keeping up with the repair debt, but when you add the dotted red line that represents missed repairs, the dark-matter repair items that form virtual debt become glaringly obvious. Virtual debt is particularly important because it represents the corpus of repair items that were never logged and will end up hurting the service down the road. When there is virtual debt, the specific TTD and TTM misses will repeat over and over until they are logged and fixed.

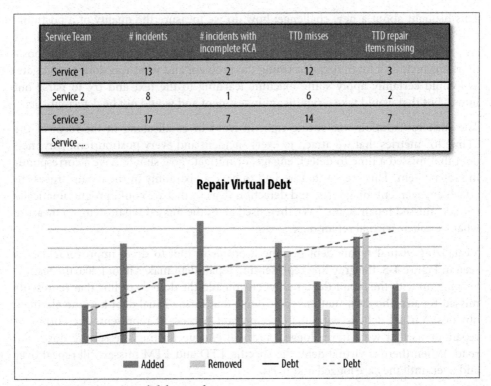

Service Team	# incidents	# incidents with incomplete RCA	TTD misses	TTD repair items missing
Service 1	13	2	12	3
Service 2	8	1	6	2
Service 3	17	7	14	7
Service ...				

Repair Virtual Debt

■ Added   ■ Removed   — Debt   - - - Debt

Figure 4-5. Repair virtual debt graph

Real-Time Dashboards: The Bread and Butter of SRE

Possibly the most important part of metrics review is bringing the metrics and insights into real-time dashboards. Looking at the data monthly or even weekly doesn't help drive change quickly enough. Every service, every component needs to be able to see in real time where they have work to do, where they are doing well, and where they can improve. This meant creating dashboards that can pivot by service, by manager, even down to the individual engineer who owns the work item.

Learnings: TL;DR

If you want to simplify everything from this chapter into a sentence, here it is: measure everything, be relentlessly curious, and don't be afraid to get dirty and wallow in your data to find the right actions to take. In many cases, getting these insights required hand curating a fair bit of data, but after we understood which metrics mattered, we could then instrument and automate them and help bring visibility to metrics that could help the services get better.

Further Reading

Blameless postmortems:

- "Blameless PostMortems and a Just Culture" (*https://codeascraft.com/2012/05/22/blameless-postmortems/*): John Allspaw, Etsy
- "Postmortem Action Items: Plan the Work and Work the Plan" (*https://www.usenix.org/conference/srecon17americas/program/presentation/lueder*): Sue Lueder and Betsy Beyer, Google
- *Beyond Blame—Learning from Failure and Success*: Dave Zwieback

Using data to derive operational insights:

- "Improving Operations Using Data Analytics" (*https://www.oreilly.com/ideas/improving-operations-using-data-analytics*): Parviz Deyhim and Arti Garg, Data-pipe
- "Incident Analysis" (*https://www.usenix.org/conference/srecon15/program/presentation/lueder*): Sue Lueder, Google
- "Measuring the Success of Incident Management at Atlassian" (*https://www.usenix.org/conference/srecon17asia/program/presentation/millar*): Gerry Millar, Atlassian
- "PDA: A Tool for Automated Problem Determination" (*https://www.usenix.org/legacy/event/lisa07/tech/full_papers/huang/huang_html/index.html*): Hai Huang, Raymond Jennings III, Yaoping Ruan, Ramendra Sahoo, Sambit Sahu, and Anees Shaikh, IBM T.J. Watson Research Center

---

Martin Check is a site reliability engineering manager on the Microsoft Azure team. He has worked on large-scale services at Microsoft for 14 years in a variety of roles, including service design and implementation, crisis response, problem management, and even leading teams through the DevOps/SRE transition. Martin is currently working as an SRE manager for global SRE teams, where he continues to leverage data insights to drive SRE improvements.

## CHAPTER 5

Working with Third Parties Shouldn't Suck

Jonathan Mercereau, traffiq corp. (formerly LinkedIn)

Over the years, the definition of Site Reliability Engineering (SRE) has evolved, but the easiest to digest is subjectively "what happens when software engineering is tasked with what used to be called 'operations.'"[1] Most Site Reliability teams consider *operations* as the applications running on their own infrastructure. These days, more and more companies rely on third parties to serve a very specific function in which they specialize. This includes things like Domain Name System (DNS), Content Delivery Network (CDN), Application Performance Management (APM), Storage, Payments, Email, Messaging (SMS), Security (such as Single Sign-On [SSO] or Two-Factor Authentication [2FA]), Log Processing, and more. Any one of these resources, if not implemented properly, is a dependency that has the capacity to bring down your site.

Are vendors black boxes that we don't control? Not necessarily. As we approach working with vendors, it's important that we apply the same suite of SRE disciplines to working with third parties in an effort to make it suck less.

Build, Buy, or Adopt?

Before we dive into the topic of working with vendors, we should discuss the decisions that would lead us to *buy* over *build* or *adopt*. Our level of involvement in this process will depend on the combination of importance and stakeholders. Determining importance is the first step in this entire process and will dictate the significance of other deciding factors, such as weight of cost, the weight of support, influencers, Service-Level Agreements (SLAs), and more.

---

1 *Site Reliability Engineering*, Introduction (*https://landing.google.com/sre/book/chapters/introduction.html*).

Establish Importance

Determining importance can be challenging for an SRE leading a project or integration. For instance, if the decision is on which JavaScript framework to use for the next version of the website, it's clear that there are going to be many stakeholders involved in the decision-making process and many more impacted, such as Data Science, Quality Assurance, Tools, and more.

However, the decision over which certificate authority (CA) to select is another story altogether. For some, the choice of certificate is as simple as saying, "Let's just use Let's Encrypt," and move ahead. There are, however, a handful of companies that must make considerations that go beyond the choice between a single name certificate and a multiname certificate.

If you're scratching your head right now, good. Let's explore this a bit more.

Depending on the SRE team, certificates might simply imply security. To other SRE teams, certificates might elicit concerns of impact on performance. Yet *other* SRE teams might question the impact to protocols and cipher suites. And beyond SRE teams comes the question of long-term ownership, integration, changes to request process, workflow, access control, revocation process, certificate rotation, and more.

Determining the importance of an integration early on will help avoid technical debt and scaling limitations down the road.

Identify Stakeholders

The smaller the company, the easier the decision-making process is. However, as companies grow, it is important to at least consider factors that will impact scale, slow growth, reduce productivity, and cause headaches down the road. Further, understanding importance also allows us to identify who might be impacted by our decisions so that they can be brought into the fold.

As SREs, we know firsthand the role collaboration plays in site reliability. The earliest SRE teams at Google were embedded with software engineering teams, provided valuable insights into scaling, and took an operational approach to building reliable services. It would only make sense that as we consider the impact of integration, we identify the stakeholders and influencers who will prove key to our project's overall success.

The sense of ownership and importance play a significant role in a project's success. It goes without saying that people don't like unplanned work and they don't like being told what to do. The earlier stakeholders are identified and consulted, the easier it will be to apply ownership and have additional people to work toward the project's success. Nothing is worse than starting a project and committing time and energy, only to have it shot down by a stakeholder whose role was not considered.

Make a Decision

After you have established importance and stakeholders, we can begin evaluating the decision to *build* or *buy*. Quite often, the build discussion is heavily dependent on the incorporation of an open source solution, which I propose is an altogether new category to be considered: *adopt*. Let's break down the differences between each option.

Build (developed in-house from scratch)
> Your needs are so custom and innovative that it cannot be done by anyone other than your company. Often, these solutions are open-sourced after battle hardening. Such examples include Kafka by LinkedIn, React by Facebook, and Envoy by Lyft.

Buy (SaaS, hosted, or licensed solution)
> Your needs are common and a paid solution exists to solve that problem.

Adopt (integration of an open source solution)
> Your needs are common and open source solutions exist.

As we deliberate whether to build, buy, or adopt, we might note that some key differences exist in when and where the money is spent. As we consider adopting an open source solution, the capital expenditure (CapEx) and operational expense (OpEx) can be difficult to predict. Evaluating and researching an open source project for a Proof-of-Concept (PoC) is relatively inexpensive; however, as the project is utilized at scale, issues such as memory utilization, computational constraints, and storage requirements can quickly exceed benchmarks captured during R&D. Additionally, skilled personnel are necessary not only for initial integration, but also for the continued operation, enhancements, and inevitable upgrades. Open source projects will have bugs that can lead to exposure to significant security vulnerabilities, memory leaks, and loss of data. In some cases, full version upgrades create incompatibilities with other integrations as a result of feature deprecation. Last, but not least, migrating between open source versions introduces *breaking changes,* often causing full configuration rewrites, loss of backward compatibility, and operational instability. These sorts of issues are generally covered in a single line item in the CapEx table, but that line item should be expanded into its own project operating expense (PrOpEx) table.

As a result, our predictions often aim low if we don't consult with an experienced project manager. In the buy case, CapEx is generally low with little integration cost, while OpEx is generally *perceived* as high—perceived because we often do not consider the personnel hours we would otherwise have to spend to produce a similarly operationally viable product. Many of the considerations involved in an open source adoption are resolved by a third-party solution, and they are on the hook for maintaining that operational stability.

Neither adopt nor buy solutions invalidate the need for documentation, maintenance, monitoring, logging, tooling, automation, and all other aspects that define a service. The difference between a PoC, a functional prototype, a Minimum Viable Product (MVP), and a first-class service with high operational integrity resembles the distance between the sun and each planet. Toward the end of this chapter, we address some of the critical facets that define a first-class service.

However, now that we're at least considering the difference between build, buy, and adopt, we can address some additional points of consideration.

Acknowledge Reality

You're a fantastic SRE. You produce eloquent code. You're a natural leader. Scalability comes naturally to you. But you aren't good at everything. It's likely that you've found a niche that allows you to excel. The next interesting project might not be something that should be built from scratch. Not because you can't, but because business decisions are rife with justifications that go beyond your personal interests. As a responsible SRE, prioritizing business objectives over personal interests can lead to success. The unfortunate reality is that working on something cool is not always what's best for business.

As we let that reality sink in, let's take a look at some other project considerations that we need to assess:

- What problem is being solved?
- How does this impact the bottom line?
- Will this impact the critical path?
- Is this a core competency?
- Maturity of a solution?
- Nice to have or need to have?
- Will this have continued adoption?
- What vulnerabilities are exposed?
- What is our CapEx?
- What are our OpExes?
- What are our PrOpExes?
- What are our abandonment expenses?
- Who are our customers?
- To whom are we a customer?
- Did we identify ancillary benefits?
- What is the delta of inception to production?
- What is the integration timeline?

- How will this be monitored?
- Who's responsible long term?
- What does escalation look like?
- What are the SLAs? Is that critical?
- What are the risks/benefits?
- What is our fallback?
- How to measure success?
- How to tolerate failure?
- What happens if I get hit by a truck?

These points are only a handful of the considerations to keep in the back of your mind when debating whether to buy or adopt. Going through each consideration with your team depends on the significance of the integration. As we consider buy options, it's worth expanding on a few of these points to provoke additional thoughts that you might not have considered.

Is this a core competency?

Always weigh whether a solution/integration under consideration is both your core competency as well as the company's core competency.

Third parties offer specialized solutions and have teams of engineers working to expand their value proposition by building additional features and services. A Software as a Service (SaaS) solution for log aggregation might be more effective in the long run than trying to adopt an open source solution such as Elasticsearch. You have to decide whether Elasticsearch is really something that you, your team, and your company need to focus on.

Integration timeline?

However long you think it's going to take to complete an integration, double it. Then add a little more. A PoC for an open source solution might be easy to implement, but this does not mean that the project is production ready. The definition of *production readiness* for SREs should encompass testing/staging, monitoring, logging, configuration management, deployment procedure, disaster recovery, and beyond.

With things like CDN, DNS, monitoring, CA, and messaging solutions, implementation of these production readiness factors can prove to be incredibly challenging, and in some cases, impossible. Fortunately, with third-party integrations, especially at larger companies, a variety of teams will evaluate the solution as we work on the integration. You should expect that Legal, Security, and Procurement[2] teams will play a role during the purchase process. Each of these teams will introduce its own processes, which can delay getting the third-party solution into production.

Project Operating Expense and Abandonment Expense

Beyond consideration for the initial cost to purchase goods and services (CapEx, such as hardware, software, and one-time licenses) and the ongoing costs to run and maintain (OpEx, such as monthly server prices, recurring service fees), additional expense categories should be a part of the consideration process.

Project Operating Expense (PrOpEx)
> Implementation costs for a solution. Typically a single line item in the CapEx table, implementation costs can prove to be a more significant factor in the decision over build, buy, or adopt choices. Implementation costs to consider include services that will be utilized as the solution is implemented, such as legal fees, vulnerability probing, additional monitoring and performance infrastructure, and professional or consulting services. These costs can also expose overlooked OpEx costs.

Abandonment expense (AbEx)
> This is the cost to abandon a solution to implement another altogether. This is sometimes referred to by the softer term *migration cost*. There is always the potential that adopting an open source solution might result in abandonment in order to buy a fleshed-out SaaS solution, or vice versa. Costs will differ between abandonment scenarios. In the *buy-to-adopt* scenario, you might be required to pay out contractual obligations such as monthly usage commitments in addition to the incurred costs of restarting a project. In the *adopt-to-buy* scenario, cost is less of an issue; however, time is a much larger factor. In the previous section, we saw that Legal, Security, and Procurement processes can prolong time to production. It's in our best interest to plan accordingly and abandon early.

> You should consider AbEx throughout the lifetime of a project. Working with third parties means that we should also consider the *buy-to-buy* abandonment scenario, as well—that is, leaving one vendor to use a cheaper, more robust vendor's solution. If you're not careful, one vendor's custom solution could cause *vendor lock-in*, ultimately increasing abandonment expense. Vendor lock-in can also tip the scales in the vendor's favor when it comes time to renegotiate contracts.

---

2 Procurement teams are the experts in handling of purchase orders and subcontracts. They purchase the goods and services required for the project and company initiatives. They pay the bills to keep the website on, but also ensure that legal and business obligations are met.

Case Study

Although LinkedIn worked with a variety of third parties for DNS, CDNs, monitoring, CAs, and the like, we always considered whether a vendor's solution would cause us to be locked in to a solution. To a less experienced engineer, DNS and CDN appear to be straightforward solutions for steering your users to your home page and accelerating your content, respectively. However, sales engineers at third parties often push features that make their product unique and cool. Even though these are often great features, they are not feasible with competing vendors. Some generic examples of this include Geo-steering provided by a DNS provider or Edge Side Includes (ESI) by CDN/Dynamic Site Acceleration (DSA) providers.

Let's dive deeper into an example. ESI allows for caching of reusable portions of a page—such as title bars, menus, footers, and so on—to be stitched together in the final delivery at the edge. Although this solution can marginally reduce page load times or improve load on origin servers, ESI implementation is inconsistently implemented across providers.[3] After you begin using one solution and its unique features, your cost to undo new and evolving workflows begins to outweigh the cost to implement a competing third party or implement alternate solutions such as server-side includes, alternate compression techniques, or client-side includes/scripting.

After deliberating the risks and benefits to every solution, you may reach the decision to buy. Therefore, it should come as no surprise to the higher-ups that there's work involved in setting up the third party beyond simple configuration. SREs have an obligation to build world-class solutions, and to that end, we should explore some best practices to move third parties from being *ancillary* to your tech stack to being an *extension* of it.

Third Parties as First-Class Citizens

In many organizations, you hear the term "first-class citizen" being thrown around in reference to some mission-critical service—for example, auth/login or ads. Rarely will you hear "third party" and "first-class citizen" in the same sentence. By and large, third parties are treated as ancillary to the tech stack. That sentiment is to be expected —if you're paying another company for its products, features, and services, it's that company's responsibility to manage its SLAs. However, your end users (your customers) do not necessarily share that sentiment, nor are they as forgiving. For all intents and purposes, your third-party integrations are an extension of your company.

---

3 Several third-party CDN providers offer ESI solutions. Some providers offer basic ESI support based on Specification 1.0 (*https://www.w3.org/tr/esi-lang*), while others offer extensions and custom solutions.

When They're Down, You're Down

Third-party integrations take many forms. As we integrate with third-party solutions, it's important to define how these can have an impact on our end users. In Figure 5-1, there are a few third-party integration points that have *direct* and *indirect* impacts to end-user experience.

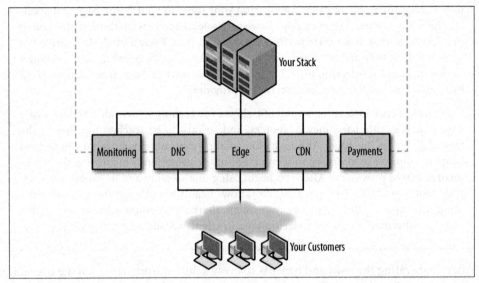

Figure 5-1. Third parties can fit anywhere around the edge of your tech stack

Direct impact

Quite often, the third-party providers that we work with have a direct impact on site availability, site reliability, and performance. In fact, these third parties are obviously impactful to the overall reliability. Here is a short list of providers with direct impact:

- DNS is the first system that end users experience. When DNS is down, you're down.
- Edge products, such as site accelerators, wide-area firewall, forward proxies/load balancers, and so on, can suffer congestion issues, human configuration error, and routing failures.
- CDNs for static objects, such as JavaScript and stylesheets, play a role in *perceived* user experience; improper configuration can lead to ineffective cacheability and high page load times, leading to increased bounce rates. The ability to

diagnose and triage performance has become increasingly complicated with Single-Page Application (SPA) frameworks.[4]

Indirect impact

Some providers impact site reliability in less obvious ways. Based on experience, these are third parties that process transactions on the backend of the technology stack. The following are examples of providers with indirect impact:

- Payment processors outages—for instance, failed API key rotation or incorrect billing codes—should not delay user experience. An optimistic approach might use previous billing history to indicate future payment processing success and will simply queue the transaction.

- Synthetic and Real-User Monitoring (RUM) are necessary for telemetry; however, use caution when utilizing either for automation.[5]

- SMS and email integrations generally have no direct touchpoints between your end users and your tech stack. However, end users have come to expect instant gratification; therefore, undelivered payment receipts or delayed two-factor verification codes will lead to a negative perception of your company.

SREs are not only seeking excellent uptimes, but also a consistent user experience overall. A theoretically simple mitigation strategy for mission-critical services is to establish redundancy. Whether direct or indirect, these mission-critical third-party integrations should be treated as first-class citizens and run like any other service in your tech stack.

But if third parties are categorized as black boxes, we shouldn't expect much from them in terms of data, right? That's simply not true in modern day. More and more third parties are building APIs that allow us to take advantage of running their infra-

---

4 SPA frameworks dynamically rewrite the current page rather than reloading the page from the server; that is, SPAs use client-side rendering instead of server-side rendering. They do so by loading HTML, JavaScript, and stylesheets in a single page load and caching those objects locally in the browser. Content is then loaded dynamically via WebSockets, polling over AJAX, server-sent events, or event-triggered AJAX calls. For a cached SPA, traditional page load timing using Navigation Timing API is incredibly low; however, the page is likely unusable without the dynamic content. Triggering a Resource Timing API in modern browsers well after expected page load times can help with the ability to diagnose and triage user experience issues.

5 Use of monitoring-based automation is growing among large companies. Synthetic monitoring solutions utilize a wide dispersion of nodes running tests on set intervals. Automation relying on consecutive event triggers from synthetic test nodes can be unwieldy and inconsistent, especially between geographies. Instead, triggers based on event consensus among test nodes can yield better results. RUM can be just as unwieldy for larger sites because the amount of data is much larger. A more surgical approach to automation is required for working with RUM-based automation.

structure as code, which means we are able to manage configuration, reporting, and a suite of other features to run our third-party products more like services.

Running the Black Box Like a Service

Third-party solutions are not like the services you run in your tech stack; therefore, the consensus view is that they're black boxes—you put stuff in and get stuff out. Each third-party vendor offers a set of products and features that provide some value propositions. Depending on the vendor, its solution could very well be a black box. However, many modern vendors have come to understand the need for transparency and have built APIs to facilitate integrations. Thus, rather than stamping a vendor as a black box, we should consider a vendor as being on a spectrum.

We can use Figure 5-2 as a way to determine where on the spectrum a third-party vendor might land. Let's take two vendors. Vendor A might have great reporting, tons of monitoring capabilities, simple configurations, access to a robust set of APIs, and high-caliber documentation to maximize self-service. Vendor B could have the best solution with simple configurations through an intuitive portal, but if we're looking for the ability to utilize Vendor B to help automate processes, limited API access will prevent us from fully implementing its solution. In this example, Vendor A is a very open box, and Vendor B is a more closed solution, perhaps closer to a black box.

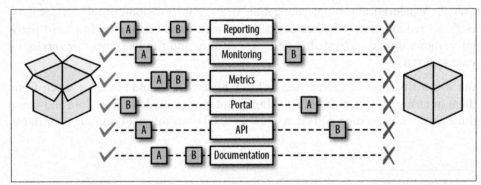

Figure 5-2. Not all third-party solutions are black box

It's often hard to determine which part of a third-party integration could possibly be treated like a custom-built service. To that end, we need to define the top-level functionality that we are attempting to achieve. After we understand that functionality well, we should refine the activities needed to manage that integration to yield a set of predictable and actionable states. Some of these states might be the following:

Fully operational
    All vendor operations working as expected.

Vendor solution is operational but performance is degraded; for example, CDN is delivering content, but objects are being delivered slowly.

Operational but limited visibility
Vendor solution is operational but telemetry does not reflect operational state. An example of this with a third-party integration could be reporting API or Log Delivery Service outage if you rely on third-party data to flag service state.

Operational but API down
Vendor solution is operational but its configuration API and/or portal are down. Vendors typically segregate configuration from operation. Fortunately, we can still be up, operationally, but this might create a bottleneck.

Hard down
Vendor solution is not operational.

With third parties, some additional states might include portal outages, processing delays, data consistency issues, regional performance degradation, regional service outages, and so on. The level of observability we have will dictate our success when we're dealing with these states. Let's dig into what it takes to help manage these states.

Service-Level Indicators, Service-Level Objectives, and SLAs

We can't talk about running a service without talking about Service-Level Indicators (SLI), Service-Level Objectives (SLO), and SLAs. But how do you capture SLIs on services that run outside of your tech stack that are seemingly out of your control? This is where we need to be creative.

SLIs on black boxes

SLIs for services within our own tech stack are objectively easy to collect. In many cases, it's a matter of running a daemon to collect operating system/virtual machine/container stats or a library/SDK that we import to emit metrics to our metrics collection cluster. Easy enough. Vendors run their services within their own tech stack. They will not typically emit server-level metrics; however, they do offer a wealth of data in a couple of different forms.

Polling API informs SLIs. If your vendor does not offer a robust reporting API, walk away. Reporting APIs will be a first step toward building your SLIs. You should not, however, trust these nor use them as if they were real time. Many vendors will try to keep their reporting APIs as close to "real time" as possible; however, there is *always* a processing delay. Any provider running a distributed network will likely suffer from some reporting latency—they will need to aggregate, process, and provide a flexible

API—and this all comes at a cost that is not necessarily beneficial to their bottom line.

Real-time data informs SLIs.   As technology has progressed, vendors are beginning to offer real-time logs delivered via Syslog, HTTP POST, or SFTP upload. In addition, log processing companies have partnered with these vendors to facilitate integration and dashboards. With these integrations in place, we can see the paradigm shift from *the vendor is a black box* to *the vendor is a partner*. With the data on hand, we are allowed to lift the weight of vendor dependency to becoming more self-reliant. If real-time data is offered as a paid service, ask that it be free. Ultimately, you, as an SRE, will utilize this to troubleshoot issues, thus alleviating their customer support.

Synthetic monitoring informs SLIs.   Trust but verify. Our providers can give us a wealth of data, and it's unlikely that our vendors would hide anything. But for services that we run that have a very broad scope, such as CDN or DNS, it can often be extremely difficult to triage and diagnose an issue. Synthetic monitoring (APM solutions such as Catchpoint and Keynote) provides an additional layer of detail that could not be seen through service metrics alone. Synthetic tests will often reveal configuration issues, delivery latency, cache efficiency, compression handling, and corner cases that would be difficult to find with log data alone. For SREs that own CDN and DNS, this is becoming critical. And if you're wondering, synthetic monitoring providers offer both real-time and polling APIs, so you can do more cool stuff with test results.

RUM informs SLIs.   Nothing is better than real-user data. With advancements made in modern browsers, there is a wealth of information that we can garner from navigation timing and resource timing APIs (client side). RUM can tell you all sorts of information about how users are experiencing your third-party services, which includes CDN, DNS, CA, payment processors, ads, and more.

SLOs

SREs typically focus on meeting their SLOs—the agreement between SRE and product owners for how often a service's SLIs can be out of spec. As an SRE working with a provider, SLOs can be difficult to calculate and even more difficult to define. It's not simply a matter of carrying over the SLA from the vendor. SREs responsible for third-party integrations might be dealing with multiple vendors simultaneously and support a broad range of product teams, as is the case with payments, ads, CDN, and DNS. In this scenario, the product owners end up being your sibling SRE teams. The SLOs we define in this scenario allow our sibling SRE teams to calculate risk and formulate error budgets.

Negotiating SLAs with vendors.   When you first sign up for service with your vendor, you sign a lot of things, including a Master Service Agreement (MSA), which covers all of the vendor's products and services, and an SLA. Historically, SREs haven't had to work with MSAs or SLAs, but with the evolution of the SRE role and broadened scope of work, these agreements are more commonplace for the SRE. That said, if you're big enough to have a legal team and a procurement team, be sure they are in the loop before signing anything.

Often, vendor SLAs provide credits for service when they fail to meet their end of the agreement. Most SLAs include 99.5% uptime. Unless there's a catastrophic event, these SLA targets are easily met. Things get tricky when we begin to consider SLAs that meet specific needs, such as throughput for large object delivery on a CDN, indexing latency for our log processing companies, or metric accuracy for our synthetic monitoring providers.

Use the same SLIs and SLOs to inform your SLAs to hold vendors accountable for their service availability and performance. Your procurement team will appreciate the transparency and validation of their hard work.

Playbook: From Staging to Production

With many of the services we run, we have to adhere to some sort of playbook—a means for running our service in production. This involves a detailed explanation of what the service is intended to do, how to test it, how to deploy it, and how to deal with it should things go sideways.

Testing and staging

Quarterly releases are ancient history. These days, Continuous Integration (CI) and Continuous Deployment (CD) are standard. We've become accustomed to maintaining a deployment pipeline similar to one that is triggered by committing code to master and allowing our automation to run a suite of unit tests, followed by deployment to a staging environment, followed by Selenium testing, followed by canary deployment, and finally production deployment.

Third-party integrations can pose a different set of challenges with regard to properly testing functionality within staging environments. It's unlikely that CDN, DNS, certificates, and edge proxy configurations are considered as part of a CI/CD pipeline. It's even less likely that your staging environment resembles production, if that staging environment even exists. Unfortunately, as these products have been seen as ancillary, little attention has been given to how these technologies play a role in the deployment process.

With the emergence of new players in the CDN, DNS, certificate, edge, and APM space, progress is being made as to how we can configure and manage their respective products via code. As a result, replication of environments has become more feasible. Additionally, some vendors offer some form of staging environment. For example, Akamai offers configuration staging as a standard part of its configuration deployment procedure; the staged configuration is triggered by modifying hostname resolution to target the staging hosts. Staging environments ultimately encourage the creation of unit, regression, and Selenium test regimens.

Case Study

For LinkedIn's CDN integrations, we maintained a suite of regression tests that were executed before and after every configuration change and mapped to a set of content profiles (static images versus JavaScript versus stylesheets). Even though a set of content might have a shared origin server[6] and edge hostname/configuration,[7] the context-path mapped to different underlying services with a variety of caching headers. Sprites and logos rarely change and are highly cacheable; therefore, query parameters can be ignored, implement long expiries, and disable edge compression. On the contrary, to optimize delivery performance, JavaScript was minified and concatenated to take advantage of a single connection. Further, JavaScript concatenation required query parameters included as part of the cache key, a long expiry, and support for edge compression.

The suite of regression tests validated cacheability, retention rules, negative testing (what happens when something goes wrong; e.g., HTTP 404 or HTTP 500), error handling, compression, and protocol because they vary between each content profile. In addition to running regression tests before and after configuration changes, these tests were also executed periodically. This allowed us to detect modifications to the underlying services acting as origins, thus allowing us to get ahead of any major performance or reliability issues.

Monitoring

There are two categories of monitoring that we should consider with third-party solutions: *integration monitoring* (is the integration working?) and *impact monitoring* (what impact does the solution have on our users?). Obviously, we want to ensure that the integrated service (CDN, message processor, etc.) is stable; hence, we should be looking at whether the third party is up or down. Additionally, we want to know when the integrated service is dropping connections, becoming overloaded, or introducing processing delays. Some third-party integrations rely entirely on APIs; thus, monitoring the integration is a bit more straightforward, as is the case with an SMS or email provider.

---

6 An origin server in the context of CDNs is simply the source of the original content.

7 A CDN edge hostname generally maps to a single configuration/protocol combination; that configuration contains a mapping to the origin server and content rules. Conditional rules (such as request headers or context-path) can trigger alternate origin server selection, caching rules, header modification, and so on.

Impact monitoring is a bit difficult. When we relinquish some control of our site to third parties—for example, content delivery by CDN or steering to data centers by DNS providers—monitoring a third party's impact on our users becomes a bit more challenging. To understand how end users are impacted by these critical path integrations, we should rely on synthetic monitoring or RUM.

Uses for synthetic monitoring. Synthetic monitoring is a dimension of end-user experience testing that relies on probes or nodes that run canned tests at regular intervals. Many third parties specialize in this type of APM solution; these include Catchpoint, Keynote, Gomez, Pingdom, and Thousand Eyes. This type of monitoring is great for things as simple as testing whether an endpoint is up or down, or as complicated as transactional workflows.

Here are some things to do:

- Utilize real-time push APIs rather than polling for aggregated test data. Polling APIs will cause delayed Mean Time to Detect (MTTD) if you're using synthetic tests to identify failures due to reporting aggregation delays. Push APIs can ensure that you get the raw results.

- Create multiple synthetic tests for each CDN/edge configuration. Each CDN can behave differently within the same region, and synthetic tests can possibly reflect regional performance and reliability issues.

- Monitor for content errors such as HTTP error codes or connection resets or timeouts on child assets (not just base page) to better understand how a CDN provider is handling your content.

- Run DNS tests against authoritative name servers so that you remain aware of issues related to your traffic steering; testing against default resolvers will not isolate issues to your DNS provider(s).

- Ensure good test node coverage over your highest-traffic geographies and maintain low test intervals to ensure maximum test data. This will allow you to flag for errors from a consensus of servers over a smaller rolling window.

And here are some pitfalls to avoid:

- Don't rely on polling of third-party reporting APIs. This data is generally aggregated.

- Don't configure long test intervals to save money. Long test execution intervals will limit granularity. Because each node will generally run a test only once within a given interval, it's unlikely that monitoring consecutive events from a single node will flag failures. Instead, consensus for a test over a given interval might prove more fruitful.

- Don't run static page tests to monitor your CDNs. Synthetic test nodes will likely hit the same CDN edge Point-of-Presence (PoP) repeatedly and artificially improve cache efficiency anyway. Therefore, static page testing will tell you only how well a CDN serves cached content; this does not represent how well a CDN serves content from origin to end user.

- Don't pick nodes for the sake of picking nodes. Some nodes might not be on eyeball networks (such as Comcast or Time Warner); instead, nodes sit on Backbone networks in data centers or peering facilities. Performance data from backbone networks might not be a reflection of what real eyeball networks experience.

- Don't select nodes that are regionally disparate from your actual users. Selecting a node in Timbuktu when most of your customers are in North America is simply illogical.

Uses for RUM.   RUM also falls within the dimension of end-user experience testing. The key distinction is that RUM is executed on the client side. The improvements in browser APIs have allowed for enhanced reporting data. We now have access to navigation timing APIs—page load time—and more interestingly, resource timing APIs —per object load times—across most modern browsers. The same third parties that offer a synthetic monitoring solution often offer a complementary RUM solution in the form of a JavaScript beacon.

Here are some things to do:

- Take advantage of both navigation and resource timing APIs to pinpoint content delivery issues.

- If using vendor-agnostic hostnames (hostnames that are not vendor specific), implement a custom header to identify which third-party vendor was responsible for object delivery.

- If your company has a Data Science/Performance team, it is likely that real-user data is already being collected and processed through a data pipeline. They might be enticed to enhance that data pipeline to include enhanced delivery details from resource timing APIs.

- Ensure Security and Privacy teams evaluate the RUM beacons that you are considering using. This is especially important because RUM can expose personally identifiable information (PII), cookies, and IP details. This might run afoul of the

EU's General Data Protection Regulation (GDPR)[8] compliance rules, which went into effect on May 25, 2018.

Again, here are some pitfalls to avoid:

- Don't reinvent the wheel; if you have a Data Science or other team concerned about RUM, it might already have a data pipeline[9] that we can utilize. Similarly, Google, Amazon Web Services (AWS), and others offer solutions for message queueing and streaming.

- Don't rely on third-party APIs as a conduit for monitoring third-party health. Third parties generally do an excellent job of performing what they're paid to do; however, their reporting APIs are not necessarily their core competency. If you rely on third-party reporting APIs, you are likely relying on data that is stale or inaccurate. This is because of data aggregation delays, processing delays, data pruning, and repackaging of that data for your consumption. Instead, we want to rely on as much real data as possible, such as data that can be pulled from logs in real time.

Case Study

Many large organization use a combination of synthetic and RUM to diagnose issues. While at LinkedIn, my team was responsible for synthetic monitoring, and we grew the suite of tests 15-fold to cover all products and detect issues. Synthetic monitoring was utilized to identify content delivery issues in a variety of ways for CDN and DNS and was a great secondary resource for identifying issues with configuration changes.

Tooling

Tooling is a critical part of our third-party integration, especially in a larger organization. As an SRE responsible for third-party integrations, we want to avoid being a choke point as much as possible. To that end, we should build systems that take advantage of everything the third party has to offer via APIs. These APIs facilitate integrations by allowing you to build the tools needed to effectively manage your third-party integrations. As these APIs are employed, we will want to consider AbEx and avoid the use of custom features that could create vendor lock-in. We can see an

---

8 GDPR applies to all foreign companies and extends current data protection regulations for all EU residents. You can find more information at *https://www.eugdpr.org*.

9 Many companies use a data pipeline for interapplication messaging following a publish–subscribe (pub–sub) architecture to trigger events. These pipelines are often also utilized for streaming data, such as page views, application logs, or real-user data.

example of this in CDN purge APIs—some vendors utilize surrogate keys, some utilize some form of regular expression, some utilize wildcards, and some utilize batching. Any of these implementations into our regular workflow could cause an issue if we need to replace or add another vendor's solution.

Further removing us from being a choke point, we want to avoid any integration that requires we play a role in access control. Managing access to vendor portals for every engineer is overly cumbersome and has the potential to lead to security issues and technical debt.

Finally, as we create tooling around our vendor's API, it's critical that we consider abandonment. Try to maintain a modular architecture to support a variety of third parties. This layer of abstraction allows for additional providers and swapability should a third-party vendor need to be replaced.

Case Study

For years, LinkedIn has worked with upward of six CDNs and three DNS providers. To prevent becoming a choke point, we implemented tools that allowed for tedious, manual processes to be implemented across all providers uniformly. Tasks such as content purge, DNS record changes, and reporting data are handled via centralized systems. Requests are abstracted and data is normalized to maximize implementations across each provider.

Automation

As an extension of tooling, we want to be able to automate some of the functionality of our third-party solutions as much as possible. The possibilities here are endless and fully depend on how you make use of your third party's APIs. To give you an idea of what we can do, let's look at the following examples:

Automating content removal on account closure
> When a user closes their account, certain privacy laws apply and require that user PII is deleted. As a result, it's possible to utilize your company's data pipeline (or similar message queue) to identify such events to automate the image removal process. This will be necessary for GDPR compliance.

Automating data center/endpoint selection
> In the event that a critical service is down behind an endpoint, we can use DNS APIs to steer traffic away from the affected endpoint.

Automating certificate renewal
> In the event that certificates are ready to expire, you could easily use your CA's API to reinstall certificates to your endpoints rather than relying on manual intervention or outage.

Logging

Third-party reporting APIs are generally not great. Often, the reporting data we receive via pull APIs are aggregated, processed, and scrubbed. Aggregation delays are common with pull API and should not necessarily be used for raising alerts. As an SRE, we need to know what's happening now, not what happened 15 minutes ago. To that end, third-party integrations have often been looked at as black boxes with little to no visibility into their operations.

But times have changed. Many third parties offer real-time data feeds that include all sorts of useful data; CDNs are offering delivery receipts for every object; DNS providers are offering query data; and synthetic monitoring providers offer granular test data.

The benefit to all of this available data is that we're able to build with it as we see fit. However, this is also a risk. Just because we have the data does not mean that it's entirely useful. As we utilize real-time logging data, we need to be sure we're utilizing what we need to supplement our monitoring as well as provide a way to track down issues. For example, CDN logs can include a browser type, extension details, client IP details, cookies, and other request headers. Much of this is unnecessary for most applications, such as regional isolation of HTTP response codes.

Finally, logging can be absurdly expensive. Not only do some vendors charge for the delivery of this data, but you're also responsible for consuming, indexing, processing, and retaining it. This can be a large undertaking in and of itself, and you should approach it with caution.

Disaster planning

Although we don't like to think about it, working with a third-party vendor incurs some risk. As part of our playbook, we will need to consider what to do when the vendor is *hard down*. Disaster planning should include considerations for the removal of the third party altogether. You will likely have to consider the following:

- Maintaining an additional (as active or standby) provider
- Having capacity to serve requests ourselves
- Queueing requests to be handled later

Removal of a CDN might require that we accept a certain amount of latency. Removal of a payment processor might require an optimistic approach to ensure a good customer experience. Some delay in a welcome message or payment receipt via email might not be entirely noticeable to an end user. Remember, slow is better than down.

Communication

With third-party integrations, it's important to not live in a silo. Talking to a solutions or sales engineer actually plays to your advantage for discussing product enhancements, discovering unknown or underutilized features, understanding their product roadmap, and preparing third parties for future events such as product releases. Additionally, it pays to maintain bidirectional communication to align priorities. Third-party vendors should be under NDA; therefore, it's helpful to communicate any upcoming projects that might alter the relationship.

Establishing a regular call cadence can be useful but might not be ideal for all SREs. Often, these calls are tedious are time-consuming, and can conflict with production issues. Additionally, there is a bit of organization required, especially when you're working with multiple vendors. To that end, it's often a good idea to work with a project manager or someone similar who can facilitate these calls and keep detailed notes. Support from a project manager will help you keep your vendors aligned with your team's and company's priorities.

Decommissioning

When it comes time to decommission a service, we consider all of our dependencies. The same is true of dealing with third parties. We obviously need to consider removal of tooling, service monitoring, alerts, and data collection services/endpoints. In addition, we are obliged to consider a few other dependencies that play a role in the integration.

Sometimes, termination is not as simple as stating "you're fired." Terms of the termination are generally stated in your service agreements. If you're deciding to terminate a contract for financial reasons, you might be able to negotiate in advance of termination. In these cases, use caution when evaluating contracts that include Most Favored Customer (MFC) clauses because these often make it harder to negotiate a better deal. Some agreements also allow for autorenewal months prior to a contract's end date. Your legal and procurement teams might have prevented this, but it's important to look at the contract and discuss termination with them.

Communication obviously played a role in the purchase and ongoing relationship of your third-party integration. Communication is even more critical during contract termination. If, for instance, the third party was not meeting SLAs but that was never communicated, it's not necessarily fair to that vendor and could prove costly for the third-party sales teams.

The tech industry is small, and stories of a bad breakup will haunt you and your company. These stories could play a role in your future integration attempts. Sales organizations remember which customers were most difficult to work with, and salespeople move between companies, especially within the same industry. Failure to communi-

rate during the decommissioning process can tarnish reputations and complicate future relationships.

The best way to avoid this is to communicate your intent to terminate a third party well in advance of the end date—at least a quarter ahead. This gives the third-party sales team an opportunity to rectify any problems that might have persisted during the integration life cycle. We vote with our dollars. Losing a large enough customer can incentivize a third party to prove themselves.

Closing Thoughts

Many SREs consider working with third-party solutions to be a disappointment from both an intellectual-challenge and career-path perspective. Not only would we rather solve large problems by building our own custom, in-house solutions, but we're often encouraged to do so to advance our professional trajectory. However, custom solutions are not necessarily in the best interest of our company or our end users.

Quite often, buy options offer as much of a challenge as the build or adopt options. We should shift our mindset away from third-party solutions getting in the way of our creativity and instead consider how a third-party solution plays a role in end-user experience and site reliability.

As we close out, you should take the following points with you:

- Third parties are an *extension* of your stack, not *ancillary*.
- If it's critical path, treat it like a service.
- Consider *abandonment* during the life cycle of an integration.
- The quality of your third-party integration depends on good communication.

Jonathan Mercereau has spent his career leading teams and architecting resilient, fault tolerant, and performant solutions working with the biggest players in DNS, CDN, Certificate Authority, and Synthetic Monitoring. Chances are, you've experienced the results of his work, from multi-CDN and optimizing streaming algorithms at Netflix to all multi-vendor solutions and performance enhancements at LinkedIn. In 2016, Jonathan cofounded a SaaS startup, traffiq corp (https://traffiq.io), to bring big company traffic engineering best practices, orchestration, and automation to the broader web.

## CHAPTER 6

How to Apply SRE Principles Without Dedicated SRE Teams

Björn Rabenstein and Matthias Rampke, SoundCloud Ltd.

Often, mid-sized organizations find themselves in a position in which a relatively small number of engineers must develop and run a relatively large number of diverse features.

SoundCloud has grown into exactly that situation. With each new feature added to the original monolithic Ruby on Rails code base, adding the next feature became more difficult. So around 2012, we began a gradual move to a microservices architecture. SoundCloud engineers have talked a lot about the various challenges that needed to be tackled for such a move to succeed.[1] In this chapter, we explore lessons learned from reliably running hundreds of services at SoundCloud with a much smaller number of engineers.

SREs to the Rescue! (and How They Failed)

In 2012, SoundCloud happened to hire a couple of former Google SREs. Although dramatically smaller in scale, SoundCloud was moving toward technological patterns not so different from what larger internet companies had been doing for a while. By extension, it was an obvious move to also run those systems in the same way Google does. We tried "SRE by the book," except that back then there was no actual book.

---

1 The SoundCloud backstage blog (*https://developers.soundcloud.com/blog/*) is a good starter to learn more.

A Matter of Scale in Terms of Headcount

What is the smallest reasonable size of an SRE team? Because SREs ought to be on-call, the team needs to be large enough for at least one on-call rotation. Following the best practices for on-call rotations,[2] we end up with a minimum team size of eight. For organizations of a similar size as SoundCloud—that is, roughly 100 engineers—even that one SRE team of minimal size would already comprise 5 to 10 percent of the total engineering population. Doubling or tripling this percentage would not be feasible, which limits us to at most one SRE team. For an even smaller organization size, the headcount requirement of a dedicated SRE team appears to be prohibitive. At Google, with two orders of magnitude more engineers, there are obviously many SRE teams dedicated to certain areas, like Search or Ads, supporting a limited number of development teams.[3] The one SRE team SoundCloud could accommodate would be in charge of everything! However, SoundCloud needs to serve a very diverse set of features to different groups of users: listeners want to stream music; creators want to upload and manage their tracks; rights holders want reports and ultimately money; advertisers want to manage their campaigns. In fact, SoundCloud already had a catch-all on-call rotation, staffed by a team called *SysOps*. Even with fairly stable, mature services (and SoundCloud's services at that time were far from that), the large number of moving parts would have led to an unsustainable pager load, violating the goal of keeping toil below 50% of each engineer's time.[4] On top of that, the wide diversity of involved services made it unlikely that the on-call systems engineer could react competently to a given page. The usual reaction to a page was to identify the right team to which to escalate. We had to conclude that, despite being large enough to sustain a dedicated SRE team, our feature diversity effectively put us into the same situation as smaller organizations: we could not just copy Google SRE verbatim, we had to adjust the approach to our circumstances.

The Embedded SRE

In a first attempt to apply SRE principles and reduce the pressure on the SysOps team on call for everything, we embedded SREs into the backend development teams. SoundCloud has always had a strong culture of software engineers controlling the deployment of their work. This was partially a holdover from the very early days when there was neither an operations team nor an on-call rotation. Later, it was perpetuated as part of a deliberate management strategy that optimizes for long-term velocity in delivering features.

---

2 *Site Reliability Engineering: How Google Runs Production Systems*, Chapter 11 (*https://landing.google.com/sre/book/chapters/being-on-call.html*).

3 Ibid., Introduction (p. 125).

4 Ibid., Chapter 5 (*http://bit.ly/2LQ4XMQ*)

The approach of embedding SREs was doomed by the numbers: because development teams consisted of no more than 10 engineers, there was at most one SRE assigned to each of them, following the assumption that about 10% of engineers would be SREs.

In this environment, individual SREs had very little leverage with which to influence the design and technical direction of new services. Even though some of them had soaked up the concept at Google, most of the other engineers and managers had not, and did not know what to do with that engineer who showed up one day and proclaimed to be "their SRE now." In most cases, they were either ignored or treated as yet another backend engineer, but working with them was not seen as an opportunity to improve reliability or productivity.

Being embedded, they also could not work together as a team on the kind of impactful, strategic projects that would later provide a framework for empowering the development teams.

You Build It, You Run It

At this point, we had to try something new. We embraced what was already present in our cultural DNA: *you build it, you run it*. Or, as we sometimes like to put it: true DevOps, where there are no separate dev and ops teams anymore and not even designated dev or ops roles within a team. Arguably, this is contrary to fundamentals of SRE. After all, an SRE team *is* an operations team on some level, albeit with the premise of solving ops concerns with the mindset and the toolbox of software engineers. To successfully apply SRE principles in our scenario, we needed to instill the SRE mindset into everybody.

The Deployment Platform

Very early in our migration to microservices, we learned that our processes and infrastructure were not ready for the resulting large number of services. Each service required dedicated servers, the configuration management code to support them, and a deploy procedure to actually get code changes out.

Application developers would deploy the code but did not control the infrastructure. Servers for new or existing services were provisioned exclusively by the SysOps team. For each new service, we needed to write configuration management and deployment scripts.[5] This led to friction and long cycle times for bringing up new services or for scaling out existing ones. For example, adding more servers to the Rails monolith, at

---

5 Because of our background in Ruby, we chose Chef for configuration management early on. Ruby services were usually deployed using Capistrano. As we began experimenting with alternatives to the Ruby on Rails monolith, many more technologies and methods came into play.

the time still the biggest single service by far, required multiple hand-offs between SysOps and the backend development team to provision the servers, add an initial set of configuration management to prepare for the deployment, deploy the code, and then change configuration management to actually create the processes.

To deal with this situation, a handful of engineers had already begun to create a container-based deployment platform that would empower all developers to build, deploy, and operate their services. It was, by design, superficially similar to the popular Heroku Platform as a Service. It supported 12-factor applications (*https:// 12factor.net/*), which was luckily not a big step for many existing services. To build a new version and make it ready to deploy, developers would push to a Git repository. This made the deployment system immediately accessible to application developers without the steep learning curve of configuration management. Its constraints shaped the design of applications and made it easy to do the right thing without stifling innovation.

The engineering management realized that a dedicated team was needed to support and further develop the new deployment platform as well as other "platform services" like monitoring. This was the birth of the Platforms team. Besides the developers of the deployment platform, the new team drew heavily on the formerly embedded SREs, resulting in a mix of engineers with very solid software engineering skills but also a good understanding of systems and operational concerns. Almost accidentally, the Platforms team became the role model for a self-sufficient, autonomous development team: from the beginning, it was on call for all the services it provided, including the supporting infrastructure.

 Historical note: our deployment platform was called Bazooka. You might still find references to it in talks and posts on the internet. At its time, it was a highly innovative container orchestration platform. Back then, there was no Docker, containers were fairly arcane stuff to most, and there was obviously no established container orchestration platform available in the open source space. Hence, building Bazooka was a necessity and not a result of a not-invented-here syndrome. Later, we migrated completely to Kubernetes. Bazooka and the Platforms team are history now.

Closing the Loop: Take Your Own Pager

Now that it was easy and quick to deploy changes and create new services, a new bottleneck became apparent: even though developers could deploy at any time, they had to be mindful and coordinate with those carrying the pager for their systems.

From the earliest days of SoundCloud, the decision of when to deploy changes had been with the developers making the change. On the other hand, the SysOps team, both from experienced systems and network engineers, had installed the first monitoring and, by default, received all of the notifications and pages.

This situation caused a large amount of friction: SysOps were regularly dealing with the consequences of code deploys over which they had no control. They were unfamiliar with the deploy mechanisms for those applications not running on Bazooka, and they did not know to which versions they could safely roll back. Because the global traffic peak usually happened just after regular work hours ended in Europe, performance regressions often hit in the off-hours. For most issues, the on-call SysOps engineer could do only one thing: find an application developer to whom to escalate. Because there was no organized developer rotation, this could at times be difficult, and the load of escalations was very unevenly distributed among developers.

It was clear that we could not have a sustainable single on-call rotation while maintaining the independence of development teams to deploy features as quickly as possible. Adding more gatekeeping was out of the question. Instead, we went the other way: spearheaded by the Platforms team, more and more teams took over on-call duties for their own services.

Starting with the health of the service itself, developers gradually extended their responsibility to all direct dependencies such as database clusters. The main incentive for teams to take up the operational burden was autonomy: they could now build and deploy new features without having to wait for any other teams.

To ease the transition for engineers who did not have on-call experience, we developed a series of interactive learning workshops. To help all engineers brush up on their operational skills, these workshops covered topics like monitoring, incident response, and conducting postmortems.

The resources freed up in SysOps were reinvested in continuously improving the tooling to support the development teams in their journey so that more ownership and alerts could be handed away. We had created a virtuous circle: the more we improved our systems and automation, the faster we could do so.

Introducing Production Engineering

As each team works within the boundaries of its own domain, overall availability suffers. Decoupling systems to such a degree that an outage in one does not influence any others can reduce this issue, but not completely eliminate it—at some point the user experience comes together to form a whole, and this is where cross-domain failures happen. The Production Engineering team's function is to counter this, champion holistic system stability, and foster exchange of knowledge and good practices throughout the organization.

As the SysOps team succeeded in handing away much of the daily operations of services and their direct dependencies, it remained primarily responsible for the buildout and maintenance of the physical layer—servers and networks. However, this position also caused it to loosely interact with almost all of the other teams. Teams would use this opportunity to gather input on system design, help with database issues, or become connected with other teams solving similar challenges.

As the SysOps team worked toward its own obsolescence, Production Engineering (or ProdEng for short) was formed by merging some of the former SysOps engineers with the aforementioned Platforms team, which had shrunk significantly after its big projects had been mostly completed. Thus, it again had the SRE-typical mix of systems and software engineers. The goal here was to increase focus by separating the consulting and data center operations functions.

A significant difference from both traditional operations teams and Google-style SRE teams is that ProdEng at SoundCloud does not have formal power to prevent feature releases, let alone any more sophisticated safeguards like error budgets. (In fact, in our early days, we only learned about our user-facing error rate from Twitter.) In contrast to a Google-style SRE team, ProdEng cannot even threaten to return the pager, because they don't carry the pager for user-facing applications in the first place. Although this was a challenge, it proved possible to overcome. As we will see in more detail later, there was no "decree from heaven" to follow ProdEng's advice, especially as our engineering culture placed a heavy focus on autonomy of teams.

From the Platforms team, ProdEng inherited ownership of the deployment platform. By providing this fundamental service that every production deployment needs, they maintain contact with all engineering teams without needing to become a gatekeeper. Working up from the bottom of Mikey Dickerson's Hierarchy of Service Reliability,[6] ProdEng offers assistance and common technologies for monitoring (so that we can detect outages before our users tweet about them), guide incident response, and facilitate the postmortem process, all with well-known SRE practices in mind.

Because of the wide variety of experiences and exposure to past choices, ProdEng is also often called upon to help with the design of new systems. This step is, however, completely optional—development teams are free to choose whether they want to engage consultations at any step or leave it be. These consultations are often informal —for example, a hallway conversation might turn into a one-hour brainstorming in the early conception of a new feature. Formal reviews also happen, but only if the team owning a service feels the need. They are a desirable service that ProdEng provides, not a requirement for launch. Reviews can happen at any point in the service life cycle, with changes in service ownership being a common reason.

---

6 *Site Reliability Engineering: How Google Runs Production Systems*, Figure 3-1 (*https://landing.google.com/sre/book/chapters/part3.html#fig_part-practices_reliability-hierarchy*).

It is up to development teams whether, and in what form, they want to engage with ProdEng. This allows them to pace feature development as it suits their needs.

Keeping development and production support within the same group creates self-regulation: a team that haphazardly ships half-baked features to production will be slowed down as a consequence of their choices, delaying future features. A team that overthinks and overdesigns will similarly be slow to deliver, but each team finds its own sweet spot on this continuum—and temporarily deviates from it if the circumstances demand it.

It is important to not damage the user experience too much while exercising this control loop. Quantifying and setting limits for the impact on the user experience is not trivial. We have set a few clearly defined high-level availability targets but rely otherwise on our common postmortem process to hold each team accountable for the impact of its choices, an approach mostly enabled by the limited size of our engineering organization and certainly helped by a strong sense of empathy with our users.

Some Implementation Details

This section provides concrete details of how we applied SRE principles in spirit while adjusting the implementation to our given situation in which a relatively small number of engineers run a relatively diverse set of features. We picked examples we deem most interesting and most suitable to illustrate how the adjustment worked out.

Developers' Productivity and Health Versus the Pager

Having a group of people on call for too many different moving parts is not only very prone to pager fatigue, it also makes it difficult to react in a competent way and thus leads to "pager monkey" devolution. However, the opposite end of the spectrum is equally dangerous. With our move to developers being on call for the systems they built, there was a natural tendency to have very small, expert-only rotations. This sounds great at first but falls into a number of traps:

- "Experts only" usually means very few engineers in the rotation, which leads to far too much time on call for a healthy work–life balance (especially if follow-the-sun is not an option and on-call times regularly span the night).
- Being on call for very few things creates a larger tolerance toward noisy pages, which would be unbearable in a rotation with more responsibilities. It is thus very easy to fall into bad habits and procrastinate improvements of the situation, given that there are usually more pressing things to work on.
- As there are only experts in the rotation, "tribal knowledge" is another bad habit to easily slip into. The incentive to write proper runbooks or even set up alerts in an easy-to-understand way becomes fairly low.

We fell into all of these traps and had countless two- or three-person rotations that were paged all the time by completely undocumented, often meaningless alerts. Getting out of that trough was not only a matter of discipline and strict guidelines; suitable technology (like Prometheus (*https://prometheus.io*) for monitoring and alerting) played an important part in enabling meaningful alerting and facilitating incident response even for non-experts.

Following our strategy of making it easy to use the right solutions, without mandating them, we added extensive Prometheus instrumentation to the preferred application framework, which wraps Finagle (*https://twitter.github.io/finagle/*). Most of our microservices work in a network-heavy scatter-gather fashion with only limited internal logic. By exposing metrics about incoming and outgoing network calls, the users of this framework get insight into the health of their services without the usually required boilerplate code. This, in turn, makes it more attractive to use the framework in the first place.

ProdEng made it easy for teams to improve their own monitoring, and additionally provided some generic high-level alerting. With these as a starting point, it is now easier for development teams to have decent monitoring than no monitoring at all—a profound shift that removes the perception of monitoring as a burden.

With the tools in place, we were ready to address the issue of small, noisy, expert-only on-call rotations. To limit the time being on call, we needed more engineers in the rotation, not only experts.

A few smaller teams began merging their on-call rotations into one. This meant that even without a dedicated SRE or Ops team, engineers were again on call for services for which they did not have a hand in writing and did not own. This was made possible by following SRE practices.

This group of teams documented and publicized their experiences as well as the ground rules they had developed for any other teams joining this rotation:

- Any team that has any service covered by the consolidated on-call rotation must have at least one engineer on the rotation. This way, teams could not hand off all operational responsibility without contributing back.

- All operational tasks for incident handling must be documented in a runbook. There must be a runbook entry at least giving context and an explanation for every alert.

- Noisy pages must be eliminated—every page to the consolidated rotation should have meaning. Unless there is a strong argument that future pages will be actionable, unactionable pages usually cause the alert to be eliminated or made less sensitive. This tends to eliminate cause-based alerts unless they are very strongly correlated with real and immediate issues.

- Mechanistic remediation actions should be automated whenever they can be.

- If the documentation is insufficient or the problem complex, incidents can be escalated to the team that owns the service. This happens infrequently enough that these teams usually do not have a separate rotation, but just spray the notification to everyone on the team.

- During the workday, the on-call engineer can delegate dealing with any pages to the team that owns the service. This relieves that engineer from figuring out what changes are being made to this service at the moment.

- It is the responsibility of the team that owns the service to prevent problems from occurring in the first place.

All of those together not only keep the shared on-call rotation viable, they also help the productivity and health of the developers who own the service. Having developers on call imposes an even stricter requirement to follow the best practices than dedicated SRE support. An SRE is at least a full-time SRE, whereas a developer with SRE responsibilities can wear their SRE hat for only small fractions of their time.

Through the framing and incentive of reduced on-call load, it was attractive for teams to invest into their documentation and monitoring. Soon, more consolidated on-call rotations formed, often by groups of teams with related features and similar engineering cultures such as language and framework choice.

That the team owning a feature is ultimately responsible for the operation of all of the services related to it provides an important safety valve in this setup. Although teams have the freedom to weigh short-term feature delivery against long-term maintenance and tech debt, they cannot neglect the latter forever. As services reach the limits of their design, or as badly designed services are created, the operational load on the team increases. This slows down future feature delivery—drastically so if the situation becomes so bad that the services are removed from the consolidated rotation and on-call is again the responsibility of one team alone.

Resolving Cross-Team Reliability Issues by Using Postmortems

Even with the best of intentions, implicit instrumentation, and generic alerts, things do go wrong between systems owned by different teams. Maintenance has unexpected side effects, alerts are missing, or a new feature critically depends on a system whose owners are unaware of the new dependency.

A company-wide, firm but lightweight postmortem process[7] is the basis for addressing these issues. All teams document serious incidents, which helps them to prioritize

---

7 *Site Reliability Engineering: How Google Runs Production Systems*, Chapter 15 (*https://landing.google.com/sre/book/chapters/postmortem-culture.html*).

and justify efforts to improve their own systems and their interactions with others. Integrated engineering teams that are responsible for maintaining their own systems have a strong incentive to address recurring causes of incidents, especially when estimating and reporting the time lost to incident response or toil that could have been used for feature work. At our size, it is possible for ProdEng to review all incidents company-wide and identify issues that occur across teams or that might be solved by a cross-team effort.

Postmortem documentation follows a specific format guided by a template in the internal wiki. We prioritize ease of use for humans over machine readability, but do also extract some automated reports.

A weekly meeting is the forum for discussing recent incidents, resolutions, and future improvements. The meetings are attended by at least one representative for each incident on the agenda, ProdEng, and anyone else who wants to join. The majority of attendees are engineers directly involved in the development of the affected services. The wider perspectives of the attendees often bring new insights into the incidents at hand, or make connections between past and current incidents.

Postmortem meetings are an efficient way to spread knowledge about the patterns and practices that cause or avoid incidents, help to resolve them, and mitigate their impact. Here, smaller organizations have a big advantage over large corporations: if there is one meeting for the entire organization, such knowledge can reach into all teams within a very short period of time, without the need for elaborate processes or enforcement through management.

If there are too many incidents to discuss in a reasonable time, ProdEng curates based on noteworthiness or impact. Incidents with a very high impact are usually discussed, but this is not absolute—often, knowledge about a close miss and why it did not become a catastrophe is more important to share than a well-understood and accepted failure scenario with a clear resolution. In the end, all incident reports undergo a review of one sort or another, even if not all of them are subject to a meeting. Meetings dedicated to a single incident are held only in extraordinary circumstances and feed into the general postmortem meeting.

In general, and especially for cross-team issues, it can be easy to become stuck on assigning blame. The postmortem guidelines take this into account by focusing on the systemic issues that led to the event, finding ways to avoid the class of problems altogether, and attempting to understand the originating context and how it might be improved. The engineers who attend the meeting take these learnings back into their teams. The meeting often inspires additional means of knowledge sharing, such as internal tech talks, documentation, or pairing sessions.

Uniform Infrastructure and Tooling Versus Autonomy and Innovation

Historically, SoundCloud's technology stack has been quite diverse, especially when it comes to languages and runtimes. This has its advantages. Freedom of choice keeps developers happy and makes recruiting easier. Tools can be picked very specifically for the project at hand.

However, in the long run there is a price to pay. Transitioning systems between owners often means that the new owners need to learn yet another new set of technologies, and a lot of wheels need to be reinvented several times. Systems in less common languages will often lack the more sophisticated instrumentation and client-side load-balancing capabilities that we need to maintain a fleet of microservices.

At SoundCloud, technical direction more often emerges from the bottom up than it is decided from the top down. In the transition away from being a "Ruby shop," we had opened up to and recruited from many different language and platform communities. In this culture, it was unlikely that simply declaring a set of allowed technologies would be accepted. However, the Cambrian explosion of technologies caused an unsustainable fragmentation of efforts around tooling and frameworks. To rein this in, management began favoring the Java Virtual Machine (JVM), Scala, and Finagle stack over others by allocating resources to maintaining this ecosystem. However, we chose JSON over HTTP as the primary communications protocol over more efficient contenders such as ThriftMux (*https://twitter.github.io/finagle/guide/Proto cols.html#mux*). This *lingua franca* of service-to-service communication allowed us to go without immediately rewriting all the nonconforming services, and leaves room for experimentation with other languages and technologies. As a direct consequence, Go has gained a foothold for certain use cases for which its simplicity and performance outweigh the disadvantage of not benefiting from all the effort that went into the Scala framework.

This approach also extends beyond language choice. By providing an easy path for anyone following the common practices, development teams have a strong incentive not to introduce new technologies—but they *can* if the benefits outweigh the costs of blazing a new trail.

This also extends into the domain of data stores. Certain database and cache technologies (Percona Server for MySQL (*https://www.percona.com/software/mysql-database/percona-server*), Cassandra (*http://cassandra.apache.org*), and Memcached (*http://memcached.org*)) are maintained as easily reusable, shared components. They allow any team to stand up a cluster very quickly and benefit from all the automation, documentation, and support of a widely used and well-understood tech stack.

As mentioned earlier, although the setup is provided for them, teams are wholly responsible for the day-to-day on-call and maintenance of their dedicated infrastructure dependencies. They do not need to ask for permission or coordinate with anyone for changing a schema or creating a new feature. Consultation for schema and capacity planning is voluntary and often not necessary. In part, this is possible by virtue of physical separation. Dedicated database clusters for each system limit the blast radius of an ill-advised change or a lack of capacity. The increase in development velocity and the more predictable planning that results from this autonomy more than make up for the slightly reduced utilization of single-tenant clusters.

Sometimes, though, a new technology can really solve a problem so much better that it is worth taking up. This is a decision that each team makes for itself. As an example, the Data Platform team adopted Apache Kafka (*https://kafka.apache.org*) to power the central event bus, replacing the well-established RabbitMQ (*https://www.rabbitmq.com*). Soon, Kafka gained traction with other teams as well, who could build on the prior work of the original explorers.

However, maintaining a generic solution that works for many teams can become a strain on the resources of a team that should be focusing on the actual product. At this time, it makes sense to hand over the technology to a team oriented toward maintaining the common technological basis. A dedicated team was founded to support the common backend framework for JVM-based languages. Monitoring is one of the main "products" of the ProdEng team, mostly in the form of templates and automation for running Prometheus.

Shared components can go a long way and make teams autonomous in areas that are often guarded by dedicated teams providing them as a service. How far you want to go in this is up to you. For SoundCloud, ProdEng provides the deployment platform to all teams as a service. It is, however, not mandatory to use it—certain applications live outside of it by choice of the teams that maintain them.

Getting Buy-In

There is a common theme in the way in which Google ensures SRE practices are followed. Rather than enforcing "golden rules," the preferred way is to create an incentive structure that aligns following best practices with the natural desire of an engineer to increase their own efficiency and productivity. The result is a low-overhead self-regulation. The proverbial example is the introduction of error budgets[8] rather than SRE-mandated stop gaps for releases. Where the self-regulation is not sufficient, a Google SRE team does not need intervention of higher management, but can simply threaten to return the pager. The privilege of SRE support outweighs the burden of following rules.

---

8 *Site Reliability Engineering: How Google Runs Production Systems*, Chapters 1 (*https://landing.google.com/sre/book/chapters/introduction.html*) and 3 (*https://landing.google.com/sre/book/chapters/embracing-risk.html*).

Does that mean management support is not needed at all? On the contrary. Although error budgets or the "nuclear option" of returning the pager foster self-regulation, putting those mechanisms in place and making them work requires extraordinarily strong management support, capable of mandating top-down decisions if need be.[9]

Introducing SRE principles into an established organization will first face the challenge of how to get buy-in by management on the various levels before even getting to the problem of how to incentivize individual engineers.

At SoundCloud, the situation was, again, a bit special. Autonomy of individual teams has been deeply rooted in our engineering culture from the beginning. Conway's law (*https://en.wikipedia.org/wiki/Conway%27s_law*) was often quoted when it came to rationalizing our move to a microservices architecture, but it was also used in reverse to justify the team autonomy as a good fit for our engineering approach. This aspect of our engineering culture was both good and bad for the introduction of SRE principles. The good part was that there was little resistance to overcome. Senior management was, in general, very open to experiments and welcomed any attempt to tackle our increasing reliability problems. The bad part was that centrally introducing and enforcing any rules or even a framework like error budgets was difficult. Getting buy-in from team leads, who cherished their autonomy, was difficult, not to mention individual engineers. This problem was not limited to SRE practices.

Enforcing anything that is contrary to your engineering culture is usually a bad idea, not only because you (hopefully) like your own culture. It's much better if you can alter your approaches so that they play well with the existing culture or even gently encourage an organic cultural evolution toward a more mature organization.

The episode of embedded SREs that we described earlier is a perfect case study. Nobody really opposed the idea. However, there was an implicit expectation that every individual team would independently change its proven habits to make good use of its embedded SRE. In hindsight, that was overly optimistic. Even during the era of the Platforms team, a frequent complaint by engineers on the team was that their advice was ignored or not even requested in the first place. Both cases prove that change is impossible if there is no incentive structure in place to drive it.

Similar to Google SRE, we needed to create an incentive structure and self-regulation rather than mandating strict rules. However, for doing so, we could not rely on centralized decisions and guidance; rather, we had to embrace a cultural environment that is very open to experiments and innovation and highly values team autonomy.

In the success stories that we've related in this chapter, you can see the repeating pattern of teams gaining *more* autonomy by following the new ways: by taking their own

---

9 *Site Reliability Engineering: How Google Runs Production Systems*, Chapter 1 (*https://landing.google.com/sre/ book/chapters/introduction.html*) (p. 7).

pager, they took things into their own hands. Subsequently, they could make better trade-offs between features and stability. By adopting the common deployment platform, they could push changes more quickly and reduce operational overhead at the same time. Introducing modern monitoring practices not only helped to detect and resolve outages, but enabled entirely new ways of debugging and optimizing code. Monitoring is seen as a necessary evil in many places. At SoundCloud, it is by now almost seen as a privilege to have tools like Prometheus well integrated in the infrastructure, with direct support by domain experts in the ProdEng team.

Some other helpful aspects of our engineering culture have evolved over time:

- There is a strong notion of "learning from one another," which sometimes counteracts or even supersedes the desire for autonomy. Soliciting and receiving help from others has always been an important part of the SoundCloud experience, but has become even more important over time. Opportunities to learn, like internal tech talks or the postmortem reviews, are well received, even without coercion by management.

- Perhaps related to the previous point, "leading by example" often works well after success has been proven. For example, the adoption of Prometheus initially required a lot of hard persuasion. It only gained traction after monitoring as the base of Dickerson's Hierarchy of Reliability was sufficiently established to visibly improve our availability.

- The lack of alignment and cooperation between teams became a constant topic of complaint during retrospectives. At some point, the collective consciousness of the company gained the insight that *some* agreement to common practices is strictly necessary. The stronger alignment was certainly helping our SRE efforts but had a much broader impact on many aspects of engineering at SoundCloud.

Conclusion

For developers at Google, one of the most attractive aspects of getting SRE support is freedom from the operational burden. At first glance, we did exactly the opposite: instead of relieving developers of the operational burden, we put them in charge of it. However, while doing so, we embraced *the* fundamental principle of SRE all the more: "SRE is what happens when you ask a software engineer to design an operations team."[10]

---

10 Ben Treynor in *Site Reliability Engineering: How Google Runs Production Systems*, Chapter 1 (*https://land ing.google.com/sre/book/chapters/introduction.html*)

The bottom line is that, in SoundCloud's scenario of a mid-sized engineering organization in charge of a relatively broad and diverse spectrum of features, dedicated SRE teams might not work out as intended. But even without dedicated SRE teams, you can, and in fact must, apply SRE principles, precisely because your software engineers must wear an SRE hat during a good chunk of their work. Comprehensive monitoring, low-noise alerting, and decent operational documentation reduce the workload so that features can be shipped without offloading operations to another team; preferring certain platforms and a common postmortem process foster cohesion and exchange of knowledge; and a well-placed team in a consultative role does not need veto powers to maintain availability.

Further Reading

- Some of the initial impulses for these developments came from former Googlers, many of them SREs. The context from which they came from is well explained in *Site Reliability Engineering: How Google Runs Production Systems* (*https://land ing.google.com/sre/book.html*).

- Our postmortem process is based on the one developed at Etsy in the early 2010s. A good starting point is the blog post (*https://codeascraft.com/2012/05/22/ blameless-postmortems/*) that popularized it. More in-depth, Etsy has also published a "Debriefing Facilitation Guide" (*https://codeascraft.com/2016/11/17/ debriefing-facilitation-guide/*). A notable differences in our version of this process is that we do not hold separate meetings for every incident.

- Decoupling production readiness reviews from the initial release of a feature was inspired by Susan Fowler's *Production-Ready Microservices* (O'Reilly, 2016). Until its release, we had struggled to come up with a definition of "good" services that would not be seen as a burden. Although we place much less emphasis on standardization, the book provides a good starting point for questions to consider when building or owning a service.

Björn Rabenstein is a production engineer at SoundCloud and a Prometheus developer. Previously, Björn was a site reliability engineer at Google and a number cruncher for science.

Matthias Rampke joined SoundCloud in 2011 to help with internal IT. As part of the Systems and Production Engineering teams, he has been operating, debugging, and frequently restarting the glue that holds SoundCloud together since 2013.

## CHAPTER 7

SRE Without SRE: The Spotify Case Study

Daniel Prata Almeida, Saunak Jai Chakrabarti, Jeff Eklund,
David Poblador i Garcia, Niklas Gustavsson, Mattias Jansson,
Drew Michel, Lynn Root, Johannes Russek, Spotify

Many people are surprised that Spotify does not actually have an SRE organization. We don't have a central SRE team or even SRE-only teams, yet our ability to scale over time has been dependent on our ability to apply SRE principles in everything we do. Given this unusual setup, other companies have approached us to learn how our model ("Ops-in-Squads") works. Some have adopted a similar model. Let us tell you a bit about how we came to this model and how it works for us so that you can see if a similar idea would work for you.

First, we need to share a little context about our engineering culture: at Spotify, we organize into small, autonomous teams. The idea is that every team owns a certain feature or user experience from front to back. In practice, this means a single engineering team consists of a cross-functional set of developers—from designer to back-end developer to data scientist—working together on the various Spotify clients, backend services, and data pipelines.

To support our feature teams, we created groups centered around infrastructure. These infrastructure teams in turn also became small, cross-functional, and autonomous to provide self-service infrastructure products. Some examples of these are continuous integration, deployment, monitoring, software frameworks, and guidelines. The vast majority of the SREs at Spotify work in these teams, using their skills and experience to make the production environment reliable, scalable, and easy to work with for our feature teams.

However, some concerns of SRE are cross-cutting and can be addressed only from a central perspective. This includes outages caused by large cascading failures, teaching best practices for deployments, incident management, or postmortems. Our SREs organize themselves in working groups across the company, but these working groups are not exclusively engineers with the SRE title. Only half of the engineers on our central escalation on-call rotation (internally referred to as Incident Manager On Call, or IMOC), for instance, are SREs; the rest are engineers with various roles.

Why have we organized ourselves in such a way? What are the benefits of doing so, and what are the trade-offs? In the following sections, we discuss how Spotify built its SRE organization from a tiny startup with servers in a Stockholm apartment to the large global company that it is today. We highlight how Spotify has made operations the default among all engineers by providing a frictionless development environment and a culture of trust and knowledge sharing.

Tabula Rasa: 2006–2007

- One ops engineer
- Seven developers, approximately nine backend systems at the time of the invite-only beta release

Prelude

We'll talk a bit about how we began to incorporate an operations focus in our early history, including:

Ops by default
Unintentionally bringing in an operations focus from the beginning has influenced our engineering culture, proving to be beneficial in the future.

Learning to iterate over failure
Although we might have had the foresight with operations, we were not impervious to the common traps that startups fall into.

One of the curious aspects about the Spotify story of operations and SRE is how the initial staffing of the six-person company included an operations engineer.

Many startups add an operations-minded person only after the first customers begin using the service. The unfortunate ops engineer might then discover a backend hobbled by undocumented scripts; services running inside of screen sessions; lack of backups; single points of failure; and layers of unfinished, good intentions. From this point on, the ops engineer might constantly be playing catch-up, trying to fight fires while keeping abreast of new developments.

Including an ops engineer from the beginning, ensured that operational soundness, by extension, was included in discussions as an equal partner, not left until the last minute. From the get-go, dev and ops worked side-by-side toward our common vision of streaming music to the entire world. This initial way of working led to a culture of collaboration and trust, which continues to thrive today.

Our backend, as originally envisioned, consists of many small services—a pattern now called *microservices*—which together provide the content for the Spotify clients. The microservices themselves are programs that do one thing and do it well.

During these first two years, work was distributed between dev and ops as follows: developers took care of the business logic in the form of client features or backend services, whereas ops owned everything else, including detecting problems in production as well as taking care of office technology.

This was a startup, and as you might imagine, almost everything was done manually, like deployment of backend services and desktop client rollouts. As Spotify grew in the beginning, tools were added to lessen the load, but these tools only helped with manual tasks; humans still needed to make all the critical decisions.

Key Learnings

Some of our key learnings from this early period were:

- Including an ops engineer from the get-go influenced the engineering culture and proved highly beneficial as we grew.
- You should introduce an operational mindset into the engineering culture as early as possible.
- Aside from business logic architecture, ensure that an infrastructural architecture is in place, as early as possible.

Beta and Release: 2008–2009

- Three ops engineers
- ~10 backend engineers
- 1 data center
- 10–20 backend services
- 4 clients: Windows, Mac, iPhone, libspotify

Prelude

In this section, we'll talk about how our "Ops by default" philosophy shifted and how that links up with our core engineering values:

Ops by default

Bringing in operations into regular discussions of scalability and reliability with developers from the start was pivotal to creating the foundation of our engineering approach. Operations was a cornerstone in every engineer's work, whether it was in developing and maintaining services, or in the intrinsic urge to help improve our infrastructure.

Core engineering values

Innately trusting engineers set the foundation for one of the most prevalent principles we continue to have in the tech organization: autonomy.

Spotify went into "invite-only beta" in May 2007, and a premium (and "freemium") option was released in 2008. During this period, Spotify experienced its first real dose of the dreaded problems that come with rapid user growth. At scale, pain points that are rare and mostly theoretical become visible. They applied not only to the backend services, but all the way down the stack. Here are a few examples:

- The backend services had capacity-related outages during peak times.
- There were disk I/O performance issues when the battery of a RAID controller failed.
- A ZFS bug caused the servers responsible for critical data to become unresponsive under high utilization.
- Racking and stacking servers was painfully slow.

Adding to the problem, the number and complexity of the backend services rose as Spotify developed new features. With time and a lot of effort, each of these technical issues was solved, and the backend continued to scale with the number of users.

However, the way in which ops engineers initially worked did not scale as well as Spotify did. There were three ops engineers at the time who owned all of the following:

- Keeping an eye on all the services that were handed over to ops from dev
- Maintaining the underlying Linux server configuration
- Responding to service disruptions
- Ensuring incident remediations were prioritized
- Keeping up with system security
- Maintaining networking equipment and configuration

- Releasing new Spotify desktop clients and monitoring for deployment failures
- Data center management including procurement, vendor relationships, and provisioning
- Maintaining and expanding storage
- Maintaining our data infrastructure and pipelines
- Owning office IT (network, firewall, staff computers and peripherals, Google apps, LDAP, Samba, Kerberos, AFS, wiki, printers, etc.)
- Serving as a support center to all of our colleagues; for example, helping with laptop setup, explaining networking configurations and how TCP/IP works, or helping our peers work with system monitoring graphs

There was quite a lot to do, but, at least initially, operations still had a little time left over for deep discussions like the future of IPv6, or bickering over the principles and pragma of the different free software licenses. However, as the different scalability issues hit us in increasingly large waves, it became clear that operations would fail spectacularly at keeping Spotify running if something wasn't done.

Bringing Scalability and Reliability to the Forefront

Until this point, there were many people at Spotify who wanted to *help* with scalability and reliability-type problems, but only the ops staff was ultimately accountable for the work. But the ops team had too many responsibilities to juggle and needed to distribute those to the rest of the organization.

A weekly meeting was introduced during which all relevant backend developers and at least one ops engineer discussed services that were dealing with scalability issues. Every week, one or more services were discussed, and developer stories to scale up a system would usually trump feature work. Through this meeting, the ops engineers got some indication of which types of servers (high in disk space, CPU, or memory) was needed for the next procurement purchasing cycle.

The flavor of this meeting changed over time as dev and ops worked together. A single service's scalability and reliability issues involved more and more dependencies on other services, so looking at each service in isolation was not enough; the focus of the meetings began to shift to the backend ecosystem as a whole.

Although we didn't know this at the time, a transformation was taking place in our organization. Gradually, the sense of responsibility for ensuring system health was moving from being an ops-only job to something shared by all engineers working in the backend, regardless of role.

At this point in the company's history, some of the original backend developers had root access. Seeing how useful this was, we gave root access to all developers who needed it. This level of access was unheard of in most traditional companies. Since the advent of DevOps, this is now common practice, but it wasn't at the time. Yet it never occurred to us to do it differently; we innately trusted our engineers. The company was young, and we were united in the belief that we would take over the world of music.

By the time Spotify went out of beta, a new service would go from idea to production in the following way:

1. A developer would write and locally test the service.
2. The developer would then ask ops for one or more production servers.
3. After the servers were provisioned, the developer would log in to the host and configure the service and its dependencies.

An unintended benefit of this new flow was that developers could now understand how their services behaved in the wild better than before. The entire problem of, "Well, it worked on my computer" was bypassed. Developers could now see how their code behaved in production, view logs as they were produced, trace running processes, and even modify the operating system if necessary.

Looking back, we were unintentionally disassociating the specialized role of the SRE from the individuals in ops into a set of skills and responsibilities that could be transferred onto anyone who was capable and motivated. Over the years to come, we reused this strategy multiple times with increasing scope and depth.

And this worked—for a time.

Key Learnings

Our key learnings from this period of high growth were:

- Make operations part of the solution life cycle. Scalability, reliability, maintainability, and other operational qualities should be discussed and addressed as early as possible.
- Granting privileged access (e.g., root) to everyone who needed it removed friction, unblocking and speeding up our iteration cycles. Reliability is about achieving trust: start by trusting your own.

The Curse of Success: 2010

- Five ops engineers
- <25 backend engineers
- 2 data centers
- A few hundred machines
- ~20 backend services
- 7 clients (Windows, Mac, iPhone, Android, BlackBerry, S60, libspotify)

Prelude

In this section, we'll talk a bit about how we had to shift our operations' mentality as we grew:

Ops by default
> Introducing the roles of dev and ops owner helped us perpetuate our natural inclination to be mindful of operations in the context of feature development.

Iterating over failure
> We could not scale ourselves as an operations team fast enough, and therefore had to divest some of our responsibilities.

Spotify continued to grow in popularity during 2010. This was reflected externally in an increasing number of registered users and concurrent active users, and internally in the number of features and corresponding backend services as well as more Spotify staff.

This twin growth conundrum—a sharp upturn in both users and staff—hit the operations team very hard. Despite growing from three to five people, ops was facing a perfect storm. The increase in users led to more pressure on the backend, magnifying the risk of edge-case failures, and ultimately leading to more incidents and cross-service failures. At this time, the increase in Spotify staff was evenly split between technical and nontechnical, resulting in a higher demand for quality support with shorter lead times.

In addition to these factors, with more skilled developers, features were being churned out much more quickly. In 2009 and 2010, Spotify released five more clients: our users could now access Spotify on an iPhone, Android, BlackBerry, S60 Nokia phones, and libspotify (a library enabling third-party developers to access the Spotify backend through their own applications). The backend saw more feature work as well, but the primary focus of 2010 was scalability and stability. Every system needed some sort of revamp, be it modification to enable easy horizontal scaling, a caching layer, or even complete rewrites.

Each frontend and backend change to the Spotify ecosystem introduced new bugs, revealed new bottlenecks, and changed how the system as a whole behaved. Adding a new feature in the client caused unmodified and historically stable services to experience sudden pressure due to changing user behavior patterns. This in turn often led yet other systems to topple in a domino-like fashion. Complex systems are unpredictable and difficult to manage, and, in our case, only a handful of people knew how the entire ecosystem fit together.

Responding to unforeseen incidents became more and more of a full-time job. When Spotify experienced periods of backend instability, developers would often show up at the desk of an ops person, needing critical support. This prevented ops from creating tools to simplify and automate work. In addition, our model of enabling the backend developers with maintenance wasn't working as well as it should have. Although developers continued to maintain their systems, pressure was steadily building to deliver features, and the informal and best-effort agreement of upkeeping their services suffered, often resulting in out-of-date components, bitrot, and security issues.

In the meantime, our developer colleagues were dealing with their own organizational problems. What was originally a small team of developers with a shared understanding on how to collaborate to deliver code grew to become multiple development teams. In this new setting, developers found that collaboration between teams was difficult without agreeing on things like sprint commitments. As a result, teams felt a greater sense of urgency to deliver what they committed to. An unfortunate side effect of this was that many developers became frustrated by not being able to fulfill their informal agreement with us to maintain their services.

At this point, operations became increasingly aware of how the success of the product translated into countless nights by the laptop, manually catching up with failing systems struggling with the load. All of this led to experimenting and, ultimately, adapting to a new reality.

A New Ownership Model

We needed to clarify responsibilities across our operations and developer roles.

The dev owner role

In early 2010, we formalized the unofficial, best-effort agreement between ops and dev by introducing the dev owner role. Each service had an owner who worked in the feature team itself. Here's what the dev owner's responsibilities were:

- Keep operating systems up-to-date with latest updates

- Think about scalability of the service on our ecosystem
- Ensuring development would be scheduled to keep up with growth

Feature developers were also allocated one day during a sprint—a "system owner day"—when they were given dedicated time to maintain, upgrade, and generally nurture their services. The dev owner for each service was expected to call on us for help if needed. This eased some of the pressure on ops. This was not a controversial change, because many backend developers were already motivated to maintain their own services; this now ensured that they had the dedicated time to do so.

The ops owner role

The dev owner role helped us to spread the responsibilities of basic maintenance onto the largest group of engineers at the company, but if something went seriously wrong, ops was still accountable.

However, there were many systems and still only five in ops. Because some of the more critical services needed more attention than others, we assigned an owner from ops to each of these important services. This way, even though every service had a dev owner, the significant ones had both a dev and an ops owner, enabling two people to focus on the services' health.

Within the ops team, everyone was an owner of at least one service. Ops was expected to know the idiosyncrasies and common failure modes of any of our services and be ready to be called at any point, day or night, to restore the service back to health. When redesigning a service, the dev and ops owner would often work together.

Formalizing Core Services

Because our backend services were deeply interconnected with one another, most incidents affected multiple services; as a consequence, often one system needed to be sacrificed to save another. One of the hardest things to do was make a decision in the middle of the night, alone and sleep deprived, that might adversely impact the entire backend ecosystem. Each of us asked ourselves multiple times every week: "Am I making the right decision? What if I don't have the complete picture?" This made work during the night very draining.

When we finally identified this as a problem, a hierarchy of services was defined: those that were *critical*, those that were *important*, and those that could wait for free cycles. Out of this process came the "core services" concept. Because Spotify's purpose was to enable people to listen to music, a core service was defined as any backend service that was in the critical path from a user logging in to client-side audio playback. This amounted to a handful of services, residing on a small cluster of servers. In addition to the core user-facing services, the infrastructural systems, such as our border routers, backend network switching, firewall, and DNS, were deemed critical.

By making these designations, we lessened the burden of nighttime work, and could deal with decision-making in a healthier way.

Blessed Deployment Time Slots

Because ops had yet to formalize an on-call procedure, we were careful with making deployments during off hours. The norm was to make sensitive deployments during work hours when many people were available to help out if and when something went terribly wrong. This applied to all of our deploys with the exception of changes to network infrastructure, which was done when most of our users and employees were asleep.

Feature teams were encouraged to avoid any deployments on Fridays. This allowed us to have an honest chance of resting during the weekends.

On-Call and Alerting

Up to this point, everyone and no one was on call. Ops had no system in place to automatically send alerts on system failure. If something went down in the middle of the night, it was left broken until the morning when someone checked the graphs and reacted. In the event of an outage we hadn't noticed ourselves, our colleagues would call one of us and we would start the work of identifying the problem.

As a result, going to sleep was difficult because we didn't know if we would be called. The stress affected our decision-making abilities at night as well as our capacity during work hours to operate well—or at all.

When ops grew to five people in early 2010, we could finally do what we should have done a long time prior to that but couldn't due to workload: install a proper alerting system. This solved one of our key issues: it didn't leave the detection of system anomalies and outages to chance.

We could now proceed with the next step in our plan, starting with defining a weekly on-call rotation. With one person on call for all backend service disruptions, the rest of us in ops were finally able to sleep, with the caveat that we might be looped in if the incident involved a core system for which we were the ops owner. Any incident concerning a noncore system was not a priority, and there was no need to fix the problem in the middle of the night. Instead, we did some basic troubleshooting to understand the problem; then, we let the service be until the following workday to be dealt with by the appropriate people. Finally, the on-call person had the mandate to call the CTO, who in turn could call anyone in the company should the need arise.

Not completely pain-free

Even though an on-call rotation was defined and alerting set up, every day was full of surprises with unplanned work, issues, and outages. Firefighting and troubleshooting took precedence over any other work. Being on call meant carrying the pager for the whole of Spotify, alerting whenever some metric went over or under statically defined thresholds. If we weren't paged while on call, it could only have meant one of two things: either we've run out of SMS credits, or our cell phone provider blocked our texts due to a high rate of alerts that we were sending.

On-call fatigue was constant, but was alleviated by the company culture and camaraderie: anyone was willing to step in if the on-call engineer was tired and needed time off after hours of firefighting. It was also fun to troubleshoot outages happening in the most unpredictable ways. Learning through failure is an essential part of a healthy engineering culture.

Spawning Off Internal Office Support

As mentioned earlier, a large part of our workload in ops until this point had been internal office IT systems and support. Due to our growth, some weeks we would have four new colleagues, each eager to get started, who needed a computer, a phone, LDAP credentials, email, an introduction to our wiki, and the usual password security lecture. On top of this, our office network and shared filesystems needed maintenance and polishing. Supporting nontechnical colleagues took time and patience and took focus away from our never-ending efforts at keeping backend entropy at bay.

To better support our use cases, Spotify finally split the ops team into two: production operations and internal IT operations. This enabled each team to concentrate on its respective work.

Addressing the Remaining Top Concerns

We'll talk a bit about some of the issues we faced at this stage and how we improved.

Long lead times

Despite splitting our internal IT support to another team, we still had a large number of requests every week, including developers needing help with the maintenance of their services, addressing network issues, coordinating with external parties of how to integrate with the Spotify backend, and maintaining communication with data center and hardware vendors.

All of these issues were dealt with in a best-effort way, which led, unsurprisingly, to very long lead times, and dissatisfied colleagues and customers.

Unintentional specialization and misalignment

We unwittingly become domain specialists by chance. If one of us solved a specific problem, the person who asked for help would inevitably return to the same person the next time they encountered a similar situation. Others would hear about this, and when *they* had questions on the topic, they would turn to this same person. Not only did we become knowledge silos, but because our respective approaches were not aligned with others' outside of SRE, our solution space become siloed as well. For example, we had multiple deployment tools that were being used outside of SRE; the authors of one set of tools didn't always know about the others' work.

Interruptions

Finally, there was a constant flow of interruptions, making our day-to-day work— sometimes requiring extended periods of time for analysis, planning, and implementation—very difficult.

Although we were becoming a larger group of engineers, the close-knit relationship between the dev teams and what was now production operations was still alive and kicking. Many tasks and requests were handled as if we were one small team: someone looking for help, seeking guidance, or needing work done would walk over to our desks and ask for anyone around. Often, this would result in more than one person interrupting their current work, listening in, and joining the discussion. It was a fantastic way of collaborating, but the amount of context switches meant that we were much slower to make progress in our improvement work than desired.

Introducing the goalie role

Our approach to solve these three problems was to introduce a new role: the goalie. The goalie was rotated weekly and served as the designated lightning rod for all incoming requests during office hours to the ops team. If the incoming requests queue was particularly low, the goalie would attempt to solve all issues on their own, occasionally asking for help from the other ops engineers. If the queue was overflowing, the goalie would then only triage, dropping some requests and passing the remaining ones to appropriate people in the team. Rotating the goalie role minimized knowledge siloing because everyone was exposed to the most common problems.

Creating Detectives

One of the more creative and rewarding aspects of our work as SREs is when we roll up our sleeves and do forensics during and after a system anomaly. This detective work requires knowledge of every service in the ecosystem and how they fit together. A typical investigation could begin with peculiar behavior in one of our Spotify clients, leading us to study a flailing backend service, which, when stabilized, proved to be innocent. We'd then find a downstream system, which initially had seemed to be a model citizen, but in reality had triggered a chain of failures.

Even though we gained more and more knowledge and experience from jumping down rabbit holes and fighting complex and interesting incidents, we couldn't keep up with the ever-growing backlog of remediations, leaving us exposed to repeating the same incidents again and again. To make matters worse, the influx of new developers and services was adding to the rate at which incidents occurred. And though we very much wanted to ask for help from our developer counterparts, given that they were experts on their respective services, most of them lacked the big picture.

There were only a handful of SRE detectives, and an increasing number of incidents to study and resolve. We needed more detectives.

A solution emerged: we could make more detectives by teaching developers how the backend system worked. Out of this insight sparked a rather popular lecture that came to be known as "Click-to-Play."

Initially, we explained the backend and how it worked to a few interested developers. We noticed that it was easier both for us to teach and them to learn if we followed a scenario that touched upon all the backend systems involved, starting when a user logged in and ending with when a song began to play. Eventually, this became a standard component in the onboarding process for engineers at Spotify, and a shorter, nontechnical version is now taught to all Spotifiers around the globe.

Key Learnings

Our key takeaways from this period of high growth were:

- Deployment windows work to protect ops, so leverage them wisely.
- Alerting and on-call need to have processes and expectations in place. Fail fast and learn through failure.
- Teaching skills and responsibilities is an essential part of operations. Hold talks on teaching how the entire system works.
- It's tempting to have a single team handle production and IT in an early stage, but to be a productive SRE team, you should split it.
- A "goalie" role or another formal way to handle interruptive work helps the team focus on proactive work.

Pets and Cattle, and Agile: 2011

- Eight ops engineers
- <25 backend engineers
- 2 data centers
- ~30 backend services
- 7 clients

Prelude

In this section, we talk about how we needed to become more agile in the way we approached operations and how our values informed that growth:

Agile ops
> We needed to move from a mindset of treating servers like "pets" to one in which hardware clusters were "cattle"; this radically changed how we approached tooling and operations processes.

Core engineering values
> Our inclination toward autonomy and trust from the start informed our ways of working. However, as we became comfortable with our operational processes, a larger shift was underway in the tech organization, which would cause us to again reevaluate our approach.

In the past, when we talked about services, we often talked about individual servers: "Server X's disks are full"; "We need to add another CPU-heavy server to lighten the load of the other login servers"; and so on. This was important to us because each server had its own character and personality, and only by knowing this could we really optimize the usage of these servers. Furthermore, each healthy server was someone's pet. You could tell which services were healthy by looking at how well the server was taken care of: for example, whether the */home* directory was regularly cleaned or the service-specific logs were nice and ordered.

Our world was server-centric rather than service-centric, and this showed in our conversations, our prioritizations, and our tools.

Forming Bad Habits

The tools initially built and used at Spotify to manage our nascent fleet assumed that a server, after it was installed and live, would continue to work in that corner of the backend until it was decommissioned. It was also assumed that provisioning a server itself would be an unusual event in the grand scheme of things—something done only a few times a month. Therefore, it was acceptable that the tool that installed a server took a few minutes to run, with frequent manual interventions. From beginning to end, the installation of a batch of servers could take anywhere between an hour to a full workday.

By 2011, we were installing new servers far more often than anticipated. Repurposing servers was a known process, but there were often gotchas that forced operations to step in and fix things manually.

This wasn't strange or wrong for a small company with a handful of servers, but at this point in our journey, Spotify already had two data centers with live traffic and a third on the way. With far more than a handful of servers, this was becoming increasingly difficult to do.

Breaking Those Bad Habits

There was a paradigm shift in the air, and though some of us saw it coming, none of us really knew what this would entail for us and the availability of our services. This paradigm shift, when it finally hit us, was simple and obvious: instead of adapting our intent to the hardware, we needed to adapt our hardware to our intent.

This shift was difficult for many of us to relate to because we were too comfortable in our routines. In fact, it took several years for this mindset to change completely, probably because it took that long for us to create the tools to make this shift in mindset possible in the first place.

Toward the end of 2011, another largely unnoticed shift began: feature developers were beginning to organize differently. Over lunches, we heard the devs talk about autonomous self-organizing teams and about which chapter they belonged to. We could still talk with them about services and users, but conversations now included a focus on products and stakeholders. The entire dev department was slowly making the transition into a scalable Agile organization, and we in ops observed this from the sidelines.

From the perspective of those of us in ops, what was most jarring about this organizational change was the ancillary effect it had on our role. The shift in nomenclature from "dev teams" to "squads" with the added emphasis on autonomy and self-organizing challenged the centrality to which we'd become accustomed. Squads were in turn grouped into so-called "tribes," which also had explicit intent in being autonomous and self-organizing.

Instead of one organization to work with, ops was now faced with multiple tribes, each structured slightly differently, with worryingly few indications of staying homogenous.

Key Learnings

Some of our key learnings from this period were:

- Switch the mindset from server-centric to service-centric and make the tooling reflect that.
- The introduction of the Agile matrix organizational model forced us to rethink operations.

A System That Didn't Scale: 2012

- <25 ops engineers
- <70 backend engineers
- Three data centers, a few thousand servers
- <50 backend services

Prelude

In this section we'll talk about our challenges scaling the ops team with the organization:

"Iterating over failure"
  Scaling effectively continued to prove difficult, and divesting our responsibilities was not enough. We needed to revisit what operations at Spotify meant.

"Ops by default"
  A central ops team doing most of the operational work doesn't scale. We needed to make ops truly default by completely shifting the operational responsibilities closer to developers.

It was now 2012 and the Spotify user base continued to grow, introducing new scalability and stability problems for us.

The ops team was composed of fewer than 10 SREs (it was, in fact, during this year that the term "SRE" was adopted), unevenly split between Stockholm and New York. As an ops owner, each SRE was operationally responsible for dozens of backend services: handling deployments of new versions, capacity planning, system design reviews, configuration management or code reviews, and maintaining operational handbooks, among several other day-to-day operational duties.

Our backend was now running in three data centers, with a fourth on the horizon, which we had to operate and maintain. This meant that we were responsible for configuring rack switches, ordering hardware, remote hands cabling, server ingestion, host provisioning, packaging services, configuration management, and deployment— the whole chain from physical space through the application environment. As a result of this widening responsibility, we formed another team to develop tooling automation, which worked closely with ops. One of the early products developed by this team was a configuration management database (CMDB) for hardware inventory and capacity provisioning.

With tailored configurations and nonuniformity, predictability was hard. An ops owner worked closely with the dev owner of a service in efforts to improve quality, follow production readiness practices, and run through a now-formalized deployment checklist to ensure that operational standards were present even during the initial service design. Concerns we regularly brought up included the following:

- Is the service packaged and built on our build system?
- Does the service produce logs?
- Is there graphing, monitoring, and alerting?
- Are backups set up and restore tests defined?
- Was there a security review?
- Who owns this service? What are its dependencies?
- Any potential scalability concerns? Are there any single points of failure?

Manual Work Hits a Cliff

Even though we deployed constantly, either manually or via configuration management, continuous delivery was not in place. We were still delivering at a good pace, continuously, at the expense of work done by hand.

Service discovery consisted of static DNS records with manually edited and maintained zone files. DNS changes were usually reviewed and deployed by ops. We achieved mutual exclusion during DNS deploys by shouting "DNS DEPLOY!" on IRC and manually executing a script.

The ops owner and dev owner regularly went through a capacity planning spreadsheet to ensure that the service had enough capacity to sustain the current increase in usage. Access patterns and resource utilization were collected and used to predict capacity needs according to the current growth. For an ops owner of dozens of services, that meant doing a lot of capacity planning.

During the second half of 2012, we hit one million concurrent users. That meant a million people listening to music connecting directly to one of our three data centers. A pretty huge feat.

Looking back, that should be attributed to some early decisions like Spotify backend architecture being designed to scale, early client/protocol/backend optimizations, and good implementation that paid off. Also, with no multitenancy, most failures could be easily pinpointed and isolated. Every backend service did one thing and did it right. We kept it simple.

As the number of users streaming music continued to increase exponentially, the ops team couldn't do the same. We found that the centralized ops SRE team was a system that could not scale.

Key Learnings

Our key learnings from this period were:

- Make ops truly default from the get-go; if you build it, you run and operate it.
- Shift operational responsibilities closer to the know-how: the developers.
- As your service ecosystem scales, make sure to revisit how operational work is scaling. What worked well yesterday might not work well today.

Introducing Ops-in-Squads: 2013–2015

- <50 ops engineers
- <150 backend engineers
- 3 data centers
- 60 backend services
- 1 cloud provider for staging environment

Prelude

In this section we talk about how a new approach to operations reduced bottlenecks and allowed the tech organization to grow more rapidly:

"Iterating over failure"
  Adopting the new model of Ops-in-Squads freed us up to focus on minimizing our amount of manual work.

Core engineering values

Squads owning their own operations unwittingly helped us to maintain our values in autonomy and trust. Engineers had the potential to inflict widespread damage but were given the tools and processes to avoid it.

At this point, the engineering organization had become too large to operate as a single team. The Infrastructure and Operations (IO) tribe was formed, the home of teams focusing on delivering infrastructure for our backend developers and tackling the problems that came with operating at scale. One part of this tribe was called Service Availability (SA), mostly consisting of our engineers previously working in production operations. By 2013, SA consisted of four squads: security, monitoring, and two squads working on any other infrastructure tooling needed to provision and run servers. The rate at which we hired new developers and started new dev teams was too high for those four SA teams to keep up. More and more, the ability to deliver new or improved features slowed down due to the pace at which we could buy and rack new servers, review and merge Puppet changes, add DNS records, or set up alerting for a service. Dozens of feature teams were impatiently waiting to get their changes out to our users but had to wait on us for code reviews or provision hardware for their services.

We were also still on call for core services, and the operational quality and stability of those services suffered as we tried to keep up with our accumulation of tasks. The global "operations backlog" just kept on growing and growing.

Lightening the manual load

After looking at data of how our backend engineers worked and where they were most often blocked, we decided to focus on removing those blockers wherever possible. It was time to bring back the small startup collaboration with mutual trust between dev and ops and enable our feature teams to iterate fast while still keeping production reliable.

One of the first areas to improve was the provisioning of servers. When servers were available in our data centers, we still had to bootstrap the operating system and configure the basic environment. We had some basic automation, but to kick off that process, the backend engineers had to create a ticket for the ops team, specifying which data center they needed, how many servers, and for what service. The goalie would then pick this up and use our set of duct-taped databases and command-line tools to kick off the provisioning process. After about 40 minutes of automated tasks, the servers were often ready for backend developers.

Our first attempt at improving this process was a tool called provgun, short for "provisioning gun." Instead of sending tickets to the ops team or hunting down an operations person, teams could now open a JIRA ticket to kick off the provisioning themselves. After a while, a cronjob would scan those open tickets and automatically kick off all the steps we previously did manually and then report back to the ticket when servers were successfully provisioned.

This freed up time for the ops team to focus on other things like working on the next iteration of this system: a custom web interface with hardware configurability and available stock exposed. This web interface would show the queue of outstanding requests, the locality of servers, rack diversity, and the current stock of available servers in every cage of the data centers, giving developers more choice and a better understanding of how we built our hardware ecosystem.

The next thing that was tackled was the DNS infrastructure. At the time, DNS records for servers were manually added and deployed by the ops team. The first thing the ops team did was to use a CMDB as the source of truth for determining what server records should be automatically added to the zone files. This helped reduce the number of mistakes made, like forgetting to add the trailing dot. When enough confidence was built that these zone files were accurate, they were automatically deployed to the authoritative DNS servers. This, again, freed up much of our time, and developer satisfaction increased.

Services in our backend discover one another using DNS SRV records. These, plus any user-friendly CNAMEs, had to be manually added to the zone files—a tedious and error-prone task that still required an operations engineer to review and deploy the changes.

To remove this bottleneck, we considered ways in which we could automate the review and deploy process. A basic testing framework (*https://github.com/spotify/ rspec-dns*) was introduced in which one could express things that would be looked for in a review, such as "is the playlist service discoverable in our data center?" We also created a bot that allowed anyone to merge a change as long as the tests passed and it had been peer reviewed.

This was a scary addition: a simple change in one file could impact an entire data center. There were some initial incidents in which a bad push by a team took down much more than expected. But our backend developers quickly learned about the power and responsibilities that came with these changes; soon the number of mistakes dropped to almost zero. Again, this reduced the time they had to wait for the ops team from days to minutes.

After the success with DNS and server provisioning, the next piece of the puzzle was Puppet, the configuration management system that installed all the software on our servers and deployed our applications. The ops team had long before accepted patches to Puppet but reviewed every commit before merging anything. For larger commits or complex systems, this meant that they could be stuck in review limbo for days until someone found enough time to review it.

We tried the approach taken with DNS: merging your own change as long as your patch had a positive review from someone else. For the first few weeks, we were all pretty anxious and monitored almost every commit that was merged. We soon found that we had little reason to. Giving backend developers a feedback cycle—of making a change, merge, deploy, find problem, and go back and do it all over again—gave them that much more insight into many common problems we had and overall led to improved code quality and fewer mistakes.

These first few steps in making the teams operationally responsible was a success. They could now get servers, add DNS records for those servers, and deploy configuration and applications to the newly provisioned servers by themselves. Not only did we remove major friction points and idle time for our developers, but the stability of the services increased as a result of this first shift from "build it" to "run it."

Building on Trust

However, as we removed these "sanity checks" previously done by the ops team, we faced a new problem. Without the guidance of the ops team, the entropy in our backend exploded. Poorly tested services and simple experimentations made it into the production environment, sometimes causing outages and paging our ops on-call engineers who now lacked the required understanding of what was running in production. We needed to figure out how to get the knowledge and operational responsibilities back into one place, paging the right people to troubleshoot an incident.

The traditional ops-owner approach worked well when Spotify was a small organization, but it had complexity and scalability issues, both technical and organizational. It became impossible to rely on a single or a pair of systems owners to figure them all out. We also realized that acting as a gatekeeper to operations meant we kept a monopoly on operational learning opportunities.

Handing this responsibility over to the backend teams seemed like the logical next step. The next question was how to proceed. We needed to actively engage the teams and figure out a way forward with the rest of the tech organization.

We started rolling out a new way of working—dubbed Ops-in-Squads—which in essence included everything needed to hand over on-call and operational responsibility for services to the teams that developed them. We needed to write tooling to do many of the things that were done by hand before; we needed better documentation and training so that developers would be able to troubleshoot production issues; and we needed buy-in from developers to drive this change.

A guild (*https://labs.spotify.com/2014/03/27/spotify-engineering-culture-part-1/*) created for developers and ops-people to share knowledge among everyone and open a bidirectional communication channel helped define some key things we needed:

- A standardized way of defining Service-Level Agreement (SLAs; we did not use the Service-Level Indicator [SLI]/Service-Level Objectives [SLO] concepts back then)
- A how-to crash course on being on call, handling incidents, performing root-cause analysis, and holding postmortems
- Guidance on capacity planning
- Best practices for setting up monitoring and alerting as well as instruction on interpreting monitoring data
- Training in troubleshooting, system interactions, and infrastructure tooling

Handing all of this responsibility over to the teams would of course be a big undertaking over a long period of time, and the infrastructure team still remained to support and build upon the core platform. We struggled with defining exactly what fell into the core platform; some things were obvious, like networking, monitoring, and provisioning, but other systems were harder to classify. Critical parts of our infrastructure, like the user login service, the playlist system, or the song encryption key system, needed to be evaluated: are they core infrastructure, or should they be handled like any other backend system?

We wanted to make a deal: we remove gatekeeping and friction points in exchange for shifting operational responsibilities into feature teams. If a team needs to deploy a change on a Friday, it shouldn't be prevented from doing so. We assumed that the knowledge for operating services is held closest to where it is developed.

This was not met with cheers and optimism from everyone in the organization; there were concerns about negatively impacting feature teams' speed of iteration. How would teams have sufficient bandwidth to deliver on features and growth if they also handled the maintenance and operational duties of their systems? The teams consisted of developers, not SREs; how much of their time would they have to devote to learning and practicing operations? Preparation, process, and tooling would be essential to convince people to take on this responsibility.

We continued investing heavily in picking blessed tooling, writing and promoting frameworks, and writing documentation to help make the transition as smooth as possible for most teams.

Driving the Paradigm Shift

We aim to make mistakes faster than anyone else.
—Daniel Ek, Spotify founder and CEO

To reach all the teams with the information and tools needed, we took several different approaches. We held presentations for developers, discussing how the systems in our backend fit together and how to use the shared infrastructure. Our principal architect internally held postmortems for dozens of developers, walking them through a large incident that had resulted from a cascading failure. We made it easier for teams to find documentation and ownership for infrastructure systems by having a central entry point. We developed an Ops-in-Squads handbook that became the standard document to which to point new developers. It contained most of the information that teams needed to get started; pointers on things to do; where to read more; and checklists of processes, technical features, or processes to implement. We embedded in backend teams for short periods to transition the host team to being on-call for their services; helped teach operations; and worked directly with improving the systems, deployment procedures, on call handbooks, and so on for teams that requested or needed it. Again, we made a deal: we'll work with the team for a few sprints and "clean house" before handing over the on-call responsibilities to them.

In 2014, this approach—embedding engineers in teams—was expanded into an Ops-in-Squads tour where some parts of our operations team went week by week to different teams, engaging with their daily work and trying to help them on anything with which they struggled.

During these embeds, we reviewed the architecture of the host teams and looked at alerting and monitoring, helping to improve these when needed. We also discussed how to do on-call and shared best practices around schedule rotation, how to escalate problems, and how to hold postmortems. Postmortems, in particular, had a reputation of being time-sink ceremonies. Teams that had a lot of incidents often skipped postmortems because the work to establish timelines, find root causes, and define remediations for 10 or 20 incidents per week seemed like too much overhead. Finding different ways of approaching postmortems proved useful in these cases, like clustering incidents after a theme, or doing short postmortems for multiple incidents at once. Often many incidents had similar root causes; exact timelines weren't as important as identifying the top remediations that would reduce the likelihood of that type of incident by 90% in the future. Throughout this shift, we retained the principle of *blameless* postmortems, emphasizing the importance of learning from our mistakes, and ensuring that no one was thrown under the bus.

Key Learnings

Some of our key learnings from this period were:

- Strive to automate *everything*. Removing manual steps, friction, and blockers improves your ability to iterate on product.
- Ensure that self-service operational tooling has adequate protection and safety nets in place.

- Teaching ops through collaboration is vital to making ops "default" in the organization.

Autonomy Versus Consistency: 2015–2017

- <100 ops engineers
- <200 backend engineers
- 4 data centers
- 120 services
- Multiple cloud providers

Prelude

In this section we'll talk a bit about how we tried to balance autonomy for squads with consistency in the tech stack:

Iterating over failure
Our first approach at introducing consistency in the technology stack caused unintentional further fragmentation. Although we continued to reiterate and address these newly exposed concerns, we found ourselves blocking teams once again.

Core engineering values
Focusing on unblocking feature teams allowed us to maintain squad independence and freedom while introducing much-needed infrastructure consistency.

In moving forward with the Ops-in-Squads model, we shifted our focus to standardizing our technology stack. With this decentralized operations model, we needed to reduce the cost of operations for teams by providing consistency across our infrastructure. High entropy meant expensive context switches and unnecessary overhead. However, striking a balance between consistency and our penchant for autonomy took thoughtfulness and foresight.

Bringing uniformity to Spotify's stack came in a few forms. Although teams were now in charge of operating their services, we needed to get out of their way by building abstraction layers in the right places. The first levels of abstraction layers were tools for ourselves, iterating on our early successes of removing friction points with provgun and DNS. Out of this work came a number of tools: moob (*https://github.com/spotify/moob*), for out-of-band management of hardware; neep, a job dispatcher to install, recycle, and restart hardware; and nonentgen, a batch job to create DNS records for all servers in use, to name a few.

Building off of the earlier legwork, in 2015 through 2016 we concentrated on creating and iterating on self-service tooling and products for feature developers around capacity management, Dockerized deployments, monitoring, and SLA definitions. No longer did developers need to plan capacity with spreadsheets or deploy via SSH'ing into servers to do an apt-get install. A few simple clicks of a button and squads got the capacity they needed with their service deployed.

We established a blessed stack in 2015, one that is explicitly supported and maintained by the infrastructure team, that became the "Golden Path" for how a backend service is developed, deployed, and monitored at Spotify. We began using the term Golden Path to describe a series of steps that was supported, maintained, and optimized by our infrastructure team. Instead of dictating a "blessed stack" as a mandatory solution, we wanted to make the Golden Path so easy to use that there was almost no reason to use anything else.

The Golden Path consisted of step-by-step guide for our developers. It included how to set up their environment; create a simple, Dockerized service; manage secrets; add storage; prepare for on-call; and, finally, properly deprecate a service. We built Apollo (*https://github.com/spotify/apollo*), our Java microservice framework, which would give a developer many features for free, like metrics instrumentation, logging, and service discovery. Heroic (*https://github.com/spotify/heroic*) and Alien, our time series database (TSDB) and frontend, allowed engineers to create prepackaged dashboards and alerts of their instrumented-by-default Apollo services. Pairing with Helios (*https://github.com/spotify/helios*) then provided a supported way to roll out Docker deployments in a controlled manner with zero downtime.

Benefits

Squads were now able to focus even more on building features because operational tasks were continuously being minimized. But developer speed was not the only benefit to improving the consistency within our infrastructure. It allowed our migration from our physical data centers to Google Cloud Platform to be fairly seamless. Most of the work happened behind the scenes from the developer point of view. Creating capacity in Google Cloud Platform was no different than on bare metal. Neither was deploying or monitoring a service. From the developer point of view, moving to a new squad or doing a temporary embed became frictionless, given a consistent set of tools to work with.

Another benefit to a consistent, blessed stack is that it prevents us from falling into potential traps of trendy technologies that come and go. We also have insights and understanding about what engineers are using, informing us how to improve our products. There is less operational complexity and fragmentation, which can be a nightmare during incidents. We're able to prescribe best practices for operating a service, and provide ongoing support. As an infrastructure team, we decided to have fewer responsibilities, but strived to handle them well.

Trade-Offs

It was not all easy sailing, though. Standardizing a technology stack still had its drawbacks. Too restrictive, and we risk losing squad autonomy and experimentation, hindering development when not all use cases are addressed. We defined the Golden Path to be an Apollo service, but hadn't yet provided explicit support for the legacy and internal Python services, frontend applications, or data pipelines and analytics. We provided the ability to easily create and destroy capacity, but we didn't yet generally support autoscaling. These unaddressed use cases indirectly contributed to the fragmentation that we were confronting as some teams created their own bespoke tools for workarounds.

In some cases, supported tools were not used. JetBrain's TeamCity used to be the only Continuous Integration (CI) system used. It became too cumbersome for back-end service developers, so squads spun up their own Jenkins instances. As evidence of team autonomy and experimentation, the use of Jenkins spread so quickly among squads that it soon became the de facto backend service CI tool. It made sense with the Ops-in-Squads model we adopted, except that teams lacked good habits to maintain their own Jenkins setup, leaving them out of date, vulnerable, and inadequately secured. It forced us to rethink our build pipeline support, where we ultimately developed an explicitly supported managed Jenkins service. Similarly, we found developers were not maintaining their Cassandra clusters, despite tools provided by our team. Fearing potential data loss and realizing maintenance was too much overhead for a feature team, we brought this, too, back into our operational ownership by offering a managed Cassandra service and related support.

Even though we had many self-service tools to unblock feature teams, the IO tribe still got in the way. In 2017, our focus shifted again to strengthening our overall infrastructure by prioritizing ephemerality, security, and reliability. We built tools for initiating controlled rolling reboots of our entire fleet, which encouraged developers to write resilient services. We automated regional failover exercises, bringing to light inconsistencies that teams have in their services' capacity across regions. As we make progress in taking advantage of products and services that Google Cloud Platform offers, teams are now needing to take time away from feature development to, for instance, migrate to a new cloud-native storage solution such as Bigtable but reap the benefits when they no longer need to maintain any infrastructure.

Although we succeeded in shifting to the Ops-in-Squads model and struck a balance between autonomy and consistency, we are now focusing on removing friction from operations—but we still have a long road ahead.

Key Learnings

Some of our key learnings from this period were:

- Golden paths provide a low-friction way of getting from code to production fast.
- Support one blessed stack and support it well.
- Giving clear incentives is essential for a blessed stack adoption (e.g., operational monitoring, continuous deployment pipelines).

The Future: Speed at Scale, Safely

When thinking about the future, we can imagine a landscape where the operational burden for feature teams has been *safely* reduced to nearly zero. The infrastructure supports continuous deployment and rapid experimentation across hundreds of teams, and there is little to no cost for the majority of developers in operating their services at scale. This is the dream, but we're not fully there yet.

There are a number of technology shifts being made as part of this zero ops dream. The first part of this strategy for us is the migration to the cloud. Instead of spending time on tasks that don't give us a competitive advantage, like data center management and hardware configuration, we can shift that problem to cloud providers and benefit from their economies of scale.

The second part is around adopting cloud primitives, shifting from bespoke solutions to open source products with vibrant communities. An example of this is our planned move from our homegrown container orchestration system, Helios, to a managed Kubernetes services (Google Kubernetes Engine). In adopting Kubernetes instead of further investing in our own container orchestration system, we can benefit from the many contributions of the open source community. Making these shifts allows the ops teams to focus on higher-level problems facing the organization, thereby delivering more value.

Even with the abstractions of the cloud, ops teams still own the uptime of the platform. Toward this end, we are adopting a mantra, *speed at scale, safely,* or s^3 for short. We want to enable Spotify to iterate as fast as possible but to do so in a way that is reliable and secure. Our move to the cloud is consistent with this message, but as infrastructure and operations engineers, we also face a more nuanced problem space. Initially, services, data centers, network, and hardware were all architected, provisioned, and managed by us; we understood the intricacies of operating and supporting these systems. With the cloud and, moreover, our ever-increasing scale, we need better insights, automation, and communication channels to ensure that we can meet our internal availability SLO of 99.95%. Therefore, we've invested in reliability as a product, which includes domains ranging from chaos engineering to black-box monitoring of services.

Another part of the challenge of *speed at scale, safely* involves how we guide feature teams through the myriad technology product offerings. We can't serve as roadblocks to innovation, but we also need to ensure the reliability of the platform, which means we need to guarantee consistency in those cases for which reliability is a core concern. This involves building the right tooling, conformity engineering, a robust developer platform that engineers use to find the right product for their needs, and a concerted teaching and advocacy effort.

Toward this end, we will also need to reevaluate our Ops-in-Squads model. Although this structure has served us well, we'll need to consider how we can further reduce the operational burden that feature squads face today. In the few years since this change was put in place, we have grown and learned as a company, and the same metrics for success that applied in the past might not be as applicable in the future. We don't know exactly what this will look like, but we know that we'll be agile and continue to experiment to find the best solution. For example, consider our incident management process. A team's on-call engineer will triage incidents affecting its services and, if needed, escalate to the IMOC for assistance with overall incident coordination and communication during high-impact situations. Although the IMOC structure has been an important mechanism to quickly swarm on high-impact issues, with our increasing workforce spread across the globe, it's not always well understood when to page IMOC and, more generally, how to handle team on-call. In such cases, we will need to improve our teaching of operational best practices throughout the organization, and how we do so—how we advocate for operational quality— might require adjustments to our original thinking behind Ops-in-Squads.

Finally, as the technology landscape changes, so do our site reliability needs. One area that we're exploring is machine learning. With thousands of virtual machine instances and systems, and more than a hundred cross-functional teams, we might find machine learning an effective way to make sense of an ever-growing, complex ecosystem of microservices. Furthermore, we also have the opportunity to revolutionize what has largely been manual tunables in the past, whether it be "right-sizing" our cloud capacity needs or detecting the next big incident before it occurs; the opportunities here are manifold. We might not only predict incidents, but also mitigate them with self-healing services or by providing automatic failbacks to a trusted state.

There are other infrastructural trends to consider; for instance, adopting serverless patterns imposes a set of challenges for our service infrastructure, from how we monitor to how we deploy and operate. We also see a shift that's both organizational and technical; our developers are increasingly working across the landscape of backend, data, mobile, and machine learning systems. To support their end-to-end delivery, we need touchpoints that are seamless across these areas. Reliability can no longer be focused on the robustness of backend-only systems but must also consider the network of data and machine learning engines that provide increasing value to our ecosystem.

We hope you've enjoyed learning about our successes and failures in building a global operations and infrastructure organization. Although we've experimented with many different flavors of SRE and now function in this Ops-in-Squads model, we believe that what has made us successful is not the model itself but our willingness to embrace change while keeping core SRE principles in mind. As the technology landscape changes, we'll also need to keep evolving to ensure that *the music never stops streaming*.

Daniel Prata Almeida is an infrastructure and operations product manager for reliability at Spotify. In a previous life as an SRE, he carried the pager and nurtured complex distributed systems. He's addicted to uptime.

Saunak Jai Chakrabarti leads infrastructure and operations in the US for Spotify. He's passionate about distributed systems and loves to study all the different ways they break or work unexpectedly.

Jeff Eklund, formerly at Spotify, is an SRE and technology historian with a passion for the arcane and quirky. He believes every computer problem can be solved by tenacity, camaraderie, and ramen.

David Poblador i Garcia, ex-SRE and product lead, now engineering lead for the technology platform at Spotify, is rumored to be the friendly face of deep technological knowledge and strategy.

Niklas Gustavsson is the former owner of Spotify's worst-behaving service and currently serves as Spotify's Principal Architect.

Mattias Jansson (Spotify) is an ex-{Dev,Teacher,SRE,Manager}, current Agile coach. He's a history geek with a passion for systems—both silicon- and carbon-based.

Drew Michel is an SRE at Spotify trying to keep the lights on in the face of chaos. In his spare time, he enjoys running long distances and walking his Australian Shepherd dog.

Lynn Root is an SRE at Spotify with historical issues of using her last name as her username, and the resident FOSS evangelist. She is also a global leader of PyLadies and former Vice Chair of the Python Software Foundation Board of Directors. When her hands are not on a keyboard, they are usually holding a bass guitar.

Johannes Russek, officially former SRE and technical product manager at Spotify, unofficially dropped-ball finder and software systems archeologist. Favorite tool is a whiteboard.

## CHAPTER 8

Introducing SRE in Large Enterprises

Sriram Gollapalli, Agilent Technologies

This chapter describes my story of how an acquired Software as a Service (SaaS) startup (founded in 2006) introduced SRE into a large enterprise (originally founded in the 1930s), including the challenges and opportunities of traditional IT, operations, support/quality teams, and distinct product engineering divisions working in concert with one another. This is intended for managers who understand that SRE is what their organization and products need but they are struggling to determine how to implement these ideas. This was adapted from a talk I gave at SRECon17 Europe in the summer of 2017 in Dublin, Ireland.

> *Quality means doing it right when no one is looking.*
> —Henry Ford

Background

As a cofounder of a small SaaS startup, joining a large organization was a thrilling experience for me. Our team was excited to share our knowledge and take advantage of the resources and infrastructure this larger company could provide to expand our business. Our startup learned that the matrixed structure—in which groups have dual reporting relationships, by function and also to the product lines—can be both flexible as well as challenging when it comes to introducing new paradigms.

Our organization, Agilent Technologies, has deep Silicon Valley roots from the late 1930s. As a large instrument manufacturer with primarily shrink-wrapped software products, we traditionally have delivered software by burning CDs and DVDs and mailing them, with major releases every 12 to 24 months. As our customers are starting to accept more electronic delivery of their products, we've introduced downloadable patches and upgrades, but size limitations still make shipping sometimes more efficient.

As Agilent acquires SaaS companies and introduces SaaS products, continuous integration and deployment pipelines offer evolving conduits for delivery, which challenge traditional processes and organizational structures and roles. Organizations such as the United States Postal Service and FedEx used to be the sole source for the reliability of our software product releases. As cloud delivery becomes more ubiquitous, we have to be that source. It becomes an integral component of our brand promise and customer experience.

Introducing SRE

It's important to understand that fundamentally SRE is a vehicle to maintain and improve the health of customer-facing products while increasing software engineering velocity. This message resonates with executives and helps to advocate for dedicated SRE resources. In order to introduce SRE, we used the following approach, which you can see in Figure 8-1.

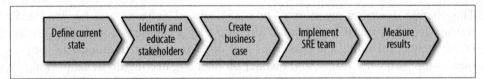

Figure 8-1. Steps to implementing SRE in an enterprise.

Defining Current State

To determine where SRE will fit in the future and how to present the business case to your leadership, you have to start by understanding the organizational structure. There are many components to consider when evaluating current capabilities and potential gaps.

Start by defining the roles and responsibilities of traditional functions in the organization to understand the landscape

Typical enterprises will have central functions such as the following:

- Information technology/central IT/information systems/help desk
- Product support and services
- Global operations

Given the unique combination of skill sets needed that span multiple groups, the cross-functional nature of SRE will present an initial challenge to determining where to position SRE in the organization. We conducted informal surveys with our peers at similar large enterprises—there isn't always a clear home for the group. To determine the best organizational structure, *identify leaders and/or executives* in leadership positions to gauge their operational experience and appetite for embracing a new approach to operations. This will later be important for SRE education and sharing the business case. Example roles could include the CIO, VP of operations, VP of support, VP of cloud, or VP of engineering. It's possible that one of these groups will be a logical fit under which your SRE team can incubate.

 To help us identify who to work with, we looked at an established SaaS product. We imagined it becoming suddenly unavailable and followed an incident to see which roles and groups would be affected. This took us to traditional product support, and IT support, and, more importantly, revealed gaps where there was neither a clear owner nor established process to comprehensively manage and monitor the product.

Prepare the business case: personalize and evaluate the cost of having engineering resources responsible for reliability

Imagine this scenario: your sprint has well-planned stories with consistent definitions of done, groomed backlog, acceptance tests approved—it's a sprint planned to within striking distance of completion with ample buffer for unplanned incidents. It's Tuesday afternoon, you're getting ready to dive into another focused coding session, and you get pinged from your support team: "Hey, I'm getting some customer tickets that they can't add items to their shopping cart, could you take a look?"

Poof! Any hope of hitting your sprint goals and velocity is out the window while you focus on trying to figure out what happened.

Sound familiar?

Context switching increasingly reduces the efficiency in task delivery. The first element of your business case can focus on the fact that without SRE resources, *traditional engineering resources cannot focus on the business-prioritized product enhancements and improvements.*

Gather stories from your support, sales, marketing, and other customer-facing teams of how engineering could have completed products more efficiently and high-level estimates of time wasted looking at outages or incidents.

Prepare the business case: calculate cost of similar resources doing duplicate work

In large organizations with multiple products (cloud and otherwise), there will likely be multiple resources or even teams with SRE-like responsibilities. Collaborating across these resources can result in knowledge sharing and cost savings by focusing these efforts in a centralized manner. *Disparate resources across the organization could be defining and developing similar processes and tools.* Identify these resources and estimate the cost of redundant work efforts.

To establish a roadmap for what products SRE will be responsible for, survey the current infrastructure landscape

As we started to identify the kinds of products that would benefit from an SRE engagement, we gathered information about the technology footprints the products were built on. We saw a wide variety, from a ready-to-release-to-cloud product with snowflake servers (*https://martinfowler.com/bliki/SnowflakeServer.html*) spread out, to a product with a complex Windows architecture and dependencies that had a history of failures and fragile ecosystem (unsupported operating system versions, limited vendor support, etc.). *Don't underestimate the complexity of operationalizing an existing environment* and include that in your assessment.

Identifying and Educating Stakeholders

Once you understand the current environment, start to have conversations and build the story of what SRE will mean to your organization and the impact it can have.

Start having conversations with leaders and champions in the organization

As identified in the previous section, leaders can include the CIO, VP of operations, VP of support, and VP of engineering. We started with one-on-one conversations to understand current responsibilities and pain points that each group was experiencing. We used this time to identify and tailor the story of how SRE could improve each of their functional areas.

Because we did our homework and understood our product footprint, we started these conversations sharing a high-level analysis of our current state and disparate product delivery models (see Figure 8-2). We used this opportunity to introduce cloud delivery concepts and how they differ from the traditional shrink-wrapped software.

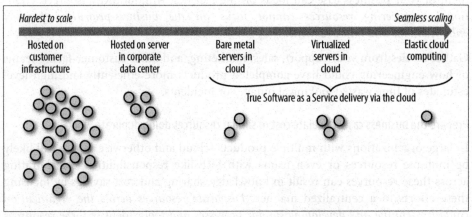

Figure 8-2. Kinds of software products and their delivery method (the dots represent a unique product).

With that context, we discussed the evolution of the delivery and operating models, which started with traditional system administrators that were usually in a central IT department. Even though our organization wasn't aspiring to be the next SaaS unicorn or hyped social media product, using examples from Google, Netflix, and so on helped to provide the background to show how the delivery models in the industry were shifting to being more integrated with the engineering organizations (see Figure 8-3). We used this to highlight the differences among traditional operating paradigms and the lack of an obvious home in an organization.

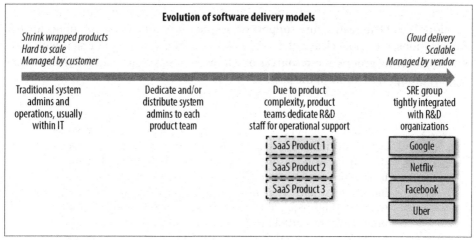

Figure 8-3. Evolution of software delivery models.

Defining SRE

This brought us to defining the key tenets of SRE as adapted for Agilent:

- The SRE team runs production services—a set of related systems, *operated for our customers*, who can be internal or external—and this team is ultimately responsible for the *health of these services*.

- Successfully operating a service entails a wide range of activities:

  — Developing and implementing monitoring systems for performance, availability, latency, and efficiency

  — Capacity planning, server management, disaster recovery

  — Emergency incident response, ensuring the root causes of outages are addressed

  — Working closely with the product team on release management

  — Setting and meeting availability targets

- When SREs engage with a service, the aim is to improve the service along these elements (improved incident response resolution time, increased availability, etc.), which makes managing production environments for the service easier.

- SREs represent the user's interest that the software product is always available and running.

- SRE's goal is to let traditional engineering resources focus on the product and *increase velocity.*

At first, some of these seemed counterintuitive and overlapping with our existing functions (i.e., IT infrastructure support or product support). However, upon further conversations, it became clearer that SRE is a unique function that interacts with software engineering groups and resources much more closely than traditional enterprise support groups have done in the past.

During these conversations, everyone agreed that engineering resources were filling this role to keep the products afloat. We also agreed that was a distraction for those resources and also prevented them from working on business-prioritized features. The initial inclination was to expand the scope of the operations team to include these SRE responsibilities. However, as we defined the technical skills required and the emerging similar needs for other products in the portfolio, it became clearer that this needed dedicated product engineering experience with an operations mindset, while staying close to the product groups.

In addition, current roles did not have the capacity or technical knowledge to take on disparate products with the level of detail necessary to support a healthy experience.

Arming ourselves with these definitions and summary, we scheduled one-on-one meetings with each of the previously identified leaders and walked them through the SRE concepts and fundamentals. This education proved to be key to allowing us to present a business case to fund a team and move forward.

Presenting the Business Case

Because we had spent a few months preparing with stakeholders, we concluded this phase by having a large group meeting during which we summarized the opportunity and presented it as a business case. In that meeting, we presented the following story:

- The current challenges/business problem we were facing
- Current effort/costs spent in similar but noncohesive functions
- Description of the approach of incubating SRE function under our technical leadership

- Potential positive impact on operations/reliability
- Proposed timeline and milestones to achieve return on the investment

Implementing the SRE Team

By this point, the business case and the "why" we are doing SRE should be answered. Now comes the "how." Start with setting goals and staffing the team. Identify the kinds of resources that are doing this kind of work already for the product(s) you're responsible for, and try to separate them into a distinct group apart from their engineering obligations so that they can now focus on SRE responsibilities.

Setting goals and defining metrics of success

Given this will likely be a unique team in the organization, consistent metrics and updates are important to define, measure, and report out to your stakeholders. A good starting point to measure the success of your SRE implementation is Google's Four Golden Signals (*https://landing.google.com/sre/book/chapters/monitoring-distributed-systems.html#xref_monitoring_golden-signals*): traffic (number of requests per minute), errors (number of incidents/errors per day, per product), saturation (number of web workers active), and latency (number of timeouts or page-load duration). Monitoring these can influence an overall product uptime metric.

Growing the team: insource or outsource?

It could be tempting to hire contractors to focus on your product's reliability and delivery (this might be the case in your organization already, in fact) to add more global coverage, redundant knowledge, support, and so on. This is a "supporting role" after all, right? Generally speaking, this wouldn't be prudent.

Although it might seem expedient and lower risk at first, we found that one of our products became too reliant on contractors for a similar supporting function. One day, the contractor had some internal turnover and it tried to manage knowledge transfer among its staff with a replacement. The contractor's transition was challenging for us because it was out of our control and the replacement didn't have the in-depth knowledge that the prior resource had about our products. More important, we realized that *we didn't even* have the details to take over the support—our product-specific knowledge had been completely outsourced.

When you're just starting to implement the SRE function, investing in a set of dedicated employees with specific product domain expertise will prove to be invaluable. Contractor turnover, and time for knowledge transfer for production systems are two reasons that using contractors as key members of your team can be challenging in the long term. When you're just starting out, *contractors could add cost and time* to have a consistent, reliable SRE function. You want to focus your efforts on building in-house capabilities and expertise, not worrying about managing an outsourcing operation.

Instances for which contractors could work include when you're looking to scale up the SRE operations, after processes are well documented and you need to add first-level triage for additional capacity.

Insourcing experienced talent: rotating engineering team members

One attribute of successful SRE team members is that they're closely tied to the engineering and development process. This kind of experience and in-depth product architecture knowledge makes current engineering team members a great funnel for resources. One way to softly recruit while spreading the SRE mindset throughout the organization is to work with engineering management to *rotate engineering team members onto the SRE team*. Find a timeframe that works for your organization; two to three months generally works well. You'll be surprised to find that sometimes resources already exist for doing this work in the product software divisions. When you bring them onto a central team, they become more exposed to the broader product portfolio and will benefit from all of the knowledge sharing.

SRE throughout the development cycle

After the team is established, it's important to start engaging with product teams during all parts of the product development life cycle, as described in Figure 8-4. The SRE function will be more effective the earlier you can involve it in each product. Informing and educating engineering, product marketing, and support teams will result in more successful relationships and implementation of the SRE function.

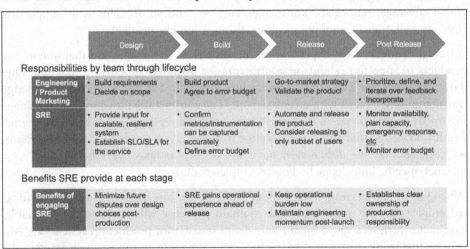

Figure 8-4. Responsibilities, sample activities, and benefits of engaging SRE at each stage of the product development life cycle

As Matt Klein, software engineer at Lyft, says, "SREs should be embedded into product teams, while not reporting to the product team engineering manager. This allows the SREs to scrum with their team, gain mutual trust, and still have appropriate checks and balances in place such that a real conversation can take place when attempting to weigh reliability versus feature."[1]

Defining the role of supporting divisions

A final component of the successful implementation will be to understand how SRE will leverage, depend on, and enhance existing divisions and functions in the enterprise. Here are some example interactions and relationships to build that could work:

- Information technology/central IT/information systems/help desk
  - These groups are likely responsible for infrastructure layers (i.e., network, data centers, corporate security) as well as running enterprise security operations centers and network operation centers. Ensure that you have *key points of contacts* and responsibilities defined to avoid duplicative effort.

- Product support and services
  - This group will usually have the front line of user-facing support, calls, and defined-incident management processes. Similarly, invest time in introducing the SRE team and its capabilities. Use it when setting up an escalation process and seamless handoff to minimize confusion. This group might also be great for handling customer-facing communications in the middle of incidents. It will be a strong partner in your successful implementation.

- Global operations
  - This group could have centralized dashboards that executives already are attuned to reviewing. Partner with them to incorporate SRE metrics and statistics of the products you're monitoring into their communications.

You will constantly be interacting with these kinds of divisions; don't replicate effort and institutional knowledge. By leveraging these existing resources and functions, you'll have an opportunity to jumpstart your SRE function. Take the time to understand these capabilities and look for the intersection points.

---

1 Matt Klein, "The human scalability of DevOps" (*https://medium.com/@mattklein123/the-human-scalability-of-devops-e36c37d3db6a*).

Lessons Learned

Following are some lessons we learned during our process of introducing SRE into our organization:

Challenge the status quo

It might not be immediately apparent that SRE is the right answer for your organization. Don't be afraid to introduce SRE as a methodology to tackle the problems you're facing. The unique blend that combines engineering, operations, IT, and support skills into a cohesive offering for next-generation products can be complex to communicate. We were fortunate to engage with leadership that had a forward-looking mindset that embraced new models of product delivery. Don't be complacent and try to slot SRE responsibilities across existing functions—use industry examples and continue to make your case.

Invest time in understanding your organizational structures

Whether you're in a small division or sit next to the CIO, take a moment to place yourself in leadership's shoes and define where you believe an SRE function would fit. If it's not immediately apparent, work with leadership to introduce the concept as described. Change is possible; after you align executive support and prove the business case, you should have the green light to incubate an SRE group. In addition, network with key leadership roles. You will need their support to introduce SRE.

Frame the SRE introduction around a business case structure

The business case will resonate with executives and provide a natural approach to the conversation with the organization's leadership. It imperative for you to have the technical knowledge to support why SRE is what your organization needs, but distilling into a business case can be effective.

Setting boundaries and focus

After you've established your group, it's imperative to set limits of what your group can deliver. Start small and focus on the reliability of a few production systems. After you're successful, you can scale and build a shared center of excellence. We were thought of as the "new kid on the block," and different groups came to us asking for assistance in improving the reliability of their systems. It was tempting to add more products to our scope; however, we realized that we needed to focus on our original set of priorities first. After you have a good infrastructure and proven set of processes in place, the next natural step will be to scale up and add more products to the SRE group's responsibilities.

Sample Implementation Roadmap

After you have established and funded your team, here are some sample activities for starting with a single product:

- Quarter 1
  - Plan overall dashboard
  - Decide on availability monitoring and error monitoring tools
  - Decide on incident management tools
  - Decide on customer-facing status site
  - Identify on-call rotation plan
  - Reduce noise from any existing monitoring tools in place (N/A if no monitoring currently in place)
  - Define the SLOs that you want to monitor
  - Investigate Continuous Improvement/Continuous Deployment tools
  - Implement 12×5 on-call rotation
- Quarter 2
  - Build/go live with dashboard
  - Implement availability monitoring tool in production environments
  - Implement 18×5 on-call rotation
  - Standardize environments configurations
  - Autodeploy to environments
  - Self-service deploy of production systems via user interface
  - Implement error monitoring across all environments
  - Monitor and manage error budgets—coordinate with product marketing teams
  - Integrate customer-facing status site to monitoring and internal chat (Slack, Stride, etc.)
- Quarter 3
  - Conduct Disaster Recovery/Business Continuity Planning test (make sure to document and test Recovery Time Objectives and Recovery Point Objectives)
  - Experiment with container management and container orchestration (as products become more complex with microservices, containers will be important to understand as a delivery vehicle)
  - Research technologies and prepare for microservice deployments by piloting test application deployments

— Confirm the environment has met resiliency and high-availability goals for key infrastructure components

— Formalize sign-off in product development life cycle process as described in Figure 8-4

- Quarter 4

— Investigate and test tools for predictive analytics from logging analysis

— Implement 24/7 on-call rotation

Closing Thoughts

Good luck on introducing SRE into your enterprise. SRE has an exciting future in small and large organizations alike.

Further Reading

1. *Accelerate: The Science of Lean Software and DevOps: Building and Scaling High Performing Technology Organizations,* by Nicole Forsgren, Jez Humble, and Gene Kim (IT Revolution Press, 2018)

2. *Increment On-Call*

3. *Starting and Scaling DevOps in the Enterprise,* by Gary Gruver (BookBaby, 2016)

4. Ideas on metrics

5. Skill sets for successful SRE team members (*https://www.atlassian.com/it-unplugged/devops/site-reliability-engineering-sre*)

6. Templates for incident management (*https://response.pagerduty.com*)

Sriram Gollapalli has spent over 15 years designing, developing, and implementing enterprise SaaS product and solutions. He was the cofounder and COO/CTO of iLab Solutions, an enterprise SaaS focused on the healthcare market that Agilent acquired in the summer of 2016. Prior to that, he spent several years as a consultant at Deloitte Consulting focusing on strategic technology enterprise solutions and at Intel as a system engineer. Sriram has a B.S. in Computer Science and masters in information systems management from Carnegie Mellon University.

## CHAPTER 9

From SysAdmin to SRE in 8,963 Words

Vladimir Legeza, Amazon Japan

If you cannot measure it, you cannot improve it.
—William Thomson, Lord Kelvin

Over the past 10 years, *Site Reliability Engineering* has become a well-recognized term among many tech companies and the SysAdmins community. In many cases, it stands as a synonym for a new, advanced way of computer systems management tightly coupled with such keywords as *distributed systems* and *containerization*, representing a set of practices that allow a variety of companies to run and support systems at large scale efficiently and cost effectively.

The fundamental property that differentiates Site Reliability Engineers (SREs) and traditional System Administrators is the point of view. The conventional approach is to make sure that the system does not produce errors or become overloaded. SRE, on the other hand, defines the desired system state in terms of business needs.

Both approaches use myriad metrics that monitor service from every angle, from individual CPU core temperature to the stack traces of a high-level application. However, the same metrics will lead the two approaches to very different conclusions. From the SysAdmin point of view, latency growth of a couple of milliseconds might not seem significant compared to a large number of errors. An SRE, on the other hand, might be led to an entirely opposite conclusion: an error might happen, but if the end users have not been affected, the service is fine. Of course, if even a negligible latency increase causes difficulties for customers, now we are dealing with a severe issue.

Let's take a closer look at where this difference is getting its roots through the following short example.

Suppose that a manager asked us to create a small new service: "A sort of a simplified web crawler. It has to receive a base URL, download its content, and find and return a list of all URLs retrieved from that page with the status of whether it is valid and accessible or not." This task is more or less straightforward. An average software developer can immediately begin the implementation using a small number of lines of high-level code. An experienced SysAdmin given the same task will, with high probability, try to understand the technical aspects of the project. For instance, they might ask questions like, "Does the project have an SLA [Service-Level Agreement]?" and "What load should we expect, and what kind of outages do we need to survive?" At that point, prerequisites might be as simple as, "The load will be no more than 10 requests per second, and we expect that responses will take no longer than 10 seconds for a single URL request."

Now let's invite an SRE to the conversation. One of their first questions would be something like, "Who are our customers? And why is getting the response in 10 seconds important for them?" Despite the fact that these questions came primarily from the business perspective, the information questions like these reveal can change the game dramatically. What if this service is for an "information retrieval" development team whose purpose is to address the necessity of content validation on the search engine results page, to make sure that the new index serves only live links? And what if we download a page with a million links on it?

Now we can see the conflict between the priorities in the SLA and those of the service's purposes. The SLA stated that the response time is crucial, but the service is intended to verify data, with accuracy as the most vital aspect of the service for the end user. We therefore need to adjust project requirements to meet business necessities. There are lots of ways to solve this difficulty: wait until all million links are checked, check only the first hundred links, or architect our service so that it can handle a large number of URLs in a reasonable time. The last solution is highly unlikely, and the SLA should therefore be modified to reflect real demands.

What we've just done is to raise the discussion to a new level—the business level. We started with the customer and worked backward. We understood the service's use cases, identified its key aspects, and established and adjusted the SLA. Only now can we begin to architect the solution. This is the exact meaning of the first of Amazon's leadership principles (*https://www.amazon.jobs/principles*): "Customer Obsession— Leaders start with the customer and work backwards." Absolutely the same idea appears in the first of Google's "Ten Things" philosophy (*https://www.google.com/intl/en/about/philosophy.html*): "Focus on the user and all else will follow."

Clarifying Terminology

At this point, I want to present a short, three-character terminology clarification to avoid confusion or uncertainty. We will use these terms in the same way as they were introduced in Chapter 4 (*https://bit.ly/2wylnP*) of Google's *Site Reliability Engineering* book.

Service-Level Indicator

Service-Level Indicator (SLI) is a single, measurable metric related to service behavior that is carefully chosen with a deep understanding of its value's meaning. Every indicator covers one specific aspect of the service. We can measure every aspect on its own terms and conditions; however, the rule of thumb is that every indicator must be meaningful.

Example list of SLIs:

- Availability (% of requests per calendar year)[1]
- Response time (milliseconds)

SLA

SLA is a combined set of SLIs that defines the overall behavior of what users should expect from the service. Every indicator gets its own particular value or a range of values. Every possible value should be clearly defined as "good" or "bad." Also, all barrier values that turn "good" to "bad," and vice versa, should be precisely specified. A good SLA not only represents a list of guarantees, but also contains all possible limitations and actions that might take place in specific circumstances; for instance, graceful degradation in a case of primary data center outage, or what happens if a certain limit is exhausted.

Example SLA: "99% of all requests per one calendar year should be served in 200 ms A request should contain 10 chunks at maximum with no more than 2 megabytes of payload per chunk. All requests that exceed the limit will be served on a best-effort basis or entirely rejected."

This agreement contains four SLIs, namely:

- Availability (% of requests per calendar year)
- Response time (milliseconds)
- Data chunk size limit (megabytes)
- Limit of the number of chunks (chunks per request)

---

1 All percentile values (99.9%) and evaluation cycle periods ("per calendar year") used in examples within this chapter are conditional and presented for demonstration purposes only. Real services might have stricter requirements, such as 99.999%, and/or shorter period, such as "per quarter."

Service-Level Objective

Service-Level Objective (SLO) is absolutely the same set of SLIs that an SLA has but is much less strict and usually raises the bar of the existing SLA. The SLO is not what we need to have, but what we want to have.

Example: For the previously mentioned SLA, the availability indicator is set to 99%. For the SLO we might raise this value to 99.9%, and definition will look something like "99.9% of all requests per one calendar year should be served in 200 ms."

The difference between SLA and SLO lies only in the strength of restrictions. Here we will use only the SLA term for simplicity; however, all the facts that we discuss further are also correct to the SLO term. We can use them interchangeably, except cases for which the difference is explicitly mentioned.

The principle that the user's perspective is fundamental is very powerful and leads us to the understanding of vital service aspects. Knowing what is valuable for the customer provides a precise set of expectations that must be finally reflected in the SLA. And by being carefully crafted, the SLA can shed light on many dark corners of a project, predicting and preventing difficulties and obstacles.

But first, the SLA is designated as a reference point to understand how well a service is performing. Let's distinguish which indicators we should use to form an agreement that serves that purpose. There might be hundreds of metrics that reflect a service's state, but not all of them are appropriate for an SLA. Although the number of SLIs tends to be as minimal as possible, the final list of SLIs should cover all major user necessities.

Only two relatively simple questions should be answered positively to indicate that an investigated metric is a good candidate to be chosen or, otherwise, should definitely not be.

- Is this metric visible to the user?
- Is this metric important enough to the user (and from their perspective as a service customer) that it needs to be at a certain level or inside a particular range?

When we add a metric to an SLA, we also need to be sure that the metric, as we express it, has the same meaning for both sides—that is, for the service owner and for the customer.

If it seems impossible to stabilize initial SLA values due to frequent project changes, we might consider revisiting the list of included SLIs to verify that all indicators are not exposed internal specifics and measurable by the user.

For example, the SLA defined as the following:

> 99.9% of all requests per one calendar year should be served in 200 ms with no more than 1,000 requests per second.

At first glance, this is all correct: we have both guarantees and limitations. In reality, this limitation (or the Throughput SLI) has a fundamental difficulty: it has more than one interpretation that can lead to agreement misunderstanding, the disclosure of internal metrics, and frequent value changes.

For the end user, the only case for which this throughput statement is meaningful is when the service is used by this customer exclusively. So they might understand this limitation as meaning that designated throughput is the one that is provisioned for them personally. But the SLA does not state this explicitly, and a user can only guess whether their understanding is correct.

Another interpretation of 1,000 RPS (requests per second) is the "required amount of overall service capacity," which might be meaningful for engineers who will design and support this service but is useless for the users, because a user will never know how much capacity is being used by others and how much of the 1,000 RPS is available for them.

Finally, the 1,000 RPS can be treated as a value that shows the current service capacity. And if the performance of the service or hardware is changed, the value in the SLA will be updated accordingly.

If we want to clearly express that we want to limit the amount of incoming traffic, we can slightly adjust the SLA and say that every customer is provided with its dedicated throughput capacity:

> 99.9% of all requests per one calendar year should be served in 200 ms with no more than 1,000 requests per second from a single user account.

Now, this number is measurable on the user side and independent from the hardware and software capabilities. We can calculate how many users we can serve and are able to add more capacity and change software without touching the SLA.

Establishing SLAs for Internal Components

What if the service is not an end-customer-facing one. Should it have its own SLA, too? To clarify the "Yes" answer, let's play with an imaginary message distribution service (see Figure 9-1) that consists of the following four main components:

Data receiver
Accepting and registering messages

Data transformer
Adjusting message content with data from separate external sources

Distributor
  Delivering messages to multiple endpoints

Consumer
  Receiving data from the endpoint over a "publisher–subscriber" model

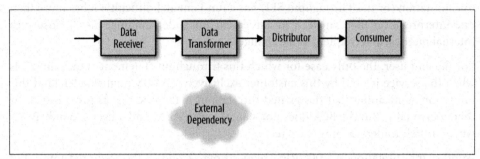

Figure 9-1. Message distribution service components relationship

At the moment, this system is working fine: no errors, no alarms.

One day, one of the top project managers comes to us and poses the following: "One of the projects we are working on now uses the 'message distribution service.' From time to time, we will need to send a huge amount of data in a short time period. Can we use this service as it is, or how should we adjust its capacity in order to handle the new traffic?

Let's work this out gradually. Having an actual number for the data amount is handy. Let's say that the forecasted traffic will be three times higher than the maximum known peak-time value. However, this knowledge will not provide us with a clear understanding of whether we will be able to handle such growth. The reason is simple: even if we know how much data is managed by the service right now during peak times, we would still need to know the breakpoint at which we reach the service's capacity limit to be able to compare it with the forecast.

Our message distribution service has several components. The slowest component is the one that dictates overall service capacity: the "strength of the chain is determined by the weakest link." So now we need to spend some time to establish a performance-testing environment and identify breakpoints[2] for every component separately and determine which component is the bottleneck.

So far, we have data that will tell us about traffic-handling possibilities: the number of messages that can be consumed without errors. And if it is fine, we are ready to go on

---

2 During performance testing, we gradually increase the traffic. The breakpoint is the amount after which the quality of responses falls lower than prescribed by requirements. Service begins to respond slower or even start producing errors.

to announce that no changes are required. That would be a great scenario if we had planned such growth in advance. Otherwise, if we can serve three times more traffic without rescaling, and service consists of more than one host (undividable resource unit), it might mean that up until now two-thirds of all allocated resources were never used, which might raise a question about cost efficiency. But that is a different story, and hopefully it is not the case.

Comparison of the test results and the forecast reveals that we can deal only with half of the expected growth. And we now, as per the new request, need to at least double throughput.

This is a relatively simple task. Traditionally, to solve such a problem SysAdmins determine the critical system resource—like CPU, memory, disk, network I/O, and so on—that is used the most, and that is the one that actually needs to be doubled. Then, they accordingly request new hardware to cover necessity. And there is nothing wrong with this approach. However, there is something else that is lying outside of its scope and hence not counted.

From the SRE point of view, we were missing additional service-specific restrictions without which we cannot scale our service accurately.

For our imaginary service, the goal is to pass a number of messages throughout from the entry point to the final consumer in a reasonable amount of time. Each component has only a limited time that it can stay inside each component before it will be sent to the next component. And this is our specific restriction: the time limit per component. Without such a limitation, during the traffic growth, some messages can be delayed or stuck for a very long time somewhere in the middle. This problem would not be visible; delayed messages are not marked as problematic because they do not raise any errors. They don't raise errors just because we don't know what duration is "good" and what isn't.

To overcome this inconvenience, we should express the overall delivery time in a particular time value. Then, we should assign the portion of it to the specific component and, again, define it in the exact time value. Here, we are correcting the meaning of a breakpoint for the performance testing procedure. What we need is not the number of messages that we can receive without errors, but how many messages this component is able to pass through such that every message been processed for no longer than the defined time limit. Establishing these limits usually decreases the previously calculated capacity even further.

Time constraint per component is nothing but another SLI ("Passing time") and its value is determined for every component individually. Also, each component has other valuable indicators such as "Availability" and "Response time." When combined they form a per-component SLA.

Now we have an SLA of two natures. The first is the one that we mentioned earlier, which covers the entire service and is exposed to the services' customers. We will use it to observe the overall service behavior.

The other one is the per-component SLA. It is not presented to the services' end users; however, it allows us to determine the relationship between components, helps to identify quickly which component caused difficulties to the overall service, and is used to precisely scale the component. Its SLI's values can (and should) be used during performance testing as limits to identify the correct breakpoint.

For our toy service, the breakpoint will be identified as a maximum throughput at which a component will meet the following demands:

- 100% of requests get responses faster than the certain limit.
- No errors occurred.
- 100% of messages are sent to the next component such that every message met its time limitations.

Keep in mind that all three criteria must be verified simultaneously, because receiving messages and sending them further might be done asynchronously by different processes, and the good condition of one metric does not mean the same status of the other.

Back to our scaling. We previously said that we need to double the throughput. Now, this statement needs to be revised because we changed the testing procedure by appending new requirements, and the results might not be the same as before.

The forecasted input will be received by the first "Data receiver" component. Knowing particular values of expected traffic and component performance metrics, we can finally estimate required capacity adjustments. We can calculate the potential maximum capacity we have now, the required capacity that can handle the maximum traffic expected, and then find the delta between the two. But this will be true only to the "Data receiver" because the forecasted input defines the size for this component only.

Do not forget that, for instance, doubling the throughput for a component does not necessarily mean that we need to double its fleet. Not all components scale linearly, so for some of them, it will be enough to add only a few machines. For others, it might require adding much more than double the number of hosts.

But what about the next component? In the same way, we can calculate its current capacity, but we don't know how much data it will receive from the previous one. We can assume that its traffic will increase according to the growth of the previous component's input, but this would be only an assumption, which might have nothing to do with reality.

Knowing what a component does, we can perform a set of experiments that will establish a ratio between the input and output of the component.

Now we can approximate the amount of input data for every individual component from the originally forecasted amount. For example, if the input/output ratio for the "Data transformation" component is 1:2, and 1:1 for the "Data receiver," it means that for every original megabyte of messages, the "Distributor" will get two.

Before we move on, we should say a few more words about the bottleneck component. We keep track of it for a single reason: the bottleneck is the first component that will experience difficulties in case of traffic growth. In other words, if this component is overloaded, the entire service has a problem. Why do bottlenecks exist if we scale every component to the maximum performance and throughput needed?

There are two factors. The first is that some components will be a bit overscaled. For example, if a single host can handle 1 million messages per minute, but the traffic is 1.1 million, adding the second host will leave 90% of its capacity (or 45% overall) unused. And this component will be fine until traffic reaches the 2 million messages per minute rate. But the other part of the service, in contrast, may already utilize its capacity up to 95% processing the same 1.1 million messages. The second factor is the input/output ratio. If for the first component the growth of incoming traffic is small but the rate is high, the input to the next component might increase significantly and might require our attention.

The bottleneck is the component that in comparison with others has minimal difference between current load and maximum available capacity, is very sensitive to traffic changes, and is the first that will be overloaded.

Returning to our story, to illustrate how the bottleneck identification works, let's imagine that the forecasted load peak is 1,000 RPS; the components' capacity after rescaling is as follows:

- Data receiver: 1,300 RPS
- Data transformer: 1,250 RPS
- Distributor: 1,100 RPS

With this information, we now have located a bottleneck; it is the Distributor because its performance is closest to the forecasted peak and, in spite of the Data receiver capabilities service, will work fine only until the load is less than 1,100 RPS. The next bottleneck is the Data transformer because it is the closest component to the current bottleneck, and so on.

So far, we know the following:

- Where the bottleneck is. And we can predict where the bottleneck will relocate from where it is now (literally this means that now we know the next slowest component, the next after that one, and so on).

- Expectations for every component (number of messages that can be processed by a single application instance and the expected amount of time that message can spend inside this component—literally an SLA).

- Per-component incoming/outgoing traffic ratio. We can predict the traffic volume between components and fit capacities accordingly.

- The overall and per-component capacity and how much of it is actually in use. We are also able to predict capacity drops in case of a variety of outages and make resource reservations accordingly.[3]

Our scaling calculations are based on the forecasted values. Keep in mind that the real traffic can have different characteristics. Continuously tracking available capacity along with the knowledge of whether all components stay within their SLAs will clearly tell us how "good" our service is doing.

The real-world scenario can become more complicated. There might be more than one SLA per service because we might have several data types, and each of them might need to be treated differently (Figure 9-2). In our case, different messages might have different priorities and processing-time restraints. Without an individual SLA for each priority, it would be tough to say what we should do if there is a growth in the load from only one of the data types even though this might affect the others.

---

3 Every host in a fleet represents a portion of a service capacity. The outage of a single host will decrease overall capacity by the amount represented by this host. Depending on the outage type that we need to sustain, we can add a number of hosts in advance so that during such an outage the overall service capacity will stay reasonable to deal with the traffic. For example, if 100% of required capacity is six hosts, but we need to withstand a data center outage, as one of the possible solutions, we will need to have nine hosts in three data centers. The disruption of any of these data centers will decrease overall capacity by three hosts, but we will still have a sufficient amount of six in the other two data centers.

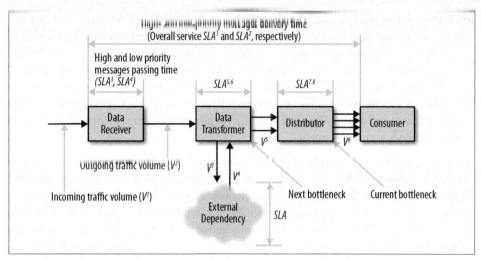

High and low-priority message delivery time
(Overall service SLA^1 and SLA^2, respectively)

High and low priority
messages passing time
(SLA^3, SLA^4)

$SLA^{5,6}$ $SLA^{7,8}$

Data Receiver → Data Transformer → Distributor → Consumer

V^5 V^6

Outgoing traffic volume (V^2) V^3 V^4

Incoming traffic volume (V^1)

External Dependency   SLA

Next bottleneck   Current bottleneck

Figure 9-2. Components relationship in terms of SLAs and traffic patterns for two message types

Here's a short example: due to high load spikes in high-priority messages, other message deliveries will be slowed down from a few seconds to several minutes. The key question then is, is a delay of several minutes acceptable?" By applying the "divide and conquer" principle, we declare specific criteria for every type separately, and if we know exact barrier values and can quickly identify "good" and "bad" values, there will be no problem taking the right action. Otherwise, we will fall into a state of not knowing and can only guess what to do or whether we should do anything at all.

Establishing SLAs for internal components helps to clarify the relationship between them and precisely coordinate their interaction. This is true not just across components but also across big services. SREs mostly focus on service efficiency and quality tracking what matters to the user. Service architecture and particular applications used are secondary, at least until a service delivers results according to a user's expectations.

And this is still not the end of the story!

Understanding External Dependencies

As you might recall, the "Data transformer" component in the course of its work adjusts messages' content with information from separate external sources. These sources are called external dependencies. The difference between a dependency and the services' components we have been discussing up to this point is that as opposed to a component, we cannot control a dependency and its behavior. Here, "Data transformer" is playing the role of a customer, and these external services are just a set of "black boxes."

From this perspective, the question is, "What capacity can these external services provide and how will their limitations affect our component's performance and scalability?" We want to know what we can expect, and, technically, we are asking for an SLA. We need this to understand whether we can use the service as a dependency, or we need to look around to find another solution for our task. The provided SLA will give us a clue about available limitations (like request size), performance (like response time), and availability, but still, how is our component performance affected by this and does it suit our needs?

If we imagine that we are SysAdmins who care mostly about service health and load and have nothing to do with SLAs—which, by the way, may not exist at all—the question we asked will be very tough to answer. However, knowing precise requirements for our own service (while we change our point of view closer to an SRE perspective), we can easily compare the values between SLAs that will direct us to the answer. Let's see. If, for example, the requirement to pass a message through the Data transformer component is 50 ms and we spend half of this time on internal manipulations only, we have 25 more milliseconds that we can designate to requesting data from the external source. By having an SLA for that source that states the response time should be less than 20 ms, we can confidently say that it is safe to use this service as a dependency.

As another example, it might be a stated capacity limitation that the dependency could serve only 900 RPS per customer account, and if the previously discussed 1,000 RPS of the forecasted peak value is still applied, we will either need to ask to raise the limit or to look for another solution.

The final case worth mentioning is when the performance of the dependency dictates our own component throughput. Suppose that without dependency the Data transformer can process 2,000 requests per second. If the performance of the external source is 1,100 RPS, the Data transformer will be limited by its performance to the same amount of 1,100 RPS. We're definitely able to use this service as it is, but we should keep in mind that the performance of our component is limited not by its own performance or capacity, but by the external dependency capabilities. This is a very important point because if we, someday, will need to scale up throughput of the Data transformer higher than 1,100 RPS, changes on its capacity will not make sense.

As is demonstrated here, we now can not only say whether we can use this service, but we're also able to predict whether we will reach the dependency's limits and if so, in what circumstances it would happen.

Another aspect of the external dependency is the tightness of a relationship between our component and this service—in other words, how an external service outage will reflect on our component performance and availability. To demonstrate the meaning of tightness, let's look at a couple of examples.

The most widely used external dependency is Domain Name System (DNS). If a component is frequently resolving domain names, an outage of the DNS might paralyze it completely and the entire service will be affected. The less expected scenario is when only a part of the service experiences difficulties. The entire service can also be affected, but this time it might be a bit more difficult to trace the source of a problem.

For the second example, we will discuss a less frequently used service called Lightweight Directory Access Protocol (LDAP). If we assume that the service calls LDAP only a few times during the start, the only moment during which our component can potentially be affected is while the service is starting or restarting.

Overall, the tightness of the relationship between the component and LDAP service is very low compared to the one between the component and DNS. Both services can affect their dependents, but the severity of a failure event is significantly different.

To visualize a dependency relationship, let's make a list of all of the external services we are using along with their SLAs and potential outage effects. Having it readily at hand in an emergency such as a fire could be critical. It could save you many priceless minutes that otherwise would be wasted figuring out influences on the fly. You should update it every time you add a new major feature or a new dependency.

From the SLA perspective, we need to make sure that our service's promised level of reliability is not higher than the lowest level among all direct dependencies. If we noticed that this might be the case, we need to either downgrade the SLA or find a technical solution to mitigate the difference. For that purpose, in some cases, we might develop a thin intermediate layer with, for example, caching or replication. Keep in mind that we may compare only directly related dependencies and that the service is depending not only on software, but also on hardware, power supplies, a network provider, and so forth, and they all have their own availability limitations that can affect us.

Even at this point, the understanding of whether the service is okay heavily depends on a personal point of view. The outage of a single dependency that blocks part of the service will be treated as a big problem by the classic SysAdmin role, but for SREs this service might appear to be only partially affected or even totally fine. For our messaging case, an outage of the "Data transformation" dependency might block this component entirely (service outage for SysAdmins). But even if we still can receive new messages and store them for a while, the high-priority messages would be affected immediately in terms of delivery timing. However, the low-priority traffic might not be affected at all (for SRE, service is only partially affected). Moreover, if there is no high-priority traffic at the moment, the service is totally fine (unless we are not breaching delivery time limits for the low-priority messages).

Now we see how the new viewpoint can dramatically change the way we understand the current service condition. Interestingly, when we actually write down the ideas of what we expect from a service and begin to collect related data to measure what we have in reality, it usually turns out that the service is not doing as well as we believed it was doing.

Measured results are different because, without an SLA, we can count only these problems that somebody complained about. And in our mind, the service is doing well because there were only a few complaints in the past that appear to have been successfully resolved. The problem is that we did not receive complaints about all of the issues we actually have and, in reality, there might be a thousand cases in which end users just leave silently with a bad taste in their mouth.

Nontechnical Solutions

Technical solutions are not the limit of an SLA's potential. SLAs will give you a hand in other fields as well. The SLA determines, for instance, the right time to hand a new service over to the SRE team to support. This can be as simple as, "If a product meets expectations (i.e., does not violate an SLA), the product is ready; otherwise, it is not."

When we talk about the handover procedures, the first thing that comes to mind is a big checklist with dozens of bullet points. It covers all possible aspects of the service, from architecture decisions and comprehensive administration documentation to monitoring alarms and troubleshooting runbooks. However, having all these bullets checked hardly gives you a strong sense of confidence that it is ready to be taken over. Unless you are freezing all activities except transition preparations, that is a very unusual thing to do; you will never be 100% sure that there will be no unpleasant surprises.

Consider the following. All new software projects will have some prerequisites long before they pass architecture review and a couple of proof-of-concept models have been built. When it is believed that an application is ready to be officially launched and begin serving live production traffic, both SLA and SLO counters are reset[4] and start to collect the real data. This is the starting point for the service condition measure. Because the SLA defines statements over time (the frequently used period is one calendar year), the project should last in this state a significant portion of this time (several months or a quarter) to collect enough data points that confirm that the service is stable enough and that there are no agreement violation risks.

If we add an "expectations reaching" goal as an additional checklist point along with the alarms limitations (amount of alarms for a service during the time period; e.g., "No more than one alarm per two weeks"), we will be much more confident that ser-

---

[4] You can set SLAs and SLOs for all environments (dev/test/prod), but they all will show the condition of the particular environment each. The metric might be the same for every environment, but values will be unique. When we launch a service, we reset all counters so that we avoid influences from the prelaunch data.

vice was not on fire for long enough before, that it is not on fire now, and that the developers team is able to maintain this state and it will not throw you a curveball.

Similar to this example, you might put any task or idea through the SLA prism to see how impactful it is for your customer and treat it accordingly. This understanding will guide you not only about the points that need to be improved, but also about where further improvements are unnecessary and therefore you can switch your attention to something else. As an example, if your SLA stated the requirement of 99.9% availability, but for the last quarter the service is running as good as 99.999%, you do not need to do any more work on that service.

Now, let's see how theory meets with practice.

Tracking Availability Level

All right, so let's assume that we've successfully defined an SLA. But from a practical perspective, how should we track all of these numbers and percentiles?

Before jumping into the arithmetic, let's clarify some meanings first.

Here, we need a list of all agreement violation conditions to take them all into account. Let's name these conditions as "failures" to distinguish them from the "errors" we have been using previously. This separation is necessary to stress that we will not use these two terms interchangeably. Failures will contain not only errors, but also a variety of other events that, one way or the other, affect the availability metric. Moreover, the spectrum of included errors also needs to be restricted, because the "404 Not Found" HTTP error, for example, is more of notification rather than an actual error caused by service internals and hence should be removed from the list.

To return to our previous example, let's say that for the high-priority traffic for the "Data receiver" component of the "Messaging bus" service the SLA is defined as follows:

> We will process all messages marked with the high-priority flag within 10 ms in 99.9% of cases over a calendar year.

The list of failures, in this case, will contain the following:

- Messages that took longer to process than 10 ms.

- Messages unable to be processed due to internal service problems but not caused by incorrect incoming requests.

To track the ongoing availability level, we need to subtract the number of failures from the total amount of messages received.

Here we are dealing with a single component and not with the entire "Message-passing bus." As a result, we need to count the total messages locally from the component perspective even if we have a set of load balancers in front of it. You should use the data from load balancers to track the overall "Message-passing bus" SLA.

The same is true for the error counters. Collecting error counters from the load balancers will definitely depict the real customer's impact; however, at the same time, it will hide the actual errors amount happening in the component level and prevent us from reacting to them before they become visible from the outside.

So, let's run the math. Our initial availability is equal to 100%. After the first 24 hours, we will collect all metrics, calculate a number of failures, and finally get the new availability value to start the next day with it.

If for the last day we receive 1 million messages and 200 of them were marked as failures for whatever reason, the availability would be reduced to 99.98%, calculated as follows:

$$100\% - (200 / 1,000,0000 \times 100) = 99.98\%$$

This calculation method will work fine to a certain extent, but it does have a few problems. The first one is that availability level changes in only one direction and once decreased will never recover.

The second is that we do not take the "over time" distribution into account, which can lead to dramatic drops where it is not expected at all. For instance, suppose the traffic is served by two hosts fronted by a load balancer and there was a very quiet time period during which only 10 messages were sent for an entire day. What would happen to the statistics if one of the hosts begins producing errors for every received message? If all 10 messages were sent back to back, they were equally spread between the hosts and half of them failed. The load balancer resent them to the other host and finally all 10 were successfully delivered. From the calculation perspective, it would be a huge availability drop:

$$100\% - (5 / 15 \times 100) = 66.67\%$$

A 33.33% drop without any customer impact!

The last obvious constraint is that we are unable to plan maintenance that requires downtime because it is unclear how to integrate this intentional downtime from the messages amount perspective.

This leads us to another difficulty: unsafe update rollouts. Any rollout with massive changes can potentially end up counting as an entire service outage regardless of the number of tests and canary stages the software passed. The problem is not the outage by itself; the problem is our inability to predict in advance whether such events will break the SLA. Even if we know how much time we need to detect an issue and perform a rollback, it is still unclear how to compare this time with the available 0.1% of cases that are left apart from that 99.9 % that we agreed to serve correctly.

The solution is hidden in the interpretation of the "99.9% cases per year" statement. The "year" is a value of time, and thus 99.9% can also be treated as a time value.

According to this statement, we can count how much time per year we have left for failures and maintenance. A single year consists of 525,600 minutes. The 0.1% that is left beyond the SLA level is equal to almost 526 minutes. Google gives this value a unique name, the *error budget*. The percentage of time that service worked correctly over the year is usually referred to as a service's "uptime," and "99.9%" specified in the SLA is the acceptable level of this metric.

Literally, we can interpret the error budget as follows: if the service does not produce even a single failure for the last 365 days, we can shut it down completely for about 8 hours and 45 minutes without violating the SLA.

Now we are able to compare rollback timing requirements against such a budget to see whether the next rollout will put availability levels at risk.

Also, availability level (uptime) now becomes recoverable. Previously, we were able only to decrease the uptime value, but the new method allows us to restore it over time up to the original 100% mark. Because "a year" is a constant duration value, every new minute of operation appends new metric values into the head of a year timeline and discards the same amount of data from its tail. If we calculate availability on a daily basis, every time we will work with 1,440 minutes of data. By subtracting all of the failure time from 1,440 daily minutes, we get a "daily uptime." To calculate new overall service availability, we need to subtract daily uptime as it was a year ago from the previous overall availability value and append it with today's uptime. For example, if we have the following:

- Yesterday's service availability level: 525,400 (99.9619%)

- Error budget size: 326 minutes

- Daily availability for the same day last year: 1,400 minutes

- Today's failures: 5 minutes

---

5 "Canary" rollout is a method wherein we gradually deploy new software over several stages that begin with a tiny portion of a fleet at first and increase distribution wired up to 100%. At every stage, the new product must perform as expected for some time before it will be pushed forward to the next stage.

Today's overall uptime is as follows:

Uptime = "Yesterday's uptime" – "Last year's daily uptime" + "Today's daily uptime"

525,400 – 1,400 + (1440 – 5) = 525,435 (99.9686%)

Here is the current error budget calculated as a difference in minutes between the current overall uptime and the SLA level:

525,435 – (525,600 – 526) = 361

As we can see, last year we had only 1,400 minutes of correct operation, which means that the 40 remaining minutes were used by failures and cut off from the error budget. After a year, these 40 minutes can be returned to the budget because the period when they were encountered is moved beyond the one-calendar-year period (our current availability scope; see Figure 9-3). So, by today, the budget increased by 40 minutes and decreased back by 5 minutes used by today's failures.

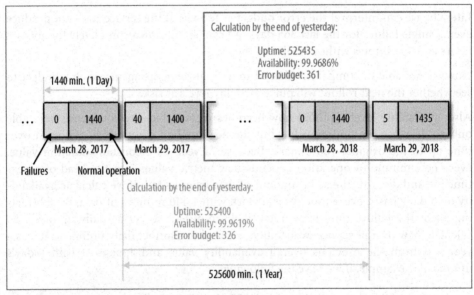

Figure 9-3. Daily availability calculation scope

Finally, the last thing we need to do is establish a way to convert our service's failure counts into error budget amounts.

To avoid the previous problem in which a very few messages reflected on availability as a 33.33% drop, we will calculate day values, not as a single data set, but gradually by the smallest possible duration between available data points. For instance, if statistics are collected once a minute, we also can analyze the data on a per-minute basis.

The conversion itself is very simple. For every analyzed minute interval, we know the number of messages and the number of failures. One interval represents 100% of the time, and the total message amount is also treated as the 100% value. From this we can derive the failures fraction and extract the same amount from the time interval.

The sum of all converted failure times should be used to adjust current uptime and error budget values.

Let's see how all that will work on the "Data receiver" example. For this component we have two types of failures:

- An error occurred, and we lost the message.
- The message is stuck somewhere for more than 10 ms.

We collect metrics on a per-minute basis, and we also produce all zero values (if there were no errors, we would produce a metric that explicitly says that "Errors=0."). We also recalculate availability once every 24 hours.

For every minute interval, we have three data buckets:

- Number of messages processed
- Timers for every message
- Number of errors

If the timers bucket is missing a data point, we don't know what exactly happened with that message and we mark it as a failure. Similarly, we do this with the number of processed messages and number of errors buckets, and if one of them is empty, we mark the entire minute as a failure.

Let's recalculate our original example with 2 hosts and 10 messages and imagine that incident happened across a minute border and that was the only 10 messages for the entire 24-hour period. Here's the calculation:

Minute 1

- Messages: 10
- Delays: 0
- Errors: 5

Minute 2

- Messages: 5
- Delays: 0
- Errors: 0

The uptime for the first minute is 0.5 minutes (50%), and 1 minute (100%) for the second minute. Overall, it is 0.5 minutes of downtime. Overall daily availability would be 1,439.5 minutes (1,440 – 0.5 = 1,439.5). In a worst-case scenario, if this incident were to spread over a longer time period and all messages happened to be delayed, we will lose only 20 minutes[6] of a budget, which is quite different from the 33.33% we saw earlier.

Do not be surprised if a freshly established error budget drains out very quickly even from tiny incidents and the real availability level is much lower than you thought initially. We were establishing the SLA primarily to reveal this difference.

At this point, we are able to derive failures from other events; we know that they are not errors only. Also, we can convert these failures into the SLA-related values to track changes in the services' availability level. And finally, we know how to calculate and use the error budget to plan time for experiments and to perform maintenance procedures without putting at risk agreements with our customers.

Now, let's see what else we should keep in mind while working with SLAs.

Dealing with Corner Cases

To avoid the impression that involving SRE and establishing SLAs is a simple and straightforward way to address various difficulties and is only beneficial, here is a brief overview of a couple of notable corner cases when SLA by itself introduces a bit of additional complexity.

An SLA is not a constant, and to bring significant benefits, it should be well maintained and sometimes needs to be changed. On the other hand, the SLA should not be violated (by design). Moreover, not all projects need to have a strict SLA or involve SRE to maintain it.

An SLA is an agreement not only with the user, but also among developers, SREs, and management that are all committed to supporting this availability level. This means that "the level, as it is set, is the one that is needed." An SLA violation is a severe incident, and to avoid it they all will need to interrupt their regular duties and put as much effort as needed to get the service back on track.

Not all agreements-related difficulties are introduced by errors and outages. Some of them are accumulated over the time span little by little. For example, take a case in which for the preceding six months the response latency gradually doubled and drew

---

6 If 10 messages at first attempt will be landed to a bad host and retransmitted to a good one only by the next minute, every one of them will drive the entire minute to be counted as a 100% failure. Next, if all retries will be delayed, they will score another 10 minutes as 100% failures. Finally, because all of these events don't share one-minute intervals, that day will be finalized with 20 minutes of downtime.

very close to the SLA limit. There might not be a single commit in the code that was responsible for that regression, but thousands of small modifications, each of which introduced its own few nanoseconds' delay, can eventually double the original value. There would be no single developer or a team responsible for that. However, it is clear that we cannot leave this situation in place.

There are only two ways to deal with the situation at that point: adjust expectations (i.e., the list of indicators included into the SLA or the values that are related to one or several of these SLIs), or get under the hood and optimize the service.

For the first way, if it somehow turns out that the problem is not severe enough to pay additional attention to it, it means that we set our SLA incorrectly and need to make corrections. This case is the most typical for startup companies. Many small organizations have a certain period of growth when releasing new features is much more important than any other metric. The number of users at that time is very small, and minor inconveniences will be forgiven in favor of new functionality. If this describes your circumstances, the recommendation will be to downgrade your SLA to the status of an SLO and return to strict requirements later when the company gains a critical mass of customers. Another possibility is that we overestimated customer needs or, even more surprisingly, there might be an aspect of a service's behavior that we previously treated as a minor one that over time became an exciting feature and a crucial part of the service.

For the second way, we need to deal with the issue from the technical perspective. The team should have a goal to return the problematic metric closer to its original state. To be clear, the goal is not to prevent latency growth caused by further product development; the goal is to reduce and keep the latency within a specified limit. We might introduce a bit of latency with a new feature, but at the same time it might be possible to decrease it again by refactoring an old component. Practically, we might dedicate one or two people to work on the optimization, while the rest of the team will continue working on ongoing projects. After a while (two weeks or a month), swap the people working on optimization with two other team members, similar to an on-call rotation.

 Choosing the exact way to go is not a technical decision but a managerial one. Changes in an SLA are a change in business priorities. And changes in business priorities can lead a company to rapid growth or immediate death. The SRE's job here is to provide management with a clear overview of the current situation and resolution possibilities to help with making the right decision.

Finally, it would be a mistake to say that every project needs to have an SRE onboard. Consider what would happen if we were involved with a project that does not require a high availability level. What if a maintained service was down for an entire weekend until developers brought it back online at the next business day and there was no negative impact at all? At the least, it would become a conflict of priorities because SREs and developers do not share the same availability goals and will drive the project in opposite directions. The number one priority for the developers might be to deliver new features as fast as they can, regardless of service availability, and the SREs will work hard to slow them down to, at least a little bit, stabilize the product. For such a project, having a SysAdmin who can help with system-level duties like initial configuration and supplementary software maintenance would be more than enough. So, before trying to apply SRE approaches to a particular service, we have to make sure that we do it in the right place. Otherwise, we will waste a lot of time and energy.

Conclusion

The SRE philosophy differs from that of the SysAdmin just by the point of view.[7] The SRE philosophy was developed based on a simple, data-driven principle: look at the problem from the user and business perspectives, where the user perspective focuses on "take care of product quality," the business perspective pays attention to "managing product cases and efficiency," and "data-driven" signifies "not allowing assumptions."[8] Identify, measure, and compare all that is important. Everything else is the result of this. This is the core of all SRE practices.

If this all sounds very difficult and complicated, start with the following short list of instructions and summarized potential outcomes, applying it step by step to the smallest service component you have:

1. Begin a new project with the following quote: "Start with the customer and work backward."

2. Divide large services into a set of components and treat each component as an individual service. That will help us to identify problematic spots easily.

3. List the vital service indicators (SLIs) that will provide us with a better understanding of what we should care about the most. Of course, we may not rely only on our beliefs and need to keep an eye on actual customers' experience.

---

7 This philosophy differs "just by the point of view" and not by practices because, having originated from this point of view, the set of SRE practices can be shared among SREs and SysAdmins. However, the successful adoption of a practice does not immediately make an SRE from a SysAdmin.

8 Having assumptions is fine. However, the assumption cannot be stated as true unless it is supported by data. For example, if it is believed that a service is working fine, it cannot be stated that it is fine unless there is a known measurable meaning of the word "fine," and a collection of data that supports this "fine" statement assumption.

4. Indicators being aggregated to a complete SLO will explicitly express the meaning of a "good" and "bad" service state.

5. If the service you're working with is already serving production traffic, try to pick values for the initial SLO such that they reflect the current service availability as close as possible. Work from that. This kind of SLO will not create an immediate necessity to change the service to match the desired level. We can raise the bar as the next step.

6. Start with a 100% uptime. Compute an error budget and make a list of all "failure" conditions that will reduce its size. It will help you track how much time is left for issues, maintenance, and experiments.

7. Enumerate all dependencies and their influence. This will be an important indicator of issue sources or performance regressions. You will need to consider whether an issue is caused by a problem with the service itself or due to a service with which it communicates.

8. Test service performance against SLO barrier values. That will indicate the relationship between traffic and required capacity.

9. During the test, measure not only how much incoming traffic the application is able to handle, but also how much additional load to external services it will generate. This will approximate the ratio between input and output (for every service separately), and precisely estimate requirements for dependent services. Repeat tests periodically, track changes in trends, and adjust capacity accordingly. Over time, an SLO will display the effective service reliability level, indicate regressions, and draw attention to problematic conditions.

10. Evaluate necessities and priorities for all technical and nontechnical decisions against the SLO and from a customer perspective.

11. Promote the SLO to SLA and establish a new objectives level; then move on to your next service.

Now, you can control your systems more accurately and can precisely know when, what, why, and how they should be adjusted. Following the "Focus on the user and all else will follow" principle, you can develop and enrich a set of your own best practices to gain efficiency, enjoy lower costs, and raise the bar for an overall positive customer experience.

Vladimir Legeza is a site reliability engineer in the Search Operations team at Amazon Japan. For the last few decades, he has worked for various companies in a variety of sizes and business spheres such as business consulting, web portals development, online gaming, and TV broadcasting. Since 2010, Vladimir has primarily focused on large-scale, high-performance solutions. Before Amazon, he worked on search services and platform infrastructure at Yandex.

## CHAPTER 10

Clearing the Way for SRE in the Enterprise

Damon Edwards, Rundeck, Inc.

"Sounds great, but how would that ever work here?"

Do you work in a medium- to large-sized enterprise? Did this question cross your mind while reading this book? Know that you are not alone.

Changing how an organization does its operations is difficult at any scale. However, it is in the enterprise where the challenges and roadblocks to change will often seem like insurmountable mountains.

Change your tools? Complicated, but doable at any size.

Teach individuals new skills? Difficult, slow work, but there are known paths for everyone to follow.

Fundamentally change how your organization works? This is where you hit that metaphorical mountain in all but the smallest of organizations.

Fear not, moving from a classic enterprise operations model to an SRE model is doable. Companies are doing it right now as you read this book.

This chapter is for enterprise leaders who are seeking to transform their traditional operations organizations to SRE. You will learn how to identify and clear the obstacles that, if left unaddressed, would otherwise undermine your SRE transformation.

This chapter comes from a compilation of knowledge gained while working with large enterprises to transform their operations organizations. These folks have taken the uncharted path to SRE so that your journey might be easier.

First, I will examine the systemic forces that will be standing in your way. Second, I will highlight techniques for clearing those obstacles so that you can start and sustain your SRE transformation.

How should you measure success? Improved reliability, improved MTTD/MTTR,[1] improved organizational agility, and fulfilled effective colleagues. What is failure? Ending up with some new "SRE" job titles, but not much else changing.

Toil, the Enemy of SRE

Toil is the hidden villain in the journey to SRE. In organizations that have already internalized the SRE way of working, spotting and eliminating toil is a natural reflex. In organizations that are coming from a traditional operations culture, spotting and eliminating toil is a organization-wide skill that often needs to be learned.

What is toil? Vivek Rau from Google (*https://landing.google.com/sre/book/chapters/eliminating-toil.html*) articulates this answer well: "Toil is the kind of work tied to running a production service that tends to be manual, repetitive, automatable, tactical, devoid of enduring value, and that scales linearly as a service grows." The more of these attributes a task has, the more certain you can be that the task should be classified as toil.

Being classified as toil doesn't mean that a task is frivolous or unnecessary. On the contrary, most organizations would grind to a halt if the toil didn't get done. The value of toil is often a point of confusion among traditional enterprise operations teams. To some, manual intervention in the running of services *is* their job description.

Just because a task is necessary to deliver value to a customer, that doesn't necessarily mean that it is *value-adding* work. For people who are familiar with Lean manufacturing principles, this isn't dissimilar to Type 1 Muda[2] (necessary, nonvalue adding tasks). Toil can be necessary at times, but it doesn't add enduring value (i.e., a change in the perception of value by customers or the business).

Instead of your SREs spending their time on non-value-adding toil, you want them spending as much of their time as possible on value-adding engineering work. Also pulling from Vivek Rau's helpful definitions, engineering work can be defined as the

---

1 Mean Time to Detect (MTTD) is the average length of time between the onset of a problem and the problem being detected. Mean Time to Repair (MTTR) is the average length of time between the onset of a problem and the resolution of the problem. Although these are commonly used operations metrics, their use is not without controversy. The first point of controversy is how precise of a judgment you can make using these metrics to evaluate operational performance. If no two incidents are alike, how valid is looking at an average? The other controversy is over which metric should take priority. Rapid detection can be an indicator of a system better instrumented and better understood, leading to more consistent resolution and better prevention. Rapid repair might indicate better automation or failover capabilities, and repairing/restoring is the ultimate goal in any incident.

2 Womack, J. P., & Jones, D. T. (2010). *Lean Thinking: Banish Waste and Create Wealth in Your Corporation.* Riverside: Free Press.

creative and innovative work that requires human judgment, has enduring value, and can be leveraged by others (see Table 10-1).

Table 10-1. Comparing characteristics of toil and engineering work

Toil	Engineering work
Lacks enduring value	Builds enduring value
Rote, repetitive	Creative, iterative
Tactical	Strategic
Increases with scale	Enables scaling
Can be automated	Requires human creativity

Working in an organization with a high ratio of engineering work–to-toil feels like, metaphorically speaking, everyone is swimming toward a goal. Working in an organization with a low ratio of engineering work–to-toil feels more like you are treading water, at best, or sinking, at worst.

A goal of "no toil" sounds nice in theory but, in reality, that isn't attainable in an ongoing business. Technology organizations are always in flux, and new developments (expected or unexpected) will almost always cause toil.

The best we can hope for is to be effective at reducing toil and keeping toil at a manageable level across the organization. Toil will come from things you already know about but just don't have the time or budget to automate initially (e.g., semimanual deployments, schema updates/rollbacks, changing storage quotas, network changes, user adds, adding capacity, DNS changes, and service failover). Toil will also come from any number of the unforeseen conditions that can cause incidents requiring manual intervention (e.g., restarts, diagnostics, performance checks, and changing config settings).

Toil might seem innocuous in small amounts. Concern over individual incidents of toil is often dismissed with a response like "There's nothing wrong with a little busy work." However, when left unchecked, toil can quickly accumulate to levels that are toxic to both the individual and the organization.

For the individual, high levels of toil lead to the following:

- Discontent and a lack of feeling of accomplishment
- Burnout
- More errors, leading to time-consuming rework to fix
- No time to learn new skills
- Career stagnation (hurt by a lack of opportunity to deliver value-adding projects)

For the organization, high levels of toil lead to the following:

- Constant shortages of team capacity
- Excessive operational support costs
- Inability to make progress on strategic initiatives (the "everybody is busy, but nothing is getting done" syndrome)
- Inability to retain top talent (and acquire top talent after word gets out about how the organization functions)

One of the most dangerous aspects of toil is that it requires engineering work to eliminate it. Think about the last deluge of manual, repetitive tasks you experienced. Doing those tasks doesn't prevent the next batch from appearing.

Reducing toil requires engineering time to either build supporting automation to automate away the need for manual intervention or enhance the system to alleviate the need for the intervention in the first place.

Engineering work needed to reduce toil will typically be a choice of creating external automation (i.e., scripts and automation tools outside of the service), creating internal automation (i.e., automation delivered as part of the service), or enhancing the service to not require maintenance intervention.

Toil eats up the time needed to do the engineering work that will prevent future toil. If you aren't careful, the level of toil in an organization can increase past a point where the organization won't have the capacity needed to stop it. If aligned with the technical debt metaphor, this would be "engineering bankruptcy," as illustrated in Figure 10-1.

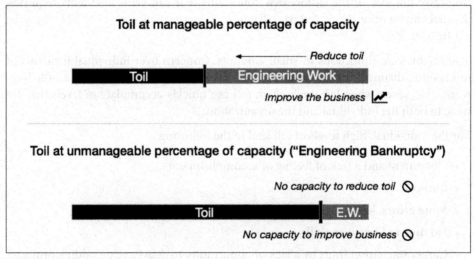

Figure 10-1. Excessive toil consumes a team's capacity to perform engineering work to both improve the business and reduce toil

The SRE model of working — and all of the benefits that come with it — depends on teams having ample capacity for engineering work. If toil eats up that capacity, the SRE model can't be launched or sustained. An SRE perpetually buried under toil isn't an SRE, just a traditional long-suffering SysAdmin with a new title.

Toil in the Enterprise

Enterprises are fertile ground for toil. First, when it comes to the concept of toil, legacy operations management philosophies were either blind ("Everybody looks busy. Great efficiency!") or indifferent ("Why are you complaining about these headaches? I pay you to have headaches."). Second, the high level of organizational complexity found in an enterprise creates toil and gets in the way of efforts to reduce it.

For this discussion, let's define an "enterprise" as any company that has had the historical success needed to accumulate a significant amount of legacy (culture, organization, process, and technology).

Enterprises have a distinct "look." From a business perspective, you'll find multiple business lines, each born or acquired during different eras that had unique context and underlying assumptions. From a technology perspective, you'll find multiple generations of platforms and tools—some brand new, some old and evolving, some orphaned—that all need to hang together to provide services to customers.

It is good to keep in mind that nothing in an enterprise lives in isolation. What you are working on is dependent on others. What others are working on is dependent on you. In classic architectures, these dependencies are fixed and obvious. In modern architectures, these dependencies are often dynamic and abstracted away, but still exist. At the human level, incentives, budgets, policies, beliefs, and cultural norms are all intertwined across the various ends of an enterprise.

This interconnectedness makes eliminating toil significantly more challenging in the enterprise. The toil of your team's own making can be eliminated with straightforward engineering work. But what about all of the toil that is due to conditions or systems that exist in other parts of the organization? Eliminating it is out of a team's control unless that team can effect solutions across organizational boundaries, which anyone with enterprise experience knows is no trivial feat.

Toil that is partially, or wholly, out of a team's control is especially dangerous. It pushes the team closer to that bankruptcy threshold at which toil crowds out all engineering work. This is a common cause of the antipattern where SysAdmin teams are rebranded "SRE teams," but the lack of engineering blocks transformation beyond the new name.

Silos, Queues, and Tickets

After you've established that excessive toil will prevent an enterprise from shifting to an SRE model, it logically follows that you are going to have to work across organizational boundaries in order to effectively contain toil. However, working across organizational boundaries is one of the great challenges in enterprise IT.

Working across organizational boundaries is difficult because of a confluence of silo effects, request queues, and the most venerable of all IT operations workhorses, tickets.

Silos Get in the Way

The silo metaphor is first attributed to Phil S. Ensor, who used it in 1988[3] to describe the organizational challenges at his employer, Goodyear Tire. Since then, the concept of "silos" has been discussed by the Lean manufacturing movement and the DevOps movement. Some people mistakenly think "silos = teams," but in reality, silos don't have that much to do with organizational structure. The idea of a silo really has everything to do with how a group(s) works within an organization.

In simple terms, a group is said to be "working in a silo" when its members are working in a disconnected manner from other groups (whether they know it or not), as depicted in Figure 10-2. When spotting silos, look for situations in which a group is working in a different context from other groups, their work is coming from a different source than other groups (i.e., different backlogs), and the group is working under different incentives or priorities (and often part of a different management chain). It is almost certain that this group is working in a silo and experiencing any number of symptoms: bottlenecks, slow handoffs, miscommunication, tooling mismatches, delivery errors, excessive rework, and conflict (usually the finger-pointing type).

---

3 Ensor, Philip. S. (1988, Spring). The Functional Silo Syndrome. *Target*. Association for Manufacturing Excellence.

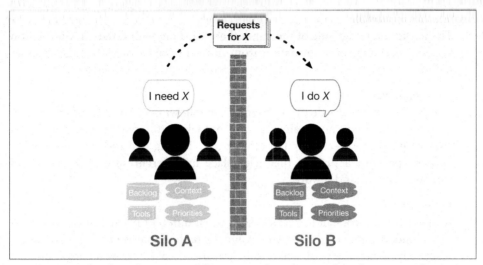

Figure 10-2. Silos describe a way of disconnected working rather than a specific organizational structure

If you've worked in operations in an enterprise, you probably recognize this condition. Some might even ruefully describe it as "the way things have always worked." It is endemic to the classic operations model in which you have lots of specialist teams divided by functional expertise and use ticket systems and a heavy reliance on project management to coordinate work and push it through the organization.

Operations teams don't set out to work in silos or suffer the consequences of silos. It is usually the natural byproduct of traditional management philosophies based on the human urge to "optimize" large-scale efforts by sorting people according to functional specialization, grouping like with like, and then incentivizing them to look inward and optimize.

Problematic handoffs (too slow, incorrect, lots of rework, etc.) are the most commonly cited problem that can be attributed to silo effects. This makes sense given that silos only become a problem when you need something from someone outside of the silo (or someone outside of the silo needs something from you).

And remember, in the enterprise, nothing lives in isolation. Doing anything significant usually means information and work is going to have to cross one or more organizational boundaries.

What goes wrong when work has to pass between siloed groups? It usually has to do with mismatches (see Figure 10-3):

Information mismatches

The parties on either side of the handoff are working with different information or are processing the information from different points of view, leading to an increase in errors and rework (i.e., repeat work due to previous errors).

Process mismatches

The parties on either side of the handoff are following either different processes or processes that are nominally the same but take a different approach and produce results not expected by the other party. Timing and cadence mismatches between parts of a process that take place in different silos also lead to an increase in errors and rework.

Tooling mismatches

An increase in errors and rework is seen when different parties on either side of silo boundaries are using different tooling or tooling that isn't set up to connect seamlessly. When the work needs to be translated on the fly by a person moving information and artifacts by hand from one tool to another, delay, variance, and errors are bound to be introduced into the process.

Capacity mismatches

Bottlenecks and delays occur when the amount or rate of requests coming from one side of the silo boundary exceeds the capacity of those fielding the requests. Requests levels often exceed or are below expectations, which has the ripple effect of disrupting the planning and flow of work for other parts of the organization.

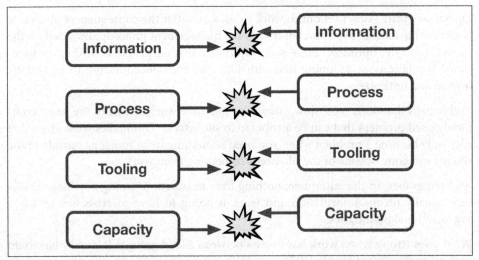

Figure 10-3. Handoffs between silos are problematic due to mismatches

Ticket-Driven Request Queues Are Expensive

For decades, the go-to countermeasure for dealing with the handoff problems caused by silos is to insert a request queue to govern the handoff (usually a ticket system). On the surface, request queues might seem like an orderly and efficient way to manage work that crosses the divides of an organization. However, if you look under the surface, you will find that request queues are a major source of economic waste for any business. Let's look at the following list, created by noted author and product development expert, Donald G. Reinertsen, that catalogs the negative impact of queues (see also Figure 10-4):[4]

Longer cycle time
> Queues increase cycle time because it takes longer to reach the front of a large queue than a small one. Even small delays can exponentially compound within a complex interdependent system like an enterprise IT organization.

Increased risk
> Queues increase the time between request and fulfillment, which in turn increases likelihood of the context of the original request changing (a race condition). If a problem does arise, the requestor is now in a different mental position (often working on something else) from where they were when they made the request.

More variability
> Longer queues lead to high levels of utilization, and higher levels of utilization amplify variability. This leads to longer wait times and a higher likelihood of errors.

More overhead
> Queues add a management overhead for managing the queue, reporting on status, and handling exceptions. The longer the queue, the more these overhead costs grow in a compounded manner.

Lower quality
> Queues lower quality by delaying feedback to those who are upstream in the process. Delays in feedback cause the cost of fixing problems to be much higher (e.g., bugs are easier to fix when caught sooner) and often mean that additional problems of a similar origin have been created before the first negative feedback arrives.

---

4 Reinertsen, Donald G. (2009). *The Principles of Product Development Flow: Second Generation Lean Product Development*. Redondo Beach, CA: Celeritas Publishing.

Less motivation

> Queues have a negative psychological effect by undermining motivation and initiative. This is due to queues (especially longer queues) removing the sense of urgency and immediacy of outcomes from the requestor's work. If you don't feel the impact and don't see the outcome, it's human nature to grow negatively disconnected from the work.

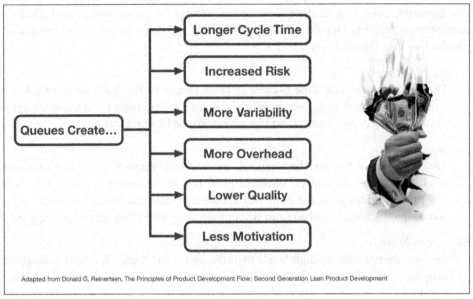

Adapted from Donald G. Reinertsen, The Principles of Product Development Flow: Second Generation Lean Product Development

Figure 10-4. Queues have been proved to be economically expensive

Looking at the science behind the impact of queues, it is difficult to justify inserting queues all over your organization. It doesn't make sense to willingly inject longer cycle times, slower feedback, more risk, more variability, more overhead, lower quality, and decreased motivation into your organization.

Despite this, what is the most common method of managing work within IT operations organizations? Request queues in the form of ticket systems.

When an organization manages the interaction between people working in other silos via tickets, you are undermining people's capacity for value-adding engineering work both directly (more wait time, more overhead, more disconnects, more errors) and indirectly (more toil). Worse still, much of this lack of capacity and increased toil is beyond their capability to fix because the cause is in another silo.

In the coming sections, I discuss how to eliminate silos, queues, and tickets—and how to avoid their harmful effects where they can't be eliminated.

Take Action Now

Hopefully, the first part of this chapter made the case that SRE demands a change to the fundamental conditions prevalent in legacy enterprise operations organizations. The following sections lay out steps that you can take to clear the obstacles to an SRE transformation.

As with any transformation, you should favor a continuous improvement approach. Your organization is a complex system. Big bang transformations of complex systems are risky and have a poor record of success. No matter how much you plan up front for an SRE transformation, it will likely go differently after you begin moving. Encourage your team to embark on a series of steady, deliberate actions.

The suggestions in the rest of this chapter should not be looked at as prerequisites to taking action or a definitive formula to follow (i.e., "the one true way"). These are patterns and lessons to apply on a continuous basis. Gather your new SRE team. Empower it to begin transforming how it works. Empower the team to reach across organizational boundaries and collaborate on improvements that will benefit everyone. Favor action and continuous improvement.

Start by Leaning on Lean

If you are going to transform how your operations organization works, you might as well leverage a proven body of transformational knowledge. The Lean manufacturing movement has produced a wealth of design patterns and techniques[5] that we can apply to improve any work process. In particular, it is the principle of *Kaizen* (which roughly translates to "continuous improvement"), born from the Toyota Production System, that speeds transformations and drives an organization's ability to learn continuously. To bring Kaizen to an organization, there is a method called *Kata*, also based on Toyota Production System.

Kata is an excellent methodology to apply to the challenge of eliminating toil, silos, and request queues. Kata encourages organizations to look at the end-to-end flow of work and methodically experiment until the desired outcome is reached. Teams are encouraged to see beyond their work silo and think holistically about problems. Kata will help you identify what stands in the way of your goals and then stay aligned as you iterate toward those goals.

It is important to point out that Kata is about teams improving *themselves*. Lasting performance improvement comes from when people know how to fix problems as part of their day-to-day work. One-off projects or external help might provide a spe-

---

5 *https://www.goldratt.com* and *https://www.lean.org*

cific benefit at a specific point in time. However, enterprises don't stand still. New challenges, large and small, will arise all the time.

SRE teams are meant to do engineering work to improve the reliability and operability of systems and reduce toil (freeing up more time for engineering work). SRE teams, by definition, must be learning teams who can spot and fix problems as part of their day-to-day work. Kata is an excellent reference to teach new SRE teams how to think and work like that.

The Kata approach is already becoming a common practice in Agile and DevOps efforts looking to improve development and delivery processes. However, operations processes are rarely deemed worthy of the effort, especially in legacy operations cultures. This oversight is unfortunate because operational quality is equal in value to any other quality measure in your organization. Even ad hoc operations processes (e.g., one-offs due to an incident or similar type of event) are processes that are worthy of study.

If you are considering the move to SRE, you should assume that your organization already knows the value of investing in improving operations work. If not, a conversation on value needs to happen among both technical and business leaders in your company.

There are many books, presentations, and other resources available to take you deep into the practice of Kata. I highly recommend the works of Mike Rother[6] and John Shook.[7] However, part of the beauty of Kata is that you don't need much knowledge to get started and begin seeing benefits. Here is an overview of the Kata process in an operations context:

1. *Pick a direction or challenge.* This is your higher-level directional goal. Where do you want to go as an organization? What is the business value that you are there to maximize? What is the ideal state of operations work at your company?

   It is critical that there is consensus on what the value of operations is to the business and what performance and reliability levels need to be in order to maximize that value. The entire organization (from frontline engineers to leadership) should know why they are embarking on this SRE transformation and how it will improve the business.

---

6 "The Improvement Kata" (*http://www-personal.umich.edu/~mrother/The_Improvement_Kata.html*)

7 Rother, Mike, and John Shook (2009). *Learning to See Value-Stream Mapping to Create Value and Eliminate Muda.* Cambridge, MA: Lean Enterprise Institute; Shook, John (2010). *Managing to Learn: Using the A3 Management Process to Solve Problems*, Gain Agreement, Mentor, and Lead. Cambridge, MA: Lean Enterprise Institute.

The answers don't need to be overly detailed or address how you are going to get there. However, if the answers end up sounding like general platitudes or a vague mission statement, that is a failure (e.g., "Delight customers with highly available and speedy services"). Keep trying until people have a decent notion of where the organization needs to go and why. There should be some recognition of both measurable operational outcomes (e.g., reducing incidents, improving response times, and increased frequency of change) and desired business outcomes (e.g., increased sales and higher net promoter score).

2. *Grasp the current condition.* Build a clear understanding of how things work today. Take an end-to-end view of the process that you want to improve and strive to understand how it is actually done today. Why does it happen this way? What is needed to get it done? Who is needed to get it done? What gets in the way? When does it go wrong?

Be sure to look at each of the types of work in your organization. Project-oriented work is an obvious choice (systems engineering, environment build outs, etc.). It is equally important to look at incidents (i.e., failure scenarios). Examining incidents as processes might sound odd because incidents rarely follow much of a standard process beyond some communication and information gathering formalities. However, if you look at enough incidents, you will find common patterns. Incidents provide a very enlightening look into how an organization is really "programmed" to work.

Remember, silos are your enemy. Doing this kind of analysis in private or limiting it to a team of "experts" delivers minimal value to your organization. Enterprises are notorious for their compartmentalization of information. Very few people will know how end-to-end processes actually happen—and even they will disagree. You are bound to open a lot of eyes and hear comments like, "Hmm, that's not how I thought that worked," or, "I never knew that," from even the longest-tenured employees. That alone is worth the effort.

Do your analysis in the open and encourage participation from as many people as possible. Look upstream and downstream for participants with knowledge to contribute. Invite developers, program managers, and other operations teams. Your transformation to SRE has the best chance of success if as many people as possible have a similar understanding of what needs to change.

Visual analysis is a very effective way to get a group of people aligned—assuming you do the visual analysis as a group. In Lean terminology, this is known as "Going to the Gemba," which roughly translates to "going to the place where the work happens," In the physical manufacturing world, this means going to the factory and directly observing the work firsthand.

In IT operations, you can't actually see most of the work happen. Other than some artifacts, the work is all abstractions and individual's mental models. So,

Going to the Gemba in our context only works if you are getting people together and aligning those mental models the best you can in a process retrospective session. Figure 10-5 shows the results of one of these sessions. This alignment is extremely important because those individual mental models are the lens through which every person in your organization evaluates and executes their daily work.

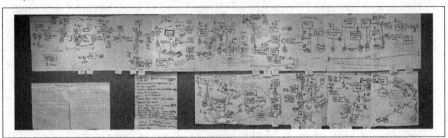

Figure 10-5. Artifacts from visual analysis created during a process retrospective session

So how do you do this? This visual analysis works best when you look at one process at a time. Pick a process (a specific delivery of project work or a specific incident). Get people together who have first-hand knowledge of the process (enough to look at it end-to-end). Draw out what actually happened (focus on the flow of work, with people and tools as second-level supporting details). Finally, get the participants to identify and discuss what got in the way. Repeat this with enough instances of the process (or group of related processes) until there is reasonable consensus on how the process happens, why it happens (if it is an incident), and what gets in the way.

There are other resources you can draw on to develop your visualization and analysis technique. Value Stream Mapping[8] and Lean Waste classification (*https://itrevolution.com/the-7-wastes-of-devops/*) are highly useful.

3. *Establish your next target condition.* This step is where you decide on the next improvement target that your organization will attempt to reach. Again, this is best done as a group. Based on the directional goal determined in step 1 and the current condition uncovered in step 2, what is the next major intermediate step we are going to try to accomplish? This is what the organization is going to focus on, so everyone should be able to articulate what it should be like when the target condition is achieved.

---

8 Rother, Mike, and John Shook. (2003). *Learning to See: Value-Stream Mapping to Create Value and Eliminate Muda.* Cambridge, MA: The Lean Enterprise Institute.

As Mike Rother advises "Setting the target condition is not about choosing between existing options or best practices. It's about aspiring to new performance. By setting a target condition and trying to achieve it, you learn why you cannot. *That's what you work on.*"

4. *Experiment toward the target condition.* Get the organization into an iterative rhythm of forming hypotheses (e.g, "If we could stop/start *x*, it would reduce/ increase *y* by *z* amount"), testing alternatives (e.g., process, tooling, or org changes), and evaluating the result. If the result moves you toward the target condition, implement whatever was tested and continue with other experiments. If you see the Scientific Method in this, you are correct. Repeat the experimentation until you've reached the next target condition.

During step 4 of this process, be sure you revisit step 2 often to make sure everyone still grasps the current condition. Also, make sure that you are reviewing the specification of the next target condition often to ensure that everyone stays aligned.

When you hit the target condition, repeat step 1 ("is the goal still valid?") and then steps 2 through 4.

Get Rid of as Many Handoffs as Possible

As was described earlier in this chapter, silos and their accompanying problematic handoffs and expensive request queues do considerable damage to an organization. So, perhaps it is obvious that the first strategy to relieve this problem is to get rid of as many silos and handoffs as you can.

Forward-thinking organizations are transforming from a traditional "vertical" structure aligned by functional skill to a "horizontal" structure aligned by value stream or product. The vertical structure is the classic divide-by-function strategy (Dev, QA, Ops, Net, Sec, etc.). The horizontal structure comprises cross-functional teams that can own the entire end-to-end life cycle of a service.

The idea behind cross-functional teams is that they will handle as much of the life cycle as possible without needing to hand off work to other teams. There are no significant handoffs or breaks in context, and everyone's work flows from a single backlog aligned by common priorities. Bottlenecks are largely avoided, feedback loops are shorter, and cycle times are quicker. If a problem does arise, it is easier for a cross-functional team to respond and rectify the problem, as illustrated in Figure 10-6.

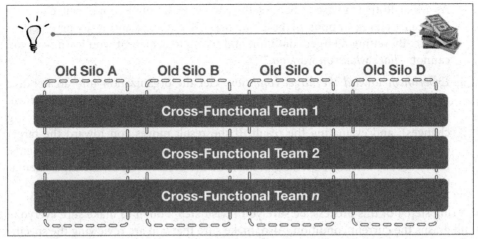

Figure 10-6. Cross-functional teams alleviate the need for many handoffs

These cross-functional teams are also often referred to as *service-oriented teams*, *product-oriented teams*, or *market-oriented teams*. These labels emphasize that the goal of these teams is alignment toward a business-recognizable delivery of value to a customer (i.e., a specific customer-identifiable service). This alignment allows for the team members to understand how their work impacts the business and then optimize the team for maximizing customer value (rather than functional efficiency).

Although the idea of cross-functional teams appears simple, implementation is a significant structural and cultural change for enterprises.

To understand why this is such a significant shift for enterprises, look no further than the rules of corporate accounting. Admittedly, this is an area in which most engineers thought they would never have to delve. However, some basic concepts provide a window into some of the most fundamental forces that shape an enterprise.

Project-based funding is often the primary flow of money in enterprise IT. After a business need is identified, there is a process to define a project and fund it with a specific budget. After funding, the project will proceed through the various functional silos of the IT organization until the project reaches production and is deemed complete. The next iteration is generally looked upon as a new project with a distinct budget.

Project-based funding increases the pressure on operations in several ways:

- First, the proliferation of services and bespoke infrastructure generates a significant amount of toil for operations. When an organization is project oriented, teams move from project to project, often leaving a trail of new software and new infrastructure behind. The movement of teams to new projects deprives the teams of learning from operational feedback. Also, as discussed earlier in this chapter, the constant creation of net new software and infrastructure (even if built following documented patterns) creates new technical debt and errors from unknown conditions. These behaviors are continuous sources of toil for the teams on which operational responsibility is dumped.

- Second, in the drive to hit a project's finish line, operational concerns are not always adequately addressed before being pushed to production. Delivering the project at or under the budget is what the delivery teams are judged on. It is only human nature that operational concerns like stability, scalability, deployability, configurability, observability, and manageability tend to get superficial treatment or are often the first thing cut in a time crunch. In the worst cases, these operational concerns are not considered at all. Although the high-value development resources are quickly recycled and reattached to projects, an operations team has to catch each project and own reliability and scale. In a traditional model, this is a continuous stream of toil that usually requires adding more headcount. However, even assuming that the operations teams are equipped with the skills to do engineering work in an SRE model, these teams are still in perpetual catch-up mode, and engineering bankruptcy is always a risk if toil levels get too high.

- Third, with projects being the primary funding vehicle, operations budgets are viewed as mostly operations and maintenance expenses, or *OpEx* in accounting lingo. OpEx is the budget category that gets the most scrutiny and cost controls because it directly impacts the current year's profitability. Teams whose funding largely comes from OpEx are naturally susceptible to management impulses for organization-by-function and efficiency mandates, both of which encourage siloed working.

Toil mostly appears around operations and maintenance work, which is OpEx. Generally, all of the project-based funding is *CapEx* (capital expenses). Engineering work to build or improve a system is usually CapEx because it is improving an asset (and can be amortized over several years, so the negative impact on current year profit is smaller). A team funded out of an OpEx budget and being managed for efficiency often won't have the budget (or the general charter) to engage in significant engineering work.

To move to an SRE model, you do not need to be an accounting expert. However, it does pay dividends to be acutely aware of how the money flows in your company. If you want your move to SRE to be more than a change in job titles, you are going to need to make the case that the SRE team should be funded to do engineering work and attached to teams who own the service life cycle, from inception to decommissioning. The move from project-based funding to product-based funding (with cross-functional teams) is already gaining traction in Agile and DevOps discussions. If this idea is making headway in your organization, try to leverage it for your SRE transformation.

Two common patterns are shaping up in enterprises experimenting with cross-functional teams and SRE. The first is to have SREs (and other functional roles) join dedicated product teams. This creates cross-functional teams that can own a service from inception to decommissioning. Development and ongoing operations all happen from within these cross-functional teams. From an enterprise perspective, this is often seen as a radical departure from traditional organization models. Sometimes, you might hear this referred to as the "Netflix" model.

The second pattern is to have SRE remain a distinct organization. Development teams have SRE skills and initially will own the full life cycle of a service. When the service has reached a certain level of performance and stability, there is a formal handoff to an SRE team that has embedded development skills. This SRE team manages the availability and scalability of the service according to performance agreements made with the development teams.

If further changes made by the development team drop the performance of the service below the agreed-upon levels, there is a mechanism to return more operational responsibility to the development team. From an enterprise perspective, the general shape of this model seems the most familiar. However, how work happens in this model is still a radical departure from traditional operations models. Sometimes this is referred to as the *Google model*.

Of course, employees from both Netflix and Google will be quick to point out that there is a lot more nuance to either model. However, these descriptions provide a possible high-level starting point for thinking about how to devise a model that works best for your company's unique conditions.

The options available to you will likely be constrained by how the rest of your company wants to operate. For example, changing organizational structure to move to product-aligned teams entirely will require buy-in from at least development and product management (which will likely need broader business discussions). Staying with a traditional development and operations organizational divide has the benefit of not upending the entrenched political structures within your company, but at the same time, those political structures can reinforce the old ways of working and unintentionally undermine improvement efforts.

The visualization techniques described in step 2 of the Kata process (grasp the current condition) can help with discussions on organizational structure changes. Not only does visualization help people understand the flow of work, but it also helps them see how organizational structure impacts that flow of work.

In any model you choose, there is still bound to be culture shock when the walls between traditionally development-only teams and operations-only teams are broken down. SREs play an essential role in bringing operations skill and experience to previously development-only teams. In the physical-fitness world there is an expression,

"Great abs are made in the kitchen, not in the gym." Likewise, "Great operations begins in development, not in production." SRE's play the critical role in bringing operations skills and discipline to previously development-only teams.

Replace Remaining Handoffs with Self-Service

There are always cases in the enterprise in which you cannot put all of the required skills and knowledge into cross-functional teams. For practical, financial, or political reasons, most companies operating at significant scale cannot avoid having functional specialist teams. Networks, platforms, security, and data management are common areas in which enterprises rely on centralized teams because of either not enough specialists to go around or the need (perceived or real) to centralize control.

The presence of these specialist teams means that handoffs can't be avoided during the normal flow of work through the organization. Either you need something from one of them to get your work done, or you are on one of these specialist teams where everyone needs something from you.

Dependencies between services (a fact of life in the enterprise) require teams to consume services from other teams and make operational requests of those teams (e.g., configuration changes, health checks, performance tuning, deployment coordination, and adding accounts). This creates yet another set of unavoidable handoffs.

As was discussed earlier, whenever there is a handoff point, and work has to move from one team's context to another, there is an opportunity for silo effects to take hold and create problems.

Because you cannot get rid of all handoffs, you need to apply techniques and tooling to mitigate the negative impact of those handoffs. Deploying the traditional solution of ticket-driven request queues is expensive, is toxic to the organization, and should only be a last resort.

Instead, the go-to solution should be to deploy self-service capabilities at those handoff points. These self-service capabilities should provide pull-based interfaces to whatever was previously needed to be done by someone on the other end of a request queue (investigating performance issues, changing network/firewall settings, adding capacity, updating database schemas, restarts, etc.).

The point of self-service is to stay out of the way of people who need an operations task completed. Rather than having someone fill out a ticket and sitting in a request queue, you give them a GUI, API, or command-line tool to do it themselves, when they need to do it. This capability eliminates wait time, shortens feedback loops, avoids miscommunication, and improves the labor capacity of the teams that previously had to field those requests, freeing them from repetitive requests so that they can focus on value-adding engineering work.

Self-Service Is More Than a Button

The idea of self-service isn't new. However, the traditional approach to self-service is to have a privileged operations team create somewhat static "buttons" for less-privileged teams to push (e.g., push-button deployment for new *.war* files). There are a limited number of scenarios in which this static approach works. Also, it still leaves the higher-privileged team as the bottleneck because they are the ones who need to build—and maintain—the button and the underlying automation. This maintenance burden alone limits the amount of static self-service capabilities an operations organization can expose.

To maximize the effectiveness of self-service, the ability to both define and execute automated procedures needs to be provided, as demonstrated in Figure 10-7. Of course, you need to put constraints in place to enforce security boundaries and help prevent mistakes, but providing the ability to define *and* execute delivers the most value.

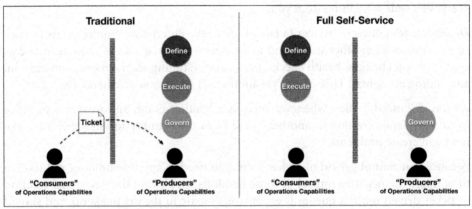

Figure 10-7. Traditional ticket-driven request fulfillment versus full self-service

For example, consider the Elastic Compute Cloud (EC2) (*https://aws.amazon.com/ec2/*) service from Amazon Web Services (AWS). The ability to press a button and get a running virtual machine was interesting. However, the ability to control your own destiny by making your own machine images (AMIs) and configuration was revolutionary. It empowered individuals and allowed teams to decouple and move at their own pace. However, it isn't unfettered access. Users are constrained for security reasons by both AWS and their own self-selected security policies (*https://docs.aws.amazon.com/IAM/latest/UserGuide/introduction.html*). Users are also constrained in their choices to provide "guardrails" to keep users of the system from making some types of mistakes or impacting performance of other users. In this example, the ability to define and execute automation is pushed to end users and governance is shared by the operators (AWS in this case) and end users.

To maximize the value of self-service in the enterprise, replicate this pattern of moving the ability to define and execute automation to wherever in the organization it will improve the flow of work.

Self-Service Helps SREs in Multiple Ways

Within an enterprise, effective self-service capabilities are a boost to SRE efforts. The following is a list of some of the benefits:

Reduces toil

With few exceptions, fielding repetitive requests is toil. Having effective self-service capabilities can help SREs reduce toil by quickly turning around automation to reduce those repetitive requests. Often repetitive requests do not follow the same pattern each time, and this can undermine an SRE's ability to set up reusable automation. If you can set up the right primitives and then give requestors the ability and permission to create their own automated procedures, you can create self-service for an even broader set of repetitive requests. Examining which self-service processes end up being built can also indicate to both SREs and developers where their current engineering efforts should be focused to reduce the need for future intervention.

Alleviates security and compliance concerns

Security and regulatory compliance are unavoidable facts of life in the enterprise. Whether it is organizational scar tissue from past problems, a response to industry fears, or a directive from an auditor, your SRE transformation will need to work within existing security and compliance requirements. I do not advise trying to introduce a new operations model and question existing security or compliance policies. Pick your battles.

Self-service capabilities can provide both a system of record for operations activity and a point of policy enforcement. You can use the same self-service mechanisms within teams and across team boundaries. This will give you both the ability to track operational activity to meet compliance requirements and a way to safely expand the distribution of access privilege. By doing so, SREs can work across a wider scope of your infrastructure than was previously permitted. This also enables your traditionally nonoperations colleagues to participate in operations activity without opening tickets for others to do it for them.

Separation of duties is a standard requirement of most enterprises. No matter if it is to comply with specific regulations (e.g., PCI DSS Requirement 6.4 (*https://www.pcisecuritystandards.org/documents/PCI_DSS_v3-2.pdf*)) or to satisfy more general regulatory controls, separation of duties can interfere with a team's plans to take cross-functional ownership of the development, testing, and operations of a service.

Self-service tooling can help by providing a mechanism through which a person in a development role can create a procedure that someone in an operations role can quickly vet and execute. Also, those in privileged operations roles can create preapproved, limited self-service capabilities that can be executed on demand by those in nonprivileged roles (e.g., development or QA roles). You can often persuade auditors that this form of self-service still meets a separation of duties requirement because the operations role sets up the procedure, grants specific access, and receives the logs and notification of its use.

Security concerns are also the culprit behind many of today's repetitive requests that can be labeled as toil. Purely for security reasons, people are currently being forced into queues and are waiting for someone to do something for them. Self-service, done correctly, gives the requesters the ability to take action themselves. You can maintain security postures through fine-grained access control, full logging, and automated notifications.

Improves incident response
Self-service capabilities are helpful for capturing a team's best practices as checklists and automated runbooks. When responding to incidents, checklists can improve both individual and team performance. Setting up checklists as automated runbooks not only encourages consistency but also allows running the checklists—and watching the output—to be a group activity.

Maximizes the value of standard services and infrastructure
It is considered a best practice for SRE teams to use some of their engineering time to build and maintain standard infrastructure (e.g., platforms and environments) and operations services (e.g., deployment systems and observability). The better the self-service capabilities are, the more an organization will be able to leverage these standard components and services.

Operations as a Service

If you examine companies that both employ an SRE style of operations and are regarded as high performers by their peers, you will find that they have often built custom-purpose tooling to enable self-service capabilities. For example, look at Netflix's combination of Spinnaker,[9] Winston,[10] and Bolt.[11] These were originally purpose-

---

9 *https://www.spinnaker.io*

10 Netflix Technology blog, "Introducing Winston — Event driven Diagnostic and Remediation Platform" (*https://medium.com/netflix-techblog/introducing-winston-event-driven-diagnostic-and-remediation-platform-46ce39aa81cc*).

11 Netflix Technology blog, "Introducing Bolt: On Instance Diagnostic and Remediation Platform" (*https://medium.com/netflix-techblog/introducing-bolt-on-instance-diagnostic-and-remediation-platform-176651b55505*)

built tools developed from the ground up for Netflix's focused, purpose-built organi zation. Enterprises will probably find that they need more generic self-service capabilities to embrace the heterogeneity that comes from decades of acquisition and accumulation.

Operations as a Service (OaaS) is a generic and deceptively simple design pattern for creating generic self-service operations capabilities. The basic idea of OaaS (*https:// www.rundeck.com/oaas-guide*) is that it is a platform for safely distributing the ability to both define and execute automated procedures, as shown in Figure 10-8.

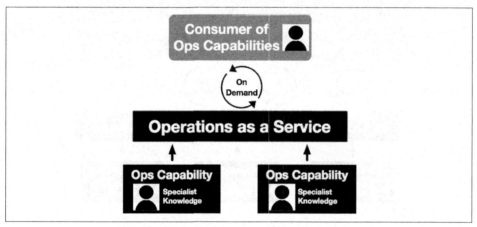

Figure 10-8. Overview of OaaS design pattern

Critical to the success of this design pattern is the requirement that the platform both is lightweight and works with any popular scripting language or tool. Forcing teams to standardize on one language or automation framework just isn't realistic given the heterogeneous nature of modern enterprises. In fact, it is not just unrealistic, it can actually slow an organization down. Teams need to be able to use the automation languages and tools that they want (or inherited) while allowing for other tools to orchestrate procedures across those underlying frameworks and languages.

Access control and audibility are also critical to the success of this design pattern. For any solution to thrive in the enterprise, ultimate control needs to remain with people and teams that are deemed to have a higher level of access privilege.

OaaS efforts have the best chance of exceeding expectations when paired with moni- toring and observability projects. Implementation projects tend to focus heavily on automation. However, when the project progresses, many organizations discover that visibility into operational health, state, and configuration is lacking. Metaphorically speaking, they are distributing the keys to the car without giving people the capability to see where there are going. To avoid this problem, put equal emphasis from the beginning on both "the view" and "the do."

The OaaS design pattern should be compatible with any operations operating model. Whether you are moving to cross-functional teams (Figure 10-9) or staying with closer to a traditional development and operations organization divide (Figure 10-10), developing your organization's self-service capabilities will pay dividends.

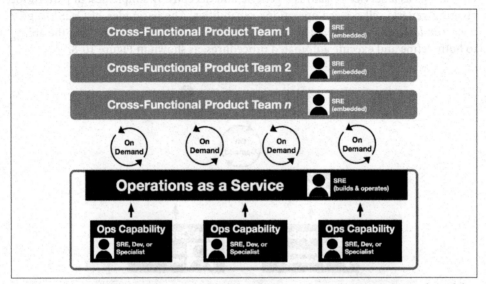

Figure 10-9. OaaS design pattern with a cross-functional teams organizational model

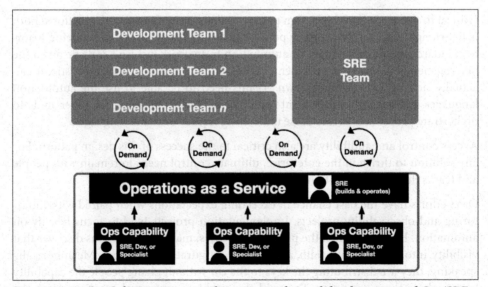

Figure 10-10. OaaS design pattern with a more traditional development and Ops/SRE split organizational model

Error Budgets, Toil Limits, and Other Tools for Empowering Humans

One of the more powerful developments to come out of the SRE movement is the popularization of a set of management concepts that formalize the expectations around an organization's operational activity. For those who work in companies that had an SRE model from inception, the following ideas might be self-evident. For those who work in traditional enterprise IT operations, these ideas often highlight how much of a departure the SRE model is from traditional operations beliefs and practices.

Error Budgets

There are often tensions in an organization over how much risk is tolerable for a particular service and who is responsible when the Service-Level Objectives (SLOs) are not met. In traditional enterprise divides, the product end of a company is incentivized to go faster, and the operations end is incentivized to avoid downtime and other performance problems. This is the type of mismatch in incentives that encourages silos to form. How do you keep both interests aligned? How do you keep all roles investing in both speed and reliability?

Error budgets are a framework for measuring, and utilizing, allowable risk. Specifically, it is the gap between theoretically perfect reliability and an acceptable SLO agreed upon by business and technology stakeholders. Error budgets provide a framework to negotiate with the business on how much failure is acceptable and still be able to meet the needs of the business.

It is not an accident that the metaphor of a budget is used. Budgets are a representation of currency that is available to be spent. That is the same with error budgets. Developers and SREs can use that budget in attempts to move the business forward. If a service has a small error budget, developers and SREs must be more conservative to favor stability. If a service has a bigger error budget, developers and SREs can be more aggressive and favor speed and production experimentation. As with other types of budgets, the negotiation is about how to best spend it—and in some cases, don't spend it at all (see Figure 10-11).

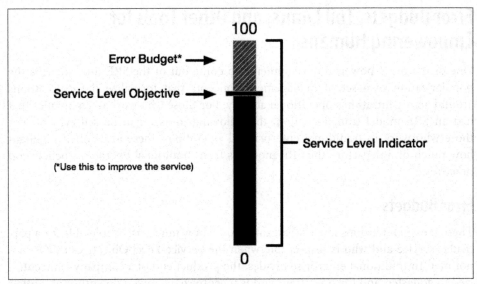

Figure 10-11. Error budget is the difference between perfection and the agreed-upon SLO

What happens if you exceed the error budget? Error budgets are attached to a service, not a particular role. All roles involved with the service must respect the budget. For example, if the error budget is violated due to aggressive or problematic change, those in development roles need to adapt their behavior (including often taking over more operational responsibility) and adapt the service to perform within the error budget allotted.

This is a sharp contrast to the traditional business-mandated Service-Level Agreements (SLAs) found in enterprise IT operations. If those traditional SLAs were broken, operations (in a service provider role) incurred the penalty and development—already on to their next project—usually did not. Also, the concept of a Service-Level Indicator (SLI; quantifiable performance measure), an SLO (performance target), and the error budget (current amount above the SLO) is more nuanced and pragmatic than traditional SLA approaches. You need to be sure that teams coming from traditional operations cultures understand the differences.

Toil Limits

Toil limits are another concept that challenges traditional operations thinking. I have already covered why toil undermines the SRE function. Defining a limit on the amount of toil that is to be undertaken by an individual SRE or team both makes a statement about priorities and protects an individual or team's capacity to do engineering work.

Toil limits are also indicators of a team's health. If a team's toil exceeds a predeter-mined threshold (e.g., Google's default limit of 50% of an engineer's capacity), the organization can swarm to the find out ways to help rectify the situation. Like error budgets, toil limits help SREs reach an agreement on expected behavior, provide clear signals when help is needed, and avoid being overrun by non-value-adding repetitive work. In a traditional IT operations culture, teams rarely have these types of protec-tions.

The concept of toil is largely absent from traditional enterprise operations culture (despite high levels of what you can now identify as toil). For people working in modern SRE-inspired organizations, toil feels bad. The urge is to find ways to elimi-nate it, and your colleagues support the effort. In traditional enterprise culture, toil is, at best, considered a "nice to fix" item and, at worst, just accepted.

When introducing toil limits, you will need to educate your people to socialize the concept of toil and to get them to understand why toil is destructive to both the indi-vidual and the organization.

Leverage Existing Enthusiasm for DevOps

Although DevOps was once the exclusive domain of web-scale startups, it has become an accepted ideal in most enterprises. Born in 2009, DevOps is a broad cul-tural and professional movement focused on "world-class quality, reliability, stability, and security at ever lower cost and effort; and accelerated flow and reliability throughout the technology value stream."[12]

There is quite a bit of overlap between the goals of DevOps and SRE. There is also quite a bit of overlap between the theoretical underpinnings of DevOps and SRE. Benjamin Treynor Sloss, the Google leader who first coined the term SRE and presi-ded over the codification of Google's SRE practices, sees a clear overlap between DevOps and SRE:

> One could view DevOps as a generalization of several core SRE principles to a wider range of organizations, management structures, and personnel. One could equivalently view SRE as a specific implementation of DevOps with some idiosyncratic extensions.[13]

Within the enterprise, DevOps has been applied most often to the limited scope that starts with software development and moves through the service delivery pipeline (from source code check-in to automated deployment). In these enterprises, the pen-

---

12 Kim, Gene, Patrick Debois, John Willis, and Jez Humble. (2017). *The DevOps Handbook*. Portland, OR: IT Revolution Press, LLC.

13 *Site Reliability Engineering: How Google Runs Production Systems*, Introduction (*https://landing.google.com/sre/book/chapters/introduction.html*).

---

etration of the DevOps transformation is minimal beyond deployment and the bulk of operations practices have remained unchanged. SRE is an opportunity to leverage the momentum started by DevOps and continue the transformation efforts throughout to the rest of the post-deployment life cycle.

I recommend looking for DevOps momentum in your organization and aligning your SRE transformation efforts. There are lessons that each can learn from the other. Working both Dev-toward-Ops (DevOps) and Ops-toward-Dev (SRE) will give your company's transformation the best chance of success.

Unify Backlogs and Protect Capacity

The concept of working from a single, well-managed backlog and protecting a team's capacity did not start with the SRE movement. These are both fundamental Lean concepts for improving the flow of work and are popular in both the Agile and DevOps communities. These concepts are a lot less prevalent in traditional operations cultures but can be extremely useful for managing the work of—and protecting —teams transitioning to SRE.

SRE work, by definition, is a mix of planned and unplanned work. This mix of work types is among the most difficult to manage. Planned and unplanned work are different modes of working and do not mix well. Having different backlogs for each type of work makes things even worse. It is like serving multiple masters at the same time. It is easy to be pulled in too many directions or to be completely run over by the competing demands.

Engineers working in traditional IT operations organizations often have multiple backlogs with different sources of work managed in different ways. There is one system through which formal project work comes to them. Then there can be another way the team maintains a backlog and manages engineering work that doesn't bubble up to a formal project. Then, of course, there is a different way that interrupt-driven requests, like incidents, are handled.

Moving each team to a single, unified (planned + unplanned) backlog pays dividends. Rather than the constant tension between valuable planned work and necessary unplanned work, unified backlogs make prioritization and trade-offs clear. Unified backlogs also make it easier to reserve capacity for unplanned work (really another type of "budget").

Kanban is a management methodology that features ideas like unified backlogs and protected capacity. Kanban has been shown to significantly improve the flow of work in organizations with mixed types of work. The writing and presentations of longtime Kanban expert and author Dominica DeGrandis (*http://ddegrandis.com*) are a good place to start, as she is one of the pioneers in the application of Kanban to operations organizations.

Psychological Safety and Human Factors

It might now seem like common sense that optimizing the performance of your most important assets, your people, is critical to the success of any technology business. However, this was not always the case. If you have been in the IT operations industry long enough, you have seen traditional operations cultures that treated its people like interchangeable cogs. If a cog wore out, it must not have been tough enough! If the machine broke, there must be a cog to blame! Cogs are just parts, so keep looking elsewhere for the cheapest supplier of cogs!

If you want to build a highly effective, fast-moving organization, you need a culture that empowers your people to engage in reasonable risk-taking, bring up bad news to superiors, engage in creativity, and support their coworkers. Psychological safety and human factors[14] are related fields of study that are much broader than IT but have a lot to offer to our industry. From examinations of airplane disasters to medical tragedies, there is a reusable body of knowledge on how to maximize human performance in stressful, complex situations.

Join the Movement

We are working during a unique moment in IT operations history. Although we often get new technologies and tools, rarely do we get an opportunity to reshape the structure, behaviors, and culture of operations. This is an opportunity to improve the work lives of operations professionals around the globe *and* improve outcomes for their employers.

SRE is a continuously evolving practitioner-led movement. The best part of a practitioner-led movement is that you can be a part of it. Whether it is online or in person at conferences or meetups, join in.

As with most of IT, the early adopters and promoters tend to not be from enterprises. Don't let this dissuade you. First, the lessons learned and the principles debated are more generally applicable than you would think. Second, enterprises might not be quick to adopt new practices, but as community acceptance grows, enterprise adoption will certainly follow. Getting involved early with SRE is a way to both prepare your skills and make your company more competitive.

It doesn't matter if you are learning from the experiences of other practitioners or validating your learnings through sharing your experiences, your participation will return more value than the effort you put in.

Now let's roll up our sleeves and get to work.

---

14 *https://www.youtube.com/watch?v=CFMJ3V4VakA* and *http://stella.report*

Damon Edwards is a cofounder of Rundeck Inc., the makers of Rundeck, the popular open source operations management platform. Damon was previously a managing partner at DTO Solutions, a DevOps and IT operations improvement consultancy focused on large enterprises. Damon is a frequent conference speaker, writer, and podcast host.

## CHAPTER 11

SRE Patterns Loved by DevOps People Everywhere

Gene Kim, IT Revolution

 This is an edited excerpt from *The DevOps Handbook* by Gene Kim, Jez Humble, John Willis, and Patrick Debois (O'Reilly, 2016).

When David Blank-Edelman asked me to contribute a chapter on the SRE body of knowledge and the impact it has had on the DevOps community, I gave a very enthusiastic "Yes!"

Although some might argue that SRE and DevOps are mutually exclusive, I argue the opposite. In my opinion, it is difficult to overstate the impact that SRE has had on framing how the operations community can best contribute to organizational goals and improving the productivity of developers. As Ben Treynor Sloss, VP of SRE at Google, famously said in his 2014 SREcon presentation: "I define SRE as what happens when software engineers create an operations group."

In that famous presentation, Treynor Sloss introduces the breathtaking concept of a truly self-balancing system, where an organization first decides on an acceptable error budget, which then guides the prioritization of nonfunctional requirements and gates the decision to deploy and release.

During the research and writing of *The DevOps Handbook* (along with my coauthors Jez Humble, John Willis, and Patrick Debois), I couldn't help but notice how many of the DevOps patterns that we love and now can take for granted were pioneered at Google.

Here are three of my favorite patterns, excerpted from *The DevOps Handbook*, that can be traced to the SRE body of knowledge. Almost any organization can integrate them into its daily work.

Pattern 1: Birth of Automated Testing at Google

Automated testing addresses a truly significant and unsettling problem. Gary Gruver observes that "without automated testing, the more code we write, the more time and money is required to test our code—in most cases, this is a totally unscalable business model for any technology organization."

Although Google now undoubtedly exemplifies a culture that values automated testing at scale, this wasn't always the case. In 2005, when Mike Bland joined the organization, deploying to *Google.com* was often extremely problematic, especially for the Google Web Server (GWS) team. As Bland explains:

> The GWS team had gotten into a position in the mid-2000s where it was extremely difficult to make changes to the web server, a C++ application that handled all requests to Google's home page and many other Google web pages. As important and prominent as Google.com was, being on the GWS team was not a glamorous assignment—it was often the dumping ground for all the different teams who were creating various search functionality, all of whom were developing code independently of each other. They had problems such as builds and tests taking too long, code being put into production without being tested, and teams checking in large, infrequent changes that conflicted with those from other teams.

The consequences of this were large—search results could have errors or become unacceptably slow, affecting thousands of search queries on *google.com*. The potential result was loss not only of revenue, but customer trust.

Bland describes how it affected developers deploying changes: "Fear became the mind-killer. Fear stopped new team members from changing things because they didn't understand the system. But fear also stopped experienced people from changing things because they understood it all too well."[1] Bland was part of the group that was determined to solve this problem.

---

1 Bland described that at Google, one of the consequences of having so many talented developers was that it created "imposter syndrome," a term coined by psychologists to informally describe people who are unable to internalize their accomplishments. Wikipedia states that "despite external evidence of their competence, those exhibiting the syndrome remain convinced that they are frauds and do not deserve the success they have achieved. Proof of success is dismissed as luck, timing, or a result of deceiving others into thinking they are more intelligent and competent than they believe themselves to be."

GWS team lead Bharat Mediratta believed automated testing would help. As Bland describes:

> They created a hard line: no changes would be accepted into GWS without accompanying automated tests. They set up a continuous build and religiously kept it passing. They set up test coverage monitoring and ensured that their level of test coverage went up over time. They wrote up policy and testing guides and insisted that contributors both inside and outside the team follow them.

The results were startling. As Bland notes:

> GWS quickly became one of the most productive teams in the company, integrating large numbers of changes from different teams every week while maintaining a rapid release schedule. New team members were able to make productive contributions to this complex system quickly, thanks to good test coverage and code health. Ultimately, their radical policy enabled the Google.com home page to quickly expand its capabilities and thrive in an amazingly fast-moving and competitive technology landscape.

But GWS was still a relatively small team in a large and growing company. The team wanted to expand these practices across the entire organization. Thus, the Testing Grouplet was born, an informal group of engineers who wanted to elevate automated testing practices across the entire organization. Over the next five years, they helped replicate this culture of automated testing across all of Google.[2]

Now when any Google developer commits code, it is automatically run against a suite of hundreds of thousands of automated tests. If the code passes, it is automatically merged into trunk, ready to be deployed into production. Many Google properties build hourly or daily, then pick which builds to release; others adopt a continuous "Push on Green" delivery philosophy.

The stakes are higher than ever—a single code deployment error at Google can take down every property, all at the same time (such as a global infrastructure change or when a defect is introduced into a core library that every property depends upon).

Eran Messeri, an engineer in the Google Developer Infrastructure group, notes, "Large failures happen occasionally. You'll get a ton of instant messages and engineers knocking on your door. [When the deployment pipeline is broken,] we need to fix it right away, because developers can no longer commit code. Consequently, we want to make it very easy to roll back."

What enables this system to work at Google is engineering professionalism and a high-trust culture that assumes everyone wants to do a good job as well as the ability to detect and correct issues quickly. Messeri explains:

---

2 They created training programs, pushed the famous Testing on the Toilet newsletter (which they posted in the bathrooms), developed the Test Certified roadmap and certification program, and led multiple "fix-it" days (i.e., improvement blitzes), which helped teams improve their automated testing processes so that they could replicate the amazing outcomes that the GWS team was able to achieve.

There are no hard policies at Google, such as, "If you break production for more than 10 projects, you have an SLA to fix the issue within 10 minutes." Instead, there is mutual respect between teams and an implicit agreement that everyone does whatever it takes to keep the deployment pipeline running. We all know that one day, I'll break your project by accident; the next day, you may break mine.

What Mike Bland and the Testing Grouplet team achieved has made Google one of the most productive technology organizations in the world. By 2013, automated testing and continuous integration at Google enabled more than 4,000 small teams to work together and stay productive, all simultaneously developing, integrating, testing, and deploying their code into production. All their code is in a single, shared repository, made up of billions of files, all being continuously built and integrated, with 50% of their code being changed each month. Some other impressive statistics on their performance include the following:

- 40,000 code commits/day
- 50,000 builds/day (on weekdays, this can exceed 90,000)
- 120,000 automated test suites
- 75 million test cases run daily
- 100-plus engineers working on the test engineering, continuous integration, and release engineering tooling to increase developer productivity (making up 0.5% of the R&D workforce)

Pattern 2: Launch and Handoff Readiness Review at Google

Even when developers are writing and running their code in production-like environments in their daily work, operations can still experience disastrous production releases because it is the first time we actually see how our code behaves during a release and under true production conditions. This result occurs because operational learnings often happen too late in the software life cycle.

When this is left unaddressed, the result is often production software that is difficult to operate. As an anonymous ops engineer once said, "In our group, most system administrators lasted only six months. Things were always breaking in production, the hours were insane, and application deployments were painful beyond belief—the worst part was pairing the application server clusters, which would take us six hours. During each moment, we all felt like the developers personally hated us."

This can be an outcome of not having enough ops engineers to support all the product teams and the services we already have in production, which can happen in both functionally and market-oriented teams.

Our potential countermeasure is to do what Google does, which is have development groups self-manage their services in production before they become eligible for a centralized ops group to manage. By having developers be responsible for deployment and production support, we are far more likely to have a smooth transition to operations.

To prevent the possibility of problematic, self-managed services going into production and creating organizational risk, we can define launch requirements that must be met in order for services to interact with real customers and be exposed to real production traffic. Furthermore, to help the product teams, ops engineers should act as consultants to help them make their services production-ready.

By creating launch guidance, we help ensure that every product team benefits from the cumulative and collective experience of the entire organization, especially operations. Launch guidance and requirements will likely include the following:

Defect counts and severity
   Does the application actually perform as designed?

Type/frequency of pager alerts
   Is the application generating an unsupportable number of alerts in production?

Monitoring coverage
   Is the coverage of monitoring sufficient to restore service when things go wrong?

System architecture
   Is the service loosely coupled enough to support a high rate of changes and deployments in production?

Deployment process
   Is there a predictable, deterministic, and sufficiently automated process to deploy code into production?

Production hygiene
   Is there evidence of enough good production habits that would allow production support to be managed by anyone else?

Superficially, these requirements might appear similar to traditional production checklists we have used in the past. However, the key differences are that we require effective monitoring to be in place, deployments to be reliable and deterministic, and an architecture that supports fast and frequent deployments.

If any deficiencies are found during the review, the assigned ops engineer should help the feature team resolve the issues or even help re-engineer the service if necessary so that it can be easily deployed and managed in production.

At this time, we might also want to learn whether this service is subject to any regulatory compliance objectives or if it is likely to be in the future:

- Does the service generate a significant amount of revenue? (For example, if it is more than 5% of total revenue of a publicly held US corporation, it is a "significant account" and in-scope for compliance with Section 404 of the Sarbanes-Oxley Act of 2002 [SOX].)

- Does the service have high user traffic or have high outage/impairment costs (i.e., do operational issues risk creating availability or reputational risk)?

- Does the service store payment cardholder information such as credit card numbers, or personally identifiable information such as Social Security numbers or patient care records? Are there other security issues that could create regulatory, contractual obligation, privacy, or reputation risk?

- Does the service have any other regulatory or contractual compliance requirements associated with it, such as US export regulations, PCI-DSS, HIPAA, and so forth?

This information helps to ensure that we effectively manage not only the technical risks associated with this service, but also any potential security and compliance risks. It also provides essential input into the design of the production control environment. See examples of the launch and handoff readiness reviews in Figures 11-1 and 11-2.

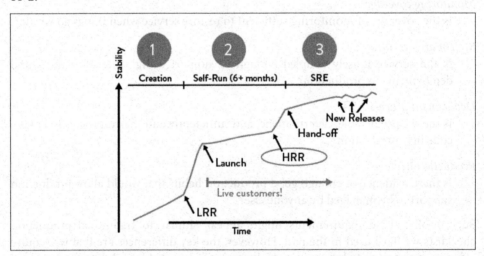

Figure 11-1. The launch readiness review at Google (source: "SRE@Google: Thousands of DevOps Since 2004" (https://www.youtube.com/watch?v=iIuTnhdTzK0), YouTube video, 45:57, posted by USENIX, January 12, 2012)

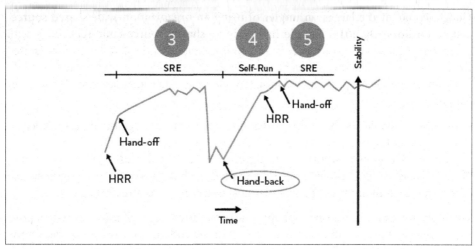

Figure 11-2. The handoffs readiness review at Google (source: "SRE@Google: Thousands of DevOps Since 2004" (https://www.youtube.com/watch?v=iIuTnhdTzK0), YouTube video, 45:57, posted by USENIX, January 12, 2012)

As Tom Limoncelli, coauthor of *The Practice of Cloud System Administration* (Addison-Wesley, 2002) and a former site reliability engineer at Google, mentions in one of his talks, "In the best case, product teams have been using the LRR checklist as a guideline, working on fulfilling it in parallel with developing their service, and reaching out to SREs to get help when they need it." Furthermore, Limoncelli once told me in 2016:

> The teams that have the fastest HRR production approval are the ones that worked with SREs earliest, from the early design stages up until launch. And the great thing is, it's always easy to get an SRE to volunteer to help with your project. Every SRE sees value in giving advice to project teams early and will likely volunteer a few hours or days to do just that.

The practice of SREs helping product teams early is an important cultural norm that is continually reinforced at Google. Limoncelli explained, "Helping product teams is a long-term investment that will pay off many months later when it comes time to launch. It is a form of 'good citizenship' and 'community service' that is valued; it is routinely considered when evaluating engineers for SRE promotions."

Pattern 3: Create a Shared Source Code Repository

A firm-wide, shared source-code repository is one of the most powerful mechanisms used to integrate local discoveries across the entire organization. When engineers update anything in the source code repository (e.g., a shared library), it rapidly and automatically propagates to every other service that uses that library, and it is integrated through each team's deployment pipeline.

Google is one of the largest examples of using an organization-wide shared source-code repository. By 2015, Google had a single shared source-code repository with more than 1 billion files and more than 2 billion lines of code. This repository is used by every one of its 25,000 engineers and spans every Google property, including Google Search, Google Maps, Google Docs, Google+, Google Calendar, Gmail, and YouTube.[3]

One of the valuable results of this is that engineers can leverage the diverse expertise of everyone in the organization. Rachel Potvin, a Google engineering manager overseeing the Developer Infrastructure group, told *Wired* (*https://www.wired.com/ 2015/09/google-2-billion-lines-codeand-one-place/*) that every Google engineer can access "a wealth of libraries" because "almost everything has already been done."

Furthermore, as Eran Messeri explains, one of the advantages of using a single repository is that it allows users to easily access all of the code in its most up-to-date form, without the need for coordination.

We put into our shared source-code repository not only source code, but also other artifacts that encode knowledge and learning, including the following:

- Configuration standards for our libraries, infrastructure, and environments (Chef recipes, Puppet manifests, etc.)
- Deployment tools
- Testing standards and tools, including security
- Deployment pipeline tools
- Monitoring and analysis tools
- Tutorials and standards

Encoding knowledge and sharing it through this repository is one of the most powerful mechanisms we have for propagating knowledge. As Randy Shoup told me in 2014:

> The most powerful mechanism for preventing failures at Google is the single code repository. Whenever someone checks in anything into the repo, it results in a new build, which always uses the latest version of everything. Everything is built from source rather than dynamically linked at runtime—there is always a single version of a library that is the current one in use, which is what gets statically linked during the build process.

In his book, Tom Limoncelli states that the value of having a single repository for an entire organization is so powerful, it is difficult to even explain.

---

3 The Chrome and Android projects reside in a separate source-code repository, and certain algorithms that are kept secret, such as PageRank, are available only to certain teams.

You can write a tool exactly once and have it be usable for all projects. You have 100% accurate knowledge of who depends on a library; therefore, you can refactor it and be 100% sure of who will be affected and who needs to test for breakage. I could probably list a hundred more examples. I can't express in words how much of a competitive advantage this is for Google.

At Google, every library (e.g., libc, OpenSSL, as well as internally developed libraries such as Java threading libraries) has an owner who is responsible for ensuring that the library not only compiles, but also successfully passes the tests for all projects that depend upon it, much like a real-world librarian. That owner is also responsible for migrating each project from one version to the next.

Consider the real-life example of an organization that runs 81 different versions of the Java Struts framework library in production—all but one of those versions have critical security vulnerabilities, and maintaining all of those versions, each with its own quirks and idiosyncrasies, creates significant operational burden and stress. Furthermore, all of this variance makes upgrading versions risky and unsafe, which in turn discourages developers from upgrading. And the cycle continues.

The single source repository solves much of this problem, as well as having automated tests that allow teams to migrate to new versions safely and confidently.

If we are not able to build everything off a single source tree, we must find another means to maintain known good versions of the libraries and their dependencies. For instance, we might have an organization-wide repository such as Nexus, Artifactory, or a Debian or RPM repository, which we must then update where there are known vulnerabilities, both in these repositories and in production systems.

Conclusion

I hope these patterns show a glimpse of the obvious bridges between SRE and DevOps—they have far more in common than most would imagine and are certainly grounded in similar principles and goals.

Further Reading and Source Material

- DevOps Enterprise Summit 2015 talk by Mike Bland: "Pain Is Over, If You Want It" (*http://www.slideshare.net/ITRevolution/does15-mike-bland-pain-is-over-if-you-want-it-55236521*), Slideshare.net, posted by Gene Kim, November 18, 2015.

- GOTO Conference talk by Eran Messeri, "What Goes Wrong When Thousands of Engineers Share the Same Continuous Build?" Aarhus, Denmark, October 2, 2013.

- Tom Limoncelli, "SRE@Google: Thousands Of DevOps Since 2004" (*http://www.youtube.com/watch?v=iIuTnhdTzK0*), YouTube video of USENIX Association Talk, NYC, posted by USENIX, 45:57, posted January 12, 2012.

- Ben Treynor, "Keys to SRE" (*https://www.usenix.org/conference/srecon14/technical-sessions/presentation/keys-sre*) (presentation, Usenix SREcon14, Santa Clara, CA, May 30, 2014).

- Cade Metz, "Google Is 2 Billion Lines of Code—and It's All in One Place" (*http://www.wired.com/2015/09/google-2-billion-lines-codeand-one-place/*), *Wired*, September 16, 2015.

- Eran Messeri, "What Goes Wrong When Thousands of Engineers Share the Same Continuous Build?" (*http://scribes.tweetscriber.com/realgenekim/206*) (2013).

- Tom Limoncelli, "Yes, you can really work from HEAD" (*http://everythingsysadmin.com/2014/03/yes-you-really-can-work-from-head.html*), EverythingSysAdmin.com, March 15, 2014.

- Tom Limoncelli, "Python is better than Perl6" (*https://everythingsysadmin.com/2011/01/python-is-better-than-perl6.html*), EverythingSysAdmin.com, January 10, 2011.

- "Which programming languages does Google use internally?," Quora.com forum, accessed May 29, 2016; "When will Google permit languages other than Python, C++, Java and Go to be used for internal projects?" (*https://www.quora.com/When-will-Google-permit-languages-other-than-Python-C-Java-and-Go-to-be-used-for-internal-projects/answer/Neil-Kandalgaonkar*), Quora.com forum, accessed May 29, 2016.

- Tom Limoncelli, Strata Chalup, and Christina Hogan, *The Practice of Cloud System Administration* (Addison-Wesley: 2002).

Gene Kim is a multiple award-winning CTO, researcher, and coauthor of The Phoenix Project, The DevOps Handbook, and Accelerate (IT Revolution). He is the organizer of the DevOps Enterprise Summit conferences.

## CHAPTER 12

DevOps and SRE: Voices from the Community

As told to David N. Blank-Edelman

Background

From almost the very beginning of my time interacting with the SRE community, I've been curious about the relationship between DevOps and SRE. I've had the pleasure of talking about this with many smart people and heard many smart things. As far as I can tell, it's not a settled question. Each person I have talked to added something to my understanding. When it came time to find a contributor on this topic, it seemed like the best thing I could do would be to invite as many voices into the discussion as possible.

Welcome to an experiment—an entirely crowdsourced chapter.

Method

At the end of February 2018, I put up a website with a page that asked the following:

> In two paragraphs or less, what do you think is the relationship between DevOps and SRE? How are they similar? How are they different? Can both be implemented at every organization? Can the two exist in the same org at the same time? And so on…

I put a call out via Twitter and LinkedIn to my professional social network for contributions (and to ask them to pass a pointer to this web page to their network, as well, which many kindly did). In the end, Google Analytics reports 1,165 people from 34 separate countries came to the contribution page.

Results

It was thrilling to see the sorts of thoughtful answers I received to these questions. I present to you now, only slightly copyedited, a sample of the responses[1] I received in no particular order and with no particular organization (so it accurately reflects the "messy" nature of the discussion as you would find it on the internet). For each reply, I've listed the person's name, title, and affiliation if they chose to share that information.

It's hardly a representative survey on the question, but I think it does an excellent job of showing both the heterogeneity and homogeneity of opinions on the subject. Hopefully just hearing this discussion will provide an opportunity for you to begin to form your own thoughts on the matter. I should also say that I am intentionally presenting these responses without my own comments or opinions. Rather than attempting to wrap this non-Newtonian fluid of a subject up in a neat bow (from which it would only escape) or impose my own impressions of the material on your thinking, I'm more interested in hearing your conclusions. Are you/we any closer to an answer on these questions?

There's obviously much more that can be said on this topic. Feel free to get in touch if you'd like to share your ideas, too, I'd love to hear them.

Replies

Site reliability is operational reliability, scalability, and efficiency. This includes business continuity (disaster recovery, high availability). The operational site becomes a product in and of itself and may include their own CI/CD for internal tooling. The automation tends toward custom tools; for example, Python with Boto library, Ruby with AWS [Amazon Web Services] SDK, and Go language rather than the use of high-level tools like Terraform and Ansible, as they are considered inefficient. Though this is not absolute, just a trend. SRE is programming the operations to create reliable and efficient infrastructure.

DevOps focuses on breaking down cultural silos and increasing efficiency or velocity of deployment (CI/CD) pipeline, from development to delivery; this includes building and pre/post artifact testing (testing before and after the artifact is built), thus CT, or *continual testing*. It takes over where Agile left off and embraces aspects of Lean. DevOps would work with optimization and integration upstream (build, test) and downstream toward deployment and delivery. There is overlap, where deployment/delivery to an operational site is a shared domain with SRE. There is also opposing

---

[1] Space constraints prohibit me from including more, but I'm grateful for each and every response I received. Thank you!

ideals where DevOps is integrated across the pipeline. SRE is only on the operational infrastructure, and would be considered a silo under strict DevOps philosophy.

—*Joaquin Menchaca, Senior DevOps engineer, NinjaPants Consulting*

◆ ◆ ◆

While many consider DevOps to be a single framework, it is in fact an umbrella for a pipeline of practices that span the organization's value stream from concept to value creation. Most DevOps practices focus on the stages from development through deployment as Continuous Integration, Continuous Delivery and Continuous Deployment. To my mind, SRE is a natural extension of DevOps as Continuous Operations.

Under that same umbrella, SRE plays a key role in aligning and evolving ITIL/ITSM processes to DevOps. Monolithic processes such as incident, problem, knowledge, change and service-level management become less of a constraint and more of an enabler when managed and executed at the SRE level in order to accommodate the faster and more frequent flow of changes. Why? Because SRE is not only a set of practices: there is a defined SRE role with a set of responsibilities. That is another fundamental difference between SRE and DevOps; there is not a clearly defined "DevOps Engineer" role.

—*Jayne Groll, CEO, DevOps Institute*

◆ ◆ ◆

DevOps is underpinned by three principles: systems thinking (looking at the whole system not just your slice), amplifying feedback loops, and a culture of continual experimentation and learning. SRE adheres to these same principles, as evidenced by SLOs, error budgets, and its involvement in all aspects of a system. In some ways, SRE is one way to go about doing DevOps, much like scrum is one way to implement Agile.

SRE differentiates itself from DevOps by its focus on engineering solutions. This focus on code enables scaling at a level other solutions cannot approach, making SRE essentially a highly scalable DevOps. Put another way, SRE is an engineering-solutions-focused implementation of DevOps.

—*Tanner Lund, Microsoft*

◆ ◆ ◆

I believe DevOps came up from the industry as an answer to the relentless increase in operational complexity driven by two huge trends in technology: the migration to the cloud, and immutable infrastructure plus infrastructure-as-code. With every company out there scrambling desperately to move to cloud providers and drastically change their cost structure and therefore valuation (cloud providers are variable operational costs, not fixed), and all companies trying desperately to catch up with the latest infrastructure-as-code breakthroughs (Docker and Kubernetes), operational complexity is increasing exponentially. Most companies lack the skill set and engineering culture treats that enable for a healthy balance of forces to release innovation and operate it reliably.

I believe SRE is just Google's, Microsoft's, LinkedIn's, Facebook's and other huge companies' efforts to tackle the same issue. These companies have been dealing with this level of operational complexity of this scale for well over a decade now, with many generations of engineering teams adopting it, executing, and moving on. Add to that a higher expectation of reliability and performance on their products, and you have a recipe for top-tier practices, well defined and polished for both learning and implementing at a team level. I believe SRE is basically DevOps, but it's ahead by a whole decade of trial and error, and it now, thanks to a few books and whitepapers, has been made available for the rest of the industry to learn and adopt.

—*Santiago Suarez Ordoñez, CTO, Blameless*

♦ ♦ ♦

I think fundamentally these roles are very similar, but the difference is more in their focus in relation to the needs of the business. For a smaller business, or newer teams in larger businesses, things may be a bit more manual as there hasn't been someone there to automate their common tasks. This may mean there is more of an immediate need for an operations engineer. I see a site reliability engineer as the natural progression after teaching an operations engineer how to apply software engineering principles to their work (DevOps), and they've automated away a sizable amount of their operational work. As part of this exercise, they've scaffolded and operated services that need to be available and reliable at scale. This gives them the necessary experience to step in to other projects and help implement improvements as well as to intuit software engineering patterns that will result in better systems.

I think these roles can be implemented at most organizations, but they will probably happen at slightly different times. The infrastructure being used to support the business should be built out, and then dedicated people can focus on building more reliable systems on top of these in a consistent way. This would really mean probably starting with operations engineers and focusing their work in a way that has them eventually acting like site reliability engineers. Starting to adopt an SRE program is not a sign that those doing Ops aren't needed, or are deprecated, but in fact they are probably needed more to help continue to iterate on the supporting infrastructure and systems to ensure it continues to meet the demands of the business. While the core focus of these two roles is slightly different, it's important to remember that they both can complement each other when used effectively within a single organization.

—Tim Heckman, senior site reliability engineer, Netflix, Inc.

♦ ♦ ♦

DevOps and SRE are engineering practices with a heavy focus on collaboration and automation in a culture where learning from failure is championed. Whereas DevOps focuses on frequent delivery of customer functionality in an Agile way, SREs concentrate on releasing products as reliably as possible by supporting DevOps teams with their expertise.

Considering they share their fundamental principles, SRE and DevOps can coexist pretty easily as long as the organization is clear on the responsibility of build and run. Within ING, BizDevOps teams are end to end responsible for their service(s) and its incident response: SREs deliver monitoring and alerting solutions, work on traffic modeling, ChatOps and introducing a blameless culture where we embrace failure to our organization via postmortems and chaos engineering. The ratio of SRE versus DevOps is 7 to 1,700 engineers for the retail bank of ING in the Netherlands, and I think our SRE team is a bit on the smaller side compared to other organizations. Hiring SREs can be more difficult than hiring DevOps engineers due to the demand of automation capabilities, full-stack engineering skills, reliability mindset and soft skills required for consulting and educating others about SRE related topics.

—Janna Brummel and Robin van Zijll, IT chapter lead SRE and SRE/product owner, ING, respectively

♦ ♦ ♦

From a purist view, in short DevOps is practice where the objective is to increase feedback cycles by reducing handoffs and increasing collaboration, whereas SRE is more aligned to actual role titles and is more engineering focused, driving change specifically through engineering outcomes. Where they are similar is that they both require a mindset, behavior and culture change. I do not agree with the term DevOps engineer, but in my mind that is what I view an SRE to be.

DevOps can and should be implemented in every organization adopting Agile or an iterative way of working so as to close the feedback loop cycle to product owners or those owning the backlog of features to ensure service management waste is known and addressed. SRE's are compatible with organizations that have or seek to foster an engineering culture and eliminate waste and find efficiencies with engineering outcomes. Both can coexist at the same time in the same organization when the organization is big enough or old enough. Organizations with what many people term as "legacy systems" can easily allow for DevOps ways of working while they form up targeted SRE teams for more green fields or evergreen systems. As the wise old proverb says, how do you eat an elephant? One bite at a time.

—*Michael Ewald, head of operations*

♦ ♦ ♦

Though my own title violates my own advice (and advice noted elsewhere), the term "DevOps" in a job title is inherently impractical. DevOps is more a philosophy, methodology, or practice one follows, much the same as Agile. Though one having a job title such as "Agile Developer" seems absurd in today's world, it's likely "DevOps Engineer" may (and arguably should) one day follow suit.

An SRE tends to generalize the functions of the job. Be it they follow DevOps principles, Agile principles, or the next hot trend, their function remains the same: ensure the reliability of the "site" in all of its components, down to the underlying infrastructure, using methodology adopted and recognized as a fit for accomplishing that task.

—*Keith McDuffee, senior manager, infrastructure & DevOps, Cardinal Health*

♦ ♦ ♦

DevOps and SRE are related, and we are all developers again. In my first job at IBM in the early 80's, three kinds of people helped us ship products ("program products" back then): product programmers, systems programmers, and electricians. People who worked on program products were developers, systems programmers were developers. We've just gone back to a good model; we're all developers. Some developers are responsible for keeping their software up and running as a platform for other developers, those developers are responsible for keeping their software up and running for other types of customers. In the modern world, both DevOps and SRE are oriented toward building and operating software, which is the concern of anyone who builds and operates a software product.

As to the differences between DevOps and SRE, and whether they can coexist, every organization will likely have a different approach, just as Agile can be practiced differently by different teams. But, whether the customers of your software product are other software developers, or people shopping for a new pair of shoes, you need to build and operate products holistically, and avoid drawing boundaries around

DevOps/SRE developers and other software developers. In some organizations, separating "DevOps" and "SRE" may be more driven by organizational or political structure rather than by a meaningful difference between the two. We are all developers, again.

—*Paula Paul, technology principal, ThoughtWorks*

◆ ◆ ◆

Site Reliability Engineering: we don't know what DevOps is, but we know we're something slightly different.

—*Mike Doherty, successful reliability escapee*

◆ ◆ ◆

If you look at job advertisements the answer is quite clear: the industry has decided that DevOps engineers focus on the SDLC pipeline with occasional responsibilities for production operations. Job advertisements for SREs focus on production operations with occasional responsibilities for the SDLC pipeline. The two are the same thing: The difference is in emphasis (Figure 12-1).

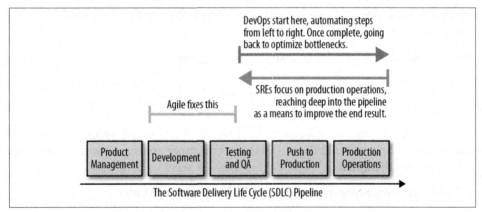

Figure 12-1. The Limoncelli model of SRE, DevOps, and Agile strategies

Google SREs can focus on the later parts of the pipeline because within Google the earlier phases are either solved problems or delegated to other teams. Over time SRE has been able to purify their focus: excellence in operations. They dive into the earlier parts of the pipeline as a means to an end. If a production problem is rooted in insufficient or sloppy CI/CD discipline, SREs will parachute into the developer area and make improvements until production is no longer affected. DevOps, historically, have emphasized the earlier parts of the pipeline because DevOps are stuck solving the entire problem and experience has shown that transforming a project to use CI/CD is a prerequisite to everything else. This is not to say that DevOps does not care about production operations, but if you look at DevOps job advertisements and stories of "DevOps Transformations" they all tend to focus on moving a company towards CI/CD. Once CI/CD enables rapid releases, the focus changes to production operations and likewise job titles often then change to SRE.

—*Thomas A. Limoncelli, SRE manager, Stack Overflow, Inc., Google SRE Alum*

◆ ◆ ◆

They are similar in that both have a heavy focus on automation around developer and operations workflows. DevOps focuses on upgrading old workflows and cultures with efficient tools and strategies that scale. SRE focuses on preventing customer downtime by autohealing on events, knowing when there's something wrong as soon as possible and load testing to plan for future capacity.

DevOps is for newer teams to Agile that need to improve tooling and culture. SRE is for established Agile teams that are looking to improve uptime, monitoring, sanity and peace of mind. To use some actual examples, moving to the cloud should be a DevOps initiative, while setting up a failover disaster recovery site would be SRE. Both can be implemented together, as there will be people and parts of your company that are in different stages.

—*Jefferson Hale, site reliability engineer, Seismic Games*

◆ ◆ ◆

An SRE typically doesn't manage infrastructure. They might manage debugging dashboards or help to build them. DevOps seems more concerned with automating toil away from all humans.

—*Adam Shannon, software engineer, Jack Henry and Associates*

◆ ◆ ◆

DevOps is, at its core, an amalgam of various IT practices from Lean, Agile, etc. Instilling a DevOps culture in an organization is a lot like embracing open source in an organization. It's a new way of doing the things you've done before. But, like open source, you can do them faster and cheaper. However, where open source is about the software, DevOps is about the people, processes, and to a much lesser extent, tooling.

SRE, on the other hand, takes a very analytical approach to service and software in production. Utilizing metrics, thresholds, SLAs, and SLOs a team can point to concrete facts about a system. There is no reason DevOps and SRE can't work together. As a matter of fact, they make a lot of sense when paired together. Taking what an SRE team learns about production use of code and feeding it back into the delivery pipeline is literally "The Third Way" in DevOps.

—Chris Short, senior DevOps advocate, SJ Technologies

◆ ◆ ◆

To me, SRE and DevOps are similar but not the same. I view SRE as being the next evolution of a more traditional operations (system/network) environment that brings what was missing most from such an environment, the view of the software engineer in the operations. It is still highly skilled and focused teams managing the infrastructure, and the SRE world still seems to be a silo, but one that has taken system administration to the next level and continues to evolve and grow with modern infrastructure, platforms, tools, and concepts. Compared to SRE, I think that DevOps is most valuable when it is used as a means to facilitate better relationships between all parts of the business. DevOps introduces an operations mindset to software developers and a software mindset and understanding to the operations team. DevOps also leverages and keeps up with modern infrastructure, platforms, tools, and concepts, but it's the cultural shifts and building of a shared sense of ownership across all teams that is the most valuable.

Can the two coexist? Yes. Should they coexist? It depends. What are the goals of the business, the organization(s), and team(s)? Not everything is one size fits all. SRE works great for very large organizations like Google, where it was born, who have very specific and very complex problems, but it might not make sense for you and your organization. The same is true for DevOps. As much as there is good that comes from DevOps, the benefits only come from everyone in the business being bought in.

—Sean Lutner, infrastructure architect, Edgewise Networks, Inc.

◆ ◆ ◆

To many large enterprises, the primary difference between DevOps and SRE are their ages as buzzwords. Outside of Google, the term DevOps is at least six years older than SRE. This means the books, blogs, conferences, and experts associated with SRE have had far less time to exert influence. So far, there have been significant overlaps in the subject matter and advice from DevOps and SRE. Both have produced great guidance on tools, processes, platforms, cultures, and places of work. Not everything SRE espouses will be entirely new, but it is all (well, mostly...) worth paying attention to, and anyone interested in the DevOps movement would be foolish to ignore it.

It is, however, wrong to think of SRE as being just another name for DevOps. Often (and slightly ironically) people talking about DevOps tend to focus more on the development and release part of the software delivery life cycle compared to the operations side. SRE, on the other hand, has an existential leaning toward improving operations. To some extent, if DevOps can be thought of as stepping in where Agile moved a bottleneck in delivery from development to releasing code, SRE is stepping in to alleviate a new bottleneck in operating and scaling the live running of systems. SRE is also comfortable being something DevOps never was: a job title (and at that, one capable of giving an instant morale boost to folks working in operations). Finally, the SRE movement provides useful new terminology to increase discussion of topics such as repetitive manual work (toil) and release management (launch configuration engineer).

—*Mark Rendell, principal director, Accenture*

◆ ◆ ◆

Reliability engineering and DevOps aim to solve the same problem set that most of the world is now realizing they are faced with: keeping digital services always online and available while improving functionality and operability over time. While DevOps remains elusive in a manifesto-type definition, reliability engineering assigns a more concrete role and responsibility to the term in many ways. At its core, site reliability engineering embodies and encourages the same exact principles that have been associated with DevOps since the term began entering the web operations lexicon. Building and operating digital services with 24/7 availability expectations has become a necessity for more than just Software as a Service vendors. Businesses, governments, and organizations across nearly every industry are faced with balancing rapid development of new functionality with maintaining the health and availability of the service.

Engineering practices, teams, and individuals lumped in to the title of SRE helps businesses assign a concrete effort to these roles. The core reason for the existence of an SRE (team, individual, etc.) is to leverage technical skills in systems architecture, automation, and problem-solving along with social skills of collaboration and communication to seek new ways to know more about the system as a whole. This then feeds engineering teams to continuously seek out new and better ways of developing software as well as improving the architecture and delivery pipelines.

—*Jason Hand, Senior Cloud Ops Advocate, Microsoft (formerly VictorOps)*

◆ ◆ ◆

At PayPal, we believe that site reliability engineers are both the ultimate enablers as well as the ideal practitioners of DevOps. To that end, we engineer for reliability in two major ways. The first, as platform providers, building and constantly improving the key tools that enable other SRE, dev, and ops teams across the enterprise. The second, as the embedded experts within business-critical product teams where dedicated reliability engineering is required to achieve world-class availability, productivity, and more.

As we've grown in our practice of DevOps, we've found that the mental model that a gifted SRE is able to develop around a complex system like PayPal is increasingly needed within the organization. This mental model is key to the development, by SRE, of highly effective tools and platforms. This mental model also enables SRE capabilities that are uniquely valuable to the wider dev and ops teams such as the exporting of systems knowledge, sharing in ownership of critical services, drawing on expertise during critical incidents, and driving insightful postmortems.

—Andrew Farmer, senior manager, SRE, PayPal, Inc.

◆ ◆ ◆

I believe SRE is a practice that can help DevOps at scale. DevOps alone worked fine for us while we scaled the company from 8 to 20 teams. However, as the number of engineering teams practicing DevOps grew, it became apparent we needed something overarching to help guide and support those teams. Lessons weren't being shared across all teams, and reliable practices weren't always getting the attention they needed.

SRE helps bring in a level of monitoring of how reliability focused our teams were beyond their recent incident history. Through testing and analysis, both manually and through tools, SRE is able to help the teams understand their reliability risks and help prioritize them. The SRE teams are also able to commit time to building cross-cutting tooling and services that support all the engineering teams in ensuring the reliability of their products. Just as DevOps and PaaS [Platform as a Service] can coexist so I believe DevOps and Reliability as a Service (SRE) can coexist.

—Bennie Johnston, head of SRE, Just Eat

◆ ◆ ◆

The largest difference is that DevOps is an approach and SRE is a specific job role. Despite that it typically manifests as a guardian of the "Deployment System," DevOps is rooted in the multidisciplinary examination of delivery flow and overall effectiveness of managing services. The SRE role is a manifestation of labor division for online services. Unlike traditional specialization which focuses on function, SRE's labor division aligns around the product regardless of function.

A key cause of confusion between the two is that both strive for multidisciplinary or cross-functional methods applied on their focuses; but it is the focus which is what differentiates them. DevOps is focused on the process, and SRE is focused on the product.

—*Chris McEniry, systems architect*

◆ ◆ ◆

SRE and DevOps have a wide scope of overlap, but they are distinct ideas. As used in practice, companies recruit for DevOps when they want their maintenance developers to also look after the production and nonproduction infrastructure as they continue to make improvements to an existing software system. In contrast to this, companies tend to recruit for site reliability engineers when they want to retain a division of labor between infrastructure management and development. The SRE will have deeper and broader infrastructure skills encompassing more of load balancers, networking, databases, and container orchestration systems like Kubernetes; whereas the DevOps developer will usually have deeper expertise in the business domain and preferred programming language.

DevOps teams are more likely in environments with either common technology stacks or cloud hosted infrastructure. In these cases, the cloud provider is taking care of the infrastructure so the developers can focus more on delivering business value. Increasingly, SREs are found in holdout companies that are biased toward self-hosting or environments that have complicated infrastructure requirements. These SREs provide the operational support that used to be the domain of systems administrators. The difference being that the SRE is expected to draw on programming skills to automate the environment buildouts and application deployments or write patches for infrastructure tools in ways that the traditional system administrator could not.

—*John Siegrist, release engineer, Deswik Mining*

◆ ◆ ◆

While DevOps and SRE roles overlap a lot technical execution-wise, the distinction likely comes from the size and scale of the organization. Since software and its eco-system do not follow economies of scale (*https://www.allankellyassociates.co.uk/ archives/date/2015/10*), it becomes imperative for teams to specialize and focus, as an organization's software and infrastructure grows with scale; that is where the proba-ble transition from DevOps to SRE comes into play. For smaller businesses and organizations, DevOps culture reduces the impedance between development and operations resulting in rapid iterations and change. As an organization grows and scales it becomes imperative to standardize how software is developed and deployed to reduce the cognitive load and effort when it comes to understating and getting things done.

Both DevOps and SRE roles can make contributions here, DevOps can focus more on developer productivity (e.g., tooling like build systems, trainings, better testing, etc.), while SREs focus on maintaining uptime, upkeep of production systems, and special-ized tooling (e.g., distributed tracing infrastructure), both the roles become a full-time job with scale. The common aim is again to deliver change from code commit to production deployment, which is as frictionless as possible, highly visible, and pre-dictable. Yes, DevOps and SRE roles can coexist, but the line is blurred and not easy to draw. It would largely depend on the organization, its business, and size.

—Pranay Kanwar, staff site reliability engineer, LinkedIn

◆ ◆ ◆

Having a lot of experience with both DevOps and operations, and now running a number of SRE teams, this topic has always been something I found a bit fascinating. I believe that the two concepts have a lot of overlap, despite the fact that they remain rather distinct. On the one hand, we have DevOps, an international software develop-ment movement that emphasizes looking at the delivery of software from a systems-thinking perspective. On the other, we have SRE, which takes an approach of managing operations from a software engineering perspective. There are many parts of SRE that fit very easily into the DevOps CAMS model, especially as it relates to things like culture with error budgets and measurement with the four golden signals.

I think for me, one of the most interesting things is that SRE brings back, from tradi-tional operations work, a bit of the "wall of confusion (*http://dev2ops.org/2010/02/ what-is-devops/*)" that we always talk about eliminating as much as possible in DevOps. This in no way means in SRE software is "tossed over the wall" like we like to bemoan from traditional software development. However, unlike developers car-rying pagers in the DevOps model, there is a clear line of responsibility in the SRE model where they are responsible for meeting the SLOs of the production systems, even if that means working on those problems with development. This is probably necessitated by scale. In some respects, SRE is a hybrid of the legacy model and the new DevOps model, bringing elements of the "Operations is a clearly distinct group" from legacy, and many components of the CAMS model from DevOps. Instead of having a wall of confusion, there is a wall of conversation or collaboration (it's a low wall!). It's no wonder we struggle to differentiate the two.

—Dave Mangot, former head of site reliability engineering, SolarWinds Cloud

◆ ◆ ◆

DevOps is really about Dev and Ops working together, with complementary and overlapping skills, but really focused on different areas. The main goal is supporting developers in their quest to rapidly develop high-quality code, features, and value to the end user. At the same time, to deploy it cleanly and quickly onto high-quality, highly maintainable, and reliable infrastructure, then support and operate it to bring reliability, scalability, performance, security, and cost savings.

SRE on the other hand, is really about building and managing highly reliable systems and applications. Thus, it operates at a higher level in the conceptual stack, in that SRE focused on the architecture, configuration, tooling, monitoring, and management plus processes so the DevOps teams can really deliver on their goals. Developers and operations tend to be buried in the day-to-day, while SRE ensures the whole system and ecosystem can meet its goals.

—Steve Mushero, CEO, OpsStack

◆ ◆ ◆

The relationship between DevOps and SRE is where an actual SRE role is defined and the methodologies from DevOps are actually implemented and practiced within that SRE team along with operations. Where DevOps/SRE become similar is asking an engineer (system/software) to apply software engineering principles to the operations of a software system that is providing a service to users or other systems. Where DevOps/SRE go in different directions is there is no manifesto with rules and regulations on how to implement DevOps. For SRE, while there is no defined prescription, organizations are making great strides to provide a playbook on how to define and implement SRE, so it doesn't get watered down. For example, public cloud companies are providing customers free services to help implement SRE within their organization.

When you implement SRE at your organization you're automatically consuming the DevOps methodologies as part of that implementation, so, in a sense, you're implementing within the organization. The idea to have both exist is to keep focus on the mission of leveraging software engineering principles when performing operational work of software systems and services the SRE team is supporting.

—*Chad Todd*

◆ ◆ ◆

SRE is DevOps when you're driven by SLOs. Both aim for the same goals but take different paths. The SLOs help steer effort and investment and there's no similar instrument in DevOps.

DevOps is more common for startups, where the incentive to reach production as fast as possible clearly outweighs reliability or availability. SRE makes more sense on well-established businesses when the conflict between innovation and reliability start to emerge.

—*Luis Mineiro, principal site reliability engineer, Zalando*

◆ ◆ ◆

In my view, DevOps is a set of practices organizations can adopt to better enable the operation and delivery of products to their customers. The simplest summary of these practices is summed up in CAMS, which stands for Culture, Automation, Measurement and Sharing. SRE (site or service reliability engineering) is a role that is generally filled by individuals or teams. In my experience these folks are broadly focused on the stability and operation of products in an organization. By and large, most SRE professionals rely on the four pillars of CAMS to do their work and influence the organization to address operational needs.

It's worth noting that not all organizations "do" SRE the same way, especially as it relates to organizational structure. The two main forms I'm familiar with are "Horizontal" SRE integration and "Vertical" SRE integration. An organization with horizontally integrated SRE staff will generally have one or more independent teams made up of folks that do SRE work for the organization. Vertically integrated staff are generally integrated directly with engineering teams and remain dedicated to said team.

—*Aaron Blew, director of service reliability engineering (SRE), iovation*

◆ ◆ ◆

DevOps 10 years ago to me was a way to express the need for a better, nonfunctional and nonpolitic agreement between who made software and changes to said software and who had the task of keeping the service up. DevOps now is a way to describe someone that has initiative and knowledge on the part of the stack that is fronting the service and feels comfortable changing that. Sadly, DevOps is a term used to indicate a skill set and a willingness to be one of the developers taking care of Ansible or Jenkins or tending to help fix package repositories and not someone to make what is called "silos" go away.

SRE to me is a methodology and a set of roles with inverse energy as DevOps—SRE keep the lights on and have the ownership, budget, and final word on what goes to production and what needs care in all aspects I mentioned before. It is the evolution of the Ops teams we saw in the last decade, fit to companies that can handle that and better adapted to survive Conway's law. In essence we all expect that developers know how their software works and their stack in [depth], but this is far from what someone tasked with running services does.

—*Gleicon Moraes, director of engineering*

◆ ◆ ◆

As the SRE nomenclature continues to grow, it is interesting that some people see it as in conflict with the term DevOps. In most cases, this would seem to require a narrow view of at least one if not both of those terms, as they are really just different responses toward a common problem; the continually increasing pressure by companies to build and deploy software within ever faster iterations. In both cases the realization that the "old ways" are not going to work is paramount, and while the SRE model takes a more tactical, engineering-focused approach to solving the problem, DevOps approaches this more from the cultural side, but still with an idea of reducing friction and getting people to work across cultural barriers.

One interesting aspect [of] both of these ideas is that they suffer from their current adoption patterns. On the DevOps side, we have seen so much hyperbole around the term, and so many companies trying to twist DevOps to fit their own (often sales-based) definition, that it has diluted what "adopting DevOps" even means. Ironically, on the SRE side, that term is now so dominated by Google's published information on the term that companies who don't operate like Google (i.e., almost everyone) may not be able to be able to pick up the practice. Working in a company that started adopting an SRE-style approach to operations almost 10 years ago, it has become harder to hire for those positions as people's expectations changed to looking for a specific set of practices rather than an agreed approach to operations to a more specific set of practices. My hope is that the conversation around these topics will continue to grow so that others can gain some of the benefits in ways that work for their organizations, whatever the form those organizations take.

—Robert Treat, CEO, OmniTI

◆ ◆ ◆

SRE is holistic at its core—everything on both Dev and Ops is connected and the approach is to identify, understand, and execute said connections by diving deep into the low- and high-level technical matters of Dev and Ops, and help the teams deploy the implementation with the provided help.

Unfortunately, SRE is often interpreted as an overseer position, like if it was an oracle where people go to ask questions, when it shouldn't. At the end of the day, SRE could be whatever your organization needs it to be to ensure that you're providing the best service possible and bringing teams together.

—Manuel Fernandez, SRE, VividCortex

◆ ◆ ◆

DevOps is a cultural term that embodies a spirit or enablement and accountability across operational and development teams. A typical team that adheres to the DevOps philosophy brings the operational mindset of service ownership to the development teams and provides the guidance and tools necessary for them to more effectively maintain a product through its full lifecycle. SRE is [a] class of operational user with a strong development background along with a deep understanding of operational principles and designs.

SRE teams should closely embody the DevOps philosophy, using its basic tenets to provide the operational integrity and stability to their environment through contact with service owners and other operational teams.

—Matt Jones, senior infrastructure security operations engineer

◆ ◆ ◆

I'm working in a medium-sized startup where I actually hold both SRE and DevOps position. For me, being the SRE is about managing the production systems, making them reliable, handling the scale, automating, etc. While for the DevOps position I rather think it is about being the junction between our Devs and the production. Being that link includes helping Devs in many aspects: having available staging env,

CI/CD pipelines, automated testing, etc. Overall I think the DevOps engineer should be everything possible to ease the Devs' life so they can focus on coding.

While the two positions are different on the scope they are similar on the implementation. It would make sense that SREs build the staging and preproduction env, make it available to Devs, which would qualify as a DevOps mission (once again, ease the Devs' life). The same goes for automation that can be implemented.

—*Julien Avenet, SRE, Kiwi.ki Gmbh*

◆ ◆ ◆

A DevOps team member is someone who is familiar with installing and maintaining software on the systems for which they're responsible. They know about an upcoming minor database upgrade, and what bug fixes and new features are part of that upgrade. They're aware that the disk space situation isn't that dire but will need addressing in the next three to six months, either by trimming the database, or at least partitioning some tables. The switch we're currently using is adequate, but might be up for an upgrade, as well. Normally, things are fine, but in high-traffic situations, it has been struggling a little.

An SRE team member is thinking about how a new piece of software will need to integrate with other systems. Some situations will require additional table space in the database, and that requirement needs to be discussed with the DevOps folks. Two classes of servers will need to have low latency and redundant network connections, which shouldn't be an issue, but will be another point to raise. And the code review should be interesting—we want to make sure that the algorithm is as smart as possible, but no smarter.

—*Alex Beamish, software developer, independent*

◆ ◆ ◆

I think of DevOps as an approach, and of SRE as a role. DevOps was a kick in the pants the infrastructure world needed. Its core message is simple: building and testing of infrastructure is something we can and should automate. It's not prescriptive about how you structure your teams, though it definitely encourages structures that support collaboration between product and infrastructure engineers.

SRE is a role whose tenets align well with the goals of DevOps. Having dedicated SREs at an organization is a bit of a luxury. You have a group of people whose sole focus is making your service run better. Not every organization needs a whole team doing this! It's perfectly fine to distribute the work around a more generalized engineering team, especially early in a company's life.

—Chris Sinjakli, site reliability engineer, GoCardless

◆ ◆ ◆

It's become repetitive for infrastructure-oriented Devs and SREs to repeat: "DevOps is a philosophy, not a job title." At their cores, DevOps and SRE are both about putting developers in charge of operations—the difference is in ownership. A small dev team can practice fantastic DevOps—automated and frequent rollouts with CI/CD, comprehensive monitoring and alerting, and a shared on-call rotation, while the Devs themselves still own the services. SRE is a way to have a separate group of developers own the production environment when its reliability is critical to the organization.

The difference is that SRE is structured, organized, and well defined, and DevOps is harder to pin down. In my opinion, organizations that want to practice DevOps are best suited to have a developer team read the SRE book and consider a few components to integrate across the entire team, not just for one or two "DevOps" people. Insofar as DevOps can be a superset of SRE, they can (and should) peacefully coexist in a healthy organization that recognizes a shared responsibility for reliability among all developers and SREs.

—Jason Gwartz, software developer

CHAPTER 13

Production Engineering at Facebook

A discussion with Pedro Canahuati, Facebook,
and David N. Blank-Edelman

David: What's production engineering?

Pedro: Philosophically, production engineering stems from the belief that operational problems should be solved through software solutions and that the engineers who are actually building the software are the best people to operate that software in production.

In the early days of software, a developer who wrote the code also debugged and fixed it. Sometimes, they even had to dive into hardware issues. Over the years, with the advent of remote software systems, the internet, and large data centers, this practice changed dramatically. Today, it's still common to see software engineers writing and developing applications, then handing off their code to a QA team for testing, and then handing that off to another team for deploying and debugging. In some environments, a release engineering team is responsible for deploying code and an operations team ensures the system is stable and responds to alerts. This works fairly well when QA and operations have the knowledge required to fix problems, and when the feedback loops between the teams are healthy. When this isn't the case, fixing and/or debugging production issues needs to work its way back to the software engineers, and this workflow can significantly delay fixes. At Facebook, our production engineering [PE] team is simply bringing back the concept of integrating software engineering [SWE] and operations.

We started the PE model a few years ago to focus on building a more collaborative culture between the software engineering and operations teams. Our goal is to ensure that Facebook's infrastructure is healthy and our robust community of users can access the platform at any hour. The PE team is a critical component in accomplishing this through automation, writing new tools to make operations easier for everyone, performance analysis, hardcore systems debugging, firefighting when necessary and by teaching others how to run their systems themselves. Facebook engineering has built common infrastructure that everyone uses to build and deploy software. Facebook's infrastructure has grown organically over the years, and while I'm confident that we will solve many of the operational problems we have today, we still haven't. Production engineers help bridge this gap to ensure teams can get back to solving the hard software problems we face and spend as little time as possible on operational problems.

The PE team not only writes code to minimize operational complexity, but also debugs hard problems in live production that impact billions of people around the world—from backend services like Facebook's Hadoop data warehouses, to frontend services like News Feed, to infrastructure components like caching, load balancing, and deployment systems. PE, working side by side with SWE, keeps Facebook running. The team also helps software engineers understand how their software interacts with its environment.

Think of production engineering as the intersection of large-scale manufacturing (hardware, automotive, industrial, etc.), expert engineering, and good operational management. A production engineer typically has wide knowledge of engineering practices and is aware of the challenges related to production operations. The goal of PE is to ensure production is running in the smoothest way. A great analogy to our role is that of a production line for manufacturing automobiles. A team of designers creates the car, a team of engineers builds the hardware and another team is responsible for the automation that puts it all together. When this process breaks, a production engineer steps in with knowledge of the whole flow of the production line, including everything upstream and downstream. They understand how the automobile was designed, how it's supposed to function, and what the software used to build it is supposed to do. Armed with this knowledge, production engineers can troubleshoot, diagnose, and fix the issue if they need to, and they also work with the entire team to prevent it from happening in the future.

At Facebook, production engineers are not line operators, but they do know how everything in the line actually operates. For example, when software is responding to user traffic, or even when it's failing, production engineers are often the ones who best understand how the code interacts with its environment, how to fix and improve it, and how to make it performant over time.

David: Can you say a little bit more about the origin story of PE?

Pedro: During its early years, Facebook applied the then-industry-accepted approach to operating its production website and services via a dedicated operations team. The operations team consisted of separate Site Reliability Engineering [SRE] and Application Operations [AppOps] teams.

The SRE team had more in common with a traditional communications provider's network operations center [NOC] than it did with solving operations problems through software. At the time, a team of less than 20 monitored the systems infrastructure for issues, reacted to alerts, and triaged problems using a three-tier escalation process with the support of AppOps. SRE worked in three shifts to provide 24/7 coverage. AppOps, on the other hand, was a small set of individuals already embedded within Software Engineering [SWE] teams. The model back then was effectively one AppOps engineer per service (for example, newsfeed, ads, web chat, search, data infrastructure) with a ratio of production engineers to software engineers of approximately 1:10 but could range as high as 1:40. Sometimes, there was one AppOps engineer assigned to multiple services. For example, data warehouse and centralized logging systems had one embedded AppOps engineer. Early on, AppOps was able to understand the full application stack well enough to react to and resolve outages quickly.

Even though the SRE team was supposed to be engaged with SWE teams developing software, SRE was often absent in the early development process and regularly found out about new software changes or new services being built as they were being deployed. The relationship between SRE, AppOps, and SWE wasn't strong. The SRE team also had to juggle the additional responsibility of lighting up new data centers and ensuring capacity needs were met during peak traffic hours. SRE ensured capacity needs were met by shifting users' loads across multiple data centers using web interfaces on enterprise-level load balancers. There was some level of automation happening through ad hoc shell scripting and lightweight tooling that incorporated APIs from these devices or from in-house written code bases.

While the SRE, AppOps, and SWE teams focused on scaling the website and infrastructure for web-based services, users started transitioning from desktop to mobile, and the whole company was reprioritized to follow a mobile-first strategy. This significantly increased service complexity and accelerated the need to provision an ever-increasing amount of infrastructure. The scaling of Facebook's services in a mobile world, combined with hyper-scale customer growth, overwhelmed the SRE and AppOps teams. The majority of the AppOps engineers had to be on call 24/7, and firefighting was the norm. As user growth and complexity increased, both SRE and AppOps were unable to focus on recruiting and couldn't hire additional staff for months, pushing the teams further underwater.

Adding to an already challenging situation, infrastructure capacity was falling behind due to a lack of automated data center provisioning from the SRE team and the constant need to fix individual servers in production. Without the necessary automation to keep up with server failures and adding new clusters, we ended up in a capacity crunch. People were overwhelmed and experiencing burnout. A better approach was clearly needed. Our management team recognized that the operations team had not kept pace with changes in the business and that the current operating model was no longer adequate.

The main challenges we faced were unclear expectations of the roles of SRE, AppOps, and SWE; an inability to balance firefighting, server failures, and turning up new capacity; weak credibility with the SWE teams when asking for changes in architecture.

We first focused our efforts in clarifying the roles for SRE, AppOps, and SWE. We understood that we needed to be involved earlier in the software process and that the embedded model had a higher likelihood of effecting change. We also needed to establish stronger working relationships and credibility between the software and operations teams and ensure that the SWE teams had stronger ownership of their services.

We executed a multistep reorganization and hired different types of engineers. To continue managing the growing infrastructure needs, we decided to split the SRE staff into two. We would retire the SRE moniker and stand up a new Site Reliability Operations [SRO] team, and we would expand the existing AppOps team with some members from the former SRE team. By moving key individuals from the former SRE team we were able to expand AppOps' operational knowledge and staffing quickly and double the team's size. Retiring the SRE moniker also helped change expectations from the SWE teams over time.

SRO's remit was to focus in two areas. The first was to continue the needed and noble effort of firefighting outages. The second was to build software and automation to reduce the human involvement in these efforts. We also moved some of the reorganized SREs into an SRO function focused on turning up new capacity.

The discussions around expectations of these roles brought to light the fact that many SWEs didn't have empathy for the role of these operational teams. Operations was a bit of a black box to many software engineers, and we needed to change this perception. The embedded model would help to make sure that the SWEs understood what it takes to operate a service at scale, and, later, as we embraced shared on-call, we would make space for SWEs to gain more empathy. However, we didn't always have the credibility needed to influence the SWE teams to change the architecture to be more stable. Part of the problem was that SWE, SRO, and AppOps didn't speak the same language of algorithms, concurrency, scalability, and efficiency that goes into building a distributed system. There were a few engineers in SRO and AppOps that had this knowledge, but it became clear that we needed additional individuals who were more like software engineers and also understood operations to help make this transition. As a first step, we actively recruited and hired several technical leaders with deep experience in operations and infrastructure, focusing heavily on candidates who demonstrated a strong cultural fit in addition to technical acumen. These new hires needed both algorithmic and practical coding skills in addition to an understanding of low-level systems and building distributed services. We also desired supportive communication and influence skills. We were successful in finding this type of engineer and adding them to both SRO and AppOps.

Changing the expectations for SRO and AppOps from SWEs is challenging. Engineers that had been at Facebook when SRE and AppOps had been established expected these teams to merely do firefighting and operational work *for* the SWE teams. A typical comment overheard in meetings when discussing remediation of issues during outages and ownership of stability would have been: "Well, that's the AppOps job. I shouldn't be doing this as a SWE." Even though there were some SWE teams that had a culture of strong ownership of stability and did firefighting or worked on solving operational problems, many did not. We needed to change the expectation of what the operations teams did and we needed the SWEs to take ownership of their stability and operational issues in production.

It wasn't enough that we had changed our hiring practices to focus more on software engineering skills, in addition to network fundamentals, systems internals, and large-scale systems designs. In order to reset the expectation bit, we needed to rebrand. We decided to remove the word "Ops" from the "AppOps" name and became Production Engineering.

Removing "Ops" from the name had two main outcomes:

- It communicated to the rest of the company that we were an engineering team building software to solve operational problems, not just traditional operators of systems.
- It helped reset the notion that SWEs could just have their services run by some other ops team.

We still had one major hurdle to overcome related to ownership of stability and operational issues. As more SWEs and, now production engineers worked on scaling services, SRO continued to be an operational backstop during service outages and responded to alerts 24/7. SRO embarked on building an automation framework we named FBAR [**F**ace**B**ook **A**uto **R**emediation] that solved one of the main pain points at the time of running a service in production: removing failing servers and replacing them with healthy ones. SRO continued to grow while this system matured with a future eye of handing over this operational work to automation written by PEs and SWEs.

After a few years of building up PE teams and hiring more SROs, the complexity of our infrastructure grew so much that our centralized SRO team no longer was able to comprehend how every service worked. Their ability to respond to outages became difficult, and SROs became worried that instead of fixing the issue, they may cause a new outage. We realized we needed to dissolve the SRO team and hand complete operational ownership 24/7 to the PE and SWE teams. SRO spent the next 18 months working with PEs and SWEs to write code that ran on FBAR to handle many of the server issues that required SRO response. Where we had PEs paired with SWEs, they created a shared on-call rotation. Where SWEs didn't work with PEs, they took on-call ownership. At the end of these 18 months, the centralized SRO team was dissolved, and its members moved over to production engineering. It took about four years to complete the transition from SRE and AppOps to all production engineering.

David: Let's talk a little bit about structures. Some SRE models have this notion that software teams get an SRE after a certain amount of work is completed by the SWEs. SREs are sourced from a completely separate group that is not part of the product group or the service group. They live in their own org. How do you think of the organization around PE? How do production engineers relate to the larger org tree?

Pedro: Our model borrows from the separate organizational structure of some companies and the embedded nature of some SRE and operations teams, where they report into the product group or the business unit. We have a *centralized reporting* structure and a *decentralized seating* structure.

The operations function needs to ensure that operations is running smoothly across all of the engineering functions. Sometimes, this may be hindered by competing priorities of the people who report to the highest C-level executive (for example, the CEO). In many companies, the highest-level operational executive (Head of Ops) usually wants to report to the CEO, and I believe this causes more problems than it solves. I believe the operational executive should instead report to the most senior software engineering executive (Head of Eng). This effectively makes the Head of Ops a peer to other software engineering groups instead of a peer to the Head of Eng. This also makes the Head of Eng responsible for the success of operations. When performance assessments are taken seriously, and if the operations team isn't succeeding, then the engineering executive is not succeeding. This, in my opinion, fixes a lot of the dynamics of "Dev versus Ops" because Ops is now part of Dev.

I recognize that there are a lot of larger companies out there that have splintered their operations teams and they each report into the head of their business unit. I'm sure in some cases this works, but it's very hard to make that work well. What I've seen happen more often is that the head of a business unit forces the operational team to do their bidding and the escalation path is very muddy when it comes time to deal with a disagreement.

So, to prevent some of these dynamics, we kept a centralized reporting structure for these main reasons:

Flexibility

Our production engineers can work on hardware design, UI, backend software, and everything in between. For example, a production engineering team designed and built out a Faraday cage for wireless mobile phone testing. We developed a specialized rack with mobile devices where engineers can run their software on various types of mobile hardware and do on-device testing. The centralized reporting structure gives us the flexibility to set our own goals and decide what kind of work we "should do" versus being told what work needs to be done by the lead of a specific business unit. The headcount for people doing PE work is managed separately from the broader engineering headcount and so the leadership in PE can ensure this work won't get reprioritized by the business lead who may have different priorities.

Motivation

PE managers are able to motivate their teams to get work done based on the problem they're trying to solve, as opposed to focusing on shipping a product or service. There's a qualitative and a quantitative aspect to evaluating production engineers, and certain things that motivate individuals in production engineering are not necessarily what motivates software engineers. The PE management team is able to give people the guidance to work on the context switching that operations-minded folks are really good at when it's needed, and the ability to solve software engineering problems when it's time to focus on them.

I've found that there are those, like me, who run toward a problem instead of away. I'm pretty sure one of the reasons I chose to not go the pure software route was because I enjoyed the context switching. I have found that even though the folks who like PE-type work may complain about context switching, they actually enjoy it. There's also a certain adrenaline-like rush they get when they finally figure out that one little detail in the system that unblocked the problem, restored the service, and allowed everyone to breathe easily and get back to work. I've always found that the best way to hire and manage a PE is to figure out what excites them about this kind of work and hire managers who can understand this aspect of their personality. Having performed the same (or similar) type of role in the past more often than not increases the likelihood that these managers will be able to successfully motivate them. I've found, conversely, that many of the managers who really just want to think about algorithms and write pure software are challenged by how to manage and motivate PEs.

Shared accountability with slight tension

We hire external software engineers that may come from a traditional Dev-to-QA-to-Ops model and believe operations should do the things software engineers don't want to do. A separate organizational structure creates a buffer for the production engineering leadership team between operational stability and features. The SWE and PE teams need to come together to build a stable, reliable, secure, efficient, and feature-rich service. If a software engineering manager and a production engineering manager have a disagreement, we need to make sure that they are working together to solve the problem. The software engineering manager can't say to the PE team, "You should do all my operations work for me." The production engineering manager also can't say to the SWE team, "You should only work on stability and reliability." There needs to be a balance between these two competing priorities. Our structure provides that healthy tension and shared accountability for doing what's needed, not what might be defined by a single manager's responsibility.

At Facebook, we have a saying: "code wins arguments." We've applied a similar model to keep teams accountable when there's disagreement between operational load and new features. When this happens, we bring the managers and tech leads of both SWE and PE together to discuss their views with senior leaders in their respective organizations. These managers and tech leads provide operational metrics that help us all understand what is not working in a system/service and what the team is going to prioritize to improve these metrics. The discussion also needs to touch on what features may be delayed based on this prioritization. This way, all the leaders understand the potential impact to the business and can make an informed decision. Ultimately, I and my counterparts on the SWE teams are held accountable by our manager to build systems that are feature-rich, stable, and operable. Since the org tree for all of us meets at the same level, if we don't do our jobs, our performance suffers. This, in my opinion, gives us the best of both worlds.

The decentralized, embedded model gives us greater abilities to influence how services are built. PEs sit right next to their SWE peers. They go to their meetings and offsites; they're available for hallway conversations and ad hoc discussions about architecture. Both the SWE and PE managers work on what the road map should look like for a service, what will make the service more reliable, and also what features are needed to enable growth. They compromise between features and stability.

With this embedded structure, the software team also gets the constant vigilance of the production engineers as well as the interaction of pointing out problems that are actively happening and need to be solved. When problems surface in production, both SWEs and PEs huddle together, shoulder to shoulder, solving the problem. When the software engineer is on call, the production engineer is sitting there with them, and the software engineer can also just lean over and ask, "Hey, I don't know how to do this operation in production right now. Can you jump in with me, help me, and teach me how to do that so I can be more effective in the future?"

I'm sure that this isn't the only way that works and there are likely other organizational models that can perform in the same way and don't need to have the same reporting structure with colocated people. This is the way that we've found works the best for us at Facebook.

David: You mentioned on-call earlier in the PE organization's origin story, but I thought you said that the software engineers were on call, and the PEs were not on call. Is that always the case?

Pedro: No, not always. A phrase I often use is: "if you write code and release it to production, *congratulations*, you own it." This meant we needed to get SWEs to take responsibility for keeping their services up in production and also taking primary on-call. PE is not primary on-call for services we don't own or build outright. We have a shared on-call model when we're embedded with an SWE team and how that on-call rotation manifests itself is situational. In most cases, it's a weekly rotation. There's a software engineer on call for one week, then a PE on call the next week, and so forth. In some cases, due to cognitive load or because the infrastructure is currently harder to manage, some teams do shorter on-call rotations of a few days. We have only two scenarios where solely software engineers or production engineers are on call:

- A software engineering team that doesn't have embedded production engineers. In this scenario, they have no choice because they have to be on call for their service.
- Places in our environment where production engineers build everything end to end.

David: Like infrastructure, the DNS team, that sort of thing?

Pedro: Yes, exactly—PE actually owns a couple of pieces of infrastructure, like the software used to provision servers, or manage server replacements in production (FBAR). FBAR (*https://www.facebook.com/notes/facebook-engineering/making-facebook-self-healing/10150275248698920/*) is an automated system that handles repetitive issues so that engineers (SWE and PE) can focus on solving and preventing larger, more complex site disruptions. We also built systems that automate service migrations during maintenance and another focused on turning up new clusters from scratch. We own and built the L4 load balancer that sits in between our L7 load balancer and our web servers. For the Faraday cage-like rack I mentioned earlier, we built Augmented Traffic Control (*http://facebook.github.io/augmented-traffic-control/*) [ATC] that allows developers to test their mobile application across varying network conditions, easily emulating high-speed, mobile-carrier, and even severely impaired networks.

In these last few examples (and there are others), we are on call 100% of the time, because we're the ones who built these systems. It follows the same model I described earlier where the team that built and deploys the software into production owns it, and the team that built it has the accountability to fix it when it breaks.

David: Given this structure, how do you manage the relationships between the PE org and other teams?

Pedro: Company-wide, we send out what we call Pulse Surveys every six months. One of the questions asked relates to how well a team collaborates with their partner teams. Facebook has built a lot of common software that is used by other teams and is critical to its operation. So teams need to collaborate well together, and this includes PEs embedded in SWE teams. The survey outputs a general favorability score that tells us if the PE team thinks it collaborates well with other teams. Often there have been signs along the way and this survey is now specific data we can use to narrow down the problem. We start by asking a bunch of questions. For example: "Is the relationship working well? Does the PE team feel like they have a voice? Are the PEs listening to the SWE team's needs to lessen operational load and building tools to solve these problems? Do the PEs feel like they're being treated as equals? Do the SWEs understand what work PE should be doing, and vice versa?"

If we find that the relationship isn't healthy, we talk to the PE and SWE managers and tech leads to gather more feedback. If the feedback points to confusion around how to work with PE, or vice versa, we educate everyone on what a successful PE and SWE team engagement looks like and what a successful healthy partnership feels like. We also discuss what shared ownership means and how SWEs need to care about the stability of their system and that more PEs potentially doing firefighting isn't sustainable. We make sure the PEs aren't being obstructionists and preventing the SWE team from innovating, if for example, they are constantly saying "No" to changes. People and relationships are challenging and sometimes value systems are just not aligned, but we can't ignore these relationships and let them become toxic.

Ultimately, if we can't come to an agreement on how to work together, we need to make a change. If the relationship problems stem from the PEs, we work on removing the individuals causing these problems, talk to them and their manager about our collaboration expectations, and begin the work to rebuild the team if necessary. If the relationship problems stem from SWEs not wanting to own their services in the way we've described or constantly dismissing the work needed to make a system more stable, we will also talk to their manager and tech leads. We'll revisit the situation sometime in the future after we've given everyone time to work things out. If the SWE team's expectations of PE continue to focus on handing off operational work, then we will gladly redeploy PEs into other SWE teams. There are plenty of places where the PE skill set and discipline will be valued, treated equally, and able to effect change.

Removing an embedded PE team is a lever we pull as a last resort and after we've exhausted all our methods to build a strong relationship. I have only done it a small number of times because we can definitely lose credibility with the SWE team and it will make it much harder to build trust in the future. That being said, I would rather not burn out PEs trying to force something. In the few cases where this has happened, the SWE teams have come back some months later asking to try to work together again. The reality is that some software teams don't have people who have an operational mindset and can quickly get overwhelmed with work due to a skills gap or the mounting operational debt. Sometimes, learning a lesson the hard way is the best way for everyone to start fresh.

David: Let's continue down this path of organizational structure for one more moment. Does every project get a PE? What do you do when you show up?

Pedro: You noted earlier that in some companies, SREs don't arrive until they hit some level of maturity or operational stability. At Facebook, our M.O. has been to ruthlessly prioritize. Not every SWE team gets to work with an embedded production engineering team and it is situational. It has to do with the service itself and its stage of development, the maturity of the service and the team. We would ideally like to enter in the nascent phase of a software team, because they're building something new and might not know exactly what it's going to become. By embedding ourselves early on, we could get some of the operational work accomplished early and quickly. Sometimes that happens, and sometimes it doesn't.

There are software engineering teams that end up building some services in the beginning that don't have production engineers. This is typically a new service that doesn't quite have a well-defined use case. It could be someone's innovative idea to solve a problem, but it will take a while to develop. Once that service is established, and they realize that they're hitting the stage where scaling is critical, they come to us looking for help. We keep a running list of these services and teams and as we hire more production engineers, we use that list to prioritize what is critical and what needs the most help.

In some cases, like when we built out live video and our generalized videos infrastructure, we knew this was going to be a legitimate use case and so we were involved from the beginning. Unfortunately, we had to pull valuable members from other teams to stand that team up, and there's always a conversation about the trade-offs we're making.

When we engage in the scaling stage of a service, we need to figure out what work the team should tackle first, and that's sometimes hard to pin down. The service may be suffering from any one of reliability problems, capacity, deployment issues, or monitoring issues. Andrew Ryan, a production engineer on our team who often helps us with organizational design, came up with a "Service Pyramid" that is loosely based on Maslow's Hierarchy of Needs. I presented about this hierarchy of needs in an SRE-Con talk about production engineering. I later found out that Mickey Dickerson also presented about a similar service reliability hierarchy of needs at an O'Reilly conference. It was nice to see that this concept for how to approach work was shared across a few other teams.

We use this service hierarchy to prioritize the type of work production engineers do when they're first engaged with a team. The bottom layer of the pyramid is focused on ensuring that the service is integrated well with standard Facebook tooling to deal with the life cycle of a server (provisioning, monitoring, replacement, migration, decommissioning) and service deployments (new deployments, integration tests, canarying, etc). Once you have the basic needs of your server and service met, you can move up the layers of the pyramid to working on higher-level components like performance tuning and efficiency, disaster recovery, anomaly detection, and failure modeling.

Only then can you efficiently work at the top of the pyramid on "weird stuff." These are things that may not happen at smaller scale but happen in our environment due to the influx of data and the amount of work done on backend systems. Every PE and SWE has an obligation to investigate these weird issues, but if the basic needs of the service aren't met, they might find themselves chasing issues that should have already been dealt with automatically instead of real problems of scalability.

David: What do you mean by stages of development?

Pedro: I see teams and services go through three phases in this order:

Bootstrap phase
Do anything and everything that you need to get the service up and running. That might mean a lot of firefighting and manual intervention to fix things. It might mean quick, iterative deployments that fail fast. It might mean just allowing a trickle of traffic at first. You build up these operational muscles and figure out what the failure modes are and how it affects other systems.

Scale phase
Once you're out of the bootstrap phase, you start to move into the scale phase. This might include deploying the service into multiple regions, getting the service used by millions or billions of people depending on the type of service. The team gets much more mature at being able to operate the service and its feature set, understanding the dependencies on other systems, and the architectural changes that may need to occur over time.

Awesomize phase
Now the service needs to become really, really awesome. Do the last 10 to 20% of work needed to optimize the service to be more efficient and more performant. I call it "awesomize" because when I try to ask people to optimize something, nobody really wants to do that. But everybody wants to make something awesome, so I call it the awesomize phase.

The people required for each of these phases might be different. There is a certain set of people on both the software and production engineering teams who really love to do the bootstrapping work. There are also those who really love the middle of this continuum. The bootstrapping is done, and they want to scale the service: make it better, more resilient, and bigger; take on more users; and deal with the consistency and concurrency problems and the big disaster recovery problems that will arrive with a higher level of maturity. There are even others that want to make something performant, efficient, and rock-solid. Some people will evolve over time and grow with each of these phases, but my experience has been that most do not stay with the service through these three phases. They'll find their sweet spot, and they'll move around in the organization to find the work that plays to their strengths. Ultimately, we want everybody to do the awesomization work, but the reality is that not everybody does and that's OK.

David: Given these phases and people's inclinations toward them, how do you create teams?

Pedro: I've seen a tendency to try to stretch people to do everything and become a jack-of-all-trades that can work up and down the stack, from lower-level hardware issues, to middle-layer protocol problems, to UI programming. This model is useful and needed in many startup environments but does not work well at scale. There is no way that one human can do that type of work and make themselves sustainable over time and not burn out, so we focus more on matching individuals to technologies. For example, on the cache team, knowledge about network protocols and debugging is needed, but understanding how the overall system works is the ultimate goal.

When we are starting up a new team, we look for four factors and ask these questions:

- Is there enough work for at least three people for the next 18 to 24 months? I came up with three because that number, to me, really defines a team. If there are only two people and one is sick or wants to take vacation, the other person has to take the entire workload. When a third person is added, then at least people can pair up on projects, define shared responsibilities, etc. It's simple team dynamics.

- Does the service fit our prioritization model? We need to understand how the service is solving a business need and that it will be something that's used and not just a prototype that may never see production scale. Is it the right time to prioritize this team over another? This one is tricky because it's much more subjective.

- Do we have a manager who can work with the production engineers and build out a larger team? The manager is a critical component, making sure that engineers are focused and getting things done. It's important that everyone is developing and growing over time. We need to ensure the team is getting the right level of context for their work and that they're learning from other people.

- Is there a local SWE team to work with on this service? This is primarily in the case where we're not the ones building the software. We need to make sure that there is an SWE team that can engage in shoulder-to-shoulder debugging and in-person discussions around architecture and problems.

These four ingredients have to come together. That filters out a bunch of nascent projects that may take up valuable people. Although it would be nice to have production engineers on every type of team, it doesn't make sense based on our prioritization model.

In order to establish a new location with production engineering teams, the four ingredients above need to exist and we add another constraint. We need to ensure the new location has the ability to sustain three different teams, of at least three people for 18 to 24 months working with SWEs locally. This means we establish PE teams later into the site's maturity.

David: It does, but what about the small stuff? The things that have to be done but aren't going to take that long? Is there a catch-all team?

Pedro: No, there's no catch-all team that does that kind of work. In general, it is the software engineering team's responsibility to manage their technical and operational debt. They do this for as long as they can, but eventually if their service needs to be prioritized and it makes sense to build a team, then we do. Oftentimes, PEs that have an affinity for certain work might see something on a team without PEs and spend a couple of weeks on it to make it better, and then come back to their original team. We think this is valuable overall and where we can, we encourage it because it can help the SWE team gain some quick operational efficiency and knowledge.

In infrastructure, we generally focus on making operational things like bootstrapping go away. We have built a lot of services that give engineers "more for free." They can use our containerization service for deployments. They will get general server health monitoring for free. We have a centralized monitoring system with built-in graphing, anomaly detection, and alerting. The service gets basic remediation for free through things like FBAR (originally built by SRO, then significantly augmented by PE). All the basics are handled for you so you can focus more on the higher-level software problems. This allows our software engineers to do rapid prototyping and work on the small things first and figure out whether there's something worthwhile building versus having to focus on the small stuff. This kind of "more for free" stuff gets you through some of the bootstrapping phase I discussed earlier without needing too much initial help because it's all self-service.

David: We've talked a little bit about how a PE gets involved with a team and the product or service. How does a PE leave the team?

Pedro: Mobility is actually a core tenet of ours.

We like to hire generalists. In addition to the core practical and algorithmic programming skills, we also look for other traits. We expect PEs we hire or train to understand network protocols and how to debug them. They need to have lower-level systems knowledge and understand how software interacts with the kernel, the hardware, and the network layer. If they are further in their careers, they need to understand how to build distributed systems. These are the general skills we look for when hiring PEs. When they join a team, they may not be experts in every one of these dimensions, but, over time, they'll gain this knowledge and experience and they'll become even stronger engineers. This knowledge allows them to move around more easily within PE.

They will also learn how to use Facebook-built tools and services. Many of these mimic services outside of Facebook, like a containerization service. If the service is using our in-house containerization system—be it Cache, Messaging, Ads, or Newsfeed, or anything else—it's still the same containerization service. The inner workings of the system they're working with and the problems that come up—concurrency, consistency, disaster recovery, for example—will vary depending on the service. That is what a PE needs to learn when they land on a team, but the general skills of managing systems in our environment and how to use the tools we've built appropriately are portable. PEs can take all of this knowledge and move to any team at Facebook as long as they are colocated with the SWE team building that service. It's a lot easier to collaborate that way rather than having the operations team and software engineering team located in different areas or even different time zones.

So, to answer the original question, we influence our managers to ask at 18 to 24 months into the PE's time on the team whether they have thought about moving to another team. Generally, the answer to that question is, "No. I love the job that I'm doing. The service that I'm building still has to mature. I like my team and the work. Go away and talk to me later." This is fine and it introduces the concept in their mind and lets them know that it's OK to consider moving at some point and that we value mobility.

We approach the question again at 24 to 36 months and we start looking for things that would complement their current knowledge. For example, if Jane, a PE on the storage team, has been there for a long time, we might ask her if she's ever thought of joining an in-memory cache team. The conversation goes something like this: "Hey, Jane, you've been on the storage team for a while, and I'd like to make sure you become a more well-rounded engineer. Have you considered moving to the cache team? They need a senior engineer like you and you have a lot of experience scaling systems rapidly. Sure, it's cache and not storage, but you should go talk to Joan about this and see what's going on." Generally, her answer is, "That sounds interesting. Let me go talk to her." Or Jane will come back and say, "You know, I've got three or four more months of work that I want to do. Let me finish this project, and then I'll consider a transfer to Joan's team or do a hack-a-month."

Hack-a-months are something that spun out of hack-a-thons when we realized that in all of our engineering teams, we needed a better way to give people the chance to learn something new. A hack-a-month serves two main purposes. One: encourage any engineer who has been on the same project for more than a year to leave their team for a month to work on something completely different. Many use these for a little break from their normal routine. Two: to find a new team and figure out if they want to move. In either case, the team has to be able to handle the person being out, so the manager needs to ensure their staffing is at a good level or needs to work on finding someone else to take their place.

To best evaluate folks in these hack-a-months, the two managers need to be in sync on performance during that period of time. In the case of someone learning something new, there's usually a well-defined project that has an end state that can be objectively measured. In the case of moving to a new team, we give people the room to ramp up into the new space and we take that into consideration in their performance evaluation.

After 36 months on the team, we more directly talk to the engineer about moving to another team. We do this because I believe that when people get stuck in a rut, they can slow down the progress of their team. When a new PE (or SWE) joins the team and proposes a new idea, they may be shot down by the engineer who is comfortable with the way the system works. The established engineer might reject this new idea because it changes their mental model and it changes their comfort with the system. This might stifle innovation. We've actually experienced this, and so we're much more prescriptive about moving engineers to new teams when they have been in the same team for three or more years. As we expand into new geographies, engineers that are hitting this three-year mark should have enough mobility to move into other teams.

We have quite a few senior engineers who have done this over and over again. And they have their own thoughts behind this, such as how managers influence them, how they influence themselves, how they talk to each other, whether it is easy to move, and how they deal with impostor syndrome if it sets in again. We encourage these engineers to share their stories candidly because it gives others insight into this process from a nonmanager's perspective. If an engineer experiences impostor syndrome but knows their manager has their back, it makes it easier. If the organization built around them provides this mechanism to try something new and not worry too much about performance, then mobility becomes a more fluid process.

David: What are the things required to be a successful production engineer?

Pedro: I'll try to list a few of the key traits that come to mind:

A focus on getting stuff done

Production engineers need to have a bias for action. When we're looking at a problem, building a system, or creating a team, there has to be a tangible problem we can work on and fix for the long term. There's definitely a reactive portion to the role and it's needed because systems break all the time. PEs need to be building sustainable solutions to these problems so there needs to be a focus on proactively addressing things. If we're stuck in one mode of operation, turning the crank on the same thing over and over again, we're not succeeding in the role.

Supportive communication and influence skills

You can't be a jerk. Jerks generally do not interact well with people. Those of us that have been in the industry for a long time remember that the image of someone in operations associated with the BOFH [Bastard Operator from Hell]. Dealing with outages and fixing things on a regular basis can wear people down and potentially turn them into angry curmudgeons, so we need to ensure we hire folks who understand when to be direct and still be civil in the way they talk to people. It really irks me when someone wants to show off their knowledge and shoot somebody down who might not have as much experience as they do. Production engineers need to be good at communicating to be successful in the role. The "no asshole" rule applies here, and when you find these folks, you should coach them to communicate differently, and if they don't, you should aggressively manage them out because their toxicity can easily permeate through the team.

Technical knowledge and skills

Production engineers not only need to speak the same language as software engineers, they also need to be able to speak the language of others. For example: network engineers, capacity engineers, data center engineers, and project managers. This means that they need to have knowledge about these different disciplines and be able to jump into any problem in the stack, whether it be a hardware problem or a UI issue. For example, in order to find a problem in the rendering layer, PEs need to be able to look at the code and understand how it renders data. Production engineers don't necessarily need to be experts at all of these disciplines, but they can't shy away from them. This is why our interview looks for a variety of technical skills and we also train engineers over time to gain more knowledge. Finding the unicorn that knows everything isn't a goal, so we're careful about expecting deep understanding of everything.

Flexibility

PEs play different roles at different times and need to understand when certain skills will be used. For example, on some teams, PEs need to be the communicator or the liaison. In other instances, they might need to be the problem solver, the debugger, or the fire fighter. Sometimes, they may need to code a critical component of a service. The role of a production engineer isn't neatly defined in a box, and this is by design. We specifically chose to have a broad definition because we engage at different stages in the service life cycle that I described earlier. The team's composition is a key factor in ensuring success in the role and we need to draw on each other's strengths in different areas to solve the problem. We really stress not falling into the "not my job" mentality, and PEs need to be open to doing things that aren't well defined in a job description.

Collaboration and compromise

Our model is that we work with the software teams, not for the software teams, and vice versa. On the one hand, we want SWEs to care about reliability, stability, and operations. On the other, we as PEs need to ensure we're not always using the stability hammer and need to care about features and delivering new services. We all need to work together to do what's right for the business, the service, and the team. Sometimes, that means that we'll need to compromise on operational issues, and sometimes that means SWE will need to compromise on features. One dimension shouldn't be the one that wins all the time. If there isn't compromise when we work together, then this could lead to unhealthy working relationships. The PE leadership often talks about this concept with PE teams because it's easy to get stuck in one mode of operating without taking the time to self-reflect and make sure that we're not actually the ones causing the rift between Dev and Ops.

Willingness to teach and not be a SPOF [Single Point of Failure]

None of the roles we play are sustainable in the long term. PEs need to be focused on building software, establishing processes, and evolving over time so they can no longer be needed. PEs need to be careful to always be the one the team calls on to solve a specific type of problem or own a specific domain on their own. PEs need to ensure they're building tools that will allow them to replace themselves.

Production engineering kind of resembles a trade within the engineering discipline, and understanding how to operate systems isn't something that's taught in school or university. Since it's something that you learn on the job and through experience, it means that we have to teach others how to do what we know how to do. I have found that in the beginning of their careers, few software engineers are constantly thinking about failure or the "what if?" scenarios and building systems that will be resilient to these failures. There is definitely a mindset that comes with being a successful PE, but I strongly believe this can be learned behavior. It's our responsibility to infuse those around us with this mindset. The more practiced software engineers know how to do this well, but the reality is that we're adding more and more new software engineers into our ranks and I believe PE helps them gain the knowledge of how to build more resilient software faster. This also means you need to make room for this kind of training and development and not just expect quantitative output from production engineers on the team.

David: Can we talk a bit about how you train new production engineers? Facebook is famous for its onboarding Bootcamp; do production engineers go through a Bootcamp? Is there a PE curriculum that is part of Bootcamp?

Pedro: How we gained a stronger position in Bootcamp is the part of the PE origin story that I didn't cover earlier. When I got to Facebook, operations wasn't allowed to join the existing software engineering Bootcamp. I had read about Bootcamp and seen the videos before joining and was excited. However, when I joined, I was told: "You're in operations, why would you ever want to commit code?" I was pretty irate. I spent the first year or so of my career at Facebook working hard to change this perception and prove folks wrong. I came from a computer science background, and I had written code my whole career. It felt unfair to be penalized because I chose to be in operations because I like to solve broad operational problems through software.

The first few weeks of an engineer's time at Facebook is where they get taught the fundamentals of operating as an engineer: how to commit code, learn about Facebook's code quality standards, work with our tools, deploy stuff into production, learn how to monitor it and add instrumentation, and more. This seemed like very relevant material that we also needed to understand, but since we weren't allowed to attend Bootcamp, we initially had to build our own version. In parallel, some of us spent more time with the Bootcamp leaders and through many conversations and by hiring more people with stronger software backgrounds, we were eventually able to gain entry.

Bootcamp has now been part of the onboarding process of all production engineers for a long time. We have influenced a lot of the classes taught to both software and production engineers, so that everyone gets some fundamental operational knowledge about systems before they land on a team.

We follow the same model for team selection that software engineering does here at Facebook. PEs spend three or four weeks getting fundamental technical knowledge in Bootcamp, and then spend two-plus weeks on team selection. We hold a career fair, for lack of a better term, where all the teams that are looking for people get together with all the Bootcampers that are looking for teams. We try to find a match based on the needs of the team and the skill set and desire of the individual. Some people have an affinity for security, for example, while others have an affinity for product-facing services or backend systems. For the most part, this works fine but this team selection process doesn't always work for everyone. Some people we hire want to know the team they'll be working on before they join Facebook. So we spend a bit more time up front learning about them and then narrowing down the set of teams to make it a little easier.

Over time, we found that there's still some type of work that doesn't necessarily apply to every software engineer joining Facebook. So, we created another mini Bootcamp that we call PE Fundamentals. That curriculum is geared specifically toward production engineers, network engineers, and other operational-like teams. In Bootcamp, we're trying to pack in a lot of information into a short period of time. I think it's overall very successful, but the content isn't as meaningful until the engineer has landed on their team and has spent a little more time understanding the infrastructure. About four weeks after PEs exit Bootcamp and have been on their team, they come back to a more hands-on set of classes that explains the nuances of our tools. Now armed with context of the system they're working on, they can make better connections in their mind about how our tools apply to their work.

We also do more cultural onboarding in PE Fundamentals. For example, we cover how to apply some healthy tension without going overboard. When we're talking to engineers about their solutions, we need to be careful about always being the naysayer because something might not be perfect. We can't always say "No." In these onboarding presentations, other PEs share their war stories so new folks can build examples in their mind for how to deal with potential disagreements on their team. PEs learn about being part of a culture that enables others to solve their problems as opposed to being a blocker to change.

David: Let's go to the wider picture around production engineering as a model. We've talked about the uniqueness of the PE organization at Facebook. Do you think that a PE organization could be implemented outside Facebook and still feel like a PE organization to you?

Pedro: Yes, I think a similar PE organization can be created elsewhere. I believe that Facebook's secret sauce is actually the people we hire and how they get things done. There are a lot of cultural factors that might need to be there, but I'd be wrong to assume that we're the only company that has a culture of autonomy, independence, empowerment, and healthy debate, among others. I do worry that other companies may adopt monikers and don't adopt the cultural implications that come with them. I've talked with a lot of teams outside some of the bigger companies that will build an SRE team, and in reality, it's just a rebranded SysAdmin team with a completely separate Ops role and no expectation of automation, collaboration, and equality. I believe it's because they want to be able to attract people externally, but the work doesn't necessarily change. The engagement model with the software engineers doesn't change. The ability to influence change isn't different. The relationship at the leadership levels and the shared accountability doesn't exist.

I strongly believe that software teams should ultimately be accountable for their operations, but I also recognize that PEs can help ensure this isn't too hectic. I want to emphasize again that PEs should not be doing operations *for* SWEs, they should be doing it *with* them. If this construct of working *with* others instead of *for* others exists, then I think this model can work in other places.

David: So how do you know whether an org is a PE org in the same way you define it?

Pedro: I want to be clear that the way we've built and run our org isn't the only way. Many companies are trying to figure out how to best run operations in their environment and it's great if they seek other models to reference—we should all be learning more from each other. However, this model isn't one-size-fits-all. When companies are trying to build their organizations, they should pick and choose the things that work for them and the things that can apply to their environment. If they choose to implement some of the concepts I've talked about, modify them, and make them their own, that's great. If, however, they try to follow some set of strict rules, I can almost guarantee that it will fail because everyone is different, every company is different, and every infrastructure challenge is different.

With that being said, if I had to quickly summarize the ways to evaluate the PE model, here are the main things to consider:

- Shared on-call with an embedded and collaborative model
- Strong relationships with technical credibility
- Balance between operations and features
- Leadership accountable to delivering a feature-rich and stable system

Let's break those down into a bit more detail.

When I want to gauge how close another team is to our PE model, the first question I ask is: "Who is on call? When things go down, who is responding to a service outage?"

If they respond that it's SRE, production engineering, DevOps, or whatever, as opposed to software engineering (or a shared on-call rotation between SWE and the operational team), then I know they're not building the PE model in the way we've defined it. In my opinion, the ultimate accountability for a service's stability needs to fall on those who are building the service. If the primary builders are SWEs, then that's who needs to be on call.

Another factor I look for in determining how closely someone's implementation resembles our model is related to equality and perception. In my experience, there are software engineering teams that look down on operational work and, conversely, operational teams that don't respect pure software work. Internally, I use a framework that highlights that Different != Bad.

Often, software engineers spend their mental time on algorithms and features instead of thinking about operational complexity. This isn't inherently bad, but it can lead to perception issues from operations. PEs, on the other hand, spend mental time and energy on other things that aren't purely software. Focusing on availability, scalability, operability, failure modes, security, deployments, reliability, and monitoring instead of software is also not inherently bad. The mental time spent is just on different things. It's everyone's responsibility to ensure there's shared context with respect to decisions and actions being taken by everyone on the team. I look for this type of shared understanding in my evaluation of whether someone else is implementing a similar model.

My typical follow-up question is about prioritization of features over operational stability. "When faced with prioritizing between features and operational stability, how often does operational stability lose?" When a team wants to build a service and repeatedly chooses to overrule the stability work even though they understand that the operational debt is going to be high, then the team is not succeeding at this model.

This leads me to another set of questions related to when the operational team is engaged in discussions regarding the architecture of a system. If the software team views the PEs, SREs, etc. as equal contributors, then discussions related to architecture will happen with both groups of people in the room. If they aren't seen as equal, and the operational team is consulted after the fact, then the implementation isn't going so well.

I don't think that any system or team will ever be perfect, but diversity of thought needs to exist in the team to build something that's going to be feature-rich and resilient under pressure. This last factor has a lot more to do with the relationship than it does with the level of technical knowledge. If the relationship is adversarial or if there's a large technical gap between the groups, the result will be a weaker system. If there's trust between the groups, there's shared technical understanding and the conversations are constructive, then a better, stronger system will be built.

When it comes to features versus stability, I think everybody should win a little and lose a little. The software team should sometimes deprioritize features to ensure stability. The PE team should sometimes deprioritize some gains in stability to ensure features are being built. Stability shouldn't regress, but sometimes it might be OK to hold the line. The software teams need to continue to innovate and PE's role is to help enable this innovation by reducing the operational load and solve operational problems through software. PE also needs to simultaneously work with the software team to reduce operational complexity. If PE is 100% focused on stability and reliability, then the software teams may dismiss them and the critical work won't happen. The work needs to be balanced over a longer time horizon. For example, some months may be heavily skewed toward features and then the following months may be heavily skewed toward operational stability. As long as this is balanced, then the implementation is working fine.

The last component is related to accountability. If the system isn't feature-rich and stable, are the leaders in software and operations held accountable together? When it comes to promotions and performance assessments, are these held to equal standards or are they different? At Facebook, for example, when we are assessing the performance of senior leaders in SWE and PE, we talk about them in the same set of discussions. Their impact, their ability to execute, work cross-functionally, and to build healthy organizations is held to the same standard.

As I said earlier, I do think that everyone's implementation might be slightly different and they should pick and choose the things that work well in their environment. I've talked to a few companies, and while they aren't doing the exact same things we are, overall, I think they're being successful in their implementation.

With over 20 years of experience in software design, architecture, and operating robust services at scale, Pedro Canahuati is the Vice President of Production Engineering and Security at Facebook. In this capacity, Canahuati is responsible for ensuring Facebook's infrastructure is stable and that the data of its over two billion users is secure. Throughout Canahuati's career, he has built and managed global engineering teams with a focus on operationally scaling companies to provide users with the best experience.

## PART II

Near Edge SRE

- Chaos engineering.
- Privacy engineering.
- Database reliability engineering.
- Durability engineering.
- Machine learning and SRE.

This is your near future…discuss.

You Know You're an SRE When...

…your personal blog can withstand multiple AWS region failures.

…you and your spouse resolve arguments by checking the error budget.

…you justify buying a Roomba on the basis of automating away routine operational work.

…you read accident reports and books about human factors for enjoyment on the beach.

## CHAPTER 14

In the Beginning, There Was Chaos

Casey Rosenthal, Backplane.io (formerly Netflix)

Services go down and people have a bad time. Customers who rely on the service become frustrated, other systems that rely on the service stop working, and the people responsible for the system are paged. History suggests[1] that even the most celebrated online services are vulnerable to outages, even with hundreds and sometimes thousands of people dedicated to their operation and uptime. As software inexorably increases in complexity,[2] old methods of preventing errors and outages prove insufficient.

In the not-so-distant past, best practices around testing, code style, and process gave us confidence that the code that we wrote and deployed would do what we expected it to do. We believe that practices like rigorous testing, Test-Driven Development (TDD), Agile feedback loops, pair programming, and many others can help reduce bugs in the long run. Practices like these are still very important, but they are not sufficient for engineering modern complex systems.

New best practices are needed to give us confidence again in the systems that we build. Best practices are emerging to meet this need, and *chaos engineering* is among them. Chaos engineering is a new discipline pioneered at Netflix specifically designed

---

1 Amazon AWS outage on 2/28/17 (*https://techcrunch.com/2017/02/28/amazon-aws-s3-outage-is-breaking-things-for-a-lot-of-websites-and-apps/*); Google Gdoc outage on 11/15/17 (*https://www.washingtonpost.com/news/the-switch/wp/2017/11/15/google-docs-is-back-after-a-major-outage/*); Facebook outage on 10/11/17 (*https://mashable.com/2017/10/11/facebook-is-down-oct-11/*); Apple iCloud outage on 1/26/18 (*http://www.businessinsider.com/apples-icloud-service-is-having-technical-issues-2018-1*)

2 The second Law of Software Evolution (*https://ieeexplore.ieee.org/document/1456074/*) states that net complexity will increase in a manner similar to entropy, and combined with the Law of Requisite Variety (*http://requisitevariety.co.uk/what-is-requisite-variety/*), we can safely assume that complexity in software will increase as long as more software is written.

to optimize for *availability* in complex, distributed systems. We can have our confidence, and engineer it, too.

I ran the Chaos Team at Netflix for three years, during the period when we formalized chaos engineering, built a community around it, and brought that definition to the industry at large. This chapter introduces the class of problems that threaten availability in complex distributed systems. Then, we review the evolution of chaos engineering to illustrate how it evolved to meet that class of problems. We list five more advanced concepts in chaos engineering and close the chapter with a FAQ curated from audiences of many presentations and workshops on the topic.

The Problem with Systems

You can think of the engineering organization at Netflix as about a hundred small engineering teams, of around five to seven people each. The service—that product that the customers use—is architected as many hundreds of microservices working together. Every microservice is owned by just one team, and that team is responsible for everything: features, roadmap, operations, and uptime for that microservice.

An example of a microservice might be a customer microservice, which for a given customer ID serves up the metadata stored with that person. Another might be a personalization service that stores information about preferences related to a customer so that when a customer looks for something to watch on Netflix, we decorate their experience with context based on what they previously watched, and so on. And, of course, proxies and an API layer and specific datastores could all be microservices.

Imagine that one day a customer is watching *Stranger Things* on a train late at night. Let's call this customer CLR. At a particular point in the show, a frightening scene surprises CLR, causing him to drop his laptop. He retrieves his laptop, and the show is no longer streaming, so he does what any reasonable customer would do and furiously refreshes his browser. It doesn't load instantaneously, so he refreshes again… about 100 times.

Now CLR is on a train and happens to be between cell towers, so he is currently partitioned from the internet. Those requests are actually being queued up in the web browser and the operating system. When internet connectivity returns, all 100 requests go through at once.

What happens on the Netflix side? The requests come in to a proxy, advance to an API layer, and fan out to multiple services like a personalization service, which extracts a user ID and requests that user from the customer service.

The customer service is large, so it spans a cluster of many nodes. It doesn't make sense to store every customer's data on every node, so instead a consistent hash of the ID directs requests for any particular customer to one particular primary node.

Because teams are responsible for the operations of their microservices, they also ensure that the clusters autoscale to responsibly use resources, and hand off data in the case that a node goes down. They also have fallbacks in place to protect from degraded performance or errors; for example, the customer service can serve data from an in-memory cache if it can't get data from disk, and the personalization service can serve a default user experience if it can't get a response from the customer service.

Getting back to CLR's case, 100 requests suddenly arrive simultaneously to the personalization service, which issues a corresponding 100 requests to the customer service. All 100 are consistently hashed and forwarded to one node in the cluster. This node can't fetch the data from disk in time, so it does the sensible thing and returns results from the in-memory cache. These results might be somewhat stale, but that should be acceptable.

The autoscaling rules look at I/O and CPU load and scale up the cluster if the average work climbs too high. Conversely, they scale down the cluster if the average work falls too low. In this case, serving from in-memory cache is much less work than fetching from disk, so the average I/O and CPU load for the customer service drops. The autoscaling rules do the responsible thing and scale down the cluster, terminating the node that was doing the least amount of work, and shifting its data to other members of the cluster.

The personalization service sees that the last request that it sent to the customer service did not complete in time (because that node was being shut down), and so it does the sensible thing and returns a fallback default user experience.

This last request is returned to CLR, the responses from the previous 99 having been thrown out. CLR looks at the default experience and can't understand why it looks so different from the personalized experience that he's used to. It doesn't even have the bookmark to the point in the show before he dropped his laptop. CLR does what any reasonable customer would do: he refreshes the browser another 100 times.

The cycle repeats: the customer service receives 100 requests, flips to serving data from in-memory cache, triggers the autoscaling policy, scales down, and the personalization service again returns a default fallback experience. Now, other customers who are assigned to those two terminated nodes are also seeing the fallback experience, so they too begin refreshing their browsers. We now have a user-induced retry storm. The additional traffic puts more pressure on the customer service, flipping the entire thing into serving from in-memory cache, dramatically reducing the average load, autoscaling the cluster down dramatically, until the remaining nodes can't serve their function with stale data, the personalization service stalls, and the entire service collapses, bringing streaming video screeching to a halt.

The above is entirely hypothetical and did not happen. But something like this *could* happen. So what went wrong?

The important lesson to learn from an example such as this one is that no human made an incorrect decision. The engineers were smart, and they followed reasonable industry best practices. They didn't make a mistake, and yet the holistic behavior of the system produced an undesirable result.

By definition, a complex system is one in which no part can understand the whole. A complex system is unreasonable: you cannot reason about it. This is one of the reasons why Netflix doesn't have a chief architect or similar role: no human (a component in the system) can hold a model of all of the moving parts in their head simultaneously and thus have any predictive power over the behavior of the system.

How, then, do we prevent or minimize the undesirable behaviors of the system? There are two logical options: reduce the complexity so as to make it not a complex system, or find another way to steer the system even without understanding how it works in intricate detail. We call this latter option *navigating complexity*.

I don't know of any practical, generalized theory for making a complex system not complex. Because many of the features we want in a system—feature velocity, performance, availability, and so on—necessarily introduce complexity, it isn't clear to me that it's even possible to make a system *uncomplex* without necessarily also making it worse.

Instead of trying to reduce the complexity, we can then focus on the other avenue: learning to navigate the complexity.

Economic Pillars of Complexity

Kent Beck, the creator of Extreme Programming and proponent of TDD, introduced me to a model (*https://www.facebook.com/notes/kent-beck/taming-complexity-with-reversibility/1000330413333156/*) that I call the Economic Pillars of Complexity (EPC). The model identifies four pillars of complexity that can confound progress when you're making a product or delivering a service. We can think of the product or service as a system. Here are the four pillars:

States
   The number and nature of configurations that the system can be in.

Relationships
   The number and nature of the ways in which parts of the system, including human operators, can interact.

Environment
   Uncertainty introduced by the environment external to the system.

Irreversibility
   The degree to which a change to the system can be easily undone.

All or none of these forms of complexity can exist in your system, but if you find that business goals are being overwhelmed by rampant complexity, it might be possible to cap one of the pillars and focus on the others where it might be more manageable. Ford is the classic example of tackling complexity in this way, limiting the states of the system by offering the Model T in only one color (black) for some years, and limiting relationships through assembly-line manufacturing.

In software systems, we can seldom limit the states. In modern systems like microservice architectures, we also don't have much control over the nature of relationships between microservices. Irreversibility is an interesting pillar to think about, though. If we can make decisions, try things, and roll them back quickly enough, we can respond to the unreasonable nature of a complex system before unwanted systemic effects take hold or cause too much damage.

Microservices help with this by decoupling deployments and allowing small parts to change and roll back asynchronously. Some development practices like XP and Agile also optimize for reversibility, putting regular checkpoints into the development process so that ideas can be tested and rolled back quickly and easily. Immutable architectures, Continuous Delivery, and, arguably, cloud deployment in general all cap this pillar of complexity, allowing us to focus on navigating the other three pillars.

For the majority of software teams, capping one of the pillars isn't an option. The decisions that could possibly constrain states, relationships, environment, or irreversibility have already been made or are thwarted by business goals and objectives. Other methods are required to confront the complexity.

Beginning Chaos

When I arrived at Netflix in early 2015, Chaos Monkey had already been around for almost five years. When Netflix moved from data centers to the cloud in 2010 and 2011, the scaling profile changed from vertical to horizontal. On the cloud, services ran on many more but smaller instances. As a result of the higher number of instances, it became much more likely that in any given hour an instance would catastrophically fail or blink out of existence.

Disappearing instances impact availability if they are Single Points of Failure (SPOFs), or if the sudden change in traffic profile causes a cascading failure. There are many easily accessible best practices that we can implement to prevent this. At Netflix, there is no CTO or, as I mentioned earlier, chief architect to pick best practices and issue an edict that all microservices must conform. The best practice solutions were at hand, but there was no efficient mechanism of delivery.

Instead of dictating best practices, the engineers at Netflix decided to take the pain that they wanted to solve—instances disappearing—and bring it to the forefront. Chaos Monkey is the result. Chaos Monkey pseudo-randomly selects about one instance of each service per day, and rudely turns it off, but only during business hours.

Suddenly many engineers couldn't work on what they had planned in their roadmap. Chaos Monkey had created a problem for them and put it right in front of their queue. Fortunately, engineers are great at solving problems right in front of them. All of those separate, small engineering teams were now all aligned to make their services resilient to instances disappearing.

And it worked: in four years, Netflix has had many, many instances disappear, but only one outage related to a SPOF. The vast majority of microservices are now resilient to that event.

In that one case where we did have an outage, it was Chaos Monkey that terminated the instance. Fortunately, the service had just been deployed and the engineers responsible were still at the office, so context was readily at hand to resolve the outage quickly. Compare that to the situation if we didn't have Chaos Monkey; that instance could become unstable months or years after deployment and none of the context would be at hand to identify and fix the issue in a timely fashion.

Navigating Complexity for Safety

The human factors expert Jens Rasmussen proposed a model that describes how systems evolve over time away from boundaries that are visible to the people doing the work. The three boundaries are Economics, Workload, and Safety. These boundaries are crossed in failure. If something becomes too expensive, for example, it crosses the Economics boundary and then maybe the company goes out of business. If something becomes too much work, the Workload boundary is crossed and nothing else gets done and everyone has a bad time, and so on.

In most software engineering situations, it's not difficult to model the team's budget or get an idea of how expensive the resources are to run an application—the overall cost captured in Economics. Likewise, with Workload, in most cases engineers will have a good intuition about how many people work on developing and maintaining the project that they work on, how many hours they put in, and how difficult it is to make progress—these are all signals. Cost overruns, coworkers complaining about how many hours they put in, expectations around urgency—these are also signals. These signals provide an awareness of the boundary.

One of the roles of management is to reinforce this and provide a strong signal to a team or organization if it drifts too close to one of the boundaries. "Hey, we are running out of money and have only two months left of runway to get this feature built," is a pixel example of a strong signal for the Economics boundary. Most software projects have strong signals for Economics and Workload boundaries.

The same cannot be said about Safety. Software engineers don't know how fragile their system is, right up until the moment that it unexpectedly breaks. In most cases, there is no signal for Safety. As a result, software projects are naturally motivated to make their system less expensive and easier to operate. They drift away from the Economics and Workload boundary, toward the Safety boundary. Over time, a system in this situation drifts to being cheaper and doing more work and, unbeknownst to the operators, less safe.

The beauty of Chaos Monkey is that it creates that signal of Safety. If the boundary for safety is crossed when an instance disappears, you will quickly discover that when it drops an instance during business hours. The repercussions of being vulnerable to an instance disappearing—whatever those repercussions may be—are exposed when that condition is forced. This is a strong signal to the service owners of just how safe they really are. As a result, the microservices at Netflix stay resilient to this type of safety issue, preventing the system from gradually drifting into a less safe arrangement.

Chaos Goes Big

Building on the success of Chaos Monkey, Netflix decided to go big. Instead of just terminating instances, we turn off an entire region. They call this *Chaos Kong*.

In case you are unfamiliar with cloud terminology, a region can be thought of as a major data center. The control plane for Netflix is deployed in three geographically distributed regions. This handles traffic for all of the devices that interact with the streaming service. The Traffic team at Netflix has built orchestration that allows us to detect a severe outage in one region and move all of those customers over to the other two regions. Because control plane traffic alone accounts for more than 3% of the bits on the internet in North America, this is quite a large shift.

Chaos Kong is exercised regularly to verify the orchestration that the Traffic team has built. More important, it verifies that all of the microservices can survive a regional outage. It generates a Safety signal for the microservice owners, to prevent the system from drifting into a less safe configuration.

Formalization

By the end of 2015, Chaos Monkey and Chaos Kong were well-understood fixtures at Netflix. These two programs generated pretty solid Safety signals for small-scale disruptions (instances disappearing) and very-large-scale disruptions (regions disappearing). Not much existed to generate a Safety signal for the systemic effects: all of the interesting interactions between microservices that lead to unforeseeable effects, both good and bad.

What would such a system look like? I was given a small budget (two headcount) to build a Chaos team. I went around the company and asked, "What is chaos engineering?" The most common answer was some form of, "That's when we break things in production." I asked around the industry and got the same reply. The problem with that answer is that it's not a definition. Many things can break in production and provide no value to business. In fact, breaking things in production from within a system is easy to do, but I suspect the Chaos team would get no appreciation within the company if that was their only goal.

I sat down with the nascent Chaos team to formalize the practice. The result is a manifesto of sorts available at PrinciplesofChaos.org (*http://principlesofchaos.org/*). We defined an empirical practice that has clear goals, boundaries, and best practices. This allows us to generate buy-in, plan, and evaluate. We now know whether we are doing chaos engineering or not, how well, and to what end.

Western science is predicated on an empirical process of falsifiability. We build confidence in an explanation for some observed phenomena by proving that alternative explanations are incorrect. Chaos engineering borrows heavily from this. A definition from the manifesto captures the essence: "The facilitation of experiments to uncover systemic weaknesses." The four steps of building an experiment are as follows:

1. Start by defining "steady state" as some measurable output of a system that indicates normal behavior.
2. Hypothesize that this steady state will continue in both the control group and the experimental group.
3. Introduce variables that reflect real-world events like servers that crash, hard drives that malfunction, network connections that are severed, and so on.
4. Try to disprove the hypothesis by looking for a difference in steady state between the control group and the experimental group.[3]

This template for building experiments can be applied to any instantiation of chaos engineering in practice. For Chaos Monkey and Chaos Kong, Netflix looks at the number of videos streaming as the steady state given that this number is fairly well defined and well understood. Deviations in that number between a control group and an experimental group are easy to spot.

Exploring the solution space of things that could disrupt the system's steady state will never be exhaustive. There are an infinite number of things that could go wrong.

---

3 Quote from principlesofchaos.org.

Because certainty isn't possible, we settle for confidence. A successful program of experimentation increases confidence. The more experiments that run without disproving our hypothesis, the more confidence we have in our system's stability.

There are many technical considerations to address when you are implementing a chaos engineering program, but most of those are going to be specific to the system of interest. The template of experimentation should be universal.

Advanced Principles

We can use the template of experimentation to know whether we are performing chaos engineering. We also defined some advanced principles to know whether we are doing it well. Here are those advanced principles:

Build a hypothesis around steady-state behavior
As engineers, we often have a proclivity to dig into a problem. We want to figure out how something works. But chaos engineering isn't about how something works. That's model *validation*. We want model *verification*. We already know that a complex system can't fit inside any individual's head. So instead of figuring out *how* something works, we want to keep the focus on *whether* it works. Focusing on steady-state behavior helps keep us closer to "whether," which helps us get the most value out of chaos engineering.

Vary real-world events
The variables in the experiments should reflect the plausible range of conditions as accurately as can be conceived. There is an art to this, because it does rely on some historical knowledge and hence expertise. This principle provides the opportunity to reflect on the risks to stability and prioritize accordingly.

Run experiments in production
Keep in mind that the point of chaos engineering is to generate new knowledge. If you know (or suspect) that running an experiment will disprove the hypothesis, don't run it. Fix the problem first. Make your system resilient to the variable you want to verify. After you think you have a sound hypothesis, run the experiment to build confidence. Staged environments can never be identical to production environments. Run experiments in production for the best, most accurate results.

Automate experiments to run continuously
Complex systems are dynamic. The confidence that you should have in a system decays with the time since the last experiment was run. To create the safety signal that you desire, you need to run experiments continuously, not just on occasion or during game-day events.

Minimize blast radius

> As the sophistication of chaos engineering tools increases, it opens the possibility of making experiments more precise. Precision becomes a cyclical positive reinforcement for more experiments, covering more of the search space. Especially when you're running experiments in a production environment, that doesn't mean you necessarily have to expose all of production to the same variable. Scoping segments of production traffic to specific variables allows you to run more experiments concurrently and makes the discovery of a hazard safer.

Frequently Asked Questions

Outside of technical considerations, there are often many techno-social questions around chaos engineering. Here are the most common questions I have received in Q&A sessions and online forums, with general answers.

Q: How do I get buy-in from management to implement a chaos program?

A: The best way to get management to buy in to the value of chaos engineering is, as Churchill said, "Never let a good crisis go to waste." The safety signal is missing in most software organizations. In a complex system, you can't know how close you are to a failure until just after you experience it. This can cause buy-in issues because the ROI of an investment in chaos engineering isn't obvious until after the system drifts so far into an unsafe condition that it crosses the line into a failure. This was the case even at Netflix. Take advantage of the insight gained from an incident and use that to make a case for chaos engineering, which can prevent future failures by revealing the safety signal early.

Q: How do I get Chaos Engineering started at my organization?

A: This is highly dependent on the technical maturity of the system and the organizational support that chaos engineering has. Nora Jones (*https://www.linkedin.com/in/ norajones1/*) has spoken at length (*https://www.infoq.com/podcasts/nora-jones-chaos- engineering*) on some of the options available to people seeking to introduce chaos engineering into their organization.

Q: Does chaos engineering apply in my industry?

A: Early on, we would hear comments from the fintech industry along the lines of, "Sure, chaos engineering is fine at Netflix, but I have actually money on the line. We can't experiment in production in fintech." This statement hides a supposition that the likelihood and scope of a failure in the future is known. If the software in question is a complex system, that supposition cannot be true. To put it another way: Would you rather discover chaos in your system in a controlled manner or do you instead want to wait until a failure surprises you? Chaos engineering is now a common practice at many fintech companies as well as large banks and financial asset institution. More recently, we would hear comments from the medical industry along the lines of, "Sure, chaos engineering is fine at Netflix or banks, but I have actual lives on the line. We can't experiment in production in medicine." The clinical trial is often held up as the pinnacle of Western science. We remind people working in medicine that clinical trials are basically chaos experiments running in production—with human lives on the line. The type of experimentation that inspires chaos engineering was in fact pioneered in medicine. That doesn't suggest that we can be careless when lives are on the line; rather, it should stand as a testament to the approach.

Q: Do I really have to run experiments in production?

A: If you aren't, you are building confidence in a system that isn't yours. The boundary that we draw around a system is arbitrary. If you experiment in a staged environment rather than a production environment, you might still learn useful things; however, by definition you can't know all of the components that go into a complex system that could lead to undesirable behavior. This means that the boundary you draw around the staged environment cannot be an exact replica of production, no matter how much time you spend certifying the similarities. There is always the possibility that the production environment will exhibit a behavior not seen in the staged environment. Running experiments in production is more accurate, and accuracy is crucial when you're building confidence.

Conclusion

Reliability is created by people: the engineers who write the functionality, those who operate and maintain the system, and even the management that allocates resources toward it. SREs have a special role in creating that reliability, bringing to bear best practices and focused attention to this property of the system. Tools can help. Chaos engineering is another tool that SREs and dedicated chaos engineering practitioners can use to create reliability.

Chaos engineering is not about creating chaos; rather, it is about exposing chaos inherent in the system. With a thoughtful discipline structured in basic principles of Western empiricism, chaos engineering can teach us about the complex systems that we build and manage. This discipline becomes increasingly relevant as more of software engineering moves into the realm of complex systems. As practitioners in this industry, our success relies not on removing the complexity from our systems, but on learning to live with it, navigate it, and optimize for other business-critical properties despite the underlying complexity.

Casey Rosenthal is the CTO of Backplane.io, providing availability and security in the form of a cloud-hosted traffic management service. Prior to Backplane.io, he managed both the Chaos Engineering team and the Traffic Engineering team simultaneously at Netflix. Casey Rosenthal co-wrote the book on chaos engineering (http:// www.oreilly.com/webops-perf/free/chaos-engineering.csp).

## CHAPTER 15

The Intersection of Reliability and Privacy

Betsy Beyer and Amber Yust, Google

 Privacy engineering is a young field in which industry players remain cautious with their public discussion. We hope that the relatively abstract concepts and approaches discussed in this chapter will spark ideas of more concrete privacy opportunities within your own organization and build an environment in which conversations around privacy innovation can thrive.

With the recent publication of Google's SRE book (*https://landing.google.com/sre/book.html*) as well as a fair number of other publications and conferences about SRE, DevOps, and related movements, there's a fairly active conversation about reliability engineering across the industry. As an inherently more sensitive topic, privacy engineering is less openly discussed, and, as a result, less well understood. Although many companies and organizations are beginning to think about many of the correct and important aspects of privacy and to consider privacy as an engineering discipline, this field is much less robust than SRE. Yet at the same time, privacy is a critically important concern for virtually every company or organization that handles private data, given that mishandling private data typically can't be undone.

After scanning the contents of this volume, you might be asking yourself, "Why does a book about SRE dedicate an entire chapter to privacy?" Sure, any organization that actually cares about its users should invest energy in both reliability and privacy. But beyond that, why is privacy so relevant to SRE?

As anyone working on reliability knows, SRE doesn't exist in a vacuum. There are many concerns that arise when performing SRE work (e.g., reliability, cost, efficiency, scalability, and security); privacy is one of these related concerns, and arguably one of the most important. Although privacy engineering, security engineering, and SRE are related disciplines, privacy engineering is a distinct field/position because it requires distinct cultural knowledge. Privacy engineers bridge social and technical work by maintaining all of the real-world context and perspective to understand what data is sensitive to whom and under what conditions. This chapter will help you build a robust privacy engineering posture in your organization based on SRE-style principles, regardless of your background.

The Intersection of Reliability and Privacy

Why, as someone in the field of reliability engineering, do you also need to think about privacy engineering, and why are you well positioned to do so?

The starting point for both reliability and privacy is the same: to deeply understand your systems before you can begin to reason about what reliability and privacy should look like in a specific environment. From the opposite end, privacy and reliability resemble each other because they share an end goal: *satisfying user expectations*. Both disciplines examine their problem space through the lens of what users expect. Users expect a company or organization's products to work, and to work most of the time; they also expect you to respect their privacy—including data—appropriately. Both reliability engineering and privacy engineering boil down to the ultimate goal of *ensuring user trust*. Both ask, "Is the system working in a way that makes sense to the user, or will the user be surprised because the system doesn't behave as expected?" One way to look at user expectations is to consider surprise a failure mode of a system: if a user can't trust a system with their data, that system might as well be down.

Reliability also intersects the privacy realm on a structural level: privacy is protected by actual technical and administrative operations. These systems need to work reliably to fulfill their mission of protecting user privacy. In terms of the software development life cycle, both privacy and reliability concerns are also analogous. Operations teams long ago realized that the earlier they are involved in the pipeline, the better the end result. The same principle holds true for privacy engineering.

As experts in reliability, SREs are already concerned with meeting user expectations when it comes to providing a reliable system or project. But when it comes to the people using your product, some of their strongest expectations (whether they realize it or not) involve privacy. Privacy issues have come to the forefront in current events and have risen in public awareness in recent years. More than ever, users expect more from service providers when it comes to privacy. Because privacy is so fundamentally tied up with user expectations and trust, there's a high demand for providers to do what they say with user data. The people tasked with safeguarding user expectations —whether that be an engineer, technical project manager, or program manager explicitly working on privacy engineering, or a counterpart in SRE who's positioned to do so—will be the guardians of this realm. These teams are responsible for meeting users' implicit and explicit expectations, fundamentally creating a reliable user experience (UX).

The good news is that there are people already doing work in the area of privacy engineering, and (as discussed in the section "Privacy and SRE: Common Approaches" later in this chapter) what they've learned can help you, as an SRE, to begin thinking about and approaching privacy in a productive way. Even better: if you're just beginning to think about how to (better) engineer privacy into your system or service, you don't need to start from scratch. SREs are already well equipped to create privacy value because SRE techniques are useful in the privacy space.

The General Landscape of Privacy Engineering

A privacy engineer's goal is to go above and beyond compliance to try to make good products. Privacy engineering is not solely about checking boxes to achieve legal compliance. Rather, it is about developing creative solutions to achieve products that people trust, often according to extremely challenging technical, administrative, and legal requirements.

There is no single checklist that answers, "Is this privacy, or not?" As a complex discipline, privacy engineering is characterized by a certain amount of subjectivity: different people (users from all different walks of life, product visionaries, governments) might have quite different desires about privacy-related matters. This is one of the reasons we tend to think about "user respect"—although user respect isn't an explicit mental model, it gets people asking the right questions: "Having seen and read the product's notices and policies, would I, as a user, feel that this product works correctly? What about another user who's not like me?" In its ideal form, privacy engineering should pursue intentional diversity, incorporating a range of life experiences, demographics, and personal philosophies. To create really good products, you must incorporate as many perspectives as possible and make sure you don't miss something that would be obvious from a different frame of reference (see the comments by Amber Yust in the Buzzfeed article, "You've Never Heard of this Team at Google—But They're Thinking of You" (*https://www.buzzfeed.com/sheerafrenkel/google-has-a-secret-team-making-sure-its-products-are-safe*)).

Google engineer Lea Kissner argues in her G+ post "Privacy, Security, and Paranoia" (*https://plus.google.com/+LeaKissner/posts/R83iUadqMUj*) that privacy engineers "stand between our users and the dark places of the internet." Privacy work tends to fall into three main categories (we'll leave security engineering out of scope for this chapter—this is a substantial topic that deserves its own thorough treatment):

Guard
    Find and solve potential privacy problems for products. Much of this work involves cultural mindset-related steps in addition to consulting and teaching good privacy practices to other teams, from product teams to business analysts to support teams.

Strengthen

Make it easy for all teams developing products to "do the right thing." These are the technological infrastructure steps that follow the cultural mindset-related steps that we looked at earlier. To this end, privacy engineers design and build infrastructure, work with teams to improve existing systems, build privacy-related product features, and develop and provide shared libraries for easy implementation of privacy concepts.

Extinguish

When a fire does arise, privacy engineers put it out. They learn from these events by finding ways to generalize solutions or avoid problems in the future—not just for one team, but for many. Note that postmortem culture is just as useful for privacy as for SRE, although it's often subject to wariness from legal departments due to the sometimes-sensitive nature of the fires.

Privacy engineers tend to think about the products and services they protect in a very specific way. When you ask a privacy engineer to evaluate a product or service, that engineer will be thinking about the following questions:

- What data is involved?
- Where is the data stored?
- How is the data used?
- What are the potential implications of having this data available?
- What are the user's expectations?
- Who has access to the data, and how?

Note that this list is somewhat aspirational—these are nuanced questions that you might not be able to answer straightaway. At the same time, this list is incomplete: a good privacy engineer considers the nuances of how a product works and its real-world implications, not just the raw flow of data.

Privacy engineers drill into aspects of a system or user behavior that aren't obvious to the untrained eye. Even though they necessarily must keep state around complexity, there's also a skill set around practicing empathy and how to factor that practice into engineering work. For example, when debugging or remediating a bug or incident, a privacy engineer thinks not only about user impact, but also about the specific intentions of users—their human motivations, desires, and goals. Furthermore, they don't just think about "typical" users, but consider the many different user audiences and their diverse assumptions and expectations around product behavior and privacy.

For example: for cases in which a system bug has resulted in unintended behavior, a fix generally consists of two parts: ensuring the specific cause/bug is fixed ("stopping the bleeding"), and then attempting to restore affected users to the intended/happy state ("cleaning up the mess"). Privacy engineers are especially useful for that second step because what the "intended state" is for a particular user is often a complex question to answer (consider: does a user mashing a button *really* want to perform the action repeatedly?). Having a clear record of explicit user interactions makes it easier to work backward to what results the user expected versus what they got. This can make a huge difference in how long it takes to restore expected system behavior. With this information, an engineer can analyze and replay inputs to return to a known-good state, even if the outputs were corrupted. This ability can be particularly crucial when the state the bug affected is privacy-critical, such as privacy preference data or access control lists (ACLs). Privacy engineers try to envision these scenarios ahead of time and ensure that this safety net infrastructure is built in from the ground up.

Privacy and SRE: Common Approaches

Given that reliability engineering and privacy engineering share the goal of ensuring user trust—a goal that requires big-picture thinking about worst-case scenarios—it's no surprise that both tend to attract people with similar mindsets and outlooks. In both disciplines, the ability to "see broken things" is a key aspect of a good engineer. Although they have different foci (availability versus respect), both good privacy engineers and reliability engineers look at a system and see how it breaks, not how it succeeds. Many of the lessons SREs have learned over time also apply to privacy engineering.

Reducing Toil

One key element that elevates SRE from straightforward operational work to a proper engineering discipline is its focus on reducing human time spent on toil. The same goal can be applied to privacy engineering: frameworks and careful selection of defaults are two opportunities to reduce human toil.

Automation

You might not think that automation—a tried-and-true core concept of SRE—applies to privacy engineering in an immediate and obvious way. Privacy-related matters are judgment calls and human decisions, which means that they can't just be automated away, right? Actually, automation can be helpful in privacy engineering.

Automation often entails writing a script, program, or service that programmatically eliminates some aspect of human toil. To apply this model to privacy, you might write a script or simple program that checks to make sure auditing settings match up rather than requiring a human to perform manual verification. A simple example: checking that only a specifically designated set of storage buckets are world-readable, and all others are not. A more complex example: enforcing mutual exclusion between access to two datasets, if policy has determined they should never be cross-joined.

Default behavior for shared architectures

Automation makes things simpler for humans, reducing the amount of effort required by humans and freeing up human time for other tasks. We can effectively "automate" many privacy improvements by building systems that "do the right thing" by default. In other words, "Make correct easy." Specifically, we can implement system defaults that handle a great deal of decision making, drastically reducing how often engineers building a product need to consciously make a decision for which an improper choice could lead to an undesirable privacy outcome.

Instead of requiring the developers building your products to repeatedly face the same questions, and make the same decisions, sound privacy engineering should have them enumerate and contemplate these decision points in advance. If, for a given situation, there's a correct or safe choice that applies to 80% of situations, make that choice your system default. Doing so relieves many people of that decision-making burden 80% of the time. For example, a shared library, a schema, or a data access layer might be good places to consider implementing defaults. As a result, you'll no longer need to spend human time dealing with decisions that could have been made in advance. Instead, you can then spend your human time on decisions that are *actually* difficult. By focusing your time, you can dig deeper into the hard problems to find better (and more repeatable) solutions.

Note that one of the creative challenges privacy engineers face is when the common choice and the safest choice are not the same. It might not always be possible to adopt the safest choice as the default, which means downstream developers will want to carefully ensure that their usage matches their intent. Make sure these cases are well documented so that other developers know they exist.

Frameworks

Reliability and privacy concerns span multiple products and services. As they encounter new systems, engineers tasked with reliability and/or privacy must either find ways to understand a large variety of systems, or ways to standardize systems so that they don't need to reunderstand them from scratch each time. Frameworks bake in reliability and privacy best practices in an efficient and scalable way. Factoring both aspects into system design also means that you don't need to invest the energy and resources to retrofit a product to meet reliability and privacy standards.

So how might you practically apply the concept of frameworks to privacy in your organization? The following examples can get you started thinking about potential approaches:

- How you handle access control should be one of the most important properties of your system. Establishing a framework for handling ACLs will ensure that all (new) systems can easily and consistently apply your recommended best practices.

- Deletion of user data is another canonical concern of privacy engineering. Having a consistent, organized system to propagate deletions throughout your system (including caches, syndication to third-party sites, etc.) helps ensure that you don't leave data orphaned.

The industry still has some work to do when it comes to frameworks. To provide just one specific example, it seems that few startups currently use Role-Based Access Control (RBAC), which is a basic and widely accepted tenet of good privacy engineering.[1] Surveying the industry for any kind of standard frameworks (for example, baking in the principle of least privilege (*https://en.wikipedia.org/wiki/principle_of_least_privilege*) for free when turning up new products or services) also turns up few results.

Efficient and Deliberate Problem Solving

As it has evolved, SRE has worked out many of the kinks that lead to inefficient, disjointed troubleshooting and problem solving. Privacy engineering can embrace these aspects of SRE culture without having to experience the same (sometimes painful) journey. Here are just a couple of examples of how SRE best practices in this area can also directly apply to privacy engineering.

Solve challenges once

When you solve a problem, prevent other people from needing to reinvent the wheel by publicizing your solution. Widely communicate what you did to investigate and solve the problem, the decisions you made, why you made these decisions, the results of your decisions, and when and why others should also adopt this solution. Be sure to document the scope of what you've solved in terms of constraints and context. For example, when you address a privacy concern for the United States, that solution might not apply when you expand to the EU.

For example, in the privacy space, you might do the following:

- Build a system to create the necessary audit trails for user consent screens and then reuse it.

---

1 Also referred to as *scoped access*: narrowing the scope of access granted (both to humans and to production roles) not only helps protect privacy, it also reduces the potential impact of a security breach or production accident. This concept is sometimes alluded to in the general sysadmin advice of "don't run everything as root," but here is taken further and structured.

- Build a differentially private experiment system and then reuse it.[2]
- Perform UX studies to determine a clear and concise way of describing the privacy implications of a feature. Then, push to have that language used across all products with that type of feature. (Note that accessibility features intersect in interesting ways here.)[3]

Find and address root causes

Merely fixing symptoms means that the same issue is likely to recur in the future. Step back, take a look at the bigger picture, and invest in the extra levels of investigation to determine the actual cause of the problem and fix it at its source. As discussed in relation to postmortems,[4] an investigation that assigns blame to people is counterproductive. Instead, fix the technical or process factor underlying the issue.

In the privacy space, you might apply this principle in the following ways:

- If a bug results in a data leak, don't just fix the bug. Sometimes you might end up revising your documentation, safeguards, or tests; sometimes you might determine that something in a library or framework makes it difficult to do the right thing and therefore needs to be revised.
- If you find the ACL on a storage directory to be overly broad, don't just fix that particular ACL. Find the tool that sets up the directories and change its default ACLs to be narrower.
- Create memorable ways to emphasize privacy concerns to other job functions early on in the design phase of a project. For example, you might have designs for sharing flows that consistently enumerate which user interface elements indicate each of "who-what-where" (who is sharing, what are they sharing, where are they sharing it). Eventually "who-what-where" will become a mantra.

Relationship Management

Although concepts like automation and root causing might be obvious wins in the reliability and privacy environments, (as previously mentioned) neither privacy engineering nor SRE exist in a vacuum—both organizations work in a larger engineering

---

2 For an example of a system that's similar in spirit, see the code for Rappor (*https://github.com/google/rappor*), a privacy reporting system.

3 Good examples of this standardization include app permission prompts on Android and iOS.

4 See the SRE Book, Chapter 15: Postmortem Culture: Learning from Failure (*https://landing.google.com/sre/book/chapters/postmortem-culture.html*) and Postmortem Action Items: Plan the Work and Work the Plan (*https://ai.google/research/pubs/pub45906*).

and product ecosystem with multiple other players, each with its own priorities and goals. Note that privacy engineering is cross-functional in ways that differ from reliability engineering in that a lot of privacy work is driven not by engineering mandates, but by legal, policy, and compliance needs and business risks. Here, we focus on product team relationships and the ways in which privacy can leverage SRE wisdom.

A key aspect of relationship management when it comes to privacy is making sure that you focus on what has the biggest pragmatic impact for the user, not features that are flashy or high profile. Privacy is unique in its potential impact and the high stakes involved. Unlike deciding on the perfect color schema or menu bar for a product, or even making sure that a service doesn't violate an agreed-upon Service-Level Agreements (SLA), most privacy-related pitfalls tend to be one-way ratchets: mishandling private data typically can't be undone.

Because of the high stakes, it's important to foster strong collaborative relationships by providing your partners with actionable and constructive feedback. When giving guidance to product teams, avoid merely pointing out why their products or processes are flawed. Instead, focus on building a shared vision. Express feedback about how to meet your goals in the context of their goals and your larger shared goals. For example, align the privacy-centric goal of transparency and control with the product team's goal of building trust in its product by describing how doing the right thing will delight users. Your feedback loop is a two-way street, as is your relationship: people on both sides of the equation can save each other time and energy by making their value propositions clear, explicitly acknowledging the other people's goals, and working together toward a shared goal.

Early Intervention and Education Through Evangelism

After your colleagues are aware that they need to factor reliability and privacy into product decisions, figure out where your talents are best applied and how to scale your expertise effectively by educating others. Spread knowledge about your goals— not just *what* your goals are, but *why* you have these particular goals. Instead of simply telling developers, "Your product needs to do x," tell them *why* their product needs to do x ("If your product doesn't do x, the fallout is y and z"). Even better, also point them to other products that do x, with proven benefits a and b.

In the reliability space, this conversation might look something like the following:

> **Not so great:** "We need you to move your service onto this RPC framework."

> **Better:** "We need you to move your service onto this RPC framework because it will allow us to better monitor requests. That way, we can understand where slowdowns are, and then work to improve product performance."

In the privacy space, this conversation might look something like the following:

Not so great: "We need your product to integrate with the new privacy settings account dashboard."

Better: "We need your product to integrate with the new privacy settings account dashboard. Products x, y, and z are already using this new dashboard, so integrating will help users find controls where they expect to find them. Our end goal here is to minimize user frustration by providing a consistent experience across products."

When it comes to both reliability- and privacy-related matters, when people understand why you're supplying them with a specific piece of guidance, both that immediate project *and* future projects will benefit. If teams understand your areas of concern up front, next time they can proactively approach your team early in the project life cycle rather than shortly before they're hoping to push to production. Again, the key to good communication here is to focus on your shared mission and assume good intent, rather than assigning blame.

Early engagement is always best, and beyond providing frameworks to engage products from the design phase (see "Frameworks" on page 250), proactive education is your best (and sometimes only) hope of getting your partners to talk about privacy and reliability at an appropriate time. Otherwise, people don't even realize that they should engage with privacy engineering until they're forced to talk to you, which tends to happen last when developing a new product or feature (if it happens at all). Failing to engage with a product from its early stages means that the product will veer into directions you don't want it to go. Having a broad network of people who understand what you care about and why also helps your partners detect outages and other potential issues earlier.

Proactively educating others about privacy also allows you to distribute load. The goal isn't to avoid work your team should rightfully be handling, but to engage in knowledge sharing that enables you to spend your time on the hard problems that only you can solve. For issues that are clear-cut, after your partners understand what you care about and how to avoid obvious and predictable problems, they won't need to come to you for these straightforward cases. The product team both saves time and avoids having to potentially redo work in light of privacy matters that they could have considered from square one.

For example, access control is a topic that every product team needs to approach strategically. Instead of starting this discussion from the basics with each and every product team, educate your developers on the benefits of having well-structured access control groups. From a reliability standpoint, this means engineers are less likely to cause an outage when making changes (for example, because some critical workflow is gated by an access path). From a privacy standpoint, it's important to have good visibility into who has access to your systems so that you can prevent unauthorized access to user data. In a similar vein, you should also make sure that developers design their products to clearly track who's talking to your service. If you can't differentiate between the clients accessing your service, you won't know who to work with to resolve a problem.

You can make better decisions about the actually important and hard questions facing your team when you don't need to waste time answering basic questions or providing standard design advice repeatedly. Your partners also benefit because they have a quicker turnaround time on their questions.

Nuances, Differences, and Trade-Offs

Despite their similarities, reliability engineering and privacy engineering have some fundamental differences.

Although neither reliability nor privacy is strictly black and white, when it comes to user expectations around reliability, you have more latitude in defining an acceptable threshold that constitutes a "reliability outage." Privacy "outages" are subject to many external factors, such as how users react to particular events and even legal and regulatory requirements. Even though users might be perfectly happy if a service is available for 99% of a year, they might not be so happy if you guarantee to handle only 99% of their data in the right way. Reliability issues are inherently also more "fixable": if your service is down, you can fix the problem by getting that service back up and running, but there's no way to "fix" a compromised database: you can't unring a bell.

Some design decisions might end up trading one of these aspects for the sake of the other; however, creating technical reliability at the cost of user surprise isn't necessarily productive. This equation is far more likely to be weighted in favor of privacy. Sometimes, it makes sense to ship a product that's not "perfectly reliable" for the sake of shipping something usable—mandating that a launch or service is 100% risk-free means that you'd never ship anything. But because of the consequences of an "outage," privacy doesn't have the same degree of flexibility. A service that goes down can be restored without lasting ill effects (customers understand an occasional outage), but a privacy incident can have permanent effects. These long-term effects should factor into operational decisions. At the end of the day, you're creating a product that actual people use, not a hypothetical technical service with abstract "users."

Conclusion

Reliability engineering and privacy engineering are fundamentally similar in many ways: both disciplines work from the same foundation and toward the same ultimate goal. Both can leverage many of the same best practices and approaches. Both are sufficiently important to users, and hard enough to get right, that they should be treated as proper engineering disciplines, not as afterthoughts. And both should be ingrained in your company or organization's culture. Although their states of maturity may differ, SRE and privacy engineering are living, breathing, and quickly evolving fields—as their core tenants gain wider adoption across the industry, they both must evolve alongside user expectations.

Google teams frequently make use of the techniques described in this chapter to build world-class products that respect user privacy. SREs are in an ideal position to advocate for user privacy, even if they don't explicitly work in the privacy space (and particularly if your organization can't dedicate specific resources to privacy engineering). Working from the base of effective problem-solving skills, privacy engineers combine those skills with empathy and societal context to tackle a different realm of user-centric challenges. As any well-seasoned SRE knows, metrics are just a means to an end; the user's experience is what really matters.

Further Reading

- OECD Guidelines on the Protection of Privacy and Transborder Flows of Personal Data (*http://www.oecd.org/sti/ieconomy/oecdguidelinesontheprotectionofpri vacyandtransborderflowsofpersonaldata.htm*)
- Google's Privacy Policy (*https://policies.google.com/privacy*) and Privacy Technology and Principles (*https://policies.google.com/technologies*)

Betsy Beyer is a technical writer for Google in New York City specializing in site reliability engineering. In addition to editing Site Reliability Engineering (O'Reilly, 2016), she has previously written documentation for Google's Data Center and Hardware Operations teams in Mountain View and across its globally distributed data centers. Before moving to New York, Betsy was a lecturer on technical writing at Stanford University.

Amber Yust worked in Google SRE before joining Google's privacy effort in 2014. As a staff privacy engineer, she now leads a team working to engineer reliable privacy into Google's products at a fundamental level.

## CHAPTER 16

Database Reliability Engineering

Laine Campbell, Fastly

 This is an edited excerpt from *Database Reliability Engineering* by Laine Campbell and Charity Majors (O'Reilly, 2017).

In this chapter, I talk about the craft of database reliability engineering as a subset of SRE. The database tier is the tier with the least tolerance for risk and is thus one of the greatest opportunities for growth through a culture of reliability engineering. Traditionally, DBAs were in the business of crafting silos and snowflakes. Their tools were different, their hardware was different, their languages were different. DBAs were writing SQL, systems engineers were writing Perl, software engineers were writing C++, web developers were writing PHP, and network engineers were crafting their own perfect appliances. Only half of the teams were using version control in any kind of way, and they certainly didn't talk or step on one another's turf. How could they? It was like entering a foreign land.

The days for which this model can prove itself to be effective and sustainable are numbered. This chapter is a view of reliability engineering as seen through a pair of database engineering glasses. I do not plan on covering everything possible here. Instead, I am describing what I do see as important, through the lens of the SRE experience. You can then apply this framework to multiple datastores, architectures, and organizations.

Guiding Principles of the Database Reliability Engineer

I have spent a considerable amount of time considering how the paradigm of reliability engineering fits in the world of database engineering. One of the first questions I asked myself was what were the principles underlying this new iteration of the database profession? If the way people approached datastore design and management was changing, a definition for the foundations of this new world was required. Thus, here are the guiding principles of the database reliability engineer (DBRE).

Protect the Data

Traditionally, this always has been a foundational principle of the database professional, and still is. The generally accepted approach has been attempted via the following:

- A strict separation of duties between the software and the database engineer
- Rigorous backup and recovery processes, regularly tested
- Well-regulated security procedures, regularly audited
- Expensive database software with strong durability guarantees
- Underlying expensive storage with redundancy of all components
- Extensive controls on changes and administrative tasks

For teams with collaborative cultures, the strict separation of duties can become not only burdensome, but restrictive of innovation and velocity. There are ways to create safety nets and reduce the need for separation of duties without impacting reliability.

The new approach to data protection might look more like this:

- Responsibility of the data shared by cross-functional teams
- Standardized and automated backup and recovery processes blessed by DBRE
- Standardized security policies and procedures blessed by DBRE and security teams
- All policies enforced via automated provisioning and deployment
- Data requirements dictate the datastore, with evaluation of durability needs becoming part of the decision-making process
- Reliance on automated processes, redundancy, and well-practiced procedures rather than expensive, complicated hardware
- Changes incorporated into deployment and infrastructure automation, with focus on testing, fallback, and impact mitigation

Self-Service for Scale

A talented DBRE is a rare commodity. Most companies cannot justify or retain more than one or two of these specialists. So, we must create the most value possible, which comes from creating self-service platforms for teams to use. By setting standards and providing tools, teams are able to deploy new services and make appropriate changes at the required pace without serializing on an overworked database engineer.

Following are some examples of these kinds of self-service methods:

- Ensuring the appropriate metrics are being collected from data stores by providing the correct plug-ins
- Building backup and recovery utilities that can be deployed for new data stores
- Defining reference architectures and configurations for data stores that are approved for operations and can be deployed by teams
- Working with Security to define standards for data store deployments
- Building safe deployment methods and test scripts for database migrations to be applied

In other words, the effective DBRE functions by empowering others and guiding them, not functioning as a gatekeeper.

Databases Are Not Special

Databases are often critical components of an organization's infrastructure. They tend to generate the most risk in terms of needs for them to be available and complexity of recovering from failure and corruption. We must strive for standardization, automation, and resilience. Critical to this is the idea that the components of database clusters are not sacred. We should be able to lose any component, and efficiently replace it without worry. Fragile data stores in glass rooms should, and can, be a thing of the past.

The metaphor of pets versus cattle is often used to show the difference between a special snowflake and a commodity service component.[1] A pet server is one that you feed, care for, and nurture back to health when it is sick. It has a name—at Travelocity in 2000, our servers were Simpsons characters. Our two SGI servers running Oracle were named Patty and Selma. I spent so many hours with those gals on late nights. They were high maintenance!

Cattle servers have numbers, not names. You don't spend time customizing servers, much less logging on to individual hosts. When they show signs of sickness, you cull them from the herd. You should, of course, keep those culled cattle around for forensics if you are seeing unusual amounts of sickness. But I'll refrain from mangling this metaphor any further.

---

1 Original attribution for this goes to Bill Baker, Microsoft Distinguished Engineer.

Data stores are some of the last holdouts of "pethood." After all, they hold "The Data" and simply cannot be treated as replaceable cattle with short lifespans and complete standardizations. What about the special replication rules for our reporting replica? What about the different configuration for the primary's redundant standby?

Why Guiding Principles?

Every day in our jobs, we find ourselves faced with an incredible number of decisions. Guiding principles reduce the cognitive overhead of these decisions, helping us to be consistent in our choices. Over time, each of these incremental decisions adds up to hopefully contribute to a coherent culture.

A Culture of Database Reliability Engineering

The reason I feel there a real need for an emphasis on reliability in not just the job title of the DBRE, but in everything they do, is because the database is one of those places where risk and chaos simply has no place. A lot of what is now commonplace in our day-to-day work came about from innovation in areas of computing where risk could be tolerated. Now that these paradigms are ubiquitous, it is up to the stewards of one of the organization's most precious resources, the data, to find paths to bring databases into the fold.

Much of the work to make persistent data stores a first-class citizen of the world of reliability engineering is still in its early phases. There is only so much risk that an organization can tolerate when data comes into play. Thus, how we introduce these concepts to the rest of the organization or how we respond to others doing so becomes an actual discipline and job function for us. It is not enough to have the vision and the intent; we must simultaneously find ways to introduce this vision in such a way as to be successful.

What does a culture of database reliability look like and how can you promote it? There are many items that people think of when they think of reliability culture that are not specific to the database world, including the following:

- Blameless postmortems
- Automating away repetitive work
- Structured and rational decision making

This all makes sense, and everyone within an operations or SRE organization should constantly be working toward this. In this chapter, I look at two specific database engineering functions that an SRE can focus on to ensure that their database infrastructure and the supporting organization gains the benefits of reliability culture. These functions are data integrity and durability, and Continuous Delivery (CD).

While these functions are only part of the work that must be accomplished by the DBRE in the world of SRE, they encompass an excellent cross-section of the approach to operations and engineering expected.

Recoverability

Let's face it. Everyone considers backup and recovery to be dull and tedious. They think of it as the epitome of toil. It is often relegated to junior engineers, outside contractors, and third-party tooling with which the team is loath to interact. I've worked with some pretty horrible backup software before. Trust me, I empathize.

Still, this is one of the most crucial processes in your operations toolkit. Moving your precious data between nodes, across data centers, and into long-term archives is the constant movement of your business's most precious commodity: its data. Rather than relegating this to a second-class citizen of ops, we strongly suggest you treat it as a VIP. Everyone should not only understand the recovery targets, but be intimately familiar with operating and monitoring the processes. Many DevOps philosophies propose that everyone should have an opportunity to write and push code to production. We propose that every engineer should participate at least once in the recovery processes of critical data.

We create and store copies of data, otherwise known as backups and archives, as a means to accomplish the real need: recovery. Sometimes, this recovery is something nice and leisurely, such as building an environment for auditors or building an alternate environment. More often, though, the recovery is the need to rapidly replace failed nodes or to add capacity to existing clusters.

Today, in distributed environments, we face new challenges in the backup and recovery realm. Now, as before, most local datasets are distributed to reasonable sizes, of up to a few terabytes at most. The difference is that those local datasets are only one fraction of a larger distributed dataset. Recovering a node is a relatively manageable task, but keeping state across the cluster becomes more challenging.

Considerations for Recovery

When first evaluating an effective strategy, you should look back to your Service-Level Objectives (SLOs). Specifically, you need to consider availability and durability indicators. Any strategy that you choose will require you to be able to recover data within the uptime constraints you have set. And you need to get data backed up fast enough to ensure that you meet the necessary parameters for durability. If you back up every day, and your transaction logs between backups remain on node-level storage, you might very well lose those transactions before the next backup.

Additionally, you need to consider how the dataset functions within the holistic ecosystem. For instance, your orders might be stored in a relational system where everything is committed in transactions and is thus easily recovered in relation to the rest of the data within that database. However, after an order is set, a workflow might be triggered via an event stored in a queuing system or a key-value store. Those systems might be eventually consistent, or even ephemeral, relying on the relational system for reference or recoverability. How do you account for those workflows when recovering?

If you are in an environment with rapid development, you might also find that data stored in a backup was written and utilized by a different version of the application than the one running after the restore is done. How will the application interact with that older data? Hopefully the data is versioned to allow for that, but you must be aware of this and prepared for such eventualities. Otherwise, the application could logically corrupt that data and create even larger issues down the road.

You must take into account each of these, and many other variables that you cannot plan for, when planning for data recovery. You simply can't prepare for every eventuality. But this is a critical service. Data recoverability is one of the most significant responsibilities of the DBRE. So, your plan for data recoverability must be able to be as broad as possible, taking into account as many potential issues as possible.

Anatomy of a Recovery Strategy

There is a reason why I say recovery strategy, rather than a backup strategy. Data recovery is the entire reason we do backups. Backups are simply a means to the end and thus are dependent on the true requirement: recovery within parameters. The simple question "Is your database backed up?" is a question that should be followed with the response "Yes, in multiple ways, depending on the recovery scenario." A simple yes is naive and promotes a false sense of security that is irresponsible and dangerous.

An effective database recovery strategy not only approaches multiple scenarios with the most effective strategies, but also includes the detection of data loss/corruption, recovery testing, and recovery validation.

Building Block 1: Detection

Early detection of potential data loss or corruption is crucial. This means that backups might even be aged out by the time the need for them is noticed. Thus, detection must be a high priority for all of engineering. In addition to building early detection around data loss or corruption, ensuring that there is as long of a window as possible in place to recover in case early detection fails is also critical. Let's look at the different failure scenarios discussed and identify some real-world approaches to detection and lengthened recovery windows.

User error

One of the biggest impacts in reducing time to identifying data loss is through not allowing manual or ad hoc changes to be executed in production creating wrappers for scripts, or even API-level abstractions; engineers can be guided through effective steps for ensuring all changes are as safe as possible, tested, logged, and pushed up to the appropriate teams.

An effective wrapper or API will be able to do the following:

- Execute in multiple environments via parameterization
- A dry-run stage, where execution results can be estimated and validated
- A test suite for the code execution
- Validation post-execution to verify changes met expectations
- Soft-deletion or easy rollback via the same API
- Logging by ID of all data modified, for identification and recovery

By removing the ad hoc and manual components of these processes, you can increase the likelihood that all changes will be trackable by troubleshooting engineers. All changes will be logged so that there is traceability and the change cannot simply disappear into the day-to-day noise.

Similarly, you can coach software developers to change how they think about the removal, or deletion, of data from their environments. Instead of deleting data, or irrevocably changing data (also known as DELETE or UPDATE operations), developers can record a continuous timeline of actions (INSERT, NEW VERSION, DELETE). This allows an application to have a full history of an object, which allows for software-level recovery and auditing, as opposed to expensive and error-prone human recoveries. This is not a guarantee; after all, manual processes can be extremely well logged, and people can forget to set up logging in automated processes, or they can bypass them.

Application errors

When engineers introduce new objects and attributes, DBREs should work with them to identify data validation that can be done downstream, outside of the application itself. Initial work should focus on quick tests that provide fast feedback loops on critical data components, such as external pointers to files, relationship mapping to enforce referential integrity, and personal identification information (PII). As data and applications grow, this validation becomes more expensive and more valuable. Building a culture that holds engineers accountable for data quality and integrity rather than the storage engines pays dividends in terms not only of flexibility to use different databases, but also of helping people feel more confident about experimenting and moving fast on application features. Validation functions as a guardrail, helping everyone feel braver and more confident.

Infrastructure services

Any catastrophic infrastructure impacts that require recovery should be caught rapidly by monitoring in the operational visibility stack. But there are changes that can cause silent data loss, data corruption, or availability. Using golden images and comparing them regularly to your infrastructure components can help identify straying from the test images quickly. Similarly, versioned infrastructure can help identify straying infrastructure and alert the appropriate engineers or automation.

Operating system and hardware errors

As with infrastructure services, the majority of these problems should be rapidly caught by monitoring of logs and metrics. Edge cases that are not standard will require some thought and experience to identify and add to monitoring for early detection. Checksums on disk blocks is an example of this. Not all filesystems will do this, and teams working with critical data need to take the time to consider the appropriate filesystems that can identify silent corruption via checksumming.

Building Block 2: Diverse Storage

An effective recovery strategy relies on data being placed on diverse areas of storage with different operating characteristics. Different recovery needs can be served by different storage areas, which not only ensures the right performance, but also the right cost and the right durability for any number of scenarios.

Online, high-performance storage

This is the storage pool most of your production data stores will run on. It is characterized by a high amount of throughput, low latency, and, thus, a high price point. When recovery time is of the utmost importance, putting recent copies of the datastore and associated incremental backups on this tier is paramount. This allows for rapid recovery for common and critical recovery scenarios, including full dataset copies after host failures or adding nodes rapidly for additional capacity. These pools often also have snapshots available.

Online, low-performance storage

This storage pool is often utilized for data that is not sensitive to latency. Larger disks have low throughput and latency profiles, and a lower price point. These storage pools are often much larger, holding more copies of data from further back in time. Relatively infrequent, low-impact, or long-running recovery scenarios utilize these older backups. Typical use cases include finding and repairing application or user errors that slipped by early detection.

Offline storage

Snapshots, tape storage, or even something like Amazon Glacier are examples of this kind of storage. Snapshots store only Input/Output (I/O) blocks that have changed, allowing for even more copies to be retained at some level of resource overhead. Snapshots, if available via your volume manager or filesystem, can allow for rapid point-in-time recovery.

Tape or Glacier is typically off-site, requiring movement via vehicle or slow pipelines to bring it to an area where it can be made available for recovery. This type of storage can support business continuity and audit requirements but does not have a place in day-to-day recovery scenarios. Still, due to the size and cost, vast amounts of storage are available here, allowing for the potential of storing all data for the life of the business, or at least for a full legal compliance term.

Object storage

Object storage is a storage architecture that manages data as objects rather than files or blocks. Object storage gives features not available through traditional storage architectures, such as APIs, object versioning, and high degrees of availability via replication and distribution. This enables easy recovery of specific objects. Amazon Simple Storage Service (Amazon S3) is a classic example of an inexpensive, scalable, and reliable object-level storage tier.

Each of these tiers plays a part in a comprehensive strategy for recoverability across multiple potential scenarios. Without being able to predict every possible scenario, it is this level of breadth that is required. Next, we discuss the tools that utilize these storage tiers to provide recoverability.

Building Block 3: A Varied Toolbox

You will note that nowhere do I discuss replication as a way to effectively back up data for recovery. Replication is blind, and can cascade user errors, application errors, and corruption. You must look at replication as a necessary tool for data movement and synchronization, but not for creating useful recovery artifacts. Similarly, Redundant Array of Independent Disks (RAID) is not a backup; rather, it is a redundancy.

Full physical backups

We know that we will need to do full restores at each level of scope: node level, cluster level and data center level. Rapid, portable full restores are incredibly powerful and mandatory in dynamic environments. A full backup can be done via full data copies over the network or via volumes that you can easily attach and detach from specific hosts or instances. To do this, you need full backups.

A full backup using online, high-performance storage is for immediate replacement into an online cluster. These backups are typically uncompressed because decompressing them takes a lot of time. Full backups using online, low-performance storage are utilized for building different environments, such as test, or for analytics and data forensics. Compression is an effective tool to allow for longer timelines of full backups on limited storage pools.

Incremental physical backups

Incremental backups bridge the gap between the last full backup and a place in time after it. Physical incremental backups are generally done via data blocks that have a changed piece of data within it. Because full backups can be expensive, both in terms of performance impact during the backup as well as storage, incremental backups allow you to quickly bring up to date a full backup that might be older, for use in the cluster.

Full and incremental logical backups

A full logical backup provides for portability and simpler extraction of subsets of data. They will not be used for rapid recovery of nodes, but instead are perfect tools for use in forensics, moving data between data stores and recovering specific subsets of data from large datasets.

Object stores

Object stores, like logical backups, can provide for easy recovery of specific objects. In fact, object storage is optimized for this specific use case, and APIs can easily use it to programmatically recover objects as needed.

Building Block 4: Testing

For such an essential infrastructure process as recovery, it is astonishing how often testing tends to fall by the wayside. Testing is an essential process to ensure that your backups are usable for recovery. Testing is often set up as an occasional process, to be run on an intermittent basis such as monthly or quarterly. Although this is better than nothing, it allows for large periods of time between tests during which backups can stop working.

There are two effective approaches to adding testing into ongoing processes. The first one is incorporating recovery into everyday processes. This way, recovery is constantly tested, allowing for rapid identification of bugs and failures. Additionally, constant recovery creates data about how long your recovery takes, which is essential in calibrating your recovery processes to meet Service-Level Agreements (SLAs).

Examples of constant integration of recovery into daily processes include the following:

- Building integration environments
- Building testing environments
- Regularly replacing nodes in production clusters

If your environment does not allow for enough opportunities to rebuild data stores, you can also create a continuous testing process, whereby recovery of the most recent backup is a constant process, followed by verification of the success of that restore. Regardless of the presence of automation, even off-site backup tiers do require occasional testing.

With these building blocks, you can create a defense in depth for different recovery scenarios. By mapping out the scenarios and tools used to recover them, you can then begin evaluating your needs in terms of development and resources.

Championing Recovery Reliability

Much of this section has been about creating infrastructure and focusing on enabling development teams to make better choices about how they store, change, and recover their data. This is the heart of reliability: leveraging the entire organization to do the right thing and giving them the best range of tools with which to do it. Next, let's discuss the function of continuous delivery.

Continuous Delivery: From Development to Production

One of the highest-value activities the SRE can do is working with software engineers to build, test, and deploy application features. The traditional DBA was a gatekeeper, reviewing each database migration, database object, and query accessing the database. When satisfied, the DBA would plan an appropriate hand-crafted change and shepherd it through into production. A gatekeeper can rapidly become a bottleneck, however, leading to burnout on the part of the DBA and frustrations in software engineering.

My goal in this section is to look at how to effectively utilize your time, skills, and experience to effectively support a software engineering process that utilizes Continuous Integration (CI) and even Continuous Deployment without becoming a bottleneck.

Education and Collaboration

One of the first steps is educating the developer population. If a software engineer can make better choices about their data structures, their SQL, and the overall interaction strategies, there will be fewer needs for your direct intervention. By taking on the role of educator, you can have greater impact on the organization while fostering better relationships, trust, and communication.

I am suggesting that regular interactions and strategic efforts enable teams to have access to resources and autonomy for most decisions around the database. Remember to keep everything you do specific, measurable, and actionable. Define key metrics for your team's success in this, and as you implement strategies and changes, see how they help the team.

This requires cross-functional interactions between people of different backgrounds, skill levels, and professional contexts to collaborate closely. Education and collaboration is a huge part of this process; it's a great opportunity to shift out of the legacy "DBA" mode and become an integrated part of your technical organization.

Architecture

I am not a fan of static documentation separate from the processes that build and deploy architecture. With configuration management and orchestration systems, you get a lot of documentation for free. Putting tools on top of these to allow for easy discovery, borrowing, and, of course, annotation of notes and comments creates a living document for teams.

Your job is to make knowledge, context, and history available to engineers who are making decisions daily while working on features without your oversight. Building a knowledge base of design documents creates the structure necessary to build context and history around the architecture. These documents might apply to full projects that require new architectural components, or they might relate to smaller incremental changes or subprojects.

Data model

Knowledge of the organization's data is also critical. Knowing what is stored and where you can find it can eliminate a significant amount of redundancy and investigative time from the development process. This is also the opportunity to give best practices for which data stores are not appropriate for certain kinds of data.

Best practices and standards

Giving engineers standards for the activities they engage in regularly is another effective method for optimizing the amount of value you are able to generate. You can do this incrementally as you help engineers and make decisions. If your organization regularly hires new engineers with no domain expertise, you can also converge these incremental decisions into an onboarding and training program. Here are some examples of this:

- Datatype standards
- Indexing
- Metadata attributes
- Datastores to use
- Metrics to expose
- Design patterns
- Migration and database change patterns

Publishing these as you work with engineers allows for a self-service knowledge base (*https://martinfowler.com/articles/evodb.html*), which teams can access at any time rather than being forced to bottleneck on you.

Tools

Giving software engineers effective tools for their development process is the ultimate enabler. You might be helping them with benchmarking tools and scripts, data consistency evaluators, templates, or even configurators for new data stores. What you are doing is enabling greater velocity in the development process while simultaneously freeing up your time for higher-value efforts.

Collaboration

If you're regularly educating, creating tools, and empowering engineers, you will naturally create good relationships. Any engineer should be empowered to reach out to you to ask for information or for the chance to pair while they work. This gives great value bidirectionally, as the SWEs learn more about how the SRE team works and what they look for, and the SRE team learns more about the software development process.

You can facilitate this further by proactively reaching out to engineers. There are features that have a large dependency and reliance on database development and refactoring. This is where the DBRE should be focusing their efforts to help guarantee success and efficiency. Ask to pair or be part of a team on these stories. Similarly, keeping an eye on migrations being committed into mainline will help the DBRE team cherry-pick where it needs to perform reviews.

Next, I discuss how to effectively support the various components of the delivery pipeline. While Continuous Delivery is not a new concept by any means, organizations have struggled to incorporate databases into the process. In each of the following sections, I will discuss how to effectively introduce the database layers into the full delivery cycle.

Deployment

It makes sense to decompose data migrations in such a way that engineers can easily and incrementally modify environments with a minimum of risk. Your goal should be to empower engineers to recognize when their database changes require analysis and management by experts in order to be effectively introduced into production. Additionally, you would be able to give those engineers the tools to safely and reliably introduce most changes into production themselves. Optimally, you would give them the ability to push changes at any time rather than during restrictive maintenance windows.

Migrations and Versioning

Each change set that is applied to the database should be given a numeric version. You generally do this by using incrementing integers that are stored in the database after a change set is applied. This way, your deployment system can easily look at the database and discover the current version. This allows you to easily apply changes when preparing to push code. If a code deployment is certified for database version 456, and the current database version is 455, the deployment team knows that it must apply the change set for 456 prior to pushing code.

So, a software engineer has committed change set 456 into the code base, and integration has been successfully run with no breaking changes. What comes next?

Impact Analysis

We discussed impact analysis in the previous section under post-commit testing. Some impacts, such as the invalidation of stored code in the database, or violation of security controls, are gates that cannot be passed. The software engineer must go back and modify their changes until these impacts have been mitigated.

Some impacts can include the following:

- Locking of shared objects
- Saturation of resources
- Data integrity issues
- Broken or stalled replication

Migration Patterns

After impact analysis, the software engineer should be able to make a decision on the appropriate way to deploy the migration. For many migrations, there is no reason to need to go through a lot of incremental changes and extensive review work to execute. New objects, data inserts and other operations can be easily pushed through to production.

After data is in the system, however, changes or removal of existing data, and modification or removal of objects with data in them, can create opportunities for your migration to impact service levels, as discussed earlier. It is at this time that the engineer should bring the DBRE in. Luckily, there is a finite set of changes that can be planned for. As you work with engineers to plan and execute migrations, you build a repository of patterns for changes. At some point, if these migrations happen frequently and painlessly enough, you can automate them.

The more flags and safeguards you put in place to enable safety in production for everyone, the more confidence you create in all teams. This results in development velocity. Now, assume that our intrepid software engineer who has checked in change set 456 has had their change flagged due to an alter that is deemed to be impactful. At this point, the engineer can use a migration pattern for that operation if it has been applied and documented. Otherwise, one should be created in collaboration with the DBRE team.

Migration testing

Even though it might seem self-evident, it is imperative to recognize that if a change set's implementation details are modified, the revised migration must be committed and fully integrated before deployment in post-integration environments, including production.

Rollback testing

In addition to testing migrations and their impact, the DBRE and their supported teams must consider the failure of migrations or deploys and the rolling back of partial or full change sets. Database change scripts should be checked in at the same time as migrations. There can be autogenerated defaults for some migrations such as table creations, but there must be an accounting for data that comes in. Therefore, I don't recommend reverting by simply dropping an object. Renaming tables allows them to still be accessible in case data was written and must be recovered.

Migration patterns also enable ease in the process of defining rollbacks. The lack of an effective rollback script can be a gating factor in the integration and deployment process. To validate that the scripts work, you can use the following deployment and testing pattern:

- Apply change set
- Quick integration tests
- Apply rollback change set

- Quick integration tests
- Apply change set
- Quick integration tests
- Longer and periodic testing

Much like testing recoveries, testing fallbacks is critical and you must incorporate it into every build and deploy process.

Championing CD

Database changes are inevitably the last blocker for truly continuous delivery. The more you enable rapid, safe, and predictable changes to the database tier, the greater the organization's ability to be competitive in the marketplace. Additionally, this is the greatest opportunity for building trust and rapport between teams. It must be a priority!

Making the Case for DBRE

Throughout this chapter, I have attempted to show how the landscape of database engineering has shifted. I'd like to thank you for taking the time to read this. I am so very passionate about helping one of the most burdensome and byzantine of technical careers to evolve. I believe that the DBRE movement is one that can drive so much value to data-driven services and organizations.

My hope is that you are inspired to explore these shifts in your organization and that you are eager to learn more. But, most important, I hope I've helped you see that there is opportunity to bring the time-honored role of DBA into the modern world and into the future. The role of DBA isn't going away, and whether you are new to this career or a tried-and-scarred veteran, I want you to have a long career ahead of you as you drive value to every organization of which you are a part. Should you be inspired to dig more into this topic, I recommend the following readings.

Further Reading

- Campbell, Laine and Charity Majors. *Database Reliability Engineering* (O'Reilly, 2017).
- Kleppman, Martin. *Designing Data Intensive Applications* (O'Reilly, 2017).
- Morris, Kief. *Infrastructure as Code* (O'Reilly, 2015).
- Humble, Jez and David Farley. *Continuous Delivery* (Addison-Wesley).

Laine Campbell works as Senior Vice President of Engineering at Fastly. She was also founder and CEO of PalominoDB/Blackbird, a consultancy servicing the database needs of companies including Obama for America, Activision Call of Duty, Adobe Echosign, Technorati, Livejournal, and Zendesk.

## CHAPTER 17

Engineering for Data Durability

James Cowling, Dropbox, Inc.

SREs live and breathe reliability, but to many engineers the word *reliability* is synonymous with *availability*: "How do we keep the site up?" Reliability is a multifaceted concern, however, and an extremely important part of this is *durability*: "How do we avoid losing or corrupting our data?"

Engineering for durability is of paramount importance for any company that stores user data. Most companies can survive a period of downtime, but few can survive losing a significant fraction of user data. Building expertise in durable systems is particularly challenging, however; most companies improve availability over time as they grow and as their systems mature, but a single durability mistake can be a company-ending event. It's therefore important to invest effort ahead of time to understand real-world durability threats and how to engineer against them.

Replication Is Table Stakes

If you don't want to lose your data, you should store multiple copies of it. You probably didn't need a book to tell you this. We'll breeze through most of this pretty quickly because this is really just the basic requirements when it comes to durability.

Backups

Back up your data. The great thing about backups is that they're logically and physically disjointed from your primary data store: an operational error that results in loss or corruption of database state probably won't impact your backups. Ideally, these should be stored both local to your infrastructure and also off-site, to provide both fast local access and to safeguard against local physical disasters.

Backups have some major limitations, however, particularly with regard to recovery time and data freshness. Both of these can conspire to leave you vulnerable to more data loss or downtime than you might expect.

Restoration

Restoring state from backups can take a surprisingly long time, especially if you haven't practiced recovering from backup recently. In fact, if you haven't tested your backups recently, it's possible they don't even work at all!

In the early days of Dropbox, we were dismayed to discover that it was going to take eight hours just to restart a production database after a catastrophic failure. Even though all of the data was intact, we had set the `innodb_max_dirty_pages_pct` MySQL parameter too high, resulting in MySQL taking eight hours just to scan the redo log during crash recovery.[1] Fortunately, this database didn't store critical data, and we were able bring dropbox.com back online in a couple of hours by bypassing the database altogether, but this was certainly a wake-up call. Our operational sophistication has improved dramatically since then, which I outline later in this chapter.

Freshness

Backups represent a previous snapshot in time and will usually result in loss of recent data when you restore from them. You typically want to store both full-snapshot backups for fast recovery and for historical versioning, along with incremental backups of more recent state to minimize staleness. Any stronger guarantees than this, however, require an actual replication protocol.

Replication

Database replication techniques range from *asynchronous replication* to *semi-synchronous replication* to full *quorum* or *consensus* protocols. The choice of replication strategy will be informed by how much inconsistency you can tolerate and, to some extent, the performance requirements of the database. Although replication is often essential for durability, it can also be a source of inconsistency. You must take care with asynchronous replication schemes to ensure that stale data isn't erroneously read from a replica database. A database promotion to a replica that is lagging from the master can also introduce permanent data loss.

Typically, a company will run one primary database and two replicas, and then just assume that the durability problem has been solved. More elaborate storage systems will often require more elaborate replication mechanisms, particularly when storage overhead is a serious concern. For a company like Dropbox that stores exabytes of

---

1 We were running MySQL 5.1 at the time; this is much less of a problem with versions 5.5 and above.

data, there are more effective ways of providing durability than basic replication. Techniques like *erasure coding* are adopted instead, which store coded redundant chunks of data across many disks and achieve higher durability with lower storage overhead. Dropbox utilizes variants on erasure coding that are designed to distribute data across multiple geographical regions while minimizing the cross-region network bandwidth required to recover from routine disk failures.

Estimating durability

Regardless of the choice of replication technique, an obvious question you might have is, "How much durability do I actually have?" Do you need one database replica? Two? More?

One convenient way of estimating durability is to plug some numbers into a *Markov model*. Let's jump into some (simplified) math here, so take a deep breath—or just skip to the end of this section.

Let's assume that each disk has a given mean time to failure (MTTF) measured in hours and that we have operational processes in place to replace and re-replicate a failed disk with a given mean time to recovery (MTTR) in hours. We'll represent these as failure and recovery rates of $\lambda = \frac{1}{MTTF}$ and $\mu = \frac{1}{MTTR}$, respectively. This means that we assume that each disk fails at a rate of λ failures per hour on average, and that each individual disk failure is replaced at a rate of μ recoveries per hour.

For a given replication scheme, let's say that we have n disks in our replication group, and that we lose data if we lose more than m disks; for example, for three-way database replication we have $n = 3$ and $m = 2$; for $RS(9,6)$ erasure coding, we have $n = 9$ and $m = 3$.

We can take these variables and model a Markov chain, shown in Figure 17-1, in which each state represents a given number of failures in a group and the transitions between states indicate the rate of disks failing or being recovered.

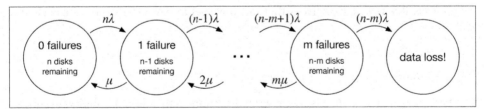

Figure 17-1. Durability Markov model

In this model, the flow from the first to second state is equal to $n\lambda$ because there are n disks remaining that each fail at a rate of λ failures per hour. The flow from the second state back to the first is equal to μ because we have only one failed disk, which is recovered at a rate of μ recoveries per hour, and so on.

The rate of data loss in this model is equivalent to the rate of moving from the second-last state to the data-loss state. This flow can be computed as

$$R(loss) = n\lambda \times \frac{(n-1)\lambda}{\mu} \times \cdots \times \frac{(n-m)\lambda}{m\mu} = \frac{n!}{m!(n-m-1)!} \times \frac{\lambda^{m+1}}{\mu^m}$$

for a data loss rate of $R(loss)$ replication groups per hour.

This simplified failure model allows us to plug in some numbers and estimate how likely we are to lose data.

Let's say our disks have an Annualized Failure Rate (AFR) of 3%. We can compute MTTF from AFR by using $MTTF = \frac{-8,766}{\ln(1-AFR)}$ (this is approximately $\frac{8,766}{AFR}$); in this case $MTTF = 287{,}795$ hours. Let's say we have some reasonably good operational tooling that can replace and re-replicate a disk within 24 hours after failure, so $MTTR = 24$. If we adopt three-way data replication we have $n = 3$, $m = 2$, $\lambda = \frac{1}{287,795}$, and $\mu = \frac{1}{24}$.

Plugging these into the equation earlier, we get $R(loss) = 7.25 \times 10^{-14}$ data loss incidents per hour or 6.35×10^{-10} incidents per year. This means that a given replication group is safe in a given year with probability 0.9999999994.

Wait, that's pretty safe, right?

Well, nine 9s of durability is pretty decent. If you have a huge number of replication groups, however, failure becomes more likely than this, because each *individual* group has nine 9s of durability, but in aggregate it's more likely that one will fail. If you're a big consumer storage company, you'll likely want to push durability further than this. If you reduce recovery delay or buy better disks or increase replication factor, it's pretty easy to push durability numbers *much* higher. Dropbox achieves theoretical durability numbers well beyond *twenty-four 9s*, aided by some fancy erasure coding and automatic disk recovery systems. According to these models, it's practically impossible to lose data. Does that mean we get to pat ourselves on the back and go home?

Unfortunately not…

Your durability estimate is only an upper bound!

It's fairly easy to design a system with astronomically high durability numbers. Twenty-four 9s is an MTTF of 1,000,000,000,000,000,000,000,000 years. When your MTTF dwarfs the age of the universe, it might be time to reevaluate your priorities.

Should we trust these numbers, though? Of course not, because the secret truth is that *adherence to theoretical durability estimates is missing the point*. They tell you how likely you are to lose data due to routine disk failure, but routine disk failure is pay in model for and protect against. If you lose data due to routine disk failure, you're probably doing something wrong.

What's the most likely way you're going to lose data? Is it losing a specific set of half a dozen different disks across multiple geographical regions within a narrow window of time? Or, is it an operator accidentally running a script that deletes all your files, or a firmware bug that causes half your storage nodes to fail simultaneously, or a software bug that silently corrupts 1% of your objects? Protecting against these threats is where the real SRE work comes in.

Real-World Durability

In the real world, the incidents that affect you worst are the ones that you don't see coming: the "unknown unknowns." If you saw something coming and didn't protect against it, you weren't doing your job anyway! Because we never know when a truck will plow into a data center or when someone will let an intern loose on production infrastructure, we need to devote our efforts to not only reducing the scope of bad things that can happen, but also being able to recover from the things that do. *Bad things will happen.* Reliable companies are the ones that are able to respond and recover before a user is impacted.

So, where do we start when guarding against the unknown? We're going to devote the rest of this chapter to durability strategies that span the four pillars of durability engineering:

- Isolation
- Protection
- Verification
- Automation

Isolation

Strong isolation is the key to failure independence.

Durability on the basis of replication hinges entirely on these replicas failing independently. Even though this might seem pretty obvious, there is usually a large correlation between failure of individual components in a system. A data center fire might destroy on-site backups; a bad batch of hard drives might fail within a short timeframe; a software bug might corrupt all your replicas simultaneously. In these situations, you've suffered from a lack of isolation.

Physical isolation is an obvious concern, but perhaps even more important are investments in *logical* and *operational* isolation.

Physical isolation

To put it succinctly, store your stuff on different stuff.

There's a wide spectrum of physical failure domains that spans from disks to machines, to racks, to rows, to power feeds, to network clusters, to data centers, to regions or even countries. Isolation improves as you go up the stack, but usually comes with a significant cost, complexity, or performance penalty. Storing state across multiple geographic regions often comes with high network and hardware costs, and often entails a big increase in latency. At Dropbox, we design data placement algorithms taking into consideration the power distribution schematics in the data center to minimize the impact of a power outage. For many companies this is clearly overkill.

Every company needs to pick an isolation level that matches its desired guarantees and technical feasibility, but after a level is chosen, it's important to *own it*. "If this data center burns down, we're going to lose all of our data and the company is over" is not necessarily an irresponsible statement, but it is irresponsible to be caught by surprise when you're unsure of what isolation guarantees you actually have.

There are other dimensions to physical isolation, like dual-sourcing your hardware or operating multiple hardware revisions of disks and storage devices. Although this is outside the scope of many companies, large infrastructure providers will usually buy hardware components from multiple suppliers to minimize the impact of a production shortage or a hardware bug. You'd likely be surprised how often bugs show up in components like disk drivers, routing firmware, and RAID cards. Judicious adoption of hardware diversity can reduce the impact of catastrophic failures and provide a backup option if a new hardware class doesn't pass production validation testing.

Logical isolation

Failures tend to cascade and bugs tend to propagate. If one system goes down, it will often hose everything else in the process. If one bad node begins writing corrupt data to another node, that data can propagate through the system and corrupt an increasingly large share of your storage. These failures happen because distributed systems often have strong logical dependencies between components.

The key to logical isolation is to build loosely coupled systems.

Logical isolation is difficult to achieve. Database replicas will happily store corrupt data issued to them by the primary database. A quorum consensus protocol like Zookeeper will also suffer the same fate. These systems are not only tightly coupled from a durability perspective, they're tightly coupled from an availability perspective: if a load spike leads to a failure of one component, there is usually an even greater load applied to the other components, which subsequently also fail.

Strong logical isolation usually needs to be designed into the underlying architecture of a system.

One example at Dropbox is region isolation within the storage system. File objects at Dropbox are replicated extensively within a single geographical region, but also duplicated in a completely separate geographical region on the other side of the country. The replication protocols within a region are quite complicated and designed for high storage efficiency, but the API between the two regions is extremely simple: primarily just put and get, as illustrated in Figure 17-2.

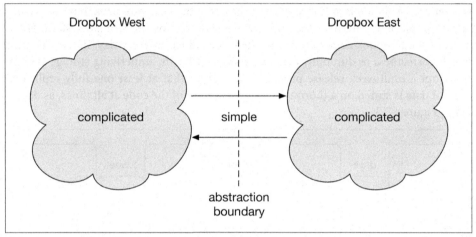

Figure 17-2. Isolated multiregion storage architecture

Strong isolation between regions is a nice way to use modularity to hide complexity, but it comes at a significant cost in terms of replication overhead. So why would a company spend more than it needs to for storage?

The abstraction boundary between storage regions makes it extremely hard for cascading issues to propagate across regions. The loose logical coupling and simple API makes it difficult for a bug or inconsistency in one region to impact the other. The loose coupling also makes it possible to take an entire region down in an emergency without impacting our end users; in fact, we take a region down every week as a test exercise. This architecture results in a system that is extremely reliable from an availability and durability perspective, without imposing a significant operational burden on the engineers who run the system.

Operational isolation

The most important dimension to isolation is operational isolation, yet it is one that is often overlooked. You can build one of the world's most sophisticated distributed storage systems, with extensive replication and physical and logical isolation, but then let someone run a fleet-wide firmware upgrade that causes disk writes to fail, or to accidentally reboot all your machines. These aren't academic examples; we've seen both happen in the early days of Dropbox.

Typically, the most dangerous component of a system is the people who operate it. Mature SRE organizations recognize this and build systems to protect against themselves. I elaborate more on protections in the next section, but one critical set of protections is isolation across release process, tooling, and access controls. This means implementing restrictions to prevent potentially dangerous batch processes from running across multiple isolation zones simultaneously.

Operational isolation is enforced at many layers of the Dropbox stack, but one particular example is isolation in the code release process for the storage system. Some parts of the Dropbox code base are pushed to production every day, in use cases for which correctness or durability aren't at stake, but for the underlying storage system, we adopt a multiweek release process that ensures that at least one fully replicated copy of data is stored on a thoroughly vetted version of the code at all times, as depicted in Figure 17-3.

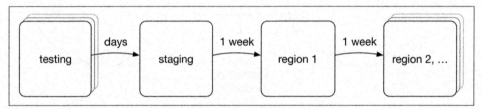

Figure 17-3. Storage system code release process.

All new versions of storage code go through an extensive unit testing and integration testing process to catch any trivial errors, followed by overnight end-to-end durability testing on a randomized synthetic workload. We also run a set of long-running version-skew tests during which different code versions are run simultaneously on different nodes in the system; code pushes aren't atomic, so we need to ensure that old and new versions of code are compatible with each other. After these tests have all passed, the release is automatically marked as "green" and is ready to be pushed to the staging cluster.

The staging cluster is an actual production deployment of the storage system that stores a mirror of a subset of production data. This is a relatively large cluster storing many tens of petabytes across multiple geographical regions. The code runs on this cluster for a full week and is subjected to the same workloads, monitoring, and verification as the rest of the storage system. After a week in staging the individual "DRIs" (directly responsible individuals—the engineers who "own" each subsystem) sign off that each software component is operating correctly and without any significant performance degradation. At this point, the software is ready to be pushed to the first real production region.

Code is pushed to the first production region and runs for another week before it can be safely pushed to the remaining regions. Recall that the multiregion architecture of the storage system ensures that all data in one region is replicated in at least one other region, avoiding any risk of data loss from a single code push. Internal verification systems are tuned to detect any anomalies within this one-week timeframe, but in practice, any potential durability issues are caught well before making it this far. The multiregion deployment model is tremendously valuable, however, at catching any performance or availability issues that arise only at large scale.

The release process is pipelined so that there are always multiple versions of code rolling out to production. The process itself is also automated to a large extent to avoid any operator errors. For practical reasons, we also support a "break-glass" procedure to allow sign-off on any emergency changes that need to be fast-tracked to production, along with extensive logging.

The thoroughness in this release process allows us to provide an extremely high level of durability, but it's clearly overkill for the vast majority of use cases. Operational isolation comes at a cost, which is usually measured in inconvenience or engineer frustration. At a small company, it can be incredibly convenient to run a batch job across all machines simultaneously, or for engineers to be able to SSH into any server in the fleet. As a company grows, though, investments in operational isolation not only guard against major disasters, but also allow a team to move faster by providing guardrails within which to iterate and develop quickly.

Protection

Your biggest durability threat is yourself.

In an ideal world, we would always catch bad things before they happen. This is an unrealistic goal, of course, but still worth investing significant effort in attempting to achieve. In addition to safeguards to prevent disasters, you need a well-thought-out set of recovery mechanisms to mitigate any issues that slip through the cracks.

Testing

The first protection most engineers think of is simply *testing*. Everyone knows that you need good tests to produce reliable software. Companies often invest significant effort in unit testing to catch basic logic errors but underinvest in comprehensive end-to-end integration testing. Mocking out parts of the software stack allows fine-grained testing but can hide complex race conditions or cross-system interactions that occur in a real production deployment. In any distributed system, there is no substitute for running the full software stack in a test environment and validating correctness on long-running workloads. In more advanced use cases, you can use *fault-injection* to trigger failures of system components during this integration testing. In our experience, codepaths that handle failures and corner cases are far more error-prone than more common flows.

Safeguards

As mentioned previously, the biggest durability risk in a system is often yourself. So how do you guard against your own fallibility? Let's begin with an example of one of the worst production issues in the history of Dropbox.

Many years ago, an operator accidentally left out a set of quotation marks when running a distributed shell operation across a set of databases. The operator intended to run

```
dsh --group "hwclass=database lifecycle=reinstall" reimage.sh
```

but instead typed the following:

```
dsh --group hwclass=database lifecycle=reinstall reimage.sh
```

This is an easy mistake to make, but the end result was disastrous. This command caused the command `lifecycle=reinstall reimage.sh` to attempt to run on every database in the fleet instead of just running `reimage.sh` on databases that were slated for reinstall, taking down a large fraction of our production databases. The immediate impact of this was a widely publicized two-day outage during which a number of Dropbox services were unavailable, but the long-term impact was a process of significant investment to prevent any such events from ever happening again.

The immediate point of reflection following an outage such as this is that *the operator is not to blame*. If it's possible for a simple mistake to cause a large-scale outage, that's a process failure, not a personnel failure. Don't hate the player, hate the game.

There are many obvious safeguards to implement in a situation like this. We added access controls that prevent rebooting a live database host—a very basic protection, but one that's often overlooked. We changed the syntax of the distributed shell command to make it less vulnerable to typos. We added isolation-based restrictions within our tooling that reject any distributed command that is run simultaneously across multiple isolation domains. Most important, however, we significantly invested in automation to obviate the need for an operator to ever need to run a script like this, and instead relied on systems more reliable than a human at a keyboard.

The need for protections must be maintained as an engineering principle so that safeguards are developed alongside initial deployment of the systems they protect.

Recovery

Failures will happen. The mark of a strong operational team is the ability to recover from disasters quickly and without long-term impact on customers.

An important design consideration is to attempt to always have an undo button—that is, to design systems such that there is sufficient state to reverse an unintended operation or to recover from an unexpected corruption. Logs, backups, and historical versions can greatly aid in recoverability following an incident, particularly when accompanied by a well-rehearsed procedure for actually performing the recovery.

One technique for mitigating the impact of dangerous transformations is to buffer the underlying mutation for sufficient time to run verification mechanisms on the new state. The file deletion life cycle at Dropbox is designed in such a way so as to prevent live-deleting any object in the system, and instead wraps these transformations with comprehensive safeguards, as demonstrated in Figure 17-4.

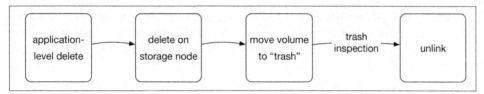

Figure 17-4. Object deletion flow

Application-level file deletion at Dropbox is a relatively complex process involving user-facing restoration features, version tracking, data retention policies, and reference counting. This process has been extensively tested and hardened over many years, but the inherent complexity poses a risk from a recovery perspective. As a final line of defense, we protect against deletions on the storage disks themselves, to guard against any potential issues in these higher layers.

When a delete is issued to a physical storage node, the object isn't immediately unlinked. Instead, it is moved to a temporary "trash" location on the disk for safekeeping while we perform further verification. A system called the Trash Inspector iterates over all volumes in trash and ensures that all objects have either been legitimately deleted or safely moved to other storage nodes (in the course of internal filesystem operations). Only after trash inspection has passed and a given safety period has elapsed is the volume eligible for unlinking from disk via an asynchronous process that can be disabled during an emergency.

Recovery mechanisms are often expensive to implement and maintain, especially in storage use cases in which they impose additional storage overhead and higher hardware utilization. It's thus important to analyze where irrevocable transformations occur in the stack and to make informed decisions about where recovery mechanisms need to be inserted to provide comprehensive risk mitigation.

Verification

You will mess up; prioritize failure detection.

In a large, complex system the best protection is often the ability to detect anomalies and recover from them as soon as they occur. This is clearly true when you are monitoring availability of a production system or when tracking performance characteristics, but it is also particularly relevant when you're engineering for durability.

The Power of Zero

Is your storage system correct? Is it really, *really* correct? Can you say with 100% confidence that the data in your system is consistent and none of it is missing? In many storage systems this is certainly not the case. Maybe there was a bug five years ago that left some dangling foreign key relations in your database. Maybe Bob ran a bad database split a while ago that resulted in some rows on the wrong shards. Maybe there's a low background level of mysterious 404s from the storage system that you just keep an eye on and make sure the rate doesn't go up. Issues like this exist in systems everywhere, but they come at a huge operational cost. They obscure any new errors that occur, they complicate monitoring and development, and they can compound over time to further compromise the integrity of your data.

Knowing with high certainty that a system has zero errors is a tremendously empowering concept. If a system has an error today but didn't yesterday, something bad happened between then and now. It allows teams to set tight alert thresholds and respond rapidly to issues. It allows developers to build new features with the confidence that any bugs will be caught quickly. It minimizes the mental overhead of having to reason about corner cases regarding data consistency. Most important, however, it allows a team to sleep well at night knowing that they are being worthy of their users' trust.

The first step toward having zero errors is knowing whether you have any errors to begin with. This insight often requires significant technical investment but pays heavy dividends.

Verification Coverage

At Dropbox, we built a highly reliable geographically distributed storage system that stores multiple exabytes of data. It's a completely custom software stack from the ground up, all the way from the disk scheduler to the frontend nodes servicing external traffic. Although developing this system in-house was a huge technical undertaking, the largest part of the project wasn't actually writing the storage system itself. Significantly more time and effort were devoted to developing verification systems than the underlying system they are verifying! This might occur surprising outside the context of a system that is required to be absolutely correct at all times.

We operate a deep stack of verification systems at Dropbox. In aggregate, these systems generate almost as much system load as the production traffic generated by our users! Some of these verifiers cover individual critical system components and some provide end-to-end coverage, with the full stack designed to provide immediate detection of any serious data correctness issues.

Disk Scrubber

The Disk Scrubber runs on every storage node and continually reads each block on disk, validating the contents against our application-level checksums. Internal disk checksums and S.M.A.R.T. status reporting provide the illusion of a reliable storage medium, but corruptions routinely slip through these checks, especially in storage clusters numbering hundreds of thousands or millions of disks. Blocks on disk become silently corrupted or go missing, disks fail without notice, and fsyncs don't always fsync.

The Disk Scrubber finds errors on disks every single day at Dropbox. These errors trigger an automated mechanism that re-replicates the data and remediates the disk failure. Rapid detection and recovery from disk corruption is crucial to achieving durability guarantees. Recall that the durability formula for *R(loss)* given earlier in this chapter depends heavily on MTTR from failure. If MTTR is estimated at 24 hours but it takes a month to notice a silent disk corruption, you will have missed your durability targets by several orders of magnitude.

Index Scanner

The Index Scanner continually iterates over the top-level storage indices, looks up the set of storage nodes that are meant to be storing a given block, and then checks each of these nodes to make sure the block is there. The scanner provides an end-to-end check within the storage system to ensure that the storage metadata is consistent with the blocks stored by the disks themselves. The scanner itself is a reasonably large system totaling many hundreds of processes, generating over a million checks per second.

Storage Watcher

One challenge we faced when building verifiers was that if the same engineer who wrote a component also implements the corresponding verifier, they can end up baking any of their broken assumptions into the verifier itself. We wanted to ensure that we had true end-to-end black-box coverage, even if an engineer misunderstood an API contract or an invariant.

The Storage Watcher was written by an SRE who wasn't involved in building the storage system itself. It samples 1% of all blocks written to the system and attempts to fetch them back from storage after a minute, an hour, a day, a week, and a month. This provides full-stack verification coverage if all else fails and alerts us to any potential issues that might arise late in the lifetime of a block.

Watching the Watchers

There's nothing more comforting than an error graph that is literally a zero line, but how do you know that the verifier is even running? It might sound silly, but a verification system that never reports any errors looks a lot like a verifier system that isn't working at all.

At steady state, the Index Scanner mentioned earlier doesn't actually report any errors, because there aren't any errors to report. At one point early in the development of the system the scanner actually stopped working, and it took us a few days to notice! Clearly this is a problem. Untested protections don't protect anything.

You should use a verification stack in conjunction with disaster recovery training to ensure that durability issues are quickly detected, appropriate alerts fire, and failover mechanisms provide continual service to customers. In our production clusters, these tests involve nondestructive changes like shutting down storage nodes, failing databases, and black-holing traffic from entire clusters. In our staging clusters, this involves much more invasive tests like manually corrupting blocks on disk or forcing recovery of metadata from backup state on the storage nodes themselves. These tests not only demonstrate that the verification systems are working, but allow operators to train in the use of recovery mechanisms.

Automation

You don't have time to babysit.

One of the highest-leverage activities an SRE can engage in is investing in strong automation. It's important not to automate *too* fast: after all, you need to understand the problem before attempting to solve it. But days or weeks of automation work can save many months of time down the track. Automation isn't just an efficiency initiative, however; it has important implications for correctness and durability.

Window of Vulnerability

As discussed previously, MTTR has a significant impact on durability because it defines the *window of vulnerability* within which subsequent failures might cause a catastrophic incident. There is a limit to how tight you can set pager thresholds, though, and to how many incidents an operator can respond to immediately. Automation is needed to achieve sufficiently low response times.

One illustrative example is to compare a traditional Redundant Array of Independent Disks (RAID) array to a distributed storage system that automatically re-replicates data to other nodes if a disk fails. In the case of a RAID array, it might take a few days for an operator to show up on-site and replace a specific disk, whereas in an automated system, this data might be re-replicated in a small number of hours. The same comparison applies to primary-backup database replication: smaller companies will often require an operator to manually trigger a database promotion if the primary fails, whereas in larger infrastructure footprints, automatic tooling is used to ensure that the availability and durability impact from a database failure is kept to a minimum.

Operator Fatigue

Operator fatigue is a real problem, and not just because your team will eventually all quit if they keep getting paged all day. Excessive alerting can cause *alert blindness* by which operators end up overlooking legitimate issues. We've observed situations in which an operator has been tempted just to pipe the Unix `yes` command into a command-line tool that asked hundreds of times whether various maintenance operations were authorized, which defeated the purpose of the checks to begin with.

Rules and training can go only so far. Good automation is ultimately a necessary ingredient to allow operators to focus on high-leverage work and on critical interrupts rather than become bogged down in error-prone busy-work.

As a system scales in size, the operational processes that accompany it also need to scale. It would be impossible for a team running many thousands of nodes to manually intervene any time there was a minor hardware issue or a configuration problem. Management of core systems at Dropbox are almost entirely automated by a system that supports plug-ins both for detecting problems within the fleet and for safely resolving them, with extensive logging for analysis of persistent issues.

Systems that have the ability to automatically remediate alerts need to be implemented extremely carefully, given that they have the power to accidentally sabotage the infrastructure that they're designed to protect. Automatic remediation systems at Dropbox are subject to the same isolation protections discussed earlier in this chapter, along with stringent rate limits to ensure that no runaway changes are performed before an operator can intervene and recover. It is also important to implement significant monitoring for any trends in production issues—it is very easy for a system such as this to hide issues by automatically fixing them, obscuring any emergent negative trends in hardware or software reliability.

Reliability

The primary motivation for automation is simply reliability; you are not as reliable as a shell script. You can test, audit, and run automation systems continuously in ways in which you can't rely on an operator.

One example of a critical automation system at Dropbox is the disk remediation workflow, shown in Figure 17-5, which is designed to safely manage disk failures without operator intervention.

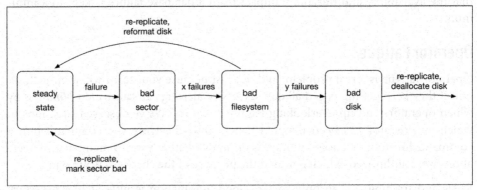

Figure 17-5. Automatic disk-remediation process

When a minor disk issue such as a corrupt block or a bad sector is detected, the data is recovered from other copies in the system and re-replicated elsewhere, and then the storage node is just allowed to continue running. Issues like this are sufficiently routine such that they don't justify further action unless disk failure rates begin shifting over time. After a certain number of errors, however, the system determines that there are serious problems with the disk or filesystem, recovers and re-replicates data that was on the disk, and then reprovisions the disk with a new clean filesystem. If this cycle repeats multiple times, the disk is marked as bad, the data is recovered and re-replicated, and a ticket is filed for data center operators to physically replace the disk. Because the data is immediately re-replicated, the replacement of the physical disk can happen any time down the track, and usually happens in infrequent batches. After a disk is removed from the machine it is kept for a safe-keeping period before eventually being physically shredded on-site.

This entire process is completely automatic and involves no human intervention up until the disk is physically pulled from the machine. The process also maintains the invariant that no operator is ever allowed to touch a disk that holds critical production data. Disks stay in the system until all the data that they held has been reconstructed from other copies and re-replicated elsewhere. Investing in development of this automation system allows seamless operation of an enormous storage system with only a handful of engineers.

Conclusion

There was a lot of stuff proposed in this chapter, and not every company needs to go as far as geo-distributed replication or complete alert autoremediation. The important point to remember is that the issues that will bite you aren't the disk failure or database outage you expect, but the *black swan* event that no one saw coming. Replication is only one part of the story and needs to be coupled with isolation, protection, recovery, and automation mechanisms. Designing systems with failure in mind means that you'll be ahead of the game when the next unknown-unknown threatens to become the next unforeseen catastrophe.

James Cowling is a principal engineer at Dropbox and served as technical lead on the project to build and deploy the multi-exabyte geo-distributed storage system that stores Dropbox file data. James has also served as team lead for the Filesystem and Metadata storage teams. Before joining the industry, James received his PhD at MIT specializing in large-scale distributed transaction processing and consensus protocols.

## CHAPTER 18

Introduction to Machine Learning for SRE

Ricardo Amaro, Acquia

Why Use Machine Learning for SRE?

In clear and simple words: because it makes sense and mostly because we (now) can.

SRE, fundamentally, is what happens when you ask a software engineer to design an operations function.[1]

This chapter is based on the presentation I did at DrupalCon Vienna (*https:// events.drupal.org/vienna2017/sessions/intelligent-automation-and-machine-learning-site-reliability-engineering*). Here we will be exploring some machine learning solutions for a few SRE open questions:

- How do we automate those repetitive tasks that just generate toil and that no one wants to do?

- How do we look at data and preview what's going to happen to our system in the future?

- How do we reinforce "applying software engineering to an operations function"?

The automation of operation processes is a critical target we pursue. As artificial intelligence (AI) and machine learning get better, the tasks that we can automate increase. If we keep the historical data to programmatically react to something new, we will be able to fix the issue beforehand because the system will alert us as to what is going to happen instead of having someone manually analyzing the past results and trying to preview the future.

---

1 Ben Treynor Sloss, Google Engineering.

I've just picked up a fault in the AE35 unit. It's going to go 100% failure in 72 hours.

—HAL 9000, *2001: A Space Odyssey*

That gives us the chance to use our time for more innovative tasks and feature development. Although this certainly is not an overnight achievement, lately we have seen the line between the work of machines and humans grow thin. Through the advances that machine learning and automation can offer, we can enable greater productivity among teams and businesses.

I've tried to make this chapter as simple as possible because it is intended for people who want to learn some basics about how to explore and improve automated response on critical systems and lower the level of manual operational work. The goal here is not to dive too deeply into machine learning (see the references at the end of the chapter) but just to give you an idea of how easy it is to get started playing with some of these techniques. Therefore, I go over the basics of AI implementations and then give some examples for using machine learning techniques, behavioral analytics, statistics, and specific tools for this domain.

Why and How Should My Company Be Engaging in This?

A few major and medium-sized companies are adopting AI and machine learning technology for its usefulness in augmenting human understanding of complex interaction and datasets by uncovering the unknowns. This enables preventing toil that could have been avoided and also frees resources to be more innovative and creative, bringing value to the businesses. That is the job of the SRE.

Some SRE Problems Machine Learning Can Help Solve

Supposedly, we could solve all the problems that arise for SREs using techniques of automatic treatment of routines and carefully observing all past events, inferring strategies for regeneration of processes and services. But that day is yet to come, and we now can foresee such horizons only by investigating innovative forms of automation that subtly arrive to our work in the form of AI.

In my day job, we have several thousands of instances running, supporting a huge number of production sites. They are generating dozens of petabytes of data transferred from several data centers and the corresponding volume of logs and metrics. Although this can seem overwhelming at first, we are continually automating and trying to find ways in which the machines can do the job for us. Nevertheless, alerts exist, in some amount, that might get out of hand if left unchecked.

Here is a list of some operational challenges that we would like to solve in order to improve the SRE function:

- Automate noise reduction to filter out a specific stream

- Look for outliers with anomaly detection—for example, cluster malfunctions.
- Automate workflows around "situations," not individual alerts.
- Automate ticket categorization based on patterns of behavior.
- Forecast short-term for service levels and long-term for capacity planning.

In addition to these are other existing solutions—for example, for text analysis like spam filtering, sentiment analysis, and information extraction.

All of these will hopefully reduce toil and alerts for humans by letting the machine do its job.

The Awakening of Applied AI

As senior site reliability engineer at my organization, I tend to search for long-term solutions that make the machine do the work for us—the best path to reach durable automation.

This is the story of an investigation that is still ongoing. It has left me sometimes frustrated, there being so many complex software options (see Figure 18-1), apart from a lot of work and hours spent collecting server data, arranging it, and processing it. But on one of those tiring nights, after putting the kids to bed, I sat down and randomly picked up a movie from 1968 to watch. This single masterpiece, produced 50 years ago, had so much to do with this research that it inspired me with a few clear ideas about what we could do. Kubrick's *2001: A Space Odyssey* has an almost encrypted message that intelligence is the higher paradigm of evolution; it combines science, technology, philosophy, history, memory—much like AI combines them. The movie's only problem was that it was too generous in foreseeing the future that would happen for the year 2001. It's 2018 and we're not quite there yet. The visionary for the movie was Arthur C. Clarke, who combined AI with a Fully Automated Service capable of forecasting system and hardware failures hours in advance. HAL 9000 is the dream (or the nightmare) of a self-sustained, self-regulated, and flawless machine that serves both the crew and the mission in order to achieve the objectives defined by humans. I strongly believe that we are now, in 2018, very close to *2001*'s incredible imagined achievements.

Data science and machine learning software have been available for some time now. The languages they use makes them more reachable by engineers to explore new ways to apply machine learning. In Figure 18-1, we see Python and the R language being the clear winners in this field. Notably, Anaconda, TensorFlow, and scikit-learn all use Python for interfacing with the user. For the hands-on section later in this chapter, we use TensorFlow, Python, and some Keras.

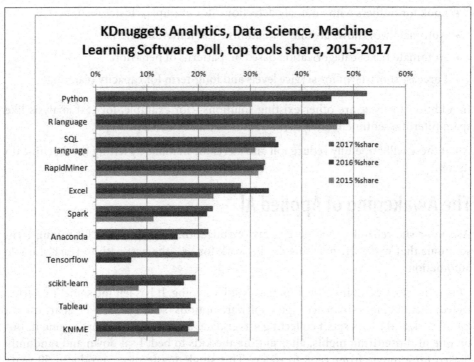

Figure 18-1. Different software for machine learning (source: https://www.kdnug gets.com/2017/05/poll-analytics-data-science-machine-learning-software-leaders.html)

What Is Machine Learning?

Machine learning refers to the statistical methods used to create algorithms that *learn* to improve performance over time, with increased emphasis on using computers to statistically estimate complicated functions and proving confidence intervals around these functions. These methods use two central approaches to statistics: *frequentist estimators* and *Bayesian inference*. The AI market is projected to swell to $3 trillion by 2024, and machine learning, which is a part of AI, is the biggest chunk of this growth.

Every time you use Google Search to find something, every time Facebook recognizes your friend's face, every time your computer marks something as spam—those are all examples of machine learning. Machine learning works by using *intelligent agents*.[2] An agent is an AI concept; it is anything that can be viewed as perceiving its environment through data or sensors and acting upon that environment through data or sen-

---

2 Russell, S. J. and Peter Norvig. *Artificial Intelligence—A Modern Approach*. Upper Saddle River, NJ: Pearson Education, 2003, Chapter 2.

sors and acting upon that environment, toward achieving goals, by actuators and displaying, sending, or writing data.

We can divide most machine learning algorithms into three broad categories: *supervised* learning, *unsupervised* learning, and *reinforcement* learning. Figure 18-2 illustrates these categories.

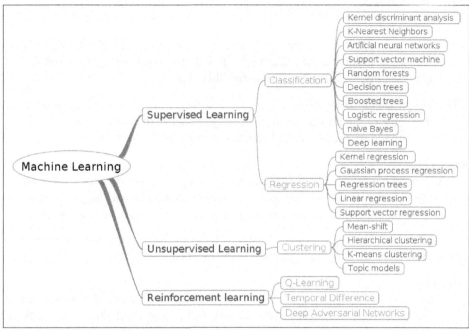

Figure 18-2. Machine learning categories

What Do We Mean by Learning?

Let's look at a modern definition of learning in terms of the machine:

> *A computer program is said to learn from experience E with respect to some class of tasks T and performance measure P, if its performance at tasks in T, as measured by P, improves with experience E.*
>
> —Tom Mitchell[3]

Let's give a clear example for learning to play checkers:

- **E** = the experience of playing many games of checkers
- **T** = the task of playing checkers.

---

3 Definition proposed by Tom Mitchell in 1998, Machine Learning Research.

- **P** = the probability that the program will win the next game

We can solve many kinds of tasks within the three main types of learning:

In *supervised learning*, the agent receives some examples of input to output and learns a function that maps from input to output. Here are some of supervised learning's common tasks:

Classification
> In this type of task, the computer program is asked to specify to which of *k* categories some input belongs. Example: find if the input server data belongs to either "Healthy," "Unhealthy," or some other class.

Classification with missing inputs
> When some of the inputs might be missing, rather than providing a single classification function, the learning algorithm must learn a set of functions.

Regression
> A regression task is a kind of machine learning problem that tries to predict a continuous (typically, floating-point) value for an input based on previous information. Example: predict storage usage given a set of features of a server dataset.

In *unsupervised learning*, the agent learns patterns in the input, despite the fact that no concrete feedback is given. Following is the most common task:

Clustering
> Clusters of useful input examples are detected. For example, a machine might gradually develop a concept of "good site traffic" and "bad site traffic" without ever having a human teaching intervention.

In *reinforcement learning*, the agent learns by using rewards (reinforcements). For example, it can be penalized for not spotting a security occurrence in a traffic stream or awarded points for every correct finding. The agent will then do better over time.

Of course, other tasks and types of tasks are possible, like anomaly detection, and there are still many being discovered as of this writing. The types of tasks we list here are intended only as examples of machine learning basics; keep in mind that AI has a larger scope than machine learning.

From Chess to Go: How Deep Can We Dive?

Historically, the reason why AI gained traction in the first place and made huge progress in dedicated computation power has been due to search algorithms and their use in games. Although solving problems using search algorithms tends to be slower, code also needs to be implemented that, most of the time, demands a lot of memory with huge time complexity (*https://en.wikipedia.org/wiki/Time_complexity*). This includes not only the MiniMax algorithm, shown in Figure 18-3 solving a simple tic-

tic tac puzzle, but also other search algorithms like *Breadth-First Traversal, Depth-First* search, A^* search, and many more, which are used in modern games. You can find more information on these in the books referenced in "Further Reading" on page 320.

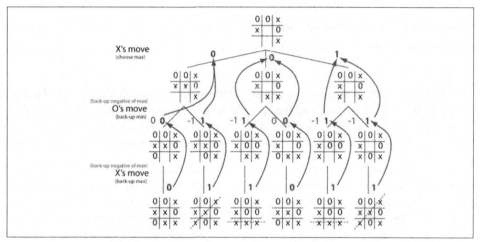

Figure 18-3. Solving problems by searching several levels of possibilities

To explain better the impact of games on AI development over the years, I would like to tell you a short story about two specific human–machine games. In 1997, in the second of two six-game chess matches, Garry Kasparov, the world chess champion, lost a chess game to Deep Blue, a machine from IBM. This outcome got everyone thinking that machines like Deep Blue would solve very important problems.

In 2015, nearly 20 years later, the ancient Chinese game Go, which has many more possible moves than chess, was won by DeepMind,[4] using a program called AlphaGo, via the application of *deep reinforcement learning*, which is a much different approach than using search algorithms. Table 18-1 compares the two machines and their methodologies.

---

4 DeepMind Technologies is a British artificial intelligence company founded in September 2010. It was acquired by Google in 2014.

Table 18-1. The two machines and their methodologies

Deep Blue; Chess; May 1997	DeepMind; AlphaGo; October 2015
• Brute force	• Deep learning
• Search Algorithm	• Machine learning
• Developer: **IBM**	• Developer: **Google**
• Adversary: Garry Kasparov	• Adversary: Fan Hui

But the first game that gripped the world's attention in AI was checkers, with the pioneer Arthur Samuel, who coined the term "machine learning" back in 1959. This first game used alpha–beta pruning. Since then, AI has been alternating between being the key to our civilization's future and tossed on to technology's trash heap.

Today it's absolutely unfair to say "human versus machine" in any of these and other games given that the machines are in a clear position of strength. Over the past few years, we've seen AI exploding, mostly due to Graphics Processing Units (GPUs) making parallel processing faster and cheaper as well as a flood of data of every stripe: images, text, transactions, logs—you name it.

Why Now? What Changed for Us?

In the SRE world, deployments are getting faster and faster, and we (humans) can react only so fast. We need to automate more and get decisions right. And we need smarter monitoring.

The rise of AI is happening now because we have enough data[5] from all of the big data initiatives out there and cheap GPUs[6] for machine learning algorithms to churn on.

In addition, what's surprising about deep learning is how simple it is. Last decade, no one suspected that we would achieve these incredible results with respect to machine perception problems. Now, it turns out that all you need is *sufficiently large* parametric models trained with gradient descent on *sufficiently many* examples.

---

5 According to a report from IBM, "10 Key Marketing Trends For 2017," every day we create 2.5 quintillion bytes of data and 90% of the data today has been created in the past two years alone. That corresponds to 10 million Blu-ray discs, which if stacked would be as tall as four Eiffel Towers.

6 Nvidia GeForce GPU cards were initially ramped up in terms of GigaFlop (GFLOP)/s capabilities by games in need of good graphical performance to satisfy the greedy processing requirements of image rendering. GPUs surpassed CPUs in terms of GFLOP/s around 2004, and today the best graphical cards are much faster than 5,000 GFLOP/s, while CPUs are much slower at around 1,000 GFLOP/s.

It's not complicated, It's just a lot of it.

> —Richard Feynman, in the 1972 interview, Take the World from a Different Point
> of View

So that gives us a fairly good idea of why we now can do deep learning in such a reachable way and who to blame for the whole thing—gamers and games.

Next, we'll explore three different machine learning techniques: *decision trees*, *neural networks*, and *long short-term memory* networks.

Decision trees
Decision support tools that use a tree-like graph or model of decisions and their possible consequences, including chance–event outcomes, resource costs, and utility.

Long short-term memory (LSTM) networks
Well suited to learn from experience to classify, process, and predict time series given time lags of unknown size and bound between important events.

Neural networks
A bit complicated to begin with, so let's take a moment to dive into them separately.

What Are Neural Networks?

In this section, we try to answer this question by briefly walking you through the basics of neural networks, deep learning techniques, and how to apply them to real data problems.

Neurons and Neural Networks

Unfortunately, it's not possible for us to jump right into some deep learning magic Python for SRE without first talking a bit about neural networks to get a basis for our code.

A neural network is composed of *artificial neurons*. An artificial neuron is just a mathematical function conceived as a model of the biological neuron. It receives one or more inputs, and sums them to produce an output. The activation function usually has a sigmoid, or step function, shape, but can also take the form of other functions. Figure 18-4 demonstrates this relation.

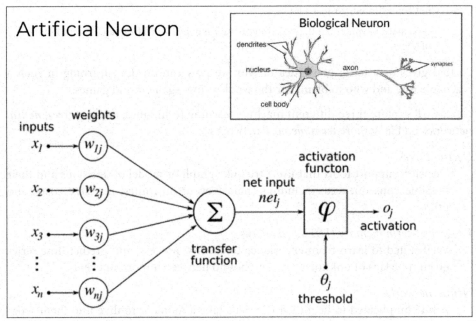

Figure 18-4. A biological neuron and an artificial neuron.

We can achieve the artificial neuron by using a simple Python function that in turn will be grouped in layers, thus creating the neural network. We directly interact with some of these layers, like the input and output layers, while some are hidden layers, as shown in Figure 18-5.

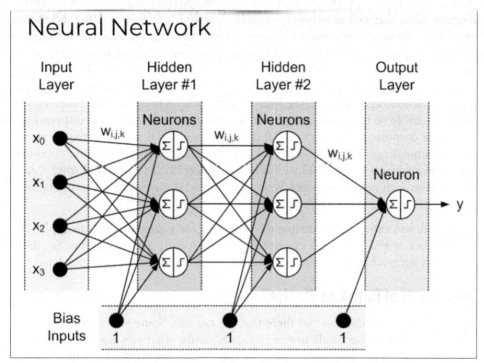

Figure 18-5. An example of a neural network with two hidden layers

How and When Should We Apply Neural Networks?

The following checklist will help you get started with using a neural network to perform machine learning tasks on your data:

1. See whether a traditional algorithm will work before applying a neural network.
2. Check whether a neural network can solve the problem.
3. Choose a library or language for that neural network architecture.
4. Format and batch the data so that is consumable.
5. Augment the data to increase the sample size for better training.
6. Feed batches to the neural network.
7. Validate during training and improve by using test data.
8. Test your model and save it for future use.

After we decide that we are indeed using a neural network or another machine learning model, we need to get the raw data, which will be unstructured most of the time. Cleaning and structuring that data will be the biggest chunk of the process, while building the model, testing, and predicting will be the last part of the process.

Keep in mind that neural networks require clear and informative data (and mostly big data) with which to train. The more training you can provide, the better your model will operate. And you need to have an appropriate type of neural network to solve the problem. Each problem has its own demands. So, the data defines the way you approach the problem. For instance, if the problem is of sequence generation, *recurrent neural networks* are more suitable. But if it is an image-related problem, you would probably be better off using *convolutional neural networks*. Last but not least, running a deep neural network model can have substantial hardware requirements. Neural networks go way back, but they are more accepted now because computational resources are better, cheaper, and more powerful. If you want to solve a real-life problem with neural networks, be ready to spend some money on computational power!

In the end, you can even decide that the best thing for your problem is to apply simple statistics or even common engineering data structure and algorithms. So, don't rush applying machine learning; first carefully analyze the problem and the data.

What Kinds of Data Can We Use?

There are plenty of datasets out there that we can use. Some are more in line with what we normally have handy in our SRE dashboards; other sets are more generic or come from the most unexpected sources. Take your time to think about what you have, what you need to assemble, and how much you have of it. Don't forget that the more data you have, the better results you can achieve. Here are the most common sources:

Machine data
    Includes log messages created by applications, trap events created by infrastructure, and alerts generated by tools.

Traffic data
    Network communications between different systems.

Agent data
    From byte-code instrumentation and call-stack sampling. Code diagnostic tools often generate this data and are commonly used by development and QA teams.

Synthetic data
    From synthetic transactions and service checks.

Human sentiment data
    The electronic coding of human communications, often in the form of service-desk tickets and social media messages, capturing perceptions and sentiment.

Practical Machine Learning

In this section, we use some tools and dive into some practical examples that we can apply to SRE.

Popular Libraries for Neural Networks

Machine learning libraries' popularity, shown in Figure 18-6, has been changing over time.

new	forks from 2018-02-10 to 2018-03-08	
#1	10836 ■■■■■■■■■■■■■■■	tensorflow/tensorflow
#2	439 ■	fchollet/keras
#3	190 ▮	BVLC/caffe
#4	185 ▮	pytorch/pytorch
#5	93	dmlc/mxnet
#6	83	caffe2/caffe2
#7	74	deeplearning4j/deeplearning4j
#8	58	PAIR-code/deeplearnjs
#9	56	Microsoft/CNTK
#10	44	davisking/dlib
#11	39	baidu/paddle

Figure 18-6. Recent GitHub popularity metrics (forks) of machine learning libraries

Popular libraries include the following:

- TensorFlow (*https://www.tensorflow.org*)
- Keras (*https://keras.io*)
- Caffe (*http://caffe.berkeleyvision.org*)
- SkLearn (*http://scikit-learn.org*)
- Theano (*http://www.deeplearning.net/software/theano*)
- Torch (*http://torch.ch*)

Over the course of this investigation we worked with all of these, but in this chapter, I focus mostly on Keras and TensorFlow.

Practical Machine Learning Examples

OK, so now let's play with some basic machine learning SRE-oriented exercises so that you get a sense of how easy it is to get started.

Installing Python, IPython, and Jupyter Notebook

For this practical guide, you need to install Python from python.org (*https://www.python.org/*), and then run the pip command, as demonstrated here (Pip is already installed on Python version 2.7.9 and above or version 3.4 and above):

```
pip install --upgrade pip
```

I also advise that you use IPython and Jupyter Notebooks in order to have your work saved in files as you proceed with testing:

```
pip install jupyter
    jupyter notebook
```

Now check your installation by creating a new notebook on the browser page that will open at *http://localhost:8888*, as illustrated in Figure 18-7. Figure 18-8 shows a Jupyter notebook solving the Fibonacci sequence.

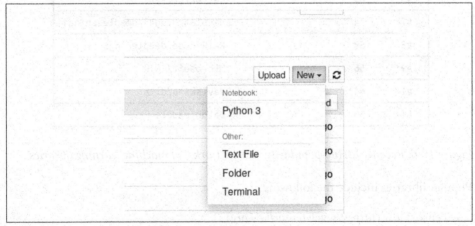

Figure 18-7. Creating a new notebook

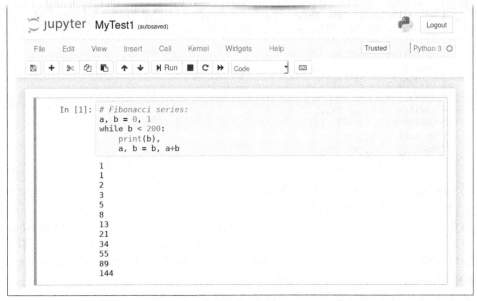

In [1]:
```
# Fibonacci series:
a, b = 0, 1
while b < 200:
    print(b),
    a, b = b, a+b
```

```
1
1
2
3
5
8
13
21
34
55
89
144
```

Figure 18-8. The Jupyter notebook solving the Fibonacci sequence

Decision trees

To give concrete examples, let's now look at some demonstrations. The first one uses a simple *decision tree* to determine whether a server is healthy or not, based on our sample data against the current CPU, RAM, and storage percent usage over the past six hours. These algorithms have always influenced a wide area of machine learning and are used both in classification and regression. In this kind of analysis, we can use a decision tree to visually and explicitly represent decisions and decision making. The model follows the branching structure of a tree as it makes decisions and is frequently used in data mining in order to reach a particular goal.

First, you need to install NumPy, SciPy, and scikit-learn from the command line:

```
pip install numpy scipy scikit-learn graphviz
```

Running the following Python code in the notebook, we will train a decision tree:

```
from sklearn import tree
import graphviz

# training data:
# Status,CPU,RAM,STORAGE
data = [
 ['healthy',45, 32, 65],
 ['unhealthy', 87, 67, 100],
 ['unhealthy', 100, 1, 1],
 ['unhealthy', 76, 70, 90],
 ['unhealthy', 1, 1, 100],
```

```
['unhealthy', 31, 100, 50],
['healthy', 12, 65, 39],
['healthy', 20, 10, 46],
['unhealthy', 100, 50, 50],
['healthy', 34, 70, 37],
['healthy', 1, 50, 50],
['unhealthy', 50, 50, 100],
['healthy', 50, 1, 50],
['unhealthy', 1, 100, 1],
['healthy', 50, 50, 1],
['healthy', 53, 53, 80],
]

metrics = [row[1:] for row in data]
states = [row[0] for row in data]
```

In this initial part of the code, notice that we begin by importing the tree model from sklearn library and also graphviz for the graph that you'll see in Figure 18-9. The data variable is populated with samples of several healthy servers. State names are given to the y-axis, and metrics to the x-axis:

```
mytree = tree.DecisionTreeClassifier()
mytree = mytree.fit(metrics, states)
```

After populating the dataset, we instantiate the mytree object with the decision tree classifier from scikit-learn and train the model with our previous data. mytree.fit takes (x-axis,y-axis) from earlier:

```
# is 10% cpu, 80% RAM, 10% Storage healthy?
print("10% CPU, 80% RAM, 10% Storage", (mytree.predict([[10, 80, 10]])))
# is 80% cpu, 10% RAM, 90% Storage healthy?
print("80% CPU, 10% RAM, 90% Storage (high)", mytree.predict([[80, 10, 90]]))
# is 60% cpu, 90% RAM, 10% Storage healthy?
print("60% CPU, 90% RAM (high), 10% Storage", mytree.predict([[60, 90, 10]]))
```

This results in the following output:

```
10% CPU, 80% RAM, 10% Storage ['healthy']
80% CPU, 10% RAM, 90% Storage (high) ['unhealthy']
60% CPU, 90% RAM (high), 10% Storage ['unhealthy']
```

Next, we test and print the results of the prediction, as illustrated in Figure 18-9. Notice that decision tree was able to figure out that the unhealthy ones have high CPU and RAM usage, as we intended with our training:

```
# Visualize the decision tree
dot_data = tree.export_graphviz(mytree,
feature_names=['CPU','RAM','Storage'],
class_names=['healthy','unhealthy'],
filled=True, rounded=True,out_file=None)

graphviz.Source(dot_data)
```

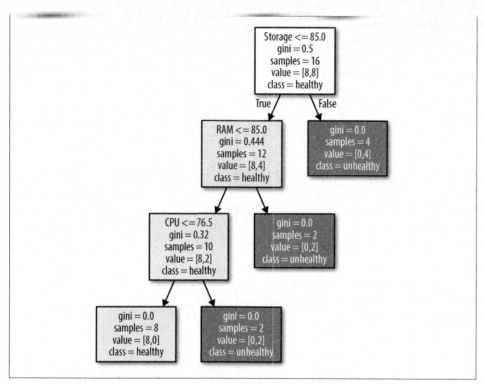

Figure 18-9. Resulting decision tree: right side branches are false, and left side branches get closer to true until the last branch

Finally, let's briefly analyze how this works. Figure 18-9 shows the decision tree we created with our training. The data upon which it made its decision passes through a series of Boolean decisions based on the values it has for comparison. If any of the checks return false, it returns `'unhealthy'`, but if all checks return true, we have `'healthy'`.

This demonstration has shown that by using a simple set of data and a decision tree, we can already do a lot.

A neural network from scratch

Next, let's explore some more examples, like some simple Python code to train a three-layer neural network from scratch. First, just using NumPy, we can construct a simple neuron using a "Sigmoid." This is the activation of a neuron, a function that will map any value to a value between 0 and 1 so that it *creates probabilities* out of numbers:

```
import numpy as np

def nonlin(x,deriv=False):
```

```
    if(deriv==True):
        return (x*(1-x))
    return (1/(1+np.exp(-x)))
```

Figure 18-10 shows the preceding code in action.

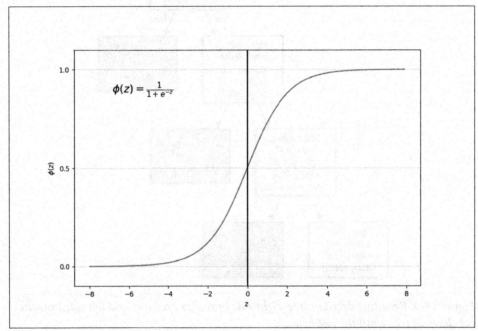

Figure 18-10. A Sigmoid function

The artificial neuron that we saw in Figure 18-4 has different inputs $(x_1...x^n)$ with different weights $(w_1...w_n)$. The weighted sum of these inputs is then passed through a Sigmoid or a Heaviside step function f, as shown here:

```
# Initialize the dataset as a matrix with input Data:
X = np.array([[0,0,1],
              [0,1,1],
              [1,0,1],
              [1,1,1]])

# Output Data with one output neuron each:
Y = np.array([[1],
              [0.7],
              [1],
              [0]])
# Seed to make them deterministic
np.random.seed(1)
# Create synapse matrices.
synapse0 = 2 * np.random.random((3, 4)) - 1
synapse1 = 2 * np.random.random((4, 1)) - 1
```

First, we initialize the dataset as a matrix with input data (X). Each row is a different training example and each column represents a different neuron. The output data (y) has one output neuron each, and we seed them to make them deterministic; this yields random numbers with the same starting point (useful for debugging), so we can get the same sequence of generated numbers every time we run the program. To complete this simple neural network, we create two *synapse matrices* and initialize the weights of the neural network. We have just created a neural network with two layers of weights:

```python
# Training code (loop)
for j in xrange(100000):
    # Layers layer0,layer1,layer2
    layer0 = X
    # Prediction step
    layer1 = nonlin(np.dot(layer0, synapse0))
    layer2 = nonlin(np.dot(layer1, synapse1))
    # Get the error rate
    layer2_error = Y - layer2
    # Print the average error
    if(j % 10000) == 0:
        print "Error:" + str(np.mean(np.abs(layer2_error)))
    # Multiply the error rate
    layer2_delta = layer2_error * nonlin(layer2, deriv=True)
    # Backpropagation
    layer1_error = layer2_delta.dot(synapse1.T)
    # Get layer1's delta
    layer1_delta = layer1_error * nonlin(layer1, deriv=True)
    # Gradient Descent
    synapse1 += layer1.T.dot(layer2_delta)
    synapse0 += layer0.T.dot(layer1_delta)
```

The training code in the preceding example is a bit more involved, where we optimize the network for the given dataset. The first layer (`layer0`) is just our input data. The prediction step performs matrix multiplication between each layer and its synapse. We then run the Sigmoid function on the matrix to create the next layer. With the `layer1`/`layer2` prediction of the output in `layer2`, we can compare it to the expected output data by using subtraction to get an error rate. We then keep printing the average error at a set interval to make sure it goes down every time.

We multiply the error rate by the slope of the Sigmoid at the values in `layer2` and do *backpropagation*,[7] which is short for "backward propagation of errors"—i.e., what `layer1` contributed to the error on `layer2`, and multiply `layer2` delta by synapses 1's transpose.

---

7 The primary algorithm for performing *gradient descent* on *neural networks*. First, the output values of each node are calculated (and cached) in a forward pass. Then, the partial derivative of the error with respect to each parameter is calculated in a backward pass through the graph.

Next, we get `layer1`'s delta by multiplying its error by the result of the Sigmoid function and do *gradient descent*,[8] a first-order iterative optimization algorithm for finding the minimum of a function, where we finally update weights. Now that we have deltas for each of our layers, we can use them to update our synapse rates to reduce the error rate even more every time we iterate. This produces the following:

```
Error:0.434545246367
Error:0.00426490134801
Error:0.00285547679431
Error:0.00226684843815
Error:0.00192718684831
Error:0.00170049171577
Error:0.00153593455208
Error:0.00140973826096
Error:0.00130913223749
Error:0.00122657710472
```

This means the error is getting closer to zero, as our neural network learns. And if we print each `layer2` and our objective:

```
print "Output after training"
print layer2

Output after training
[[ 0.99998867]
 [ 0.69999105]
 [ 0.99832904]
 [ 0.00293799]]


print "Initial Objective"
print Y

Initial Objective
[[ 1. ]
 [ 0.7]
 [ 1. ]
 [ 0. ]]
```

we have successfully created a neural network using just NumPy and some math, and trained it to get closer to the initial objective by using backpropagation and gradient descent. This can be useful in bigger scenarios in which we teach a neural network to recognize patterns like anomaly detection, sound, images, or even certain occurrences in our platform, as we will see.

---

8 A technique to minimize *loss* by computing the gradients of loss with respect to the model's parameters, conditioned on training data. Informally, gradient descent iteratively adjusts parameters, gradually finding the best combination of *weights* and bias to minimize loss.

Google's TensorFlow is nothing but the NumPy we just looked at with a huge twist, as we will see now. The major difference is that TensorFlow first builds a graph of all the operations to be done, and then when a "session" is called, it "runs" the graph. It's built to be scalable and takes advantage of the GPU via CUDA. Keras, another library, simplifies TensorFlow's coding (see Figure 18-11).

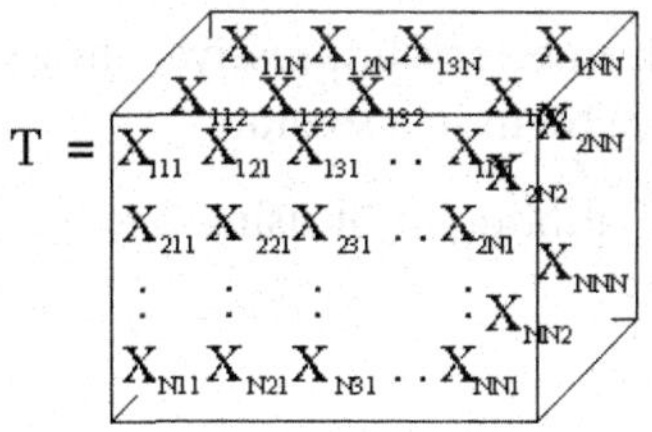

$$T = \begin{bmatrix} X_{111} & X_{121} & X_{131} & \cdots & X_{1N1} \\ X_{211} & X_{221} & X_{231} & \cdots & X_{2N1} \\ \vdots & \vdots & \vdots & & \vdots \\ X_{N11} & X_{N21} & X_{N31} & \cdots & X_{NN1} \end{bmatrix}$$

Figure 18-11. A tensor[9]

Keep in mind that TensorFlow doesn't have "neurons," per se, but it does love linear algebra. The neuron is a past fixation on the biological metaphor. Everything is just *matrix math*—or, for arbitrary dimensions, *tensor math*. This is the choice Tensor-Flow makes. It makes TensorFlow really flexible and lets it achieve efficient computation that would be more difficult otherwise.

You can install TensorFlow from the `pip` package manager:

```
pip install tensorflow
```

To test the installation, you can run this set of commands:

```
import tensorflow as tf
a = tf.constant(1.0)
b = tf.constant(2.0)
c = a + b
sess = tf.Session()
print(sess.run(c))
```

The resulting operation is diagrammed in Figure 18-12.

---

9 In mathematics, *tensors* are geometric objects that describe linear relations between geometric vectors, scalars, and other tensors. Elementary examples of such relations include the dot product, the cross product, and linear maps. (Source: *https://en.wikipedia.org/wiki/Tensor.*)

Figure 18-12. Resulting operation

Ignore any warnings about the CPU. The result of our TensorFlow run should be 3.0.

The preceding test, although not very impressive, shows how TensorFlow declares things, before actually running them in a session.

The following Python code,[10] although not using a real dataset, does some data neuron training using TensorFlow:

```
1  import tensorflow as tf
2
3  x = tf.constant(1.0, name='input')
4  w = tf.Variable(0.8, name='weight')
5  y = tf.multiply(w, x, name='output')
6  y_ = tf.constant(0.0, name='correct_value')
7  loss = tf.pow(y - y_, 2, name='loss')
8  train_step = tf.train.GradientDescentOptimizer(0.025).minimize(loss)
9
10 for value in[x, w, y, y_, loss]:
11     tf.summary.scalar(value.op.name, value)
12
13 session = tf.Session()
14
15 summaries = tf.summary.merge_all()
16 summary_writer = tf.summary.FileWriter('log_simple_stats', session.graph)
17
18 session.run(tf.global_variables_initializer())
19 for i in range(100):
20     summary_writer.add_summary(session.run(summaries), i)
21     session.run(train_step)
22     if (i % 10) == 0: print (session.run(y))
23
24 summary_writer.close()
```

This code imports TensorFlow and creates a graph on it using the definitions from lines 3 through 8.

Initially, the system takes the input 1.0 and returns 0.8, which is wrong because the 'correct_value' is 0.0. We need a way to measure how wrong the system is. Let's call that measure the "loss" and give our system the goal of minimizing the loss in the

---

10 *https://www.oreilly.com/learning/hello-tensorflow*; credit: Aaron Schumacher.

training_step using the gradient descent optimizer to make the neuron learn what the value should be.

On line 13, we start our TensorFlow session. Then, we prepare some summaries to visualize on the TensorBoard, and we finally run our session optimizing in a 100-step loop at line 19.

The run shows the output getting closer and closer to 0 as expected by the optimization:

```
0.76
0.45504
0.272449
0.163125
0.0976692
0.0584782
0.035013
0.0209636
0.0125517
0.00751515
```

TensorBoard is a graphical dashboard that displays the summaries saved during the execution of one or more TensorFlow programs. You can obtain and visualize the graph and the values of this operation there:

```
25  !tensorboard --logdir=log_simple_stats

    Starting TensorBoard b'54' at http://localhost:6006
    (Press CTRL+C to quit)
```

Notice that we ran the preceding optimization before starting TensorBoard, while the values are kept on log_simple_stats for later usage by TensorBoard. The results are now as expected, as demonstrated in Figures 18-13 and 18-14.

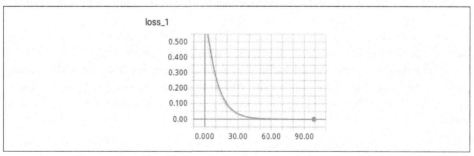

Figure 18-13. The loss function being minimized

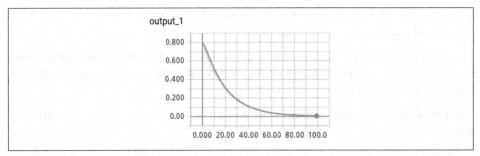

Figure 18-14. The neuron's output training 100 times

Looking at the Graphs tab on TensorBoard, we see our Main graph and an auxiliary GradientDescent graph that was used to find the minimum of our function, as depicted in Figure 18-15.

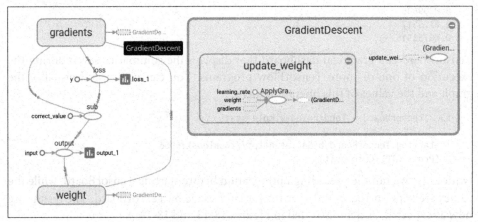

Figure 18-15. Main graph and an auxiliary GradientDescent graph in TensorBoard

Besides visualizing graphs and scalars data, TensorBoard also allows you to see image data, audio data, distributions, histograms, embeddings, and text. That's why I think it's a great tool that you should include in your machine learning for SRE learning path. TensorBoard produces both powerful and somewhat complex graphs. However, using TensorFlow with graph visualization can help you understand and debug them.

There are a lot of ready-to-use TensorFlow models that you can find in the Tensor-Flow GitHub repository, together with a CPU and a GPU Dockerfile, at *https://github.com/tensorflow/models*, including:

Mnist
    A basic model to classify image digits from the MNIST dataset.

A deep residual network that you can use to classify both CIFAR-10 and Image-Net's dataset of 1,000 classes.

Wide_deep

A model that combines a wide model and deep network to classify census income data.

Time series: server requests waiting

Up to this point, we haven't yet seen the best out of machine learning for SRE. In my opinion, I believe that distinction rests with time series. A time series is a signal that is measured in regular time steps. In this example, we see a set of server requests that experiences a huge jump around May 2017, as shown in Figure 18-16.

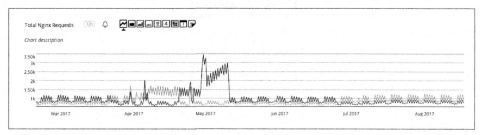

Figure 18-16. A time series example

How nice would it be if we could do the following:

- Use anomaly detection to find and trigger responsive automation
- Forecast server requests a few hours in advance

Before we can use this data, there are a few important points to keep in mind:

- The estimation of future values in a time series is commonly done using past values of the same time series.
- Notice that the time step of a series may be of any length, for example seconds, hours, days, years, and so on.
- We need to choose a correct time step for what we want to predict, and, for that, it needs to be tested. It needs to be tried several times and with different values before we get to a final choice.
- Deep learning, despite being a data science, has a lot of trial and error before getting to a good solution, mostly because it deals with probabilities.

In the example that follows, shown in Figure 18-17, we grab several months of nginx requests data and try to predict the tendency over the next 20 hours. This model is experimental right now, and like weather prediction, it can fail. This is a recurrent neural network with sequential model, used in the Keras code using TensorFlow backend, which is available online:

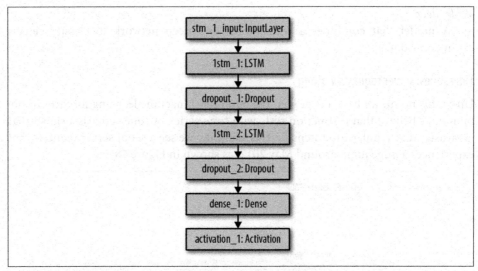

Figure 18-17. Recurrent neural network with sequential model. (source: https:// github.com/ricardoamaro/MachineLearning4SRE/blob/master/ demo_predicting_nginx_requests-Final.ipynb)

The provided code in the repository loads the data, normalizes it, predicts sequences, and plots the results, which you can see in Figure 18-18. The actual training is done in 100 epochs.

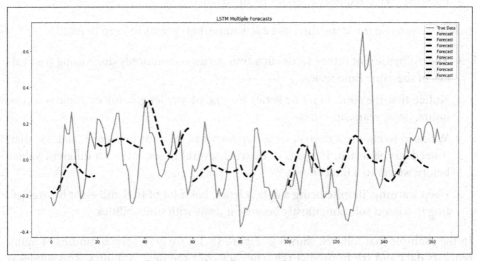

Figure 18-18. Time series forecasting based on past data

The output graph shows a sample of 100 hours of traffic from the past data we obtained, which we call the test set. The model was trained using 120 days of data against a cross-validation set of also 160 hours. This was the ratio that returned the best results. The black dashed lines represent around 20-hour predictions in the future, which are not perfect but clearly give an idea that the model was able to predict the tendency of the traffic.

In conclusion, these results clearly show good progress in forecasting within a certain time frame in the future, including a presence of a spike, such that we could actually provision new hardware if needed, avoiding an outage problem. For SRE, this type of analysis can be useful—for instance, in incident response and capacity planning.

Success Stories

There are a few areas of enterprise IT for which AI has and will have a significant impact:

- Log analysis
- Capacity planning
- Infrastructure scaling
- Cost management
- Performance tuning
- Energy efficiency
- Security

Recently, Google started managing data center cooling through DeepMind. In one instance, it managed to *reduce the amount of energy used by 40 percent*, as illustrated in Figure 18-19.

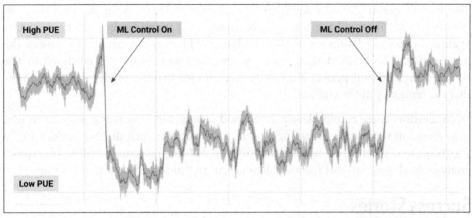

Figure 18-19. Reduction of 40% spent on data center energy using DeepMind (source: https://deepmind.com/blog/deepmind-ai-reduces-google-data-centre-cooling-bill-40)

It accomplished this by using the historical sensor data, such as temperatures, power, pump speeds, setpoints, and so on, that were already collected by thousands of units in the data center. This data was then used to train an ensemble of deep neural networks on the average future Power Usage Effectiveness (PUE), and the model was used and tested directly on the data center cooling system.

Neural networks are also being used extensively in image recognition. For example, data center security is using it to spot nonauthorized personnel by analyzing video frames from surveillance cameras in real time.

Apart from neural networks and deep learning, there are, of course, other machine learning success examples out there, such as Naive Bayes classifiers, that filter email spam automatically and have been used in the industry for a long time with great success. Your email provider is probably using this today.

Another field of IT where we have seen good results from machine learning is in security, where anomaly detection, for instance, is used for credit card fraud detection and many other applications that improve the security automation immensely with outlier detection.

Further Reading

This chapter has taken a very light approach to the subjects of machine learning and AI. If you want to go deeper into your investigation, I suggest exploring some open source code, some of which you can find in my repository and two reference books. *Deep Learning* you can read online for free at *deeplearningbook.org*, or get the print version. It's time to apply machine learning in your organization.

My GitHub Repository

- *https://github.com/ricardoamaro/MachineLearning4SRE*

Recommended Books

- Russell, Stuart J., Peter Norvig, and John F. Canny. *Artificial Intelligence: A Modern Approach.* Upper Saddle River, NJ: Pearson International (2003).
- Goodfellow, Ian, Yoshua Bengio, and Aaron Courville. *Deep Learning.* Cambridge, MA: MIT Press (2016). *www.mitpress.mit.edu/books/deep-learning.*

Ricardo Amaro is currently performing senior site reliability engineering functions in Acquia, one of the largest companies in the world of Free Software with around 20,000 servers in production. Ricardo is president of ADP—Associação Drupal Portugal and had his first contact with open technologies and especially Linux in the '90s. Ricardo started applying Agile techniques and encouraging the DevOps culture very early. He is also a passionate advocate of free software, digital rights, and is a frequent speaker at IT events.

## PART III

SRE Best Practices and Technologies

- SRE needs better ways to do documentation.
- Can you teach SRE through a game?
- Your SLOs are measuring the wrong thing.
- How do you know when SRE is a success?
- What are the SRE antipatterns?
- Immutable infrastructure, scriptable load balancers, and service meshes can makes SRE easier.

Discuss.

You Know You're an SRE When...

...you find yourself buying extras of everything because two is one and one is none.

...you are involved in a new feature from design to deploy.

...Production readiness reviews are something to look forward to.

...you wonder what your power company's SLO is.

## CHAPTER 19

Do Docs Better: Integrating Documentation into the Engineering Workflow

Ríona MacNamara and Shylaja Nukala, with Stas Miasnikoŭ,
Aaron Gillies, Jeremy Sharpe, Google, and Niall Richard Murphy,
Microsoft

Across the software industry, confidence in engineering documentation is low. Stack Overflow's 2016 developer survey (*https://insights.stackoverflow.com/survey/ 2016#work-challenges-at-work*) ranked documentation as the number two challenge facing developers.

This is a problem. Missing, incomplete, or stale or inaccurate documentation hurts development velocity, software quality, and—critically for SREs—service reliability. And the frustration it creates can be a major cause of job unhappiness for developers (*https://arxiv.org/pdf/1703.04993.pdf*).

Documentation takes time and effort, and this is especially challenging for SREs. SREs often spend 35% of their time on operational work, which leaves only 65% for development. Time spent on documentation needs to come out of the development budget, and this is challenging if there's a perception that creating and maintaining documentation is grunge work that might not be recognized or rewarded during performance review and promotion processes.

How can this be changed? How do you make your organization understand the value of engineering documentation, encourage engineers to create and maintain it, and convince management and leadership that doing so is an activity worthy of recognition, funding, and reward?

At Google, we're lucky to have a strong technical writing organization, but our writers tend to focus on high-impact, high-visibility projects. The truth is that most engineering and SRE teams need to create and maintain their own documentation, and they have not always found this easy or appealing. However, since 2015 we have made significant progress in improving the quality and availability of internal engineering information. In this chapter, we share what we've learned and provide recommendations in the hope that they will be useful to the SRE, SWE, or technical writer looking to do docs better. In particular, we focus on the following:

Defining documentation quality
> We propose a framework and vocabulary for defining documentation quality and show (with a focus on SRE operations) how you can use these to define documentation requirements.

Integrating documentation into the engineering workflow
> Documentation is a core part of engineering work. *In theory!* In practice, the creation and maintenance of documentation often requires expensive context switching and, as a result, tends to be neglected. We share our experience of integrating documentation with our code base and workflow tools.

Communicating the value of documentation
> To drive change in an organization and to convince leadership that documentation is worth the investment, you need to be able to communicate the business impact of your documentation work.

It might be true that documentation is not fully integrated into engineering practices today. Luckily, there is a precedent we can look to for inspiration, vocabulary, and models: software testing. Ten years ago, testing was very much in the same situation that documentation is now: ad hoc, unstandardized, and unpredictable. Today at Google, unit testing, regression testing, and integration testing are all so deeply integrated into engineering processes and tooling that pushing untested code to production simply isn't practical. Testing at Google is a rigorous, highly accepted practice that is fully integrated into the engineering workflow. We can do the same for documentation.

Defining Quality: What Do Good Docs Look Like?

The definition of documentation quality is, essentially, simple:

> A document is good *when it fulfills its purpose.*

But before we can measure or report on documentation quality, we need a vocabulary for describing it. In this section, we propose a vocabulary lifted directly from the field of software testing, where it is used to describe various aspects of software quality. Essentially, there are two aspects of documentation quality—*structural quality* and *functional quality*—that each contribute to the overall quality of a document.

Structural quality is what usually comes to mind when one is describing technical documentation, and it's definitely the quality that is being invoked when technical writers refer to themselves as "wordsmiths." Structural quality describes *what the documentation should be like*. A document or document set has high structural quality if it meets the following criteria:

- Spelling and grammar are correct
- It complies with style and usage guidelines
- It uses proper voice and tone
- It's well organized and easy to navigate

Structural quality can be relatively easy to determine: spelling is either correct or it isn't; style is followed or it isn't; links work or they don't. This ease of measurement makes it tempting to use structural quality as the default measure of quality for your doc set. If you're measured and evaluated on the basis of the structural quality of your docs, it's tempting to overemphasize it at the expense of overall quality. Docs need only be good enough for their purpose, and internal-facing docs describing a system that is constantly in flux require a lower level of polish and style than customer-facing content.

Functional quality, on the other hand, describes the *effectiveness* of your docs. A document with high functional quality is one that satisfies its stated requirements. These requirements generally reflect business goals. For example, outages cost money and erode customer experience, so they need to be resolved quickly. Therefore, playbooks relied on by SREs need to be complete and up to date; service overviews need to cover the basic information required to understand a service; and postmortems need to include information needed to understand what happened and provide a list of action items for reducing the possibility of recurrence and/or make recovery more straightforward.

For example, for a playbook, we can ask whether it provides all the information an SRE needs to handle an emergency or outage:

- Does the playbook provide 100% coverage of alerts?
- Can the team rely on the playbook to perform on-call duties?
- Is the playbook reliable (highly available)?
- Is it easy to create and update entries?
- Is each alert description accurate and complete?
- Does each entry give enough information to understand and resolve the alert?
- Does the entry give guidance on escalation?

Now, it's definitely true that functional quality often depends on structural quality. The most effective instructions in the world won't be useful if SREs can't navigate to them, or their links are broken, or the language is unintelligible. But the truth is that functional quality is *always* more important:

- High structural quality + low functional quality = poor overall quality
- OK structural quality + good functional quality = good overall quality

Of course, high functional quality + high structural quality is ideal. But it might not be worth the effort. SRE doesn't strive for 100% reliability in production, and we shouldn't strive for perfection in documentation. Perfection costs too much, and its pursuit comes at the cost of work that could improve other documentation or even your service itself. What's important, especially for internal documentation, is that critical information exists and is clearly conveyed.

Because it's so tightly tied to business and product goals, functional quality has a much stronger relationship to what we perceive as *value*. We believe that to meet the goals of our business, functional quality must be our primary goal.

Functional Requirements for SRE Documentation

In this section, we look at what SRE documentation must deliver to support the core SRE functions, including the following:

Monitoring and metrics
Establishing desired service behavior, measuring how the service is actually behaving, and correcting discrepancies

Emergency response
Noticing and responding effectively to service failures in order to preserve the service's conformance to the Service-Level Agreement (SLA)

Capacity planning
Projecting future demand and ensuring that a service has enough capacity in appropriate locations to satisfy that demand

Service turnup and turndown
Instantiating and deleting service capacity in a predictable fashion, often as a consequence of capacity planning

Change management
Altering the behavior of a service while preserving desired service behavior

Performance
Design, development, and engineering related to scalability, isolation, latency, throughput, and efficiency

To do their job, SREs need to be effective across two domains (development and operations), and they need documentation to understand and run services in production. However, in this section we limit ourselves to discussing examples of the core documents SREs rely on to run production services. These include *service overviews*, *playbooks* and *procedures*, *postmortems*, *policies*, and *SLAs*. A comprehensive discussion of all types of SRE documentation is unfortunately beyond the scope of this chapter—as are the general requirements for project developer documentation—but you can apply the principles we describe to all technical documentation.

Service overviews

These are critical for SRE understanding of the services they support. SREs need to understand the system architecture, components and dependencies, and service contacts and owners. Service overviews are a collaborative effort between the development team and the SRE team. They are designed to guide and prioritize SRE engagement and uncover areas for further investigation. These overviews are often an output of the production readiness review (*https://landing.google.com/sre/book/chapters/evolving-sre-engagement-model.html*) process.

A basic service overview provides SREs with enough information about the service to dig deeper, which is particularly important for onboarding new SREs. A complete service overview provides a thorough description of the service and how it reacts with the world around it as well as links to dashboards, metrics, and related information that SREs need to solve unexpected issues.

Playbooks

Playbooks are quintessential operational docs, and they enable on-call engineers to respond to alerts generated by service monitoring. Playbooks contain instructions for verification, troubleshooting, and escalation for each alert generated from monitoring processes. Playbooks typically match alert names generated from monitoring systems. They contain commands and steps that need to be tested and reviewed for accuracy. They often require updates when new troubleshooting processes become available, and when new failure modes are uncovered or dependencies are added.

Playbooks are not exclusive to alerts and can also include *production procedures* for pushing releases, monitoring, and troubleshooting. Other examples of production procedures include service turnup and turndown, service maintenance, and emergency/escalation.

Postmortems

SREs work with large-scale, complex, distributed systems, and they also enhance services with new features and addition of new systems. Therefore, incidents and outages are inevitable given the velocity of change. Postmortems are an essential tool for SRE, and they represent SRE's formalized process of learning from incidents.

A postmortem describes a production outage or paging event, including (at minimum): a timeline, description of user impact, root cause, and action items and lessons learned. The postmortem is written by a member of the group that experienced the outage, preferably someone who was involved and can take responsibility for the follow-up. A postmortem needs to be written in a blameless manner (*https://land ing.google.com/sre/book/chapters/postmortem-culture.html*). It should include the information needed to understand what happened, and a list of action items that would significantly reduce the possibility of recurrence, reduce the impact, and/or make recovery more straightforward.

Policies

These are documents that mandate specific technical and nontechnical policies for production.

Technical policies can apply to areas such as production change logging, logs retention, internal service naming (naming conventions engineers should adopt as they implement services), and use of protocols governing emergency access.

Policies can also apply to process. Escalation policies help engineers to classify production issues as emergencies and nonemergencies, and provide recommendations on the appropriate action for each category. On-call expectations policies outline the structure and responsibilities of team members.

SLAs

SRE teams document their service(s) SLA for availability and latency, and monitor service performance relative to the SLA.

Documenting and publishing an SLA and rigorously measuring the end-user experience and comparing it to the SLA allows SRE teams to innovate more quickly. This also results in less friction between SRE and SWE teams because they can negotiate targets and results objectively and avoid subjective discussions of risk.

Defining success metrics

As you define your documentation requirements, it's also important to define how you will *measure* the functional quality of your docs. This is important both for ongoing maintenance and improvement for your docs, but it's also essential if you want to be able to communicate the value of your work to the rest of your organization.

For example, a playbook should enable an on-call SRE to respond to an alert or complete a procedure. A playbook has high functional quality if an SRE was able to handle an alert without the need for escalation, and if the postmortem did not identify documentation as a contributing factor to the incident. A service overview has high functional quality if it provides the SRE the context needed to handle an outage.

Integrating Docs into the Engineering Workflow

Based on our experience, we strongly recommend that SWE and SRE keep documentation in source control, alongside its associated code. We discuss this in more detail in the rest of this chapter, but in summary: when documentation is written in a simple format and stored in source control next to the code it describes, engineers can create and update that documentation as part of their regular engineering workflow, using their existing tools. In addition, this approach enables integration with the engineering toolchain, such as code search and review tools, and IDEs; and because the relationship between code and docs is explicit, it supports automation and better discovery of content.

The Google Experience: g3doc and EngPlay

Back in the spring of 2014, a couple of Google technical writers with some time on their hands decided to do something unprecedented: talk to their customers (internal engineers) and understand the challenges that they faced with respect to documentation. As expected, they found most engineers were deeply unhappy with the state of internal engineering docs. But almost universally they felt bad about feeling bad. They *understood* docs were important, they *knew* it wasn't possible for every team to have a technical writer, and they *wished* they could do a better job.

Some of the issues came from mismatched expectations. For users, documentation is *urgent*: they need answers now. But for creators, documentation is often low-priority, especially given the obstacles to its creation. At Google, almost all of these obstacles stemmed from fragmentation: documentation was scattered across multiple repositories, including our internal wiki, Google Docs, our intranet, and internal Google Sites (*http://sites.google.com*). This meant that in order to create or edit docs, engineers had to leave their development environment, find the right doc location, and spend time on formatting, layout, and other issues. Context switching like this is expensive. A 20-minute interruption while working on a project entails two context switches; realistically, this interruption results in a loss of a couple hours of truly productive work.

Given limited time and tough requirements, how could you justify work on documentation, especially when you weren't confident that this work would be rewarded at performance review, and particularly when it stole focus from your primary task, coding? Something had to give. Generally, it was the docs.

Granted, Google is an extreme case. Our code base, google3, is described as having more than 2 billion lines of code (*https://www.wired.com/2015/09/google-2-billion-lines-codeand-one-place/*), and might be the biggest code base in the world. Many tens of thousands of engineers work with it and Piper (the version control system that sits on top of the code base), submitting tens of thousands of changes every day, modifying millions of lines of code each week. The workflow tools engineers used every day were deeply integrated with google3 and with Piper. Coding, building, testing, and releasing software in a system like this provides extraordinary efficiencies. But these efficiencies had no impact on documentation, which lived pretty much anywhere you wanted it to and had *no* explicit connection to the project code or standard engineering workflow and tools.

What would be possible if documentation was written in a simple portable format called Markdown and stored next to its associated code? After all, GitHub's documentation model—in which docs were written in Markdown and stored with the code—worked well. Why couldn't we do the same at Google? Our initial idea was very simple: enable engineers to find, create, and maintain docs by keeping documentation in a *simple portable format* (Markdown), *next to its associated code*, and *rendering it at a URL that reflected its location in the code base*. This strategy had some obvious benefits:

- Markdown is easy to learn and easily readable in source. Its simplicity also means that it's portable: If what we designed didn't work, it would be simple to take our Markdown content and move it somewhere else.

- SWEs and SREs could edit their docs, send them for review, and submit them to source control using the exact same tools they used to create and edit code.

- Keeping the docs with their associated code would make it much easier for engineers to find them. Instead of leaving their IDE and hunting around in Sites, wiki, or Docs, engineers could just edit a Markdown file in their regular IDE and send it for review along with the code that triggered its update.

- It created the very powerful possibility of integrating rendering into our internal IDEs, generating a default expectation that at least a minimal document—a README—would be present.

- Rendering the page at a URL that reflected the location of the doc in Piper would make the association between the doc and the project clear to users searching for information on our intranet.

Our original prototype did very little other than render plain Markdown. We tested it with a couple of teams. "Wow, that's ugly," they said. "But the idea? It's...interesting." Give us a better look and feel, they said, and some navigation, and better formatting for things like code blocks, and we might use it.

The g3doc team went away and began adding these basic features as well as theming that removed the need for authors to think about formatting and look and feel. Quietly, we began working with a small number of teams to help migrate their content to the new platform. Slowly, word began spreading. As interest grew, several things happened:

- The g3doc team was joined by engineers and writers from across Google who found that g3doc was missing features crucial to their teams and who volunteered to build those features. This grass-roots, bottom-up model of development was, we believe, critical to ensuring that the platform reflected the requirements of a very broad set of users.

- Other engineering tools, such as our internal code search and review tools, and our internal IDEs added g3doc-based features such as the ability to preview a file before it was submitted to the depot. These changes were small in and of themselves, but they removed friction from the workflow and made it far more seamless to create and edit files with regular engineering workflow tools.

- The platform acquired champions: highly visible engineers and leaders who promoted its usage to their teams and organizations posted on internal social media and began requiring their teams to use g3doc.

For the first few months, adoption was slow, but about six months in, interest exploded. Adoption was largely viral: teams discovered g3doc and chose to migrate to it. Three years later (October 2017), almost all engineering documentation at Google (thousands of projects) use g3doc and its less engineering-centric cousin, Company-Doc. As a result, Google deprecated its internal wiki, resulting in less fragmentation of engineering knowledge across the company.

But even though adoption figures like these are gratifying, anybody can create documentation; what's important is that the documentation is maintained up to date, and that requires a change in developer behavior. Our theory was that if you made it as simple as possible for engineers to create and maintain documentation, and if you enabled them to do that as part of their regular workflow, and if you created a cultural expectation that docs existed, the quality of engineering documentation would improve. And it appears to be working. About 75% of all Google engineers submit doc changes monthly; an average doc file is updated several times a month; and, crucially, around a third of all changelists containing code also contain documentation files. These metrics indicate that developer behavior is changing and that documentation is in fact becoming a standard part of internal engineering practice at Google.

We also launched EngPlay, a version of g3doc intended for SRE playbooks. EngPlay provides centralized hosting for playbooks within Google. EngPlay is more resilient than g3doc, to ensure that content is available in case of outages. EngPlay also has additional features to ensure that playbooks are complete and reflect the current state of the system:

- Each alert has its own documentation page. A tool automatically compares alerts from the monitoring configs to the playbook entries and throws a warning if an alert is undocumented *or* documentation exists for a missing alert.

- If a page is not found at its expected URL, a minimalistic mechanism checks likely variants of that URL, increasing discoverability.

- Support for variables allows EngPlay to adjust alert documentation pages with information from our monitoring, such as the ID of the job that generated the alert, the ID of the affected cluster, and even live graphs that reflect the current state of the system.

Both g3doc and EngPlay use the same (EngDoc) server as a backend. EngPlay hosts playbooks with the sole focus of being extremely reliable, while g3doc is meant for general documentation. Therefore, the core differences between g3doc's capabilities and EngPlay's capabilities are conceptual.

EngPlay's reliability was a top priority from its beginning. It can survive almost all outages and is available if and when there is an emergency. Due to this need for extreme reliability, which requires EngPlay to be a separate job and have its own dedicated path in Piper to serve, its features are limited in comparison to g3doc.

What We Learned

This section outlines some of our core principles around documentation, based on our experience with g3doc and EngPlay.

Where possible, documentation should live in source control, alongside its associated code

This enables SWEs and SREs to edit their docs, send for review, and submit to source control using the same tools they use to create and edit code. As a result, engineers are far more likely to maintain the docs they do create. In addition, a predictable location for docs makes those docs more discoverable by humans and systems.

But we also discovered that keeping documentation alongside its associated code enabled new features and functionality that removed much of the toil from creating and maintaining documentation. For example:

- A Markdown linter and a formatter, eventually integrated into our IDEs and into the presubmit pipeline, removes the need to manually tinker with Markdown

- The ability to expose project metadata (such as project code locations and key contacts) from code configuration files on documentation sites

- The ability to automatically detect broken links in the documentation corpus and notify owners

- The ability to include live code in documentation instead of relying on static code blocks that are destined to decay as the underlying code changes

Our experience tells us that the best solution is for docs to live alongside code; however, we realize it's not always possible. If this g3doc-style system doesn't work for your project, the most critical step is to *choose a canonical repository for your documents.*

Pick the simplest markup language that supports your needs

The two core principles behind g3doc's decision to use Markdown are that *content must be easy to edit and read in source,* and that *content should be separated from display.* In our system, the g3doc server handles rendering and formatting. It should always be possible to ditch the renderer and read the content in source, and, in fact, in the case of certain outages, it might be essential that SRE playbooks are readable in source. Raw HTML is allowed but not encouraged for reasons of readability.

However, depending on your requirements, you might have different guiding principles. DocBook (*https://en.wikipedia.org/wiki/DocBook*) is a nightmare to read in source, but it supports a lot of flexible output. Not everyone shares our love of Markdown. People often choose it because GitHub supports it, but GitHub also supports an awful lot of other formats such as reStructured Text (RST) and ASCIIdoc. There are a lot of different flavors of Markdown (g3doc uses GitHub-flavor with some added customizations, and our renderer is based on Hoedown). Just remember that your goal is to remove as much friction as possible from the task of creating and editing documentation. Any complexity in your choice of markup language must be justified by the real benefit you get from it.

Integrations are key to adoption

Our first integration was extremely simple: the ability to preview a rendered version of a document before it was submitted to source control. Yet adding this link to our code review tool was critical to adoption, and g3doc usage surged immediately after its launch. Similarly, we made it easy to view a rendered version of a doc directly from our code search and browse tool. Many smaller integrations (such as support for short links for internal URLs and syntax highlighting) followed; none of them was critical in itself, but each removed a small piece of friction from the documentation process and made the platform far more attractive as a result. Newer integrations have focused on removing much of the toil from the process of writing documentation. For example, a linter checks files for style and formatting issues, and a formatter automatically formats Markdown files so that they comply with the g3doc style guide. Both of these tools can be invoked from all IDEs used internally.

Essentially, the most important lesson we learned is that *engineers will create and maintain documentation if you make it as simple as possible for them to do so.*

Doing Docs Better: Best Practices

In this section, we cover recommendations for documentation practices to improve the quality of the documentation for your organization.

Create Templates for Each Documentation Type

After you've determined the functional requirements and quality indicators for each document your service delivers, codify those requirements by building them into a set of templates.

Templates make documentation easier to create and far easier to use.

- *They make it easy for authors to create documentation* by providing a clear structure that they can populate quickly with relevant information. With a good template, creating a simple document can be as easy as filling out a form.

- *They ensure that documentation is complete* by including sections for all required pieces of documentation. If a certain piece of information is not yet available or doesn't apply, it's fine to mark these as "TBD" or "N/A," but each section should be addressed.

- *They make it easy for readers* to quickly understand the topic of the doc, the type of information it's likely to contain, and how it's organized. In addition, your template should ensure that the reader knows when the doc was last updated and by whom.

The *Site Reliability Engineering* book (*https://landing.google.com/sre/book/index.html*) contains several examples of documentation templates. Here's a sample Playbook template that provides structure and guidance for engineers filling in the content:

```
Title
The title should be the name of the alert (e.g., Generic Alert_AlertTooGeneric).
Author:
Last updated:

Overview
Address the following:
What does this alert mean?
Is it a paging or an email-only alert?
What factors contributed to the alert?
What parts of the service are affected?
What other alerts accompany this alert?
Who should be notified?

Alert Severity
Indicate the reason for the severity (email or paging) of the alert
and the impact of the alerted condition on the system or service.
```

Identification
Provide specific instructions on how to verify that the condition is ongoing.

Troubleshooting
List and describe debugging techniques and related information sources here.
Include links to relevant dashboards. Include warnings. Address the following:
What shows up in the logs when this alert fires?
What debug handlers are available?
What are some useful scripts or commands? What sort of output do they generate?
What are some additional tasks that need to be done after the alert is resolved?

Solution
List and describe possible solutions for addressing this alert.
Address the following:
How do I fix the problem and stop this alert?
What commands should be run to reset things?
Who should be contacted if this alert happened due to user behavior?
Who has expertise at debugging this issue?

Escalation
List and describe paths of escalation. Identify whom to notify (person or team)
and when. If there is no need to escalate, indicate that.

Related Links
Provide links to relevant related alerts, procedures, and overview documentation.

Better > Best: Set Realistic Standards for Quality

A core SRE principle is that Google strives to make our systems reliable enough to keep our users happy, but no more reliable than that. Increasing reliability comes at a cost: maximizing stability limits how fast new features can be developed and how quickly products can be delivered to users, and it dramatically increases their cost, which in turn reduces the numbers of features that a team can afford to offer.

Requiring high standards of writing can be counterproductive, intimidating engineers from creating docs. Similarly, polishing a document past the point where key information is up to date, discoverable, and clearly conveyed is a waste of time that could be spent improving other parts of the documentation (or your service itself). Just as code is an iterative process, so too is documentation.

Learn to embrace what Anne Lamott describes as the "shitty first draft": an imperfect document is infinitely more useful than a perfect one that does not yet exist. Ask yourself this: Does this doc meet its functional requirements and is the required information present and clearly conveyed? If the answer is yes, hold the doc changes to the minimum reasonable standard. After a document has met that quality bar, *move on*. Good writing is *great* to see, but don't block changelists because the author used the passive voice in a doc. Don't be that engineer.

Require Docs as Part of Code Review

Documentation is like testing: nobody really wants to do it. But in other cases, code reviewers have power: we can withhold approval until the docs are sufficient. Do this!

Not all changes require doc updates, of course. Here's a good rule of thumb:

> If a developer, SRE, or user of your project needs to change their behavior after this change, the changelist should include doc changes.

On the other hand, if a change doesn't require tests, it probably *doesn't* require documents either. Examples include refactors and experiment tweaks. Use your judgment.

As always, simplify and automate this process as much as possible. At Google, teams can enforce a presubmit check that either looks for a flag that indicates a doc update isn't necessary (presubmit checks for style issues can prevent a lot of arguments, too). We also allow owners of a file to submit changes without a review.

If your team balks at the requirement, remind members that simple project documentation is about saving the information in your head so that others can access it later *without bothering you*. And doc updates aren't usually onerous; generally, the size of your documentation change scales with the size of your CL. If your CL contains a thousand lines of code, you might need to write a few hundred lines of documentation. If it contains a one-line change, you might just need to change only a word or two.

Finally, remember that docs don't need to be perfect; they need merely be *good enough*. What's important is that key information is conveyed clearly.

Ruthlessly Prune Your Docs

A small set of fresh and accurate docs is better than a large assembly of "documentation" in various states of disrepair.

Every line of documentation, just like every line of code, should serve a purpose. When documentation isn't serving a useful purpose, it should—like code—be archived or deleted. Unnecessary or unhelpful documentation is a tax; it's a kind of technical debt, adding complexity and uncertainty and often obscuring or even contradicting useful information.

At Google, we encourage SWEs and SREs to fearlessly delete no-longer-useful documentation. The magic of source control means that we can easily restore them if the need occurs, but it rarely does.

If you don't have a way to restore deleted documents, for the love of all that's holy move them to an "Archived" directory, mark them as "Deprecated" (possibly the only legitimate use of <blink>), and ideally provide a link to the new version.

Recognize and Reward Documentation

Documentation, as we have already noted, takes time and effort. One of the barriers to better documentation is that it has often been perceived as toil: drudge work that is not recognized or rewarded at performance review or in the promotion process. But documentation is core engineering work that reduces toil (*https://landing.google.com/sre/book/chapters/eliminating-toil.html*) and improves the reliability of a service. If SREs are to do docs right, that work needs to come out of the 50% time they have budgeted for development.

This is a reality that needs to be faced. It requires managers and leads to rigorously identify documentation requirements, establish baseline standards for quality, and ensure that this work is budgeted for in the project schedule and recognized during performance review and promotion time.

Because leadership support is so important to driving change, the next section focuses on how to best communicate the value and impact of documentation work in your organization.

Communicating the Value of Documentation

If you want to convince fellow engineers and leadership to invest time and resources in documentation, it's essential that you gather data that accurately demonstrates the *quality*, *effectiveness*, and *value* of your documentation.

Avoid the temptation to rely on structural quality data. Such data can be easy to collect, but it's uncompelling and provides a weak statement of impact that is unlikely to support your case; for example:

- "I submitted 90 changelists that updated the documentation."
- "I wrote 37 pages of a service overview."
- "Everything was spelled correctly."
- "My style and usage conform to our style guide."
- "My documentation was mostly task based."

Sure, those stats are a bad way to evaluate the work of a very junior writer who is just beginning to learn the craft of technical writing. But they're a *terrible* way to demonstrate the value and impact of the noble work you have undertaken to improve documentation in your organization.

Remember, when you talk about the impact of your doc work, you're talking about the *business value of your output*. While structural data is unpersuasive, functional data is convincing.

Although structural quality is generally pretty easy to measure, functional data has a different shape and can be trickier to gather. It typically falls into three buckets:

Measurable success

> If an alert was successfully handled using your documentation, and no documentation-related issues are revealed in the postmortem, your documentation has high functional quality.

User behavior

> Your product team wants people to try out a new feature. If you can test how many users read the docs and try the feature, you can measure how well you satisfied this requirement.

Sentiment data

> This is trickier, is prone to misunderstanding, and can be too easily dismissed. "Not statistically significant!" "It's just someone's opinion!" But sentiment data is real data, and it can sometimes be the only data you can get. When a user tells you that they like your doc, they are explicitly telling you that the doc met their requirements. When a team adopts your documentation platform or uses your documentation templates, they are telling you that the platform or templates are useful to them. You can gather sentiment data via surveys, bug and issue tracking, feedback mechanisms on the page itself, or by talking to the teams you support.

Functional quality data enables you to build a compelling story around documentation, like this:

- Our SRE team had a goal to decrease the time it takes for a new engineer to go on call.

- I pitched a proposal to create a playbook with complete documentation for all alerts.

- The team accepted the proposal. I worked with the engineers to revamp the playbook so that each entry clearly conveyed what the alert meant and provided ways to immediately address and mitigate any negative effect.

- As the result of the document effort, the revamped playbook received five times more visits.

- Engineers reported that they could rely on the playbook during on-call.

- A follow-up study indicated that there was an x% decrease in the time it takes for a new engineer to go for on-call.

Here's another example, demonstrating how Stas communicated the value of moving SRE playbooks to EngPlay:

With EngPlay, I developed an improved version of our playbook service, but the adoption wasn't great. People preferred to stay with the old clunky but battle-tested implementation. After six months, only 10% moved onto the new version. Moreover, I was constantly dragged into explaining to people why I've done what I've done, why and how they should move onto a new version. I started feeling like I increased fragmentation instead of cleaning the mess. At that point, I wrote a *very* basic set of documents outlining the most common questions:

- Why the new platform for playbooks?
- What are the benefits?
- How to migrate to it?

As a result:

- The stream of private conversations almost entirely drained. In the rare case that someone would ask, I could just send them a link to a document. I finally could concentrate on improving the platform itself.
- When the documentation was available, new adopters began contributing to it. This created a chain reaction of more users → more improvements to the documentation → more users.
- In the next three months, 30% more projects migrated to EngPlay—a six-fold increase in the adoption rate.
- Six months later, almost all services had adopted EngPlay for their playbooks.

This is a story we can communicate in all sorts of ways:

- With other SREs and with technical writers, who might be interested in learning from your experiences and adopting your processes.
- With our managers, who need to be able to understand why we're spending our time on documentation.
- At performance review and promotion time, when you need to be able to build a case for recognition.
- With the other teams we work with and collaborate with on documentation.

Functional data is compelling. Gather it and use it to state a case for impact and convince your team, your organization, and your leadership that investing in documentation is worth doing.

Because it is.

Further Reading

- ZWISCHENZUGS, "Things I Learned Managing Site Reliability for Some of the World's Busiest Gambling Sites" (*https://zwischenzugs.com/2017/04/04/things-i-learned-managing-site-reliability-for-some-of-the-worlds-busiest-gambling-sites/*).

Ríona MacNamara is a senior staff technical writer at Google who has focused extensively on internal engineering documentation and process, and believes that documentation is as fundamental to the discipline of software engineering as testing.

Shylaja Nukala is a technical writing lead for Google Site Reliability Engineering, where she has worked for 12 years. She leads the documentation, information management, and select training efforts for SRE, Cloud, and Google engineers. Prior to Google, she was a staff technical writer at Epiphany and Sony Electronics. She holds a PhD in communication studies from Rutgers University.

Stas Miasnikoŭ is a site reliability engineer at Google.

Aaron Gillies manages a software documentation group in Google Cloud in New York City.

Jeremy Sharpe is a senior software engineer at Google. Over six years with Google, he's worked on ads, shopping, and cloud, but some of his favorite contributions have been to engineering documentation tools and education as part of his 20% time.

Niall Richard Murphy has been working in internet infrastructure for over 20 years, and is currently Director of Software Engineering for Azure Production Infrastructure Engineering in Microsoft's Dublin office. He is a company founder, an author, and a photographer, and holds degrees in computer science and mathematics and poetry studies. He is the instigator, coauthor, and editor of Site Reliability Engineering and The Site Reliability Workbook (both O'Reilly).

## CHAPTER 20

Active Teaching and Learning

Laura Nolan, formerly Google

Spoon feeding in the long run teaches us nothing but the shape of the spoon.
   —E.M. Forster

The distributed datastore is down. Writes are failing on all replicas and reads are timing out. The SRE on call checks the monitoring; there are no clues as to the cause, yet it's clear this key production service is in a bad state: the errors and latency graphs are the only ones going up and to the right. Revenue is being lost. The on-caller declares a production incident.

The VP of engineering storms in, demanding to know what's going on.

The other SREs in the room just laugh. Why? Because this is *Incident Manager*, a game designed to teach incident response skills and teamwork, and the current player just drew a bad card.

Incident management is a key SRE skill that can be learned—and it's much better for your organization's SLO budget (and the stress levels of your SRE team) to learn it via a fun and effective game rather than during an actual production incident.

Because SREs are both generalists and experts (one of the major reasons why it is difficult to hire them), they are constantly learning.

The skillset of an SRE can span operating system internals, networking, monitoring and alerting, troubleshooting, debugging, incident management, software engineering, software performance, hardware, distributed systems, systems administration, capacity planning, security, and many other areas. Not all SREs are expert in all of these areas, of course; most SREs are "T-shaped": broad in many areas, and deep in one, or a few.

This broad set of skills is channeled into a vast array of job functions, some of which might be new territory, such as the following:

- Onboarding a new team member (or a few)
- Onboarding a new service (or a few)
- Making major changes to at least one existing service
- Dealing with changes in the systems with which our systems interact
- Dealing with explosive growth or some other major systems challenge

New team members are learning both their team's systems and key SRE skills that they might not yet have. More established team members are developing their skills and knowledge as they deal with change and as they dive deeper into different areas of expertise.

If we must be learning all the time, we should make our learning effective, and more importantly, fun.

Active Learning

> *I am convinced that the best learning takes place when the learner takes charge.*
> —Seymour Papert

Seymour Papert, the inventor of the Logo programming language and the inspiration for Lego Mindstorms, said that learning was "building knowledge structures," and that this works best when the learner is creating something. He also said that learning through play doesn't mean that the material being learned is easy; it means it's engaging. In Seymour Papert's studies, learners called their learning fun because it was hard.

Trying to solve problems, either successfully or unsuccessfully, and receiving timely feedback seems to be key to the learning process. Games are ideal for this.

Chess Is One of the Oldest Educational Games

This isn't a new idea. Chess is said to have originated over a millennium ago as a way to teach strategy to noblemen.

Kriegsspiel (which means "wargame" in German) was a system created in 1812 to train officers in the Prussian and German armies. It is a role-playing game, with a grid, gaming pieces and dice, and ways to simulate fog of war and communication difficulties. Players on either side act as commanders, and a gamemaster acts as umpire and decides the effects of player action.

---

games are still used in education today. In March 2017, the CIA showed some of its internal training board games at SXSW.[1] The games are designed to encourage problem solving and collaboration. One, designed by Ruhnke, is designed to teach players about the political situation in Afghanistan, and he believes it gives players a much more nuanced mental model of the issues in the region than just reading briefs.

There are lots of examples of games in computing education in recent times, including *Regex Golf* (*https://alf.nu/RegexGolf*), in which players write regular expressions to match given inputs accurately, and *Deadlock Empire* (*http://deadlockempire.github.io*), in which the players attempt to reveal concurrency problems by acting as a scheduler.

Games are effective learning tools because people enjoy them. They are a way to get effortlessly into a flow without fear of failure posing a distraction. They can be social. They have inbuilt and instant feedback, and they have rewards or scoring systems when players get things right. These are all great features of any learning experience.

Other forms of active learning exist. Tutorials and discussion groups are a common example. These sorts of learning structures don't have scores and levels like games do, but they do include active and creative engagement with the material, and feedback should come from tutors and students in the group.

Active Learning Example: Wheel of Misfortune

Wheel of Misfortune is one of the best training tools we at Google have for getting new SREs, or SREs new to a system, up to speed. And it's a game—basically, a role-playing game. There's no board, or simulator, or any equipment needed (although a laptop and a whiteboard usually come in handy).

Wheel of Misfortune starts out with a gamesmaster and a team member playing the on-call engineer. The gamesmaster describes some event happening to the on-caller, generally a page or maybe some escalation from another team. The engineer playing the on-caller then responds as they would in a real situation, mitigating, root-causing, fixing the issue, and escalating, as required. The gamesmaster acts as an oracle and will answer the on-caller's questions about what the monitoring, logging, and so on would show.

This is a deceptively simple but incredibly valuable exercise for everyone involved. As the gamesmaster, you generally spend some time beforehand getting your scenario

---

1 "The CIA Is Training Its Officers With D&D-Style Tabletop RPGs" (*http://io9.gizmodo.com/the-cia-is-training-its-officers-with-d-d-style-tableto-1793295549*) by Beth Elderkin and "Why the CIA uses board games to train its officers" (*http://money.cnn.com/2017/03/13/technology/cia-board-games-training/*) by Selena Larson.

ready, and you need to have thought it through in considerable detail before you put it to your colleagues. As the engineer playing the on-caller, or as another colleague observing, you likewise learn about your system's behavior, and also about its monitoring, any recovery tools, points of escalation, and so on.

There are also skills to be learned, like techniques for troubleshooting and root-cause analysis as well as incident management. *Wheel of Misfortune* is a great way to practice these in a low-risk and (relatively) low-pressure environment.

We take *Wheel of Misfortune* so seriously that in the Dublin (Ireland) Google SRE building, we have a room that was specially designed for it. It has amphitheater-style seating, enough for the largest team or a set of related teams; a whiteboard, and a large screen. The best part is that we SREs got to name it: it's called Kobayashi Maru, after the fictional no-win training exercise from *Star Trek* (and yes, it is styled as a starship bridge). Luckily, our *Wheel of Misfortune* exercises generally have a much happier ending than the Kobayashi Maru scenario does (usually it involves noting some action items to improve dashboards or playbooks and going for coffee, rather than the Klingons destroying your starship).

Active Learning Example: Incident Manager (a Card Game)

Incident Manager is a card game that I've used as the basis of workshops to teach incident management (*https://landing.google.com/sre/book/chapters/managing-incidents.html*) skills (it ran at SRECon Europe 2016 and I've run it within Google). Solid incident management practices can mean the difference between a minor outage and a prolonged and a major outage of the kind that hurts user trust. They are key to the success of any SRE team.

Incident management skills are about communication and coordination, and a separation of responsibilities. The difficult thing about incident management is that the techniques need to be applied during incidents, which are often stressful and confusing moments. The incident manager game was devised to give people practice in applying incident management in something approximating how dealing with production incidents can feel.

One common example of the sort of thing that can go wrong while responding to an incident is simply lack of structure—responders jump in, don't coordinate or communicate with the rest of the organization, and collectively miss something vital, or all end up investigating the same potential root cause.

Another well-known incident response antipattern is when a junior member of a team sees a potential problem but isn't confident enough to point it out. Worse, sometimes when one person does point out an issue, others might still ignore it. I have seen postmortems describing more than one serious outage that was unnecessarily prolonged because the correct answer was suggested but no one listened. Experience (as provided in this game) can help teach confidence, and it can also help people to learn to listen to other team members who might have valuable insights.

Like *Wheel of Misfortune, Incident Manager* presents a production system and an outage scenario, with a gamesmaster presiding. With a team that works together on a real service, you could use that service. Running this with mixed groups, I use a short system description for a distributed storage system that looks much like the Google File System (*https://research.google.com/archive/gfs.html*) (GFS), including some notes about its monitoring and other deployment information.

Participants split into two teams (representing two shifts, Europe/Middle East/Asia [EMEA] and US, of an on-call rotation for the service suffering the outage) and are dealt playing cards. The cards add the structure of a game, which a *Wheel of Misfortune* session lacks. They also provide useful prompts about the incident management process—their real purpose. The scenario adds the sorts of distraction from incident management processes that a real production incident does.

There are four card types: basic rules, roles, keepers, and actions, all shown in Figure 20-1.

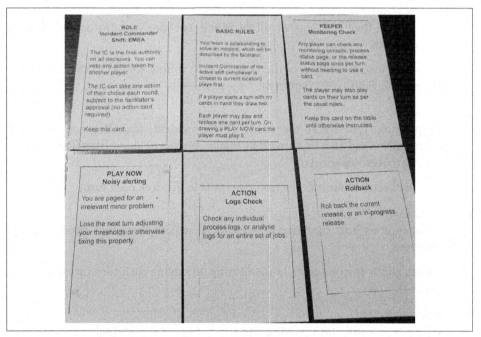

Figure 20-1. Cards from the Incident Manager game

Here are the basic rules:

- Your team is collaborating to solve an incident, which will be described by the facilitator.
- The Incident Commander of the active shift (whichever is closest to the current location) plays first.
- If a player starts a turn with no cards in hand, they draw two.
- Each player may play one card per turn. On drawing a PLAY NOW card, the player must play it.

Each player gets one role card, which they keep for the duration of the game. As in real incident management situations, roles come with responsibilities and with special powers. Each role card belongs either to an EMEA or US shift. The gamesmaster removes responder cards from the deck as needed to ensure that each shift has critical lead roles staffed.

Here are the roles:

Incident commander (IC)
> The IC is the final authority on all decisions. You can veto any action taken by another player.
>
> The IC can take one action of their choice each round, subject to the facilitator's approval (no action card required).

Planning lead
> The planning lead tracks the status of the incident, including actions taken, efforts under way, and anything that might need to be done later (for instance, undoing mitigation efforts).
>
> You can check and reorder the next five cards in the deck each turn.

Operations lead
> The operations lead coordinates responders, making sure that efforts are not duplicated.
>
> You can check any one piece of monitoring or logging each turn (no action card required).

Communications lead
> You are responsible for updating any affected teams or external users about the status of this incident.
>
> You can communicate with users or escalate internally to another team or a business owner each turn (no action card required).

Responder

The responder has no special abilities.

Yours is but to contribute to the effort as your cards allow and as the IC thinks best.

As in real life, the incident commander should start an incident document describing the progress toward resolving the "incident" (this could be a shared document or a whiteboard/flipchart).

Each player on the active shift takes a turn, as described by the basic rules. They draw action cards—some of these can be kept, but some must be played immediately. The actions are the sort of things that might happen during an incident—some of these are helpful and some are not.

Here are some examples of actions:

- Check monitoring
- Query a running process
- Query logs for a given job
- Roll back a process
- Modify load-balancing configurations
- Develop a new utility or script (the facilitator decides how many turns this will require, and the player who plays this will be out of the game for that number of turns)
- Modify a job (change flags, number of instances, etc.)
- Bug fix, cherry-pick and roll-out—again, requires a number of turns to be decided by the facilitator
- Escalate to developers (played by the facilitator)—the player who plays this loses a number of subsequent turns depending on how well the facilitator feels the SRE team did on investigating the situation before escalating
- Escalate to business owners (for an answer about any decision impacting users)

Here are some examples of PLAY NOW cards:

- Shift change: active shift loses all their cards; the other shift takes over
- An unspecified terrible thing happens (the gamesmaster decides)
- Noisy alerting: paged for an irrelevant minor problem, lose a turn
- Interfering executive: communications lead misses their next turn dealing with it (also a planning lead variant)

- Engineers not involved in the incident response overload your monitoring: lose all your monitoring check cards

This game teaches incident management skills quickly, without being dull (and really, very little is duller than sitting through a bunch of slides about processes). Here, people get to actually use the process, with time and resource constraints like in a real incident. It builds confidence that they can use the incident management processes under stress. The cards reinforce real-world problems that arise in incident management (such as the interfering executives who can descend if communication isn't good, or bystanders overloading monitoring if the operations lead isn't coordinating who is working on different tasks).

This game requires preparation to work well. It won't work well if the group size is larger than around 12. The group also needs to have a shared understanding of the system that the game is based on, either because it's their actual system or via a description. Like *Wheel of Misfortune*, it needs careful preparation of the scenarios by the gamesmaster, so that the gamesmaster can answer the questions that players will ask about system behavior. You should also organize props, like a shared incident document, ahead of time.

Active Learning Example: SRE Classroom

SRE Classroom isn't a game. It's a workshop that a number of Google SREs (including me) have been running since 2012. We've run it at many public conferences (including USENIX LISA (*https://www.usenix.org/blog/non-abstract-large-system-design-sysadmins*), USENIX SREcon, O'Reilly Velocity, and FLOSS UK) and we've run it by invitation at Google offices. It has been run in two formats: half day, with only design exercises, and as a full day, which includes some talks.

SRE Classroom is intended to teach people how to do practical distributed systems design and basic capacity planning. This is quite an ambitious thing; it's a complex area of practice, and people attend with radically different levels of experience.

I'm one of the very few SREs who have been on both sides of the fence for this particular event. Before I joined Google I attended one of the very first versions of this workshop, at the Google office in London in 2012. After I started at Google, I was quite active in updating the content of the workshop along with several others, and I taught it many times. Recently, I developed a more in-depth version of it (it's around three days long if run continuously) for new Google SREs without systems design experience, or for non-SRE Googlers who are interested in joining SRE.

In the workshop, we throw the participants in at the deep end of the pool, to sink or swim. At the beginning of the workshop we split the participants into groups of around five, each group having a facilitator. They get a problem statement and some nonfunctional requirements around scale and resilience to failure. These scaling and resilience requirements are really the heart of the problem. One of our problems uses business logic that is as simple as a SQL join, but the system being designed must scale to roughly the number of page views that Google serves daily—which is a lot!

Then, each team is asked to design the system and to come up with some initial capacity estimates for the hardware needed to run it. At the end, we run through a design that meets the goals and then discuss.

Teams work together on the design. The facilitator's job isn't to give answers. The facilitator's job is to clarify anything in the problem that isn't clear, to help the team by asking the right questions when needed to avoid spending too much time down rabbit holes, and to make sure that no one person is dominating the conversation. The team does the work together, because what we are trying to do is to develop their ability to design distributed systems (and that is not quite the same thing as coming up with a correct design for this particular system). In many ways, it doesn't really matter if the team actually gets all the way to the "correct" answer. The process is the point. What really matters is that people have spent time wrestling with the problems and thinking about the trade-offs that different solutions imply.

As I mentioned earlier, I've been on the nonteaching side of the fence as well, and it is in some ways hard work. But my experience of it, as both learner and teacher, is that it's possible to lose yourself in the work so deeply that you and your team will entirely lose track of time working and discussing the problems. Like Seymour Papert's students, they find that it is fun because it is hard. The large majority of those who have attended have enjoyed it and found it useful (as reported on post-session surveys). Participants are certainly significantly more skilled and confident at systems design and capacity estimation at the end of the workshop. Only a small minority of students (low single-digit percentages) strongly disliked the active learning experience. Those participants tended to be people who wanted to sit back and let someone read slides to them rather than learning through experience.

This sort of exercise is also quite an effective way of learning the reasons for the architecture of a system. We've used different system designs as the basis of this workshop at different times, but one we've used quite often is Photon (*https:// research.google.com/pubs/pub41318.html*), a log-joining pipeline. The reason we like using this one is that for most workshop attendees, it's different from the sorts of systems they work on day to day, so it's more of a challenge. Photon is a fairly complicated beast—I was on the SRE team that owned the service. I noticed that going through an exercise like the SRE Classroom workshop yields a much deeper and better understanding of Photon than just reading about it or watching someone talk about it. Putting in the effort to wrestle with the problems yourself really works. This really pays dividends when you are an SRE and trying to figure out the latest failure mode that your system is currently exhibiting.

This is a technique I use myself now when I need to learn a new system: first figure out the functional and nonfunctional requirements, then sketch a design myself, and only then read about how the system actually works. Regardless of whether what I came up with was close to reality, I find I understand its constraints and trade-offs much faster than I can just by learning about it passively. It takes longer, but in many cases the time investment is well worth it.

If your team is taking on a new service, or using a new piece of infrastructure, you can do this sort of thing with your entire team, a whiteboard, and a little preparation, and it's a lot more fun than sitting through a presentation. The downside of it is that it's not a great technique for remote teams; being in a room together really helps.

The Costs of Failing to Learn

SRE teams are sometimes going to learn things the hard way. We might cause or extend an outage. Much worse, we might cause a security breach; we might lose user data. Production problems are going to bite us sometimes, but it's a very, very expensive way to learn and we can't afford to repeat the lesson. We need to do better. SRE organizations must therefore be training and learning organizations.

There are other tangible costs to any SRE organization that isn't a good training organization. The first cost is a longer time for new hires or for those switching between teams to become productive. In larger organizations with multiple SRE teams, you might also find less cohesion between SRE teams. If they don't share a common training and learning system and share knowledge, teams will diverge in their mindset, techniques, and approaches to the job. Teams are likely to create or adopt different tools and processes for the same purpose, increasing development cost and adding barriers for those switching between teams.

SRE teams that can't share knowledge won't work as effectively with other non-SRE engineering teams in their organization. SRE teams are, in effect, constantly training development teams and their own junior members about good production practices. They do this via design reviews, launch readiness reviews, postmortems, and maybe other avenues like formal training or rotations working with the SRE team.

Another major cost for SRE teams who aren't strong in training is that newer team members who aren't confident in their skills and in their knowledge of their service can find themselves under increased stress, particularly when they are on call. This is a major risk factor for burnout, and it's awful for team effectiveness and morale. Furthermore, a burned-out SRE team is a far less effective SRE team, and that can pose an existential risk to the entire enterprise. We owe it to ourselves and our teams to be good at both teaching and learning.

SRE teams that don't learn and don't teach are ineffective. Learning and teaching are therefore core SRE skills; but they're skills in which many of us aren't specifically trained. They're also skills that most of us don't really think about as being vital to SRE.

In recent years, we have explicitly added teaching and education to the SRE job description at Google in order to recognize that it should be one of core competencies.

Learning Habits of Effective SRE Teams

Learning isn't only about onboarding new team members or services. Effective SRE teams incorporate learning into their regular working practices. The two most widespread learning habits for SRE teams are regular production meetings and postmortem incident analysis. It is very difficult to run a large and complex service reliably without implementing both of these practices.

Production Meetings

You can view a weekly production meeting, in which developers and SREs meet to discuss the state of their service (*https://landing.google.com/sre/book/chapters/ communication-and-collaboration.html*), partly as a process of learning. The team as a whole learns new things about how the service is performing and what problems are occurring. Individuals on the team usually learn some new things about how the service operates, too. Most well-run production meetings tend to spawn sets of follow-up actions that require people to go and find answers that weren't known during the meeting.

There are a couple of ways to maximize the value of your production meeting as an active learning opportunity.

For engineers new to the team, consider having them keep a list of anything that comes up in the production meeting that isn't clear to them. In most organizations, the new engineer should have a team member designated as a mentor to help them get up to speed. After each production meeting, that mentor can explain items noted from the production meeting to the new engineer. This is also a good opportunity to make sure your team documentation is up to date.

When issues arising in the production meeting are not clear to experienced members of the team, another learning opportunity presents itself. One engineer (either someone who does understand the issue or who is tasked to research it) can bring the knowledge back to the rest of the team, perhaps during the next production meeting. These sorts of poorly understood corners of your systems are also among the best sources of ideas for your *Wheel of Misfortune* sessions.

Postmortems

Postmortems are another great (if sometimes expensive) learning opportunity. Both the process of writing them and the final artifacts are really valuable for learning curious corners of your systems and technologies (as well as for the headline purpose of actually avoiding repeating the incident).

Postmortems, however, are not very active in and of themselves. You can activate them, though.

I set up a postmortem reading club as a key avenue for a number of closely related SRE teams to share understanding about the systems we run. Every fortnight we choose the most interesting postmortem from the recent past, and we have a semi-structured discussion. There is a rotating chairperson, whose responsibility is to lead the discussion and keep notes. We generally use a whiteboard to describe the sequence of events to everyone's satisfaction, drawing on the knowledge of the people in the room to fill in any blanks or required context. When that is complete, we look at action items, again drawing on the collective wisdom of the room to add meaning.

Attending one of these sessions is a much richer learning experience than simply reading a document.

Operations reviews are a lighter-hearted incarnation of the same sort of idea—pager-carriers and on-call people of all varieties come together for sociable and humorous discussions of recent problems and outages. Frequently at Google, we encourage attendance at such events with bribes such as cake. Expensing the weekly ops review donuts might be one of the best financial investments an SRE manager can make in their team's development.

A Call to Action: Ditch the Boring Slides

In this chapter, I've talked about a variety of ways that I and other Googlers have used active methods to teach and learn. You can apply these sorts of techniques to your own team's tools, systems, and processes, too.

There is almost nothing more critical to the success of any SRE team than the ability of its members to learn. Active learning methods are among the most effective (and often the most engaging and fun) ways of achieving that. So, why not ditch the slides and use some of these techniques next time you need to run some kind of training?

Laura Nolan taught herself to program in her teens, did a CS degree, and worked as a developer and as a software performance engineer before joining Google SRE in early 2013. At Google, she worked mainly on large data processing pipelines and the network, so all tubes basically. She was co-chair of USENIX's SREcon EMEA conference in 2017 and 2018.

The Art and Science of the Service-Level Objective

Theo Schlossnagle, Circonus

You can't meet or exceed expectations if no one agrees what the expectations are. In every job, you must understand your objectives to measure your success. In this chapter, we learn what it looks like when an SRE sets goals.

Why Set Goals?

The main objective of an SRE is to maintain the reliability of systems. Service-Level Objectives (SLOs) are the primary mechanism used by SREs to determine success in this objective. I'm sure you can see that it is difficult to "do your job well" without clearly defining "well." SLOs provide the language we need to define "well."

You might be more familiar with Service-Level Agreements (SLAs), so let's begin there. SLAs are thought of by some as the heart of darkness, and by others as the light of redemption. Why the disparity? I believe it's because of how they are defined. They can be defined in a way that enables producers and consumers to level-set their expectations, or they can be tool for despair, false assurances, or exposing one to dangerous financial liability. Let's not spend too much time in the darkness.

Oftentimes today, the term SLO is used, and for the purposes of this text, an SLA is simply an SLO that two or more parties have "agreed" to. SLO and SLA are used fairly interchangeably herein, but we make an effort to consider SLAs as "external" multiparty agreements and SLOs as "internal" single-party goals.

Although the concept of an SLA is quite generic and it simply outlines in clear terms how a service will be delivered to a consumer, at least in the world of computing, they tend to focus on two specific criteria: availability and quality of service (QoS). Now, QoS can and should mean different things depending on the type of service. Note that *producer* and *consumer* ultimately means *business* and *customer*, respectively, but oftentimes, as we define the SLO between components in an architecture, it can mean *producing component* and *consuming component*. Examples of a producing component would be a network accessible block storage system and an authorization microservice API; each would have many disparate customers and make promises to those other services about availability, performance, and sometimes even safety.

SLAs are actually quite simple in that you aim to limit your risk by not over-promising and appeal to customers by providing assurances that make them feel comfortable consuming your services. The devil is in the details; while the concept is straightforward, there is art in choosing what to promise and science in quantifying how to promise it.

In an SLA, you're always promising something over time. This time is often monthly, sometimes daily. The time period over which you promise tends to align with your standard billing cycles but matches your refund policy perfectly. This last part is important. If you are promising something over the course of a day and fail to deliver, you are likely going to back up that promise with a refund for that day's service. The implications are quite clear when that promise is for a month.

Obviously, many SLAs use multiple time windows to provide a balance between exposure and assurance. For example, if the SLA is violated for 1 minute in a given day, that day will be refunded, and if the SLA is violated for 1 hour in a given month, the entire bill for that month is forfeit. I will talk no more of the ramifications of SLA violation in terms of refunds, but instead of just violation. How you choose to recompense for a broken promise is out of the scope of this book; good luck.

The takeaway here is that SLAs make sense only when considered in fixed time-frames, which are called *assurance windows*. Given how services are trending today and how major service providers disclose their outages (a simplified term for SLA violations), I'll assume that we use a daily context. All the concepts herein can be applied if that window is different, but do the math and understand your exposure when changing that assurance window.

Now, let's look at this in context instead of the abstract. I'll tackle availability before QoS because that's easier to reason about.

Availability

Availability simply means that your service is available to consume. It functions in only the most basic sense of the word. It does not mean that consumers get the answers they expect when they expect them. I'll give a few examples of availability that might help illustrate the point.

If you send a package via a major carrier, I would consider it available if the driver comes and picks up your package and it is delivered to the destination. The driver could show up late to pick it up, the contents could be exposed to extreme temperature and thus be damaged, and it could show up three weeks later instead of two days, as requested. It's available, but utterly unsatisfying. Imagine for a moment the opposite assurance: your package would be delivered on time in pristine condition every time it shipped, but the carrier never showed up to take the package. Now we have perfect QoS, but an utterly unsatisfying experience because it is unavailable.

Availability in computing systems seems like it would be simple to quantify, but there are many different ways to measure availability, and if you articulate them incorrectly, you are either exposed horribly or effectively promising nothing to the consumer. The latter might sound great, but you'll eventually face the music: higher standards lead to success and consumers are smart.

The most common ways to measure availability are the marking of time quanta or counting failures. The classic SLA language of "99.9% uptime" can put into these terms.

Time Quanta

The idea of time quanta is to take your assurance window (one day) and split it up into pieces. If we were to choose minutes, we'd end up with 1,440 time quanta in that day (unless it is a daylight saving time shift that leads you to question why you work in this field and how, given our bad ideas, humans are still alive at all).

Within each of those time quanta, you can measure for failure. If any failures are detected, the specific time quantum is marked as bad. At the end of the day, your availability is simply the unmarked (good) time quanta over the total (1,440): $1,439/1,440 = 99.930\%$ and $1,438/1,440 = 99.861\%$. So, with a 99.9% uptime guarantee, you are allowed 1 minute of downtime in that day, but 2 and you've violated your SLA.

This seems simple enough, but it has some flaws that can expose you unnecessarily or provide no acceptable assurance to your consumers—or both. I'm going to use an API service to articulate how this is. Let's assume that we have a shipping-calculator API service that takes package weight, source, and destination postal code and provides a price.

If we do 100 million transactions per day, that would average to almost 70,000 per minute. If we failed to service one each minute, we'd violate every time quantum of our SLA and have 100% downtime. At the same time, we've only failed 1,440 out of 100 million transactions, which is a success rate of 99.998%. Unfair!

On the flipside, if the consumers really use the app only between 10 AM and 10:30 AM when they're scheduling all of their packages for delivery, we fail every single transaction from 10:20 to 10:21 and still meet our SLA. From the customer perspective this is doubly bad. First, we've met our SLA and disappointed more consumers (3,333,333 failed transactions versus 1,440) and we've had an effective uptime of 1 minute out of the 30 that is important to them: a perceived uptime of only 96.666%.

If your usage is spread evenly throughout the day, this approach can work and be simple to understand. Most services do not have an even distribution of transactions throughout a day, and, while simplicity is fantastic in SLAs, this method is too flawed to use.

Transactions

Another common method is to use the raw transactions themselves. Over the course of our assurance window, we simply need to count all of the attempted transactions and the number successfully performed. In many ways, this provides a much stronger assurance to a client because it clearly articulates the probability for which they should expect to receive service.

Following the earlier example, if we have 100 million transactions and have a 99.9% uptime guarantee, we can fail to service 100,000 without breaking our SLA. Keep in mind that this might sound like a lot, but at an average 70,000 per minute, that is identical to a continuous 2-minute outage resulting in an SLA violation. The big advantage should be obvious; it allows us to absorb aberrant behavior that affects a very small set of consumers over the course of our entire assurance window without violating the SLA (mutual best interest).

One significant challenge is that it requires you to be able to measure attempted transactions. In the network realm, this is impossible: if packets don't show up, how would we know they were ever sent? Regarding online services, they are all connected by a network that could potentially fail. This means that it is impossible for us to actually measure attempted transactions. Wow. So, even though this is clearly an elegant solution, it allows for too much deniability on the part of the producer to provide strong assurances to the consumer. How can we fix this?

Transactions over Time Quanta

The best marriages expose the strengths of the partners and compensate for their weaknesses. This is certainly the case for the marriage of the previous two approaches. I like to call this "Quantiles over Quantums" just because it sounds catchy.

By reintroducing the time quantum into transactional analysis, we compromise in the true sense of the word. We remove the fatal flaw of transactional quantification in

---

that if the "system is down" and attempted transactions cannot even be counted, we can mark a quantum as failed. This tightly bounds the transaction method's fatal flaw. On the flip side, the elegance of the transactional method allowing insignificant failures throughout the entire assurance window is reduced in effectiveness (precisely by the number of time quanta in the assurance window).

Now, in our previous example of 100 million transactions per day, instead of allowing for up to 100,000 failures throughout the day, we now have an additional constraint that can't have more than 69 per minute (assuming that we preserve the 99.9% to apply to the time quantum transaction assurance).

The articulation of this SLA would be as follows:

> The service will be available and accept requests 99.9% of the minutes (1,439 of 1,440) of each day. Availability is measured each minute and is achieved by servicing a minimum of 99.9% of the attempted transactions. If a system outage (within our control) causes the inability to measure attempted transaction, the minute is considered unavailable.

All of this is just a balancing act; this is the art of SLAs. Although it is more difficult to achieve this SLA, when you do miss, you can feasibly make statements like, "We were in violation for 8 minutes," instead of, "We violated the SLA for Wednesday." Calling an entire day a failure is bad for business and bad for morale. SLAs do a lot to inspire confidence in consumers, but don't forget they also serve to inspire staff to deliver amazing service.

For many years, we've established that "down" doesn't mean "unavailable." The mantra "slow is the new down" is very apt. Most good SLAs now consider service times slower than a specific threshold to be "in violation." All of the previously discussed methods still apply, but a second parameter dictating "too slow" is required.

On Evaluating SLOs

The first and most important rule of improving anything is that you cannot improve what you cannot measure; at least, you cannot show that you've improved it.

We've talked about the premise of how SLOs should be designed. I'm in the "Quantiles of Quantums" camp of SLO design because I think it fairly balances risk. The challenge is how to quantitatively set SLOs. SLAs are data-driven measurements, and the formation of an SLO should be an objective, data-driven exercise as well. Too often, I see percentiles and thresholds plucked from thin air (or less savory places) and aggressively managed too; this approach is fundamentally flawed.

It turns out that quite a bit of math (and largely statistics) is required to really understand and guide SLOs—too much math, in fact, to dive into in a single overview chapter. That said, I'll try to give the tersest summary of the required math.

First, a Probability Density Function (PDF) is a function that takes a measurement as input and a probability that a given sample has that measurement as an output. In our systems these "functions" are really empirical sets of measurements. As an example, if I took the latency of 100,000 API requests against an endpoint, I could use that data to answer an estimation to the question: "What's the probability that the next request will have a latency of 1.2 ms?" The PDF answers that question.

A close dancing partner of the PDF is the Cumulative Density Function (CDF). It is simply the integral (hence the name "cumulative") of the PDF. The CDF can answer the question: "What's the probability that the next request will have a latency *less than (or greater than)* 1.2 ms?"

Probabilities range from 0 (nope) to 1 (certainly), just as percentages range from 0% to 100%. Percentiles (like 99th percentile) use percentages as their terms; "quantiles" are the same thing, but they use probabilities as their terms. The 99th percentile is the 0.99 quantile or *q(0.99)*. The quantile function is simply a mapping to the CDF; in a typical graph representation of a CDF, we ask what is the x-axis value when the y-axis value is 0.99? In Figure 21-1, *q(0.99)* (or the 99th percentile) is about 270.

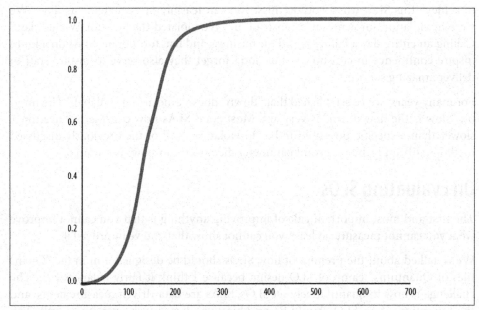

Figure 21-1. CDF function, 0.99 (y-axis) 270 (x-axis)

Oftentimes in computing, you'll hear *normal* or *Pareto* or *gamma* distributions, which are different mathematical models that indicate how you expect your measurement samples to be distributed (Figure 21-2). The hard truth is that you will almost never see a normal distribution from a real-world computing system; it just doesn't happen. Things sometimes look like gamma distributions, but computers and systems of computers are complex systems and most sample distributions are actually a composition of several different distribution models. More important, your model is often less important than the actual data.

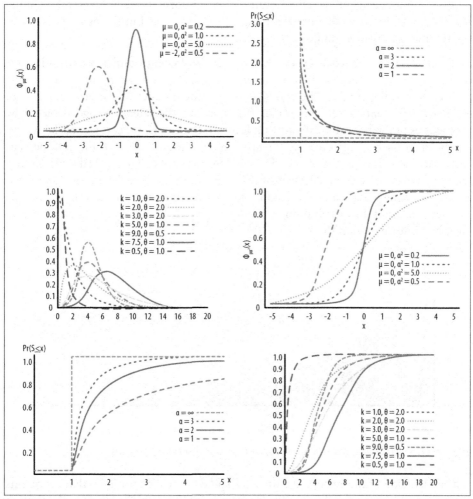

Figure 21-2. Common PDFs and CDFs

Pareto distributions model things like hard disk error rates and file size distributions. In my experience, because slow is also considered down, most SLAs and SLOs are articulated in terms of latency expectations. We track the latencies on services to both inform the definition of external SLAs as well as assess our performance to our internal SLOs.

Histograms

Histograms allow us to compress a wealth of dense information (latency measurements) into a reasonably small amount of space informationally while maintaining the ability to interrogate important aspects of the distribution of data (such as approximating quantile values).

In Figure 21-3, we see what represents the seconds of latency under real-world usage. The x-axis is in seconds, so the measurements of 1.0 m and 1.5 m are in milli-units (in this case milliseconds). The y-axis represents the number of samples. The area of each bar represents a set of samples that fall into the latency range depicted by boundaries of the bar on x-axis. Just underneath the x-axis, we can see markers indicating "quantile boxing" showing the $q(0)$ (the minimum), $q(0.25)$ (the 25th percentile), $q(0.5)$ (the median), and $q(0.75)$ (the 75th percentile). The $q(1)$ (the maximum) isn't visible on the graph, as much of the long tail of the distribution is outside the right side of the viewport of the graph. The vertical line (m) indicates the arithmetic average (mean) of the distribution. The graph in Figure 21-3 packs a punch! There's a wealth of information in there.

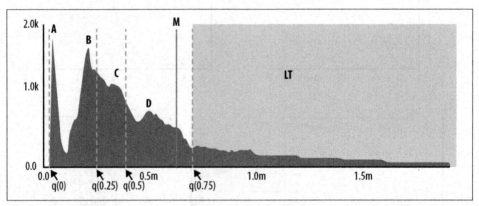

Figure 21-3. An example latency histogram for data service requests

On the left side of the histogram, we see a spike (A), called a mode, that represents services that were served fast (likely entirely from cache) and the distribution between (A) and 1.0 ms looks composed of several different behaviors (B), (C), and (D). If you refer to the gamma distribution PDF graph, this looks a bit like several of those graphs stacked atop one another. The largest samples in this histogram are actually "off the graph" to the right in part of the distribution's long tail (LT), but the blue underbox indicates that $p(100)$ (our "maximum") is 120 ms. It's important to recognize that most real-world distributions have complex cumulative patterns and long-tail distributions, making simple statistical aggregates like min, max, median, average, and so on result in a poor understanding of the underlying data.

Given the data that is used to draw this histogram (bins and sample counts), we can estimate arbitrary quantiles (and inverse quantiles) and more advanced characteristics of the workload such as modal cardinality (the number of bumps in a histogram).

In addition to some typical 99th percentile SLA, we might also want to establish internal SLOs that state 75% or more of the requests against this service should complete in 1 ms or less. The histogram in Figure 21-3 happens to comprise samples over a 1-second period and contains more than 60,000 samples. If you've been looking at "averages" (which happens to be vertical indicator line) of your data over time, this visualization of 1 second's worth of data should be a wake-up call to the reality of your system behavior.

The more challenging question in setting an SLO around this service is "how fast should it be for most consumers?" The graph should inform us whether we're succeeding, but the business and technical requirements around the service should be the driver for the answer to that question. In this particular case, this is a data-retrieval API and the applications that it powers have negotiated that 99% of the requests they make should be services within 5 ms. Doing analysis on the data, the previous example has a $q(0.99) = 3.37$ ms. Yay!

Where Percentiles Fall Down (and Histograms Step Up)

Knowing that our $q(0.99)$ is 3.37 ms, we're currently "exceeding" our SLO of 5 ms at 99%. But, how close are we to the edge? A percentile grants no insight into this. The first sample slower than the 99th percentile sample could be 10 ms or (more likely) could be less than 5 ms, but we don't know. Also, we don't know what percentage of our consumers are suffering from "slow" performance.

Enter the power of histograms, given the whole histogram to work with, we can actually count the precise number of samples that exceeded our 5-ms contract. Although you can't tell from the visualization alone, with the underlying data we can calculate that 99.4597% of the population is faster than 5 ms, leaving 0.5403% with unsatisfying service, or 324 of our roughly 60,000 samples. Further, we can investigate the distribution and sprawl of those "outlier" samples. This is the power of going beyond averages, minimum, maximums, and even arbitrary percentiles. You cannot understand the true behavior of your systems and think intelligently about them without measuring how they behave. Histograms are perhaps the single most powerful tool in your arsenal.

Parting Thought: Looking at SLOs Upside Down

As an industry, we have arbitrarily selected both the percentile and the performance for which we set our SLOs. There should be more reason to it than that. If you are measuring at $q(0.99)$, is that really because it is satisfactory that 1% of your consumers can receive a substandard experience? This is something to think about and debate within your team and organization as a whole.

It has also been standard to measure a specific quantile and construct the SLO around the latency at that specific quantile. Here is where I believe the industry might consider looking at this problem upside down. What is special about that 1% of consumers that they can receive worse than desirable performance? Would it be better if it were 0.5% or 0.1%? Of course it would. Now, what is special about your performance criteria? Is it the 5 ms in our data retrieval example (or perhaps 250 ms in a user experience example)? Would it be better if it were faster? The answer to this is not so obvious? Who would notice?

Given this, instead of establishing SLOs around the $q(0.99)$ latency, we should be establishing SLOs around 5 ms and analyze the inverse quantile: $q-1(5\ ms)$? The output of this function is much more insightful. The first just tells us how slow the 99th percentile is, while the latter indicates what percentage of the population is meeting or exceeding our performance target.

Ultimately, SLOs should align with how you and your potential consumers would expect the service to behave. SLOs are simply the precise way you and your team can articulate these expectations. Make SLOs match you, your services, and your customers; another organization's SLOs likely make no sense at all for you.

Another advantage of SLOs is that by exceeding your SLOs they quantitatively play into your budgets for taking risk. When you're close to violating an SLO, you turn the risk dial down; if you have a lot of headroom, turn the risk dial up and move faster or innovate!

Further Reading

- Navidi, William. (2009). *Statistics for Engineers and Scientists*. New York: McGraw-Hill Education.
- Limoncelli, Thomas A., et al. (2014). The Practice of Cloud System Administration: DevOps and SRE Practices for Web Services, Vol. 2. Boston: Addison-Wesley Professional.

Theo Schlossnagle has been architecting, coding, building, and operating scalable systems for 20 years. As a serial entrepreneur, he has founded four companies and helped grow countless engineering organizations. Theo has had about 200 speaking engagements on software, operations, and many meta issues related to the tech industry.

## CHAPTER 22

SRE as a Success Culture

Kurt Andersen, LinkedIn

If you read much about the practices of Site Reliability Engineering (SRE) or the professional concerns discussed by site reliability engineers (also SRE), you could quickly gain the impression that the central concept is failure, or the results of failures, or having fewer failures, or avoiding failure in distributed computing systems. However, SRE is most productive and valuable when focused on achieving business success than when focused on preventing or mitigating failure. Peter Senge captured some of the key mental shifts that characterize site reliability engineering:

> [a] shift of mind from seeing parts to seeing wholes, ... from reacting to the present to creating the future.[1]

Unlocking the full benefit of SRE involves cultural changes to empower teams to optimize the full-service life cycle toward successfully delivering the business metrics (service level) to delight their users. SRE teams and practices are most effective when aligned with a supportive corporate culture. To get the full value from the SRE work in your company, it is also important to ensure that site reliability is considered proactively throughout the life cycle of services—from ideation through retirement.

Where Did SRE Come From?

The idea of SRE coalesced sometime around 2003 to 2007. This is roughly the same period when the idea of the "DevOps" movement came into being, and both originated in the tech sector of Silicon Valley. Although DevOps focuses on the leading edge of how to reliably create and deploy software into production, the companies that

---

1 Senge, Peter M. (1990). *The Fifth Discipline: The Art and Practice of the Learning Organization.* London: Random House.

were the innovators for SRE already had effective practices which would be labeled Continuous Integration (CI) and Continuous Deployment (CD) today. With these fundamentals already in place, SRE practice was able to focus later in the value chain on customer benefit.

> SREs work at the intersection of software and systems engineering to sustain highly reliable and scalable distributed systems engineering and all of the necessary disciplines to support those practices.[2]

The complete ecosystem of any given product or service includes not just the utilities (equipment, software, third-party functions) that are used to provide the service, but also the data, other service providers, the users, and the complex interplay among all of those components. All of these components are in the purview of a mature SRE team. To accomplish their work, SREs rely on measurement and data rather than guesses or instinct, following Lord Kelvin's dictum:

> When you can measure what you are speaking about, and express it in numbers, you know something about it; but when you cannot measure it, when you cannot express it in numbers, your knowledge is of a meagre and unsatisfactory kind; it may be the beginning of knowledge, but you have scarcely, in your thoughts, advanced to the stage of science, whatever the matter may be.[3]

SRE uses measurement to define and track the adherence to Service-Level Objectives (SLOs) and leading indicators that are traditionally known as Key Performance Indicators (KPIs). It is still somewhat challenging to directly measure "user satisfaction," but SREs are ultimately focused on increasing user satisfaction and business success through providing the right levels of reliability and responsiveness that allow the rest of the development teams to deliver a continuously improving feature set to the users.

Tim O'Reilly described SRE in *WTF? What's the Future and Why It's Up to Us* (*https://www.oreilly.com/tim/wtf-book.html*) as "...its core [is] the practice of 'debugging' the disconnect between software development and operations...building new connective tissue." This is particularly the case with regard to the complexities that arise as systems move from the domain of being complicated into being complex/chaotic as distributed architectures. Even though this characterization is true—SREs are highly capable of debugging complex distributed systems—that capability comes as a byproduct of focusing on entire system aggregates and, at the same time, being able to zoom in to critical minutiae that affect the behavior and performance of systems. In the most effective engagements, site reliability considerations are engineered

---

2 Tim O'Reilly, *WTF? What's the Future and Why It's Up to Us* (*https://www.oreilly.com/tim/wtf-book.html*)

3 Lecture on "Electrical Units of Measurement" (May 3, 1883), published in *Popular Lectures* (*https://archive.org/stream/popularlecturesa01kelvuoft#page/73/mode/1up%7C*), Vol. I, p. 73 (*https://archive.org/stream/popularlecturesa01kelvuoft#page/73/mode/1up%7C*).

[illegible] from their initial conceptual stages just like bugs are most cheaply fixed early in the software life cycle (*https://www.researchgate.net/figure/255965523_IBM-System-Science-Institute-Relative-Cost-of-Fixing-Defects*).

SRE practices have arisen among groups and organizations supporting service delivery models that have been "born in the cloud." The lifeblood of these organizations is the continuous delivery of online value. With an online service, users are impacted in near real time by changes to the system rather than being removed in both time and place via some intermediate software distribution mechanism. If the site is not "up" and performing correctly with adequate response speed, it is not being reliable and it is not delivering the intended benefit to the end users. This immediate or near-real-time feedback loop facilitates reliability engineering at a whole-site level. Rapid feedback for large-scale system behaviors enables a qualitatively different approach, analogous to the way that unit tests and Test-Driven Design (TDD) changed software engineering and increased the reliability of individual pieces of software. Reliability engineering is a broader discipline that encompasses safety disciplines. SRE practices, as applied to computing functions, are extending beyond their cloud-origin cultures to be implemented in other contexts, including critical internal-facing IT services, banking, manufacturing and other segments.

Key Values for SRE

There are four key values for the practice of site reliability. Different organizations might phrase them slightly differently or have different relative rankings, but they are widely spread in the zeitgeist of the profession. Without establishing these as fundamental cultural values SRE will not exist in the way it is currently known. Just as *Effective DevOps* focused on the crucial importance of "building a culture of collaboration, affinity, and tooling at scale," SRE is much more than a collection of techniques and practices. The techniques and practices organically grow out of core cultural values. Here are those fundamental values:

- Keeping the site up
- Empowering dev teams to "do the right thing"/distributed decision making
- Approaching operations as an engineering problem
- Achieving business success through promises made, measured, and fulfilled

Keeping the Site Up

For SRE teams, keeping the site (or website) "up" is the ultimate goal of all of their day-to-day work efforts. Although the use of the phrase "site up" and even the use of the term "site" within SRE hearkens back to the origins of the SRE practice, SRE work and skills are being employed on a growing basis to keep services, networks, internal and external-facing infrastructure, and products reliable. As "software is eating the world"[4] and capabilities that were once the province of custom silicon move to horizontally scaled general-purpose hardware complemented with the right software, SRE practices become more important than chipset design or assembling the right constellation of unique hardware. For the sake of terminology, I will stick with the term "site" (or "website") in this chapter, but please read that term in a widely inclusive sense. Nothing constrains the value of SRE practices to the HTTP protocol.

As pointed out in "Gray Failure: The Achilles' Heel of Cloud-Scale Systems"[5], for modern websites, there can be a lot of nuance in what "up" means. Distributed systems can fail in catastrophic ways, such as the British Airways incident on May 27, 2017,[6] and further notes a week later,[7] but generally the influence of reliability engineering will serve to mitigate the impact into what might more appropriately be called "gray failures" or a "brown out" rather than a full "black out" outage. Some of the techniques that SREs use to keep as much as possible of the functionality operational include the following:

- Isolated failure domains
- Redundant systems
- Graduated degradation of service under load

Isolated failure domains

If a site is built using a monolithic code base and with a single backing database, it will be vulnerable to a full "black-out" experience if any of those single points of failure experiences an outage. To guard against such a scenario, site reliability practices will segment the code (using either a microservice architecture or through functional segmentation across different failure domains) and also the underlying data store so that a failure in any critical component will not take everything down. Note that in this aspect, as in a variety of others, SRE is extending good software engineering prac-

---

4 Marc Andreessen [paywall], "Why Software Is Eating The World" (*https://www.wsj.com/articles/ SB10001424053111903480904576512250915629460*), republished at Andreessen Horowitz (*https://a16z.com/ 2016/08/20/why-software-is-eating-the-world/*).

5 Peng Huang, Chuanxiong Guo, Lidong Zhou, Jacob R. Lorch, Yingnong Dang, Murali Chintalapati, Randolph Yao, "Gray Failure: The Achilles' Heel of Cloud-Scale Systems" (*https://www.microsoft.com/en-us/ research/wp-content/uploads/2017/06/paper-1.pdf*)

6 Jude Karabus, "BA's 'global IT system failure' was due to 'power surge'" (*http://www.theregister.co.uk/ 2017/05/27/ba_it_systems_failure_down_to_power_supply_issue/*).

7 Gareth Corfield, "BA IT systems failure: Uninterruptible Power Supply was interrupted" (*https://www.there gister.co.uk/2017/06/02/british_airways_data_centre_configuration/*).

---

tiees to a "system" or more "macro" level. At each level, similar principles apply, but the tools that are available differ as the scale changes.

Highly reliable system design includes a constant awareness to avoid single points of failure. As the use of horizontally scaled services across commodity hardware became more economical and commonplace than investing in "big iron," distributed system principles became much more important to the proper execution of systems. Perhaps foremost among those principles is the conclusion drawn from the fallacies of distributed computing (*https://en.wikipedia.org/wiki/Fallacies_of_distributed_comput ing*) that anything can fail at any time, even things that used to be considered, in simpler environments, rock solid. Working at scale has another consequence, too: problems affect only "1 in a million" are painfully frequent when dealing with hundreds of millions or billions of events. In such an environment, minimizing the losses from expected failures becomes a critical design guideline. The goal has to shift away from failure *avoidance* toward reducing or containing failure *impact*.

Redundant systems

Just like hardware teams have learned to employ multiple fallback redundancies, site reliability teams also employ redundancy to protect their sites. Redundancy can be through multiple locations, multiple copies of data, and multiple providers of services at every level of the stack, from Domain Name System (DNS) through Content Delivery Network (CDN).

Graduated degradation

Not all features are equally important and not all users need to use the same sets of features. As part of engineering reliable performance, economic and business trade-offs can be made to ensure the most important features continue to operate while sacrificing less important features when there are problems within the environment. Ideally, well-designed boundaries exist between "sacrificial" systems and "essential" systems, and continuing to work with development teams to ensure that graceful degradation under failure conditions is a key function for site reliability teams.

Empowering Teams to "Do the Right Thing"

SREs focus on the operation of distributed systems, and the best teams recognize that they themselves are also subject to the same stresses and failure modes that they work to manage in their sites. To achieve the "Holy Grail" of scaling their own teams and effectiveness, SREs need to strive toward both educating their development counterparts and empowering them to find the right information and make the right choices: fostering a shared ownership around the importance of "site up." A lot of this happens by cultivating shared values as well as demonstrating the ongoing value that SRE teams bring to the table.

When a company grows to have distinct development teams, the individual development teams usually end up being highly focused on the particular portion of the whole site "stack" for which they are responsible to deliver features. The rest of the stack will fade into a peripheral awareness, but for the SRE, the way in which the individual pieces of the site fit together and interoperate is fundamental. This important perspective is stewarded by SREs as individual teams make design decisions.

By providing tooling frameworks to instrument and visualize site and individual (micro)service performance, SREs help the development teams to identify both good and bad aspects of their individual pieces of the website. With the right tools to facilitate observability as well as monitoring and alerting around the measurements, SREs enable developers to respond to how their code is performing in near real time with live user interactions. This enables rapid iteration toward the achievement of business goals for each component of the website or service.

Giving development teams the capability to understand the effect of their pieces in the context of the whole is both fundamental to the effectiveness of the SRE teams and to promoting a culture of self-responsibility in which problems are not "thrown over the wall" in an oppositional us-versus-them dynamic.

Approaching Operations as an Engineering Problem

Brian Koen describes engineering as follows:

> pursuing a strategy for causing the best change in a poorly understood or uncertain situation within the available resources.[8]

Site reliability as a role has emerged to handle the complexity of modern distributed systems along with the near-real-time feedback loops that are enabled by online service delivery. Computer systems and networks used to be within the realm of personal comprehensibility—as reflected in the naming patterns that would encompass the entire group of machines within the span of the "seven dwarves." As systems in aggregate grew from being treated like pets to the scale where they need to be managed more like a herd of cattle (*http://cloudscaling.com/blog/cloud-computing/the-history-of-pets-vs-cattle/*), and now people are suggesting that they need to be considered even more transitory (or prolific) like poultry (*https://dzone.com/articles/cloud-computing-pets-cattle*), the combinatorial complications have undertaken a phase change into being not just complicated, but complex.

Complex distributed systems do not necessarily respond in intuitive ways and require tooling to both expose inner state information as well as to exert control over the sys-

---

8 Cited by John Allspaw: Koen, Billy V. (1985). *Definition of the Engineering Method*. Washington, DC: American Society for Engineering Education, p. 5 (*https://www.kitchensoap.com/2017/08/12/multiple-perspectives-on-technical-problems-and-solutions/*).

tems. Complex systems are also characterized by nonlinear effects, so tooling is critical for safe management of the larger systems. Only through this tooling can a team have any opportunity to handle the ever-expanding number of systems and software services that execute upon them, often coming into existence, performing activities for a short time, and then going away again while other services take their place.

This ever-shifting and growing landscape is why "engineering" is a key discipline for strategically working toward site reliability. As Dave Zwieback wrote in *Beyond Blame* (O'Reilly):

> The root cause for both the functioning and malfunctions in all complex systems is impermanence (i.e., the fact that all systems are changeable by nature). Knowing the root cause, we no longer seek it, and instead look for the many conditions that allowed a particular situation to manifest. We accept that not all conditions are knowable or fixable.

Mathias Lafeldt summarized this "single root cause" as: "All things are compounded objects in a continuous change of condition."[9]

The daily task for an SRE team is to deal with the inconstant nature of the systems that they support: a point-in-time snapshot gives one an impression of a solid network of interrelated services, but the reality is that the relationships between the services and even the composition of the services themselves are an ever-shifting matrix of changeable components. These changeable components are further obscured from true understanding by the nature of the human–computer interface and even basic physics.[10]

As described in the *Stella Report* (*https://stella.report*) and shown in Figure 28-1 (also from the *Stella Report*), people are critically dependent upon the tools that they build to represent information about their systems. Tim O'Reilly describes this in *What the Future?* as follows:

> Every Silicon Valley firm builds two intertwined systems: the application that serves users, and a hidden set of applications that they use to understand what is happening so that they can continually improve their service.

Building and maintaining the "hidden set of applications," or tooling—which can ensure that an up-to-date mental model is readily available to everyone who needs it —is a significant function of the SRE team.

---

9 Lafeldt, Mathias. (2017). "Impermanence: The Single Root Cause" (*https://medium.com/production-ready/ impermanence-the-single-root-cause-bd9ebadf1e8e*), Medium.com.

10 Watch Grace Hopper illustrate a nanosecond (*https://www.youtube.com/watch?v=JEpsKnWZrJ8*). Understanding the state of a computer system that executes multiple instructions per nanosecond when your view of that system is an indeterminate length of time removed from the real execution means that the interface through which you come to understand the system is, at best, seeing "through a glass darkly."

Achieving Business Success Through Promises (Service Levels)

All of the work that goes into SRE must be oriented toward the fundamental core business objectives and the contributing enablers for the achievement of those objectives, or it will be wasted. As Peter Drucker wrote:

There is surely nothing quite so useless as doing with great efficiency something that should not be done at all.[11]

Successful SRE teams both understand the business metrics and have developed frameworks of measurement that can help achieve those goals, supporting both site performance and usage patterns. The treatment of Service-Level Agreements (SLAs), objectives, and indicators covered in *Site Reliability Engineering* (*https://landing.google.com/sre/book/index.html*) is probably the canonical framing of these topics. The most important aspects of service levels (agreements, objectives, and indicators) have to do with the alignment of objectives between the development teams and their SREs. The goal is for both groups to work together to define the targets, achieve them, and maintain performance on a daily basis, in spite of the ongoing evolution in site components and user demand.

Setting these benchmarks and then developing and executing plans to achieve them distinguishes SRE from other related disciplines such as software engineering. It is also the mechanism within the mantra: "Hope is not a plan."

Progression in Service-Level Execution

Initial efforts at service-level monitoring often start because of contractual obligations. At this level, the SLAs are extrinsically driven and often reflect only gross measures such as availability or some components of response times. The monitoring is often highly selective or ad hoc, generating contractually mandated reports on a periodic basis and motivated by the desire to avoid financial penalties. Neither insight nor understanding of the service execution is an objective at this level of execution.

As an organization progresses, it will begin to understand the limitations of ad hoc SLA reporting and the mandatory measurements that support the reports, and will develop internally motivated SLOs that will begin to provide some insights about the execution characteristics of its services. Usually these SLOs will start by measuring parameters that are relatively easy to determine or measure.

More advanced organizations will develop a set of "leading indicators" or KPIs that will enable them to proactively respond to threats that can endanger the achievement

---

11 Drucker, Peter F. (1963). "Managing for Business Effectiveness," Harvard Business Review. (*https://hbr.org/1963/05/managing-for-business-effectiveness*)

of their SLOs as well as provide more nuanced understandings of how their services operate and depend on related services (internal or external). Over time, the continuous monitoring of KPIs and SLOs will provide a baseline from which experienced SRE teams can make educated inferences about the services that they support and the relationships with adjacent services throughout the entirety of their stacks.

Critical Enabling Functions of SRE

The achievement of service levels is a difficult task for organizations that do not have them ingrained as a cultural tenet. To support a service-level-oriented practice, SRE teams work across five pillars of practice:

- Monitoring, metrics, and KPIs
- Incident management and emergency response
- Capacity planning and demand forecasting
- Performance analysis and optimization
- Provisioning, change management, and velocity

Monitoring, Metrics, and KPIs

As noted previously, if you can't measure it, you really don't understand whatever the "it" is. Having a robust set of metrics that relate to what really matters for the business (KPIs) is critical to developing service-level definitions and reporting against those definitions.

Because metrics are so fundamental to the practices of SRE, SRE teams will often be involved in the core enabling technologies within their companies or organizations that allow and encourage the larger development community to instrument their code in consistent reliable ways.

SREs are often also involved on the "export" end of the metrics pipelines in making the data visible and usable by whoever needs access to it, whether software engineers managing their own code or business executives needing high-level overviews.

Incident Management and Emergency Response

Because SRE teams are often at the intersection of multiple software development teams and involved with the system-level dynamics between different services, they play a key role in incident response. Often SREs will be involved in incident command and coordination roles, and their system-wide perspectives can be key to effective learnings in postmortem analysis following incidents. SRE teams can also help with the meta-task of ensuring an effective on-call function within the engineering teams such as with the open sourced Iris and Oncall tools (*https://engineer ing.linkedin.com/blog/2017/06/open-sourcing-iris-and-oncall*) from LinkedIn SRE organization and integrating code commit responsibilities into a distributed response framework, as detailed in this blog post (*https://engineering.linkedin.com/blog/ 2018/01/project-star-streamlining-our-on-call-process*).

Capacity Planning and Demand Forecasting

Frequently, software engineers will not understand exactly how their software is being in practice. The gap between the designed usage and the actual usage can have huge effects and impacts on capital expenditures (CapEx) and operational expenditures (OpEx) to implement and maintain a service. SRE teams are well positioned to measure, report, and forecast both what the system can deliver (capacity) and, when looped into business discussions and ongoing design strategy, a sense of what future usage requirements will be (demand).

Performance Analysis and Optimization

A big part of understanding capacity involves knowing how a service (or constellation of services) performs, both with and without stress (aka failure). With the measurement frameworks available to them, SREs are well equipped to assist their development partners to characterize the performance of services in aggregate and use their system-level point of view to suggest optimizations that can increase capacity or performance.

Provisioning, Change Management, and Velocity

Although different organizations will have varying approaches to provisioning hardware and services and managing change within their environment, the SRE teams play a key role by improving automation whenever possible to maximize the velocity of change while preserving performance within the boundaries of the established service levels. Sometimes this means that SRE teams help to establish or strengthen CI/CD frameworks and pipelines or that they apply automation tooling ideas to "racking and stacking" or reliably operating warehouses and other logistical entities.

An equally important component of provisioning is tearing down (deprovisioning) obsolete services. Unfortunately, no one likes to plan for retirement (of their services) so the SRE teams, looking across the landscape of functions and services, are frequently the ones who have to push for the removal of the "walking dead"—zombie services with no effective engineering support that consume resources without contributing to the benefit of the business.

Phases of SRE Execution

Many organizations will go through three or four major phases[12] as they implement the cultural shifts necessary to achieve a functional SRE practice that spans the full life cycle of the service. This progression follows a move from the reactive end of the value chain back toward the earlier phases of the service life cycle. As SRE teams become more effective along this spectrum, the quality of their interactions with corresponding development teams improves and their participation becomes more highly desired and sought after.

Phase 1: Firefighting/Reactive

In the first phase, teams are starting from a reactive stance. Too many moving parts, overwhelming complexity, unexpected interactions that cascade in unanticipated ways lead the teams to feel like it will never again see the light of day, much less have a hope of being able to apply any "engineering" to a chaotic situation.

In this firefighting/reactive stage, teams have little recourse but to keep struggling to respond to each crisis while at the same time trying to reserve enough attention and energy to gain leverage within the untenable situation. Calling a halt to feature development so that teams can collectively focus on wrestling the bugs in the system down to a manageable level is one strategy for getting some relief. Teams can also be supplemented with extra personnel to help structure automation that can reduce the load of manual toil.

This phase can be the hardest one for a team to overcome because it requires a dual perspective: on one hand "keeping the lights on," while at the same time building a new approach through automation and enabling adjacent teams.

Being reactive, this phase is also reflective of SRE teams that are engaged late in the process of releasing a new service. Perhaps they were called in to clean up the mess of a service that is already in production but performing badly, or perhaps the service is just about to go into production without having reliability engineered into it during the design phase.

Phase 2: Gatekeepers

As the crisis-driven approach wanes, and the team gets past the worst of the reactive toil, the gatekeeping phase of team evolution can happen. The temptation for SRE teams in this phase is to set themselves up as a gatekeeper, a single choke point through which changes to production systems must pass and be approved. At small

---

12 See Benjamin Purgason's presentation, "The Evolution of Site Reliability Engineering" (*https://www.usenix.org/conference/srecon18asia/presentation/purgason*) for more on the subject.

scales, this can be mostly functional, but as scale increases, teams will be under growing pressure to get out of the way and must cede control by empowering the development teams to do the right thing. SREs in this stage need to become partners, not doors.

The gatekeeping phase is also a common next step for teams that are looking to become engaged with their dev partners earlier in the process. It can be implemented as a "launch control," "operational readiness review," or "release to production" process. Even though those terms can reflect positive engagement with the development teams, they most often indicate a gatekeeper mentality that can lock teams in an us-versus-them struggle. If SREs position themselves as the gatekeepers, this sets them in opposition to the feature teams and incentivizes feature teams to circumvent the process (and the SREs) whenever they interfere with the feature priorities.

Phase 3: Advocates/Partners

By building jointly agreed-upon frameworks, such as the error budget concept explained in *The SRE Book*, (*https://landing.google.com/sre/book/index.html*) Chapter 3 (*https://landing.google.com/sre/book/chapters/embracing-risk.html*), SREs are able to remove their teams from the critical path for service releases and rely on an objective measure. When everyone agrees on adhering to this measure, the SRE team is freed up to partner with the dev team(s) to help them achieve the agreed target and then to continue to meet it. The SRE team is also involved with continually evolving the components of the service measured to include all important aspects that impact the user experience.

The partner phase sees SRE teams involved much earlier in the development process for upcoming services. They work to ensure that the designs consider reliability in their architecture and build defenses against the most likely or expensive failures.

SRE teams become much more effective because the engagement is less antagonistic with the dev teams, and design changes that are introduced early are less expensive to implement and provide longer-term value. Teams often have much higher satisfaction among their members because they feel that their work is valued by their partners. The SRE team has become an important contributor rather than being viewed as the "cleanup crew" or a gatekeeping roadblock. SRE services become sought after by the dev teams who recognize this value.

Phase 4: Catalytic

The final stage for SREs to operate within their organizations is in a catalytic role. Just as a chemical catalyst facilitates reactions and can guide the process of those reactions, SREs serve to consult with development teams, bringing a consistent mindfulness of the business goals, reliability, and security into the full life cycle of every service component. SREs should be involved from conception through decommis-

planning of every service and help to provide the right tools so that the development teams are intimately familiar with the effects that their code has on the overall site or service function.

Executing SRE at this level provides the greatest leverage for the SRE teams, enabling their influence to scale beyond their headcount increase. SRE engagement with the dev teams has moved fully into a "pull" model with dev teams seeking SRE input rather than the Phase 1 and 2 "push" model that is usually imposed by management. Voluntary, value-based engagement is more enjoyable for all of the participants and sustains a virtuous circle of ongoing benefit to the company both internally and externally.

Complications of Differing Phases

Teams in different phases of execution have significantly different priorities and allocate their attention in very different ways. This can cause a lot of friction because teams will seem to be speaking different languages. It is important to understand a team's context in order to avoid misunderstandings. If a Phase 4 team talks to a Phase 1 team about engaging during the design phase with their development counterparts, the Phase 1 team is likely to consider that completely unrealistic.

From discussions with a variety of people across the industry, it appears that there are few shortcuts that can enable a team to leap from the fires of Phase 1 to the bliss of Phase 4 without progressively growing through the various stages of engagement. With high-level management support, it is possible for SRE teams to engage only in Phase 3 and above engagements, but even then, it requires significant fortitude to withhold support from struggling development teams. This fortitude is usually only found in fairly mature SRE organizations who have experienced the benefits of engaging with willing development partners.

Focus on the Details of Success

Having a holistic view of each service as well as the overall site, understanding aspects of networking and system performance that are taken for granted by most feature-oriented developers, and being able to develop and execute on plans for mitigating risk to a site and its services are all daily aspects of SRE. The most effective SREs epitomize a growth mindset.[13] SREs need to be able to analyze problems in the context of the bigger picture of the business metrics that are relevant. Like rock climbers or alpinists, they need to be able to take issues that appear to be insurmountable and work to overcome them step by step. SREs also need to be able to uncover and solve the

---

13 Dweck, Carol. (2007). *Mindset: The New Psychology of Success*, updated edition. New York: Ballantine Books; *https://hbr.org/2016/01/what-having-a-growth-mindset-actually-means* or *https://mindsetonline.com/*

problems that turn up around the edges of all of the leaky abstractions (*https://www.joelonsoftware.com/2002/11/11/the-law-of-leaky-abstractions/*) that most of the development teams don't want to know or worry about—all in pursuit of site reliability. If the site is not "up," nothing else much matters. Business success for an online service relies fundamentally on the effective work and the continual focus on site reliability through engineering attention and skill while features that delight the users are brought into being.

Further Reading

1. Victor Chircu, "Understanding the 8 fallacies of Distributed Systems" (*http://www.simpleorientedarchitecture.com/8-fallacies-of-distributed-systems/*).

2. Carol Dweck at TEDxNorrkoping, "The power of believing that you can improve" (*https://www.ted.com/talks/carol_dweck_the_power_of_believing_that_you_can_improve*).

3. Carol Dweck, "What Having a 'Growth Mindset' Actually Means" (*https://hbr.org/2016/01/what-having-a-growth-mindset-actually-means*), Harvard Business Review.

4. Senge, Peter M. (1990) *The Fifth Discipline. The Art and Practice of the Learning Organization.* London: Random House.

5. McChrystal, Stanley (2015). *Team of Teams: New Rules of Engagement for a Complex World.* New York: Penguin Group.

6. The paradigm shift to view SRE as focused on success rather than failure parallels the change in other industries, such as air traffic management; see Erik Hollnagel et al. "From Safety-I to Safety-II: A White Paper" (*https://www.skybrary.aero/bookshelf/books/2437.pdf*). EUROCONTROL 2013.

Kurt Andersen started his career dealing with big data at NASA's Jet Propulsion Laboratory. He's been involved with shared standards since the early '90s instigating the PERL DBD/DBI specification and now works on various IETF standards. Kurt is currently the senior individual contributor for the Product SRE team at LinkedIn. He also works as one of the program committee chairs for the Messaging, Malware, and Mobile Anti-Abuse Working Group (http://www.M3AAWG.org). He has spoken at M3AAWG, Velocity, SREcon, and SANOG on reliability, authentication, and security.

## CHAPTER 23

SRE Antipatterns

Blake Bisset, Dropbox, Inc.

Human brains are built and trained for threat avoidance. We might be terrible at weighing relative risk,[1] but we're excellent at picking out the one thing in a pile of other things that looks like a failure mode that we've seen before.[2]

Let's face it. Failure is fun![3] And failure makes a good story (*https://blog.buffer app.com/science-of-storytelling-why-telling-a-story-is-the-most-powerful-way-to-activate-our-brains*). So, it can often be both easier and more effective to catalog the things you shouldn't do rather than just the things you should.

But "antipatterns" are not your average "this one time, at Foo camp" Tale of Fail. They're the things we've seen go horribly wrong not once, not twice, but over and over again. Antipatterns are attractive fallacies. Strategies that succeed for a little less time than you will find you needed them to. Common sense that turns out to be more common than sensible.

Throughout the rest of this book, you'll find examples of things that you should do. That's not what I'm about here in this chapter. Think of this section as your "Defense Against the 'D'oh!' Arts" glossary. Or just sit back and enjoy imagining all the stuff I and a host of colleagues past and present had to screw up in order to get to the point

---

1 Perhaps not even as reliably as plants! See this article about Hagai Shemesh and Alex Kacelnik (*https://www.nytimes.com/2016/07/01/science/pea-plants-risk-assessment.html*) and the accompanying link to a Society for Risk Analysis article (*http://sds.hss.cmu.edu/risk/articles/WhyStudyRiskPercep.pdf*).

2 For a great reading list on risk perception, check out Bruce Schneier's bibliography for his Psychology of Security essay (*https://www.schneier.com/essays/archives/2008/01/the_psychology_of_se.html*).

3 As long as it's someone else's. Including sufficiently-long-enough-in-the-past-you, because, let's admit it, in the immortal words of Bugs Bunny: "What a maroon!"

where I could share this short list with you. SREs are not perfect. Some of these mistakes I've even made more than once myself. That's why they're antipatterns.

Antipattern 1: Site Reliability Operations

A new mission cannot always be achieved with old tools and methods.

Site Reliability Operations: The practice of rebranding your operations as Site Reliability without fundamentally changing their approach to problems and the nature of the work they are expected and empowered to accomplish.

Site Reliability Operations is not a thing. Site reliability is a software, network, and systems engineering discipline. You cannot take a bunch of technicians sitting in a Network Operations Center (NOC), give them a GitHub account and a public cloud budget, tell them to move some stuff to containers, and magically rebrand them as SREs.[4]

The NOC is an outgrowth of several outmoded ideas. The first is that there are specific people whose job is to keep the systems that have already been built running at all costs. SREs don't do this. SREs build systems to require less human intervention and to fail less often, and they modify existing systems to remove emergent failure modes. They do not babysit, or feed the machine with blood, sweat, tears, dinosaur grease, or any other biological product.

SREs should spend more than half their time building better systems, rather than conducting or documenting operational tasks. In a word, they should be *engineering*. Good engineering requires flow. Flow dies in an interruptive environment. Give your teams the time and space they need to keep ahead of the technical problem set by doing engineering, and you will get increased efficiency in all things, even as you increase scale, velocity, and scope.

We've seen a lot of people coming in to SRE conferences talking about the NOC they've built for their SREs. NOCs are cool. They're inspirational. The best of them can make you feel like a hero with the fate of the world—or at least the business— riding on your shoulders. But hero culture is an antipattern in and of itself, and SREs don't work in a NOC, even though NOCs originally evolved for very understandable reasons.

Sometimes, you can't beat the communications bandwidth that comes from having everyone working on a problem in the same physical space, but the tools they're

---

4 Well, you can, of course. Minus the magic part. But it isn't going to end up any better than your existing system. This does not seem to stop people from taking this approach time and again. And then giving talks about it. All of which seem to end right at the point of the rebranding, as though that were "Mission Accomplished!" in and of itself without actually effecting measurable changes in reliability.

going to do that work shouldn't be tied to that room and neither should the jobs and/or people. NOC's aren't conducive to good engineering work.

The NOC is the most open of open plan offices, with extra blinky and noisy distractions thrown in on top of the sea of coworkers to boot. And it is incomprehensible how our industry, which prides itself on being data driven, remains so willfully data-blind to the growing scientific evidence of how utterly unsuitable the open-plan office is for the work conducted by engineering teams.[5]

Don't spend your time and treasure building rooms that try to bring ops people closer to the machines and each other 24/7.

The key here is distributed sharing and collaboration from anywhere, so that just the engineers who should actually be on call at the moment can respond immediately without leaving the productive comforts of their home, office, or really well-designed cube.[6] If you want to share a link to a particular plot of a time series, you should be able to post it into a chat or an incident response tool where everyone interested in the incident can then look at the same plot with the same filters for traffic, start and end time, resolution, and so on.

Ideally, this tooling should share live data, not just a static graph or a screenshot, so that folks can use it as a starting point to play with theories, and to dig in and find discrepancies or alternate explanations for whatever is being held up as odd or offered as a cause. Any ephemeral data from these live links should be preservable with a checkbox/flag-type operation so that it will be available later for your postmortem.

Having to have everybody who wants to discuss something have to put it up on a shared monitor where other folks can't poke at it—like you do in an NOC or an old-school war room—isn't as good. More brains and hands able to manipulate information directly while still preserving collaboration and sharing will get you to a remediation of your issues faster and more consistently. And freeing your engineers from the NOC will improve their ability to deliver on actual engineering work.

---

5 Decreased Productivity (*https://onlinelibrary.wiley.com/doi/10.1002/9781119992592.ch6*); Decreased Well Being (*http://www.jstor.org/stable/255498*); Increased Sick Days (*https://www.ncbi.nlm.nih.gov/pubmed/21528171*); 2014 New Yorker review of literature (*https://www.newyorker.com/business/currency/the-open-office-trap*); Memory performs better if we have our own consistent space (*http://www.bbc.com/capital/story/20170105-open-offices-are-damaging-our-memories*); Effects of interruption on engineer productivity (*http://blog.ninlabs.com/2013/01/programmer-interrupted/*).

6 Anything's better than endless tables with no visual or auditory separation, and even cubes can be cool. (*https://www.hermanmiller.co.uk/research/research-summaries/forward-thinking-why-the-ideas-from-the-man-who-invented-cubicles-still-make-sense.html*)

Antipattern 1: Site Reliability Operations | 381

Antipattern 2: Humans Staring at Screens

If you have to wait for a human to detect an error, you've already lost.

Humans Staring at Screens: Any practice for which the detection of a problem condition relies on a human noticing that a particular series of data is abnormal, or a combination of several datasets is problematic, or that a particular condition is relevant to a known error or outage rather than relying on thresholds, correlation engines, velocity metrics, structured logs parsers, and other tooling to detect those conditions and surface them for analysis by only the relevant humans.

Another old NOC paradigm is that having human beings looking at data—even partially aggregated or correlated data—is a good way to detect and respond to potential problems before they get too bad. It is not. It is an adequate way, but it is not good. Machines are much better at finding patterns in large datasets, and they should be used to do so whenever possible.

Even modeling large amounts of data in statistically valid and yet still humanly understandable ways is difficult, let alone consuming it in any quantity or over any prolonged period. Don't spend your innovation and attention on getting a feel for constantly evolving complex systems. Machines don't need lots of tricky user experience (UX) to consume structured data. Feed it to them and then focus on grooming only the bits that matter for human consumption.

Instead of watching graphs and manually feeding an alert or ticket into a server to document and coordinate response when you detect a problem (people feeding worthwhile work to machines), build systems that can watch data for you and detect when something is going wrong. Preferably systems that can attempt some form of automated response to it, before alerting a human if the canned playbook response doesn't resolve the condition (machines feeding people worthwhile work), both to prevent interruptions and to speed recovery, because humans can't process incident detection and response fast enough without it as Service-Level Objectives (SLOs) begin to creep above four-9s.

Build tools that make it easier for engineers who spend most of their time doing engineering work in good engineering conditions (not NOCs or open-plan offices) to be notified reliably and immediately when something needs human attention and to achieve rapid access to information, systems, and one another as necessary.

Antipattern 3: Mob Incident Response

Keep your eyes on the ball, but your feet in your zone.

Mob Incident Response: All-hands-on-deck incident handling with little thought to coordination of effort, reserves, and OSHT[7] troubleshooting, sleep cycles, human cognitive limits, or the deleterious effect of interrupts on engineering work.

One of the other problems engendered by carrying over the NOC model to SRE teams, or even of using distributed systems that don't carefully scope the alerts they generate, is that the natural human tendency is for everyone within the reach of an alert or a troubling graph to sort of pile on and begin poking at the problem. Or, at the very least, they are pulled out of their flow and have the condition taking up attention at the back of their brain until it is resolved.

Not only is this disruptive to engineering work, but without extremely good policies and discipline surrounding incident response, you can actually increase the time to analyze and resolve an issue. This is especially true if multiple people begin making changes to test multiple hypotheses simultaneously, creating unplanned interactions that prevent anyone realizing they'd found the solution to the original problem or hiding/destroying evidence that would help in tracing the sources of the issue.

Even if you avoid such complications through good coordination, teams can end up in situations where a problem drags on without an imminent resolution, and because everyone piled on immediately, there's no fresh set of eyes or second shift to come in and manage the situation as the first responders' effectiveness begins to wear down.

The Incident Command System (ICS)[8] provides a good procedural framework for handling such situations and learning and implementing something similar[9] can help no matter what your tech stack or working environment looks like.

That said, we all know that relying on humans to follow procedure consistently in abnormal situations is not the best choice for avoiding problems. Why place the burden on the people you work with to do the right thing every time?

Build your detection and alerting and incident management systems to allow the necessary people to engage fully with managing the problem while protecting and pre-

---

7 1. Observe the situation. 2. State the problem. 3. Hypothesize the cause/solution. 4. Test the solution.

8 Wikipedia entry on Incident Command System (*https://en.wikipedia.org/wiki/Incident_Command_System*).

9 pagerduty incident response "Being On-Call" (*https://response.pagerduty.com/*) and "Incident management at Google — adventures in SRE-land" (*https://cloudplatform.googleblog.com/2017/02/Incident-management-at-Google-adventures-in-SRE-land.html*) by Paul Newson.

---

serving the attention and energies of the others until they are needed. Sooner or later, you will be glad for the foresight.

Antipattern 4: Root Cause = Human Error

If a well-intentioned human can "break" it, it was already broken (https://codeas craft.com/2012/05/22/blameless-postmortems/).

Root Cause = Human Error: Blaming failures upon the well-intentioned actions of a human who came to an erroneous conclusion as to the probable outcome of a given action based upon the best understanding of the system available at that time or, more generally, reducing the explanation for any unwanted outcome to a single cause.

When systems break, it is good and right to look for factors contributing to the failure so that we can seek to reduce the likelihood that the system will fail in that same manner again. The desire to prevent such recurrent failures is a very powerful incentive to identify causes that can be understood and remedied. When, in the course of such an investigation, we arrive at a human making a choice that brings about an unintended and harmful consequence, it is very tempting to stop there, for several reasons.

It allows us to feel we can shift from an investigative mode to "fixing the problem," which gives us closure and the thought we might be protected from a future problem.

It is also objectively harder to map all of the possible chains of contributing factors inherent in a person as opposed to a machine. Figuring out the context in which that person was operating—their knowledge, the exact actions they took, and the myriad possible inputs and factors they bring with them, not only from the work environment, but even from their life outside the immediately relevant interaction—is toilsome and imprecise at best and can produce outright misleading and erroneous data and conclusions at worst.[10]

We have collectively cut our teeth on decades of dualistic explanations seeking to determine whether the "cause" of an incident was a hardware failure or a human screw-up. But even "purely" mechanical failures could probably be traced back to a human error of commission or omission by an omniscient investigator. The bearing that seized wasn't lubricated properly, or cooled too quickly during manufacturing,

---

10 Assuming the human is even available to interview afterward, which in a severe accident is not always the case, the disturbing evidence of the past few decades is that many of the things we remember never actually took place: "The movie that doesn't exist and the Redditors who think it does" (*https://www.newstates man.com/science-tech/internet/2016/12/movie-doesn-t-exist-and-redditors-who-think-it-does*) by Amelia Tait and "Why Science Tells Us Not to Rely on Eyewitness Accounts" (*https://www.scientificamerican.com/article/ do-the-eyes-have-it/*) by Hal Arkowitz and Scott O. Lilienfeld

or was dropped, or inserted with too much force, or should have been replaced more frequently, or, or, or.

And the same is true conversely for "human" causes. If a human didn't perform any of those actions appropriately, there was probably a mechanical test that could have caught it, or a greater tolerance that could have been built into the part or the system, or a more visual checklist indicator that could have made the failure to perform maintenance an immediately apparent and recoverable error rather than a catastrophic production failure.

There are two seductive but unhelpful tendencies at play here. The first is the misperception of human or hardware or software or any other particular class of error as a cause of failure rather than an effect of a flawed system that would inevitably generate failure again, given a chance.

The second is the notion that post hoc incident analysis can or should actually be reduced to a "root cause" at all. Postmortem analysis should have as a goal a thorough understanding of all aspects of a failure, not the search for a discrete smoking gun.

All too often, the "root cause" is just the place where we decided we knew enough to stop analyzing and trying to learn more, whether because it was difficult to go further or because the step in question matches well with a previous condition we think we understand or for which we have a likely solution.

Instead of a root cause, or even causes, I like to think of contributing factors, whereby any one of them might not be enough to cause the observed behavior, but they all contributed to a pattern of failure that ultimately became perceptible to users of the system. Analysis needs to allow for systems where a surprising and/or undesirable emergent behavior is the result of a web of many separate conditions, all of which are necessary but none of which is sufficient to bring about or initiate the problem rather than flowing from a linear causal chain of consequences back to the first toppled domino.

The traditional postmortem template has spaces for both, but the most interesting things always turn up in the contributing factors. That's where we find things that might not even have been the most critical flaw to directly influence the outcome currently under investigation but which might have much more profound and far reaching influence on a broader group of systems and teams and outcomes in the overall organization.

So, don't hate on those horrible humans, and don't race to root. Causal analysis is not Capture the Flag. Even if you think you already know what happened and where things "went wrong," take your time and explore the system as a whole and all the events and conditions leading up to a problem you're trying to analyze.[11]

Antipattern 5: Passing the Pager

On-call can't be off-loaded.

Passing the Pager: Assigning ultimate responsibility for responding to system failures to teams or individuals who did not create the system generating the failures.

Another hangover from the old operations world is that a lot of product developers hear about the way Google SREs take the pager for services and think that means incident response isn't still the product team's job—that they should get one of those SRE teams so they don't have to be on call.

This isn't the first or last time I will say this, but reliability engineering is velocity engineering. One of the key characteristics of highly performant organizations is rapid feedback loops from the moment production code is created, through integration, testing, and deployment, right up to the performance of that production code in the real world.

Divorcing the creation of software from the production consequences of that software by off-loading the pager entirely breaks that feedback cycle, prevents rapid learning and iteration on the part of the product team, and sets teams up for an antagonistic relationship as production teams attempt to gain some measure of control over the behavior of systems created by product developers who have no incentive so strong as the delivery of features.

This is not the SRE paradigm. On-call is a shared responsibility. There are a lot of different patterns for how to share it (product devs rotating through SRE stints, product taking secondary on-call, both product and SRE in the same on-call rotation, etc.), but even where SREs completely own the primary pager response, the product development team needs to participate in the form of a product on-call that can be contacted by the SRE team to speed resolution of any problems that aren't purely the result of deployment or infrastructure issues.

In all cases, ultimate responsibility for handling production incidents remains at all times with the team developing a service. If the operations load becomes too heavy,

---

11 Most of my theory in this area comes from Allspaw's writings and from the cross-disciplinary sources to which they have introduced so many production engineers. For a more detailed discussion of this topic, see John Allspaw's "The Infinite Hows (*https://www.oreilly.com/ideas/the-infinite-hows*)" and Woods/Dekker/Cook/Johannesen/Sarter's *Behind Human Error* (*https://www.amazon.com/Behind-Human-Error-David-Woods/dp/0754678342*).

the product team needs to take the overflow, fix the technical debt, or might even end up losing pager support entirely.

Of course, if the load is just the result of a healthy service whose operational load is growing sublinearly beyond the capacity of the SRE team, growing the SRE team is an option as well. Some people are tempted to do this even when they know the system is overburdened with technical debt: "Let's just add some folks for now, and then we'll fix it down the line."

But good SREs are even harder to hire than good product developers, so it's not really possible to hire ahead of the operational load of an undesirably burdensome service without dragging a team down into an operational quagmire from which the organization you end up with will be unable to recover.

It is almost impossible to hire your way out of technical debt. You need to commit your organization to valuing and pursuing reliability and scalability with whatever resources you have, and that means not accepting bad scaling models, whether technical or human.

Antipattern 6: Magic Smoke Jumping!

Elite warrior/hero culture is a trap.

Magic Smoke Jumping (*https://en.wikipedia.org/wiki/Magic_smoke*): valuing incident response heroics over prudent design and preventive planning. This includes situations where all three are being done, but it is the IR heroics that receive the only or the most effusive public praises and rewards.

Most of us have been guilty of this. SREs are not Smokejumpers (*https://www.fs.usda.gov/detail/r5/fire-aviation/?cid=FSEPRD494036*). They are not Systems SEALs. Yes, it is a calling that requires a rare combination of skills and knowledge. Yes, we continually prepare and drill and train to handle outages when they do come.

And yes, it feels good when people from all through the organization—especially senior people and business or product development folks not even in your department—recognize *you* as the responder who saved the day and thank you for everything you endured in order to prevent the End of the World. Plus, we get these neat patches and achievement badges and get to tell "war stories" about "fighting fires."

But the hero culture concept that lauds and rewards responders for personal sacrifice in the face of system failures is destructive. Not only does the response itself suffer, but rewarding operational endurance rather than good engineering and prevention provides the wrong incentives and leads directly to ops churn and engineer burnout.

Unrested engineers are unproductive engineers and, on the whole, more unhappy people than they would be without prolonged or frequent interruptions in their work and personal life.

Being on call is a good way to learn how complex services fail and keep in touch with the as-built characteristics of your systems. But it should be once or twice a quarter, not once or twice a week, and it shouldn't involve sprinting a marathon because the team is too small and there's no one else on it or outside of it to whom you can hand off.

The incident load per shift should be low enough so as not to overwhelm the time available for work, sleep, family, or any other critical component in a sustainable life —a couple a week at most on average, and when someone gets blasted with more than that in a shift, there should be no shame in rotating in other engineers to pick up the overflow or to pick up other duties while the on-call catches up on sleep...or life.

Instead of praising someone who takes on an entire outage themselves, we should be questioning why we didn't rotate in additional personnel as needed, and asking whether the system design is as simple, reliable, resilient, and autonomous as possible.

If you're a leader in the site reliability function at your organization, you need to do everything you can to promote a culture throughout the company or institution, all the way to the highest levels, that models sustainable work and incident response, and praises engineering work that improves scale, resilience, robustness, and efficiency above responders who throw themselves into the breach left by the company as a whole not prioritizing such work.

Antipattern 7: Alert Reliability Engineering

Monitoring is about ensuring the steady flow of traffic, not a steady flow of alerts.

Alert Reliability Engineering: Creating a monitoring/logging infrastructure that results in a constant flow of notifications to the system operators. Often a result of adding a new alert or threshold for every individual system or every historically observed failure.

Alerts need to scale sublinearly with system size and activity just like everything else SRE does. You should not become uneasy because you haven't heard any low-level, nonurgent, spammy system notices from your logs and monitoring in the last hour and it's quiet; too quiet, and you need to begin looking for magic smoke signals and fire up those jump planes.

Stop paging yourself for anything other than UX alerts. Or, at the very most, those user-facing outages plus any imminent failures on whatever Single Points of Failure that you might not yet have engineered out of your organization. For critical failures that are not immediately customer detectable, velocity-bounded thresholds are your friends here. If you are losing systems at an unsustainable rate, or if you get down to three replicas out of five, or if your data store detects corruption that you need to head off before it ends up replicated into your clean copies, by all means page away. But don't do it naively at every failure or sign of trouble.

There's no shame in accommodating a system with a mixed maturity model where necessary. You start with the hand you're given, and work to change out the jokers as you're able. But you'll never get to a big payday if you don't accept that it's more important to focus effort on improving your systems than it is to burden people trying to achieve a state of flow and do effective engineering work with a stream of constant alerts and attention interrupts.

Outside of that, however, host alerts are worse than no alerts. Focus on alerting for system- or at least site-wide metrics. Otherwise, you will either end up with alert fatigue and miss critical issues, or the vital project work that can get—and keep—you out of operational churn will be buried under an avalanche of interrupts, and you will never start the virtuous cycles of productivity/efficiency that are at the heart of SRE.

In a reasonable system, outages page. Lower-grade problems that can't be resolved automatically go into your ticketing system. Anything else you feel you have to note goes into logs, if anywhere. No email spam. Email is for high-value, actionable data created by your colleagues,[12] like meeting invites and 401K renewal notices.[13]

Don't accept the noise floor and either alert too much or stop alerting on it. You can fix this with aggregation and velocity trending.

Antipattern 8: Hiring a Dog-Walker to Tend Your Pets

Configuration management should not be used as a crutch.

Hiring a Dog-Walker: Using advanced configuration-management tools like Puppet or Chef to scale mutable infrastructure and snowflake servers to large numbers of nodes, rather than to help migrate to an "immutable" infrastructure.

Configuration management is great. It is a prerequisite for doing real reliability engineering, but we've seen people presenting on how they've managed to scale it to support hundreds of configurations for thousands of hosts.

This is a trap. You will never be able to scale your staff sublinearly to your footprint if you don't instead use configuration management as a tool to consolidate and migrate

---

12 Artificial intelligence does not count as a colleague. Yet.

13 High-value examples courtesy of my ranting partner Jonah Horowitz, who also contributed to this book.

to immutable infrastructure. And if you're not scaling your staff sublinearly, you're not doing SRE. Or not successfully, anyway. Sublinear scaling is the SRE watchword, for people, processes, systems—everything.[14]

Pets < Cattle[15] < Poultry.[16] Containers and microservices are the One True Path.[17] At least until they are potentially replaced by "serverless" functions.[18] In the meantime,[19] get your fleet standardized on as few platforms as possible, running idempotent pushes of hermetic build and config pairings. I could throw some more buzzwords at you here, but instead I'll just tell you to read Jonah Horowitz's chapter on immutable infrastructure, right here in this very book (Chapter 24).

Antipattern 9: Speed-Bump Engineering

Prevention of all errors is impossible, costly, and annoying to anyone trying to get things done.

Speed-Bump Engineering: Any process that increases the length of the time between the creation of a change and its production release without either adding value to or providing definitive feedback on the production impacts of the change.

Don't become a speed bump. Our job is to enable and enhance velocity, not impair it. Reliable systems enhance velocity, and systems with quick production pipelines and accurate real-time feedback on system changes and problems introduced enhance reliability.

Consider using error budgets to control release priorities and approvals.[20] If you aren't, define explicitly what criteria you're using, instead, and how they provide an effective mechanism for controlling technical debt without requiring political conflict between production and product engineering.

---

14 Except, hopefully, compensation. :-)

15 Thank you, Randy Bias.

16 Thank you, Bernard Golden.

17 Except, of course, where they aren't.

18 Leading to the inevitable addition "Poultry < Insects." Or whatever slightly less bug-related mascot we eventually land on FaaS offerings like Lambda, GCF, Azure Functions, and OpenWhisk. Protozoa perhaps?

19 Which given how much shorter the reign of each successive paradigm in the Mainframe > Commoditization > Virtualization > Containerization timeline has been—and how much less mature when production services began shifting to it—should be approximately 8:45 AM next Tuesday.

20 Error budgets have been covered extensively in O'Reilly's first SRE handbook as well as in an inordinate number of conference talks (of which I am perhaps guilty of having given an inordinate percentage). If you don't know about them already, find the book or one of the many videos, and prosper.

Whatever it is needs to be nonsubjective, and not require everyone in the conversation to have an intimate technical understanding of every aspect of every component in the service. Change Control Boards fail both of these tests, and generally fail at satisfying reliability, velocity, and engineering time efficiency as well.

Studies have shown that lightweight, peer-review-based release controls (whether pair coding, or pre- or post-commit code reviews) achieve higher software delivery performance, while additional controls external to the engineers creating the changes are negatively correlated with feature lead time, deployment frequency, and system restore time in the event of a failure. They also have no correlation with the rate of change-induced failures.[21]

There are legitimate reasons to gate releases, but they should only be around concerns not related to the contents of the releases themselves, such as capacity planning and so forth. They should also be ruthlessly pruned and analyzed regularly to make certain they apply only to the minimum set of circumstances possible (completely new product launches rather than feature releases on existing products, for example, or capacity planning requirements for launches on services over a certain percentage of total system capacity) and only for as long as the constraining circumstances that require them are applicable (so long as the company is building its own data centers/ clusters rather than contracting with third-party cloud providers that can provide capacity on demand, perhaps, or only until a standardized framework can be created to automatically handle the implications of new privacy legislation appropriately).

Be very careful about placing any obstacle between an engineer and the release of a change. Make certain that each one is critical and adds value, and revisit them often to make certain they still provide that value and have not been rendered irrelevant by other changes in the system.

Antipattern 10: Design Chokepoints

Build better tools and frameworks to reduce the toil of service launches.

Design Chokepoints: When the only way for every service, product, and so on in an organization to be adapted to current production best practices is to go through a non-lightweight process involving direct consultation with a limited number of production engineering staff.

Your reliability team should be consulting with every product design. But your reliability team cannot scale sublinearly if they do consult on every product design. How do you resolve this?

---

21 Forsgren, Nicole, Jez Humble, and Gene Kim. (2018). *Accelerate: The Science of Lean Software and DevOps.* Portland, OR: IT Revolution Press.

Many teams use direct consultation models, either through embedding the engineers working on production tooling and site reliability within their product development organization or by holding office hours for voluntary SRE consults and conducting mandatory production reviews prior to launch.

Direct or embedded engagement has many things to recommend it, and I still use it for building new relationships with product teams or for large, complex, and critical projects. But, eventually, we reach a point where even temporary direct engagements like tech talks, developer production rotations/boot camps, production readiness reviews, and office hours can't scale.

That's no reason not to do them, because they are incredibly beneficial in their own right to collaboration, education, and recruitment. But we need something more.

If you're not looking at creating and maintaining development frameworks for your organization that incorporate the production standards you want to maintain, you're missing a great opportunity to extend SRE's impact, increase the velocity of your development and launch processes, and reduce cognitive load, toil, and human errors.

Frameworks can make certain that monitoring is compatible with existing production systems; that data layer calls are safe; that distributed deployment is balanced across maintenance zones; that global and local load balancing follow appropriate, familiar, and standardized patterns; and that nobody forgets to check the network class of service on that tertiary synchronization service cluster or comes out of a production review surprised to learn that they have three weeks' worth of monitoring configurations to write and a month-long wait to provision redundant storage in Zone 7 before they'll be able to launch because of a typo when they filled out the service template.[22]

Antipattern 11: Too Much Stick, Not Enough Carrot

SRE is a pull function, not a push function.

Too Much Stick: The tendency to mandate adoption of systems, frameworks, or practices, rather than providing them as an attractive option that accomplishes your goals while making it easier for your partners to achieve theirs at the same time.

A common theme uniting the previous two antipatterns but extending beyond them is that you will not get any place you want to go by trying to be the gatekeepers of production, or by building a tool and then trying to force people to use it.

---

22 Hypothetically. Nothing like this has ever actually happened to anyone I know who wasn't using SRE supported frameworks at any major internet company.

Worse, it has been scientifically verified that you will do harm. Organizations where teams can choose their own tooling, and which have lightweight, intrateam review processes, deliver better results faster than those trying to impose such decisions on their teams externally.[23]

Security and production engineering teams that make it harder for people to do their jobs rather than easier will find they haven't eliminated any risk; they've only created a cottage industry in the creative bypass of controls and policies.

At Dropbox, the mascot for one of our major infrastructure efforts around rearchitecting the way teams deploy services is an astronaut holding a flag emblazoned with a carrot emblem (Figure 23-1). It's not just cute, it's an important daily reminder to the teams involved.

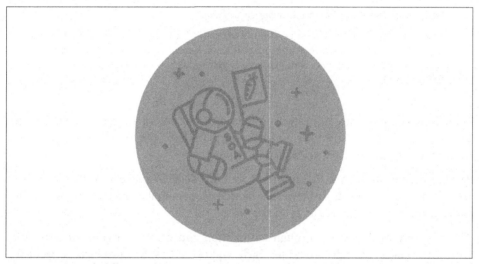

Figure 23-1. To boldly grow[24]

You should focus on building better developer infrastructure and production utilities such that product teams will see productivity wins from adopting your tools and services, either because they are better than their own, or because they are "good enough" for the 80% use case while still offloading significant development effort, and significant operational load as well, for turning up and supporting services.

Your goal is to be building cool-enough stuff by listening to your colleagues' pain points that they will see better advantage and an increase in their ability to execute

---

23 Forsgren, Nicole, Jez Humble, and Gene Kim. (2018). *Accelerate: The Science of Lean Software and DevOps.* Portland, OR: IT Revolution Press.

24 Thanks to Maggie Nelson and Serving Platform for being more awesome than a box of carrot cupcakes.

from adding an engineer to the SRE team than they would to their own, and will begin lamenting that you can't find more people to hire rather than fighting over funding.[25]

The only way to do this is to build good tools and collect good metrics about the real productivity benefits they provide. The good news is that reliability engineering is also velocity engineering. You are not a cost center. You are not a bureaucrat. You are not a build cop. You are a force multiplier for development and a direct contributor to getting the customer what they want: reliable, performant access to the services that make their lives better and more efficient.

Antipattern 12: Postponing Production

Overly cautious rollouts can produce bigger problems.

Postponing Production: The imposition of excessive lead time and testing delays in a misguided attempt to prevent any possibility of system failure, especially where it interferes with the capability for engineers to get feedback on the real impacts of their changes rapidly and easily.

Sometimes, in our desire to protect production from potentially bad changes, we set up all sorts of checks and tests and bake-in periods to try to detect any problems before the new bits ever see a production request.

Testing before production is important, but we need to make sure that it doesn't introduce a significant delay between when developers make changes and when they get real feedback on the impact of their release.

The best way to do this is through automation and careful curation of tests, and, where possible, through providing early opportunities for production feedback through dark launches, production/integration canaries, and "1%" pushes, potentially even in tandem with the execution of your slower and more time-consuming tests (load, performance, etc.), depending on your service's tolerance for, or ability to retry, errors.

We need to make it possible for product developers to know the actual impacts of their release as soon as possible. Did error rates go up? Down? How about latency? We should expose these kinds of impacts automatically as part of their workflow, rather than making them go look for information.

Product developers are part of your team. They should be able to see what results their efforts are producing in production in as close to real time as possible.

---

25 Amusingly, any sufficiently large carrot is also functionally a stick.

Focus on shortening the feedback loop for everything you can, from early development testing to performance testing to production metrics. Faster feedback delivers greater velocity while actually increasing safety, rather than imperiling it, especially if you are doing automated canary analysis and performance/load testing. Computers are better at finding patterns in large datasets than humans. Don't rely on humans.

The ability to quickly roll forward or backward, in conjunction with the ability to slice and dice your traffic along as many meaningful distinctions as possible and control what portions get delivered to which systems, reduces the risk of these practices because when a problem is discovered you can react to it. When coupled with the ability to automate rollback of changes that are detectably bad or not performant, the risk drops almost to nothing.

Antipattern 13: Optimizing Failure Avoidance Rather Than Recovery Time (MTTF > MTTR)

Failure is inevitable. Get good at handling it, rather than betting everything on avoiding it.

MTTF > MTTR: Inappropriately optimizing for failure avoidance (increasing Mean Time to Failure [MTTF]), especially to the neglect of the ability to rapidly detect and recover from failure (Mean Time to Recovery [MTTR]).

Delayed production rolls are essentially a variant of a broader antipattern, which is spending disproportionate design and operational effort to keep systems from failing, rather than ensuring that they can recover from the inevitable failures quickly and with minimal user impacts. But resilience trumps robustness except where entropy prevents it.

The truth is, there are applications for which it is not possible to recover from some kinds of failures. To take a page from medicine, when someone experiences brain death, we can't bring them back. So, it makes sense to try to make the body as robust as possible through exercise and healthy diet and do everything we can to prevent an organ failure or other breakdown that might cascade into a "negative patient outcome."

Exercise and diet can improve resilience and work to prevent the occurrence of, say, a heart attack that will cause the heart to stop. But even a single lifetime ago, we used to be unable to bring people back from acute hypothermia or cardiac arrest. This was followed by laborious manual resuscitation in the 50s, then centralized defibrillation by doctors dispatched from hospitals in the 60s, then rapid response decentralized portable defibrillation by paramedics in the 70s, then even more rapid automated highly distributed defibrillation by EMTs in the 80s, and ubiquitous automated defibrillation by the general public in the 90s and the implantable/wearable units that followed.[26]

Now, we have recovery mechanisms that can help restore function for people suffering those traumas even where prevention failed. We can even use the planned inducement of one failure (hypothermia) to help increase the survivability of other traumas (drowning, heart stoppage), or even cause a controlled heart attack to help us prevent a larger, more damaging unplanned one in the future. Every year, we get better at replacing all sorts of organs we couldn't prevent from failing. We haven't cracked the problem yet, but we're already seeing rapid detection, response, and recoverability averting catastrophes that prevention could not.

We're much further along that path when it comes to computing. The companies whose site reliability efforts I have knowledge of experience failure every day. But they expect it, anticipate it, and design everything in the sure and certain knowledge that things will break, traffic will need to be rerouted without pause, and failed systems will need to be brought back into play in short order, with automated redeployments rather than extensive administrative effort.

Chaos Engineering is a critical tool of modern service planning and design. One hundred percent uptime is a myth, because all change introduces risk into your system. But freezing changes removes your ability to address existing risk before it results in failure, and there is always risk.

Either way, your systems will fail, so it's important to accept that failure will occur and seek to minimize the size of your failure domains. Introduce capabilities to tolerate failure and provide degraded service rather than errors where possible. Sufficiently distribute your service so that it can use that capacity for toleration to continue service from the portions of your infrastructure outside the failure domain. And minimize the time and degree of human intervention needed to recover from failure and—where appropriate—reprocess any errors.

One of the best ways to ensure that these design principles are adhered to in practice is to introduce survivable failures routinely into your system.

An interviewer once asked me, "What are the characteristics of a good SRE?" One answer is that SREs need to be good at writing software, debugging systems, and imagining how things can fail.

That last one is part of what defines the difference for me between a software engineer working primarily on reliability and one working primarily on product develop-

---

26 Seattle was a pioneer in cardiac response as well as cloud computing, so these dates might not match up exactly with what you know from your own history, but the gist is probably the same: *https://en.wikipedia.org/wiki/History_of_cardiopulmonary_resuscitation*.

---

ment. We play a game sometimes in which we'll take a running instance of production, isolate it, and then try to guess what will happen if we break something in a particular way.

Then we go ahead and do it and see whether we get the predicted behavior or some other failure mode that's maybe a little more exciting and unexpected. We try to find the thresholds and the tipping points and the corner-case interactions and all the wonderful ways in which a complex system you thought you knew intimately can still surprise you after several years.

It's a lot like hacking or software testing, just with a different focus, and so a different set of attack surfaces and leverage. After a while, we become connoisseurs of failure. And then we get to try to figure out how to keep the things we discover from affecting the users of the service, and then try to break those fixes all over again. It's a good time, if you're into that sort of thing.

When you've played that game, though, the best thing is to take the most impactful of the lessons you've learned from it and incorporate them into your automated stress/canary/production testing—your Chaos Monkey or whatever tooling you're using—so that these kinds of tests are applied to the system regularly over time and help make sure that future system changes don't result in degraded robustness or resilience. This is possible only if you have good resiliency, and specifically, detection, rollback, and recoverability, so that production traffic can be shielded from the consequences of any newly introduced weaknesses/regressions.

When we work to make sure that systems will face these kinds of tests regularly, it forces site reliability developers to think more about product design and what infrastructure help they can provide to product teams. It also forces product developers to think more about designing for scale and survivability and making sure they take advantage of the reliability features and services that SRE helps provide for them. This keeps the explicit contract at the genesis of SRE—to prioritize reliability as a technical feature wherever it is required—front and center in everything the organization undertakes, without extraneous effort from either group.

Antipattern 14: Dependency Hell

Dependency control is failure domain control.

Dependency Hell: Any environment in which it is difficult or impossible to tell what systems depend upon one another, to tell whether any of those dependencies are circularities, or to control or receive notification of the addition of new dependency relationships, as well as any impending changes to the interoperability or availability of entities within the dependency web.

In any mature organization, where the software development life cycle (SDLC) has reached the point that old projects and tools are being deprecated and retired as new platforms and components and launched, unless care is taken, it will inevitably reach the point at which the interdependence of those components grow beyond the easy knowledge of any one person. The ability to predict what might be affected by your changes or what other changes might affect the systems under your control and plan accordingly becomes humanly impossible.

Make sure you have a facility to detect in an automated way what dependencies are being added to your services in something akin to real time (so that you can have timely conversations ahead of launching with the new dependency, if necessary) and to make sure that your disaster plans and road maps are updated accordingly.

Chaos engineering—or even simply business as usual—will point this out to you eventually, of course, but it's far better to track and plan for this before things get to that point. As an added bonus, explicit tracking of this can be used bidirectionally and can save service owners a great deal of time and energy in the process of migration, deprecation, and turndown.

Antipattern 15: Ungainly Governance

You can't steer a mosquito fleet like a supertanker.

Ungainly Governance: It is difficult, if not impossible, to run an Agile service delivery and dev/prod infrastructure group within a larger organization that is unwilling to adopt Lean and Agile principles in its other operations as well, or at least at the point of demarcation.

If your larger organization is locked into an antique structure of traditional IT governance, in which approvals, budget, and deliverables are tied to specific large projects or project bundles, you're going to have a hard time realizing the kind of continuous development, improvement, and release processes that are at the core of SRE, even if you are Lean and Agile within your own purview. Rigid money buckets, inadequate or unused features, zombie projects, and all manner of pervasive capacity misallocation will inevitably result.

Budget should be something that flows to organizations, not projects. And organizational leadership should be held accountable for outcomes—the results delivered across the company for the resources invested in the organization—rather than which hardware was purchased for what prices and how many hours were spent on what tasks.

Incentivize leaders to deliver quality results efficiently, and then trust them to budget and drive that process within their own organization rather than pushing down requirements and prescriptions. Prefer tracking the metrics of how you're improving current or eventual business outcomes continually over the course of work rather than judging or enforcing outcomes by adherence to the original plan or budget and use those metrics to guide you in updating your planning and execution as you go. Look at using strategic alignment techniques like Hoshin Kanri (*https://www.leanproduction.com/hoshin-kanri.html*), Catchball (*https://kanbanize.com/lean-management/hoshin-kanri/what-is-catchball/*), and Objectives and Key Results (OKRs) (*https://www.atiim.com/google-okr-objectives-key-results-video-transcript/*) to transmit broad goals to your reliability engineering organization, rather than fully enmeshing them in any more rigid systems that might pertain elsewhere in your enterprise.

Honestly, this is one of those implicit assumptions that nobody talks about because most SRE organizations exist in a culture that has already abandoned the old governance models, and SREs don't realize we're swimming in the water until we wash up on the shores of some brown-field opportunity and suddenly find ourselves wide-eyed and gasping.[27]

Getting these kinds of foundational, cultural alignments in place is critical to getting an effective reliability engineering culture and teams under way in an existing technology organization, right up there with not Passing the Pager (Antipattern 2) or (re-)inventing Site Reliability Operations (Antipattern 1).

Antipattern 16: Ill-Considered SLOh-Ohs

SLOs are neither primarily technical nor static measures.

Ill-Considered SLOh-Ohs: SLOs set or existing in a vacuum of user and business input and either not tied bidirectionally to business outcomes, priorities, and commitments, or not updated to reflect changes in the same.

SLOs are business-level objectives. They should not be set based on what you can deliver but based on what you need to deliver in order to be successful with your customers, whether internal or external.

Time after time, we see teams slap a monitor on their system, measure all sorts of things for a month, and then pick some Service-Level Indicators (SLIs) and set their SLOs based on what they measured over that period. And then never think about those levels again.

---

27 I've dealt with both systems before, but it's been so long I would never have thought to call this out to people if Mark Schwartz hadn't made a point about it after coming back to Amazon following his stint in government.

The SLO process begins when you're designing a system. It should be based on the business case and deliverables for the system, as discovered through product management, customer support, developer relations, and any number of other channels.

SLIs should be chosen based on intelligent engineering discussion of what things matter in a system and how appropriate operation of those things can be proven.

SLOs should be set through reasoned analysis of what performance and availability are needed to be useful to (and preferred by!) customers over the other options already or soon to be available to them.

If you're not doing this, you'll end up optimizing for the wrong things, and find that adoption is stunted in sectors that you were counting on, even though your service has good adoption in others. You'll also find that you've made the wrong choices in instrumentation, so that when you conduct some kinds of maintenance, or experience certain transmission problems, service errors, or capacity degradation, your system becomes useless to customers without you even being aware that anything is wrong until it shows up on Twitter or Reddit.

SLOs should be a living document. If you don't have a mechanism for revisiting them periodically or as needed, they are going to become irrelevant. If your targets don't keep up with users' changing needs, they will abandon your service. If you're exceeding the promised level of service significantly and consistently, you're going to surprise users in unpleasant ways when you make decisions about what strategies are acceptable for migrations, maintenance, production testing, or new rollouts.

Most important of all, your entire business needs to be aligned behind your SLOs. Everyone needs to know explicitly how they tie to revenue or other business goals. The SLO is not simply a stick with which to beat SREs when goals are being missed. It is a lever that should be able to elicit support and resources from the larger organization as necessary as well as driving design decisions, launch schedules, and operational work. These are business commitments, not just SRE commitments.

Capital and operational budgets need to reflect the priorities expressed in these metrics. Staffing, design decisions, and work prioritization will, at the root, flow from this data every bit as much as market research or product brainstorming sessions.

Decisions need data, and if everything is working properly, the data about how current resource allocation is affecting service and how service is affecting revenue—or work outputs, or patient outcomes, or whatever top-level organizational goal it ultimately ties to—is one of the most fundamental decision inputs that will drive your organization. So make sure these key metrics and targets are well chosen, appropriately scoped, and broadly understood and accepted.

At their heart, SLIs and SLOs are a tool for reasoning and communicating about the success of an organization. That organizations inevitably produce systems that reflect their organizational communication structures is received truth at this point.[28]

We don't have experimental evidence for causality in the other direction, but in the case of SLOs, it seems likely that organizations inevitably evolve to reflect their established communication structures every bit as much as do the systems they produce.

Antipattern 17: Tossing Your API Over the Firewall

Server-side SLOs guarantee customer outages.

Tossing Your API Over the Firewall: Failing to collaborate and integrate with key external parties using the well-established methods by which SREs collaborate and integrate with their internal customers and partners, and not measuring, sharing responsibility for, and attempting to remediate risks from outside your own systems to successful customer outcomes.

At the core of what the DevOps philosophy teaches us is the realization that *operational silos result in missed SLOs.* The effects of laggy communication boundaries and "Somebody Else's Problem" between distinct organizations are not as different as we would like to believe from the effects they create between the distinct teams within them.

Tossing your API over the internet to your customers—that is, handing them a Service-Level Agreement (SLA) for response times at the edge of your network, cashing their check, and then waiting for their inevitable support tickets—is as much an antipattern as tossing your code or binaries over the wall to the ops team was a decade ago, and for the same reasons.

Before you become too indignant about this statement, remember: tossing requirements and code over the wall was a conscientious, disciplined, and accepted business practice a decade ago, just like defining SLIs and SLOs based only on the systems controlled by your own company is today.

I'm going to steal some math here for a moment,[29] but over a 30-day window, hitting a 99.99% reliability target means you can miss your SLO for only 4.32 minutes. If you want to hit 99.999%, that drops to 26 seconds.

---

28 See Conway's Law (*https://en.wikipedia.org/wiki/Conway's_law*).

29 Dave Rensin did a great presentation laying out all the technical principles behind this calculation at SRECon Americas in 2017. If you haven't seen it, go check out the recording and slides (*https://www.usenix.org/confer ence/srecon17americas/program/presentation/rensin*).

What this math means is that without shared metrics and alerting, in which you are paying attention to the performance of the clients that are ultimately consuming your service, and any intermediate partners that own those clients and depend on you in order to service them, there is no way for your customers to consistently meet even a four 9s SLO for their own users, even if your system achieves that threshold itself.

Just the time needed for them to get paged, investigate, file a ticket that pages you, and have you investigate—even without repair time—will blow their error budget for the month. Likely for the entire quarter.

After your own house is in order and you can deliver four 9s or higher, you need to get out ahead of this. Look at your traffic. Talk to your PMs. Figure out who your critical customers are. Integrate and establish cooperation in advance.

Decide on shared metrics. You can't have a conversation if you aren't talking about the same things. Make sure everyone understands what the SLOs really mean, and that the on-call response guarantees make sense with the SLOs. Put shared communication and incident response procedures in place before you have a problem, so you can have the same kinds of response patterns to your critical customers' issues as you have to the issues of other teams within your organization.

When I onboard significant external customers, we sit down and look at what they are measuring versus what we are measuring, and at what the system as a whole, both our parts and theirs, needs to deliver to their customers rather than just to them. We determine any changes needed to grow gracefully together, and we roll them out in conjunction.

To do that, we need to commit to immediate alerting without first establishing that the problem is on one end or the other, and we have to provide remote pathways to shared integration testbeds and production canaries. Always, of course, keeping in mind that SRE's customers must be good partners regardless of whether they are internal or external, and unresolved tech debt and unsustainable operational burdens will result in devolving this kind of unmediated engagement.

It is *not* just the Googles and the Amazons that need to think about this sort of thing. As demand for ubiquitous services grows, and more companies build interdependent offerings, we're going to have to collaborate more with our most valuable customers and partners. The level at which Google CRE[30] is doing this might be beyond the scope needed today by most organizations, but the ideas are readily applicable to many services.

---

30 Dave Rensin, "Introducing Google Customer Reliability Engineering" (*https://cloudplatform.googleblog.com/2016/10/introducing-a-new-era-of-customer-support-Google-Customer-Reliability-Engineering.html*).

Antipattern 18. Fixing the Ops Team

Organizations produce the results that they value, not the results their components strive for.

Fixing the Ops Team: The mistaken belief that service delivery can be improved by bringing SREs to do SRE "to" a company, rather than for a company to start doing SRE.

This is another of those broad fallacies that people embracing the SRE brand for the first time don't always initially understand. It's basically the opposite end of the spectrum from Site Reliability Operations (Antipattern 1) in which the organization thinks that SRE is just a buzzword they can rebrand with and use to try and keep up in the recruiting competition with other companies.

At this end, people think they have an ops problem that is centered in their ops team, and if they just replace those ops engineers with SREs who have the secret sauce, they'll get the kind of results that Google and Facebook and the like get from their production engineering. But the problem isn't the ops team, it's the systemic structure that makes their operations mission impossible to achieve at scale.

SRE is not about fixing ops. It isn't just an ops methodology. Successful SRE requires fundamentally reordering how the entire company or institution conducts business: how priorities are set; how planning is conducted; how decisions are made; how systems are designed and built; and how teams interact with one another.

SRE is a particular formula for doing "DevOps" in a way that is organizationally more efficient and sustainable, and more focused on production service quality. It's not just a job or a team. It's a company-wide cultural shift to get away from gatekeepers, shadow operational costs, and institutionalized toil, and to create a healthy feedback system for balancing the allocation of engineering resources more effectively and with reduced conflict.

At the core of it is the commitment to appropriately scoped reliability as a core feature of any systems the organization creates or relies upon; to relentlessly winnowing out operational toil, delay, and human error through process and software engineering; and to shared responsibility for outcomes.

As with Lean and DevOps, both of which SRE ideally has many characteristics in common, it is an ongoing process that requires dedicated attention not just from the expert team responsible for coordinating the efforts, but also from all the other business units upon which the value stream depends.

Thus, absent commitment from the very top of the organization[31] to driving this model, your ability to realize the benefits will be limited. You can still make substantial improvements in your team processes and systems. With enough grassroots support from other teams, you might even end up with a fairly functional DevOps model.

But if you want to reliably create virtuous cycles of productivity through prioritizing engineering over toil, even at the potential cost of an SLO shortfall now and then; to establish well-aligned priorities across the organization that won't be repeatedly abandoned or regularly mired in the *conflict du jour*; to create and safeguard the sustainable work balance and systems needed to attract and retain top talent then; the further up the organization that understanding and buy-in to SRE principles goes, the closer you will come to realizing your goals. Do whatever work you must in order to make certain the entire organization subscribes to the same strategy.

So, That's It, Then?

That's all of them? We've got it all figured out?

So, what does this all mean? What do we do with this information, with these hard-won lessons in unintended consequences? Just a handful of little dead ends to watch for, and as long as we avoid these we'll never have a problem, right?

Sadly, not. Because each unhappy technology or business is unhappy in its own way, and because I haven't been around to see even more than a fraction of them, we have to expect this list to keep growing and changing as the industry does.

The important thing here is the process—the most fundamentally SRE process—of continuing to look at the places we and our peers have run into trouble, and then not only creating learning opportunities for our own organizations, but turning those catalogs of failure into stories that we can share across the industry as well.

In fact, I think the time might even be ripe for an antipattern repository where peers can share, discuss, and categorize potential new patterns or variations. If you have one that we've left out, we definitely want to hear from you before we stub our own toes on it. So @BlakeBisset me on Twitter, #SREantipatterns. Even if we do not find anything new, at least we might perhaps find the conversation very pleasant?

Spes non consilium est![32]

---

31 CEO is best, C-level is decent. At the least, the heads of your product development and production engineering teams should agree on budget, staffing, on-call, toil, change control, and epic schwag.

32 Hope is not a strategy!

Blake Bissel got his first legal tech job at 16. He did three startups (one biochem, one pharma, and this one time a bunch of kids were sitting around wondering why they couldn't watch movies on the internet) before becoming an SRM at YouTube and Chrome, where his happiest accomplishment was holding the go/bestpostmortem link at Google for multiple years. He currently serves on the USENIX SRECon program committee and as Head of Reliability Engineering at Dropbox.

## CHAPTER 24

Immutable Infrastructure and SRE

Jonah Horowitz, formerly Netflix and Stripe

Immutable infrastructure can significantly reduce the amount of toil required to maintain a large fleet of production servers. It does this by reducing the number of variables in the system and making it easier to swap pieces out because all instances of a service are identical.

Scalability, Reliability, and Performance

SRE has perhaps become overloaded, but at its core, the definition boils down to a few things: driving scalability, reliability, and performance for web operations at scale. A challenging, but incredibly powerful, piece of that is through *immutable infrastructure.*

Immutable infrastructure is the practice of starting each build of a software component with a small base image and then installing your software onto that image. For every release, this image is rebuilt before being released to production. After it is released, the image is never changed or updated. It is only replaced with a new image. The process is called "immutable" because the released software is frozen and never changed, only replaced. The running instances are never updated via a tool like Puppet, Chef, or even Secure Shell (SSH) after they are launched (they might still have SSH running for debugging purposes).

Immutable infrastructure delivers scalability and performance by allowing horizontal scaling of your infrastructure. One of the challenges of adding and removing nodes from a running cluster is making sure that every node has the correct and identical configuration. It is possible to manage a 10-node cluster when you log in and hand-configure each node, but it is toilsome and prone to error. It is silly to hand-administer 100 nodes, and with 1,000 nodes or more, it becomes literally impossible for one person if they have to spend more than 10 minutes per machine per week. In the face of such toil, organizations turn to a configuration management tool to handle large clusters of servers. Chef and Puppet are two of the more popular choices, but there are many more—including writing one from scratch (which I do not recommend).

Configuration management systems like Chef and Puppet work well initially, but they ultimately fall short when the cluster size grows, particularly when you start needing to scale it dynamically. When each node must boot and run another tool—first, to install and afterward to configure your software—you end up wasting considerable time. If the nodes already have the software ready to go, they are constrained only by their boot time. With the movement to containers, the boot times become even faster.

If you can rapidly add nodes when you need capacity, this allows you to save resources, because you need only enough capacity online at any given time to support your current traffic load. Most websites serve significantly less traffic at 3 AM than at 7 PM. If you can expand capacity within minutes of seeing increased load, you can run with a smaller buffer, and you can be more confident in scaling down when your load is lower.

Failure Recovery

Another thing enabled by immutable infrastructure is the ability to recover quickly from failure. If the hardware underlying an individual node fails, you can rapidly start another node with the immutable image to replace it. This new node does not need additional configuration or software installation because it boots from the same image that every node in your cluster already uses. Also, this allows you to take advantage of tools like Netflix's Chaos Monkey to induce failure into your system, ensuring your ability to handle that failure.

Simpler Operations

Simplicity is a fundamental component of velocity. An advantage of an immutable system is that it makes changes simpler. Components are replaced instead of modified, so you no longer need to manage careful state transitions between an old state and a new state. That is regardless of whether you are rolling out a new release of the application that runs on your servers, a configuration change to your operating system, or an update to an underlying library. In any case, you run through the same process to release the change into production.

This simplicity is an important point to stress. Not needing to worry about modifying state in place increases the velocity and reliability of your deployments. When your infrastructure is managed traditionally, so much code is dedicated to checking the current state before a change and then making sure that a change influenced that state in the way you expected it would.

Consider a simple update of a DNS server in /etc/resolv.conf. Without immutable infrastructure, you must make sure that the line for the old DNS server is removed, and then make sure that the line for the new DNS server is inserted in the correct place. With immutable infrastructure, you just release a new build that points to the updated DNS server—a significantly simpler operation.

Faster Startup Times

When I started working in tech, it took us about a day to get a new server into the rotation in the load balancer. With configuration management, I was able to get that down to less than an hour, but with immutable infrastructure, it is down to 5 minutes. There's a trade-off. It takes longer to build a new image, but each image launches significantly faster. It mirrors a lot of other trade-offs we make; for example, we exchange compilation time with runtime using gcc -02.[1]

Faster startup times allow us to scale our systems more efficiently. If your startup time is an hour, you need to anticipate the load that your system will be under at least an hour in advance and start scaling to anticipate that. If your startup time is only 5 minutes, you need to predict only 5 minutes into the future. As with all predictions, the shorter your time horizon, the more accurate you are likely to be. This gives you the ability to scale down confidently, too. If your traffic is trending downward and you expect it has peaked for the evening, you can confidently scale down your cluster, knowing that you can get capacity back online quickly if your predictions were incorrect.

Faster startup time allows more real-time or immediate capacity management, but what it really gives us is added resilience to failure. The ability to replace nodes quickly means that when they die, either due to external events like a node going offline, or internal events like a Chaos exercise, we can promptly and automatically replace the node without manual intervention. Without immutable infrastructure, adding deliberate failure to your infrastructure can end in true chaos.

Known State

One of the biggest concerns of both SRE teams and security teams is unknown dark corners in their infrastructure. If a machine has been up long enough, you never really know its true state. Without immutable infrastructure, a machine can stay in

---

1 The -02 flag in gcc *increases both compilation time and the performance of the generated code* (*https://gcc.gnu.org/onlinedocs/gcc/Optimize-Options.html*).

production for years, receiving upgrades and patches and getting new software installed, and old software can be removed without a full reimage. You cannot know the full state of an instance like this.

This is scary from a security perspective because you do not know whether the machine was compromised long ago and has a persistent piece of malware on it. It is also scary from an SRE perspective because you do not know whether there's a latent bug lurking on the system. Maybe one of your libraries was not upgraded, or one of your patches was not installed. Maybe another engineer at your company manually installed a package or an individual binary. With immutable infrastructure, you never have an instance running for more than a few weeks, optimally less than a few days.

Like everything in complex systems, configuration management itself is not perfect. It sometimes fails, so even with the best-maintained infrastructure, you end up with a few systems that didn't receive the latest updates. This could be because the agent on the box crashed in a bad state or because there was a network problem, but regardless of the reason, it does not deliver on the promise that all systems are configured in the way you expect.

With immutable infrastructure, you can be sure that machines booted from the image, and that the configuration is correct and up to date, because there's only one configuration for the entire life cycle of the instance. If an instance is misbehaving for any reason, you can just shut it down and replace it with a new instance.

Continuous Integration/Continuous Deployment with Confidence

In a traditional infrastructure, your software is installed on Dev, then Test, then maybe Staging, and then Prod. In each case, the software can be deployed slightly differently, particularly if the servers are reused between installations. The cruft and differences between servers compound over time. You cannot trust that a change that works in Test or Staging will perform the same way when it gets into Production. When you move to immutable infrastructure, this risk is significantly reduced. The image used is exactly the same for each environment, and you never hear a developer saying, "It worked fine in Test!"

The best way of deploying immutable infrastructure is to use a blue/green deployment. The way this works is that if you have a cluster of 200 instances delivering a service, which we'll label blue, you spin up 200 instances of the new release image, which we'll label green. When the 200 new instances are up and serving traffic, you stop the traffic to the old instances. After a waiting period to determine that they're healthy, perhaps an hour, you terminate the old instances. This process allows for very smooth rollouts and rollbacks. If there's an increase in errors with the new release, you just move the traffic back to the old release.

Security

Immutable infrastructure has advantages when it comes to security as well. Because each instance is built from scratch every time, you have a far lower risk of cruft accumulating on a node. This means that programs installed for temporarily troubleshooting an issue or old libraries that aren't in use anymore won't increase your attack surface.

If an attacker gains control of a node, they have a limited window where they can utilize the node before it is replaced, so they cannot install long-running exploits.

When rolling out a security patch, you can use the same release process as for application code changes. This minimizes risk because a well-exercised and understood process is less likely to fail.

One of the more painful types of security updates is kernel patches. In a traditional infrastructure, they are risky because you must reboot each server and hope that the server comes back online. This can fail for any number of reasons. You can have a configuration problem that went unnoticed until you attempted the upgrade, you can also find latent hardware problems that you did not know were there. With immutable infrastructure, you build new server images with the kernel patch already applied and then push that through your normal release pipeline. It is safer, it is faster, and it does not require the manual tending (or painful scripting) of your servers as they reboot.

Multiregion Operations

Immutable infrastructure simplifies multiregion operations. Instead of having to propagate a different configuration management stack to all of your regions and keep them synchronized, you can deploy a single image to all of your regions. Deploying configuration management to multiple regions can be challenging to manage on its own. Each configuration management master node must maintain synchronization with the master nodes in other regions, which is an additional level of complexity. This is still true if you deploy a masterless configuration management tool because you still need to copy and keep some management artifact like a *.tar* file synchronized.

When using immutable infrastructure, you need to add only a step to your deployment pipeline that copies your new image out to each region before launching servers based on that image. With blue/green deployment, you can have confidence that your deployment succeeded in one region before you roll it to additional regions. If your architecture requires that you run the same exact version in all regions at all times, you can accomplish that, too, by synchronizing the blue/green flips.

Release Engineering

Configuration management tools are scary to developers and organizations because of how powerful they are. One misconfiguration and you can disable your entire infrastructure. Because of this, many companies do not trust their developers to roll out changes to their configuration management without review by an operations team. Every configuration management software also uses its own domain-specific language, which developers are not as familiar with as their primary language. It is an additional burden on these developers to ask them to learn and use this language, and they'll never be fully fluent in it because they don't use it often.

With immutable infrastructure, you remove these concerns. You never alter the state of any running instance. This significantly reduces the risk to your infrastructure of a bad change, even more so because all changes will affect only one type of instance, and with blue/green deployments, changes are trivial to roll back in the event of a problem.

With these changes, you can enable developers to deploy code and configuration changes to production with confidence that you can trivially repair any damage caused by an unforeseen bug.

Building the Base Image

The first step to implementing immutable infrastructure is to create a good base image. This image is then used for every running instance in your infrastructure. If you run a small shop, you might do this by using a default release image from an upstream Linux distribution and then installing the latest security updates. That would be the easiest option.

If you have a team with a little more bandwidth, you can optimize the base image by doing some of the following:

- Removing packages that you know you do not need in your production environment
- Hardening the image by changing the security settings
- Tuning the network stack
- Installing common libraries and internal packages that are used throughout your infrastructure

Taken to the extreme, the base image can be entirely built from signed source code using a dedicated build and release pipeline that is immutable as well. Building an image in this way produces a bit-for-bit reproducible image that you can trust and verify. This exceeds the requirements of most organizations, though.

After you have an image you are happy with, you use that image to build all other images that you release to production. The cadence for rebuilding this image is up to you, but I recommend doing it weekly, and having an exception process so that you can build and deploy this image immediately after a security vulnerability affecting your systems is discovered.

For releasing your new image, you should find a few applications in your organization that are less critical and have more capable operations teams to *canary* each release before you roll it to your mission-critical applications. A canary is a small subset of your systems that you can deploy new code on to see whether there are issues that were not caught by your automated testing. In this way, you have both a canary and a release version available at any given time.

You can configure the base image by using a configuration management tool or even just a shell script. This is completely different than running a configuration management tool in production because you are using it only as part of the deployment pipeline, and not on your running infrastructure. Optimally, you should need to run the tool only once, bringing the upstream image into compliance with your desired configuration before the image is frozen. The team that is responsible for building and maintaining the base image should take input and collaborate with the developers who will build applications that run on the base image. The developers in your company will never need to care or even know about the configuration management tools you use to build your base image.

Deploying Applications

When each developer is ready to deploy, each application should go through an automated multistep deployment process. First, you should compile and package the code using either the packaging system for your operating system (OS) or a language-specific packaging system. After that is complete, the package, along with its dependencies, can be installed on the base image. HashiCorp has an open source tool for this called Packer. Netflix also released an open source tool called Aminator. If you are running a container infrastructure, there are many tools to build Docker images. Docker images still need to run on a base OS. You should launch this base OS from an immutable system image. The Docker images should be pulled at runtime with the version managed by your container orchestration tools. When you deploy this way, you'll have immutable Docker images running on immutable system images.

When the image or Docker container is ready, you need to test it before deployment. Initially, you will want to launch it in a development or integration environment. After it passes your tests, run it in your Test or Staging environments before launching a canary instance taking production traffic. Finally, you can either launch a new autoscaling group or Docker cluster with the new image or grow the canary cluster into the target of your next blue/green deployment.

The idea is for the SRE team to enable any developer to deploy a new version of a service safely and quickly.

Disadvantages

So far, this chapter has covered the advantages and techniques for deploying immutable infrastructure, but there are cases when it is not a good fit. It can be hard, if not impossible, to use immutable infrastructure on your persistent data layer. Some databases like Cassandra are designed to work in an immutable environment. It requires that you use a rolling release, in which you replace one node at a time instead of a blue/green release. Other databases are hard to use in an immutable way without significant modification. Depending on the application, it might be easier to run immutable on nodes outside the data layer, and a more traditional configuration-managed infrastructure for the data layer.

Immutable infrastructure can also increase the iteration latency. Building a new image, even if it's just a Docker image, takes much longer than just copying a few files of code to a development instance. This iteration latency can decrease developer productivity, chiefly when your code base can be run on only a server and can't be developed locally on the developer's workstation. One way to mitigate this is to facilitate synchronizing code from the developer workstation to a temporary dev server before the code is packaged and shipped to a Test or Staging environment. This approach balances the need for developer productivity with the advantages of immutable infrastructure.

Conclusion

When adopted, immutable infrastructure reduces toil, allowing your developers to focus on product features; your SRE team can increase developer productivity and reduce time to deploy new code, leading to happier, more productive developers while simultaneously leading to a safer and more reliable infrastructure.

Jonah Horowitz is a senior site reliability engineer with 18 years' experience building and scaling production applications. He's worked at several startups and large companies including Quantcast, Netflix, and Stripe.

## CHAPTER 25

Scriptable Load Balancers

Emil Stolarsky, DigitalOcean (formerly Shopify)

When scalability problems occur, there's no time to go back and rearchitect or refactor an entire web service. Inevitably the service you're responsible for will go down as a result of being overloaded. Sometimes, you're hoping for a miracle in the form of an easily fixable, bad database query. Or maybe you're able to simply scale up the number of workers. But what about when you don't have the time, money, or people needed for solving the problem at hand? Luckily, there's a new suite of tools that are making a name for themselves in small corners of our industry that can forever change the way we approach scalability and our roles as SREs: *scriptable load balancers.*

Scriptable load balancers are proxies that can have their request/response processing flow modified through a scripting language such as Lua. This opens new ways for infrastructure teams to shard applications, mitigate Distributed Denial of Service (DDoS) attacks, and handle high load. Small teams can now solve difficult or seemingly impossible problems in novel and elegant ways. The ability to add high-performance, custom logic to a load balancing tier isn't new; however, the ability to do that at an organization of any size is. And that's why scriptable load balancers could be game changing.

Scriptable Load Balancers: The New Kid on the Block

Look at almost any web service, and often you'll find a load balancer being the first thing a request hits, as Figure 25-1 depicts.[1] These servers act as proxies, receiving

---

1 Limoncelli, Thomas A., Strata R. Chalup, and Christina J. Hogan. (2014). "Application Architectures." In *Practice of Cloud System Administration: DevOps and SRE Practices for Web Services.* Boston: Addison-Wesley Professional.

requests (HTTP or otherwise) and forwarding them to a specified pool of upstream servers. They have become ubiquitous for their value in improving resiliency and performance. Today, they're often used for not much more than Secure Sockets Layer (SSL) offloading, simple caching, and distributing load across multiple upstreams.

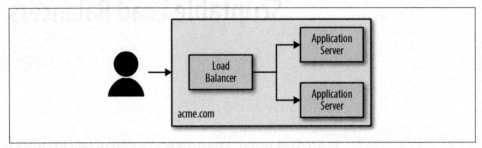

Figure 25-1. Architecture of a typical web application with a user request hitting a load balancer before being routed to an application server.

Load balancers are highly capable, specialized components in our architecture. Their ability to process requests quickly and serve orders of magnitude more traffic than their upstreams is a powerful trait. Unfortunately, any attempt at adding complex application logic is quickly shut down by the restrictive configuration languages shipped with load balancers. There are application-aware load balancers (e.g., Facebook's Proxygen[2]) that are able to peer into the content of a request (e.g., read headers) and act on it, but you need to custom-build these. The goliaths of the industry (Facebook, Google, etc.) recognize the value that application-aware load balancers can bring and have taken to writing their own. For the rest of the industry that can't spare a team of people, we're left without them entirely.

A few companies in the industry have begun to realize that there doesn't need to be this dichotomy between traditional load balancers or application-aware, custom-built load balancers that take a team to support. This middle ground can be filled by *scriptable load balancers*. With scriptable load balancers you can modify the request/response processing flow (e.g., by modifying outgoing headers) through a scripting language such as Lua. You can write extensions in a high-level language to add application-aware functionality on top of the load balancer's existing features.

The market for scriptable load balancers is still young. There are currently two main scriptable load balancer projects: OpenResty and nginScript. OpenResty is an Nginx C module with an embedded LuaJIT, created by Yichun "agentzh" Zhang. A steady community[3] has grown around it, producing multiple libraries/modules; it's been

---

2 Shuff, Patrick. (2015). "Building a Billion User Load Balancer." (*https://www.usenix.org/conference/srecon15europe/program/presentation/shuff*) Talk at SREcon15 EU.

3 Netcraft. (2016). "September 2016 Web Server Survey."

adopted by companies such as Cloudflare, Tumblr, and Shopify. Of the two, OpenResty has the largest community and powers upward of 10% of internet traffic.[4] Closely following is nginScript, Nginx Inc.'s implementation of a JavaScript scripting engine in Nginx.

Why Scriptable Load Balancers?

Scriptable load balancers have numerous advantages over custom-built and conventional load balancers.

For starters, only a select number of organizations can spare the time and people necessary to build their own production-ready load balancer. More practically, few engineers have experience building a load balancer from scratch. Rather than spending time improving resiliency or performance, engineers will spend their time reinventing the wheel, building routing and request processing engines.

At the end of the day, the custom logic you add to the edge only makes up a fraction of what load balancers can do. Rebuilding that functionality is in no one's best interest. Especially, when current capabilities are a moving target with constant improvements from the open source community.

Traditional load balancers don't offer the same capabilities as scriptable load balancers. One drawback is that traditional load balancers ship with declarative configuration languages that make it difficult to express application logic. Sometimes, it's even impossible to specify the desired behavior. Additionally, logic expressed through configuration is difficult to fully validate for correctness with tests. To compensate, many load balancers ship with a C-based plug-in system that allows developers to augment existing functionality through modules. These plug-in systems address many concerns, but they come with substantial, unnecessary downsides when compared to using an embedded scripting language. Without built-in memory safety, C is prone to memory faults (e.g., buffer overflow and segmentation faults), making it inherently unsafe. In contrast, a scripting language, such as Lua, can be sandboxed with strict runtime and memory guarantees. When writing a C module, developers can't ignore lower-level details that aren't immediately relevant to the logic at hand, a problem scripting languages don't have.

Making the Difficult Easy

Load balancers act as gatekeepers to services, with every request passing through them. Their position in our web architecture enables powerful abstractions. This

---

4 Roberts, John. (2016). "Control Your Traffic at the Edge with Cloudflare." *https://blog.cloudflare.com/cloudflare-traffic/*.

allows for solutions that aren't typically available to SREs or infrastructure developers. For example, the ability to pause requests during deploys to avoid returning errors to customers or proxying requests to the correct data center is powerful for an SRE team, but difficult to achieve with existing frameworks and applications. Typical web frameworks such as Rails or Django are designed for serving traditional CRUD/REST requests. Although they can perform nontraditional operations, it comes at the cost of resiliency. The rest of this section will show how you can use scriptable load balancers to solve common infrastructure problems to great effect.

Shard-Aware Routing

When applications grow sufficiently large, their data becomes too big to be stored on a single node. The solution is to break the data into manageable chunks, referred to as *shards*, and spread it out among multiple nodes and/or databases. Sometimes, this is done internally by the database, and all that's required to scale is adding more nodes to the database cluster. For the majority of applications, the data has to be logically partitioned depending on data models and access patterns.[5]

After an application is sharded, there's no guarantee that processes can access every shard. To render a response, therefore, you need to ensure that a request is routed to a process that can access the required data. How a particular request is routed becomes an important problem to solve. Let's now look at some common ways that you can route requests to the correct shard and how you can use scriptable load balancers to solve this tricky problem.

Routing requests with DNS

For data models that can be sharded by domain name (e.g., multitenant applications), you can use DNS to route to the correct shard. Every shard is given a unique domain that resolves to a process which can serve requests for the shard, as shown in Figure 25-2.

---

5 Matsudaira, Kate. (2012). "Scalable Web Architecture and Distributed Systems." In *The Architecture of Open Source Applications Volume II: Structure, Scale, and a Few More Fearless Hacks.* Ed. Amy Brown and Greg Wilson. (CC BY 3.0.)

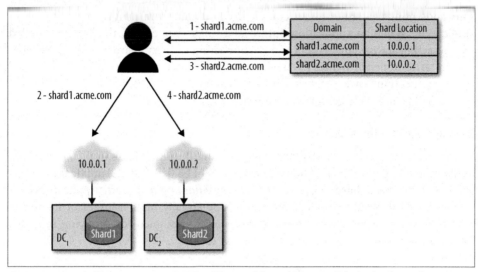

Figure 25-2. 1) Client requests DNS address of domain on a shard. 2) Client directs request to the IP returned by the DNS server to the location of the first shard. 3) Client requests DNS address of domain on a separate shard. 4) Client sends request to the corresponding DC.

The clear benefit of this method is its simplicity. Any application on the web is already using DNS. But, as we're all too familiar, DNS comes with a whole host of problems. Convergence in changes to routing information can take unpredictably long times. Using DNS also limits what can be used to distinguish between shards (i.e., only a domain name).

Routing queries in the application

You can avoid the problem of ensuring that a request is routed to the correct process if every process can access all shards. As Figure 25-3 shows us, the logic of connecting and communicating with the correct database then becomes a responsibility of the application.

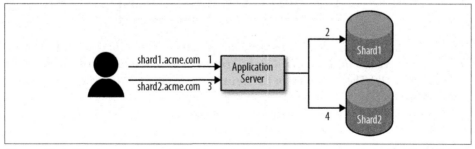

Figure 25-3. For every request, the app server connects to the necessary shard on the fly.

This adds nontrivial amounts of complexity and compromises the scalability of an application. When an application outgrows a single data center, the latency entailed in connecting across data centers makes connecting to every shard an expensive decision in terms of performance. Even when the added latency isn't a problem, the number of connections each database and application process must manage leads to its own sets of problems (e.g., max connection limits).

Routing requests in the application

At the cost of added complexity, you can place shard routing logic in the application, as illustrated in Figure 25-4. When a request cannot be handled, the application proxies it to the correct shard. This is known as *backhauling a request*. Applications are now required to be able to backhaul traffic—potentially high volumes of it—to the correct process. Traditional web frameworks aren't designed for proxying requests. To top it off, this sort of functionality isn't easy to add.

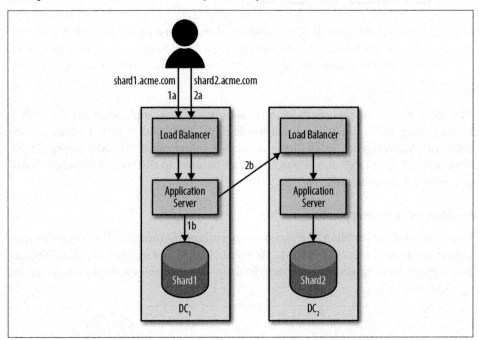

Figure 25-4. 1a) Client sends a request for shard 1 to the closest data center. 1b) The app server connects to the local shard. 2a) Client sends a request for shard 2 to the closest data center. 2b) The app server in DC$_1$ proxies the request to DC$_2$, where step 1b is repeated locally.

Scriptable load balancers allow you to move all shard routing logic into the load balancing tier, enabling new routing possibilities and giving you the ability to completely abstract away the idea of sharding from applications. Processes are never made aware of requests they can't serve, as depicted in Figure 25-5.

With full control of the request routing logic, you're able to extract the desired shard from any combination of attributes or properties (e.g., Host, URI, and client IP). It's even possible to query a database that gives insight about the shard to which a request belongs. With the other approaches to routing, the process directly affects how data models can be partitioned. For example, if you use DNS routing, data models without their own domain can't be partitioned. Infrastructure concerns shouldn't dictate the design of an application. Embedding routing logic in load balancers removes the leakiness of that abstraction.

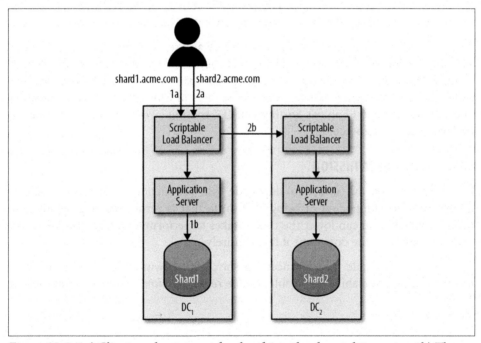

Figure 25-5. 1a) Client sends a request for shard 1 to the closest data center. 1b) The load balancer in DC₁ proxies the request to the local shard. 2a) Client sends a request for shard 2 to the closest data center. 2b) The load balancer in DC₁ proxies the request to DC₂ where step 2 is repeated locally.

Ideally, applications are minimally aware of their own sharding. With routing in the load balancer, an application is able to hold little to no awareness of its own sharding. By separating these concerns, you can reuse sharding logic among multiple applications. Google's Slicer[6] is a prime example of this approach. Slicer is an autosharding service for applications. A core component is the transparency to upstream applications in how requests are routed to a particular shard through Google's frontend load balancers and RPC proxy. The service is in production today, routing 7 million requests per second.

Harnessing Potential

The power in scriptable load balancers comes from the reuse of existing functionality. You don't need to rewrite Transport Layer Security (TLS) negotiation or health checking when your load balancers already excel at these tasks. Oftentimes, internet specifications will even make room for modifications. HTTP caching is a good example of this. The RFC allows for custom Cache-Control header extensions that modify how and when a request is cached.[7] Instead of writing a new caching proxy for fine-grained cache key control (e.g., including specific cookies in the cache key), a simpler script running in the load balancer can reproduce the exact same functionality.

Furthermore, load balancers specialize at routing and serving requests. An enormous amount of effort is invested in ensuring that they're able to do this quickly, at high volume. With little effort, these same properties can be inherited by the modules added to scriptable load balancers. You can see this in Cloudflare's Web Application Firewall (WAF)[8] and Shopify's Sorting Hat (L7 routing layer),[9] which both measure performance in microseconds.

Case Study: Intermission

For most services, the ability to ship code into production quickly and easily is important. One component of being able to do that is zero-downtime deploys. As much as automation can lower the time it takes to perform disruptive maintenance, you can't eliminate the downtime it takes entirely.

You can use scriptable load balancers to solve zero-downtime deploys or maintenance by adding the ability to enable/disable *request pausing*. Take, for example, an

---

6 Adya, Atul, et al. (2016). "Slicer: Auto-sharding for Datacenter Applications." In *Proceedings of the USENIX Conference on Operating Systems Design and Implementation. https://www.usenix.org/system/files/conference/osdi16/osdi16-adya.pdf.*

7 Fielding, R., M. Nottingham, et al. (2014). "Hypertext Transfer Protocol (HTTP/1.1): Caching" (*https://tools.ietf.org/html/rfc7234*). IETF Standards Track RFC.

8 Graham, John. (2014). "Building a Low-Latency WAF Inside NGINX Using Lua." (*https://www.youtube.com/watch?v=nlt4XKhucS4*) Talk at NginxConf.

9 Francis, Scott. (2015). "Building an HTTP Request Router with NGINX and Lua." (*https://www.youtube.com/watch?v=Cw6Ci9AF23k*) Talk at NginxConf.

application that errors on any request during maintenance, as demonstrated in Figure 25-6.

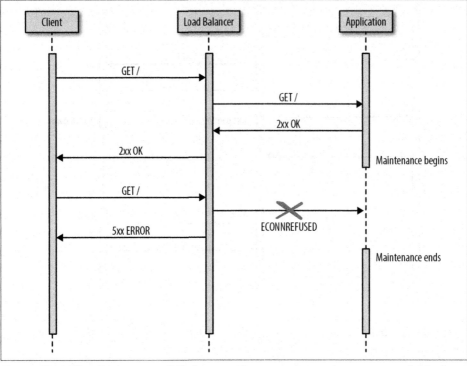

Figure 25-6. The client request fails because the upstream service was unavailable during the maintenance window.

Request pausing is when a proxy waits before forwarding the request to the desired upstream. A request can be paused for a specified amount of time or toggled by a flag stored in a datastore. When the proxy resumes, requests are forwarded to their original target, as shown in Figure 25-7.

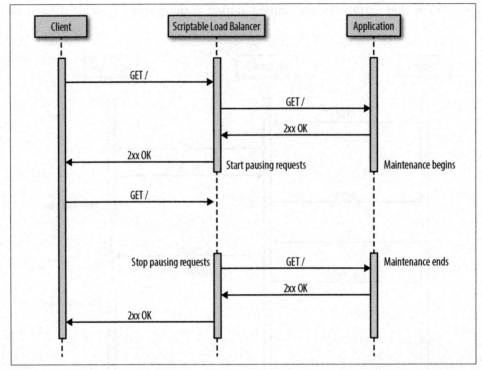

Figure 25-7. When the client request hits the load balancer, the load balancer waits until request pausing is disabled to forward it to the application.

Rather than failing a request, clients receive a slower response. Depending on the Service-Level Objectives (SLO), this can be the difference between staying within this month's error budget or bursting through it. Scriptable load balancers can be programmatically instructed to start pausing requests for a service, track whether clients have disconnected, and slowly forward requests as the service comes online to avoid overloading upstream services.

Service-Level Middleware

Eliminating toil is one of the core principles in SRE.[10] As organizations continue to adopt SRE best practices, more teams are moving to a product or service model to kick the ticket/ops cycle.

---

10 Beyer, Betsy, et al., eds. (2016). "Part II. Principles." (*https://landing.google.com/sre/book/chapters/part2.html*) In *Site Reliability Engineering* (O'Reilly).

In the traditional ops model, engineers deploy and operate dependencies for each application. A traditional example of this would be a database. The ops teams would set up, and babysit, SQL servers for the applications they're operating. With the product or service model, a dedicated team builds out an application-agnostic database as a service. This service is then exposed by an API/UI (e.g., what's offered by cloud providers).

Although a product–service model is substantially better than toil and "operating snowflakes," it still pushes the burden of interoperating with a provisioning service to applications. In some cases, this can quickly lead to high overhead. Calling out to a service requires that an application be aware of its existence. Picture an identity service that every application uses in order to authenticate requests. Each application is forced to hold awareness of the identity service, which leads to an increased maintenance burden and the overhead of calling to an outside service. With scriptable load balancers, product/service models aren't the only way SRE teams can eliminate toil.

Middleware to the Rescue

Scriptable load balancers are typically the first component that touches a request. This makes them an ideal location for logic that affects multiple services. Rather than making RPC calls to outside services, applications can read headers added to the request before it was proxied. You can think of this model as middleware similar to those found in most web frameworks. A service-level middleware transparently operates on requests before they hit the upstream application. Product developers can free themselves of the overhead and complexity of calling to an outside service.

For certain problems, a middleware is a more natural solution.[11] Take, for example, the identity service mentioned earlier. Rather than calling out directly to the identity service, an application can assume any request that has a certain header that has already been authenticated. The header could contain the scope and access the client has. The identity middleware removes the latency and complexity overhead of calling to outside services from within upstream services.

APIs of Service-Level Middleware

All but the most trivial of middlewares require some application-specific configuration (e.g., specifying a different cache key on a particular page). The immediate go-to solution might be to hardcode this configuration in the middleware code base. But, over time, the hardcoded configuration will likely diverge from reality and lead to easily avoidable outages.

---

11 Agababov, Victor, et al. (2015). "Flywheel: Google's Data Compression Proxy for the Mobile Web" (*https:// www.usenix.org/system/files/conference/nsdi15/nsdi15-paper-agababov.pdf*). In *Proceedings of the USENIX Symposium on Networked Systems Design and Implementation*.

To prevent divergence, it's important to establish clear APIs through which applications can constantly communicate to downstream middleware. You can use custom HTTP request and response headers as the communication bus over which configuration is communicated. For data that doesn't fit into the request/response flow, you can use an out-of-band message bus to propagate state to all load balancers.

Case Study: WAF/Bot Mitigation

It's only a matter of time before a web service is targeted by a Distributed Denial-of-Service (DDoS) attack or exploited through automated bots.[12] DDoS attacks can cause nasty outages, with serious downtime. Automated bots beating out human customers often leads to unhappy customers. Rather than developing the same antibot or DDoS mitigation tooling in each application, you can use scriptable load balancers to build a layer of protection against these threats and use them on all web-exposed services.[13]

Cloudflare has built a business providing such a layer with its web application firewall functionality. Any service behind its middleware gains the same benefits of protection against Open Web Application Security Project (OWASP) vulnerabilities, common DoS vectors, and zero-day exploits. When the danger or authenticity of a request is ambiguous, the middleware is able to redirect to a challenge-response test to validate that the request comes from a legitimate source.

Whereas previously protection against attacks below the application layer would require making a decision based on the scope of a single packet, scriptable load balancers allow you to make decisions after analyzing the entire transaction. Now you can optimize for user experience while keeping your services secure. The most important takeaway is that a WAF middleware, such as that offered by Cloudflare, allows for the concentration of work into a single service, from which benefits are reaped across multiple applications.

Avoiding Disaster

When SLOs are defined, they're often focused on the internal failures of a service. SLA inversion is the idea that in order to get an accurate SLO of a service, you must take into account all direct (e.g., database) and indirect (e.g., internet routing) com-

---

12 Kandula, Srikanth, et al. (2005). "Botz-4-Sale: Surviving Organized DDoS Attacks That Mimic Flash Crowds" (*https://www.usenix.org/legacy/publications/library/proceedings/nsdi05/tech/kandula/kandula.pdf*). In *Proceedings of the USENIX Symposium on Networked Systems Design and Implementation.*

13 Majkowski, Marek. (2016). "Building a DDoS Mitigation Pipeline." Talk at Enigma.

components on which the service depends.[14] In many architectures, the load balancing tier is shared by multiple applications and services. Any resiliency compromises made in the load balancers affects the SLOs of *all* upstream applications. Given this reality, it's paramount to focus on maintaining a high level of resiliency in scriptable load balancers.

With the numerous benefits offered by scriptable load balancers, it's easy to overload load balancers with logic. The load balancers go from being a powerful solution for difficult problems to a hammer that's looking for nails. As in all architectures, it's important that logic placed into scriptable load balancers doesn't add single points of failure or negatively affect availability. A particularly dangerous pitfall when you are using scriptable load balancers is mismanaging state. The rest of this chapter discusses how to best handle state on the edge.

Getting Clever with State

Through the previous examples, we've seen how powerful scriptable load balancers can be. Although past examples have focused on individual requests, in reality, when clients interact with our services, it's typically through a series of requests that we often refer to as a session (e.g., a customer browses a shop, adds items to their cart, and then goes to checkout).

To be able to properly reason about a request, it's important to know the context in which it's being made. A single request to a slow-loading page can be business as usual, while a hundred in quick succession is a DoS attack. Storing state allows you to distinguish between these two events. If the way state is stored and accessed isn't cautiously reasoned about, it can quickly lead to compromising the availability of our edge tier by adding a single point of failure or drastically increasing complexity.

Depending on which load balancers share the same database, the state stored represents a different snapshot of the world. If each load balancer were to talk to the same database on every request and the database offered consistent guarantees, we'd have a perfect understanding of the world. Depending on the number of processes, nodes, and data centers, such a setup would have impractical overhead and latency costs. Instead, it's important to modify how you approach certain problems that require consistent, global views of the world.

Let's take a throttling mechanism as an example. As Figure 25-8 illustrates, the throttle passes requests up to a certain limit for a given amount of time and blocks all subsequent requests until the next block of time. This sort of throttle typically requires

---

14 Nygard, Michael T. (2007). "SLA Inversion." In *Release It! Design and Deploy Production-Ready Software* (O'Reilly).

having a single, consistent source of truth shared between all potential throttling points.

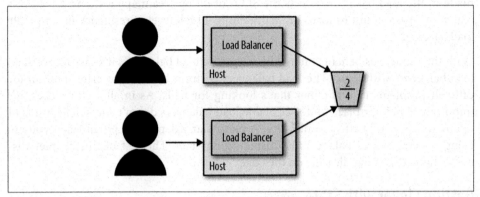

Figure 25-8. Each request is registered in a database shared by both load balancers.

An alternative to storing a counter in a shared data store would be to store the counter on each load balancer, as depicted in Figure 25-9, but divide the maximum throttle size by the number of load balancers receiving requests. If a single load balancer reaches the limit, all other load balancers are likely to have reached the same limit as well. What we lose in precision, we gain in resiliency.

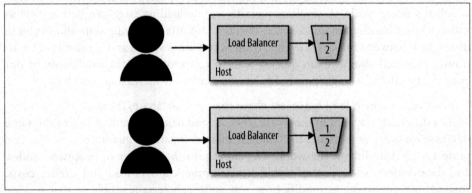

Figure 25-9. Requests are only registered on the load balancer accepting the request.

Case Study: Checkout Queue

Online shopping websites will have checkout queues, similar to a brick-and-mortar store, as a form of back pressure to ensure the service doesn't fail during high-write traffic events (e.g., a sale). Shopify has had to implement such a checkout queue to handle large flash sales brought on by high-profile merchants. The instinctive approach is to store a queue in a database that can be accessed by all load balancers. The queue would store the order of customers attempting to check out with a cart.

Unfortunately, this queue database adds another potential source of failure and increases complexity.

Instead of storing the queue of customers in a database shared between multiple load balancing nodes, Shopify implemented a prioritized throttle that behaved similarly to a queue. This was done without any shared database, only a checkout queue entry timestamp, paired with some session state, stored in each customer's browser through signed cookies.

Each load balancer has a throttle, similar to what we described earlier, deciding whether there's enough capacity for a customer to check out. Customers are assigned a checkout entry timestamp when they first attempt to proceed to checkout. If the service is overloaded, customers poll in the background on a queue page. Figure 25-10 illustrates the flow of a customer going through a throttled checkout process.

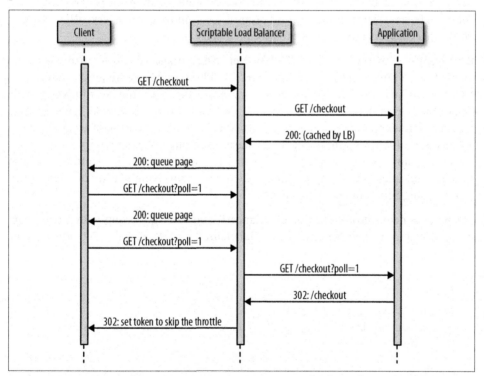

Figure 25-10. Request flow of a customer attempting to checkout, being throttled, and then eventually making it through the queue.

With each poll, individual load balancers modify their view of how long the queue is. They do this by updating the internal node timestamp that decides whether a customer is allowed to attempt to pass the throttle to checkout. The node timestamps are modified with a Proportional-Integral-Derivative (PID) controller that aims to maximize the number of requests passed to the throttle without exceeding its limit. With slight shifts in thinking of how and which state to store, suitable solutions for scriptable load balancers with better resiliency present themselves.

Looking to the Future and Further Reading

As with all new technology, scriptable load balancers aren't perfect. Adding logic to the load balancing tier is a double-edged sword. Without effort and focus on resiliency, the consequences could be disastrous, lowering the availability of the applications we support. A byproduct of being new is that there isn't a clear consensus on best practices.

Despite speed bumps, the ability for scriptable load balancers to improve resiliency and performance can't be argued. There's a real opportunity for scriptable load balancers to be a watershed moment and become a common tool in every SRE's toolbelt. I hope this chapter convinces you to give them a try.

If you enjoyed the examples in this chapter, I encourage you to learn more about them. Scott Francis's talk at NginxConf, "Building an HTTP request router with NGINX and Lua," goes into detail about building a shard routing layer in Nginx with OpenResty. John Graham-Cumming as well as Marek Majkowski have spoken numerous times on how Cloudflare implements its WAF systems with scriptable load balancers.[15,16] Intermission, the request pauser example, was inspired by a project by the same name built by Basecamp.[17] Finally, I've written more in-depth about how the checkout queue throttling mechanism works in "Surviving Flashes of High-Write Traffic Using Scriptable Load Balancers."[18]

For more general resources on load balancers, you can't go wrong with Vivek Panyam's "Scaling a Web Service: Load Balancing,"[19] Matt Klein's "Introduction to

---

15 Graham, John. (2014). "Building a low-latency WAF inside NGINX using Lua" (*https://www.youtube.com/watch?v=nlt4XKhucS4*). Talk at NginxConf.

16 Majkowski, Marek. (2016). "Building a DDoS Mitigation Pipeline" (*https://www.usenix.org/node/193951*). Talk at Enigma.

17 Intermission.

18 Stolarsky, Emil. (2017). "Surviving Flashes of High-Write Traffic Using Scriptable Load Balancers Part II" (*https://shopifyengineering.myshopify.com/blogs/engineering/surviving-flashes-of-high-write-traffic-using-scriptable-load-balancers-part-ii*). Blog post.

19 Panyam, Vivek. (2017). "Scaling a Web Service: Load Balancing" (*https://blog.vivekpanyam.com/scaling-a-web-service-load-balancing/*).

Modern Network Load Balancing and Proxying,"[20] and the "Application Architectures" chapter in *Practice of Cloud System Administration: DevOps and SRE Practices for Web Services.*[21]

Emil Stolarsky is an infrastructure engineer with a passion for load balancers, performance, and DNS tooling. When he's not analyzing flame graphs, you can find him listening to Flume and fighting his fear of heights in a nearby rock climbing gym.

---

20 Klein, Matt. (2017). "Introduction to Modern Network Load Balancing and Proxying." (*https://blog.envoy proxy.io/introduction-to-modern-network-load-balancing-and-proxying-a57f6ff80236*)

21 Limoncelli, Thomas A., et al. (2014). "Application Architectures." In *Practice of Cloud System Administration: DevOps and SRE Practices for Web Services.* Boston: Addison-Wesley Professional.

## CHAPTER 26

The Service Mesh: Wrangler of Your Microservices?

Matt Klein, Lyft

Over the past 5 to 10 years, microservices have become all the rage in distributed systems design and operation. Once relegated to only the infrastructures of the largest internet companies, the technosphere now buzzes with phrases such as "immutable container provisioning and scheduling," "continuous integration and deployment," "decentralized control," and "polyglot language implementations." It is absolutely true that microservice architectures do allow large development teams to operate with more agility. However, often overlooked is the harsh reality that large internet companies have typically invested hundreds of person-years in development and operational effort to make distributed architectures work well in practice. Reliability engineers are left wondering how to grapple with the myriad operational problems that come up when attempting to move away from our monolithic applications and deploy such an architecture in practice. How do services find and communicate with one another? How are distributed services observed and debugged? How are services packaged and deployed? What kind of complex failure scenarios can happen?

As on-the-ground microservice practitioners soon realize, the majority of operational problems that arise when moving to a distributed architecture are ultimately grounded in two areas: networking and observability. It is simply an orders-of-magnitude-larger problem to network and debug a set of intertwined distributed services versus a single monolithic application. What does this fact ultimately mean for reliability engineers? *A giant confusing mess that is difficult to reliably operate.*

Over the past few years, a new paradigm[1] has emerged that is most commonly known as the *service mesh*. The service mesh offers a reprieve for those attempting to build and operate microservice architectures by creating a generic substrate on which applications communicate. Developers can write applications in any language, largely unaware of how the distributed network is implemented, instrumented, and, most important, reliably operated. This chapter explores the reasoning behind the introduction of the service mesh as well as the architectural benefits to microservice developers and reliability engineers alike. The chapter ends with a case study of the deployment of an Envoy-based service mesh at Lyft.

Ready to Get Rid of the Monolith?

Before anyone starts thinking about microservices, they typically already have a functioning monolithic application composed of the following pieces, as shown in Figure 26-1:

- Internet load balancer (e.g., Amazon Web Services [AWS] Elastic Load Balancer [ELB])
- Stateless application stack (e.g., PHP or Node.js)
- Database (e.g., MongoDB or MySQL)

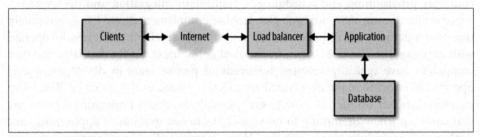

Figure 26-1. Monolithic architecture

Very well-known internet applications (e.g., Twitter, Salesforce, Snapchat, and many others) became extremely large and handle high-traffic loads with only small variations on the items in this list. Why? Because it is vastly simpler to understand and operate such an architecture versus a fully distributed one. This chapter does not go into detail on why companies eventually almost always make the switch from monolith to microservice architecture; much has already been written about that topic.[2]

---

1 "New" is used here in a very loose sense. Nothing is really ever new in computing. Service meshes have origins going all the way back to mainframes and Enterprise Service Buses (ESBs).

2 The writings of Martin Fowler (*https://martinfowler.com/microservices/*) are probably the most well known on this topic.

However, from a networking and observability perspective it's instructive to discuss some of the operational problems that are already typically visible even with this very basic architecture. Let's look at some here:

Lack of networking visibility
> In Figure 26-1, the client needs to communicate with the load balancer, the load balancer with the application, and the application with the database. Thus, in actuality the simple monolith is already a distributed application with networking and observability complexities. If something goes wrong, how does an engineer determine the source of the problem? They will rely on whatever stats, logging, and tracing is available. Odds are, the debugging tools and data are meager, hard to access, and different across all of the components, making diagnosis extremely difficult.

Application layer connection handling inefficiencies
> Many monolithic web applications make use of an application language that is very productive but not necessarily well performing—for example, Ruby, Python, and Node.js. These languages typically do not deal very well with asynchronous computation and in particular network latency. As request volume increases, the chance of a network stall also increases. When a stall occurs, and without the aid of proper asynchronous back pressure, these platforms can quickly become overwhelmed and fall over.[3]

Even with this relatively "simple" architecture, practitioners are already seeing operational and reliability pain primarily due to networking issues and observability (or rather lack thereof). When a decision is made to move away from the monolith toward a distributed microservice architecture (often for good reasons), the nascent networking and observability issues already seen become substantially worse almost immediately. In fact, it is not uncommon for microservice architectural rollouts to be aborted because of network reliability concerns. Without the proper substrate in place, developers do not understand the network or how to debug it and thus they do not trust it. Developers then typically return to adding features to the monolith, leaving a few "noncritical" microservices running. This is a vicious cycle. In some sense, making the network reliable, transparent, and easy to operate is *the* requirement for a successful distributed architecture rollout.

---

3 The typical solution to this problem is to install a high-performance proxy such as HAProxy alongside the application. This pattern has been used for many years, and in some sense, it can be considered a precursor to the full-service mesh.

Current State of Microservice Networking

At this point, it would be useful to step back and look at the current state of microservice networking in the industry. At a high level, the following components are involved:

Languages and frameworks

Almost all modern applications are *polyglot* (multilingual). It is very rare these days to find an organization that is capable of restricting the set of languages in use to only one or two. Instead, it is much more common to find a monolith written in Ruby, PHP, or Node.js, while services are written in Python, Go, Java, and C++. With each language comes wildly different performance characteristics as well as one or more frameworks on which applications are built (e.g., REST via Flask in Python and gRPC).

Protocols

Modern distributed applications are composed of many protocols related to real-time remote procedure calls (RPC) (e.g., REST, gRPC, HTTP/1.1, and HTTP/2), messaging (e.g., Kafka and Kinesis), caching (e.g., Redis and memcached), and databases (e.g., MySQL and MongoDB).

Infrastructures

Across the industry we now see applications deployed across on-prem assets, virtual machines within Infrastructure as a Service (IaaS; e.g., AWS Elastic Compute Cloud [EC2] and Google Compute Engine [GCE]), Containers as a Service (CaaS; e.g., AWS Elastic Container Service [ECS] and Google Kubernetes Engine [GKE]), and "serverless" or Functions as a Service (FaaS; e.g., AWS Lambda and Google Cloud Functions).

Load balancers

Load balancers are a primary component of a distributed architecture. Deployed solutions range from traditional hardware devices by F5 and Juniper to virtual devices by the same companies as well as cloud solutions such as the AWS ELB and the Google Cloud Platform (GCP) Internal Load Balancing (ILB).

Service discovery

Distributed applications need to find each other. Mechanisms range in complexity from Domain Name System (DNS) to fully consistent solutions like Consul.

Distributed system best practices

At a theoretical level, microservice practitioners are told that they need to employ best practices such as retries with exponential back-off, circuit breaking, rate limiting, and timeouts. The actual implementations of these best practices are usually varied or missing entirely.

Although most internet architectures utilize edge encryption via Transport Layer Security (TLS) and some type of edge authentication, the implementations vary widely, from proprietary to OAuth. For service-to-service authentication and authorization, many deployments do nothing. Others use HTTP basic authentication, while a small percentage have extremely complex systems that make use of mutual TLS, a centralized certificate authority, and Role-Based Access Control (RBAC).

Networking libraries

Trying to stitch all of these things together is a huge variety of in-process networking libraries in every language. These libraries range in complexity from simple HTTP request and response libraries such as the Python requests and PHP cURL libraries, to the gRPC libraries in 10+ languages, to the Java Virtual Machine (JVM) only but hugely feature-rich Finagle. Each library attempts to make transparent one or more of the previously described networking features. One thing common to in-process library solutions is the pain of upgrade; large deployments might have hundreds of services, and typically the only way to upgrade a library across every service is to get them all to deploy. This is painful but not debilitating for feature upgrades. However, for security issues, the number of needed deploys leads to tremendous operational burden.

Observability

Ultimately, developers and reliability engineers need to operate the entire system. They do this via a combination of logging, metrics, and, if they are lucky, distributed tracing. However, all of these components typically output *different* combinations and formats of logs, metrics, and traces (and sometimes nothing!). The cognitive load of trying to piece together the outputs of all of these disparate systems into a coherent debugging and operations story is extremely difficult, if not impossible.

What do all of the previously described components yield for most practitioners? As stated in the introduction, *a giant mess*. Another important takeaway is that even though all of these listed items are important, ultimately the most critical thing is observability. As I like to say: *observability, observability, observability*. Without easy and consistent introspection into the system, debugging the inevitable problems that arise is almost impossible. This leads directly to the general perception that distributed networking is unreliable for application development. To have a successful distributed microservice rollout, it is absolutely critical that all deployed services can access a consistent set of features and observability. As an industry can we do better?

Service Mesh to the Rescue

In the face of the confusing networking landscape presented in the previous section, how can developers and reliability engineers take control and bring sanity back to microservice application development? They have two real options:

Option 1

Limit the number of languages used within the organization and introduce extremely complex libraries that encapsulate all of the required features in a consistent way. This is a hugely expensive option, but many of the largest internet companies, including Google, Facebook, and Twitter, have used it successfully (when I mentioned hundreds of person-years in the introduction, this is where many of those years end up).

Option 2

Deploy a "sidecar" high-performance proxy alongside every application as shown in Figure 26-2. This proxy is written once in a single language, encapsulates all of the required features, and aims to make the network transparent to applications —no matter the language in which they are written. When every application is deployed alongside a sidecar proxy, applications talk only to the proxy, and the proxies are responsible for discovering and communicating among themselves, the architecture is now a *mesh*. A service mesh, to be exact.

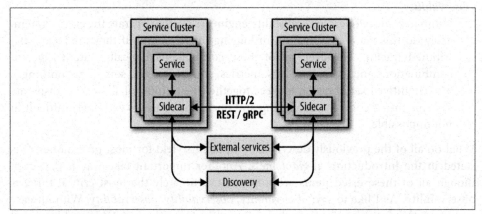

Figure 26-2. Service mesh architecture

The Benefits of a Sidecar Proxy

Initially, the benefits of a sidecar proxy architecture are counterintuitive. How can introducing an entirely new component into the system increase developer efficiency and overall reliability? In fact, the benefits of this approach are numerous and include the following:

Out-of-process architecture
The fact that the sidecar proxy is an independent server means that a large variety of complicated features can be implemented once. You can then use these features alongside any application language, whether it be Java, Go, Python, or Haskell.

High-performance code base
Because of the self-contained server, it is reasonable for the proxy to be implemented in as high-performance a way as possible, typically still in C/C++. Applications written in less-performant languages still have access to a high-performance substrate (more on the implications of this in a moment).

Pluggability
You can make the proxy pluggable such that it supports different protocols and functionalities. For example, in addition to HTTP, the proxy also can support Redis and MongoDB. You can add connection and/or request-level global rate-limiting to both HTTP and MongoDB traffic. Economies of scale (only one code base!) make it possible to support a large variety of protocols and scenarios.

Advanced protocol support
The sidecar will support the most advanced protocols more quickly than many languages and frameworks; for example, HTTP/2, QUIC, and TLS 1.3.

Service discovery and active/passive health checking
Distributed systems typically make use of multiple kinds of service discovery and health checking. The proxy can implement them all and hide them from applications.

Advanced load balancing
Having consistent and reliable implementations of retry, timeouts, circuit breaking, rate limiting, shadowing, outlier detection, and so on is critical for any moderately large system. When applications can entirely offload these functionalities to the proxy, the application code is far simpler to write, and operators can be assured that every application has access to the same functionality.

Observability
As has already been written several times (and I'll expand upon shortly), consistent observability is by far the most important thing that the sidecar proxy provides. Operators have access to consistent stats, logs, and traces for every hop in the distributed system. This 100% coverage enables the automatic generation of per-service dashboards and alarms and a high level of operational consistency across every service and the entire organization.

Additional use as an edge proxy

As it turns out, 90% of what an edge proxy and a sidecar proxy do are the same. The operational efficiency gained from using the same software in both locations is large. Why learn how to deploy and monitor both an edge and a sidecar proxy if a single component can do both jobs?

Ease of deployment and upgrade

The sidecar proxy is easy to deploy and upgrade because it is not embedded into applications. Should operators deploy a new binary or configuration of the proxy across all hosts over a period of a few minutes? Probably not. Is it possible with an out-of-process solution? Yes. (Further consider the example of deploying a TLS upgrade to patch a security vulnerability when TLS is embedded in each application.)

The rest of the chapter covers some of the more interesting fine points of the sidecar or service mesh architecture.

Eventually Consistent Service Discovery

In distributed systems, service discovery is the mechanism by which distributed processes find one another. There are many varieties of service discovery, ranging from statically configured IPs, to DNS, to systems the rely on fully consistent leader election protocols such as Zookeeper. Over the past 5 to 10 years, it has become fairly common to use fully consistent leader election stores such as Zookeeper, etcd, and Consul for service discovery.

The problem with fully consistent systems is that although required for certain use cases, they are extremely complex and require a large amount of thought and care to run, especially at scale with a high volume of data. It is not uncommon for large companies to have entire teams dedicated to running Zookeeper or etcd. Logic would say that unless a problem truly requires full consistency (e.g., distributed locks), you should not use full consistency! However, historically, even though service discovery is really an eventually consistent problem (does an operator really care whether every host has the same view of the network as every other host as long as the topology eventually converges?), fully consistent stores have been used, leading to many outages when the store goes down.

The optimal service mesh design assumes that an eventually consistent service discovery system is used from the beginning. The data from the discovery system is cross-checked with *active* as well as *passive* health checking. Active health checking is the act of sending out-of-band pings such as an HTTP request to a */healthcheck* endpoint. Passive health checking is the act of monitoring in-line request/response data to determine remote endpoint health. For example, three HTTP 503 responses in a row might indicate that a remote endpoint is unavailable.

Table 26-1 shows how the sidecar proxy uses the union of service discovery data and active health checking to yield an overall health status for a backend host. Active health checking is considered to be more reliable than service discovery; this means that if service discovery data is lost but active health checking is still passing, the proxy will still route traffic. Only for the case in which active health checking has failed *and* the backend is absent from service discovery will the backend be purged. This yields high reliability because the service discovery data can be eventually consistent and come and go without affecting production.

Table 26-1. Service discovery and active health checking matrix

	Active HC OK	Active HC failed
Service discovery present	Route	Don't route
Service discovery absent	Route	Don't route and purge

The combination of active and passive health checking alongside an eventually consistent discovery store (e.g., every host checking in once per minute into a cache with a time to live [TTL]), yields extremely high reliability for possibly the most critical component of the entire distributed system.

Observability and Alarming

As I have already mentioned several times, observability is ultimately the most important thing that the sidecar proxy and service mesh architecture provides. Problems at the network layer *will* happen. What's most important is giving reliability engineers the tools so that they can identify the problem, work around it, and fix it as quickly as possible. To this end, the proxy provides the following features:

Consistent statistics for every hop
> Because the sidecar proxy handles both ingress and egress traffic for every application in the system, it follows that every hop in the mesh has coverage by the same robust set of statistics. These range from relatively simple things like requests per second, connections per second, and so on to fully dynamic statistics such as number of HTTP 502s per second and number of Mongo update commands per call site per second, etc.

A persistent request ID that can join logs and traces across the entire system
> The proxy can form the trace/request ID root such that a single ID is propagated throughout the system for all network hops. This allows traces to be generated, logs to be joined, and consistent sampling to be done. (1% sampled logs are much more useful if the sampling is done across the entire system and captures entire request flows versus completely random sampling).

Consistent logging for every hop

As with statistics, if all applications are outputting the same request logs regardless of language, it's substantially easier for humans and tooling to process the data and understand it quickly.

Distributed tracing for the entire system

Tracing is an incredibly powerful tool to visualize distributed system request flows. Typically, however, it's quite complex to introduce it into a microservice architecture because every application must be modified to create spans, forward context, and so on. The service mesh can provide 100% tracing coverage with no involvement from the application whatsoever.

Consistent system-wide alarming

Instead of relying on every application developer to set up basic alarming around service call success rate, latency, and so forth, the service mesh provides statistics, logging, and tracing, allowing basic alarms to be created automatically for every service. This is an incredibly powerful tool for reliability engineers who can now more easily enforce and audit system-wide behavior.

Using the previously described tools, you can build custom autogenerated dashboards and tooling to expose the generated information to engineers in a way that makes it much easier to sort through everything and determine the root cause of a problem. These include things like "service to service" dashboards, which allow engineers to select a source and destination service from a drop-down list and see statistics, traces, and logs for that hop. The UI/UX possibilities are broad and could be the subject of an entire other chapter!

Sidecar Performance Implications

By now, hopefully it is clear that the sidecar or service mesh design offers tremendous benefits to developers and reliability engineers. A common concern often follows, however: What about performance? Doesn't adding all of these extra hops slow things down a lot?

It's true that adding extra hops into a distributed system will add more latency and utilize more machine resources (CPU and RAM). Because of this, it's important that the sidecar proxy be written in an extremely efficient manner. Many proxies are still written in native C/C++. However, it's important to unpack the performance question a bit and dig into the details.

In discussions of performance, there are two primary metrics that are of interest:

Throughput

How much data can be pushed through a component per unit of time (requests per second, connections per second, transactions per second, etc.)?

As throughput ramps up, how does the component perform at the "tail" of the latency histogram? That is, how do per-transaction latency numbers at P50 compare to P99 or even P99.9?

Although throughput is important, in practice it really matters for only the largest companies. This is because for smaller companies, developer time is almost always worth more than infrastructure costs. It's only at very large scale that overall throughput really begins to matter when considering total cost of ownership (TCO).

Instead, tail latency ends up being the most important performance metric for both small *and* large companies. This is because the causes of high tail latency are hard to understand and lead to a large amount of developer and operator cognitive load. Engineer time is typically the most precious resource for an organization, and debugging tail latency issues is one of the most time-intensive things that engineers do.

As a result, the sidecar proxy ends up being a double-edged sword. The proxy adds a tremendous amount of functionality to the system, so much that for all but the most performance-intensive applications, no one will notice an extra millisecond here or there as long as the tail latency properties *are not highly affected by the proxy itself*. This is primarily why the performance and, in particular, tail latency properties of the proxy are so important. If the proxy forms the basis by which the entire distributed system is observed, how can you trust the data if the proxy itself has a large amount of variability? This is why the best proxies are still written in native code with performance objectives similar to operating systems and databases.

Thin Libraries and Context Propagation

The benefits that the service mesh can provide to applications without the application doing anything at all are very large. However, this chapter has so far glossed over the unfortunate reality that no matter what, applications still have a role to play, primarily around context propagation.

Context propagation is the act of taking context from an ingress network call, potentially modifying it, and then passing it to an egress network call. How this is done is language or platform specific and not something that the sidecar proxy can provide. Although propagated context has many uses, the primary use as it relates to the service mesh is propagation of request IDs and trace contexts. For HTTP-based architectures this is primarily done via HTTP headers such as `x-request-id` and the Zipkin `x-b3-traceid` header. Users of a service mesh need to provide application- and language-specific thin libraries to enable users to easily propagate the required HTTP headers. Although it is out of scope for this chapter, I would expect to see some convergence of the libraries that developers use for this purpose over the next several years.

The astute reader might now be asking: "But you said that the service mesh is magic! I still have to do something?"

It is true that developers are still required to participate in the mesh at the application layer if full functionality is desired. However, this is still many orders of magnitude less code and functionality that would otherwise need to be duplicated in every language and framework.

Configuration Management (Control Plane Versus Data Plane)

So far, we have discussed many of the features that the service mesh can provide when building reliable microservice architectures. We have not discussed how the entire system is configured, which can become quite complicated. First, though, a few definitions:

Data plane
> This is the portion of the system that actually participates in forwarding network traffic. This includes load balancing, connection pooling, request and response modification, and so on. The data plane touches every byte of every request and response.

Control plane
> This is the portion of the system that sets up a topology and provides high-level configuration over what happens at any given time. This includes route tables, backend host registration, traffic modification rules, quotas, and so forth.

To use a subway analogy, the data plane is the actual subway cars going from point A to point B. The control plane is the high-level switching system that occasionally switches tracks, says how many trains should be moving at any one time, and so on.

When deploying a service mesh architecture, it is important to separate the different components in the system. The sidecar proxy itself is the data plane. However, a control plane is required that can take user-defined configuration, which is generally fairly opinionated and depends on the deployment and configuration management system in use, and translate that configuration into a format that the sidecar can understand. The configuration must then be distributed to all of the sidecar proxies.

Typically, the further away from the proxy you get, the more opinionated the system becomes. For example, a user who runs on-prem in a data center on bare-metal machines will have a vastly different service discovery process than someone running inside a CaaS system hosted by a cloud provider. The goal of the sidecar proxy/data plane is to provide a consistent configuration API that can be targeted. In the simplest form, a centralized configuration generator might work like this:

1. Look for global system changes that require data plane modification.
2. Generate new configuration for every proxy in the system.

3. Deploy the configuration changes to every proxy in the system via some mechanism.

4. Force the proxies to reload their configurations.

SmartStack based on HAProxy essentially works as previously described and has been deployed successfully by many companies.

More complex sidecar proxies provide a dynamic configuration API, as shown in Figure 26-3. The API is used to deliver route table changes, backend host changes, what ports to listen on, and what to do when a new connection is received. This architecture allows a centralized management service to control all of the proxies, much like a central control room oversees a subway network (to continue with the subway analogy). In general, the more logic that can be moved to a central location, the easier the system is to manage; a fleshed-out API allows the bootstrap configuration of each sidecar proxy to be trivial and essentially just know how to talk to the management server. All configuration from then on is centrally governed and thus avoids any extra infrastructure to deploy configuration files, drain traffic, force the proxy to restart, and so on.

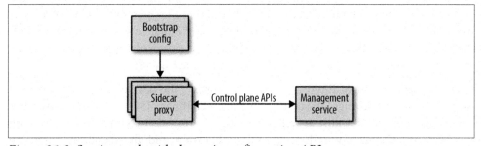

Figure 26-3. Service mesh with dynamic configuration APIs

The Service Mesh in Practice

Although the service mesh concept has only recently gained favor among the microservice community, there are already several competing solutions and large deployments. Proxy solutions include HAProxy, NGINX, Linkerd, Traefik, and Envoy. Fully managed solutions include SmartStack (built on HAProxy) and Istio (built on Envoy and now also supporting Linkerd). What follows is a short description of Lyft's transition from a monolithic application to a complete service mesh architecture built on top of Envoy. This is by no means the only service mesh success story, but it's one I am familiar with (I am the creator of Envoy) and will hopefully provide some flavor to the generic service mesh architecture description that most of this chapter has endeavored to describe.

The Origin and Development of Envoy at Lyft

By early 2015, Lyft had a primarily monolithic PHP application backed by MongoDB along with tens of microservices written in Python. The application at that time was deployed in a single region within AWS. Lyft had decided to make the jump to a microservice architecture for the same reasons that almost everyone else does: decoupling and increased agility. However, early attempts at decomposition were not going well, primarily due to all of the reasons already laid out in this chapter. *The network is inherently unreliable.* Lyft developers were having a tremendous amount of trouble debugging network failures and tail latency issues. In some cases, planned services were aborted and more features were added to the monolith because the network was deemed too unreliable to support the workloads. It's important to also note that Lyft does not currently have an SRE-like job title; all developers are expected to operate their services at a high level of reliability. (The industry move toward DevOps is extremely interesting and worthy of its own chapter; I touch on some of the implications as it relates to Lyft's service mesh migration in a few moments.)

Envoy began development in the same early 2015 timeframe. The goal of the project was to build a very high-performance network substrate that Lyft developers trusted and would ultimately be fully transparent. This did not happen overnight. Envoy was first deployed at Lyft as an edge proxy to replace and enhance the existing AWS ELB fleet. Immediately, the enhanced observability and protocol support proved to be immensely valuable for triaging and debugging product issues.

After the deployment of Envoy as Lyft's edge proxy, the development effort moved on to helping with MongoDB stability. We added a Binary JSON (BSON) parser that can inspect MongoDB traffic as well as a raw TCP proxy that could help with limiting the number of connections between our application and the database. Later, we added global rate-limiting support between our applications and the database. Envoy allowed these enhancements to be immediately provided across all of our application stacks without modification.

Over time, Envoy was deployed as a sidecar alongside every application at Lyft. During this time, we removed all internal centralized load balancers, built an eventually consistent service discovery system and API, and deployed a dense HTTP/2 mesh between all Envoys. The presence of the service mesh unlocks a tremendous number of features for Lyft developers, all of which have already been described in this chapter.

How Lyft configures and operates Envoy has also evolved over time. Originally, all configurations were handwritten and deployed alongside the binary via an eventually consistent deploy process and using Salt. Over time this switched to templated and partially machine-generated configurations using Python and Jinja. As of this writing, Lyft (and most other users of Envoy) is moving toward a fully centralized configuration system supported by a complete set of *discovery* APIs.

The net result of deploying Envoy at Lyft has been that *developers no longer consider the network when building applications.* When network problems do occur, developers have the tooling in place to help discover and remediate the issue quickly. The networking substrate deployed at Lyft has increased developer productivity, increased overall success rate, and decreased Mean Time to Recovery (MTTR) during incidents.

Operating Envoy at Lyft

As I already described, for better or worse Lyft does not have an SRE-like job title. Instead, all developers are expected to be reliability engineers as well. I lead the network team at Lyft, and in addition to developing Envoy we also operate it. Although I have strong opinions about the emergence of DevOps culture in general (out of scope for this chapter), for a system component such as Envoy, I think having the developers of the system also operate it has been a forcing function toward making sure the service mesh truly lives up to the hype of creating a transparent network. In the following subsections, I briefly summarize a few of the more interesting learnings in this regard.

Operational learnings

Automated creation of default dashboards, traces, logs, and alarms

At Lyft, we have machine created dashboards for every service that includes Envoy-related stats, logging, and tracing. Off of this data, we automatically create alarms for each service. This creates an operational baseline for every service, which makes it much easier to dive in and begin debugging issues. Additionally, we have a service-to-service dashboard that allows the user to select both the egress and ingress service from drop-down lists and immediately see pertinent statistics for that hop. Finally, we have a "global" Envoy dashboard, which aggregates service mesh-wide statistics into a single place and allows trivial inspection of system-wide health.

Documentation

I can't state enough how important documentation is and how much we under-invest in it within the industry. Documentation is even more important in a DevOps environment; although we expect all developers to be reliability engineers, in reality the base of knowledge in the field varies greatly. My team spends a tremendous amount of time helping debug system-wide issues, and without quality documentation that we can point developers to, we would be overrun. This primarily equates to an entire set of Lyft internal Envoy documentation about Lyft-specific dashboards, alarms, runbooks, FAQs, configuration guides, and so on, which are more specific than the public Envoy documentation and more accessible to developers without networking experience.

Templated configuration generation

Envoy configuration is extremely complex. We allow development teams at Lyft the flexibility to alter only a tiny portion of it via templates that the network team controls. This allows there to be consistency for most of the system, making it easier to understand in aggregate, while still allowing local flexibility where appropriate (e.g., custom circuit-breaking settings per service).

Hot restart for easy roll-forward and rollback

Lyft, like many organizations, does not currently have access to an immutable container deployment system in production. Envoy has robust "hot restart" functionality, which means that it can be fully restarted, including both configuration and binary, without dropping any connections. This allows us to deploy and roll back quickly and easily.

Administration endpoint for on-node debugging

Envoy provides a robust set of local administration endpoints that are designed to be human readable and easy to interact with. Although it's nice to aim to never have to log into a host and look at something, in reality reliability engineers do this all the time, and having easy access to runtime information is critical for operational agility.

Development learnings

Decoupled sidecar deploy process

To truly realize the benefits of the sidecar proxy model in terms of development agility, we allow Envoy to be deployed fully through staging, canary, and production independent of every application. This allows us to roll out new features, fixes, and debugging tools independent of the application deploy process.

Technical learnings

Address resolution protocol (ARP) tables

Why am I bringing up ARP? This is the most interesting bug that we faced when deploying Envoy at Lyft and something any large service mesh deployment will need to be aware of. ARP is the process by which IP addresses are converted into next-hop MAC addresses (L3 to L2). Kernels contain an ARP cache, which stores the most recently used mappings. In general, any thrashing in this cache will lead to horrendous performance because re-resolution will need to occur repeatedly as cache entries are flushed. The kernel cache size typically defaults to a relatively small value that is tuned for traditional IP-based networks in which the number of immediate L2 neighbors that a node talks to is small. *This is not necessarily true for a service mesh!* Some modern network designs utilize large and flat L3 IP subnets. In these designs, if a host can communicate with any other host in the subnet (especially if not using intermediate load balancers), the number of neigh-hors might be large. At Lyft, we had to increase the default size of the per-node ARP cache to account for this reality. On Linux this involves tuning kernel parameters such as `net.ipv4.neigh.default.gc_thresh1` (and other related values). Other operating systems have similar settings.

File descriptor limits

Somewhat related to ARP table size, it's also important that the sidecar proxy be allowed to create a large number of file descriptors because the proxy will end up creating a large number of mesh connections. Additionally, and primarily based on one extremely bad production outage, Envoy treats a failure to create a file descriptor the same as an out-of-memory (OOM) condition: a fatal crashing error. At runtime, exhausting the number of allowed file descriptors can be extremely difficult to diagnose. Making the condition (which should never happen, given proper configuration) a fatal error leads to greater visibility into a serious problem and ultimately greater reliability.

Overall, the deployment and operation of a service mesh via Envoy at Lyft has been relatively smooth given the focus on incremental delivery, ease of operations, and the points that we just discussed.

The Future of the Service Mesh

Service mesh development across both sidecar proxies as well as management systems is going to see a large amount of investment over the next 5 to 10 years across both software vendors as well as the large cloud vendors. The benefits to application developers and reliability engineers are tremendous; after an engineer uses and operates a microservice built on top of a well-functioning service mesh, it is very unlikely that they will ever want to deploy an application without one again. The benefits obtained for free are too large.

Further Reading

- Envoy proxy (*https://www.envoyproxy.io/*)
- "Service mesh data plane vs. control plane" (*https://medium.com/@mattklein123/service-mesh-data-plane-vs-control-plane-2774e720f7fc*)
- Istio service mesh (*https://istio.io/*)
- "Lyft's Envoy dashboards" (*https://blog.envoyproxy.io/lyfts-envoy-dashboards-5c91738816b1?gi=8f2449271a3d*)
- "The universal data plane API" (*https://blog.envoyproxy.io/the-universal-data-plane-api-d15cec7a*)

- "Microservices Patterns With Envoy Sidecar Proxy: The series" (*http://blog.chris
  tianposta.com/microservices/00-microservices-patterns-with-envoy-proxy-series/*)
- "Introduction to modern network load balancing and proxying" (*https://
  blog.envoyproxy.io/introduction-to-modern-network-load-balancing-and-
  proxying-a57f6ff80236*)
- "Embracing eventual consistency in SoA networking" (*https://blog.envoy
  proxy.io/embracing-eventual-consistency-in-soa-networking-32a5ee5d443d*)

---

*Matt Klein is a software engineer at Lyft and the creator of Envoy. Matt has been work-
ing on operating systems, virtualization, distributed systems, and networking, and
making systems easy to operate, for more than 15 years across a variety of companies.
Some highlights include leading the development of Twitter's C++ L7 edge proxy and
working on high-performance computing and networking in Amazon's EC2.*

## PART IV

The Human Side of SRE

- How do we keep SRE teams safe for the people in them?
- We used to think humans were the cause of most reliability and resiliency problems, but what if they are actually the solution? What is going on in their heads anyway?
- What are the mental health aspects to SRE that we are not paying (sufficient) attention to?
- On-call is a terrible idea; we should stop.
- How do people relate to complex systems?
- Can we do more with SRE than just make things better for the computers; can it be used to make our world better, too?

Discuss.

You Know You're an SRE When...

...you get a text in the middle of the night and your partner isn't even curious because they know your other bae is just PagerDuty.

...you text "hello" and the reply is "uh oh!"

...you get confused for a second every time HR tells you that you have "Time Off In Lieu" (TOIL) coming.

...you write a postmortem every time dinner doesn't turn out right.

...talking with your family you use the phrase, "What are the metrics of success?" and then they look at you funny.

Psychological Safety in SRE

John Looney, Facebook (formerly Google)

 This work was previously published in Intercom (*https://blog.inter com.com/psychological-safety/*) and in *;login:* magazine before being reworked specifically for an SRE audience.

The Primary Indicator of a Successful Team

When I worked for Google as an SRE, I was lucky enough to travel around the world with a group called "Team Development." Our mission was to design and deliver team-building courses to teams who wanted to work better together. Our work was based on research later published as Project Aristotle (*https://rework.withgoogle.com/blog/five-keys-to-a-successful-google-team/*). It found that the primary indicator of a successful team wasn't tenure, seniority, or salary levels, but psychological safety.

Think of a team you work with closely. How strongly do you agree with these five statements?

1. If I take a chance and screw up, it will be held against me.
2. Our team has a strong sense of culture, and it's difficult for new people to join.
3. My team is slow to offer help to people who are struggling.
4. Using my unique skills and talents comes second to the objectives of the team.
5. It's uncomfortable to have open honest conversations about our team's sensitive issues.

Teams that score high on questions like these can be deemed to be "unsafe." Unsafe to innovate, unsafe to resolve conflict, unsafe to admit they need help. Unsafe teams can deliver for short periods of time, provided they can focus on goals and ignore interpersonal problems. Eventually, unsafe teams will underperform or shatter because they resist change.

Let me highlight the impact an unsafe team can have on an individual, as seen through the eyes of an imaginary, capable, and enthusiastic new college graduate.

This imaginary graduate—we'll call her Karen—read about a low-level locking optimization for distributed databases and realized it applied to the service for which her team was on call. Test results showed a 15% CPU saving! She excitedly rolled it out to production. Changes to the database configuration file didn't go through the usual code-review process, and, unfortunately, it caused a hard-lock-up of the database. There was a brief but total website outage. Thankfully, her more experienced colleagues spotted the problem and rolled back the change within 10 minutes. Being professionals, the incident was discussed at the weekly postmortem meeting.

1. "If I take a chance, and screw up, it will be held against me"

At the meeting, the engineering director asserted that causing downtime by chasing small optimizations was unacceptable. Karen was described as "irresponsible" in front of the team. The team suggested ways to ensure that it wouldn't happen again. Unlike Karen, the director soon forgot about this interaction.

Karen would never try to innovate without explicit permission again.

2. "Our team has a strong sense of culture, and it's hard for new people to join"

The impact on Karen was magnified because no one stood up for her. No one pointed out the lack of code reviews on the database configuration. No one highlighted the difference between one irresponsible act and labeling someone as irresponsible. The team was proud of its system's reliability, so defending its reputation was more important than defending a new hire.

Karen learned that her team, and her manager, didn't have her back.

3. "My team is slow to offer help to people who are struggling"

Karen was new to being on call for a "production" system, so she had no formal training in incident management, production hygiene, or troubleshooting distributed systems. Her team was mostly made up of people with decades of experience who never needed training or new-hire documentation. They didn't need playbooks. There were no signals that it was OK for a new graduate to spend time learning these skills. There were certainly no explicit offers of help, other than an initial whiteboarding session that seemed to spend more time on how it used to work than it did today.

Karen was terrified of being left with the pager. She didn't understand how she passed the hiring process and frequently wondered why she hadn't been fired yet. We call this impostor syndrome (*https://en.wikipedia.org/wiki/Impostor_syndrome*).

---

4. "Using my unique skills and talents comes second to the goals of the team"

Karen's background was in algorithms, data structures, and distributed computing. She realized the existing system had design flaws and could never handle load spikes. The team had always blamed the customers for going over its contracted rates, which is like a parent blaming their infant for eating dirt. Karen rightly expected that her nonoperations background would have been a benefit to the team. It's not always clear whether a problem will require understanding a database schema, Ruby debugging, C++ performance understanding, product knowledge, or people skills.

Karen proposed a new design based on technology she'd used during her internship. Her coworkers were unfamiliar with the new technology and immediately considered it too risky. Karen dropped her proposal without discussion. She wanted to write code and build systems, not have pointless arguments.

5. "It's uncomfortable to have open, honest conversations about our team's sensitive issues"

When a large customer traffic spike caused the product to be unavailable for a number of hours, the CEO demanded a meeting with the operations team. Many details were discussed, and Karen explained that the existing design meant it could never deal with such spikes, and then she mentioned her design. Her director reminded her that her design had already been turned down at an Engineering Review, and then he promised the CEO they could improve the existing design.

Karen discussed the meeting with one of her teammates afterward. She expressed dismay that the director couldn't see that his design was the root cause of their problems. The teammate shrugged and pointed out that the team had delivered a really good service for the past five years and thus had no interest in arguing about alternate designs with the director.

Karen left work early to look for a new job. The company didn't miss her when she left. After all, she was "reckless, whiny, and had a problem with authority." They didn't reflect on the design that would have saved the company from repeated outages that caused a customer exodus.

How to Build Psychological Safety into Your Own Team

What is special about operations that drives away so many promising engineers and suffers others to achieve less than their potential?

We know that success requires a strong sense of culture, shared understandings, and common values. We need to balance that respect for our culture with an openness to change it as needed. A team—initially happy to work from home—needs to colocate if they take on interns. Teams—proud that every engineer is on call for their service

—might need to professionalize around a smaller team of operations-focused engineers as the potential production impact of an outage grows.

We need to be thoughtful about how we balance work that people love with work the company needs to get done. Good managers are proactive about transferring out an engineer who cannot make progress on a team's workload due to a mismatch in interest or skills. Great managers expand their team's remit to make better use of the engineers they have, so they feel their skills and talents are valued. Engineers whose skills go unused grow frustrated. Engineers who are ill-equipped to succeed at assigned work will feel set up to fail.

Make respect part of your team's culture

It's difficult to give 100% if you spend mental energy pretending to be someone else. We need to make sure people can be themselves by ensuring that we say something when we witness disrespect. David Morrison (Australia's Chief of the Army) captured this sentiment perfectly, in his "The standard you walk past is the standard you accept" speech (*https://vividmethod.com/transcript-the-standard-you-walk-past-is-the-standard-you-accept/*).

Being thoughtless about people's feelings and experiences can shut them down. Here are some examples in which I've personally intervened:

- Someone welcomed a new female PM to the team on her first day but made the assumption that she wasn't technical. The team member used baby words to explain a service, as an attempt at humor. I immediately highlighted that the new PM had a PhD in computer science. No harm was intended, and the speaker expressed embarrassment that their attempt at fun could be taken any other way. It's sometimes hard to distinguish unconscious bias from innocence.

- In a conversation about people's previous positions, one person mentioned they had worked for a no-longer-successful company. A teammate mocked this person for being "brave enough" to admit it. I pointed out that mocking people is unprofessional and unwelcome, and everyone present became aware of a line that hadn't been visible previously.

- A quiet, bright engineer consistently was talked over by extroverts in meetings. I pointed out to the "loud" people that we were missing an important viewpoint by not ensuring everyone speaks up. Everyone becomes more self-aware, though I had to stress in 1:1s that I expect all senior people to speak up.

It's essential to challenge lack of respect immediately, politely, and in front of everyone who heard the disrespect. It would have been wonderful had someone reminded Karen's director, in front of the group, that Karen wasn't irresponsible, the outage wasn't a big deal, and the team should improve its test coverage. Imagine how grateful Karen would have been had a senior engineer at the Engineering Review offered to work on her design with her so that it time more acceptable to the team. Improve people's ideas rather than discount them.

Make space for people to take chances

Some companies talk of 20% time. Intercom, where I worked, has "buffer" weeks in between some of their six-week sprints (*https://blog.intercom.com/6-week-cycle-for-product-teams/*). People often took that chance to scratch an itch that was bothering them, without it having an impact on the external commitments the team had made. Creating an expectation that everyone on the team has permission to innovate and at the same time encouraging the entire team to go off-piste sends a powerful message.

Be careful that "innovation time" isn't the only time people should take chances. I worked with one company in the automotive industry that considers "innovation time" to be 2:30 PM on Tuesdays! Ideas that people think are worthy should be given air-time at team design reviews, not just dismissed. Use them as an opportunity to share context on why an idea that seems good isn't appropriate.

Make it obvious when your team is doing well

One engineer describes his experience of on-call as "being like the maintenance crew at the fairground. No one notices our work, until there is a horrible accident." Make sure people across the organization notice when your team is succeeding; let team members send out announcements of their success. Don't let senior people hog the limelight during all-hands meetings.

I love how my team writes goals on Post-it notes at our daily standups and weekly goal meetings. These visible marks of incremental success can be cheered as they are moved to the "done" pile. We can also celebrate glorious failure!

Many years ago, when I was running one of Google's storage SRE teams, we were halfway through a three-year project to replace the old Google File System. Through a confluence of bad batteries, firmware bugs, poor tooling, untested software, an aggressive rollout schedule, and two power cuts, we lost an entire storage cell for a number of hours. Though all services would have had storage in other availability zones, the team spent three long days and three long nights rebuilding the cluster. After it was done, the team members—and I—were dejected. Demoralized. Defeated. An amazing manager (who happened to be visiting our office) realized I was down and pointed out that we'd just learned more about our new storage stack in those three days than we had in the previous three months. He reckoned a celebration was in order.

I bought some cheap sparkling wine from the local supermarket, and along with another manager, took over a big conference room for a few hours. Each time someone wrote something they learned on the whiteboard, we toasted them. The team that left that room was utterly different from the one that entered it.

I'm sure Karen would have loved being appreciated for her uncovering the team's weak noncode test coverage and its undocumented love of uptime-above-all-else.

Make your communication clear and your expectations explicit

Rather than yelling at an engineering team each time it has an outage, help the engineers build tools to measure what an outage is, a Service-Level Objective (SLO) (*https://en.wikipedia.org/wiki/Service_level_objective*) that shows how they are doing, and a culture that means they use the space between their objective and reality to choose the most impactful work.

When discussing failures, people need to feel safe to share all relevant information, with the understanding that they will be judged not on how they fail, but how their handling of failures improved their team, their product, and their organization as a whole. Teams with operational responsibilities need to come together and discuss outages and process failures. It's essential to approach these as fun learning opportunities, not root-cause obsessed witch hunts.

I've seen a team paralyzed, trying to decide whether to ship an efficiency win that would increase end-user latency by 20%. A short conversation with the product team resulted in updates to the SLO, detailing "estimated customer attrition due to different latency levels," and the impact that would have on the company's bottom line. Anyone on the team could see in seconds that low latency was far more important than hardware costs, and instead drastically over-provisioned.

If you expect someone to do something for you, ask for a specific commitment—"When might this be done?"—rather than assuming that everyone agrees on its urgency. Trust can be destroyed by missed commitments; this is why a primary responsibility of management is to set context, to provide structure and clarity.

Karen would have enjoyed a manager who told her in advance that the team considered reliability sacred, and asked her to work on reliability improvements, rather than optimizations.

Make your team feel safe

If you are inspired to make your team feel more psychologically safe, there are a few things you can do today:

- Give your team a short survey (like the questions posed at the beginning of this chapter), and share the results with your team. Perhaps get a trusted person from outside the team to do 1:1s with them, promising to summarize and anonymize the feedback.
- Discuss what "safety" means to your team; see if they'll share when they felt "unsafe," because safety means different things to different people (*https:// hbr.org/2017/07/being-the-boss-in-brussels-boston-and-beijing*)—it can mean hav-

ing confidence to speak up, having personal connections with the team, or feeling trained and competent to succeed at their job.

- Build a culture of respect and clear communication, starting with your actions.

Treat psychological safety as a key business metric, as important as revenue, cost of sales, or uptime. This will feed into your team's effectiveness, productivity, and staff retention and any other business metric you value. Don't optimize for it exclusively— if someone who feels unsafe quits your team, your metrics go up, which does not indicate success!

Why are operations teams more likely to feel unsafe than other engineering teams?

Let's unpick the melange of personality quirks and organizational necessities that put operations teams, and specifically SRE, into danger.

We love interrupts and the torrents of information.   Humans suck at multitasking. Trying to do multiple things at once either doubles the time it takes to complete the task or doubles the mistakes.[1] A team that's expected to make progress with project work while being expected to be available for interrupt work (tickets, on-call, walk-ups) is destined to fail. And yet, operations attracts people who like being distracted by novel events. Do one thing at a time. "Timebox" inbound communications as well as interrupt time.

Operations teams are expected to manage risk and uncertainty for their organization. We build philosophies for reasoning about risk; strategies for coping with bad outcomes; defense in depth, playbooks, incident management, escalation policies, and so on. When humans are exposed to uncertainty, the resultant "Information Gap" results in a hunger for information, often exaggerated past the point of utility.[2] This can lead to information overload in the shape of ludicrously ornate and hard-to-understand dashboards, torrents of email, alerts, and automatically filed bugs. We all know engineers who have hundreds of bugs assigned to them, which they cannot possibly ever fix, but refuse to mark them "Won't Fix." Another pathology is subscribing to developer mailing lists, to be aware of every change being made to the system. Our love of novelty blinds us to the lack of value in information we cannot act on.

---

1 Paul Atchley, "You Can't Multitask, So Stop Trying" (*https://hbr.org/2010/12/you-cant-multi-task-so-stop-tr*), Harvard Business Review.

2 George Loewsenstein, "The Psychology of Curiosity" (*https://www.cmu.edu/dietrich/sds/docs/loewenstein/PsychofCuriosity.pdf*), Psychological Bulletin.

Admit that most information is not actionable; be brutal with your bugs, your mail filters, and your open chat apps. Tell your team that it's OK to assume anything urgent will page; any other work can be picked up after they finish tasks.

On-call and operations.   The stress of on-call drives people away from operations roles. Curiously, 24/7 shifts are not the problem. The real problem is underpopulated on-call teams, working long, frequent shifts. The more time people spend on call, the more likely they are to suffer from depression and anxiety.[3] The expectation of having to act is more stressful than acting itself.[4] It's one thing to accept that on-call is part of a job; it's another thing altogether to tell your five-year-old daughter that you can't bring her to the playground.

We can mitigate this stress by ensuring on-call rotations of no less than six people, with comp time for those with significant expectations around response times, or personal life curtailment. Compensate teams based on time expecting work, not time doing work. Having per-shift on-call payments (or giving comp time)—as opposed to including on-call compensation in the base compensation package—implies employers value the sacrifice of their employees' personal time. Incident management training or frequent "Wheel of Misfortune" drills can also reduce stress, by increasing people's confidence. Ensure on-call engineers prioritize finding someone to fix a problem when multiple incidents happen concurrently.[5]

Cognitive overload.   Operations teams support software written by much larger teams. I know a team of 65 SREs that supports software written by 3,500 software engineers. Teams faced with supporting software written in multiple languages, with different underlying technologies and frameworks, spend a huge amount of time trying to understand the system and consequently have less time to improve it.

To reduce complexity, software engineers deploy more and more abstractions. Abstractions can be like quicksand. Object/relational mappers (ORMs) are a wonderful example of a tool that can make a developer's life easy by reducing the amount of time thinking about database schemas. By obviating the need for developers to understand the underlying schema, developers no longer consider how ORM changes impact production performance. Operations now need to understand the ORM layer *and* why it impacts the database.

---

3 Anne-Marie Nicol and Jackie Botterill, "On-call work and health: a review" (*https:// www.ncbi.nlm.nih.gov/pmc/articles/PMC539298/*), Environ Health.

4 J. Dettmers et. al., "Extended work availability and its relation with start-of-day mood and cortisol" (*https:// www.ncbi.nlm.nih.gov/pubmed/26236956*).

5 Dave O'Connor, "Bad Machinery" (*https://www.usenix.org/conference/srecon15europe/program/presentation/ oconnor*), SREcon15 EU.

Monolithic designs are often easier to develop and extend than microservices. There can be valid business reasons to avoid duplication of sensitive or complex code, and they have simpler orchestration configuration. However, because they attract heterogeneous traffic classes and costs, monolithic architectures are a nightmare for operations teams to troubleshoot or capacity-plan.

Most of us understand that onboarding new, evolving software strains an operations team. We ignore the burden of mature "stable" services. There is rarely any glamorous work to be done on such services, but the team still needs to understand it. The extra care required not to impair mature services while iterating on newer ones must be accounted during time-and-effort estimation.

Ensure teams document the impact of cognitive load on development velocity. It has a direct and serious impact on the reliability of the software, the morale and well-being of the operations team, and the long-term success of the organization.

Imaginary expectations. Good operations teams take pride in their work. When there is ambiguity around expectations of a service, we will err on the side of caution and do more work than needed. Do we consider all of our services to be as important as each other? Are there some we can drop to "best effort"? Do we really need to fix all bugs logged against our team, or can we say, "Sorry, that's not our team's focus"? Are our Service-Level Agreements (SLAs) worded well enough that the entire team knows where their effort is best directed on any given day? Do we start our team meeting with the team's most important topics, or do we blindly follow process?

Ensure that there are no magic numbers in your alerts and SLAs. If your team is being held to account for something, verify that there is a good reason that everyone agrees with and understands.

Operations teams are bad at estimating their level of psychological safety. Finally, I'll leave you with a thought: people who are good at operations are bad at recognizing psychologically unsafe situations. We consider occasionally stressful on-call "normal," and don't feel it getting worse until we burn out. Over-emphasizing acts of sacrifice during work normalizes sacrifice, and turns sacrifice into expectations.[6] The curiosity that allows us to be creative drives us to information overload. Despite being realistic about how terrible everything is, we stay strongly optimistic that the systems, software, and people we work with will get better.

I've conducted surveys of deeply troubled teams for which every response seemed to indicate everything was wonderful. I'd love to hear from people who have experience

---

6 Emily Gorcenski, "The Cult(Ure) of Strength" (*https://www.usenix.org/conference/srecon17europe/program/presentation/gorcenski*), SRECON.

uncovering such cognitive dissonance in engineers. After all these years, I'm still surprised when I uncover it.

Further Reading

- Kim Scott, *Radical Candor* (*https://www.radicalcandor.com/the-book/*).
- Kerry Patterson, Joseph Grenny, Ron McMillan, and Al Switzler, *Crucial Conversations* (*https://www.vitalsmarts.com/resource/crucial-conversations-book/*).

John Looney is a production engineer at Facebook, managing a data center provisioning team. Before that, he helped built a modern SaaS-based infrastructure platform for Intercom, one of the fastest-growing technology companies in the world. Before that, he was a full-stack SRE at Google who did everything from rack design and data center automation through ads-serving, stopping at GFS, Borg, and Colossus along the way. He wrote a chapter of the SRE book on automation and is on the steering committee for USENIX SRECon.

## CHAPTER 28

SRE Cognitive Work

John Allspaw and Richard Cook, Adaptive Capacity Labs

> *...irony that the more advanced a control system is, so the more crucial may be the contribution of the human operator.*
> —Bainbridge, 1983.

Introduction

The modern "system" is a constantly changing melange of hardware and software embedded in a variable world. Together, the hyperdistribution, fluctuant composition, constantly varying workload, and continuous modification of modern technology assemblies comprises a unique challenge to those who design, maintain, diagnose, and repair them. We are involved in exploring this challenge and trying to understand how people are able to keep our systems working and, in particular, how they make sense out of what is happening around them. What we find is both inspiring and worrisome. Inspiring because the studies reveal highly refined expertise in people and groups along with novel mechanisms for bringing that expertise to bear. Worrisome because the technology and organization are so often poorly configured to make this expertise effective.

Together with our colleagues, we have studied people doing SRE work, the problems they face, the approaches they take, and the issues that arise in the middle. From a distance this work is often imagined as narrowly technical, even mundane. Examining the work as done, in contrast, reveals that SRE work is often stormy and sometimes dangerous.

This chapter gives a brief overview of what we think we now know about modern technology and the work of people who design, maintain, diagnose, and repair it. There are similarities between groups doing SRE work and those in working in other high-consequence domains. We conclude with some general suggestions about ways to better support the work and more specific suggestions about how to better characterize work in this demanding, conflicted environment.

What Do SRE People *Do*?

The names given to physical and virtual places where people congregate to confront incidents[1] (e.g., "war room" and "command center") suggest that incidents sometimes have existential qualities that merit comparison to being at the center of a cyclone. Yet, even in the midst of the cyclone, we find people acting deliberately, thoughtfully, and (at least outwardly) calmly to cope with what is happening. These people are *working*—doing purposeful things that employ a specific type of expertise and doing them because that is their job. Table 28-1 shows some of the duties of SREs around the time of an incident.

Table 28-1. Some activities of SREs during incidents

Activity	Example
Decoding reports and observed behaviors into meaningful patterns that "explain" the event and its consequences	Some (but not all) locations reporting outage could mean a networking problem or a software version problem
Acting to keep the technologies working	Adding more compute instances to reduce pressure on connected subsystems or components
Weighing available courses of action, *many of which cannot be rolled back*	Bouncing the server
Making decisions to protect the system, often decisions involving sacrifice of one or more goals	Forcing a network partition to allow recovery; killing slow-running database queries until they can be fixed in code
Gathering and directing resources that are needed or might be needed	Coordinating with SaaS vendor technical staff; traffic shedding or rerouting during a DDOS attack
Anticipating and avoiding future bottlenecks in the response	Planning on-call shift handoff to rest the working team
Providing assessments of the immediate situation and its likely and possible future trajectories	Conference call with CIO; public-facing web page updates about the incident

---

1 *A note about terms:* Use of terms like *anomaly, event, incident,* and *accident* tend to evoke strident debates about their exact meanings. They are used inconsistently in tech and elsewhere. Frustration with their variable interpretation has led some to try to give them crisp definitions. Despite these efforts, *none of these terms have fixed meanings.* The situation is made even more difficult when word choice has significant consequences. For example, some tech firms have formal processes for handling an *incident* that do not apply to an *event* or an *anomaly.* (We have witnessed extensive discussions during event response about whether that event meets the organization's threshold criteria for an *incident*! Declaring an *incident* would bring additional resources to bear, generate auditable documentary trails, and involve substantial future work.) The situation cannot be resolved by fiat. Instead, we need to pay attention to how these terms are used in context and especially to the consequences of the choice of term. In this chapter, we use the term *incident* as a pointer to a set of activities, bounded in time, that are related to an undesirable system behavior.

Like cyclones, incidents in complex systems reverberate, sometimes for long periods. Repairing the damage, restoring the capacity, and making changes to avoid future incidents can take weeks or even months to complete. Understanding the deep sources of an incident is frequently impossible while the cyclone is raging. Many organizations have both formal and informal methods for incident review intended to surface and identify these deep sources. SREs have duties here as well. Engagement with postmortems and the assignment of action items are examples.

The activities shown in Table 28-1 are *cognitive* activities. The work is taking place inside the heads of SREs and expressed by their words and actions. To understand the work that they do requires understanding the *cognition* of the SREs. Understanding human cognition in complex work domains is challenging but possible.

Useful techniques have been developed in other fields such as aviation, nuclear power, and other intrinsically hazardous domains. It is interesting to note that, although the examples on the right side of Table 28-1 are specific to the network-connected information technology, the left-side activities are more generic. We find similar activities going on in a host of other high-consequence domains, from air traffic control to intensive care units (Nemeth et al., 2004) There are groups of people doing SRE-like cognitive work across a variety of domains.

Why Should We Care About Practitioner Cognition?

It was once thought that systems could be designed and built so that their operation, maintenance, and repair could be reduced to well-defined tasks, capable of being specified in all important aspects. The notion that work can be reduced to a narrowly specified best way was popularized by Fredrick Winslow Taylor (1856–1915). The idea of a well-structured, carefully regulated workplace was best exemplified by the automobile assembly lines of Henry Ford (1863–1947).

Experience during the second World War, especially with airplanes, began to undermine deterministic views of human performance. Although some assembly processes might be completely specified, *operational* situations brought humans into contact with diverse situations and settings that demanded expertise that went beyond written procedure following. In retrospect it is clear that there were very few situations where work could be reduced to a set of unambiguous rules.

The expertise needed to make things work, to fix them when they are broken, and to manage the consequences of failure is often arcane, subtle, and tacit. Understanding where this expertise comes from, how it is deployed, and how it is sustained in communities of practice (Lave and Wenger, 1991) is inherently the study of cognition in the wild (Hutchins, 1995). As Bainbridge (1986) observed, one of the ironies of automation is that increasing its sophistication and power does not reduce the need for expertise but instead increases it. Building a thorough, grounded understanding of how practitioner cognition works is critical to the operation of modern systems and will only become more so as the complexity and reach of those systems expand.

Critical Decisions Made Under Uncertainty and Time Pressure Cannot Be Scripted

The modern view of human engagement with complex systems arose from a confluence of ideas and research threads in the 1970s and broke into the open following the nuclear accident at Three Mile Island (TMI) on March 28, 1979. Prior to TMI, it was widely believed that nuclear power plants had invested so heavily in safety that major accidents were virtually impossible. Safety was encoded in design, the automated systems, and the procedures. Plant operations were regarded as simply a matter of following those procedures, which were thought to be objective and completely specified. TMI showed that this idea was fundamentally flawed. Complexity and circumstance could and would combine to create novel situations for which procedures were underspecified and inadequate. These challenging situations would require operators to build understandings of the specific situation, to weigh the risks of different approaches, to track the evolving condition of the plant and revise their understandings, and redirect attention and effort.

The 15-year period after TMI was one of rich and rancorous debate about safety complexity, automation, and human performance. It spawned multiple, productive research threads that continue to bear fruit today. And the idea of "error" as a discrete type of human performance that could be counted, channeled, and trained away simply collapsed. The approaches we use to study SREs at work were developed in large part because of TMI.

What TMI made clear is that engineers, operators, and others involved in the moment-by-moment workings of complex systems need to have the means and opportunity to understand how those systems are working and to predict how actions taken will play out—especially when the systems are breaking or broken. Achieving this depends on being able to understand their cognition in the real world of work.

Human Performance in Modern Complex Systems: The Main Themes

There is an extensive literature about human performance in complex systems, the analysis of such systems, and the sources of successful and unsuccessful operations of these systems. There are several main themes that come from this work (see Table 28-2). Some of these have obvious application to SRE work, but even the most promising among them require careful preparation if they are to be made truly useful.

Table 21-2. Themes for human performance in complex systems

Theme	Examples
Critical decision	• How does combining uncertainty, high-stakes, and time pressure influence decisions?
	• How do decision makers evaluate alternatives?
	• What makes work hard?
Sense making	• How are anomalies recognized?
	• How does troubleshooting work?
	• How do experts keep track of evolving situations?
Coordination across multiple agents	• How does cooperation happen?
	• How do people and machines interact?
	• How are the costs of coordination managed?
Resilience	• What is needed for adaptation to novel situations?
	• What trade-offs are available?
	• What degrees of freedom are worth sustaining?

Although there are general results associated with each theme, these comprise mostly a guide for the further examination of specific work areas. Each work domain is different in ways that matter. An approach that is useful in one domain might be useful in another but will always need careful tailoring to the specifics of the new domain if it is to be helpful. Simply mimicking across domains seldom produces the desired result.

Instead, the research is useful in framing explorations of a new domain and interpreting the results of empirical studies in that domain. The situation is somewhat analogous to the way that "patterns" are useful in software. Patterns are not solutions but frames that allow solutions to be developed.

Observations on SRE Cognitive Work Around Incidents

Incidents are complex system failures (Cook, 1998; Cook, 2010). They result from the combination of multiple, individually innocuous flaws, each individually incapable of producing an overt failure but, in combination, sufficient to do so. But the theory of complex system failure is too narrow to encompass SRE work, which includes managing the descent into failure, the repair and reassembly of a (sometimes partly) functional system, channeling the immediate aftermath response to limit collateral damage, and constructing meaningful, useful descriptions of what has just happened.

Every Incident Could Have Been Worse

Even when an incident seems to have begun abruptly, a review of its evolution will show many forks. Even when the outcome is terrible, a cursory review will show it might have been worse. Even if they cannot forestall a breakdown, from their vantage point inside the center of the cyclone, SREs might have opportunities to shift the trajectory of the failure so as to preserve useful elements or cushion the blow.

Especially for cascading failures, where component failures multiply to expand the area of damage, it is sometimes possible to, for example, disconnect portions of the distributed system to avoid extending the failure. Simply warning those (people and machines) using the system that it is failing can give those agents time to achieve safe shutdown in anticipation of a loss of service.

Guiding a failing system toward a less painful outcome depends on the expertise of SREs and also on the design and implementation of the technology. These events often happen quickly and the window of opportunity might be small, putting additional pressure on those trying to limit the damage.

Only the most public, high-profile incidents are reviewed in sufficient depth to reveal how the intra-incident choices made things better or worse. Two historical examples are relevant, both involving the nuclear power industry.

TMI

During the accident at Three Mile Island, the operators became concerned that the extra cooling water flowing into the reactor would fill the pressurizer and cause the reactor to "go solid"—a catastrophic condition that would result in loss of control. This led them to reduce the water flow, which exposed the reactor core and stopped cooling it, resulting in a meltdown of the core.

Fukushima

Reactor cooling water is highly purified to prevent corrosion of the reactor piping and parts. During the accident at Fukushima, the power failure stopped cooling water flow over the reactors. An option available to the operators was to pump unpurified water into the reactor, making the reactor forever unusable but avoiding core damage. Operators for one reactor took this option early, bring the reactor to a safe shutdown. Operators of another reactor continued efforts to restart the pure water cooling but were unsuccessful. That reactor core melted, resulting in a major leak of radiation to the environment.

Sacrifice Decisions Take Place Under Uncertainty

Rarely do incidents arise with clear-cut boundaries, obvious solution pathways, and predictable repair times. In most cases—and in *all interesting* cases!—the primary feature of an incident is uncertainty. The normal operating system is complex; the breaking or broken one is doubly so. Systemic complexity and uncertainty are closely linked; as complexity increases, uncertainty increases.

SREs frequently face situations in which there are only bad alternatives. Losses have already been sustained, more losses are accumulating, and cascade to enormous or even catastrophic loss is a real possibility. Although there might be temporizing measures that can reduce or defer consequences ("let's spin up another instance and see if that helps"), it's common to confront rather stark, painful sacrifice choices.

A sacrifice decision occurs when the decision is made to accept one loss in order to avoid another, more significant one. Typically, sacrifice decisions accept a well-defined loss in order to reduce the possibility of a more severe loss. In almost all cases, the loss that is accepted is better characterized than the loss that is being avoided (Woods, 2006).

Post-incident reviews are good for clarifying sacrifice decisions, but not as good at capturing the uncertainties, pressures, and conflicting data that commonly swirl around such decisions. Ironically, when a sacrifice decision is successful—that is, the bigger, more threatening loss is avoided—there is a strong tendency to be critical of the sacrifice decision. After it is avoided, the bigger loss seems less likely and the decision to accept the sacrifice seems ill-considered. Symmetrically, after a catastrophic failure, the inability to perceive an available sacrifice decision or unwillingness to make it can evoke similar criticism. Let's take a look at two more examples that demonstrate choosing the sacrifice.

New York Stock Exchange Outage

On July 8, 2015, the New York Stock Exchange (NYSE) stopped trading for three hours because automated stock quotation processes failed. Although most of the automated exchange was working at the time of the shutdown, NYSE management decided to halt all trading. "It's not a good day, and I don't feel good for our customers who are having to deal with the fallout," NYSE President Thomas Farley said, according to Reuters. NYSE later paid a penalty of $14 million to the Securities and Exchange Commission for this and "similar computer-related problems."

Knight Capital Collapse

On August 1, 2012, the trading firm Knight Capital lost $440 million when newly installed software interacted with testing code already in the system. Initial sudden losses were recognized and concern was raised about the system, but it was allowed to continue running until it had accumulated crippling losses. The company was sold a few weeks later, effectively going out of business.

Repairs to Functional Systems

SRE work in failed and failing systems produces a narrow but deep understanding of how the sources of the failure are related. This understanding is especially important as plans to repair the system are developed. Broken but still-functional systems have properties different than the "nominally working" system. New vulnerabilities and dependencies arise, often with implications for approaches to repair.

The complicated problem of rollback illustrates this clearly. Large, highly regulated systems with tight change controls (e.g., financial processors) often implement a group of changes together. When one of these changes breaks some part of the system, there are sometimes debates about the wisdom of reverting that change package. Because the entire change package was subjected to testing, the consequence of reverting a single change puts the system in an untested state. Some organizations require that any rollback include all the changes in the package. What if some changes in a package are urgently needed? More discussion and debate.

Untangling the skein of changes and effects in large systems can be challenging, especially when an incident has just demonstrated how flawed and incomplete understandings of the system are. We have observed quite vigorous discussions about how the system works [!] and about how to proceed with repairs.

Because these issues can have important and even existential consequences, SREs rarely decide them alone. Unlike the situations described in the sections "Every Incident Could Have Been Worse" on page 470 and "Sacrifice Decisions Take Place Under Uncertainty" on page 471 earlier in the chapter, repairs have a distinctly lower tempo and broader engagement of stakeholders. SREs are often called upon to examine proposed repair schemes, to critique them, and to explain the workings of the system to stakeholders with authority but who lack the deep technical knowledge of SREs.

We note that the concept of *rollback* is becoming difficult to sustain. As distributed systems include more external services and elaborate patterns of usage, the possibility of reverting to a "known state" becomes less feasible. Modern distributed system design emphasizes the need to build systems that do not depend on maintaining state. The result is that we now have systems that lack unique state. In such a world, reverting a software change can make the system take on a more familiar appearance, but it might not restore the world to the way it once was.

Special Knowledge About Complex Systems

The situation facing SREs is seldom simple. The fault-tolerance mechanisms built into the design of distributed systems and related automation handle most problems that arise. Because of this, incidents represent situations that fall outside of the "most problems" boundary. Reasoning about cause and effect here is often challenging.

For example, simply observing that a process is failing does not necessarily mean that fixing that process will resolve the incident. Processes might simply be unable to handle the extreme conditions produced by the failure of other processes. In other cases, actions intended to mitigate or break further propagation of issues can return with results that do more to shed new light on the issues than containing them as intended. Terms like "back pressure"[2] strongly suggest that SREs have special, conditional knowledge about system behaviors.

Managing the Costs of Coordination

SREs seldom work alone. Operating and supporting large distributed systems involves many people and activities that have diverse and shifting connections. The course of an incident might engage a handful or hundreds of people acting as information contributors, troubleshooters, consequence limiters, and liaisons (internally, with customers, with regulators, etc.). Garnering and directing resources, coordinating them, tracking the progression of the incident, and coping with the consequences—often while the genesis and further progression of the event remain uncertain—are themselves demanding tasks. Many organizations have sought to "manage" the dense, noisy, intra-incident situation with varying degrees of success.

Two popular methods of managing the costs of coordination are the use of classification schemes to parcel out resources and the assignment of formal roles for personnel during the incident.

Classification schemes

Many incidents have only minor impact on customers or business process. Fewer incidents have major impact. Addressing incidents can be expensive and disruptive.

---

2 Originally, the term *backpressure* referred to network traffic faults derived from switch failures. These manifested as growing message queues being accumulated in upstream components. We now use the term more broadly to refer to any disruption of interprocess communication that results in queue growth in the upstream process. Because displays of queue size are ubiquitous, increasing queue size is a conventional signal that a downstream process is failing.

By classifying incidents, organizations seek to manage resource consumption: more important incidents get more resources, while less important ones get fewer. It is sometimes quite difficult, however, to understand the significance of an incident in progress. Severe incidents might initially manifest as mild disturbances. Cascades can propel a minor event into a major one. Ordinal scales (e.g., a 1 to 5 severity scale) are difficult to apply, especially early in the event evolution when resources are being gathered and assigned. A classification scheme based on immediate customer impact might not reflect the importance or difficulty posed by an event.

Formal role assignments

Some organizations now use formal assignment of intra-incident roles. Examples are "incident commander," "communications manager," and so on. These expedients are intended to delineate authority and responsibility within the group addressing an incident and to allow for smooth coordination across the resources being brought to bear. We have seen this approach work well and also not so well. Experienced groups work well while inexperienced ones struggle, and we note that the success of leaders depends critically on the composition of the work group. One important function of the leader is to be accountable for critical decisions that have operational consequences.

These methods of managing the costs of coordination have appeared because incident management is challenging. Very little research has been done to validate their use. The actual effects of these methods is an area ripe for study.

SREs Are Cognitive Agents Working in a Joint Cognitive System

SREs' work is never accomplished without interaction with other people and machines. All these actors—human and machine—function as *cognitive agents*. It is impossible to adequately describe one actor's work in isolation. Their interactions are based on each other's capability, intention, and understanding of the situation. They coordinate, cooperate, and reason about others intentions. Together they form a *joint cognitive system* (JCS) (Hollnagel and Woods, 2006).

Much of SRE work during incidents requires reasoning about automation. What is the automation doing? What will it do next? How does it understand the situation? What will happen if we tell it to do *this* or *that*? Typically, automation is strong, silent, and hard to direct (Woods, 1997). Efforts to make automation a more useful cognitive "team player" have focused mainly on safety critical systems, such as airplane cockpits (e.g., Billings, 1996) or medical devices (e.g., Nemeth et al., 2005). The growing importance of internet-facing business systems has raised the stakes around automation in this realm.

SRE stories are filled with examples of automation-related troubles. Anyone who has deployed to production when they meant to deploy to test will have experienced this firsthand! Ironically people are so used both to balky, awkward automation and to making up for it that they regard it as normal.[3]

When automation is a poor team player, human cognitive agents must make up the deficiency by doing extra cognitive work. When this work is required at already busy times, the automation is "clumsy" (Cook et al., 1991). A lot of automation presently deployed for use during incidents has this quality.

Although we know how to make automation a team player (Klein et al., 2004), the effort required and the rapid change of technology make it difficult to accomplish for all but the most critical systems. It is clear, however, that the improving overall performance of a JCS depends on making all the cognitive agents better team players (Klein et al., 2004).

The Calibration Problem

SRE work depends on knowledge of how things work, how they don't work, what interventions are available, and the consequences (likely and possible) of these interventions. This will include general knowledge (e.g., about a particular operating system feature), specific knowledge (e.g., how this particular system's Redis is configured), and quite diverse knowledge (e.g., the code "freeze" scheduled for tomorrow will encourage people to deploy in advance and so today might be more challenging than usual).

How do people know whether this knowledge is current or stale? What triggers a reassessment? In a fast-changing, complex world, no person can have a complete and detailed understanding. How can someone know that their current view is adequate for the immediate work they're performing? What investments in improving that view are worthwhile?

Mental Models

Researchers often use the term *mental model* to describe the collected knowledge about how a system works (Gentner and Stevens, 1983; for a discussion, see Cook, 2018). Although general knowledge can age gracefully, rapid change ensures more specific knowledge will quickly become stale. Engineers know this and update their mental models. They compare their understanding of how components, subsystems,

---

3 The suit joke illustrates this well. A man goes to buy a suit. Trying it on, he notices that the arms are too long. "No problem," says the salesman, "just bend them at the elbow and hold them out in front of you." He does but then notices that the jacket is long in back. "Just bend over a bit," the salesman says. He does but now notices that the right pant leg is too short while the left one is too long. "Just rotate your hips a little," the salesman says. "There, now you look perfect." So, the man buys the suit and walks down the street past two old ladies sitting on a bench. "Oh," says one, "look at that poor man, isn't it sad that he is so twisted up like that." "Yes, it is sad" replies the other, "but doesn't his suit fit well!"

networks, and applications connect and interact, and so on, with evidence from a multitude of sources.

But this raises an important problem: how do engineers know when their mental models are stale *in ways that matter*? Modern systems change continuously. New code is deployed, new users stress the system in new ways, outside services stop working as expected, subtle factors combine to generate new interactions. It is impossible for any individual to keep up with all these changes—indeed, the agile paradigm reflects this. Given that so much change is happening and so much of it is taking place out of view, when should an engineer decide to spend time and effort to update their mental model and how should an engineer decide where to focus that attention? This is *the calibration problem*.

Woods' Theorem states: "As the complexity of a system increases, the accuracy of any single agent's own model of that system decreases rapidly." No amount of effort will be sufficient to make a mental model accurate and precise for the whole system. Even a partial system model that is "good enough" at one moment becomes stale as the system changes. The best that an individual can do is to attempt to maintain a mental model that is *sufficiently* accurate and *sufficiently* precise for the needs of the moment.

Each person has a unique mental model, often quite different from the models of others. This is both an asset and a problem. It is an asset because the many different mental models present in an organization provide coverage of more aspects of the system than a single model could possibly give. It is a problem because the models are likely, where they overlap, to be incongruent. It is quite possible for individual mental models to disagree, which, in turn, creates a need to identify and resolve discrepancies across mental models.

This situation is shown schematically in Figure 28-1 (see Woods 2018, section 2.3). Significantly, all the interaction with computing technology takes place through display artifacts. Together these create a "line of representation" that provides access and shows images of that technology. We cannot directly perceive the technology itself—the computers, programs, APIs, networks, and so on. Instead, the technology is represented by text and images displayed on screens. People take action on the underlying technology using keyboards, mice, and so forth and assess their impact via the representations. They interpret the responses via their mental models, inferring the composition and function of the underlying technology from these interactions.

Broadly, people work "above the line" of representation, while the technology that they work on is "below the line."

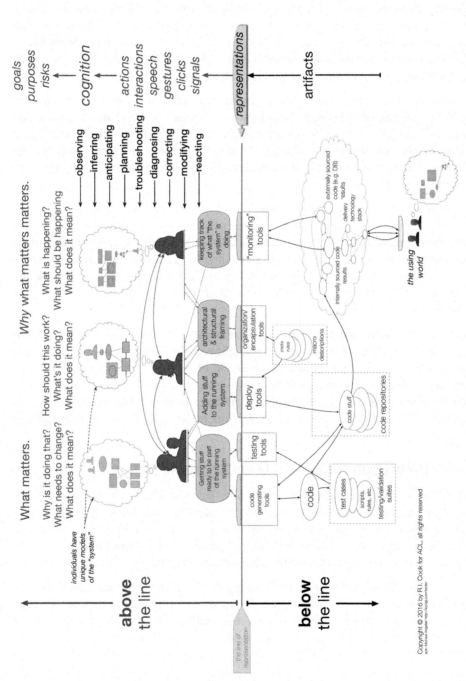

above the line

What matters.

Why is it doing that?
What needs to change?
What does it mean?

*individuals have
unique models
of the "system"*

Why what matters matters.

How should this work?
What's it doing?
What does it mean?

What is happening?
What should be happening
What does it mean?

observing
inferring
anticipating
planning
troubleshooting
diagnosing
correcting
modifying
reacting

goals
purposes
risks

cognition

actions
interactions
speech
gestures
clicks
signals

representations

artifacts

Getting stuff
ready to be part
of the running
system

Adding stuff
to the running
system

Keeping track
of what "the
system" is
doing

architectural
& structural
framing

code
generating
tools

testing
tools

deploy
tools

"monitoring"
tools

organization/
encapsulation
tools

meta
rules

macro
descriptions

code

code stuff

code repositories

test cases

scripts,
rules, etc.

testing/validation
suites

externally
sourced
code (e.g. DB)

delivery
technology
"results
stack

internally sourced code
results

*the using
world*

*the line of
representation*

below the line

Figure 28-1. Schematic drawing of a system including elements above and below the line of representation. (copyright © 2016 by Richard Cook, used by permission)

Incidents Trigger Individual Recalibration

An incident begins when an individual encounters anomalous behavior and begins exploring its sources and consequences. Incidents are first and foremost *anomalies*. The difference between what is expected and what is observed is the driver for what happens next. This difference is a signal that the observer's mental model is out of calibration with *this part* of the system. That mental model can be either coarse or highly precise, but the anomaly is evidence that it is not accurate.

Incident response is, in a large sense, a process of recalibrating the observer's mental model for *this part* of the system. Searching for a "cause" of the anomaly is driven by the mental model and serves to update it. Note particularly the emphasis on *this part* of the system. Complexity and change will foil any attempt at broad mental model updating. An observer's recalibration of their mental model is bounded by the incident and focused by the process of inquiry.

We hypothesize that experts have fine-grained, accurate mental models of specific parts of the system that they understand are critical or likely to fail. They can exploit these mental models to solve problems quickly and, in solving them, update their mental models in ways that are likely to serve their future needs. Even though novices and less expert practitioners begin with coarser, less accurate mental models, the experience of an incident can allow them to enhance their mental models of *this part* of the system.

Incidents also serve as platforms for developing expertise. Significant incident responses are rarely carried out by solo practitioners. Involvement of novices in incident response appears to promote development of expertise. Observing exploration of the anomaly provides novices with opportunities to refine their mental models in tandem with the expert. Incident handling has sharp focus and takes on the complexity of the real world in ways that are seldom matched by more formal training activities.

Incidents Are Opportunities for Collective Recalibration

The problem facing the individual practitioner has a parallel in the larger organization: *how can an organization know when its collective understanding of a complex system needs updating?* Given the limited resources available, how should an organization devote time and effort to maintaining people's appreciation for the way that the system really works, what its vulnerabilities are, and what to expect in the future?

We can use incidents to focus attention here as well. Incidents are messages from the underlying system about where trouble lies. Examining these events more broadly can provide useful insights into how the system really works, allowing the individuals involved to update their mental models. Incidents point to parts of the system where trouble has occurred. They are the most relevant indicators of what part of the system is *this part*.

The idea that incidents might be broadly useful to the organization is not new. Accident research has long emphasized the value of incidents as pointers (cf. Woods et al., 2010) and quality theory encourages the use of incidents and windows into processes and problems (cf. Deming, 1982). The use of postmortems (Allspaw, 2012) can provide insights into systems and their operations that would not be otherwise available.

The key idea here is that complexity and change make broad, generic efforts at "understanding" existing systems relatively inefficient. In contrast, incidents point to specific places where mental models of the system are in need of recalibration. Incidents are timely, relevant information about where effort and attention should go.

We acknowledge that this view is diametrically opposed to the approaches most often used to manage incidents. In many organizations, incidents are collected, reduced to a database entry, and quickly forgotten. Management "by the numbers" demands swift resolution of incidents and rewards their reduction to a set of categories. This has the effect of ignoring (or at least diminishing) the value of incidents as starting points for deeper and more thorough investigation. It is ironic that such expensively purchased data is so quickly discarded.

What Are the Implications of All This?

Incidents are remarkably frequent. For many systems the organizationally acknowledged incident rate is one or two *per day*. We know of some places where the rate is much higher. In many firms, coping with incidents is a constant struggle that consumes resources and attention. It is clear that this will continue and that, as the complexity and significance of systems increase, the consequences of incidents are likely to increase. Because the systems and environment are continuously changing, the loci, character, and impact of incidents will change. However, it's equally true that incidents are valuable sources of information that can—under the right conditions and with effort—be harvested.

Incidents Will Continue

This situation is not going to get better. Instead it is likely that the problem will become even more difficult. The stakes for system operations are rising as more business functions are embedded into systems and daily business operations become more dependent on them. The complexity of these systems continues to grow. Attempts to tame this complexity have sometimes shifted the locus of human operator attention but have not and will not eliminate the need for operators to make sense of what is happening.

As in other industries, technological progress appears to simultaneously reduce the number of major incidents while also *increasing* their consequences. The result is that major events occur less frequently but, when they do happen, have greater effects than in the past. The connectedness and responsiveness of modern systems makes disturbance propagation faster and more widespread than in the past.

We note that much of the industry dialog around development of large systems implicitly assumes that future systems will be, practically speaking, "incident free." This is a dangerous technofantasy, an *idée fixe*. The history of systems of all sorts, and especially that of information technology, does not support this idea. Incidents will continue to occur, to threaten, and to demand attention. Failure to build systems—technical and organizational—with features suitable to incident management is malpractice.

Incidents Will Impose Costs

The cost of incidents is difficult to measure but certainly may be large. Back-of-the-envelope calculations suggest that a day's outage for a major airline can generate losses in excess of $200 million. It is practically impossible to calculate cost of existential events such as the Knight Capital collapse in 2012.

The direct costs of incidents include their immediate effects on revenue, costs of response, and so on. Table 28-3 lists some of these.

Table 28-3. Some direct costs of incidents

Incident	Costs
Downtime	• Revenue loss
	• Service penalty payments
	• Restoration effort
Response	• Staff salary for incident response
	• Opportunity cost of diverting staff attention to incidents
	• Cost of implementing post-incident action items
Organizational overhead	• Maintaining incident tracking systems
Regulatory	• Compliance reporting
	• Financial penalties
	• Regulatory interference in dev/ops

Although these costs are certainly significant the indirect costs of incidents are equally disturbing. Table 28-4 shows some of these costs. Reputational injury, distraction, brittleness, and what we call "developmental drag" are not easily quantified. Even so, these indirect costs of incidents have the potential to be crippling. Again, there is an ironic quality here: the importance of the existing code base to successful operations is so great that modifications are shunned for fear of damaging that base. Any incident arising from or related to that code base reinforces that fear. Over time, that base becomes brittle and the number of people left in the organization willing to tackle it decreases.

Table 28-4. Some indirect costs of incidents

Incident	Costs
Reputation injury	• Customers lose confidence in the product and firm
	• Other products and firms gain competitive advantage
	• Downward pressure on pricing
Organizational distraction	• Management takes more active role in addressing problems and "handling" events
	• Incidents feed into (and can shape) internal political agendas
Increasing brittleness	• Fear of triggering hidden vulnerabilities or introducing new ones creates reluctance to repair/migrate/refactor legacy code or infrastructure
Developmental drag	• More uncertainty about cost of adapting to new situations
	• Efforts to control change to prevent failures (CABs, code freezes, etc.) undermine agility
	• Technical staff lose confidence in management, develop covert work practices, or leave the firm

Of particular importance is the developmental drag that results from organizations seeking to manage vulnerability. Change "review" or "advisory" boards are an organizational reflection of the desire to avoid future failures. Although this mechanism might indeed forestall some ill-conceived changes, the burden it imposes can be great. Such boards consume valuable resources, generate delays in addressing problems, lead to release clumping, and can even produce covert work systems (Hirschhorn, 1998; p. 61).

Even though these costs are real, they are difficult to quantify and can escape from management view.

From a management perspective, incidents are best regarded as unplanned investments in system performance. The challenge to managers is to find ways to extract the greatest return on investment (ROI) from incidents.

Incident Patterns Will Change

The complexity of systems and diversity of the surrounding environment continue to increase. New connections will be made and old ones will be severed. The pattern of incidents will necessarily change, as well; like the financial disclaimer says: "Past performance is no guarantee of future results."

Although much is invested in incident tracking systems, there is little evidence that these methods predict the locus or nature of future failures. For larger systems the associated administrative bureaucracy produces little of value. Instead, it appears to function largely as a kind of sea anchor—a drag from behind that the captain hopes will keep the organizational bow pointed in a safe direction.

Incidents Point to Specific Calibration Problems and Locations

The calibration problem (see "The Calibration Problem" on page 475) is a fundamental challenge. Successfully troubleshooting, repairing, and modifying a system requires an accurate model of that system. Complexity and change ensure that any system model will become stale. No single agent (human or machine) can maintain an accurate model of such a system. Instead, the need to troubleshoot, repair, and modify a system demands continuous effort to improve the accuracy of the agent's model.

But the sheer scale of modern systems makes any generic effort at maintaining calibration an exercise in futility. No one can possibly read and digest all of the code, all of the manuals, all of the protocols that comprise a modern system. Instead, we need to focus the limited resources available for recalibration on what is most relevant.

Incidents are salient guides to where recalibration is needed. Incidents are the *only* unambiguous information available about a lack of calibration. They are pointers (albeit *untyped* pointers) to areas of the system where recalibration is needed (Cook, 2017). Incidents are messages sent from the underlying system about our miscalibration. They are the most efficient means of knowing where to direct efforts at restoring calibration.

What Should Happen Next?

Harvesting the value of incidents is not easy, but it is possible. Some promising approaches to gleaning and sharing insights from incidents have been identified. Much of the value of incidents comes from comparison and contrast across incidents. The many difficulties of incident management and post-incident reconstruction and analysis are ripe for innovative approaches. The value of incidents as *efficient* pointers to the need for calibration strongly suggests that learning how to learn from incidents will be crucial to developing the adaptive capacity to weather new forms of challenge and to grasp new opportunities.

Build a Corpus of Cases

Through efforts such as the SNAFU Catcher consortium, there is a clear need to identify and build a corpus of cases from modern software organizations. We have experience in doing this in other domains, such as healthcare (e.g., Cook, Woods, MacDonald, 1991). Although it requires effort and expertise, it's the basis for exploring the settings and challenges of software service worlds.

There are, of course, many existing case collections. Indeed, every enterprise has large datasets recording many incidents that have occurred. But these collections are mostly mute about the human performance, problem representations, and cognitive processes that took place. The descriptions are, in terms of Figure 28-1, about "below the line." The corpus of cases that is needed now explicitly and in detail characterize "above the line" processes.

A corpus of cases will allow us to see how different types of "incidents" unfold and are managed from multiple perspectives, and allow for asking questions that probe for the similarities and differences between events, organizations, type of business, and so on. Examples of questions include the following:

- How does the flow of attention move and/or migrate as an incident evolves?
- How do different teams of responders describe their vantage point and understand one another?
- What do people *actually do* during the response to incidents and anomalies that they don't make explicit? What tricks or shortcuts do they use that others aren't aware of? What tools are useful? Which ones are distracting?
- What influence does time and consequence pressure have on the management of a given incident? How do structured responses (e.g., incident handling training, assigning authority to specific individuals) work in practice?
- How do teams perceive what parts of their application or systems are "risky" to touch? How did this view arise? How accurate is it?

A corpus of cases does not provide answers. Instead, it helps identify lines of inquiry likely to prove useful.

Focus on Making Automation a Team Player in SRE Work

The SRE work world is a JCS, which is composed of cognitive agents, mostly people but, increasingly, automation as well. Making automation a team player in a JCS is challenging (Klein G. et al., 2004).

There is already a lot of automation in systems, and SREs (and others) make sense of system behaviors by reasoning about how it works and fails. Load balancers, failovers, rate limiters, alerters, and a host of other automatic processes are essential to making systems work. Some incidents are simply unexpected interactions of these processes. Such incidents can be difficult to understand, especially when the individual processes are "doing" their jobs correctly.

More recently a new layer has appeared: automation intended to keep track of and direct the automation. When difficulty managing automation spurs the development of new automation, systems become even more difficult for SREs to understand and direct. The situation has an analog in medicine: the widespread use of antibiotics in hospitals promoted development of resistant microorganisms that produce *nosocomial*—that is, "hospital acquired"—infections that, in turn, led to development of even more potent antibiotics. The term *nosocomial automation* is sometimes used to describe automation intended to handle the problems caused by automation (Woods and Cook, 1991).

Ironically, although intended to relieve SREs of work, automation adds to systems' complexity and can easily make that work even more difficult (Cook and Woods, 1996). This is likely to become an even more challenging issue for SREs as layers of automation (e.g., artificial intelligence) are added to the operational elements of our systems. The need for team play has never been more acute.

Address the Calibration Problem

Software engineering teams (SREs as well as others) continually build and calibrate their models of how systems are connected and behave. The need to keep these models up to date extends across the entire organization and is especially acute for SREs. The calibration problem is critical to enterprise success. Support for SRE calibration would promote learning about narrow technical details and also broader relationships that nourish and constrain work above the line.

Concentrating on SRE calibration alone is unlikely to produce enterprise success. SRE work takes place inside the framework of the enterprise and depends on resources, guidance, and goals the SRE workforce does not control. The problems confronting SREs are intimately connected to development, infrastructure, marketing, and customer support activities.

We have argued that incidents point to where calibration is needed. This need is not, however, restricted to the SRE workforce. Incidents are the most relevant empirical data about how the system works, what it is capable of, and what is likely in the future. As technical systems become more complex, the need for calibration becomes more acute. Experience with incidents and their meanings needs to be shared across the organization. Building environments that support the development of coherent, relevant descriptions of incidents and their meanings is essential if the "above the line" part of the system is to make progress on the "below the line" part.

Especially when an incident has significant bottom-line consequences, extracting meaning from it is likely to take place in a charged and even acrimonious atmosphere. Efforts to "spin" interpretations of the event become attractive, especially in highly bureaucratic organizations. Internal political strife can lead actors to shape incident stories to their purposes. In such settings, the need for solid, carefully conducted and presented incident investigations takes on even greater organizational significance.

There are opportunities for significant improvements in understanding how people work at the sharp end of practice and how to better support that work, both technically and organizationally. Our studies indicate that the industry is more attuned to the need for calibration than in the past and that experiments that combine organizational and technical components are underway in many firms. The presence of these experiments is encouraging. Capitalizing on these experiments to achieve velocity is hobbled by difficulties in sharing results, the "spin" that seems to follow every effort, and the paucity of tools for extracting the lessons learned from them. More efforts like the SNAFU Catchers consortium will be welcome.

This chapter was not intended to slay any particular dragons that the SRE world faces; it only sketches them and points to where they sleep.

What Can You Do?

"Incident" is a neutral-sounding word that suggests detachment and a dispassionate analytical stance. But a real "incident" is often accompanied by strong emotion and its aftermath can be devastating for individuals, organizations, or whole firms. As companies become more dependent on technology for their success, disruptions of that technology pose ever-greater threats. Meeting this challenge requires the capacity to not just survive incidents but to exploit them as resources. Doing this requires some practice, some resources, some management buy-in, and some courage, but it is well within the reach of most organizations.

To start, here are four suggested activities that, experience shows, are likely to provide the early successes that will encourage further work:

Build your own internal resources to do incident analysis
  Expand on the current SRE practice around postmortems to develop this deeper practice of inquiry about cognitive performance. Recognize those who do this work as resources and encourage them to engage with others outside the organization.

Select a few incidents for closer and deeper analysis
  Even a few incidents examined closely can provide great value. Close examination and deep analysis is often easier with medium-value incidents; high-value incidents evoke managerial and regulatory attention that can make exploratory

study difficult or even hazardous. *Start small.* Demonstrate what a more thorough analysis looks like and what insights you can generate by it. Cases that contain elements of surprise, uncertainty, or ambiguity are likely to be particularly rewarding. Try to avoid "filing off the rough edges" in order to build a single, coherent account. Instead, emphasize and capture individual perspectives of responders and participants. Look for a forum for discussion with others in the organization and ask the responders to participate in any discussion.

Build or adjust tooling to capture data streams from incidents
Many data streams are already available to aid post-incident reconstruction of the intra-incident period. Few of these are well configured for post-incident work. Even a small amount of effort directed toward expanding, collating, and capturing these data streams is likely to be useful. Chat transcripts, video calls, database query logs, and other sources can all be useful if the effort needed to wrangle them into a coherent account is not too large. A bigger challenge is to record actions people took that were *not* explicit during the event, especially those that turned out to be unhelpful. It can be especially valuable to identify and characterize the (ultimately) useless "trips down the rabbit hole."

Make company-wide postmortem sessions regular events
Incidents are *unplanned investments*; gaining the full value of these investments should be a business priority. Presentation and discussion of incidents is one way of building a shared mental model of the system and the organization that runs it. Opening post-incident debriefings also emphasizes the organization's primary commitment to learning.

Conclusion

We're excited about the possibility of understanding SRE cognitive work. Making cognitive work explicit for this group exposes a great deal of the system, both above and below the line. The continuing stream of incidents reminds us that calibration is important and difficult. The attention and effort being lavished on technical and organizational tools to support SREs during and after incidents is testimony to the aspirations of many who understand this.

We have confidence that the methods and approaches used in other high-consequence and high-tempo domains are applicable in the SRE world. Applying those methods takes time and skill and is not for the faint-hearted! Even so, there appears to be a growing cadre of practitioners and researchers adopting the mantle of cognitive systems engineer, many of them with direct experience in our industry. This bodes well for our collective future.

References

1. Allspaw, J. (2012). *Blameless PostMortems and a Just Culture*. (Etsy Code as Craft blog.) *https://codeascraft.com/2012/05/22/blameless-postmortems/*, accessed June 18, 2018.

2. Bainbridge, L. (1983). Ironies of Automation. *Automatica* 19(6): 775–779.

3. Billings, C. E. (1996). *Aviation Automation: The Search for a Human-Centered Approach*. Boca Raton, FL: CRC Press.

4. Cook, R. I. (2010). How Complex Systems Fail. In Allspaw, J., ed. *Web Operations: Keeping the Data On Time*. Sebatopol, CA: O'Reilly, 108–116.

5. Cook, R. I. (2017). Medication Reconciliation is a Window into "Ordinary" Work. In Smith, P. J. and Hoffman, R. R., eds., *Cognitive Systems Engineering: The Future for a Changing World*. Boca Raton, FL: CRC Press, 53–78.

6. Cook, R. I. (2017). *Where Complex Systems Fail*. (SNAFUcatchers blog.) *https://www.snafucatchers.com/single-post/2017/11/14/void-Incidents-as-Untyped-Pointers*, accessed July 2, 2018.

7. Cook, R. I. (2018). *Medication Reconciliation Is a Window into "Ordinary" Work*. In Smith, P. J. and Hoffman, R. R., eds. *Cognitive Systems Engineering: The Future for a Changing World*. Boca Raton, FL: CRC Press, 53–75.

8. Cook, R. I., Woods, D. D., and MacDonald, J. S. (1991). *Human Performance in Anesthesia: A Corpus of Cases* (Tech. Report CSEL91.003). Columbus, OH: Ohio State University, Cognitive Systems Engineering Laboratory. *https://www.dropbox.com/s/arojonf2q6bcne9/Cook.1991.CorpusOfCases.pdf*, accessed May 1, 2018.

9. Cook, R. I., Woods, D. D., McColligan, E., and Howie, M. B. (1991). Cognitive Consequences of Clumsy Automation on High Workload, High Consequence Human Performance. NASA, Lyndon B. Johnson Space Center, *Proceedings of the Fourth Annual Workshop on Space Operations Applications and Research* (SOAR 90), 543–546, accession number N91-20702. *https://ntrs.nasa.gov/search.jsp?R=19910011398*.

10. Cook, R. I. and Woods, D. D. (1996). Implications of Automation Surprises in Aviation for the Future of Total Intravenous Anesthesia (TIVA). *Journal of Clinical Anesthesia* 8: S29–S37.

11. Deming, W. E. (1982). *Out of the Crisis*. Cambridge, MA: MIT Press.

12. Gentner, D. and Stevens, A. (1983). *Mental Models*. Mahwah, NJ: Lawrence Erlbaum Associates.

13. Hirschhorn, L. (1998). *Reworking Authority: Leading and Following in the Postmodern Organization* (Vol. 12). Cambridge, MA: MIT Press.

14. Hollnagel, E. and Woods, D. D. (2006). *Joint Cognitive Systems: Foundations of Cognitive Systems Engineering.* Boca Raton, FL: CRC Press. [ISBN 9780849339332]

15. Hutchins, E. (1995). *Cognition in the Wild.* Cambridge, MA: MIT Press.

16. Klein, G., Woods, D. D., Bradshaw, J. M., Hoffman, R. R., and Feltovich, P. J. (2004). Ten Challenges for Making Automation a "Team Player" in Joint Human-Agent Activity. *IEEE Intelligent Systems* 19(6): 91–95. [DOI: 10.1109/MIS.2004.74]

17. Lave, J. and Wenger, E. (1991) *Situated Learning: Legitimate Peripheral Participation.* Cambridge, UK: University of Cambridge Press.

18. Nemeth, C. P., Cook, R. I., and Woods, D. D. (2004). The Messy Details: Insights from the Study of Technical Work in Healthcare. *IEEE Transactions on Systems Man and Cybernetics, Part A: Systems and Humans, 34*(6), 689–692.

19. Nemeth, C., Nunnally, M., O'Connor, M., Klock, P. A., and Cook, R. (2005). Making Information Technology a Team Player in Safety: The Case of Infusion Devices. In: Henriksen, K., Battles, J. B., Marks, E. S., et al., eds. *Advances in Patient Safety: From Research to Implementation (Volume 1: Research Findings).* Rockville, MD: Agency for Healthcare Research and Quality (US). *https://www.ncbi.nlm.nih.gov/books/NBK20467/.*

20. Roth, E. M, DePass, E. P., Scott, R., Truxler, R., Smith, S. F., and Wampler, J. L. (2017). Designing Collaborative Planning Systems: Putting Joint Cognitive Systems Principles into Practice. In Smith, P.J. and Hoffman, R.R., eds., *Cognitive Systems Engineering: The Future for a Changing World.* Boca Raton, FL: CRC Press: 247–268.

21. Woods, D. D. and Cook, R. I. (1991). Nosocomial Automation: Technology-induced Complexity and Human Performance. *Proceedings of the 1991 IEEE International Conference on Systems, Man and Cybernetics,* Charlottesville, VA, 13–16 October 1991, Vol 2., 1279–82. *https://ieeexplore.ieee.org/document/169863/.*

22. Woods, D. D. (1997). Human-Centered Software Agents: Lessons from Clumsy Automation. In Flanagan, J., Huang, T., Jones, P., and Kasif, S., eds., *Human Centered Systems: Information, Interactivity, and Intelligence.* Washington, DC: National Science Foundation, 288–293.

23. Woods, D. D. (2006). Essential Characteristics of Resilience. In *Resilience Engineering: Concepts and Precepts.* Aldershot, UK: Ashgate Publishing, 21–34.

24. Woods, D. D., Dekker, S., Cook, R. I., and Johannsen, L. (2010). *Behind Human Error.* Boca Raton, FL: CRC Press.

25. Woods, D. D. (2017) *STELLA: Report from the SNAFUcatchers Workshop on Coping With Complexity*. Columbus, OH: The Ohio State University. *https:// snafucatchers.github.io/*.

John Allspaw heads Adaptive Capacity Labs and is the former CTO of Etsy. He is the coauthor, with Jessie Robbins, of Web Operations (O'Reilly, 2010) and The Art of Capacity Planning (O'Reilly, 2017).

Richard Cook is a principal at Adaptive Capacity Labs and a research scientist at Ohio State University. His most often cited paper is "How Complex Systems Fail".

## CHAPTER 29

Beyond Burnout

James Meickle, Quantopian

Content warning: *This chapter discusses mental disorders and their impact on life and work. Topics covered include medication and the medical system, coercive treatment, slurs, crisis, and laws and the legal system.*

Please note that I am not a mental healthcare professional, nor am I a lawyer or an expert in employment law. This chapter reflects my own analysis and opinions based on my own extensive research and experience. My goal is to inspire thought, dialog, and appropriate action. You need to assess whether the strategies and suggestions in this article fit your situation. Depending on where you are doing business, and the nature of your work, some of the strategies and suggestions described in this article might not comply with the laws that apply to you. If you are interested in implementing any of these suggestions or strategies, in addition to making sure that they are right for your organization, you should consult a diversity and inclusion professional with sufficient expertise to ensure that your inclusivity initiatives comply with applicable law.

Decades of research have highlighted many ways in which our jobs, as well as the broader system of capitalism, make us all sicker. There are well-documented physical impacts from sedentary workplaces, open office plans, and even artificial lighting. Psychologists agree that these unnatural working conditions also directly harm our mental health, as do the psychological demands of the modern workplace, such as frequent interruptions or performing emotional labor[1] for coworkers and customers.

SRE wouldn't exist in its present form without human-factors research. The discipline has been defined by findings from psychology, industrial accident analysis and

---

1 Emotional labor refers to work managing the emotions of others, such as being expected to keep up a smile or politely respond to aggression. This work is often expected of retail and service employees, particularly women, and is usually uncompensated.

prevention, cybernetics, and many other fields. This research has helped SREs converge on an understanding that all human operators are fallible, that blaming or shaming them doesn't lead to improvements, and that truly resilient systems must be built in ways that respect human limits.

Discussing and managing these limitations is considered an SRE best practice, and conferences frequently feature presentations about topics like burnout or hero culture that provide a blueprint for building more sustainable team cultures.[2] Not all companies have adopted these best practices yet, but it has been heartening to see so many SREs working to build a culture that values mental health. I'm proud to work in an industry in which some of my most technically respected colleagues are also some of the most confident voices in support of a cultural shift toward sustainability and caring.

What Is Mental Health?

Within this chapter, I use the term "mental health" to describe the overall state of your mind and emotions. It refers to your general condition of well-being, rather than any specific diagnosis. You can be in poor mental health without any disorder or diagnosis. And having a mental disorder does not by itself indicate poor mental health. Your mental health can be impacted by any diagnoses, but also by your stress, personal life, and coping strategies.

Unfortunately, many SRE best practices implicitly treat job duties (such as pages or toil) as the primary stressor that needs managing. These recommendations tend to assume that, if only enough unpleasant work could be automated or improved, perhaps everyone could have great mental health in the workplace. That might sound very far away indeed for SREs with mental disorders, who have typically lived with them before their current jobs and likely will after. Discussions about mental health as a workplace goal are powerful and necessary, but they're also incomplete when they're held without consideration for the specific needs of people with mental disorders.

This chapter guides you through refactoring your SRE organization to be more inclusive of people with mental disorders. I begin by providing a working definition of mental disorders to use throughout the chapter. With that in hand, I explain why mental disorders are an important part of any inclusivity initiative, and why high-

---

2 Jennifer Davis on hero culture (*http://confreaks.tv/presenters/jennifer-davis*) (DevOpsDays Boston 2014) , John Sawers on emotions (*https://youtu.be/Mc5HJSsYB7A*) (DevOpsDays Boston 2017), Emily Gorcenski on strength and emotional labor (*https://www.usenix.org/conference/srecon17europe/program/presentation/gorcenski*) (SREcon17 EMEA), Jaime Woo on psychological safety (*https://youtu.be/AttVD__QrAo*) (SREcon18 Americas), and *many* others.

performing arts teams need to allow every member to be their whole self. I close out
the chapter with inclusivity recommendations (and antipatterns) for each stage of the
employee life cycle, as well as resources for further reading.

Defining Mental Disorders

In this chapter, I use the term "mental disorder" as a catch-all that includes both
mental illnesses and neurodevelopmental disorders.[3] These terms aren't unanimous
even among practitioners, so I define them, too.

Mental illnesses are changes in thinking, emotion, or behavior that result in distress
or difficulty in life. They often occur in adolescence through early adulthood but can
do so at any age. Mental illnesses have highly varied severity and prognosis and can
range from intermittent episodes to lifelong conditions. Major depressive disorder,
generalized anxiety disorder, bipolar disorder, and eating disorders are examples of
common mental illnesses.

What's not a mental illness? Short-lived reactions to work or life stressors, such as job
burnout or grieving, are not mental illnesses. Neither are political views, or emotional
reactions that are stressful but provoked or justified. Finally, "eccentric" behavior that
doesn't cause a person distress or harm the people around them is not considered a
mental illness.

Neurodevelopmental disorders are deficits in cognition or memory that relate to specific brain processes or regions, which are often present from infancy. A disorder
might manifest as one highly specific deficit or a range of affected abilities. Many
neurodevelopmental disorders are compatible with a high quality of life, and people
who live with them often suffer only when society is reluctant to make appropriate
accommodations. Learning disorders, autism, and attention-deficit/hyperactivity disorder (ADHD) fit into this category.

Mental illnesses and neurodevelopmental disorders have very dissimilar etiology and
prognosis, but within the context of the workplace it makes sense to talk about them
collectively as mental disorders. Both categories of conditions can result in similar
symptoms, which means that people living with them might require similar accommodations. Unfortunately, people with mental illnesses and people with neurodevelopmental disorders are also united by having to struggle for equal treatment in the
face of discrimination.

---

3 Note that there are also many brain disorders that can cause mental symptoms—for example, stroke, Alz-
heimer's disease, and traumatic brain injury. Although not classified as mental disorders due to the different
cause and prognosis, they are likely to benefit from similar accommodations in the workplace.

At any point in time, approximately 25% of people have one or more diagnosable mental disorders.[4] Approximately 50% of people will meet the criteria for one or more mental disorders at some point during their lives. Poor accessibility of mental health services means that many will never receive diagnosis or treatment of their symptoms.

Mental Disorders Are Missing from the Diversity Conversation

More people in the United States will have a mental disorder in their lives than will have cancer,[5] yet people with mental disorders are one of the most stigmatized groups in America. Employment discrimination against Americans with mental disorders is largely illegal, but still encouraged by a culture that jokes about "not dating crazy"[6] and horror films about asylum escapees. It's therefore unsurprising that mental disorders are concentrated among poor people, and that poverty is concentrated among people with mental disorders. People with severe[7] mental disorders (such as schizophrenia or borderline personality disorder) are almost absent from public life due in part to the intense stigmatization of these diagnoses. For people with mental disorders, there is an inclusivity crisis—not just in tech, but everywhere.

Because people with mental disorders often face significant interpersonal and systemic discrimination, it's unsurprising that most will choose to hide their status when they have the option to do so. Far too few feel able to discuss these conditions with their friends and family, and even fewer will opt to disclose them in a workplace where they might face retaliation. With so few visible data points, it can be hard to even notice larger discriminatory trends, leaving mental disorders as a hidden inclusivity problem in engineering.

---

4 Different sources cite a range of numbers; I have seen reported lifetime rates from 15% through 70% depending on what specifically is being measured and how. For instance, it is common to study mental illnesses apart from neurodevelopmental disorders; also, studies that monitor rates of self-reported symptoms will differ from studies that monitor rates of diagnosis. For further reading on these numbers, see *https://www.cdc.gov/mentalhealth/learn/index.htm*.

5 In a typical life span in the United States, you have about a 1 in 2 chance of being diagnosed with any mental disorder, and about a 1 in 3 chance of being diagnosed with any cancer. (Source: *https://www.cancer.org/cancer/cancer-basics/lifetime-probability-of-developing-or-dying-from-cancer.html*.)

6 Crazy is considered a slur by mental disorder advocates, who discourage its use under any circumstances other than by those with mental disorders describing themselves (i.e., "reclaiming" it). Also regarded as slurs are any other terms that use a mental disorder as a negative comparison: "insane," "nuts," "retarded," and so on.

7 Any mental disorder can vary in severity from person to person. Referring to a disorder as severe is a statement about trends across the population, rather than any statement about particular individuals.

Mental disorders are also important to the diversity conversation because they can so readily intersect with other identities that have struggled to reach parity in engineering. Women tend to be diagnosed with mental illnesses more often, and with different proportions of diagnoses.[8] Race has a dramatic impact on availability of care, especially as it pertains to difficulties in obtaining care that is culturally sensitive and appropriate. LGBTQ+ people face rates of mental illness up to three times as high as the general population due to intense stigmatization that often starts in childhood and is frequently perpetuated by their own families.

But just how pervasive is a lack of inclusion for SREs with mental disorders? In my experience, most engineering managers are not aware of *any* employees with mental disorders. Given the numbers presented earlier, this is quite improbable. What is the most likely explanation for that gap between perception and reality? The best case is that engineering culture hasn't made engineers feel comfortable talking about their disorders. I describe this as the best case because the alternative is even worse: engineers with mental disorders are finding it challenging to get or stay employed.

Sanity Isn't a Business Requirement

Discrimination against people with mental disorders is unfortunately quite real. People do not hide their mental disorders simply out of a personal sense of shame; they also choose to hide them because they know that there are economic consequences to letting their employer find out. Intense stigmatization both discourages hiring people with mental disorders and then encourages them to stay "closeted"[9] if they do manage to secure a position.

But sanity isn't a business requirement. Mental disorders can affect workplace performance, but for most people with most mental disorders, this variation is much smaller in scale than what's inherent to all humans. Most mental disorders are manageable chronic health conditions wholly compatible with SRE positions if the right support structures and team culture are in place. In fact, the ability to absorb people with different cognitive and emotional traits is a strong indicator of a healthy SRE team. Instead of expecting SREs with mental disorders to stay closeted and perform, SRE organizations should build a culture that unlearns stigma, actively includes, and makes accommodations.

---

8 For example, women are up to twice as likely to be diagnosed with depression or anxiety as men. (Source: *http://www.who.int/mental_health/prevention/genderwomen/en/*.)

9 A term originating in the LGBTQ+ community, referring to hiding parts of your identity that society discriminates against. Living a closeted life is incredibly psychologically harmful, but so is discrimination, forcing people who can hide into choosing between two bad options.

What does stigma look like? People with mental disorders are often considered "unreliable." If phrased as not being capable of working a "regular nine to five": yes, they might not be. But that likely also applies to your employees who are raising children, managing chronic physical illnesses, or even just traveling for work. Inability to cope with flexible schedules indicates a rigid organization or an unhealthily low bus factor.[10] A healthy SRE team does not need 100% uptime from its SREs any more than a service needs 100% uptime from its servers.[11]

Another common form of stigma is to assume that people with mental disorders can't handle intellectually or emotionally challenging work. It's true than an employee with ADHD might miss a step on a checklist, but the lack of automation is what made that business process fragile. Anything that requires a human brain to store information *will* fail eventually, whether that's because of a mental disorder affecting concentration or because that brain's owner is awake at 3 AM or hungry or has three other pager alerts firing. (Or all three.) Ultimately, *everyone* has cognitive and emotional limitations, and expecting flawless operators is a poor strategy for success.

The most extreme form of stigmatization is to see people with mental disorders as prone to irrational or frightening behavior, such as emotional dysregulation or episodes of mania. This simply isn't the everyday experience of most people with mental disorders. When it does occur, it is likely to be successfully treated as an acute health crisis. The mandate of SREs is to build reliable systems from unreliable components, and it's not acceptable to build an SRE organization that fails when an employee experiences a medical emergency.

Thoughts and Prayers Aren't Scalable

Ask around, and many or even most engineers will express their desire to support their colleagues with mental disorders. How can that be reconciled with the limited progress on inclusion? My take on this is that the most common strategies are some of the least effective.

Companies and foundations promote awareness campaigns for mental disorders, but increased attention always comes at a cost to something else. A few brave individuals publicly share their own experiences with mental disorders, but that doesn't necessarily help people with different diagnoses. Many people speak out about ending stigma and stereotypes, but that won't guarantee that all barriers to inclusion have been removed. Almost everyone agrees that discrimination against people with mental dis-

---

10 The risk of over-concentrating responsibility or knowledge in a team such that it would be vulnerable to a particular member having a bus-related accident. (Source: *https://en.wikipedia.org/wiki/Bus_factor*.)

11 Thanks to Marianne Bellotti for the phrasing.

orders is wrong and that they'd never do it, and yet it's possible for a system to be discriminatory even when everyone taking part in it believes they're against that outcome.

Ultimately, individualistic solutions cannot fully include people who have been excluded by systems. Caring a lot about people is one of the most beautiful ways to express humanity, but it isn't inclusion—not by itself. Inclusion requires organizational change to remove exclusionary policies, barriers to access, and unintentional discrimination.

As SREs, we spend our entire career thinking about systems, and we're well aware that manual effort won't scale. Let's use our analysis skills on the right question: instead of "How can I support engineers with mental disorders," let's ask, "How can I make engineering workplaces more inclusive for people with mental disorders?"

Full-Stack Inclusivity

The rest of this chapter is a deep dive into pro-inclusion patterns as well as a few anti-patterns that you should make sure your SRE organization is avoiding. Every organization is structured differently, but there's a convenient common thread to follow: the employee life cycle. For each stage of employment, I'll suggest ways that your team can be more inclusive of people with mental disorders.

Some of these recommendations focus on not excluding people with mental disorders or exacerbating their symptoms, or, in other words, not being a hostile workplace. But a lack of workplace hostility is simply tolerance of someone despite their differences. Other recommendations will focus on making people with mental disorders feel included. Inclusion is the positive sense that someone is welcome because of who they are, which includes but is not limited to their differences.

What every recommendation has in common is that it focuses on systemic change that you can push your team, organization, or company to make. Many of these recommendations take the form of policies that you can implement without reference to any specific person, before anyone asks for accommodations. That being said, you should also consider which interpersonal steps you can take on your own time, like learning more about specific mental disorders or changing how you communicate.

It's important to note that most of these recommendations are *not* mine. I have compiled them from a variety of sources: governmental entities, professional diversity and inclusion specialists, neurodiversity self-advocates, activists for marginalized people, conference organizers and speakers, and so many more. The work that I have done to adapt these recommendations to an SRE workplace is inconsequential compared to the hard work that these organizations engage in every day to change minds and build a better world for everyone.

Application

Applicant résumés are expected to leave a good first impression, but hiring managers rarely return the favor with well-crafted job postings. Solicit your entire team's feedback when writing a new job posting, and make sure to free enough time in their schedule for them to meaningfully contribute. These few paragraphs might be the first time an applicant has heard of your company, after all!

Clearly identify essential job functions prominently in your job listings. Rather than declaring your stance on tabs versus spaces, talk about what a typical work week looks like. How much time will be spent coding versus attending meetings versus writing documentation? Will employees be expected to contribute to project management or user interviews? How many hours will they be expected to work, and how often can you take vacation?

Your job listings should also include specific information on compensation and benefits (particularly insurance and sick leave).[12] Finding out that a job won't support your mental health needs after you're already at the interview means that everyone involved has already wasted hours of time. Be as up front as possible so that jobseekers can avoid unsuitable companies or teams—it's really in everyone's best interest.

Joblint[13] is an automated tool to scan your job postings for problematic language such as gendered assumptions or over-competitiveness. You should run all your job postings through joblint; but remember, the goal isn't to "fix" your postings! Try to understand why joblint warned you about your phrasing, and how your team's culture influenced your choice of words. Do you need to fix a word or do you need to fix your team?

Ultimately, be as honest as you can be about what your job will require out of employees and what it will provide them in exchange. People with mental disorders know their needs and limits, and it's up to you to provide them the information they need to make the right choice.

---

12 As a former employee of Harvard University, I want to call that institution out as doing this very well. Each job listing contains enough information to look up salary ranges, available insurance plans, union membership, tuition coverage, and any other benefits before you even apply.

13 Joblint (*http://joblint.org*) is available online, or runnable locally from this GitHub page (*https://github.com/rowanmanning/joblint/*). The GitHub project also accepts pull requests if you want to add further rules.

Is On-Call an Essential Job Function?

There's no hard definition for what makes a job function "essential," but the US Equal Employment Opportunity Commission (EEOC) considers three factors: the degree of skill required to perform the task, whether the job was created to perform the task, and whether other employees could perform it, instead. Do any of these apply to on-call?

Being on call is an extremely skill-dependent task in a high-skill industry, so I'll give that a firm "yes." If I'm being honest, many SRE teams exist because someone needs to be on call; at the same time, the team's goal is to end it! That sounds like a "maybe." Finally, because SRE teams should have pager rotations and high bus factors anyways, that's a clear "no."

I interpret that mixed rating as on-call being essential for many SRE teams but that it's not essential that every SRE carries a pager. Consider whether your team could structure on-call as an opt-in duty with extra compensation. For more thoughts along these lines, check out Liz Frost's presentation about on-call equity (*https://www.youtube.com/watch?v=31EBLV_Bpwg*).

Interviewing

Interviewing is where prospective employees get their first close look at your team and company culture. Unfortunately, this means that it's often where they first notice signs that your workplace is not welcoming or inclusive.

Determine your interview questions and success criteria in advance and communicate that information to both the interviewers and interviewee. You don't need to share every question with an interviewee in advance, but you should make sure that they know what to expect from the process and what you are looking for them to demonstrate. When drafting your own engineering interview policies, consider reading through 18F's (*https://eng-hiring.18f.gov/*) as an outstanding example from which to draw inspiration.

You should hire a diversity and inclusivity professional to help you write your interview policies and to conduct antibias trainings for your hiring managers. Psychology research has repeatedly demonstrated that even people with the best intentions subconsciously stereotype others; worse yet, *being aware of these biases is not sufficient to negate them*. A skilled trainer will teach you structural strategies to mitigate the impact of your biases, such as anonymizing résumés or avoiding subjective criteria (e.g., "friendliness" and "culture fit").

Don't structure your interview like an exam. Level of coding skill is a relevant job qualification, but pseudocode on a whiteboard is approximately no one's favorite language or editor, and coding is just one part of engineering. Instead of asking "whiteboard-friendly" algorithm questions like inverting binary trees or implementing sorts, ask higher-level questions that test a broad range of skills like systems design, writing tests, or interpersonal communication. People with mental disorders often work around impairments by leaning into other areas, so make sure that your interview provides opportunities to demonstrate a range of abilities.

Never interview using "puzzles" or other artificially stressful situations, which can be very unwelcoming to people with anxiety disorders. A particularly egregious example saw interviewees playing a simulated bomb defusal video game, with the interviewers giving disarmament instructions. Skill at a video game you've never played before is neither a fair representation of job duties nor a sensible factor in hiring decisions, anyways.

Compensation

It's engineering tradition to use multiple job offers as leverage for negotiating higher pay at the place you actually want to work. But high-stakes negotiation is so stressful that it can force a choice between mental health or salary. Removing negotiation from the picture can help people with anxiety, depression, and many other disorders. It's also helpful to the many other groups of marginalized people who are negatively impacted by having to argue for their right to fair compensation.

Start by creating objective criteria for determining a candidate's offer. If you give a set of reviewers these criteria and a résumé, they should agree to within a few thousand dollars of one another. This is far from an impossible change; many workplaces (particularly in government and academia) already grade salaries by job description and limit pay differences within the same grade.

Make sure that you never base salaries on prior compensation, or better yet, just don't inquire about prior compensation at all.[14] This disturbingly common trend *amplifies* any prior discrimination! Taken over the duration of a career, even a small initial disparity can easily compound to a shortfall of millions of dollars of lifetime earnings.

If you work at a large company, encourage it to share anonymized demographic and compensation data.[15] Publishing regular reports on how mental disorders are associated with compensation is a great way to hold your company accountable as well as to drive change throughout the entire industry.

---

14 This might even be illegal, depending on your state, as many are moving to ban the question outright.

15 Privacy engineering principles apply here, too, of course.

Benefits

It's an unfortunate reality of America's for-profit healthcare system that many job seekers have to make employment decisions on the basis of whether their conditions will be covered appropriately. But what does "appropriately" mean? As anyone with a chronic condition can tell you, not all insurance plans are created equal.

When evaluating which health insurance plan to offer to your employees, choose one that includes comprehensive mental healthcare coverage. Many insurance plans "cover mental health," but are low quality or high cost. Closely examine what treatment options are covered, whether there are any lifetime limits, and even whether the copays for therapist visits and psychiatric medications are excessive.

As previously discussed, society's treatment of LGBTQ+ people results in higher rates of mental disorders, which means that availability of mental healthcare is *also* an LGBTQ+ rights issue. And although being transgender is not a mental disorder, availability of care is still a pressing mental health need. You should consider transgender inclusivity when evaluating insurance plans, which might exclude necessary procedures or require excessive and invasive documentation. Consult with a specialist to figure out what's best for your transgender employees, and do so *before* they ask you to. Remember, your workplace policies are a huge factor in when and how your employees decide to undergo gender transition!

Even if your benefits are inclusive, there is another problem: America's lack of single-payer healthcare has resulted in a system so complex that it can be difficult to understand how to receive care, how much it will cost, and how much of that will be covered by your benefits. People with chronic illnesses, including mental disorders, often invest so much time into navigating the healthcare system that they may even joke about being "professional patients." Unfortunately, the symptoms of many mental disorders can make it even harder to understand medical billing or make lengthy phone calls to dispute errors. Dedicate additional resources to helping your employees with mental disorders fully utilize their benefits and avoid disruptions in care.

Employees with mental disorders are often unaware of their options for taking time away from work. You should clearly document that sick days can be applied to mental disorders. Also make sure to document how longer leaves such as short-term disability or unpaid leave apply to employees with mental disorders.

It's unfortunately the case that employees with chronic conditions will resort to using their "vacation" days to cover their health needs. This is especially common for employees with mental disorders who might prefer to hide why they're taking time off due to stigmatization. Needing to reserve vacation time for health purposes can interact quite poorly with the current trend toward unlimited vacation policies.[16] How "unlimited" is your policy in practice, and are certain types of time off seen as more legitimate than others? Consider the impact on people with mental disorders prior to making any changes in your vacation policy. If you do adopt an unlimited vacation policy, consider pairing it with a *minimum* number of vacation days that you expect employees to take per year. If you're not convinced, you can also think of minimum vacation days as an SRE best practice: you need your teammates to take time off in order to detect whether they're single points of failure for any critical services.[17]

Onboarding

Make sure to consider mental disorders when putting together onboarding packets. At a minimum that means including mental health information and resource documents, as described in the previous section. Companies can go a step further by providing social aids that describe the culture and people that new employees will interact with. Having a seating chart or dictionary of in-jokes is low cost, but they could make someone's first day among strangers that much more comfortable to navigate.

Conduct post-hiring interviews for all your new employees and actively ask about needs and accommodations, making clear that you provide accommodations for both physical and mental disorders. If you make accommodations only for employees who ask, you'll be leaving out the many employees who aren't aware of the existence of the Americans with Disabilities Act (ADA) or that it also applies to mental disorders. During this interview, give examples of accommodations to employees so that they have an idea of what they can ask for. Remember, some accommodations might require ordering equipment or reshuffling offices, so it's important that you have this conversation *before* an employee's first day. You should also ask whether the employee wants to designate any emergency contacts to call in case of a medical emergency.

If your employees do ask for accommodations, first focus on meeting their needs, and then examine whether any "exceptions" you're making could become new policies that cover anyone else in a similar situation. This will help future employees who want an accommodation but are unaware that they can receive it or uncertain whether it is safe to ask. This helps to create a company culture in which making accommodations is just another aspect of continuous improvement.

---

16 Unlimited vacation policies have seen rapid adoption because they avoid the accounting liability from accrued vacation days. They are not inherently pro-employee, and although evidence is limited, they might even result in employees taking fewer vacation days.

17 Thanks to Amy Tobey for this suggestion.

Finally, don't bring your employees alone. If the accommodations that they're asking for are more than what you can provide, you need to be honest with them so that they can evaluate their next steps.

Working Conditions

The modern workplace can be stressful; thus, minimizing unnecessary noise and distractions can be incredibly important to people with post-traumatic stress disorder (PTSD) and/or ADHD. Open office plans can make this challenging, but you can make a difference even if you're stuck with one. You're best off asking your employees what they need from their office space, but likely requests include requiring meetings to be held in noise-isolated rooms, avoiding bells or gongs, and banning Nerf-gun fights.

Flexible scheduling and remote work can make anyone's life better, but they can be particularly important for people with mental disorders. A person with agoraphobia (the fear of being in situations where escape might be difficult or help wouldn't be available) might find it very draining to leave the house, or in a severe case, might be *unable* to; someone in a depressive episode might spend hours just mustering enough energy to face their commute. Create a policy that formally details what flexibility your employees have in where and when they work.[18] Make sure that your policy sets clear expectations for check-ins, meeting attendance, and other work duties that implicitly assume a shared office. It's also critical that this policy documents how in-office employees must adjust their own workflows to support their remote coworkers.

Don't expect employees to be their own project managers (unless you stated that as a job requirement when hiring). Executive dysfunction is a symptom of many mental disorders, and it can manifest as "simple" tasks (like making a checklist) being far more difficult than "complex" tasks (like writing code). By breaking work into actionable tasks and prioritizing them appropriately in a task tracking system, you're helping your employees get back to using the skills you actually hired them for.

Let employees socialize on their own terms. Social team-building exercises can build trust, but that can come at the cost of excluding anyone who doesn't or can't participate. By all means, hold the occasional outing, but make sure that "beers with the team"[19] isn't the only pathway to feeling included and trusted by your colleagues. Also, make sure to never describe an event as "optional" if it comes with professional

---

18 A full discussion of remote workplaces deserves a chapter in its own right, but consider *https://www.remo teonly.org* and *https://stackoverflow.blog/2017/02/08/means-remote-first-company/* as a starting point.

19 This is a very intentional example: events centered around alcohol consumption are often unsafe for people with mental disorders. Alcohol can be a mental disorder symptom trigger, many people with PTSD feel unsafe around alcohol consumption, and many mental disorders are a risk factor for developing substance-abuse disorders.

consequences when missed. Implicit social expectations can be especially harmful for many autistic people.

One final note: if someone insults or jokes about mental disorders, make it known that this is unacceptable workplace behavior. If the person persists, fire them and let the rest of the company know why you did. The exception to this is people making jokes about *their own* mental disorders. This can be an important coping strategy for many, and yet it is often met with concern or even punishment. It's completely reasonable to decide that this style of "gallows humor" isn't appropriate for your workplace, but just make sure to apply that prohibition evenly: would you equally discourage employees from joking about their experiences with blindness or cancer?

Job Duties

Evaluate employees on the value they contribute rather than on whether they can perform each duty that is expected of the team. It's already common for SRE teams to hire their way into new technology skills, but the same can be done for job duties, like giving presentations or writing documentation. Ideally, an SRE team should be a safe place to have a discussion about whether and how to distribute work according to the interests and abilities of the team members. Covering for each other is why you're a team, after all!

As a corollary, you should value and promote many forms of contribution. Teams often overvalue debate, public speaking, and releasing new features. In contrast, they tend to undervalue collaboration, mentoring, and maintenance and documentation work. Call out major milestones that aren't as "impressive" as winning an impassioned debate or giving an all-hands presentation. Make sure that everyone doing good work on your team has a chance to get a round of applause.

Contributing to team decisions is worth a special note because it's an important part of both daily duties and career progression. Many teams rely on adversarial decision-making styles in which each side advocates strongly for their opinion until someone "wins." Open conflict is challenging and unpleasant for *most* people, and it can also be a trigger for some mental disorders (e.g., complex post-traumatic stress disorder [C-PTSD][20] or bipolar disorder). Make sure that your team is also open to other decision-making styles where appropriate, such as consensus or voting.

While you're at it, make most meetings and presentations optional; better yet, stream or record them. This is an important part of including remote employees and

---

20 C-PTSD is a form of PTSD resulting from prolonged abuse or neglect, often during childhood. People with C-PTSD usually have different symptoms and triggers than those whose PTSD stems from experiences like battlefield trauma or survivor's guilt.

---

employees on different schedules, and, as we've seen earlier, there are good options for many employees with mental disorders.

Training

Whereas anyone might express a preference for interactive example code over prose documentation (or vice versa), that preference might instead be a necessity for a programmer with dyslexia or ADHD. Provide an independent training budget to let people learn at their own pace from their choice of materials; alternatively, purchase seats for a subscription service that provides a wide range of content.[21]

Consider starting a mentorship program at your company. By taking a more holistic view of skills and career goals, a mentor can help someone grow beyond the immediate needs of their team, with an eye toward the future. A meeting with a mentor can also be a safer place to discuss personal topics than with your immediate manager, who might treat you differently based on what you disclose.

Note that marginalized people tend to see the most benefit from mentoring when it comes from someone like them. It can feel pointless to discuss career advancement with someone who does not understand your mental disorder(s); "speak at conferences" may be inaccessible to someone with a panic disorder, and "improve your focus" might be completely out of reach to a person with ADHD. An inclusive mentorship program requires diverse mentors and, to keep it sustainable, appropriate compensation. The surest way to kill a diversity initiative is to expect a day's work and then *also* unpaid diversity and inclusion work (which is deeply emotionally taxing).

Promotion

Treating your employees well means providing opportunities for their achievements to be recognized. However, it's crucial to examine whether your criteria for advancement have implicit ability requirements. Unfortunately, this is often the case: key criteria often focus on coordinating or managing people, presenting at conferences, or working long or irregular hours. A more egalitarian approach is to offer multiple promotion tracks for different skill sets (i.e., manager versus IC), and to value multiple types of contributions during performance reviews.

Of course, your employees won't be recognized for their achievements if they don't get to achieve. Many attempts to include people with mental disorders end up "protecting" them from career-enhancing work, such as not giving them assignments that you think they'd find stressful. Don't let your good intentions stifle someone's career! Avoid paternalism, which is the idea that you know what is best for someone else or can make decisions for them. Instead, practice informed consent. Check in privately

---

21 Such as O'Reilly Safari (*https://www.oreilly.com/safari*).

with them and have an honest discussion about what the assignment will require and how important it is likely to be to the team and to the rest of the company.

That being said, don't treat advancement as a requirement on your team or think less of employees who don't take on more responsibility over time. Many managers exhibit an unfortunate tendency toward devaluing employees who don't have an upward trajectory within the organization, such as assuming that they lack a "growth mindset." But career growth is just one type of growth, and in the face of constraints on mental health or ability, an employee might quite reasonably choose to focus on other areas. Make sure not to evaluate performance at anyone's *current* job by their level of interest in pursuing a *different* job. What gets interpreted as "lacking ambition" is often "knowing what's healthy."

Leaving

Whether by choice or not, employees will eventually leave your team or your company. Their stated reasons for departure might omit more sensitive topics such as their stress or health. You should conduct exit interviews with any departing employees, and that interview shouldn't be conducted by their manager or mentor. You need to do this work to discover whether your employees are leaving for other companies because you failed to provide appropriate accommodations for their mental disorders.

Of course, mental disorders can be serious conditions, and depression in particular is one of the leading causes of disability in the United States. When accommodations on the job are no longer enough, you should offer a variety of options for medical leave or disability. Even so, an employee might find unemployment preferable depending on the particulars of their situation. Work with them to find the best solution.

If an employee does need to take leave due to their mental disorder(s), you should go out of your way to offer them a chance to return to work as soon as they've recovered. But remember never to make an offer that you can't follow through on: this means that, first, you need to build a culture in which someone *can* come back and feel included when their mental health improves.

A Note on Crisis

Crisis does not define mental illness, but, unfortunately, it can be a component of it. A mental health crisis can be frightening not just for that person, but for everyone around them. It's completely reasonable to be distressed or scared by someone acting erratically, exhibiting sudden personality changes, or making threats about themselves or others.

The most common response to a mental health crisis is to call the police. Unfortunately, officers typically do not have mental healthcare training. Also, undergoing coercive psychological treatment can prevent a crisis from escalating but often at the cost of permanent harm such as PTSD or a legal record of involuntary commitment. Do not call the police unless you are comfortable with the consequences, *up to and including death*. There have been many interactions with police (particularly in America) where a person with a mental disorder ended up dead, and this is especially true for people of color.

It takes advance planning to create strategies that avoid having to call the police. Respect the mental health of your employees and do your best to avoid triggering a crisis. Make information on phone and digital helplines available to all employees. Ask about emergency mental health contacts in advance, preferably during the onboarding interview. Train your managers to recognize and respond appropriately to mental health crises.

If a crisis does occur, weigh all of your options. Could you call their therapist, one of their friends, or another emergency contact they provided you during your onboarding process? Are any other employees willing to volunteer to take them to a hospital? If they are causing a disruption, could you close the office for the day rather than calling the police? *Always keep consent and autonomy in mind, even when it's not convenient!*

Inclusivity for Anyone Helps Everyone

Most workplaces will already have implemented some of these recommendations while still having room to make progress on others. I hope that you're fired up to contribute to that progress! But I encourage you to think of this as a marathon, not a sprint. These changes are deeply necessary, but you're making them to encourage a healthy and sustainable workplace, so I implore you to promote change in a healthy and sustainable way. Burnout in SRE is nothing compared to burnout among activists.

What does healthy and sustainable progress look like? It means not trying to do all of this work yourself. It's just as important to document and track the work yet to be done, to talk about it openly, and to convince others to help. It's crucial to build relationships with teams outside of your SRE organization who have influence over relevant policies, because a recommendation that would be an uphill fight for you to put into place could be resolved with a single email from the right stakeholder. This chapter might be oriented toward SREs, but your biggest contribution might be talking about it with HR.

Healthy and sustainable also means treating these recommendations as starting points for conversation rather than rigid policy requirements. There is no "average employee" or "average workplace," and there will always be exceptions and history and context. You need to be aware of what people with mental disorders actually want from your workplace and not impose your expectations or assumptions onto them. Mental disorders don't strip away someone's dignity; that's something that a person does by treating another person as something less than human, and that includes insisting on providing unwanted help. Coming to an individual understanding of needs can require more effort, but it is effort well spent.

At the end of the day, inclusivity for anyone helps everyone. Changing your policies to help people with depression can also help those who are grieving. Providing multiple types of training material to support your employees with learning disorders is also great for the next junior engineer that joins your team. Improving your leave policies will help people who need inpatient psychiatric care but also people who want to have children or take time off to work on a political campaign.

In fact, the person who benefits most from your work on inclusivity might one day be *you*!

Mental Disorder Resources

If you are experiencing a mental health crisis, the National Suicide Prevention Lifeline has trained counselors available 24/7, either via phone at 1-800-273-8255 or via web chat (*https://suicidepreventionlifeline.org/*).

Trans Lifeline is staffed by transgender people, for transgender people. You can reach them at (877) 565-8860 or online (*https://www.translifeline.org*).

For mental health and mental disorder resources that focus on the needs of software engineers:

- Open Sourcing Mental Illness (*https://osmihelp.org*)
- mhprompt (*http://mhprompt.org*)
- burnout.io (*http://burnout.io/en/latest/furtherReading.html*)

For general reading on mental health and mental disorders:

- National Alliance on Mental Illness (*https://www.nami.org*)

- American Psychiatric Association (*https://www.psychiatry.org/patients-families/what-is-mental-illness*)
- National Institutes of Mental Health (*https://www.nimh.nih.gov/health/topics/index.shtml*)
- Autism Women's Network (*https://autismwomensnetwork.org*)
- Autistic Self Advocacy Network (*http://autisticadvocacy.org*)

James Meickle is a site reliability engineer at Quantopian, a Boston startup making algorithmic trading accessible to everyone. Between NYSE trading days, he advises DevOpsDays Boston and conducts Ansible trainings on O'Reilly's Safari platform. What free time remains is dedicated to cooking, sci-fi, permadeath video games, and Satanism.

## CHAPTER 30

Against On-Call: A Polemic

Niall Richard Murphy, Microsoft

On-call, as we know it, must end. It is damaging to the people who do it,[1] and ineffi-cient as a means of keeping systems running. It is especially galling to see it continu-ing today given the real potential we have at this historical moment to eliminate it. The time for a reevaluation of what we do when we are on call and, more important, *why* we do it, is long overdue.

How long overdue? I can find evidence of on-call-style activities more than 75 years ago,[2] and in truth there have been people tending computers in emergencies for as long as there have been both computers and emergencies. Yet, though there have been huge improvements in computing systems generally since then,[3] the practice of out-of-hours, often interrupt-driven support—more generally called on-call—has continued essentially unaltered from the beginning of computing right through to today. Ultimately, however, whether the continuity is literally from the dawn of com-puting or whether it is merely from the last few decades, we still have fundamental questions to ask about on-call, the most important of which is *why*? Why are we still doing this? Furthermore, is it good that we are? Finally, is there a genuine alternative to doing this work in this way? Our profession derives a great deal of its sense of mis-

---

1 See, for example, "How on-call and irregular scheduling harm the American workforce" (*http://theconversa tion.com/how-on-call-and-irregular-scheduling-harm-the-american-workforce-46063*) from The Conversation, or "Why You Should End On-Call Scheduling and What to Do Instead" (*https://wheniwork.com/blog/on-call-scheduling/*) from When I Work, outlining the impact on income and family; the costs to the systems them-selves are hard to estimate, but "friendly fire" in on-call situations is estimated to occur in over 1% of on-call shifts.

2 Bletchley Park and its complement of WRNS (Women's Royal Naval Service) on-call operators.

3 According to, for example, Tom's Hardware (*http://www.tomshardware.com/reviews/upgrade-repair-pc, 3000-2.html*), around the Bletchley Park era, "in a large system, [a vacuum tube] failed every hour or so."

---

sion, urgency, and, frankly, individual self-worth, from incident response and resolving production problems. It is rare to hear us ask if we *should*, and I think the evidence clearly shows us that we should not and that a genuine alternative is possible.

But first, let us look at the rationale for doing on-call in the first place.

The Rationale for On-Call

Many SREs have an intuitive idea of why on-call is necessary: to wit, getting a system working again, and we shall come back to that shortly. However, for a fuller understanding, it is useful to look at the role of on-call in other professions, to focus our idea of what is unique to our case. Let us look at examples from medicine.

First, Do No Harm

In a medical context, the person on-call is the person on duty, ready to respond.[4] In emergency medicine, the function of the on-call doctor is in some sense to be a portable decision-maker, with appropriate expertise where possible, and the ability to summon it otherwise. The first function is to perform *triage*, in which the doctor figures out from the signals available whether or not the patient should be in A&E[5] in the first place and otherwise attempts to make the patient better. Not necessarily cure them; that is not the domain of emergency medicine. The goal of emergency medicine is to stabilize the situation so the patient can be moved to ward medicine, to manage a cure, the treatment of slow decline, or otherwise non-life-threatening, non-immediate situations.

Parallels with SRE

Emergency medicine is strongly interrupt-driven work, and the broad context of bringing people with expertise to fix a problem is exactly the same as with the SRE on-call context. Those are the strongest point of correspondence. Another parallel is the act of triage, which is also performed in the SRE context, although usually by software deciding that some metric has reached an unacceptable threshold and paging

---

4 See, for example, this MedicineNet article (*https://www.medicinenet.com/script/main/art.asp?article key=39965*) or this free medical dictionary (*https://medical-dictionary.thefreedictionary.com/on-call*), making specific reference to being reachable in 30 minutes of being paged.

5 "Accident & Emergency" in the UK/Ireland; Emergency Room (ER) in the US.

---

rather than manual actions.[6] A similar act is also performed when an SRE on call operator decides some alert is not actually important enough to bother with. (Broadly, you could look at the overall emergency medicine challenge as how we can deliver relatively well-understood treatment plans in an efficient way while wrestling with many other simultaneous demands.)

Preparations for an on-call shift are similar, too. A demanding—potentially longer than 24-hour—work shift[7] requires physiological preparation, and in on-call preparation documents I have also seen the equivalent of an SRE playbook, which is to say, a list of specific, somewhat tactical suggestions, for how to respond to different kinds of known failure in human biological systems.

 In the case of *On Call Principles and Protocols*, sixth edition (Elsevier), for example, the bulk of the chapters are about specific "subsystem" failures (e.g., abdominal pain, chest pain, seizures), with a seemingly strong Pareto Principle (*https://en.wikipedia.org/wiki/Pareto_principle*)–style assumption that 80% of cases arise from 20% of the total causes.[8]

Finally, when a system is restored to an everyday working state, but serious cleanup work is necessary, that can be left to a normal daytime activity—or ward work, in other words.

Differences with SRE

Strong though the parallels are, working with software is fundamentally different. In some ways, the frightening thing about SRE on-call is that because so many of the systems we look at are changing so quickly, the act of being on call for a particular system in January is not hugely relevant when it comes to being on call for it in June. This is not the case in A&E, where people's bodies and the life-threatening traumas

---

6 Note that doctors get a lot of automatic alerting as well, it's just that it seems that a lot of it is very low quality; see, for example, this Washington Post article (*https://www.washingtonpost.com/national/health-science/doctors-are-overloaded-with-electronic-alerts-and-thats-bad-for-patients/2016/06/10/0cae6b4a-20fa-11e6-9e7f-57890b612299_story.html*).

7 See, for example, this article (*http://www.medicalprotection.org/ireland/new-doctor/volume-2-issue-1/surviving-on-call*) from Medical Protection Ireland, emphasizing not eating junk food, paying bills in advance of a week of night-shift work, and double-checking calculations made during night shifts.

8 For example, this article (*https://journals.lww.com/em-news/Fulltext/2013/03211/News__Beating_the_80_20_Rule_in_the_ED.1.aspx*) claims that 5% of their ER admissions gave rise to 22% of their costs; this piece (*https://www.medscape.com/viewarticle/835473*) argues more broadly that Pareto Principle–style effects are distributed throughout medicine; and this article (*https://citations.springer.com/item?doi=10.1007/s00228-014-1665-2*) showed that adverse drug effects obeyed a Pareto Principle–like distribution across a sample of 700-plus cases.

that befall them tend to have quite well-understood manifestations and diagnoses, wide genetic variety and environmental factors notwithstanding. Although that rate of change can fluctuate given particular team or industry circumstances, it is almost never zero, and if it is, the software environment itself is almost always changing, too. (An SRE approach enables fast change, so this is to be expected.)

A useful analogy would be that SRE on-call is like dealing with entirely new kinds of human beings every A&E shift, in which the patient presents with an additional unexplained internal organ for which someone is still writing the documentation. If medicine had this to cope with, the treatment plan would have to be derived from first principles every time. That unbounded quality—that the causes and extent of the emergency might involve arbitrarily novel situations every time[9]—seems to be unique to software.

Of course, despite this, most adjacent shifts, and the problems encountered therein, are quite similar. But the worst-case scenario—that almost everything could have changed since your last shift—can and does happen.

Underlying Assumptions Driving On-Call for Engineers

So, the rationale for on-call in other professions is to bring expertise and resources to a problem as quickly as possible, to resolve that problem, and (often) to prevent a similar or larger problem from developing.[10] Today, we place humans in those situations because the complexity of the world remains such that a robot programmed as well as we know how to do it today could not effectively act as, for example, a medic.[11]

However, the highly restricted environment inside a machine or machines, although complicated under certain conditions, is not as complicated as the real world. If the argument is that the real world is complicated enough to need a human doing the on-call, the same argument applied to the datacenter is not as clearly true.

Yet we continue to put engineers[12] on call for services. Why?

---

9 As best I can tell, this situation is unique to software: industries that deal with very complex hardware, such as airplanes, do have problems related to complexity, and uncover latent problems with particular revisions of sensors, and so on, but the nature of software being changed *all the time* is found, as far as I know, nowhere else.

10 On-call in the medical professional also serves as a triage function, which is partially outsourced to monitoring software in the SRE case.

11 Leaving aside the considerable problems with persuading the public, this would be a good idea.

12 This applies to operations engineers generally, and sometimes to product software engineers.

Lest into us be brutally frank, fellow operations engineers, we are sometimes put on call for bad reasons. One well-known bad reason is because *it is cheaper than solving the real problem*; that is, it is cheaper to pay a human to just react and fix things manually when problems happen, rather than extend the software to do so. Another bad reason would be because *on-call work is perceived to be awful*. Therefore, product engineers who are not trained for it are very reluctant to do it, and the desire grows to pass this work off to a lower caste: operations engineers. Yet another one is the assumption that mission criticality (however critical that turns out to be), a "keep the site up" mentality, and cultivating a sense of urgency around production state all require being on call. Ultimately, however, these are dogma: firmly and long-held beliefs, which might or might not be useful.

I take a different approach and use the language of risk management for the purposes of outlining the valid reasons why we are on-call today. This allows us to be focused on matters relating to the impact on the supported systems rather than beliefs that might or might not be true or might change over time.

Let us therefore group the reasons into the following categories:

Known-knowns

Consider a system that has known bugs, and the circumstances under which they are triggered are known, their effect is known, and the remediation is known, too. Many on-call professionals today will be familiar with the sensation of being paged for something fitting this description. Of course, the obvious question is then, why are humans fixing this at all? As discussed, sometimes it is cheaper, sometimes not, but it is typically a decision made by business owners that the particular code paths that recover a system should be run partially inside the brains of their staff rather than inside the CPUs of their systems. (I suppose this is externalizing your call stack (*https://queue.acm.org/detail.cfm?id=2956643*) with a vengeance.) In this bucket, therefore, engineers are put on call because of *cost*; in reality, the problem is perfectly resolvable with software.

Known-unknowns

Many software failures result from external action or interaction of some kind, whether change management, excessive resource usage beyond a quota limit, access control violations, or similar. In general, failures of this kind are definitely foreseeable in principle, particularly after you have some experience under your belt, even if the specific way in which (as an example) quota exhaustion comes into play is not clear in advance. For example, these problems can sometimes be related to rapid spikes in traffic or other exceptional events. Although you can't necessarily predict why in advance, it's usually essentially statistically guaranteed that you'll have a few really big spikes a year. Engineers are therefore put on-call because the correct automation or scaling is not currently available; the problem is again perfectly resolvable.

Unknown-unknowns

Despite theoretical positions to the contrary,[13] systems and software do indeed fail. Today, certain kinds of failure can be automatically recovered from or otherwise responded to without human intervention—if not self-healing, then at least non-self-destroying. But there are large classes of failures that aren't, and, what's worse, these failures typically change as a system itself changes, its dependency list grows, and so on. In the language of engineering risk management, these are *unknown unknowns*:[14] things that you don't know that you don't know, but you do know that you don't know everything, so you can foresee their theoretical existence. Engineers are therefore put on-call because of the system potentially failing in ways that could not have been seen beforehand and therefore seemingly *requires* the kind of context-jumping response that only a human can give; the thing that makes this hard to respond to automatically is the complexity of what could have gone wrong.

The Wisdom of Production

This is conceptually very similar to our first two reasons; the difference is mostly in intention. We choose to put engineers on-call for a system to learn *real things* about how it behaves in *real situations*. We might learn unpleasant things about it or we might learn pleasant things, but we are doing it explicitly to gather information and to decide on where to put our effort for how to improve it.

It seems clear to me that most of the significant opposition to removing on-call as a job responsibility for SREs is because of the third category: unknown-unknowns.

On-Call Is Emergency Medicine Instead of Ward Medicine

But, actually, the only valid reason to put engineers on-call is the last one: The Wisdom of Production. The other categories are ultimately distractions.

The first category, known-knowns, involves humans executing procedures to fix things that could (by definition) be done perfectly well by machine; it merely happens to be cheaper or simpler for some set of particular humans to do it at that moment. This category is about expediency, cost control, and prioritization, not engineering. There is nothing here preventing a completely automatable approach other than

---

13 For the purposes of this footnote, I want to attack the notion that failure is unavoidable and that everything in computing is wobbly stacks built on soggy marshes of unpredictability. This is not the case. There are large classes of software systems that run without issue for years. In fact, we might propose (say) a Murphy's First Law of Production: a system operating stably in production continues to operate stably in production unless acted on by an external force. This is true for many embedded systems, disconnected from the internet. It is not largely true for non-embedded, internet-connected systems. Complexity is surely part of the answer why, but there is something we are missing.

14 See this definition (*https://academic.oup.com/jxb/article/60/3/712/453685*) of the phrase.

---

money and time, which are obviously crucial things but not a barrier in principle. Yet this category persists as a source of outages today, perhaps because of a widely held practice in the industry of treating operations as a cost center, meaning that no business owner will invest it in, because it is not seen as something that can generate revenue for the business, as opposed to simply accumulate costs.[15]

For known-unknown problems, the path away from manual action is generally more resources or pausing normal processing in a controlled way, with some buffer of normal operation before more-detailed remediation work is required. Indeed, the conditions in which the full concentration of an on-call engineer are legitimately needed to resolve a known-unknown problem usually involve a flaw in the higher-level system behavior. An application layer problem, such as a query of death[16] or resource usage that begins to grow superlinearly with input, is again amenable to programmatic ways of keeping the system running (automatically blocking queries found to be triggering restarts, graceful degradation to a different datacenter where the query is not hitting, etc.). The important questions, then, are how flaws in higher-level systems are introduced and whether there is a meaningful way of working around this.

The situation is even more dispiriting for, as an example, system-level change-control problems: perhaps a problematic Access Control List (ACL) prevents access to a critical dependency; or maybe a runtime flag changes startup servers to a set that no longer exists or are vastly slower; or possibly a GRANT command accidentally removes access to the systems for the entity performing the GRANT. Although these might seem outside of the domain of automated response, it is canarying,[17] which is the actual solution: it allows us to pilot a variety of difficult-to-reason about changes and observe the effects in a systematic way, and it does not require a fundamental rewrite in core systems, merely the ability to partition activity. Yet, instead, we typically pay for humans to make a change and watch a process; perhaps reasoning that if

---

15 See, for example, this wonderful article (*http://www.leanessays.com/2017/11/the-cost-center-trap.html*).

16 See, for example, this definition. (*http://www.doublecloud.org/2010/11/what-lessons-you-can-learn-from-google-on-building-infrastructure/*)

17 Note that I am being deliberately careful with my wording here. Canarying has limits: for example, you shouldn't canary in a nontransactional environment in which each operation is "important" (as opposed to a simple retryable web query); an operation will irrevocably alter state (perhaps with some monetary value attached) and yet can't be rolled back. You also can't canary in an environment in which fractional traffic isn't routable safely to a subset of processors. Running a canary fleet is more expensive, too, unless you're cannibalizing your production serving capacity, which is problematic on its own, and, finally, your cloud/colo/etc. provider might not provide easy hooks for canarying. But I (carefully) don't say, "canarying can solve everything." I say, "It's hard to think of a situation where you can't canary to good effect." Those are different statements, and I expect that canarying could solve a very wide array of problems that it doesn't solve today, mostly because we put people on call rather than go to the time and expense of setting up a canarying infrastructure.

we must have someone around to handle unknown-unknowns, we might as well have them do the other ones, too.

So, it really does come down to the problem of unknown-unknowns: what are the lurking unanticipatable problems present in the system that prevent us from turning an emergency situation into plain-old ward medicine? Surely, runs the argument, we can't know these in advance, and therefore we need a human around in order to be able to observe the system in its entirety and take the correct response?

The situation is more nuanced than that, however. Not all problems that could result in outages happen to a system: only some of them will. Not all of the lurking difficulties can be hypothesized in advance, but that's actually OK because we don't need to have a solution for every possible problem in advance. Instead, we need to translate problematic states of the system (requiring emergency medicine) into ones requiring business hours intervention (ward medicine). There is a very big difference between solving the general case of all unanticipatable problems and the specific case of constructing software to be much more resilient to unexpected problems within their own domain. Perhaps a little like the halting problem (*https://en.wikipedia.org/wiki/Halting_problem*), solving the general case is certainly intractable because modeling program state in order to predict halting is too big; but predicting when a simple FOR loop will halt is trivial. It is absolutely true that there have been many sizeable incidents in which extremely delicate effects have played a part in major outages. However, most people do not ask themselves why those delicate effects emerged in the first place, and this is partially because the state of the industry does not seek to build reliable systems out of well-known building blocks that fail in particularly well-understood ways; instead, unfortunately, the state of the art today is that most successful application layers, whether for startups or for huge multinationals, are reinvented time and time again from the ground up.[18]

This leads to a situation in which a number of building blocks are indeed composed together, typically in some kind of microservice architecture, but because each organization does it from first principles every time, there is no meaningful industry-wide cooperation on a single stack for serving, data processing, and so on that could produce resilient and well-tested software units. It's as if the construction industry derived bricks from first principles every time it built a house, and a row of houses would only share bricks because the team members happened to sit next to each other at lunch.

To put it another way, part of the reason we see unknown-unknowns to having bad effects on systems in the first place is because the fine detail in how systems and code interact is poorly understood. And the reason they are poorly understood is not

---

18 In this context, "ground" often equals POSIX libc, although it shouldn't.

because people are stupid or software is hard (neither of which is *necessarily* true) but because each team needs to understand things from the beginning. If we had a consolidated set of components that behaved in well-understood ways, we could offset these risks significantly, perhaps completely depending on the domain. Or, putting it in the language of solutions rather than problems, *we need a safe cloud stack*—or at least cloud components that behave in safe ways.

Another way to think about this problem is to think about the set of postmortems you've assembled for your service over the years. When you look at the set of root causes and contributing factors over a long enough period, you can ask yourself the questions: what proportion of those outages were genuinely unforeseeable in advance, and what proportion of them would have been remediated if fairly simple protections had been put more consistently in place? My experience suggests that, as per the earlier analysis of the ER, 80% of outages are caused by 20% of root causes; the rest is in the unknown-unknowns bucket. We can attack those in turn by building more resilient systems that fail safely, can allow for canarying, and separate application logic from a solid systems layer.

Counterarguments

An important counterargument is that the previous observations are all very well, but here in the current universe, with bespoke software aplenty and limited budgets, there is no prospect of avoiding unknown-unknowns, and so we are still locked into on-call for the indefinite future.

This might well be true, in the sense of there being lots of software and not enough money, but almost every piece of software everywhere does go through a rewrite cycle at some point. The prospect of adopting key reliability frameworks for cloud consumers, particularly if they are easy to use and cover very common cases (HTTP servers, storage, etc.) is not as far removed as you might think. It will take time, certainly, but it is not impossible.

Another counterargument is that this will prevent on-call engineers from understanding and effectively troubleshooting problems when they do arise; therefore, we should continue to do on-call across the industry. Well, as outlined earlier, it is true that one valid reason for doing on-call is the wisdom of production, and electing to do so is perfectly fine. However, if the objection is to the idea of an industry population of SREs that is increasingly feeble at on-call, the idea of this article is to move away from on-call as emergency medicine, and toward on-call as ward medicine, where observation over time and support from colleagues is available. I do not think we will remove every failure from every piece of software ever, just that it is certainly more possible to remove enough of them that we don't need to suffer the costs of being on-call that we do today.

Some commentary states that[19] machine learning might be an effective substitute for human on-call. Permit me, for a moment, a more skeptical view. Although I would gladly welcome a piece of software able to cope with anything, in my opinion an arbitrarily complicated unknown-unknowns failure situation would require the machine learning software to fully understand the stacks it is working with, which is not possible today and might never be possible.

Finally, it could be pointed out that building blocks exist today and are being used by engineers everywhere for specific tasks (Kafka, Spark, Redis, etc.), and yet we still have this industry-wide problem. Of course, the adoption of one framework or toolset might help with one class of problem, but there is nothing today that matches the description of a hardened cloud stack with known good choices for each functional element. As many of the use cases must be covered as possible, or too much is left to chance.

The Cost to Humans of Doing On-Call

A more pointed counterargument to SREs performing on-call is perhaps to be found in human factors analysis, cognitive psychology, and the general effect of stress on the human being.

In general, humans perform quite poorly[20] in stressful situations, which is overwhelmingly what on-call is. Not only that, it is extremely costly to the individuals involved. I will cover this in more detail shortly.

But the larger picture is that, yes, this matters because of the human toll, but also because it undermines the argument that there is no effective substitute to human on-call. This in turn is because the industry, outside of operations engineers themselves, has very much an incomplete understanding of the costs of doing on-call. Furthermore, because of the rationale underpinning the "necessity" for human on-call—to wit, unknown-unknowns—business owners believe that whatever the cost is, they are committed to paying it because they see no alternative. Precisely because people assume that there is no alternative to human on-call, it is rare to see these costs fully outlined, except at operations conferences and in one-to-one conversations. Which at the very least is a pity, because if we do not know precisely what we are paying, we cannot know if it is worth it.

---

19 See, for example, this devopsdays talk (*https://www.devopsdays.org/events/2017-oslo/program/hannah-foxwell/*) by Hannah Foxwell.

20 Poorly in comparison to what, is a valid question: here, I mean compared with a notional resolution that involves no mistakes or blind alleys, but does involve the usual delays in detection, starting analysis, and so on.

Let us leave the vexed definition of "stressful" to one side for a moment, and, for the purposes of this paragraph presume the typical properties of SRE on-call fulfill that definition—to wit, out-of-hours requirements to work; potentially large or unbounded financial/reputational impact to the organization as a whole, depending on your individual performance; sleep disrupted, truncated, or in extreme circumstances, impossible for the duration of the incident; and, if in an out-of-hours context, potential difficulty obtaining help from one's colleagues.

Humans are not in fact natural smooth performers in stressful situations. Studies of human error, specifically of stress in the context of on-call, are rare; there are many precedents in similar domains, however, including programming itself, chess, and industrial situations, such as nuclear power plant meltdown situations. Ultimately, of course, most of these are in some way inaccurate proxies for real-world performance, but remain, for the moment, the best that we have. The more generic studies on human error seem to arrive at a background rate of between 0.5% and 10% for various "trivial" activities, including typing, reading a graph, and writing in exams.[21] Similarly, *A Guide to Practical Human Reliability Assessment* (Kirwan) shows a table that lists "Stressful complicated non-routine task" as having an error rate of about 30%. Dr. David J. Smith's *Reliability, Maintainability, and Risk* states a similar rate, 25%, for complicated tasks, and somewhat depressingly, a 50% error rate for "trivial" things such as noticing that valves are in the wrong position.[22] In a paper on the subject,[23]Microsoft shows that middle-rank chess players double their chance of a serious blunder as they move from 10 seconds to 0 seconds left on their clock, and background error rates for programming—in the absence of any particular stressor— range between <1 and >13% in this comparison table (*http:// panko.shidler.hawaii.edu/HumanErr/ProgNorm.htm*).

Any way you look at it, it is clear that to err is very definitely human.

Another potentially large effect on on-call performance is cognitive bias, which (if you accept the overall psychological framework), strongly implies that human beings make errors in stressful situations in very systemic ways. A write-up goes into this in more detail here (*http://hopes-and-strategies.blogspot.de/2018/02/cognitive-bias-in-on-call-evidence-on.html*), but suffice to say that if you read *Thinking, Fast and Slow*

---

21 See, for example, Ray Panko's site for a comparison table (*http://panko.shidler.hawaii.edu/HumanErr/ Basic.htm*).

22 More shocking and yet also completely believable is a line item stating that failing to act correctly within 1 minute of an emergency situation developing has a probability of *90%*; see this article (*https://www.lifetime-reliability.com/cms/tutorials/reliability-engineering/human_error_rate_table_insights/*) for more.

23 Ashton Anderson, Jon Kleinberg, Sendhil Mullainathan, "Assessing Human Error Against a Benchmark of Perfection" (*https://www.microsoft.com/en-us/research/wp-content/uploads/2016/06/assessing-human-error.pdf*).

and wonder if there's any evidence SREs are affected by cognitive kinks of some kinds, there is indeed quite a lot of evidence to support it; for example, anchoring effects (*https://en.wikipedia.org/wiki/Anchoring*) in the context of time-limited graph interpretation, closely matching the awkward constraints of on-call.

But most of what we've been discussing merely (perhaps loosely) supports what you more or less knew already about the human condition, being human yourself. There is also a subtler effect, which is that the *fear* of on-call is often enough by itself to radically change people's behavior. Entire development teams reject outright the notion of going on call, because of the impact on their personal lives, family, and in-hours effectiveness. Many such teams are perfectly happy for operations teams without the authority to actually fix problems to keep things ticking over "during the night shift" as best they can—as long as those developer teams don't have to do on-call themselves.

Additionally, diversity and inclusion in SRE therefore suffers as caregivers—of whatever kind, parental or otherwise—deliberately opt out of a situation that promises to place them in direct and certain conflict with their other responsibilities.

When we turn our attention to the actual *effects* of serious on-call work on human beings, it makes for similarly, if not more, sobering reading. There is evidence to suggest that even the *possibility* of being called increases the need for recovery in on-call workers[24]; sleep deprivation has a long list of negative effects and there is serious evidence suggesting that it shortens life expectancy[25]; and finally, this survey of papers (*https://www.ncbi.nlm.nih.gov/pmc/articles/PMC539298/*) examining the effects of on-call generally suggests excellent evidence that on-call work can and does have a variety of effects on physical health (e.g., gastrointestinal and reproductive) and mental health (e.g., anxiety and depression). There's simply no meaningful upside for the practitioners.

All of this is not even to mention the *experience* of on-call, which is often dispiriting. Not every team looks after their monitoring and alerting as assiduously as they should, so an on-call engineer can be assailed on their shift with noisy alerts, alerts that are mainly or wholly unactionable, monitoring that doesn't catch actual outages and actual users that do, poor or nonexistent documentation, blame-laden reactions when things inevitably go wrong, a complete lack of training for doing it, and, worst of all, a systemic lack of follow-up to any of the issues discovered, meaning that one braces oneself each shift for the structural unsolved problems that paged one the last

---

24 See this paper (*https://www.sciencedaily.com/releases/2015/08/150804074052.htm*) on on-call fatigue.

25 Mark O'Connell, "Why We Sleep by Matthew Walker review – how more sleep can save your life" (*https://www.theguardian.com/books/2017/sep/21/why-we-sleep-by-matthew-walker-review*).

shift. And in some companies, you do all of this without either extra financial compensation or time-off-in-lieu.

Clearly, as a species, we don't like doing on-call, we're not terribly good at it, it's actively harmful for us, and it can often be one of the most unpleasant experiences we have.

Given all that, I ask again: why aren't we talking about meaningful alternatives?

We don't need another hero

Perhaps part of the reason is us.

The mission SRE has—the protection of products in production—mixes well with that cohort of people motivated to "step up" and work hard at resolving production incidents. But throwing oneself relentlessly against a production incident, although in some ways admirable, and in another sense what we are paid for, has at least as many drawbacks as it does merits; in particular, the negative consequences of heroism.

The bad consequences of heroism are simultaneously subtle and coarse. Many people like the approval of their peers, and also like the satisfaction of knowing that their work has had a direct (even positive) effect on their team, the system they support, their company, and so on. So, there is a direct psychological link between stepping in to be The Hero fixing the problem and the approval one can get from fellow team members, the product development team, one's manager, and so on. Both explicit and implicit incentives to repeat hero-like behavior can evolve. Perhaps company management comes to expect it; you kept the system going last time in this way, why aren't you doing it this time? Worse than management in some ways, perhaps your *peers* come to expect it, particularly in positively oriented cultures like Google where peers can award each other small bonuses at the click of a button.

But worse than that in turn, when a heroine steps up and fills a particular role, often out of hours or in demanding circumstances, this means they're not doing work they'd otherwise been scheduled to do. Therefore, a replacement heroine is required to do the things that wouldn't otherwise get done, and another in turn, and so on. Granted, a team often must make do with what it can, but a long-running production incident has definite physiological effects and *someone* has to pick up the slack. If this can't be the directly affected team member, it's someone else from the team, and so on. Not to mention the bad effect of modeling hero culture[26] to the rest of the team and seeing it being rewarded.

---

26 See, for example, Emily Gorcenski's talk (*https://www.usenix.org/conference/srecon17europe/program/presentation/gorcenski*) at SRECon Europe 2017.

Finally, it is worth noting that there can be a dichotomy in how we see ourselves versus how our value is perceived by others. As we just discussed, the profession takes on-call very seriously and tries to be good at it; yet, it is very, very rare to be promoted as a function of on-call performance. In 11 years at Google, I never saw it. It was difficult to be promoted if you were *bad* at on-call, but it was impossible if you were *good* at on-call and bad at other things. Alice Goldfuss talks about this in her 2017 Monitorama talk (*http://vimeo.com/221050366*). The peculiarity of being rewarded in small ways for heroic behavior and yet being denied larger rewards as a consequence of that same behavior is unsettling.

Yet, despite all of this, it is still seen in many quarters as a sign of weakness when someone dislikes on-call. Perhaps this is connected to our unwillingness to even think about alternatives to on-call, other than leaving the profession for a role without it.

Actual Solutions

Summarizing everything up this point, the chain of argument is as follows.

If we accept the preceding facts—that on-call is used for many things, but primarily to cover the availability gap during software failures provoked by unknown-unknowns, and that humans are not in fact very good at it and it is bad for them to do it, it seems natural to ask if there's anything else we can do.

Broadly speaking, we can try to make the existing situation better, or we can try to do something fundamentally new.

For making the existing situation better, let us subdivide this into training, prioritization, accommodations, and improving on-the-job performance.

Training

Training is one of the worst problems, which is surprising given that it is also, in theory, one of the easiest to solve. Part of the reason for this is because of the vexed question about when in a career we might expect such training to take place. For example, there is, as far as I'm aware, no academic-level treatments of on-call in the course of any computer science degree anywhere.[27] Do please correct me if I'm wrong. So, people new to the sector often come to the on-call portion of a job completely unequipped to either support, critique, or modify the on-call situation they find when they get there. It is easy and very understandable to chafe at that responsibility and decide that the right thing to do is to (effectively) have others suffer. This does of course set up a lot of the bad relationships and contributes to incentive struc-

---

27 In contrast with medicine, as discussed earlier.

turn that end up making it worse for everyone. The good news is that multiple venues where best practices are discussed, so even if there is a dearth of publicly reshareable material—perhaps *Site Reliability Engineering*'s chapters on on-call (*https://landing.google.com/sre/book/chapters/being-on-call.html*) and troubleshooting (*https://landing.google.com/sre/book/chapters/effective-troubleshooting.html*) are a reasonable place to start, although PagerDuty's training materials (*https://response.pagerduty.com/oncall/being_oncall/*) perhaps assume less about what the reader knows—it's still possible to improve. In any event, there are useful, widely available supports on how to do so.

Prioritization

But the larger part of improving is actually *wanting* to improve. That is firmly in the domain of culture, as Cindy Sridharan controversially but not unfairly pointed out.[28] In this context, a better culture would involve teaching product developers that actually, the way to have a better system while on call is not to sternly resist any attempts to be put on call, but instead to *prioritize* the fixes and engineering effort required to make it better when one *does* go on call. A piece of software that is improved in its operational characteristics is a universally better piece of software

 For some nonexhaustive arguments why, see the SRE book's chapter on automation (*https://landing.google.com/sre/book/chapters/automation-at-google.html*).

However, if a dichotomy emerges where product developers are the group most capable of improving a system's behavior, and yet are the most insulated from when the behavior is bad, nothing good will result from this broken feedback loop. The business might happen to be successful, but it will always be paying a cost for decoupling that loop—whether it is in resource costs, staffing attrition costs, or agility costs—and fixing that eternal cost is, in a way, part of what SRE promises. A similar argument applies to postmortem follow-up actions.

Accommodations

Making accommodations for folks who are on call is also a key remediation. If more accommodations were made, on-call would inspire less fear, and more people would be able to do it. If more people were able to do it, the work would be spread across more people, which means more progress could be made. If more progress could be

---

28 Cindy Sridharan, "On-call doesn't have to suck" (*https://medium.com/@copyconstruct/on-call-b0bd8c5ea4e0*), Medium.com.

made, some time could be spent on operational clean-up work, and on-call would inspire less fear. A virtuous circle.

Accommodations include but are not limited to: compensation for on-call work, particularly out of hours; reasonably flexible schedules so caregivers and others can move on-call work around (depending on how onerous the shift is, it can make even running the simplest of errands very hard); support for recovery and follow-up afterward; and mechanisms for those who are literally unable to do it to be excluded without backlash.

Compensation

Many people still work in roles for which there is no on-call compensation, or certainly no *formal* scheme. It is certainly immediately cheaper to run a company without one, but it is very much short-sighted. It is neither a good use of people's lives nor morally correct. It's also not even good for the business, despite short-term savings. *Instead, we should have a well-articulated industry-wide model*, or series of models so that each organization can pick the one that's best for it, *and* the engineers working for it can pick and choose accordingly. A huge advantage of acknowledging the domain of human obligation in on-call (by providing supports for it) would be increasing the pool of people who elect to do it, with consequent benefit for team diversity, team members' lives, and so on.

Flexible schedules

To enable flexible schedules, you should address the sources of inflexibility. Management might need to be convinced that performance will improve and hiring will be easier with more flexible schedules. Hours of coverage can vary, depending on when the statistical likelihood of outages happens. A formal Service-Level Agreement (SLA) helps immensely with not only Service-Level Objectives (SLO)–based alerting, which often lowers raw paging numbers, but even the act of negotiating one from where there was none before can help business owners to figure out that they don't actually need to try (fruitlessly) for 100% availability. This in turn enables more flexible schedules.

Recovery

Most on-call compensation schemes that I've seen focus on enabling compensation or time-off-in-lieu, but this does not necessarily happen immediately after a tiring shift. Companies could move to offering a morning off from the night before, after the activity during the shift had passed a certain threshold, outside of the terms of any time-off-in-lieu arrangement that might operate.

Making sure people feel safe on your team—no matter what their attitude to on-call is or capability to do it—is mostly part of successful line management rather than company policy. But companies could signal in advance that they adopt a "opt-out of on-call without retaliation" policy, which would again help to attract more diversity in their workforce.

Improving On-the-Job Performance

On-the-job performance is in many ways the least important component of attacking the problem of on-call. For a start, it doesn't actually advance the agenda of getting rid of it. Additionally, bad but passable on-call performance is unlikely to get you fired. If it did, an organization might well end up removing more people from an on-call rotation than are needed, resulting in an ever-increasing spiral until the subset of people left behind burn out and quit.

Instead, typically speaking, what happens is that only the people who make egregious mistakes are let go, and what most management cares about is a good faith effort to solve a problem, not consistently low Mean Time to Recovery (MTTR) metrics in a Taylorist-style[29] scheme. Therefore, after the on-call person shows up and makes a good effort, there's usually little enough incentive within the system itself to get better at it beyond not wanting to write yet another postmortem this week.

Having said that, there are many techniques one can use to improve.

Cognitive hacks

For a start, there are many cognitive "hacks" that can improve performance in on-call situations; for example, frowning can help us to feel less powerful, which in turn makes us less likely to "anchor" on specific scenarios to the exclusion of all else; reading John Allspaw's materials on blameless postmortems (*https://codeascraft.com/2012/05/22/blameless-postmortems/*) can also help to shake out assumptions about what is actually at fault when things go wrong in distributed systems, and helps to increase self-reflection, which is a crucial component of avoiding pure reactivity. As discussed earlier, reacting is a serious impediment to finding out complex truths, and there are no other types of truth in distributed systems.

Another potential hack is doing *pair on-call*; it has the very useful effect that when you need to explain yourself to someone else, having to articulate your idea often helps you figure out if you're wrong, just by saying it. This is different from active/inactive primary/secondary shifts because it implies that the people are working

---

29 Frederick Taylor was a scientific management theorist who introduced the all-too-successful idea of dehumanizing people in work situations by closely managing metrics.

closely together interactively during the shift. (This is most tractable during business hours and is hard to organize with small teams.) Aggressive hypothesizing, which is the technique of tossing out idea after idea about what's going wrong, all as different as possible, can also be useful. This is particularly so when a number of things go wrong at the same time, due to the fact that increased stress narrows the mind. It also helps to correct for cognitive bias problems like anchoring. Finally, good discipline, such as always maintaining hand-off documents and following a well-drilled incident management procedure (*https://landing.google.com/sre/book/chapters/managing-incidents.html*), is necessary to coping effectively with rapidly moving incidents; the "guide rails" provided by extensive drilling on a procedure helps you to react correctly in uncertain situations.

We Need a Fundamental Change in Approach

As useful as all of these practical recommendations are, there is something fundamentally unsatisfying with always chasing something you'll never catch up with. A more interesting question, then, is what different things can we do to *fundamentally* change this situation?

Of course, this depends on how you characterize the problem. Recall the central conflict at the heart of software systems: we know that they are deterministic,[30] yet they continually surprise us, in the worst of ways, in how their complexity and their behaviors interact to produce outages.

But how does that unreliability arise? A survey of Google outages in *The Site Reliability Workbook* suggests that binary and configuration pushes together constitute almost 70% of factors leading to an outage, with software itself and a failure in the development process turning up in almost 62% of root causes, and "complex system behaviors" being in only around 17% of postmortems. Remember these numbers, or at least the fact that analyzed outages have a structure to their causes.

At this point, let me introduce two positions that I refer to in the rest of this chapter; Strong-Anti-On-Call (SAOC) and Weak-Anti-On-Call (WAOC).

Strong-Anti-On-Call

Strong-Anti-On-Call (SAOC) runs as follows.

Software systems are deterministic. We have two possible approaches to attacking the problem of outages. We can either remove the sources of the outages, or we can prevent outages from having a catastrophic effect. Because software systems are deter-

---

30 So they keep saying, anyway.

minimal. If we remove all control of outage, the system will not fail. (SAOC does not believe that doing *both* of these things is useful.)

Let us take a moment to recapitulate what the sources of unreliability are when constructing a software system. We can make a simple programming error, a typo, or equivalent. We can make a design error, constructing something that is guaranteed to go wrong. We can insulate ourselves from the environment incorrectly (libraries, dependencies, or simply parsing data incorrectly). We can treat remote dependencies incorrectly—for example, behaving as if they will always be reachable or will always return correct data.

As discussed earlier, the maddening thing about outages is that so many of them are entirely avoidable. The SAOC position involves preventing each of the identified sources of error in the list of categories in "Underlying Assumptions Driving On-Call for Engineers" on page 514 from manifesting in your system. Although there is too much to address in detail here, the good news is that many of the difficulties of change management are already well understood, and what we are trying to do is more successfully implement something that is already relatively well understood.

The bad news is that, if we keep getting it wrong, there might be a reason for that.

However, to SAOC, this does not matter. We'll get it right eventually. But we do have one hurdle to overcome first, which is the causes of outages that result from larger interactions, not necessarily system failures within the system itself or from simple "one-step" interactions, such as ingesting bad data.

So, we need to take the complexity out of our systems. Practically speaking, there are really only two known ways of doing that: building simple subcomponents with verified, known behavior, composed in deterministic ways; and running systems for a very long time to see where we were mistaken about their stability and then fixing those problems. Today, as an industry, we make it too easy to write unreliable software, by not consistently taking advantage of those two techniques and facilitating the fact that it's still software engineers finding it easier to write code than read it that creates unreliable code.

Instead, I argue we need to change the basic *layer* at which we build software. Today that is POSIX libc, win32, or the logical equivalent; in the future, particularly the distributed future, it must be at a higher level, and with more cross-cloud (or at least, cross-platform) features. To write a server, a product developer should pluck a well-known class off the shelf, with good monitoring, logging, crisis load handling, graceful degradation, and failure characteristics *for free* and *enabled by default*. It should be actively *difficult* to write something bad. Innovation long ago moved out of the platform layer, yet we pay so much for the right to rewrite from the ground up, and gain so little in return, it is difficult to understand why we tolerate it.

Simultaneously, we need better ways to insulate bad application layer logic from the rest of the platform; today, across the industry, such insulation is essentially infinitely gradated across the spectrum—from none at all, which is unfortunately common, to completely isolated, which is unfortunately uncommon. Again, this speaks to a pre-existing toolkit that is easier to use than not.

Thus, SAOC finds itself arguing for a methodical approach to eliminating sources of error and a toolkit approach, not because of resilience, but because of eliminating complexities of interaction. There are a number of weaknesses to this position, but one glaringly obvious one is that the methodical elimination is only ever going to happen after a software system is deployed; ideally, we would be reusing only pieces of software to which this elimination had already been applied. That argues for a toolkit approach again, except one in which the software components have already been "ground down" to deterministic subcomponents.

Weak-Anti-On-Call

If you have come this far but do not agree that the strong case is either practical or worth striving for, allow me to convince you of a slightly weaker but still useful position.

In this view of the world, you might indeed believe that software is deterministic, but you are convinced that we will never be able to react successfully and programmatically to unknown-unknowns and that interaction between arbitrarily complicated systems will always produce failure of some kind. We can still make progress on eliminating on-call, except we need to look at it in a different way.

Unlike with SAOC, we are not trying to eliminate emergency medicine by replacing it with ward medicine. Instead, we are trying to implement *driverless trains*: systems for which we know we cannot control the environment completely, but we more or less have one useful reaction (stop the individual train, if not the entire system), and the question is to what extent we can stop the train and not imperil the system as a whole until the human driver arrives.

This approach therefore relies not on attempting to prevent human intervention from occurring, but on delaying it until some notion of "business hours" arrives, or otherwise removing it from the domain of emergency medicine.

In this view of the world, the most important thing to do is not to prevent outages, but to insulate the system against failure better. The strange thing is that this position actually looks quite similar to the previous one: we need the same thing, reusable standardized toolkit software, except instead of optimizing for complexity reduction, we optimize for the equivalent of driverless train failure: we automatically stop in the safest way possible, depending on what we can learn about the circumstances. It is interesting to consider how much thought a typical engineer puts into having a software system fail safely as opposed to making forward progress successfully. Failure cases are often disregarded in the hazy optimism of a favored editor, and there is every reason to suppose that we would be more successful at engineering resilience if this was more of a focus or, more important, if more guide rails were provided to do so.

The details of safe failure would vary so much from domain to domain it is not efficient to talk about them here, but the key principle is again that the work performed should be amenable to partitioning such that components of the system that encounter fatal errors can be safely removed, with no significant impact on system capacity, or at least a limited one; enough to give the human operator a little leeway to deal with it in the office. Then it is a matter of scaling the system such that the failure domains meet this goal, and then you can avoid on-call, safe in the knowledge that you might be drastically over-dimensioned in hardware, but at least you won't be paying attrition-related staff costs.

A Union of the Two

Yes, there is nothing to stop us combining the viewpoints of both approaches. In fact, even though the theoretical positions are quite different, you have already seen that both of them call for same remedies: in particular, standardized toolkits for the construction of software, albeit for different reasons.

It seems clear to me as, a result, that the industry needs put effort into making very reliable subcomponents, out of which most services could be composed; they might even be proved formally correct,[31] harking back to the cloud stack conversation outlined earlier. Yet I agree that it feels a little unrealistic to suggest this in a world where a startup can become wildly successful with some hacked-together Ruby that just happens to be a good product-market fit for a particular use case: today, what drives usage is the product-market fit, not the operability.

Furthermore, as long as a huge multinational corporation finds it cheaper to hire operations engineers to take pagers and reboot systems than to fix real problems with their software operability, there cannot be any real change. For real change, we must fix the problem at its point of origin: we must change how easy it is to write unreliable software. We must make it, if not impossible, then *actively hard* to write poorly operable software. Anything else will not lead to a fundamental change.

The benefits of *standardization on a cloud stack* also play to the assumption of the SAOC position: it is way easier to methodically eliminate sources of error if you're not rediscovering them separately inside your company each time. A single attack

---

31 This is not as ridiculous as you might think; for example, AWS uses formal methods (*http://lamport.azureweb sites.net/tla/formal-methods-amazon.pdf*).

surface, inspected by many eyeballs, will surely converge more quickly than multiple attack surfaces inspected by fewer.

Conclusion

To get rid of the scourge of on-call will require an industry-wide effort, given that what we are proposing is collaboration on toolkits explicitly designed to be rewritten as little as possible, yet used by as many people as possible.

But if we *did* do this, the benefits would be incalculable: an industry-wide set of architectures so stable they could be taught in schools; a consistent approach to layering business logic; a more welcoming environment for caregivers and minorities; a set of methodically applied best practices and consistent data processing across companies, never mind within teams in the same company, never mind within individuals in the same team!

It might sound impossible, but in essence is a task of convergence. As an industry and indeed in society, we have in the past converged on odder things: VHS, the x86 instruction set, and English come to mind, but there are surely more. Now the task is to push for it, because it would be of benefit to all, even if it is only us right now who see what the future could be.

Niall Richard Murphy has been working in internet infrastructure for over 20 years, and is currently Director of Software Engineering for Azure Production Infrastructure Engineering in Microsoft's Dublin office. He is a company founder, an author, a photographer, and holds degrees in computer science and mathematics and poetry studies. He is the instigator, coauthor, and editor of Site Reliability Engineering and The Site Reliability Workbook.

## CHAPTER 31

Elegy for Complex Systems

Mikey Dickerson, Layer Aleph (formerly
United States Digital Service)

March 19, 2018: Farmhouse Motel, Paso Robles, California. Diverted here and lost
a day on the way south, because of a rainstorm that was too much for a motorcycle.
18 hours left to make it 220 miles to the next appointment. This isn't going to plan.
Nothing ever goes to plan.

Six years ago, I was a middle manager in SRE at Google. I was about three years into
an enormous, and mostly unnecessary, project to reinvent MySQL on Google storage,
and my last two promotion applications had not been read by anyone. I was, in the
phrasing that our HR person liked to use, "loose in the saddle." The high-energy col-
lision that sent me completely out of orbit was that I was asked by President Obama
to attempt a last-ditch rescue of healthcare.gov, the so-called "federally facilitated
marketplace" that was threatening to sink the Affordable Care Act, and with it, the
concept of universal healthcare for another generation.

The healthcare.gov rescue grew into a round-the-clock effort by a couple dozen SREs,
mostly from the Bay Area. Most of them today agree they would not trade the experience for anything, and also that they would never wish a similar experience on anyone else. The rescue in turn grew into a new government entity, the US Digital
Service. And we were set loose on the most stubborn IT issues in the US government,
most of which started out as an attempt to replace one large and complex system with
another.

There's a linguistic clue to the first major challenge: Who talks about "IT" anymore?
Well, an enormous, sprawling, "enterprise"-industrial complex does. The federal government alone spends more than $80 billion a year on what it calls "IT." The Nation
of IT was founded approximately in the post-WWII era, the idea being to replace the
paper and analog processes of every big bureaucracy with computerized versions.

Forms became screens, filing cabinets became databases, memos became emails. Tremendous improvements in efficiency were realized and then gradually forgotten as the infrastructure became geriatric and developed its own, all-new problems.

The Nation of IT's jargon, job titles ("CIO," "enterprise architect"), and technology (mainframes and PCs) calcified and did not adapt to the discovery of the internet, an event which has made a lot of people angry and is widely regarded as a bad move. Those of us at Google or Facebook in the 2010s belonged to what might as well be another nation. The Nation of Tech has new buzzwords and new technology fads. Culturally, it claims not to care about job titles, hierarchy, or fashion; none of these claims stands up to scrutiny, but they are important to an understanding of how Tech sees itself.

The Nation of Tech refers to anything from the Nation of IT as "legacy." IT refers to anything from Tech as a "fad." Lost somewhere in the middle is the fact that the core problem—the problem that hobbles the best efforts of both nations—is unchanged: we are much better at building complexity than at managing it.

Somewhere between Google, the IRS, Medicare, the Department of Defense, the FBI, electronic medical records, and a dozen others, I have become convinced that all sufficiently complex systems have a number of behaviors in common.

The Computer and Human Systems Cannot Be Separated

It was 1967 when Mel Conway asserted that "all organizations which design systems are constrained to produce designs which are copies of the communication structures of the organizations." It seems as if every organization since 1967 has considered "Conway's Law" an affront and has attempted to disprove it.

They rarely succeed. And by "rarely," I mean "never, only I don't feel like arguing about it." There are good reasons why software components end up arranged like human components. In either case, the large system cannot function unless the interfaces between components are carefully defined and change slowly. Whatever they may be called, they are contracts that let each side rely on an abstraction that tells them what to expect from the other side.

When a system falls into chronic dysfunction, the technical problems and people problems are inevitably congruent. Show me two software components that fail to interoperate, and I will show you two teams that do not interact. A week ago, I interviewed people at a large team whose project has a basic requirement of being able to execute transactions on a DB2 database on a mainframe. In two years, no one has been able to do this. With some difficulty, we located one of the contractors that maintains the database. He arrived about 10 minutes late and explained that it took him a while to find the conference room because he'd never been to this end of the building before.

If you are called on to diagnose a system that does not have a tidy issue with a "root cause," but rather seems to be misfiring all over and not quite right anywhere, a great place to start is by drawing two diagrams, an org chart and a system flow diagram, to see how badly they have diverged. Remember that they are both mutable, and a solution can arise from changes in either one.

Decoherence and Cascading Failure

Any system of any size can get a simple question wrong, such as rendering an incorrect decision on an insurance claim, or the wrong billing address for a customer. But only a large, distributed system can disagree with itself. This special failure mode in which the system is not able to render any answer at all is sometimes called *decoherence*.

As always, there are abundant examples in humans and software. Anyone who works on distributed storage is accustomed to the problem where multiple replicas, chunk servers, or tablet servers have become desynchronized. In such a situation, the answer to a query depends on which server you ask, which violates the abstraction the designers have tried to create. Typically, the solution is some sort of voting scheme in which one version of the data wins, and the minority opinion is quietly deep-sixed, never to be spoken of again. Theory papers usually assume that the majority opinion will be "correct."

Human examples are even easier to find. At the time of this writing, the US legal system is unable to answer the question "is marijuana legal." The answer is both yes and no at the same time, and it depends on which court you ask. Thousands of veterans are both alive and dead according to the VA and its computers. Errors in the voter registration records are everywhere, and also almost nonexistent.

Decoherence has a well-known relative called *cascading failure*. When a system is tightly coupled, a failure in one component tends to cause failures in others that are connected. These days, half the fun of the job derives from the fact that "connected" can have many surprising definitions. You probably know how your software components exchange data according to the architecture diagram. Do you know which ones run on the same machines? Or share a network switch? Or a power distribution unit? Or BIOS version? If you are responsible for a large system for long enough, you will.

When debugging incorrect outcomes rendered by a complex system, always remember that it is not enough to look for a "root cause," popping out of hiding now and then to flip bits—probably while cackling and twirling its mustache. You might be looking at nonintuitive results of the error-correction algorithms that protect the system against disagreements with itself. These algorithms are only sometimes designed on purpose.

Always in a State of Partial Failure

Working backward through the wreckage of cascading failures in systems that you maintain, you will realize that various parts of the system had already failed before the catastrophe. Large systems exist in a state of partial failure at all times. This is an inescapable fact of the interaction between Mean Time Between Failures (MTBF) and Mean Time to Repair (MTTR).

Operations groups often take on big projects to increase MTBF and decrease MTTR, usually at the level of hardware components, because this is the only level at which assumptions of rationality hold well enough for "mean time to anything" to be well defined.

It's certainly worthwhile for a team to optimize within one "accountability domain" like this. Even so, when you're looking at the entire system, an increase in fault tolerance beyond "barely acceptable" tends to be immediately eaten up by another layer.

Suppose that you have a distributed storage system that was deployed to tolerate three simultaneous disk failures in an array. Then the hardware team, full of gumption and wishing to be promoted, takes clever measures to "guarantee" that the array will never have more than one disk down. Check back in a year, and you will find that the application has been reoptimized and can now tolerate only one failure. Why not? A statistical retrospective showed that this would "always" be good enough.

The right hand giveth nines, and the left hand taketh them away.

A large number of teams (and system components, which are the same thing) interacting will exhibit many examples of this give-and-take, and since human accountability is diffused, the laws of evolution take over. Just as in biology, evolution does not produce the optimum solution; it produces a solution just good enough to get by. The natural state of such a system is "one failure away from catastrophe."

A great illustration of the cycle of how safety margins are created and consumed and how failures accumulate unnoticed in the progression toward "one failure away from catastrophe" is found in the after-accident investigations of both the *Columbia* and *Challenger* space shuttle disasters. These were tightly managed works of complex engineering, in which every component was over-built to ensure incredible reliability. And the final safety record of the shuttle system was two catastrophic failures in 135 flights.

If you should be so lucky as to review the design of a new application before it is launched, watch out for plans that assume infrastructure components will perform to published Service-Level Agreements (SLAs). To do so is to consume all of the safety margin of the underlying layers. At the very least, try to design for the performance measured and documented in the historical record.

Novelty Priority Inversion

I have mentioned engineer promotions twice now, and not (merely) to be facetious. Because the human system and the computer system are isomorphic, the human incentive structure is the invisible hand that drives the change in the computer system over time. The desire of the hardware maintainers to optimize for MTTR is predictable because it will get them promoted. The desire of the storage operators to optimize the new safety margin away, and cut costs, is predictable because it will get them promoted.

As someone who was once responsible for staffing dozens of engineering projects that meant life or death to thousands of people, I have recruited on "mission" as much as anyone. Mission will carry you a good distance, and when you have little money to work with, a good one sure helps. Someday burnout will catch up with even the most pure-hearted, and quality-of-life concerns become dispositive.

The values of the Nation of Tech being what they are, it is rare for a successful engineer to be rewarded with less work to do. That leaves us with "quality of life" defined as money. This is not a culture that is leading to great outcomes, but it is what the Nation of Tech has.

Money, in turn, is governed by bureaucratic, heavyweight, bonus and promotion processes. So, these processes determine the long-term behavior of your company and every system you manage. What do they reward? Ignore what the company says it rewards; instead, look at the list of who was promoted. Behaviors associated with these people will be emulated. Behaviors associated with those left behind will not. This evolutionary pressure will overwhelm any stated intentions of the company leaders.

This is the oracle to consult any time you wonder whether to start a new project, or help an adjacent team, or pay the cost of adopting the latest new thing. You can still choose to row against the tide. For a while. But it will always help to know which way all the other boats are going to drift.

Nobody Anticipates the Overhead of Coordination

Heavyweight promotion processes bring to mind the last point, which is that nobody, ever, anticipates how expensive it is to communicate across a large system.

Legend has it that the Pentagon was designed so that it is possible for a messenger to travel from any location in the building to any other location in about 8 minutes. No one is quite sure if this is true. But it was built under the existential crisis of World War II and meant for coordinating decisions as fast as possible across a large organization. The first thing that might strike you about the building is the corridors are as much as 40 feet wide along main routes. This gives a clue to how many people and objects the architects expected to be in transit at a given moment.

The Pentagon reminded me of Google designs for internal cluster networking, which were meant to offer wire-speed transfers between any two points in the cluster (a similar constraint). These ended up being phenomenally expensive to implement. It is likely that there were more watts and more CPUs routing packets than doing any other work in the cluster.

Tech companies introduce new tools or programming languages all the time. An engineer might need to spend a couple dozen hours in a quarter, or fewer, to learn shiny new things, yet plans will be made for training, classes, workshops, announcements, and support staff.

The same engineers will spend a couple dozen hours a week on meetings, video conferences, and phone calls. I have never seen a curriculum designed to teach the effective use of any of these tools, much less a training or workshop to help cope with the introduction of a new remote office, possibly in a different company, with a different culture.

If you are responsible for the smooth operation of any large human or computer system, pay attention to these costs. They become the largest sink of your watts, or calories, much sooner than you think.

Your healthcare.gov Is Out There

These few ideas will not be everything you need to know to maintain and repair large complex systems. They are ones that I think tend to be overlooked and under-appreciated. And they are by no means specific to the narrow concept of "large complex system" that SREs usually look at.

A few of us, former SREs from the Nation of Technology, found that to be true and left those settled posts in the hierarchy a few years ago. Now we spend our time at the uneasy frontier between IT and Technology, studying and occasionally solving problems for large and important human–machine systems.

This is how I came to leave Mountain View for a godforsaken beige office park in Virginia, then Maryland, then the White House Situation Room, and last week, Sacramento to look at the California child welfare system. Which is how I come to be in this motel, on the road between the Bay Area and Los Angeles. Where it is time to go to sleep, because I have to get up early enough to make it 220 miles tomorrow. Tomorrow there will be another important system that is a deeply entangled human–machine hybrid, one step away from catastrophe.

Maybe I'll see you there.

To Get Involved

If these sorts of problems interest you, and you are looking to work on harder problems in much less comfort, consider getting in touch with any of the following: Layer Aleph LLC, Ad Hoc LLC, Nava PBC, or Truss (*http://truss.works*). Each group is a little different, but they all contain fine people that often run into one another at the scene of a big-old tire fire.

Further Reading

Let me be the first to say that I might not have written a single original idea in this chapter. If you would like to read more, and in the original English, please consider the following:

- *Inside Bureaucracy* by Anthony Downs, published by the RAND Corporation in 1967. It's out of print, but you can usually find it on Amazon (where I have personally driven up the price by 300%; sorry). Do not confuse this with the 36-page paper published with the same title in 1964. The paper is also good, and you can download it from RAND for free, but it is a tiny fraction of the book. If you read only one book, read this one.

- *The Tyranny of Structurelessness* by Jo Freeman (aka Joreen), 1970. Printed, reprinted, edited, and copied in dozens of places in subsequent years, but currently canonically available at *jofreeman.com*. If you read only one article, read this one.

- *The Mythical Man-Month* by Fred Brooks, 1975. Of course. Covers Conway's Law and a lot more.

- The *Rogers Commission report* on the *Challenger* disaster, published in 1986. But mostly Appendix F, being the "personal observations" of Richard Feynman, who could not reach any agreement with the rest of the committee and threatened to remove his endorsement from the report if his chapter was not included. (In homage, and out of the same necessities, there are a handful of Obama-era internal policy papers that include an appendix singly authored by one Mikey Dickerson. I don't think anyone ever realized what I was doing.)

- *How Complex Systems Fail* published by Richard Cook at the University of Chicago in 1998, available online. Also presented at O'Reilly Velocity 2012, which is on YouTube.

- *Engineering a Safer World* by Nancy Leveson, MIT Press, 2012. Professor Leveson has published dozens of papers on "systems safety," across three decades, which you can find on her web page. She has taught workshops and consulted for dozens of companies and government agencies.

- And anything you can find on the history of nuclear accidents will be fascinating—two good surveys are *Command and Control* by Eric Schlosser, 2014, and *Atomic Accidents* by James Muhaffey, 2015.

Mikey Dickerson graduated with a math degree from Pomona College. After various odd jobs, he was hired by the obviously desperate Google Site Reliability Engineering department in 2006. He was eventually promoted into middle management. Having thus achieved every child's dream, he was ready to move on to help the Obama administration repair healthcare.gov in 2013, then accepted a White House appointment to run the US Digital Service from August 2014 until the end of the administration.

## CHAPTER 32

Intersections Between Operations and Social Activism

Emily Gorcenski and Liz Fong-Jones

Measurement, risk mitigation, crisis response, and managing long-term follow-up are well-accepted parts of SRE and broadly of the discipline of software operations. We do design reviews to head issues off early, measure key service indicators, use incident management structures to manage complexity during outages, write post-mortems, and guide our future work, based on what we learn. Our focus on measurement and data enables us to better advocate for users.

The collaborative, multidisciplinary approach of SRE involves coordinating many different stakeholders, and requires individuals to work together to avoid becoming overwhelmed by complexity or burned out. Managing human factors is often the most important skill that SREs learn.

But our job as engineers does not stop purely with adherence to Service-Level Objectives (SLOs). A service that does a reliable job of harming people, exacerbating injustices, or excluding marginalized groups is not a service worth building and maintaining. Technology is poised to change the world, for good or for ill, and engineers of all kinds share a responsibility to ensure that their work is "for the public good" and "does not diminish quality of life, diminish privacy, or harm the environment."[1]

Therefore, we must turn our attention to *how* we ensure that our work is just and serves the public interest. Fortunately, successful activism for social change requires the same skills of measurement, risk mitigation, crisis response, and managing

---

1 ACM Code of Ethics (*http://ethics.acm.org/code-of-ethics/software-engineering-code/*)

follow-up as SREs have honed through our professional practice. We can apply these skills to advocating for justice in the products we build, the broader industries we work in, and the communities we live in.

In this chapter, we provide an overview of how social activism movements such as those that Emily participated in as an antiracist organizer in Charlottesville, Virginia, collectively organize; describe their similarities to SRE; and then suggest ways to participate in social change that is meaningful to readers according to their own principles, both in the spheres of technology and the broader world. Emily approaches this case study from the perspective of an activist in tech and data ethics and who lives in a city where a deep legacy of anti-Black racism has left enduring scars. Liz's career as an SRE has included forays into product inclusion and working-conditions advocacy, for which SRE skills better prepared her. Through this case study, we also see how activists have learned similar lessons as SREs about scaling incident response, developing empathy, and managing burnout.

Before, During, After

But Mousie, thou art no thy-lane,
In proving foresight may be vain:
The best laid schemes o' Mice an' Men
Gang aft agley,
An' lea'e us nought but grief an' pain,
For promis'd joy!
—Robert Burns, "To a Mouse"

To an outsider, the roles and responsibilities of organizers and engineers might not appear to have much in common. When we see media coverage of protest movements, strikes, and other popular demonstrations, we witness the result of weeks or months of behind-the-scenes labor. Political organization often relies on the tireless efforts of experienced people with diverse skills. But, just as developers cannot build a product requiring no operations, even talented planners with broad skills cannot foresee every possible circumstance. Good organizers, like good engineers, will not optimize for the elimination of errors in the moment, but rather position themselves to build resilient structures that will respond most effectively when unforeseen breakdowns occur.

The workflows of political organization can be examined through the same lens as those of software engineering. These efforts are often broken down into pre-action, action, and post-action phases, much like software engineering cycles can contain sprint planning and launch preparation, development and deployment, and retrospective phases. Larger demonstrations, like major software releases, are often built up through series of smaller, more granular efforts leading up to the main event.

Creating the Perfect Plan

All efforts must begin somewhere, and planning is a critical aspect of designing, building, and launching anything, whether it be a piece of software or an advocacy campaign.

Political actions are the result of tireless dedicated hours spent planning, organizing, staging, and coordinating people, groups, institutions, and resources. The problems organizers of these events face will be familiar to any engineering manager: asymmetric distribution of talents, scarce resources (usually in terms of time, money, and labor), contingency planning, and so forth.

In the summer of 2017, local political activists in Charlottesville became acutely aware of these planning issues. In June of that year, the community learned of the two major events that would go on to shock the community: the Ku Klux Klan rally on July 8, and the "Unite the Right" rally on the weekend of August 12. Charlottesville is a small city with an even smaller activist community; the task of planning nonviolent counter-demonstrations for these events fell to a few dozen people. The local community knew that the August 12 Unite the Right rally would be bigger, more dangerous, and potentially more violent than the KKK rally. As a result, local activist organizations spent very little time preparing for July 8 until just a few days before.

Nevertheless, organizers were able to quickly marshal community resources and scale operations to oppose the KKK. By engaging with groups and organizations rather than individuals, planners could delegate critical work to people who were not necessarily central to the planning process. This work included preparing and transporting food, water, and other wellness needs (to prevent hypoglycemia and dehydration); planning legal support in the event of arrests; preparing medical and mental health support; creating and distributing educational materials; in-action communication/coordination training; offsite support (from those not in physical attendance at the rally); social media monitoring; press and conventional media engagement; and more.

Many of these efforts have parallels in the engineering world: we coordinate meals for our engineers on release day; we prepare legal teams to review copy and terms of service; we create documentation and prepare marketing materials; we have external and internal comms plans; we staff people to watch Twitter to track social trends and identify bugs; and we work with the media to ensure product launches receive appropriate coverage. Indeed, the modern project manager has a very similar role to the modern political organizer.

However, activists often speak fondly of nonhierarchical organizing models. This may seem odd to engineers accustomed to being held accountable by managers, shareholders, clients, and teammates. It is important to note that a lack of hierarchy does not necessarily imply a lack of accountability. In fact, by holding organizations rather than individuals accountable for specific, measurable tasks, activists are often able to get work done through the process of *coalition-building*. A central element to this concept is an implicit understanding that not every organization will share every outlook or value, but that in the context of the present struggle, the organizations occupy enough common ground to get work done.

A common model used by activists is a *spokescouncil*. In this model, organizations are held accountable to their commitments as groups, rather than individuals. The organizations involved are each represented by a *spokesperson*, who shares their concerns, needs, and capabilities, and receives those of other organizations, as well. When this model operates well, each organization is able to voice its concerns and offer its best gifts, even when some of those are in conflict with other groups. Structuring responsibility and action around groups, rather than individuals, helps avoid placing the blame on specific people in what is sure to be a high-stress, often dangerous or deadly, environment. Importantly, it empowers autonomy and allows people to work most closely with those in whom they trust the most.

Principles of Organizing

In 2008, activists organizing protests against the Republican National Convention in St. Paul, Minnesota, developed a set of operating guidelines to encourage disparate groups to work toward a common goal. Known now as the St. Paul Principles,[2] these guidelines seek to aid coalition building. Although one may not agree with the politics of their originators, the St. Paul Principles generally provide a set of guardrails for preparing for high-stress, high-conflict scenarios. The four principles are as follows:

- Our solidarity will be based on respect for a diversity of tactics and the plans of other groups.

- The actions and tactics used will be organized to maintain a separation of time or space.

- Any debates or criticisms will stay internal to the movement, avoiding any public or media denunciations of fellow activists and events.

- We oppose any state repression of dissent, including surveillance, infiltration, disruption, and violence. We agree not to assist law enforcement actions against activists and others.

Although the vast majority of the services we operate as SREs are not as life-or-death critical as situations encountered by protesters, they still have immense impact upon the world. Therefore, we similarly need to ensure that we have psychological safety

---

2 D'Arcy, Steven. (2014). *Languages of the Unheard: Why Militant Protest Is Good for Democracy*. London: Zed Books.

(see Chapter 27), have trust among our teams, and have planned out how we will bring chaotic situations under control.

Principles 1 and 2 (interfaces and incident command)

SREs can interpret the first two principles as an equivalent to our understanding that teams need to respect one another's scope of responsibilities and plans. In incident management, each individual is empowered with a specific scope, and random free-lancing outside of the parameters of engagement is discouraged. In organizing, this often means keeping your tactics and actions physically separated from others' so as to contain risks.

Model-View-Controller paradigms, virtual machines, containers, and microservices are all highly specific variations on this theme. SREs define clear interfaces between, and SLOs for, systems and ensure that each component has a specific role, to avoid a tangled web of interdependencies or dependence upon implementation details. The operational principle is of isolation of the consequence of failures.

Principles 3 and 4 (blameless retrospectives and psychological safety)

The parallels of Principles 3 and 4 to SRE lie in how we approach postmortems and blameless interactions with each other during and after an incident. We must agree to avoid blameful behavior and keep our discussions about how to prevent future failures constructive. If we do not foster this atmosphere of collaboration, our colleagues will be unable to fully trust one another and we will fail.

Principle 3 involves acknowledging the realities that people are susceptible to the outside world. Our teams, coalitions, companies, and communities must be aware of this in the lead-up to major events. Solidarity is the goal, even when things go badly. Honoring the good-faith commitments of our teammates or comrades is necessary. In practice, upholding Principle 3 means that hard discussions are often required early and often, before the magnitude of failure makes it more difficult to keep the underlying issues private. This can be a very unpleasant process, and it has sundered many a relationship in organizing spaces. Managing interpersonal conflict is universally challenging.

To activists, it is critically important to manage interpersonal conflicts *before* the action. Life-altering outcomes are expected in political activism; in the worst of cases, lives have been lost. Activists must be able to trust one another and must be held accountable to one another. Proper preparation will instill a clarity of roles so that individual actors can focus on their own responsibilities to avoid making chaotic situations worse.

Managing Crisis: Responding When Things Break Down

Despite the best planning and best intentions, reality is messy. Indeed, the purpose of planning is less about having a prescribed set of behaviors with foreseeable outcomes and more about developing the habits, intentions, and trust to drive a dynamic scenario toward the most favorable result.

Handling chaos: contrast in responses during the July 8 KKK rally

On July 8 in Charlottesville, almost 2,000 community members arrived at Justice Park to oppose the messages of bigotry and hate being brought to the Charlottesville community by 50 or so members of the Loyal White Knights of the Ku Klux Klan. The vast majority of these counter-demonstrators did not attend planning sessions and did not train for the event. As a result, organizers could not coordinate their actions and responses. In technology terms, the community counter-demonstrators were our customers of our process, behaving in often inscrutable and frustrating ways. But this behavior was not entirely unpredictable.

Local activists prepared for the community response through role differentiation and relied on experience with managing (potentially angry and violent) crowds. Activists came prepared with extra banners and signs for people to carry. Outreach volunteers distributed educational materials explaining elements of social justice and activism. And chant-leaders corralled and led the crowd in ways that ensured that large gatherings of people didn't linger long, avoiding violent encounters on a hot summer day.

Additionally, activists had a plan for civil disobedience and prepared to physically blockade the KKK from entering the park by standing in front of the entrance and interlocking arms. Blockading, an act of unlawful but nonviolent resistance, is a long-standing tradition in the movement for social justice. Local organizers alone were not enough to accomplish the task, but by inspiring impassioned local counter-demonstrators to join the picket, the community realized an effective action of civil disobedience.[3]

The counter-demonstration on July 8 was initially peaceful and effective. At one point during the afternoon, almost everything was operating perfectly according to plan.[4] Media team members were giving interviews, education and outreach team members were distributing materials and holding conversations about social justice

---

3 On this day, 23 arrests were made, the majority of them related to the blockade action. After a local Black activist was found not guilty for obstructing a public passage, the remaining obstruction charges were dropped. The legacy of being willing to risk arrest and break minor laws in the pursuit of justice is a proud one and in doing so one acknowledges that civility and order are meaningless virtues in the face of racial injustice and white supremacist terror.

4 Experienced SREs reading this are likely thinking, "Uh oh..."

---

and the racial history of Charlottesville, and the snack squad was distributing protein bars and bottled water to keep people fed and hydrated. For the moment, it appeared as though the afternoon would pass without major incident.

But after the KKK departed, the heavily armed and armored police turned on the crowd. Within minutes of the Klan's departure, police declared an unlawful assembly. Shortly after, the police deployed tear gas against the peaceful crowd, injuring bystanders, media, and several of their own officers in the process.

Organizers had to pivot rapidly to address a situation with increasing tension to keep it from spiraling out of control. An injured and immobilized counter protester was in the path of advancing riot police. People who had been arrested earlier in the day had been processed and released and were seeking their friends and loved ones amidst the confusion. Uncertain and confusing messages were being exchanged as people were trying to figure out what was happening.

This pattern may be familiar to any SRE who has experienced a system in crisis. Seemingly smooth operations suddenly fail. Alerting fires a storm of pages at on-callers. Incident response is spun up. There is no way to stop time to fix the issue in place, and the longer the outage lasts, the more disappointed our customers become.

Managing crisis response is a skill unto itself. The ability to triage information, prioritize work tasks, and handle communication is critical to successful crisis recovery. An after-action report commissioned by the City of Charlottesville[5] identified several issues with the police response, including a lack of interagency communication and unclear chains of command. Lacking proper oversight, an officer without the authorization to do so gave the order to deploy three tear gas grenades into the crowd. When confronted by his superiors about this decision, the officer who gave the order exclaimed, "You are damn right I gassed them; it needed to be done!"

The impact of this decision had unintended long-lasting impacts: in trying to escape the noxious fumes, three counter-demonstrators covered their faces with t-shirts and bandanas and were consequently arrested on felony masking charges.[6]

The July 8 KKK rally showed in great relief the differences between proper and improper response. While activists were able to handle the rapidly escalating scenario, providing medical aid to people, clearing vulnerable adults and children from the tear gas, and providing support to arrestees, the police response demonstrated

---

5 Final Report: Independent Review of the 2017 Protest Events in Charlottesville, Virginia (*https://www.charlot tesvilleindependentreview.com/*)

6 All three felony charges for unlawful masking were later dropped by the Commonwealth, citing the required element of intent to disguise one's identity. Given the use of chemical weapons, these arrests could have been avoided had police adequately trained for the expected response to chemical deployments.

poor communication and a lack of ability to process dynamic information in real time.

Preparing for the worst: handling terror at Unite the Right

During Unite the Right, a terrible and tragic event occurred when James Alex Fields allegedly attacked a crowd of counter-demonstrators with his car,[7] killing Charlottesville resident Heather Heyer and injuring 35 others in an apparent act of white-supremacist terror.

The attack occurred when an antifascist crowd marched up Fourth Street SE, several blocks away from the rally, in a "victory march" celebrating the fact that the authorities had shut down the rally after hours of brutal street violence. Because of the expected crowd size, Fourth Street SE was supposed to be closed all day; the street should have been blocked off to any vehicle traffic and open to pedestrians. These road closures were well-publicized before the event; in the moments prior to the attack, local activists were trying to move the march off of Water Street, which was open to traffic, and onto Fourth Street SE for safety and to avoid potential police escalation.

Although this event made national news due to Heyer's death and the overt Nazi imagery present throughout the weekend, there are elements of the story that the public has overlooked. The crowd that Fields attacked had many experienced political activists who have been through dramatic, chaotic, and violent events before.

Immediately following the incident, dozens of injured people were left lying on the street. Well-trained medics immediately began to render emergency care while other activists helped clear the street to make way for ambulances and other first responders. But other skills in that moment proved just as critical.

One of the cars damaged in the attack contained young children; preschool teachers in the crowd were able to calm and protect them while their parents received medical care. Clergy members nearby immediately ran toward the attack to provide comfort and support in a moment of deep trauma and uncertainty. And activists used their large banners and signs to create a "medic wall" that helped protect the privacy and safety of the injured. Each person had a job and each person had to do that job. Without that preparedness and that sense of trust, it is certain that the aftermath of the attack would have been far worse.

Although the average SRE (hopefully) does not have to prepare for armed engagement with private militias and neo-Nazi terrorists, the parallels are nevertheless easy

---

7 At the time of this writing, Fields has been charged with first degree murder and eight charges of aggravated malicious wounding, among others. He awaits trial in late 2018 and is presumed innocent until proven guilty in a court of law.

---

to draw. The success or failure of a company can depend on the ability to deliver on its promises. Failures in critical services can lead to millions or billions of dollars in productivity losses. As "Internet of Things" development continues and we integrate connected technology into spaces like healthcare, transportation, and more, it does not require a stretch of the imagination to envision an environment when reliability that deviates from the specification literally leads to life-or-death outcomes. As in activism, proper planning and preparation in the form of incident management protocols and predeveloped safeguards are necessary to be ready to address crisis situations.

In the independent review of the Unite the Right rally, investigators found that Fourth Street was guarded only by a single police school resource officer. When police declared an unlawful assembly and cleared the park, rally-goers and counter-protesters were forced to disperse in the direction of Fourth Street. The officer, fearing for her safety, requested and was given permission to leave the area. This left the entrance to Fourth Street unprotected save for a single small plastic barrier, easily bypassed. The Public Works Department for the City of Charlottesville had offered dump trucks and school buses to provide a hard physical barrier to the closed streets; city officials planning the event did not respond.

The political events of the summer of 2017 in Charlottesville should be seen as a lesson in preparedness. Not every outcome could have been predicted, but it is evident that individuals were able to plan for many possible outcomes, and that planning was able to prevent bad situations from being much worse. The crises were managed by individuals who developed frameworks of trust and who had diverse skills. The failures that enabled the crises to happen in the first place can largely be characterized by lack of trust and communication. It may not be possible to plan for every potential crisis. But it is possible to prepare mitigation and reaction strategies for when crisis inevitably strikes, particularly when a major event, whether it be a political rally or a software release, has a firm fixed date at some point in the future.

The corollary to trust is forgiveness

Chaotic situations are naturally stressful. To manage this stress, it is often necessary that one relinquish some control. The act of triage is, ultimately, the acknowledgment that some problems must be solved now, some problems can be solved later, and some problems cannot be solved at all. For engineers, this can be an emotionally difficult position to be in. Many engineers find it hard to let go of a problem they know they can solve given enough time. They lack the cognitive space to coordinate and plan while they are deep in the weeds problem solving.

Fundamentally, crises are simply a scarcity of time and attention. In a crisis environment, one must optimize for mitigating damage and minimizing lost time. The time-cost of poor decisions made under stress is measured both by the time invested in the wrong decision but also the additional time needed to mitigate the damage done by that wrong decision and reorient along the right path.

Activists have acknowledged this cost in the Second St. Paul Principle: the actions and tactics used will be organized to maintain a separation of time or space. In political action, it is possible to perform a justifiable act at an unjustifiable time or place. This is doubly true when one is faced with life-or-death crises in political movements. When a planned action starts going badly, it is necessary to choose actions that minimize harms while maximizing impact. It does the movement no good to endanger people who cannot share the consequences of those actions, who cannot be endangered.

Ultimately, successful triage depends on having a team of people with diverse skill sets who can be depended on to recognize the boundaries of their own expertise. Not every activist is a medic, not every medic is a media representative, not every media representative is arrestable. Trust is critical.

Think of managing a large-scale outage. Each principal in the incident (incident commander, communications lead, operations lead) plays a distinct role, and may further delegate and coordinate even more specialized responders. And in a situation spanning multiple teams or companies, hundreds of people might be organized according to the incident command system playbook, each fulfilling a critical role in the process of identifying the fault in the system, repairing the damage, and fortifying it against similar failures. Each party needs to trust the other to do their job, so they can focus on doing their own jobs.

As Picard teaches,[8] it is possible to make no mistakes and still lose. Nowhere is this truer than in the quest for social justice. Oppression is not the result of people failing to make the right decisions to unlock the secrets of success, but rather the result of deliberate and patterned efforts to deny privilege and power. Decisions made in chaotic moments with limited information ultimately may not look like the right decisions when the complete truth is laid bare. When in a triage environment, people and things get left behind who do not deserve it. We will lose allies, customers, comrades, clients, safety, data, freedom, money. A crisis is a condition in which not everyone and everything can emerge unscathed.

We must recognize and hold sacred the ability to forgive each other in the chaos. Without this, we can never truly achieve trust. It is possible, and even likely, that we will make mistakes when things go badly. The ability to forgive mistakes is the key to sustainability. Forgiveness allows us to act with conviction in the moment; without it, we may be pushed to brashness or frozen by inaction. It is not enough to be blameless in the retrospective; we must be free to act with our best gifts.

---

8 *Star Trek: The Next Generation*, "Peak Performance," Season 2, Episode 21

Writing Our Own History: Making Sense of What Went Down

A commonly held perspective is that the real work begins when the crisis ends. Crises expose flaws that were previously unknown, or to put it another way, every user is also a QA analyst. Likewise, every activist becomes a historian, as the true and complete stories of political movements are rarely told in the newspapers and history books. Reflecting on the events and writing our own histories is important in activism as well as engineering.

In our careers as SREs, we would be exceptionally lucky to experience only a single crisis. Anyone wishing for a long career as an SRE, or as an organizer, should expect to handle multiple major incidents. How we respond and reflect in the days, weeks, and months following a major event is as important as how we planned for it and acted during it. Retrospective analysis is the necessary step of "closing the loop" and establishing productive feedback cycles that help educate and inform behaviors to prepare for the next crisis.

Charlottesville in review: assigning and avoiding blame

How did this play out for activists and police authorities in Charlottesville? Following the white supremacist rallies in the summer of 2017, the City of Charlottesville commissioned an independent review of the city's handling of the events. This review was conducted by a former US attorney—a prosecutor not commonly known for antipolice or antistate sentiments. Nevertheless, the review criticized how the city and the police handled the events.

The report correctly identified many of the matters addressed earlier in this chapter, particularly with regard to police training and preparation. With respect to the July 8 rally, the report says:[9]

> Unfortunately, the [three other law enforcement] agencies that did send personnel to assist CPD [Charlottesville Police Department] on July 8 were not well integrated. The disconnect between the agencies' respective approaches to the Klan event began well in advance of July 8. There were no joint trainings for all personnel detailing the rules of engagement for this event. VSP [Virginia State Police] and CPD operated under separate operational plans on July 8. While CPD shared their plan with VSP leadership, VSP did not disclose its plan to CPD. The CPD officers and VSP officers who were assigned to work together in particular zones did not meet each other or have any communication prior to July 8. This represents a failure in preparation that undercut operational cohesion and effectiveness during the event.

Although these failures would be damning if July 8 was the only event of the summer, the fact that the police forces failed to properly learn from these events led to the

---

9 Final Report: Independent Review of the 2017 Protest Events in Charlottesville, Virginia, page 66 (*https://www.charlottesvilleindependentreview.com/*).

chaos that ultimately ended in the death of Heather Heyer and the injuries of 35 others during the August 12 rally. Quoting again from the investigation report:[10].

> [T]he men and women tasked with preparing for the Unite The Right event did not sufficiently appreciate the challenge presented. They did not ask for advice or assistance from fairly obvious potential sources. They "didn't know what they didn't know," which in part led to the inadequate preparation for this event.
>
> Despite the obvious similarity between these prior events and the Unite The Right rally, CPD planners did not sufficiently consult with officials in other jurisdictions as they planned for August 12. While they had brief discussions with officers in other jurisdictions, they did not make any attempt to incorporate lessons learned in their own operational plans. They did not travel to other jurisdictions, obtain other departments' operational plans for similar events, or share their thoughts about Unite The Right with counterparts with more experience. This failure represents a tremendous missed opportunity.

Any engineer working in a dysfunctional environment would see similarities in these failures to learn from errors. This reflects a culture of nonaccountability; when a group is unwilling or unable to accept or address its own failures, it is doomed to repeat those failures. The police refused to acknowledge any mismanagement or wrongdoing on July 8. As a result, they failed to engage in practices that could have corrected those flaws between then and August 12.

Beyond culpability: building capacity instead of assigning blame

Engineering lately has adopted the concept of the blameless retrospective. The goal is to avoid turning individual engineers into scapegoats or pariahs. But blamelessness does not imply an absence of future accountability, and indeed it is necessary to address failures and flaws in the act of writing our own histories so that we will not repeat the same failures more than once. Learning requires periodic failure, and equally importantly, the ability to learn from the failures of others. Engineering teams that implement blameless retrospectives can learn from failure while building trust and sustainability.

This is an area where political organizing and social activism communities can learn from the engineering world. Many activist communities have difficulty sustaining activist energy. Deep divides have grown between communities, organizations, and individuals, in part as a result of the high stakes in the quest for social justice. Francis Lee writes:[11]

---

10 Ibid, page 153

11 "Lee, Francis (2017). Excommunicate Me from the Church of Social Justice (*https://www.autostraddle.com/kin-aesthetics-excommunicate-me-from-the-church-of-social-justice-386640/*)," Autostraddle, July 13.

Black Lives Matter cofounder Alicia Garza gave an explosive speech to a roomful of brilliant and passionate organizers. She urged us to set aside our distrust and critique of newer activists and accept that they will hurt and disappoint us. Don't shut them out because they don't have the latest analysis on oppression, or they aren't using the same language as us.

If we are interested in building the mass movements needed to destroy mass oppression, our movements must include people not like us, people with whom we will never fully agree, and people with whom we have conflict.

Sustainability and healing does not mean we have to get everyone on the same page as ourselves. It means honoring the objectives, struggles, and expectations of others who work alongside us. It is easy to celebrate their victories when it suits our objectives; it is harder to avoid blaming their failures when the outcomes are not as favorable to ourselves. But to sustain and grow requires us to be uncomfortable.

This may mean accepting that we own suboptimal environments, accepting that things would be better if they were done differently in the past, and that while we seek to mitigate the damage of factors outside of our control, those factors are ultimately outside of our control. Trust and forgiveness are as important now as in the moment, because the purpose of recovery is not to avoid the next crisis, but to ensure that we are ready to address the next one at full strength.

In the cloud world of critical dependencies upon others' services, the principles of trust and forgiveness are especially important to the functioning of digital businesses. Demanding that engineers actively working an incident update an uninvolved stakeholder, rather than trust that engineer to do their best possible work, slows resolution of the underlying issues. Transparency and forgiveness have become key cornerstones of reassuring technological partners that causes of the failure in services are well-understood and will not recur once mitigations are put into place. There are no perfect systems, and empathy is the best way to build interconnected systems. #hugops is a common refrain between customers and suppliers, and between competitors, precisely because it emphasizes our own humanity and that any day it could be one of us in the hot seat solving an outage.

The Long Tail: Turning Action into Change

Activism can be the journey rather than the arrival.
—Grace Lee Boggs

In the technology industry, we work toward building better products and services as our sustained, long-term goal; toil, on-call shifts, and release days are necessary steps along the way, but it would be disingenuous to treat release days as the *raison d'être* of the average engineer's career. For activists working on social justice, their goal is to bend the moral arc of the universe toward justice through intentional action, sustained growth, and faithful optimism—which takes time. In reality, both planned and spontaneous action are but a fraction of the meaningful work contributed toward the movement. The majority of an activist's time is spent fostering and growing communities based on mutual support, love, and protection.

Managing the moments between the capital-M Moments is perhaps the most vital part of sustainable activism. In these times, we learn hard lessons about who we are and whom we are among. In the period of time after a major incident, we are often beset by doubts, feelings of guilt, and an urge to assign blame. Relationships, particularly those that were tenuous before the incident, can be strained or broken.

In the long tail after an incident, it is worthwhile to reflect on which of those relationships we wish to maintain, which we wish to repair, which we wish to strengthen, and which we wish to sever. But broken trust is not an indication of a lack of worth or ability. The reality is that sometimes trust is broken beyond the point of repair. A broken relationship is unlikely to mend during the next crisis. Instead, the breakdown of trust will lead to a dysfunctional dynamic that may cause internal tension and lead to forces working against each other that should be working for each other. It may be better to address these difficult truths during the downtimes between crises than to risk exacerbating failure at an inopportune moment.

On the other hand, downtime (in the human sense) provides a fantastic opportunity to strengthen relationships that work well. If a team works well in its response to a crisis, it's a worthy investment to reflect on what elements of those interpersonal relationships are strong and strive to improve them. Chances are, building on those strengths will have an impact in more areas than crisis response. And sharing best practices with other groups will strengthen their resiliency.

In the wake of the summer of 2017, it is certain that some relationships between activists will never be repaired, and that some have strengthened immensely. By all indications, Charlottesville will remain a target for white supremacist activity. The work continues, and the community will have to build on its effective trust models and relationships to keep moving forward.

One approach is to use relatively stable periods to integrate new people into the work. By bringing in new people, which can include junior team members learning the ropes for the first time, or seasoned veterans coming onto a new team or new role, skills are refined through continuous training. The old saying, "the best way to learn is to teach," holds true. Teaching allows us a chance to revisit our retrospectives with fresh perspectives.

Teaching also allows us to hold close another truth: that we must accept imperfection. All people are imperfect, whether they be activists, engineers, organizers, or managers. We should always be interrogating our weaknesses, and the downtime between major events is a good time to allow ourselves to probe those weaknesses.

Ultimately, the best use of downtime is preparation. There will always be a next crisis, a next release, a next action. The status quo should never be considered the default state of affairs. In the social justice world, maintaining the status quo means living with injustice and inequality. In the world of technology, maintaining the status quo means features aren't shipping fast enough, our response skills are becoming rusty, or we aren't making progress on reducing operational load. There always are postmortem action items to finish to make the system more resilient for the next time. We must reorient our thinking that the default is chaos separated by long periods of learning, not stability punctuated by brief bursts of chaos.

This can be a difficult proposition to accept, and it is as exhausting as it sounds. Ultimately, we must see this as shift work. We must allow ourselves to take breaks, to shelve our desire to get involved, to control the action, or to know everything. If we have done our jobs well, we have ensured that others are capable of doing our work. There is no movement or organization that finds long-term success by burning out its best.

Activism and Change Within a Company

Not all activism looks like protesting in the streets. As technology workers, we possess influence that can be spent to the benefit of our coworkers, our customers, and the world at large. The simple steps include changes such as revising technical documentation to remove microaggressions or changing service-level indicators to measure availability for a wider range of users. More complex efforts include doing product advocacy in our role as trusted advisors in the design and launch process of software. But what about if you aren't heard at first?

If you encounter resistance from colleagues or from management in trying to address issues of equity in your company's products, policies, or working conditions, there are several important considerations that will serve you well in advocating for equity.

First, keep ears to the ground about things happening within your company so that you don't find out after it's too late to change easily. It's a lot easier to change a decision that's being contemplated or not yet implemented compared to a shipped product. Listen carefully to emotional and rational content of what others are saying. Listen to your colleagues when they have concerns and figure out whether they want empathy or problem-solving. Band together and form coalitions so you have a broader collective voice.

Second, keep your venting separate from engaging in constructive problem solving. There is a place for each of them, but constructive problem-solving with leadership requires minimizing emotional temperature. Vent to friends privately or find someone else who can advocate neutrally while you vent. Avoid saying things you'll regret having attributed to you in a lawsuit or newspaper. You aren't personally accountable for pushing the rock all the time.

Third, make sure that you've identified the right person to escalate your concerns to; it may not be the messenger or team directly working on the issue you disagree with. Addressing feedback to someone who can't do anything frustrates you and them; figure out who the decision-maker is. Once you've found the right decision-maker, assume at least initially that they're also trying to act in good faith for the best interest of your company and users, but potentially with different axioms or priorities. Identify who they listen to that you can persuade to ally with you. Keep their trust and cultivate a positive working relationship; chances are that you'll wind up needing to escalate to them in the future. And make sure that, rather than having a hundred different conversations, that you have a smaller number of liaisons working to proxy concerns to avoid defensiveness against a mob. Don't allow rogue bystanders to get in the way.

Fourth, try to understand what factors influenced the decision-maker's choice and explain your concerns in language that directly attempts to change the variables of the original decision. Your instincts about others' rationales may be naive and quite off the mark; don't argue against a nonexistent strawperson. Understanding the context around decisions and goals is critical. Framing of concerns requires explaining who is impacted in what situations, what specific interactions with your company's products will result in a negative outcome for those people, and what the net harm is. Demonstrate that the company's goals can still be met with a less harmful option.

If all else fails, there are options to try before giving up. Employee petitions/open letters can be effective at getting the attention of executives if carefully worded and succinct. Less than 5% of a company openly dissenting can be effective, but only works if your employer tolerates internal dissent. Be cautious about undermining trust/ progress by talking to the press; leaks can result in negative press and subsequently entrench the status quo due to defensiveness. The threshold of effort and badness to achieve enough negative press to force a change through is too high to be practical in many cases. If that last resort tactic doesn't succeed, you can always vote with your feet if you can afford to.

Change can take a long time, and ensuring that your activism work is sustainable over time is critical. Burnout must be managed, and initial bursts of energy devoted to creating pressure can be used to empower a small, focused group working on long-term objectives with the mandate they need to succeed. Once chartered, working groups need trust and some breathing room; negotiations tend to be more successful when kept confidential until a mutually agreeable solution is finalized.

Whether by quiet resolution via 1:1 chat, formation of a working group without semi-public pressure, or a large crisis as a forcing function, employee voice is a way of ensuring that your company's products conform to engineering ethics. The same communication and escalation skills that keep SREs adept at juggling product development, product management, and other SREs as stakeholders are great for doing internal activism. It's a small step from the culturally ingrained and supported prac-tice of pushing back on launches due to reliability concerns to pushing back on a launch for ethical reasons. It's the least we can do for our industry and for society.

Conclusion

As SREs, we have an interest in ensuring that our customers can use our products, but we often limit ourselves to the technical aspects of that rather than considering the social implications of our products and who can use them to full effect in prac-tice. Our SLOs need to consider the experiences of all users and provide a positive experience across the board.

Applying our skills to social activism can make the world a more just place *and* enable users to have more equal access to the products that we build. You can start small by ensuring that service level indicators are inclusively measuring the experien-ces of *all* users, not just able-bodied users with fast, low-latency internet connections. Expanding your reach further, you can advocate for equity in products you contrib-ute to. And your SRE skills come in useful if you choose to participate in social move-ments.

Emily Gorcenski is a data scientist and anti-racist activist from Charlottesville, Vir-ginia, who now lives in Berlin. Her passion is the intersection of technology, regulation, and society, and she is a tireless advocate of transgender rights.

Liz Fong-Jones is a developer advocate, activist, and site reliability engineer (SRE) with 14+ years of experience based out of Brooklyn, New York, and San Francisco, Califor-nia. She lives with her wife, metamour, and a Samoyed/Golden Retriever mix. In her spare time, she plays classical piano, leads an EVE Online alliance, and advocates for transgender rights as a board member of the National Center for Transgender Equality.

## CHAPTER 33

Conclusion

We have to get on, we have to get on. We have so much time and so little to do. Strike that. Reverse it.

  —Gene Wilder as Willy Wonka

I don't want the book to end here, either.

Let's pretend instead that it is a pause. A "you don't have to go home, but you can't stay here" moment.

It is up to you to keep these discussions going.

Please talk to your fellow and future practitioners about anything you found interesting in this book or omitted from it. Submit talks to conferences (<cough> <cough> SREcon <cough>). Reach out to me and other members of the SRE community over Twitter (DMs at @otterbook always open!) and other social media and introduce yourself. Write a book, compose an opera, or create an interpretive dance about SRE —whatever lets you contribute from your whole self. We need you.

Thank you for reading this book. I look forward to being part of your conversations.

Index

data durability engineering and, 275
logical, 266
physical, 265
    (see also recovery/recoverability of data)
Bainbridge, Lisanne
    on automation, 467
    on human operators and advanced systems,
        465
base image, 412
Bayesian inference, 296
Beamish, Alex, 204
Beck, Kent, 236
benefits, for job applicants with mental disor-
    ders, 501-502
Beyer, Betsy, The Intersection of Reliability and
    Privacy, 245-256
biases, in job interviewing, 16
Bisset, Blake, SRE Antipatterns, 379-404
black boxes
    running like a service, 52
    SLIs on, 53
blame
    assigning/avoiding, in reviews of social acti-
        vism, 551
    in cross-team postmortems, 74
blameless retrospectives
    in social activism, 552
    SRE/social activism parallels, 545
    (see also postmortems)
Bland, Mike, 178, 180
Blank-Edelman, David
    Context Versus Control in SRE, 3-13
    DevOps and SRE, 187-205
    Production Engineering at Facebook,
        207-229
Blew, Aaron, 201
blind resume review, 16
blue/green deployment
    about, 410
    rolling release vs., 414
Boggs, Grace Lee, 553
Bootcamp, at Facebook, 225-226
bot attacks, 426
bottlenecks, 131
breakpoints, 128
Brummel, Janna, 191
build/buy/adopt decision, 43-49
    assessing project considerations, 46
    core competencies and, 47

deciding which option to take, 45
determining importance of an integration,
    44
integration timeline, 47
LinkedIn case study, 49
project operating expense and abandon-
    ment expense, 48
stakeholder identification, 44
Burns, Robert, 542
business case, for SRE
    preparing, 113
    presenting, 116
buy-to-adopt abandonment scenario, 48
buy-to-buy abandonment scenario, 48

C
calibration problem, 475-479
    addressing, 484
    incidents and recalibration, 478
    incidents and specific calibration problems,
        478
    mental models, 475
Campbell, Laine, Database Reliability Engineer-
    ing, 257-272
CAMS (Culture, Automation, Measurement
    and Sharing), 201
Canahuati, Pedro, Production Engineering at
    Facebook, 207-229
canary rollout method, 139
canarying, 517
capacity planning, 374
capacity, team, 174
capital expenditure (CapEx), 45, 163, 374
cascading failure, 535
catalytic role SREs, 376
certificate authorities (CAs), 44
Chakrabarti, Saunak Jai, SRE Without SRE,
    81-109
Challenger space shuttle disaster, 536
champions, for SRE, 114
change management
    parallels between social activism and tech-
        nology industry, 553-557
    SRE teams and, 374
chaos engineering, 233-243
    advanced principles, 241
    and Chaos Kong, 239
    and Economic Pillars of Complexity, 236
    FAQs, 242

cross-team reliability, 73
cultural fit interviews, 20
culture (see success culture, SRE as)

D

dashboards, 40
data durability, engineering for, 275-291
    automation, 288-290
    backups, 275
    estimating durability, 277-279
    freshness, 276
    isolation, 279-283
    protection, 283-285
    real-world strategies, 279-290
    recovery, 284
    replication, 275-279
    replication techniques, 276-279
    restoration, 276
    safeguards, 284
    testing, 283
    verification, 286-288
    window of vulnerability, 288
    zero-errors system, 286
data loss
    application errors and, 263
    detection of, 262-264
    infrastructure services and, 264
    operating system/hardware errors, 264
    user error and, 263
data plane, 444
database reliability engineering, 257-272
    anatomy of a recovery strategy, 262-267
    best practices and standards, 268
    collaboration, 269
    considerations for recovery, 261
    continuous delivery and, 267-269
    culture of, 260
    data protection, 258
    deployment of CD, 270-272
    documentation, 268
    educating developers, 267-269
    guiding principles, 257-260
    impact analysis, 270
    making the case for, 272
    migration patterns, 270-272
    migration testing, 271
    migrations and versioning, 270
    organization's data model, 268
    pet vs. cattle servers, 259

    recoverability, 261-267
    rollback testing, 271
    self-service for scale, 258
    tools for, 269
de-provisioning, 374
Debois, Patrick, SRE Patterns Loved by
    DevOps, 177-185
decision trees, 301, 307-309
decision-making, uncertainty and, 468
decoherence, 535
decommissioning, 62
Deep Blue, 299
deep reinforcement learning, 299
DeepMind, 299, 319
degradation, graduated, 369
demand forecasting, 374
dependencies, external, 133-136
deployment process, immutable infrastructure
    and, 413
dev owners, 88
development teams
    embedding SRE teams into, 66
    interaction with SRE teams, 27
DevOps
    and enterprise operations model–SRE tran-
        sition, 173
    and SRE origins, 365
    automated testing at Google, 178-180
    creating shared source code repository,
        183-185
    defined, 173
    DevOps and SRE, 187-205
    favorite SRE patterns, 177-185
Dickerson, Mikey, 217
    Elegy for Complex Systems, 533-539
disaster planning, 61
Disk Scrubber, 287
Distributed Denial-of-Service (DDoS) attack,
    426
DNS (Domain Name System)
    as external dependency, 135
    at Spotify, 100
    routing requests, 418
Docker images, 413
documentation
    archiving/deleting unnecessary docs, 338
    best practices for, 336-339
    communicating value of, 339-341
    database reliability engineering and, 268

joint cognitive system (JCS), 474, 483
Jones, Matt, 203
Jupyter Notebook, 306

K

Kaizen (continuous improvement), 157-161
Kanban, 174
Kanwar, Pranay, 199
Kasparov, Garry, 299
Kata method, 157-161
Kelvin, Lord (William Thomson), 123, 366
Key Performance Indicators (KPIs), 366, 373
Kim, Gene, SRE Patterns Loved by DevOps, 177-185
Kissner, Lea, 247
Klein, Matt, 119
    on service meshes, 433-449
Knight Capital, 472
known-knowns, software failure and, 515
known-unknowns, software failure and, 515
Kobayashi Maru, 346
Koen, Brian, 370
Kriegsspiel, 344
Kubrick, Stanley, 295

L

Lafeldt, Mathias, 371
Lamott, Anne, 337
large enterprises, 111-122
    defining current state, 112-114
    defining SRE for, 115-116
    DevOps–SRE relationship, 195
    identifying/educating stakeholders, 114
    implementing the SRE team, 117-119
    introducing SRE into, 112-122
    lessons learned from process of introducing SRE, 120
    preparing business case for SRE, 113
    presenting business case for SRE, 116
    sample implementation roadmap, 121
launch readiness review (LRR), 180-183
leaders, as advocates for SRE, 114
Lean manufacturing movement, 157-161
learning, active (see active learning)
Lee, Francis, 552
Legeza, Vladimir, From SysAdmin to SRE in 8,963 Words, 123-145
LGBTQ+ inclusivity, 495, 501

Lightweight Directory Access Protocol (LDAP), 135
Limoncelli, Thomas A.
    on DevOps–SRE relationship, 194
    on LRR, 183
    on shared source repository, 184
LinkedIn, 56, 59
load balancers (see scriptable load balancers)
logging, 61
logical backups, 266
logical isolation, 280
long short-term memory (LSTM) networks, 301
Looney, John, Psychological Safety in SRE, 453-462
Lund, Tanner, 189
Lutner, Sean, 195
Lyft
    operation of Envoy at, 447-449
    origin and development of Envoy, 446

M

machine learning, 293-320
    AI background, 295
    basics, 296-301
    current SRE environment and, 300
    decision trees, 307-309
    defined, 296
    enterprise IT areas affected by, 319
    human–machine games, 298-300
    modern definition of learning in terms of machine, 297
    neural networks, 301-305
    on-call substitute, 520
    practical examples, 306-319
    Python/IPython/Jupyter Notebook installation, 306
    reasons for company to use, 293-320
    reasons to use, 293
    Spotify and, 108
    SRE problems addressed by, 294
    TensorFlow and TensorBoard, 313-317
    time series: server requests waiting, 317-319
    training a neural network from scratch, 309-312
MacNamara, Ríona, Do Docs Better, 325-341
Mangot, Dave, 200
Markdown, 332, 335
market-oriented teams, 162

Markov model, 277

Markup language, 555

Maslow's Hierarchy of Needs, 217

Master Service Agreements (MSAs), 54

McDuffee, Keith, 192

McEniry, Chris, 198

Mean Time Between Failures (MTBF), 536

Mean Time to Detect (MTTD), 148

Mean Time to Failure (MTTF)

    in Markov chain, 277

    inappropriate optimization of, 395-397

Mean Time to Recovery (MTTR), 395-397

Mean Time to Repair (MTTR), 536

    defined, 148

    window of vulnerability and, 288

Mediratta, Bharat, 179

Meickle, James, Beyond Burnout, 491-509

Menchaca, Joaquin, 189

mental disorders, persons with

    and diversity conversation, 494

    benefits for, 501-502

    business environment, 495

    compensation in job application process, 500

    crisis and, 507

    defined, 493

    importance of detailed job postings, 498

    inclusivity as beneficial to all, 507

    ineffectiveness of common workplace strategies towards, 496

    interviewing for job, 499

    job duties, 504

    leaving a job, 506

    on-call work and, 499

    onboarding packets, 502

    pro-inclusion patterns/antipatterns, 497-509

    promotion, 505

    resources, 508

    training, 505

    working conditions, 503-504

    workplace inclusivity and, 491-509

mental health, 491-509

    crises, 507

    defined, 492

mental models, 475

mentorship programs, 505

Mercereau, Jonathan, Working with Third Parties Shouldn't Suck, 43-63

Messeri, Eran, 179, 184

metrics, 28, 117, 373

    (see also incident metrics)

Miasnikoŭ, Stas, Do Docs Better, 325-341

Michel, Drew, SRE Without SRE, 81-109

microservices

    context vs. control at Netflix, 3-13

    current state of microservice networking, 436

    service mesh and (see service mesh)

mid-sized organizations (see Soundcloud, SRE at)

migration cost, 48

    (see also abandonment expense)

migrations, database reliability engineering and, 270-272

Mineiro, Luis, 201

Mitchell, Tom, 297

money (see compensation)

monitoring

    SRE teams and, 373

    third-party integrations, 56-59

monolithic architecture

    disadvantages of, 434

    service mesh vs., 434

Moraes, Gleicon, 202

Morrison, David, 456

Most Favored Customer (MFC) clauses, 62

multiregion operations, immutable infrastructure and, 411

Murphy, Niall Richard

    Against On-Call, 511-532

    Do Docs Better, 325-341

Mushero, Steve, 200

N

Netflix

    chaos engineering at, 233-243

    context vs. control in SRE, 3-13

Netflix model (cross-functional teams), 164

Network Operations Center (NOC), 380

neural networks, 301-305

    artificial neurons and, 301

    datasets for, 304

    popular libraries for, 305

    training from scratch, 309-312

    when to apply, 303

New York Stock Exchange outage (2015), 471

nginScript, 416

Nolan, Laura, Active Teaching and Learning, 343-354
normal distribution, 360
nosocomial automation, 484
Nukala, Shylaja, Do Docs Better, 325-341

O

O'Reilly, Tim
  on complex systems, 371
  on SRE, 366
Obama, Barack, 533
object stores, 266
object-relational mapping (ORM), 460
observability, service mesh and, 437, 441
on-call
  accommodations for on-call personnel, 525
  alternatives to current approach, 524-528
  arguments for keeping current system, 519
  at Spotify, 90
  cognitive hacks, 527
  cost to humans, 520-524
  emergency medicine/SRE differences, 513
  emergency medicine/SRE parallels, 512
  emergency medicine/ward medicine distinction, 516-519
  exclusion backlash and, 527
  flexible schedules and, 526
  improving on-the-job performance, 527
  industry-wide compensation model, 526
  need for fundamental change in approach to, 528-532
  negative consequences of heroism, 523
  opt-out policy, 527
  pager fatigue, 71-73
  pair on-call, 527
  persons with mental disorders and, 499
  prioritization, 525-527
  production engineering team at Facebook, 215
  psychological safety and, 460
  rationale for, 512-520
  reasons to end, 511-532
  recovery time immediately after on-call shift, 526
  Strong-Anti-On-Call position, 528
  Strong/Weak-Anti-On-Call position, 531
  training, 524
  triage function, 512
  underlying assumptions, 514-516

  Weak-Anti-On-Call position, 530
onboarding packets, 502
onsite interview, 19
  coding and system questions, 20
  cultural fit interviews, 20
  deep dives and architecture questions, 20
OpenResty, 416
operating system errors, data loss and, 264
operational debt, 37
operational expenditures (OpEx), 45, 163, 374
operational isolation, 281-283
operations
  approaching as engineering problem, 370-371
  intersections between social activism and, 541-557
  Spotify's early focus on, 82, 85
  Spotify's growth and, 87
Operations as a Service (OaaS), 168
operations organization (see enterprise operations model–SRE transition)
operator fatigue, 289
ops owners, 89
Ops Teams
  at Spotify, 91
Ops-in-Squads
  balancing squad autonomy with tech stack consistency, 104-107
  benefits, 105
  expansion of concept, 102
  rollout, 101
  Spotify's use of, 98-104
  trade-offs, 106
outsourcing, 117
  (see also third parties)
overhead of coordination, 537

P

pager fatigue, 71-73
pair on-call, 527
Papert, Seymour, 344
Pareto distribution, 361
partner phase of SRE execution, 376
patterns
  automated testing at Google, 178-180
  creating shared source code repository, 183-185
  DevOps and, 177-185
    (see also antipatterns)

R

Rabenstein, Björn, How to Apply SRE Principles Without Dedicated SRE Teams, 65-79

Rampke, Matthias, How to Apply SRE Principles Without Dedicated SRE Teams, 65-79

Rasmussen, Jens, 238

Rau, Vivek, 148

reactive phase of SRE execution, 375

real-time dashboards, 40

Real-User Monitoring (RUM)
  SLIs informed by, 54
  third-party integrations and, 51, 58

recovery time (see Mean Time to Recovery (MTTR))

recovery/recoverability of data
  championing recovery reliability, 267
  considerations for, 261
  database reliability engineering and, 261-267
  detection of data loss/corruption, 262-264
  diverse storage, 264
  full physical backups, 265
  incremental physical backups, 266
  logical backups, 266
  object stores, 266
  testing, 266
  varied toolbox for, 265

recurrent neural networks, 304

Redundant Array of Independent Disks (RAID), 289

redundant systems, 369

Reinertsen, Donald G., 155

release engineering, 412

remote work, 503

Rendell, Mark, 196

repair debt, 37

replication techniques
  data durability, engineering for, 276-279
  estimating durability, 277-279

reporting APIs, 53, 59, 61

Republican National Convention protests (2008), 544

request pausing, 422-424

request queues, 152-154

respect, team culture and, 456

resumes, blind review of, 16

roles, formal assignment of, 474

rollbacks, 271

rolling release, blue/green release vs., 414

root access, 85

root causing
  privacy engineering, 252

Root, Lynn, SRE Without SRE, 81-109

Rosenthal, Casey, In the Beginning, There Was Chaos, 233-243

Rother, Mike, 161

routing, shard-aware (see shard-aware routing)

Russek, Johannes, SRE Without SRE, 81-109

Ryan, Andrew, 217

S

sacrifice decisions, 471

St. Paul Principles, 544, 550

Samuel, Arthur, 300

scaling, 33-40

scheduling, flexible, 503, 526

Schlossnagle, Theo, The Art and Science of the Service-Level Objective, 355-364

Schwartz, Mark, 399

scriptable load balancers, 415-430
  about, 415-417
  advantages of, 417
  checkout queue case study, 428-430
  defined, 415
  future issues, 430
  harnessing the potential of, 422
  maintaining resiliency, 426-430
  problems solved by, 417-424
  request pausing, 422-424
  routing requests with, 421
  service-level middleware, 424-426
  shard-aware routing, 418-422
  state and, 427

security
  immutable infrastructure and, 411
  self-service and, 167
  third-party vendors and, 44

self-service
  and OaaS, 168
  benefits to SREs, 167
  database reliability engineering and, 258
  maximizing effectiveness of, 166
  replacing handoffs with, 165-170

separation of duties, 167

servers as cattle vs. servers as pets, 259

service discovery, 440

service meshes, 433-449
  configuration management, 444

principles of organizing, 544
software engineering as analogous to, 542
turning action into change, 553-557
Soundcloud, SRE at, 65-79
  deployment platform, 67
  embedded SREs, 66
  failure of team approach, 65-67
  getting buy-in, 76-78
  implementation details, 71-78
  need to adjust approach to circumstances,
    66
  on-call rotations and pager fatigue, 71-73
  postmortems for resolving cross-team relia-
    bility issues, 73
  Production Engineering team, 69-71
  uniform infrastructure/tooling vs.
    autonomy/innovation, 75-76
  you build it, you run it approach, 67-71
source control, documentation in, 334
source-code repository, Google, 183-185
space shuttle disasters, 536
speed at scale, safely (s3), 107
Spotify, 81-109
  balancing squad autonomy with tech stack
    consistency, 104-107
  beta and release period, 84-86
  bringing scalability and reliability to the
    forefront, 85
  challenges in ops team scaling, 96-98
  deployment time slots, 90
  dev owner role, 88
  engineering culture, 81
  excessive server growth, 94
  forensics, 92
  formalizing core services, 89
  future of SRE at, 107-109
  goalie role, 92
  growth and early success (2010), 87-93
  growth-related challenges (2011), 94-95
  interruptions, 92
  lead time issues, 91
  lightening backend engineers' manual load,
    99
  limits to manual deployments, 97
  moving away from Ops-owner approach,
    101-102
  new ownership model, 88
  on-call and alerting, 90
  operations focus in early history, 82

ops owner role, 89
Ops-in-Squads (2013-2015), 98-104
reorganization of dev teams/op teams, 95
splitting ops team into Production Ops and
  Internal IT Ops, 91
unintentional specialization/misalignment,
  92
SRE (generally)
  antipatterns (see antipatterns)
  defining for larger enterprises, 115-116
    (see also enterprise operations model–
    SRE transition)
  DevOps and, 177-185
  origins of, 365-367
  phases of execution, 375-377
  success culture and (see success culture,
    SRE as)
  without teams (see Soundcloud) (see Spo-
    tify)
SRE Classroom (workshop), 350
SRE teams (see teams)
staging of third-party integrations, 55
stakeholder identification
  in build/buy/adopt decision, 44
  in large enterprises, 114
state, immutable infrastructure and, 409
Stolarsky, Emil, Scriptable Load Balancers,
  415-430
Stone, Luke, So, You Want to Build an SRE
  Team?, 25-30
storage
  and database recovery strategy, 264
  object storage, 265
  offline, 265
  online, high-performance, 264
  online, low-performance, 264
Storage Watcher, 287
structural quality, of documentation, 327-328
Suarez Ordoñez, Santiago, 190
success culture, SRE as, 365-378
  advocate/partner phase of SRE execution,
    376
  approaching operations as engineering
    problem, 370-371
  business success through promises (service
    levels), 372
  capacity planning/demand forecasting, 374
  catalytic stage of SRE execution, 376

About the Editor

David N. Blank-Edelman has over 30 years of experience in the SRE/DevOps/sysadmin field in large multiplatform environments. He currently works for Microsoft as a senior cloud operations advocate focusing on site reliability engineering. He is a cofounder of the wildly popular SREcon conferences hosted globally by USENIX, and is the author of the O'Reilly Otter book (*Automating Systems Administration with Perl*).

Colophon

The animal on the cover of *Seeking SRE* is an Eastern lesser bamboo lemur (*Hapalemur griseus*), also known as a gray bamboo lemur or gray gentle lemur. It is native to the island of Madagascar. Lemurs somewhat resemble primates, but evolved independently of monkeys and apes after Madagascar broke away from the African continent; the divergence point is estimated to be about 58 to 63 million years ago.

The Eastern lesser bamboo lemur has gray fur and is about 11 inches long on average (in addition to a tail length of 12–15 inches). Its diet is largely made up of bamboo shoots (from 75–90%), supplemented with fruit, flowers, and other plant matter. The lemurs have very keen hand-eye coordination and dexterity, and leap vertically from one stalk to another within dense bamboo groves.

Bamboo lemurs use a wide range of vocalizations in the wild, including distinct calls for aerial predators, ground predators, mating readiness, and identification. They live in small groups of 6–9, typically made up of one male, breeding females, and dependent offspring. Females usually have one infant per year, which will be weaned after four months. Though they do transport babies in their mouth or on their back, mother bamboo lemurs more often leave their young hidden within bamboo stands for short periods while they are away foraging.

Some lemur populations may actually benefit from deforestation, as bamboo thrives as secondary growth in cleared land. However, this species is threatened by overhunting, especially for the pet trade.

Many of the animals on O'Reilly covers are endangered; all of them are important to the world. To learn more about how you can help, go to *animals.oreilly.com*.

The cover image is from the *Natural History of Animals*. The cover fonts are URW Typewriter and Guardian Sans. The text font is Adobe Minion Pro; the heading font is Adobe Myriad Condensed; and the code font is Dalton Maag's Ubuntu Mono.

Learn from experts.
Find the answers you need.

Sign up for a **10-day free trial** to get **unlimited access** to all of the content on Safari, including Learning Paths, interactive tutorials, and curated playlists that draw from thousands of ebooks and training videos on a wide range of topics, including data, design, DevOps, management, business—and much more.

Start your free trial at:

oreilly.com/safari

(No credit card required.)